W9-CHO-794

PEARSON

my World GEOGRAPHY™

EASTERN HEMISPHERE

PEARSON

Boston, Massachusetts
Chandler, Arizona
Glenview, Illinois
Upper Saddle River, New Jersey

Acknowledgments appear on pages 836–840, which constitute an extension of this copyright page.

ISBN-13: 978-0-13-363807-3
ISBN-10:   0-13-363807-3
11 12 13 14   V011   18 17 16 15

Program Authors

Gregory H. Chu, a native of Hong Kong, is Professor and Chair of Geography at the University of Wisconsin-La Crosse and Editor of *FOCUS on Geography,* a journal published by the American Geographical Society. He earned his Ph.D. degree in geography from the University of Hawaii and has served as Program Director of Geography and Regional Science at the National Science Foundation, on the Editorial Board of *Cartographic Perspectives,* and Board of Directors of the North American Cartographic Information Society.

Susan Hardwick is a geography professor at the University of Oregon. She is an expert in the human geography of North America and is the past president of the National Council for Geographic Education. She is best known as the co-host of *The Power of Place,* an Annenberg geography series produced for public television. Professor Hardwick was awarded the Association of America's Gilbert Grosvenor Award in Geographic Education, the National Council for Geographic Education's Outstanding Mentor Award, and the statewide California Outstanding Professor Award when she taught at California State University, Chico, before moving to Oregon. She is the parent of four grown sons who all live on a west coast.

Don Holtgrieve received his Ph.D. degree in geography from the University of Oregon and was a professor of geography and environmental studies in the California State University system for 30 years. He now teaches geography and environmental planning at the University of Oregon. His attraction to geography was the interdisciplinary nature of the field and the opportunity to do research out-of-doors. Dr. Holtgrieve enjoys bringing his "real-world" experiences as a high school teacher, community planner, police officer, and consultant to government agencies into his writing and teaching.

Program Consultant

Grant Wiggins is the President of Authentic Education in Hopewell, New Jersey. He earned his Ed.D. degree from Harvard University and his B.A. from St. John's College in Annapolis, Maryland. Wiggins consults with schools, districts, and state education departments on a variety of reform matters; organizes conferences and workshops; and develops print materials and Web resources on curricular change. Over the past 20 years, Wiggins has worked on some of the most influential reform initiatives in the country, including Vermont's portfolio system and Ted Sizer's Coalition of Essential Schools. He is the coauthor, with Jay McTighe, of *Understanding by Design* and *The Understanding by Design Handbook,* the award-winning and highly successful materials on curriculum published by ASCD. He is also the author of *Educative Assessment* and *Assessing Student Performance*, both published by Jossey-Bass.

Academic Reviewers

Africa
Benjamin Ofori-Amoah
Department of Geography
Western Michigan University
Kalamazoo, Michigan

Australia and the Pacific
Christine Drake, Ph.D.
Department of Political Science
   and Geography
Old Dominion University
Norfolk, Virginia

Peter N. D. Pirie
Department of Geography
University of Hawaii at Manoa
Honolulu, Hawaii

East and Southeast Asia
Jessie P. H. Poon
Department of Geography
University of Buffalo
State University of New York
Buffalo, New York

Susan M. Walcott
Department of Geography
University of North Carolina
   at Greensboro
Greensboro, North Carolina

Europe
William H. Berentsen
Department of Geography
University of Connecticut
Storrs, Connecticut

Nancy Partner
Department of History
McGill University
Montreal, Quebec, Canada

Charles Rearick
Department of History
University of Massachusetts
Amherst, Massachusetts

Middle and South America
Connie Weil
Department of Geography
University of Minnesota
Minneapolis, Minnesota

North America
Mark Drayse
Department of Geography
California State University
Fullerton, California

South and Central Asia
Dr. Reuel R. Hanks
Department of Geography
Oklahoma State University
Stillwater, Oklahoma

Pradyumna P. Karan
Department of Geography
University of Kentucky
Lexington, Kentucky

Southwest Asia
Michael E. Bonine
School of Geography and
   Development
Department of Near Eastern
   Studies
University of Arizona
Tucson, Arizona

Shaul Cohen
Department of Geography
University of Oregon
Eugene, Oregon

Religion
Brent Isbell
Department of Religious Studies
University of Houston
Houston, Texas

Gordon Newby
Department of Middle Eastern
   and South Asian Studies
Emory University
Atlanta, Georgia

Robert Platzner, Ph.D.
Emeritus Professor
   of Humanities and
   Religious Studies
California State University
Sacramento, California

Master Teachers and Contributing Authors

George F. Sabato
Past President, California Council for
  the Social Studies
Placerville Union School District
Placerville, California

Michael Yell
President, National Council for
  the Social Studies
Hudson Middle School
Hudson, Wisconsin

Teacher Consultants

James F. Dowd IV
Pasadena, California

Susan M. Keane
Rochester Memorial School
Rochester, Massachusetts

Timothy T. Sprain
Lincoln Middle School
LaCrosse, Wisconsin

Marilyn Weiser
North Dakota Geographic
  Alliance Coordinator
Minot State Univesity
Minot, North Dakota

Reviewers

Carol Bacak-Egbo
Waterford Schools
Waterford, Michigan

John Brill
Bellevue School District
Bellevue, Washington

Helene Brown
Gwinnett County Public Schools
Lawrenceville, Georgia

Sherry Echols
Hartselle Junior High School
Hartselle, Alabama

MaryLynne Fillmon
George N. Smith Junior High
Mesa, Arizona

Douglas Fillmore
Bloomington Junior High School
Bloomington, Illinois

Chad Hayes
Beadle Middle School
Omaha, Nebraska

Bill Huser
Prairie Catholic Middle School
Prairie du Chien, Wisconsin

Steve Missal
Saint Peter's College
Jersey City, New Jersey

James Reed
Caledonia High School
Caledonia, Mississippi

Gina S. Rikard
Greenwood Middle School
Goldsboro, North Carolina

Chuck Schierloh
Lima City Schools
Lima, Ohio

Welcome to my World Geography™!

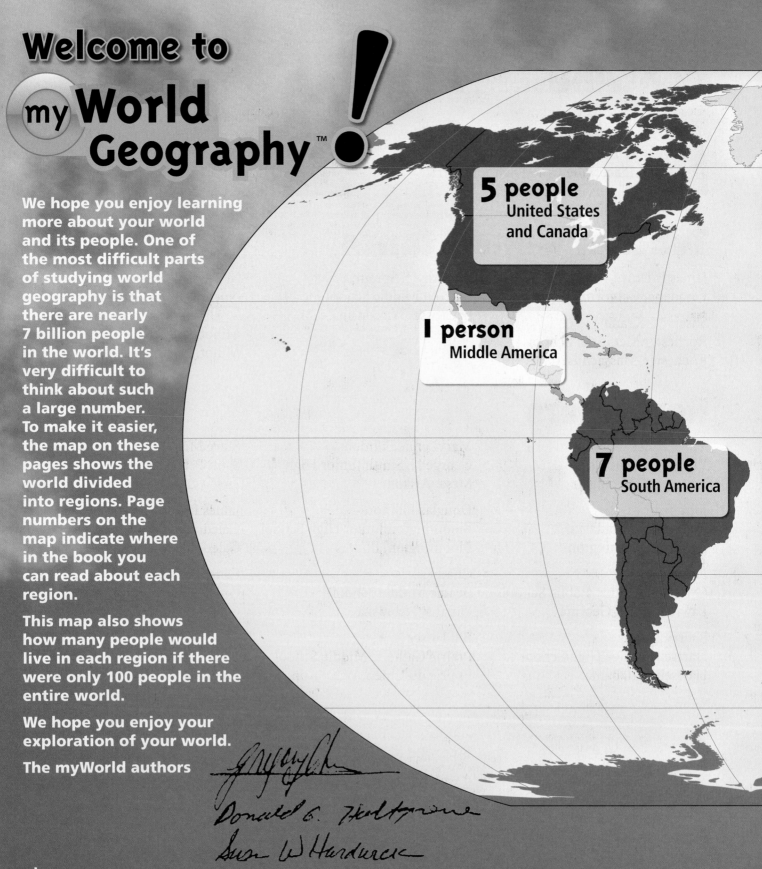

We hope you enjoy learning more about your world and its people. One of the most difficult parts of studying world geography is that there are nearly 7 billion people in the world. It's very difficult to think about such a large number. To make it easier, the map on these pages shows the world divided into regions. Page numbers on the map indicate where in the book you can read about each region.

This map also shows how many people would live in each region if there were only 100 people in the entire world.

We hope you enjoy your exploration of your world.

The myWorld authors

5 people United States and Canada

1 person Middle America

7 people South America

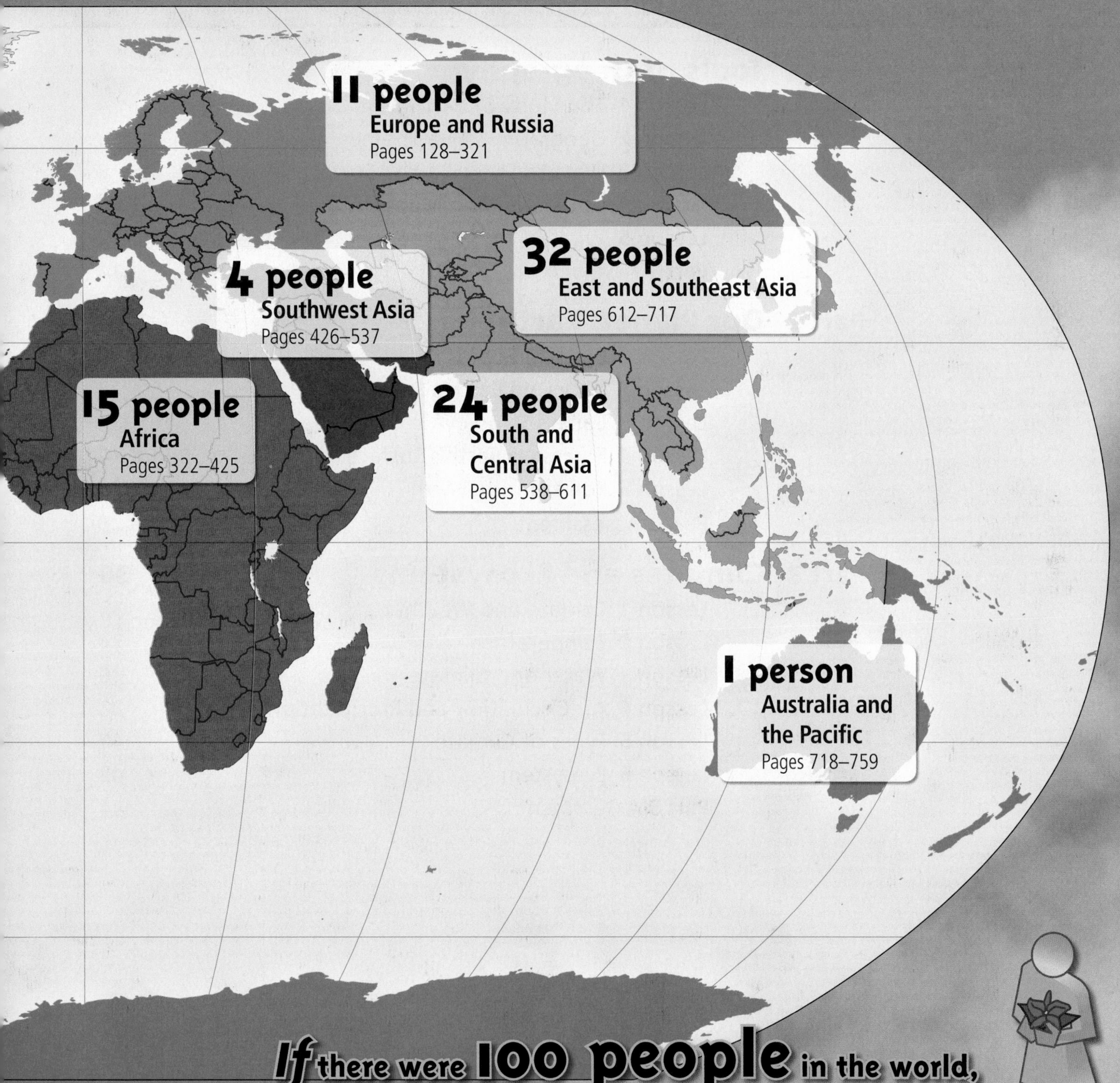

11 people
Europe and Russia
Pages 128–321

32 people
East and Southeast Asia
Pages 612–717

4 people
Southwest Asia
Pages 426–537

15 people
Africa
Pages 322–425

24 people
South and
Central Asia
Pages 538–611

1 person
Australia and
the Pacific
Pages 718–759

If there were **100 people** in the world, *where* would they *live* **?**

Contents

Core Concepts Handbook

<table>
<tr><td>Part 4</td><td>Human-Environment Interaction</td><td>46</td></tr>
<tr><td></td><td>Lesson 1 Environment and Resources</td><td>48</td></tr>
<tr><td></td><td>Lesson 2 Land Use</td><td>50</td></tr>
<tr><td></td><td>Lesson 3 People's Impact on the Environment</td><td>52</td></tr>
<tr><td></td><td>Part 4 Assessment</td><td>54</td></tr>
<tr><td>Part 5</td><td>Economics and Geography</td><td>56</td></tr>
<tr><td></td><td>Lesson 1 Economic Basics</td><td>58</td></tr>
<tr><td></td><td>Lesson 2 Economic Process</td><td>60</td></tr>
<tr><td></td><td>Lesson 3 Economic Systems</td><td>62</td></tr>
<tr><td></td><td>Lesson 4 Economic Development</td><td>64</td></tr>
<tr><td></td><td>Lesson 5 Trade</td><td>66</td></tr>
<tr><td></td><td>Lesson 6 Money Management</td><td>68</td></tr>
<tr><td></td><td>Part 5 Assessment</td><td>70</td></tr>
<tr><td>Part 6</td><td>Population and Movement</td><td>72</td></tr>
<tr><td></td><td>Lesson 1 Population Growth</td><td>74</td></tr>
<tr><td></td><td>Lesson 2 Population Distribution</td><td>76</td></tr>
<tr><td></td><td>Lesson 3 Migration</td><td>78</td></tr>
<tr><td></td><td>Lesson 4 Urbanization</td><td>80</td></tr>
<tr><td></td><td>Part 6 Assessment</td><td>82</td></tr>
</table>

ix

Core Concepts Handbook (continued)

Unit 1 Europe and Russia

Unit 2 Africa

Unit 3 Southwest Asia

Unit 5 East and Southeast Asia

Unit 6 Australia and the Pacific

my Story

Connect to stories of real teens from around the world.

21st Century Learning

Learn new skills through interactive activities.

Closer Look

Photographs, maps, charts, illustrations, and text help you take a closer look at the world.

Rulers of the Seas	140	The Economies of Israel and Its Neighbors	493
A New Form of Government and Justice	142	Iranian Art and Architecture	525
The Black Death	170	The Shrinking Aral Sea	565
To the Far Horizon	189	Climate and Culture	581
Divided Europe	210	The Mughal Empire	590
Understanding the European Union	243	Bollywood	597
Coal or Nuclear: Difficult Energy Choices	266	Women in South Asia	600
		The Three Gorges Dam	644
The Westernization of Russia	300	Japan's Popular Culture	678
European Colonization in Africa	343	Effects of Colonization	700
Darfur Refugee Crisis	382	Land and Culture	705
Agriculture and Civilization	405	Disappearing Islands	746
Arab Culture, Old and New	458		

xix

Case Studies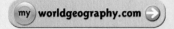

Go online to explore and investigate important global topics.

Primary Sources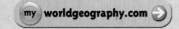

Go online to compare viewpoints through eyewitness accounts and documents.

Chapter 1	Ancient Greek Literature	146
Chapter 1	The Fall of the Roman Empire	154
Chapter 1	Learned Women of the Middle Ages	162
Chapter 2	Renaissance Views of Rulers	186
Chapter 2	The World Wars in Art	206
Chapter 2	Democracy in Eastern Europe	216
Chapter 3	A Sense of Identity	248
Chapter 4	Ethnic Conflict in Bosnia	282
Chapter 5	The Russian Revolution	306
Chapter 6	Things Fall Apart	356
Chapter 7	Literature of Southern and Eastern Africa	378
Chapter 8	Reform in Morocco	420
Chapter 9	The Roles of Men and Women in Islam	452
Chapter 10	Voices of Fear and Hope	498
Chapter 11	The Iranian Revolution	520
Chapter 12	Samarqand: A Silk Road City	560
Chapter 13	Nonviolent Protest	594
Chapter 14	Confucianism and Imperial Law	636
Chapter 15	Japan's Occupation of Korea	670
Chapter 16	Southeast Asia in the 1200s	702
Chapter 17	Aborigines Under British Rule	740

Charts, Graphs, and Diagrams

Diagrams and data help you visually access important information.

Charts, Graphs, and Diagrams (continued)

Maps

Interactive Maps help you actively learn and understand your world.

XXV

Maps (continued)

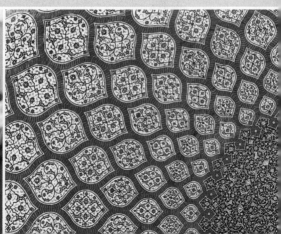

xxvi

Maps (continued)

CONNECT EXPERIE

Welcome to a new and exciting way to learn about world geography. The *myWorld Geography* program is a blend of technology, hands-on activities, and student books that will take you on a one-of-a-kind journey around the globe and through history. Get ready to connect, experience, and build an understanding of the world in a whole new way.

my Story

Xiao
Age: 18
Home: Wutang village, China

Chapter 21

CONNECT
to Different Cultures and People

Develop a deeper understanding of your world by making personal connections to the people and places in *myWorld Geography*.

my*Story* videos introduce you to the stories, families, hopes, and challenges of 23 real teens from around the world.

Regional Overview

East and Southeas...

East and Southeast Asia are regions of mountains, vast plains, dense forests, and crowded coastlines. These regions are densely populated. The largest country in these regions is China, which has more inhabitants than any other country on Earth.

The Unit Ahead
- Chapter 21 China and Its Neighbors
- Chapter 22 Japan and the Koreas
- Chapter 23 Southeast Asia

Unit 8 East and Southeast Asia

my worldgeography.com

Plan your trip online by doing a Data Discovery Activity and watching the myStory Videos of the region's teens.

my Story
Xiao
Age: 18
Home: Wutang village, China
Chapter 21

my Story
Asuka
Age: 18
Home: Yokohama, Japan
Chapter 22

my Story
Ridwan
Age: 19
Home: Bukittinggi, Indonesia
Chapter 22

Rice fields in Bali, Indonesia

See for yourself at myWorldPearson.com/learnmore

XXX

UNDERSTAND

EXPERIENCE
the World in New Ways

Travel across regions and through time—without a passport. *myWorld Geography's* interactive approach using technology, student books, and classroom activities will make learning geography fun and exciting.

Take a virtual and interactive trip around the world with myWorldGeography.com.

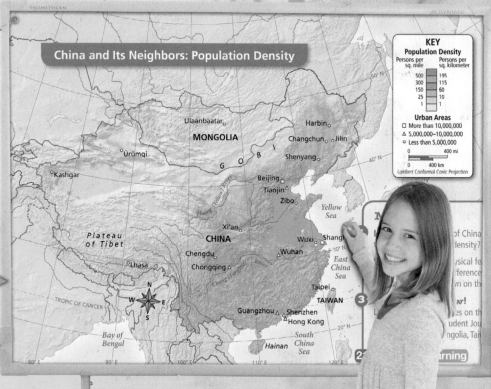

China and Its Neighbors: Population Density

UNDERSTAND
and "Own" Your Learning

myWorld Geography isn't just about reading content—it's about providing you with the tools so you really "get it."

Finding answers to the Essential Questions—found throughout the print, digital, and hands-on activities—helps you understand the key ideas of world geography.

Name _____ Class _____ Date _____

? Essential Question

How can you measure success?

Preview Before you begin this chapter, think about the Essential Question. Understanding how the Essential Question connects to your life will help you understand the chapter you are about to read.

Connect to Your Life

1. Think of some ways to measure success in the categories shown in the chart below. List at least one way in each column. For example, under school you could list grades.

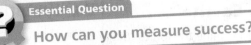

Measures of Personal Success			
Family	Friends	School	Other (Sports, Arts, Chores)

Core Concepts Handbook

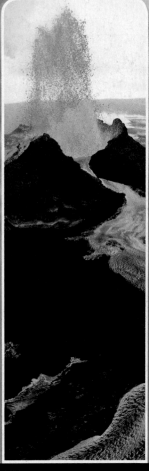

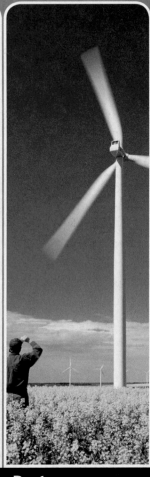

Part 1

Tools of Geography

Learn about the study of Earth.

page 2

Part 2

Our Planet, Earth

Examine the forces that affect Earth.

page 16

Part 3

Climates and Ecosystems

Learn about how climate and weather affect the world and its lifeforms.

page 30

Part 4

Human–Environment Interaction

Explore the ways in which people use resources and affect the environment.

page 46

Part 5

Economics and Geography

Study how people make economic decisions.

page 56

Part

6

Population and Movement

Learn how and why people live in certain places.

page 72

Part

7

Culture and Geography

Understand how the practices of a people make up their culture, and how culture can change over time.

page 84

Part

8

Government and Citizenship

Learn about how people organize governments and what governments do.

page 102

Part

9

Tools of History

Examine the ways in which people study history.

page 116

1

Tools of Geography

Several Maijuna people study a map.

A Peruvian toucan overlooks mountains and rain forest. The Maijuna live in a rain forest area.

2

Maijuna men use a GPS device.

Jason Young

Jason Maps in the Rainforest

Story by Miles Lemaire for myWorld

There were a number of things that took some getting used to for Jason Young when he first traveled to Peru. There was no electricity in the village where he was living, which meant that there was no place to charge his cell phone. The same was true for his computer, which he could not use much since there was no Internet connection.

He was alone in a foreign country, eating food that the hunters of the village provided for him. He ate toucan and piranha. "It is an entirely different world," Jason says. "The people there are living off the rainforest, so they go hunting and whatever they catch is what I eat."

Nothing about this place on the edge of the Amazon jungle felt like home to Jason. However, it was home to the people of the Maijuna (mai HU na) tribe and he was going to help them prove it.

According to Jason, the Maijuna "do not own the land where they live, and it is being threatened by things like logging. The Peruvian government wants to construct a road right through some of their traditional territory."

Fortunately, there is a way for the Maijuna to keep their land if they can prove their ownership of it. To do this, they need accurate maps of the area.

That is where Jason comes in. Jason studies geography, which deals with the human and nonhuman features of Earth. Using his geography skills, he has created maps to help the Maijuna prove their case. He used a GPS device, which uses satellites to locate places on Earth's surface.

Jason says, "I went down there and worked with them for four months over different field seasons. I worked with them to do what is called participatory mapping. It is where you have them draw what they believe is their territory on their traditional land. You use that to go out with a GPS unit and collect [data] points from each of the different spots. I actually took video interviews of them talking about the history of the spots that we went to."

Maijuna people took pictures of the spots, and Jason is working on putting them online in an interactive map. Eventually, users will be able to click on traditional sites to view videos or pictures.

"We are hoping to use that mostly as a teaching tool for safeguarding the Maijuna's traditions, as well as using it as a tool with which to speak to the government."

Jason's involvement with the Maijuna came to an end in 2009. Still, his bond with the Maijuna is so strong that he wants to revisit his new friends as often as he can. He feels that he has learned a lot from his experience.

"The level of poverty opened my eyes to how privileged I have been and how much potential I have to give back to the world," Jason says.

3

Geography: The Study of Earth

Key Ideas
- Geographers use directions to help locate points on Earth's surface.
- Geographers have drawn imaginary lines around Earth, dividing it into parts to help pinpoint locations.

Key Terms
- geography
- degree
- cardinal direction
- hemisphere
- sphere
- longitude
- latitude

 Visual Glossary

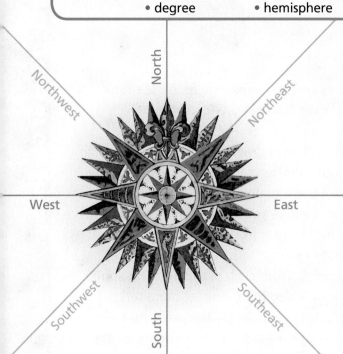

North
Northwest
Northeast
West
East
Southwest
Southeast
South

Geography is the study of the human and nonhuman features of Earth, our home. Geographers try to answer two basic questions: Where are things located? Why are they there? To answer these questions, geographers study oceans, plant life, landforms, countries, and cities. Geographers also study how Earth and its people affect each other.

Directions

In order to study Earth, geographers need to measure it and locate points on its surface. One way to do this is with directions. Geographers use both cardinal and intermediate directions. The **cardinal directions** are north, east, south, and west. Intermediate directions lie between the cardinal directions. For example, northwest is halfway between north and west.

Latitude

Earth is an almost perfect **sphere** (sfeer), or round-shaped body. Geographers have drawn imaginary lines around Earth to help locate places on its surface. One of these is the Equator, a line drawn around Earth halfway between the North and South Poles. The Equator is also known as the 0-degree (0°) latitude line. **Latitude** is the distance north or south of the Equator. It is measured in degrees. **Degrees** are units that measure angles. Minutes (') measure smaller units. On this map, lines are drawn every 20° of latitude.

Lines of latitude form east-west circles around the globe. Lines of latitude are also called parallels, because they are parallel to one another. That means they never cross.

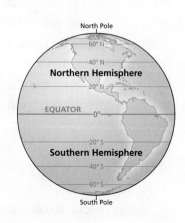

North Pole
60° N
40° N
Northern Hemisphere
20° N
EQUATOR — 0°
20° S
Southern Hemisphere
40° S
60° S
South Pole

The Equator divides Earth in half. Each half of Earth is called a **hemisphere.** The half of Earth north of the Equator is known as the Northern Hemisphere. The half of Earth south of the Equator is the Southern Hemisphere.

Longitude

Geographers have also drawn imaginary north-south lines that run between the North Pole and the South Pole on Earth's surface. One of these lines is the Prime Meridian, which passes through Greenwich, England. The Prime Meridian and the other north-south lines measure **longitude,** or the distance in degrees east or west of the Prime Meridian. Lines of longitude are also called meridians.

The half of Earth east of the Prime Meridian is known as the Eastern Hemisphere. The half of Earth west of the Prime Meridian is the Western Hemisphere.

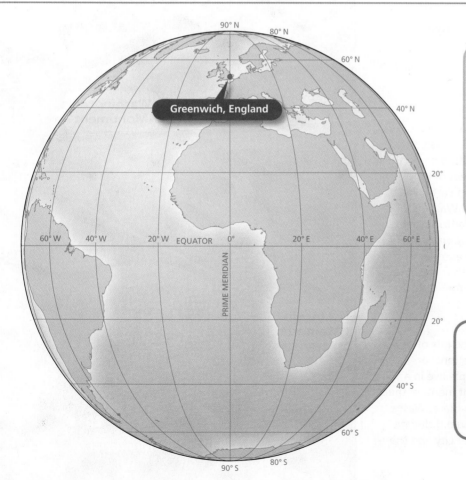

The Global Grid

Latitude and longitude form a global grid. You can describe the location of any point on Earth's surface using degrees of longitude and latitude. For example, Greenwich, England, is located at $0°$ longitude and about $51°29'$ north latitude.

Assessment

1. What do geographers study?
2. Based on the diagrams shown here, in which two hemispheres do you live?

5

Geography's Five Themes

Key Ideas
- Using five themes can help you make sense of geography.
- The theme of location is used to describe where a place is found, while the other themes describe features of a place.

Key Terms
- absolute location
- relative location
- place
- region
- movement
- human-environment interaction

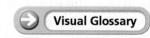
Visual Glossary

Geographers use five different themes, or ways of thinking. These themes are location, place, region, movement, and human-environment interaction. They can help answer the geographer's two basic questions: Where are things located? Why are they there? You can see how the five themes work by looking at the example of our nation's capital, Washington, D.C.

Location

Geographers begin to study a place by finding where it is, or its location. There are two ways to talk about location. **Absolute location** describes a place's exact position on Earth in terms of longitude and latitude. Using degrees of longitude and latitude, you can pinpoint any spot on Earth. For example, the absolute location of the center of Washington, D.C., is at the intersection of the 38°54' north latitude line and the 77°2' west longitude line. **Relative location,** or the location of a place relative to another place, is another way to describe location. For example, you can say that Washington, D.C, is about 200 miles southwest of New York City.

Place

Geographers also study place. **Place** refers to the mix of human and nonhuman features at a given location. For example, you might talk about how many people live in a place and the kinds of work they do. You might mention that a place is hilly or that it has a wet climate. As a place, Washington, D.C., is on the Potomac River. It has a humid climate with cool winters and hot summers. It is a major city and the center of government for the United States.

6

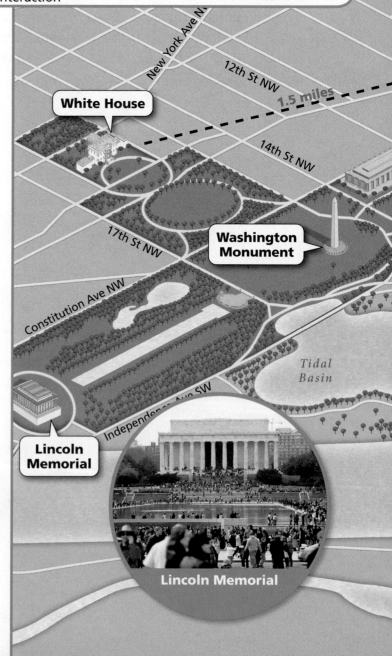
Lincoln Memorial

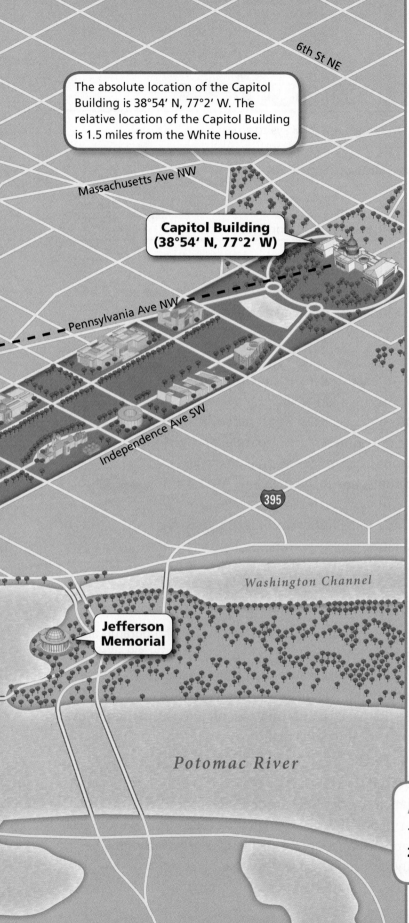

The absolute location of the Capitol Building is 38°54' N, 77°2' W. The relative location of the Capitol Building is 1.5 miles from the White House.

Capitol Building (38°54' N, 77°2' W)

Jefferson Memorial

Washington Channel

Potomac River

Region

Geographers use the theme of region to group places that have something in common. A **region** is an area with at least one unifying physical or human feature such as climate, landforms, population, or history. Washington, D.C., is part of a region called the Washington Metropolitan Area, which includes the city of Washington and its suburbs. This region shares a job market and a road and rail network. New technology, such as high-speed railroads, may give places new unifying features and connections. This can change the way people see regions.

Movement

The theme of **movement** explores how people, goods, and ideas get from one place to another. A daily movement of trucks and trains supplies the people of Washington with food, fuel, and other basic goods.

Human-Environment Interaction

The theme of **human-environment interaction** considers how people affect their environment, or their natural surroundings, and how their environment affects them. The movement of water from the Potomac River into Washington's water system is an example of human-environment interaction.

Assessment

1. What are the five themes of geography?
2. What is the difference between your hometown's location and your hometown as a place?

7

Ways to Show Earth's Surface

Key Ideas
- Globes, photographs, computer images, and maps are all ways to show and view Earth's surface.
- Each way of showing Earth's surface has advantages and disadvantages.

Key Terms
- scale
- aerial photograph
- satellite image
- geographic information system (GIS)
- distortion
- projection

Visual Glossary

▲ An aerial photo taken in Antactica (top) and a satellite image of Antarctica (above).

Geographers use a number of different models to represent Earth's surface. Each model has its own strengths and weaknesses.

Globes

A globe is a model of Earth with the same round shape as Earth itself. With a globe, geographers can show the continents and oceans of Earth much as they really are. The only difference is the **scale,** or the area a given space on the map corresponds to in the real world. For example, one inch on a globe might corespond to 600 miles on Earth's surface.

A globe would have to be hundreds of feet high to show the streets of your town. Such a globe would be impossible to carry around. Instead, people use flat maps to help them find their way.

Photographs

Geographers use photographs as well as maps. **Aerial photographs** are photographic images of Earth's surface taken from the air. **Satellite images** are pictures of Earth's surface taken from a satellite in orbit. They show Earth's surface in great detail. However, it can be hard to find specific features, such as roads, on a photograph. For this reason, maps are still the main way to show information about Earth's surface.

Geographic Information Systems

Geographic information systems (GIS) are computer-based systems that store and use information linked to geographic locations. GIS is useful not only to geographers and mapmakers but also to government agencies and businesses. It offers a way to connect information to places.

Map Projections

Flat maps and photos have one major problem. Earth is round. A map or photo is flat. Can you flatten an orange peel without stretching or tearing it? There will be sections that are stretched or bent out of shape.

Showing Earth on a flat surface always brings some **distortion,** or loss of accuracy in the size or position of objects on a map. Something is going to look too large, too small, or out of place.

To show a flat image of Earth's round surface, mapmakers have come up with different **projections,** or ways to map Earth on a flat surface. A few examples show how they differ.

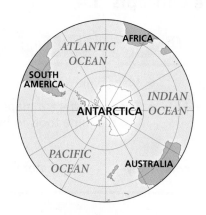

▲ This projection shows the size and shape of Antarctica nearly correctly.

HOW TO SHOW OUR ROUND EARTH ON A FLAT MAP

The Equal-Area Projection

An equal-area map shows the correct size of landmasses. However, their shapes are distorted.

The Mercator Projection

The Mercator (mur KAYT ur) projection shows correct shapes and directions but not true distances or sizes. Mercator maps make areas near the poles look bigger than they are.

The Robinson Projection

The Robinson projection shows nearly the correct size and shape of most land areas. However, even a Robinson projection has distortions, especially in areas around the edges of the map.

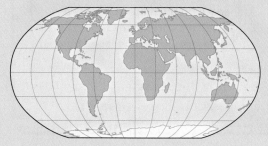

Assessment

1. How are maps different from globes?
2. What are the strengths and weaknesses of each of the three projections in showing Antarctica?

9

Understanding Maps

Key Ideas
- Maps have parts that help you read them.
- Though different maps show different things about a place, you can use the same tools to help understand them.

Key Terms • key   • locator map   • scale bar   • compass rose

 **Visual Glossary**

Look at the maps on these two pages. One is a physical map of the state of Colorado. The other is a road map of Colorado. These maps cover the same area but show different kinds of information. Despite their differences, both maps have all of the basic parts that you should find on any map.

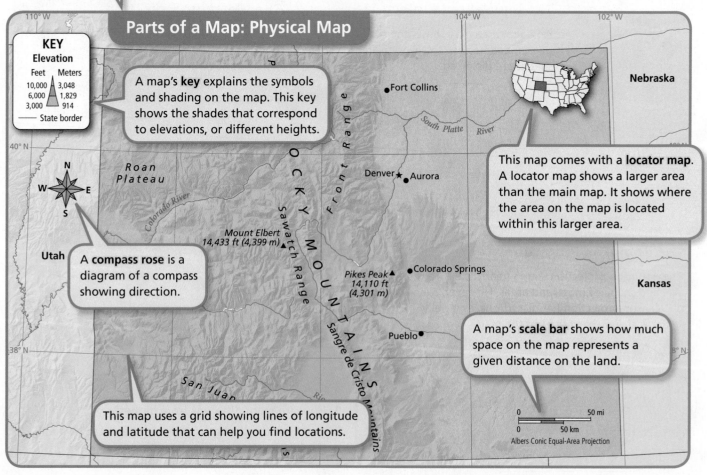

The map has a title that tells you the subject of the map.

Parts of a Map: Physical Map

KEY
Elevation

Feet	Meters
10,000	3,048
6,000	1,829
3,000	914

— State border

A map's **key** explains the symbols and shading on the map. This key shows the shades that correspond to elevations, or different heights.

This map comes with a **locator map**. A locator map shows a larger area than the main map. It shows where the area on the map is located within this larger area.

A **compass rose** is a diagram of a compass showing direction.

A map's **scale bar** shows how much space on the map represents a given distance on the land.

This map uses a grid showing lines of longitude and latitude that can help you find locations.

0   50 mi
0   50 km
Albers Conic Equal-Area Projection

Mount Elbert 14,433 ft (4,399 m)

Pikes Peak 14,110 ft (4,301 m)

Roan Plateau

Front Range

ROCKY MOUNTAINS

Sawatch Range

Sangre de Cristo Mountains

San Juan

Colorado River

South Platte River

Fort Collins

Denver • Aurora

Colorado Springs

Pueblo

Utah   Nebraska   Kansas

110° W   104° W   102° W

40° N   38° N

Reading a Map

Look at the map below. It is a highway map of the state of Colorado. This map looks different from the physical map of Colorado that you have just studied. However, it has the same parts that can help you read it. In fact, you can read most maps using the key, scale bar, and other map tools that you have learned about.

Find the key on this map. Using the key, can you find the route number of the Interstate highway that connects Denver and Colorado Springs, Colorado? Using the scale bar, estimate the number of miles between these two cities. Using the compass rose, find the direction that you would need to travel from Denver to Colorado Springs. Now you have learned to read a highway map!

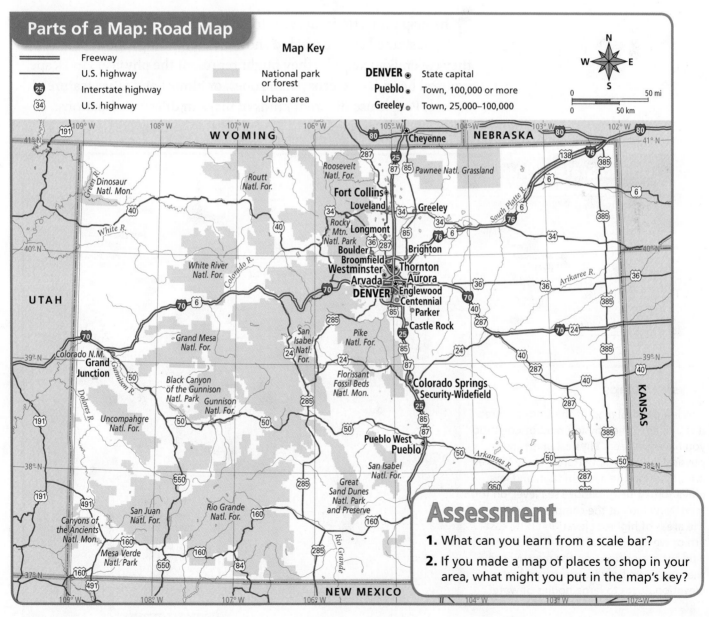

Parts of a Map: Road Map

Assessment

1. What can you learn from a scale bar?
2. If you made a map of places to shop in your area, what might you put in the map's key?

Types of Maps

Key Ideas
- Maps can show many different kinds of information.
- Political, physical, and special-purpose maps are the main types of maps.

Key Terms • physical map • elevation • political map • special-purpose map  Visual Glossary

The map projections, or ways to represent Earth's surface, that you have studied can be used to show different things about the area they cover. For example, they might represent the physical landscape, political boundaries, ecosystem zones, or almost any other feature of a place. People use different kinds of maps in different situations.

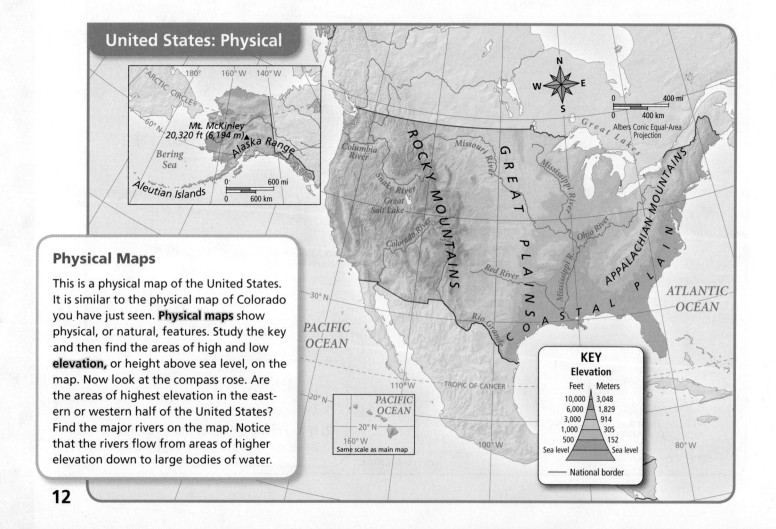

United States: Physical

Physical Maps

This is a physical map of the United States. It is similar to the physical map of Colorado you have just seen. **Physical maps** show physical, or natural, features. Study the key and then find the areas of high and low **elevation,** or height above sea level, on the map. Now look at the compass rose. Are the areas of highest elevation in the eastern or western half of the United States? Find the major rivers on the map. Notice that the rivers flow from areas of higher elevation down to large bodies of water.

KEY
Elevation

Feet	Meters
10,000	3,048
6,000	1,829
3,000	914
1,000	305
500	152
Sea level	Sea level

— National border

12

United States: Political

Political Maps

This is a political map of the United States. **Political maps** show political units, such as countries or states. They may also show capitals of countries, or centers of government, and other major cities. Study the key and compass rose of this map. Now look at the map. Which state is directly west of Georgia? How many states border Canada?

United States: Election 2008

Special-purpose Maps

Maps can show many different kinds of information. **Special-purpose maps** show the location or distribution of human or physical features. This map shows the results of the 2008 presidential election. A highway map is another kind of special-purpose map. Other special-purpose maps may show a region's weather patterns or other features. Study this map's key. Which presidential candidate won your home state in the 2008 election?

Assessment

1. What are the elements of a physical map?

2. What are the elements of a political map?

13

Part 1 Assessment

Key Terms and Ideas

1. **Compare and Contrast** What is the difference between **latitude** and **longitude**?

2. **Describe** What are some features of **place** and **region**?

3. **Analyze Cause and Effect** Why do map **projections** lead to **distortion**? Give a specific example.

4. **Discuss** What does the **scale bar** of a map show?

5. **Compare and Contrast** How do **aerial photographs** and **satellite images** show Earth's surface? What differences do you find between these types of images?

6. **Recall** What are the basic parts of a map, and what does each part show to readers?

7. **Categorize** What kind of map shows elevation?

8. **Summarize** What does a **political map** show?

Think Critically

9. **Problem Solving** Which kinds of maps could you use to choose a new city as your home? How would you use them?

10. **Decision Making** Which kinds of projections would best show the distance between your hometown and Washington, D.C., on a map of the United States? Explain.

11. **Synthesize** What can you learn from the latitude and longitude lines on a map?

12. **Categorize** Match each feature to the correct theme of geography: very flat landscape, four trains in and out of town every day, factory waste enters a local river, large Hispanic population across three states, and 42° S 147° E.

Identify

For each part of a map, write the letter from the map that shows its location.

13. title
14. compass rose
15. latitude line
16. longitude line
17. scale bar
18. key
19. What type of map is this?

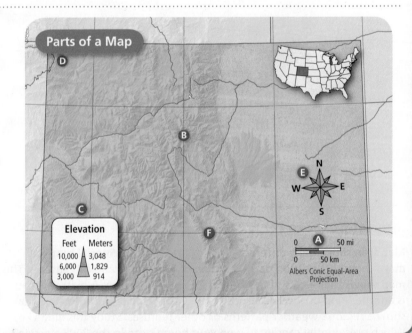

Journal Activity

Fill in the graphic organizers in your student journal.

Demonstrate Understanding Complete the Sum-It-Up activity in your journal to demonstrate your understanding of the Tools of Geography. After you complete the activity, discuss your map with a partner. Be sure to support your completed map with information from the lesson.

21st Century Learning

Evaluate Web Sites

Find three different web sites that generate maps. Compare the sites and rank each according to the following criteria:
- clarity and appearance of the maps
- option to create directions for drivers or walkers
- ability to locate addresses from incomplete information

Document-Based Questions

Success Tracker™
Online at myworldgeography.com

Use your knowledge of the tools of geography and Documents A and B to answer Questions 1–3.

Document A

Document B

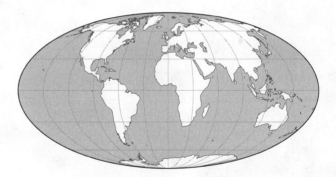

1. Which of the five themes of geography is best represented by this map?

 A location

 B place

 C region

 D human-environment interaction

2. What kind of projection does Document B show?

 A Mercator

 B equal-area

 C Robinson

 D global grid

3. **Writing Task** What are the advantages and disadvantages of the map shown in Document B? Explain your answer.

myworldgeography.com   Self-Test

15

Our Planet, Earth

The volcano Kilauea erupting

▲ Looking down into the crater of an active volcano, you can almost glimpse the interior of our planet, Earth.

16

A road destroyed by an earthquake in Indonesia

Lava flowing into the sea (left)
Tamsen Burlak (right)

Tamsen Studies a Volcano

Story by Miles Lemaire for myWorld

As 21-year-old Tamsen Burlak watched the volcano Kilauea, in Hawaii, blow lava and ash into the sky she had only one thought: "This is pretty cool."

When she was a young girl, Tamsen didn't know much about what makes up our planet, Earth, only that she loved to collect rocks during nature hikes with her parents.

"I would always pick up rocks from everywhere that we went—anything that looked cool," she says. "It was probably around middle school or high school while I was looking at the rocks that I realized I wanted to know what they were called and how they formed. So I went out and bought a bunch of those field guides, geology dictionaries for rocks. That's when I found out the field name was geology." Tamsen knew what she wanted to study.

When she went to college, Tamsen studied geology, the field of science that deals with the structure of Earth. She concentrated on volcanoes and fault lines, places where earthquakes are likely to happen. Geologists like Tamsen investigate earthquake zones to find out how likely another earthquake is, and how destructive it will be. Earthquakes sometimes occur where volcanoes are erupting.

Tamsen was able to go to Hawaii to study. The islands that make up the state of Hawaii were formed by volcanoes. Lava flowed out of volcanoes, cooled,

and formed new land over millions of years. Some of the islands still have active volcanoes. Tamsen visited Kilauea, where lava has been flowing since 1983.

"The active area I went to was part of a summer course I took on the big island of Hawaii. At that time Kilauea had just started erupting, so we were there for the first days of it," Tamsen said.

"It was really exciting," she added, but not always easy, "because of the volcanic gasses in the air. That sort of stuff can itch the throat and cause irritation, but I loved every second of it!"

Tamsen, who now has a degree in geology, says that she has been studying dormant, or inactive, volcanoes and earthquake zones for years. Her experience in Hawaii is something that she and her fellow geologists dream of.

"We'd all be really excited if there was an actual earthquake that we all got to study," says Tamsen, "but we just look at faults in the area, offsets, and the different rock types, and measure how much displacement has gone on and how big a threat we think it might be."

As Tamsen learned firsthand, studying the structure of Earth can be very exciting. Geologists face down erupting volcanoes in order to learn how to predict earthquakes and save lives. Understanding Earth may someday make that possible.

17

Earth in Space

Key Ideas
- Planet Earth moves around the sun.
- This movement causes places on Earth's surface to receive varying amounts of sunlight from one season to the next.

Key Terms
- orbit
- axis
- solstice
- revolution
- equinox

→ Visual Glossary

Earth, the sun, the planets, and the stars in the sky are all part of our galaxy, or cluster of stars. We call our galaxy the Milky Way because its stars look like a trail of spilled milk across a dark night sky. Our sun is one of its billions of stars.

Earth, the Sun, and the Seasons

Even though the sun is about 93 million miles (150 million km) away, it provides Earth with heat and light. To understand how far Earth is from the sun, consider that this distance is nearly 4,000 times the distance around Earth at the Equator.

Earth travels around the sun in an oval-shaped **orbit,** which is the path one object makes as it revolves around another. Earth takes 365 1/4 days, or one year, to make one **revolution,** or complete journey, around the sun.

Earth's **axis,** an imaginary line between the North and South Poles, is tilted relative to its orbit. Therefore, as Earth makes its revolution, the sun shines most directly on different places at different times. That is why seasons occur.

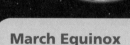

March Equinox

About March 21, the sun is directly overhead at noon on the Equator. At this point in Earth's orbit, its axis is tilted neither toward nor away from the sun. An **equinox** (EE kwih nahks) is a point at which, everywhere on Earth, days and nights are nearly equal in length. This is the spring equinox in the Northern Hemisphere and the fall equinox in the Southern Hemisphere.

June Solstice

About June 21, the North Pole is tilted closest to the sun. This brings the heat of summer to the Northern Hemisphere. This is the summer **solstice** in the Northern Hemisphere and the winter solstice in the Southern Hemisphere. A solstice (SOHL stis) is a point at which days are longest in one hemisphere and shortest in the other.

December Solstice

About December 21, the South Pole is tilted closest to the sun. The area north of the Arctic Circle is in constant darkness, while the area south of the Antarctic Circle has constant daylight. This is the winter solstice in the Northern Hemisphere and the summer solstice in the Southern Hemisphere. The lack of sunlight in the Northern Hemisphere brings the cold of winter.

September Equinox

About September 23, the sun is again directly overhead at noon on the Equator, and all of Earth has days and nights of equal length. This is the fall equinox in the Northern Hemisphere and the spring equinox in the Southern Hemisphere. Less-direct sunlight in the Northern Hemisphere brings the chill of fall.

Assessment

1. If it is summer in the Northern Hemisphere, what season is it in the Southern Hemisphere?

2. How can days be short and cold in one hemisphere when they are long and hot in another?

Time and Earth's Rotation

Key Ideas
- Earth's spinning movement causes day and night.
- This spinning also causes it to be different times in different places on Earth's surface.

Key Terms • rotation • time zone

 Visual Glossary

You have learned that Earth revolves around the sun in an oval-shaped orbit. Earth also moves in another way. This motion explains why day and night occur.

Rotation of Earth

As Earth revolves around the sun, it is also rotating, or spinning, in space. Earth rotates around its axis. Each complete turn, or **rotation,** takes about 24 hours. At any one time, it is night on the side of Earth facing away from the sun. As Earth rotates, that side of Earth turns to face the sun, and the sun appears to rise. The sun's light shines on that side of Earth. It is daytime. Then, as that side of Earth turns away from the sun, the sun appears to set. No sunlight reaches that side of Earth. It is nighttime.

Time Zones

Because Earth rotates toward the east, the day starts earlier in the east than it does farther west. Over short distances, the time difference is small. For example, the sun rises about four minutes earlier in Beaumont, Texas, than it does in Houston, 70 miles to the west. But if every town had its own local time, people would have a hard time keeping track. So governments have agreed to divide the world into standard **time zones,** or areas sharing the same time. Times in neighboring zones are one hour apart.

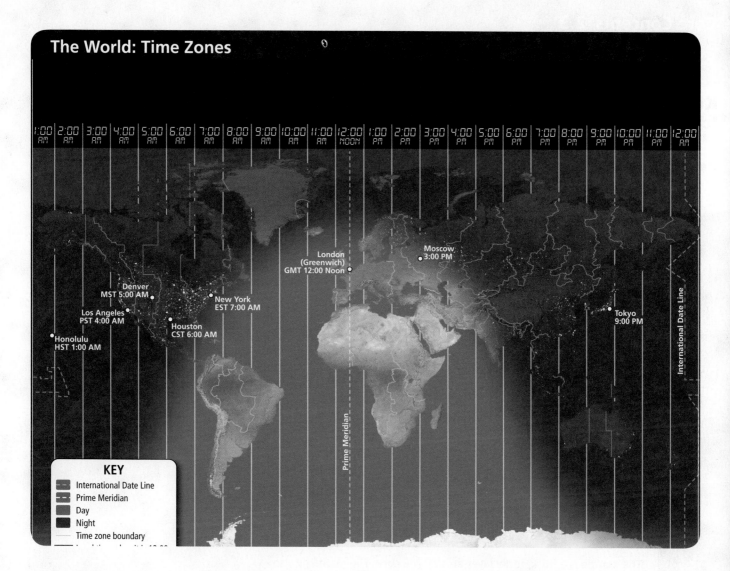

The World: Time Zones

| 1:00 AM | 2:00 AM | 3:00 AM | 4:00 AM | 5:00 AM | 6:00 AM | 7:00 AM | 8:00 AM | 9:00 AM | 10:00 AM | 11:00 AM | 12:00 NOON | 1:00 PM | 2:00 PM | 3:00 PM | 4:00 PM | 5:00 PM | 6:00 PM | 7:00 PM | 8:00 PM | 9:00 PM | 10:00 PM | 11:00 PM | 12:00 AM |

Denver MST 5:00 AM
Los Angeles PST 4:00 AM
Honolulu HST 1:00 AM
Houston CST 6:00 AM
New York EST 7:00 AM
London (Greenwich) GMT 12:00 Noon
Moscow 3:00 PM
Tokyo 9:00 PM

Prime Meridian

International Date Line

KEY
- International Date Line
- Prime Meridian
- Day
- Night
- Time zone boundary

The Prime Meridian

The Prime Meridian, in Greenwich, England, is at the center of one of these zones. The time in that zone is sometimes known as Greenwich Mean Time or Universal Time (UT). Other time zones are sometimes described in terms of how many hours they are behind or ahead of UT. (For example, Central Standard Time in the United States is UT – 6, or six hours behind UT.)

Assessment

1. What is the rotation of Earth?

2. If it is 8 P.M. in New York, what time is it in Los Angeles?

21

Earth's Structure

Key Ideas
- Earth is made up of different parts, above and below its surface.

Key Terms
- core
- mantle
- crust
- atmosphere
- landform

 Visual Glossary

The diagram to the right reveals Earth's interior, or the parts beneath its surface. It also shows some of the parts above its surface. Understanding Earth's inner and outer structure will help you to understand the forces that shape the world we live in.

Earth's Core

A sphere of very hot metal at the center of Earth is called the **core**. Despite temperatures greater than 5,000°F (3,000°C), the inner core is solid because of the great pressure of the layers above it. The outer core is hot liquid metal.

Mantle

The **mantle** is a thick, rocky layer around the core. The mantle is also hot, with temperatures greater than 3,300°F (1,800°C). The mantle is solid, but its temperature makes it fluid, or able to flow. If you warm a stick of butter, you can move the top in one direction and the bottom in another. Even though the mantle is rock, its high temperature allows it to move something like a stick of warm butter.

Crust

The thin layer of rocks and minerals that surrounds the mantle is called the **crust**. The surface of the crust includes the land areas where people live as well as the ocean floor. The crust is thinnest beneath the ocean floor. It is thickest beneath high mountain ranges, such as the Himalayas, in Asia. In effect, it floats on top of the mantle. The great heat deep inside Earth and movements within the mantle help to shape Earth's crust.

Atmosphere

Above Earth's surface is the **atmosphere,** a thick layer of gases or air. It includes life-giving oxygen. Earth's atmosphere acts like a blanket. It holds in heat from the sun, which makes life possible.

Landforms

Only 25 percent of Earth's surface is land. There are many different **landforms,** or shapes and types of land. Two kinds of processes shape these landforms: processes beneath Earth's surface that push Earth's crust up, and processes on Earth's surface that wear it down.

Water

Water covers about 75 percent of Earth's surface. This water forms a layer above Earth's crust. The oceans hold about 97 percent of Earth's water. This water is salty. Most fresh water, or water without salt, is frozen in ice sheets around the North and South Poles. Only a tiny portion of Earth's water is unfrozen fresh water. People need this water for many things. Fresh water comes from lakes, rivers, and ground water, which are fed by rain and snow.

Assessment

1. What are Earth's three main layers?
2. What part of Earth's structure are oceans located on?

23

Forces on Earth's Surface

Key Ideas
- Forces such as wind, water, and ice shape Earth's surface.
- These forces produce a variety of different landforms.

Key Terms
- weathering
- valley
- erosion
- deposition
- plateau
- plain
- delta

Visual Glossary

Forces on Earth's surface wear down and reshape the land. Along with forces inside Earth, which you will read about later, forces on Earth's surface help create the landforms we see around us.

An eroded landscape in the southwestern United States. ▼

Wearing Away Earth's Surface

Weathering is a process that breaks rocks down into tiny pieces. There are two kinds of weathering: chemical weathering and mechanical weathering. In chemical weathering, rainwater or acids carried by rainwater dissolve rocks. In mechanical weathering, moving water, ice, or sometimes wind breaks rocks into little pieces. Mechanical weathering can happen after chemical weathering has weakened rocks.

Weathering helps create soil. Tiny pieces of rock combine with decayed animal and plant material to form soil. Soil and pieces of rock may undergo **erosion,** a process in which water, ice, or wind remove small pieces of rock. Soil is required to sustain plant and animal life, and for agriculture. Because of this, weathering is very important to human settlement patterns.

Shaping Landforms

Weathering and erosion have shaped many of Earth's landforms. These landforms include mountains and hills. Mountains are wide at the bottom and rise steeply to a narrow peak or ridge. Hills are lower than mountains and often have rounded tops. While forces within Earth create mountains, forces on Earth's surface wear them down. An area in which a certain type of landform is dominant is called a landform region.

The parts of mountains and hills that are left standing are the rocks that are hardest to wear away. Millions of years ago, the Appalachian Mountains in the eastern United States were as high as the Rocky Mountains of the western United States. Rain, snow, and wind wore the Appalachians down into much lower peaks.

Rebuilding Earth's Surface

When water, ice, and wind remove material, they deposit it farther downstream or downwind to create new landforms. **Deposition** is the process of depositing material eroded and carried by water, ice, or wind. Deposition creates landforms such as sandy beaches. **Plains,** or large areas of flat or gently rolling land, are often formed by the deposition of material carried downstream by rivers. Through deposition on the floor of the sea, rivers can create new land.

A **plateau** is a large, mostly flat area that rises above the surrounding land. At least one side of a plateau has a steep slope. At the top of this slope is usually a layer of rock that is hard to wear down.

Valleys are stretches of low land between mountains or hills. Rivers often form valleys where there are rocks that are easy to wear away.

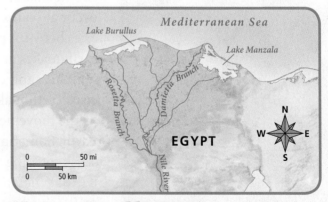

This map shows the **delta** of the Nile River in Egypt. Deltas are flat plains built on the seabed where a river fans out and deposits material over many years.

Assessment

1. How is erosion different from weathering?
2. How do plains form from the tops of worn-down mountains?

25

The volcano Kilauea in Hawaii spews molten rock. ▼

Core Concepts 2.5

Forces Inside Earth

Key Ideas	• Movements of hot, soft rock in Earth's mantle affect Earth's surface, forming volcanoes and pushing continents together or apart.

Key Terms
• plate tectonics • plate
• magma • fault

Visual Glossary

Forces deep inside Earth are constantly reshaping its surface. The theory of **plate tectonics** states that Earth's crust is made up of huge blocks called **plates.** Plates include continents or parts of continents, along with parts of the ocean floor. Earth's continental plates sit on streams of molten, nearly melted, rock called **magma.** Some scientists believe magma acts as a conveyor belt, moving the plates in different directions. Plates may move only an inch or two (a few centimeters) a year.

This movement slowly builds mountains. When two plates of crust push against each other, the pressure makes the crust bend to form steep mountains.

Earthquakes and Volcanoes

Earthquakes occur when plates slide against each other. They often occur at seams in Earth's crust called **faults**, often near the boundaries between plates. Earthquakes cause the ground to shake. Some earthquakes are too small for people to feel. But others can destroy buildings and cause great harm. For example, the 1906 San Francisco earthquake killed more than 3000 people.

The movement of continental plates creates great pressure inside Earth. Sometimes this pressure forces magma up through Earth's crust, forming volcanoes. Volcanoes spew magma from inside Earth. When magma erupts out of a volcano, it is called lava. Ash, rocks, and poisonous gasses also explode out of volcanoes during an eruption. Volcanic eruptions can be very dangerous for people. But volcanoes also serve an important purpose. When lava cools, new land forms. Undersea volcanoes even grow into islands after thousands of years of eruptions.

26

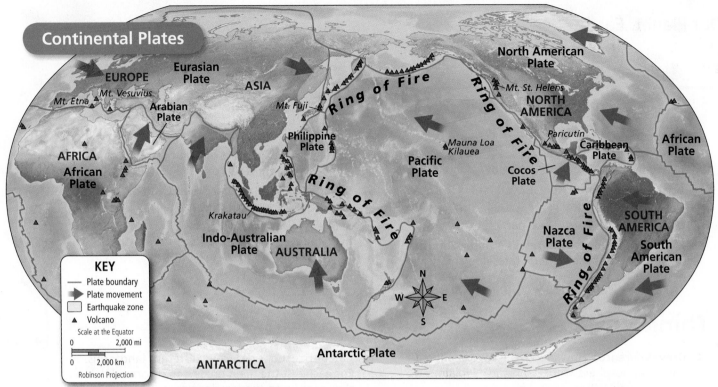

Continental Plates

KEY
— Plate boundary
→ Plate movement
☐ Earthquake zone
▲ Volcano

Scale at the Equator
0 ——— 2,000 mi
0 ——— 2,000 km
Robinson Projection

The Plates of Earth's Crust The map above shows how Earth's plates fit together today. It also shows the directions in which plates are moving. As you can see on the map, earthquakes and volcanoes occur along plate edges.

Natural Hazards

Volcanoes and earthquakes are examples of natural disasters. They are also called natural hazards, meaning dangers. Other natural hazards include hurricanes, tornados, landslides, and floods.

These events threaten lives and property. But people can take steps to prepare for natural disasters, so that damage will not be as severe when they strike. For example, architects can design buildings that will not collapse when the ground shakes. Local governments can set routes for people to leave affected areas during a hurricane. Citizens can practice what to do during an earthquake, and keep emergency supplies at home.

Preparing for a Natural Hazard
Above: Damage caused by an earthquake
Right: Students hide under their desks for an earthquake drill

Assessment

1. How do forces inside Earth shape Earth's surface?

2. What are some ways people prepare for natural hazards?

27

Part 2 Assessment

Key Terms and Ideas

1. **Compare and Contrast** What is the difference between an **equinox** and a **solstice**?

2. **Analyze Cause and Effect** How does Earth's **orbit** influence climate on Earth?

3. **Describe** How is Earth's **axis** part of its **rotation**?

4. **Identify Main Ideas and Details** What is sunrise? In which part of the United States does sunrise occur earliest?

5. **Categorize** Which part of Earth's structure is the thinnest? Where is this part?

6. **Summarize** How do **weathering** and **erosion** shape Earth's surface?

7. **Sequence** Describe the process that causes movement of the continents.

Think Critically

8. **Draw Inferences** How would our lives change if Earth's atmosphere were damaged? Explain.

9. **Draw Conclusions** Which parts of Earth's orbit are best for warm-weather activities in the Northern Hemisphere? For cold-weather activities? Explain using the terms *equinox* and *solstice*.

10. **Ask Questions** To choose a safe location for a new town, what questions about Earth's structure and movement would you ask? Explain.

11. **Categorize** Consider three different landforms. For each, list the main process that formed it. Was that process on the interior or exterior of Earth? How are the different processes related?

Identify

Identify the time in each location if it is noon GMT.

12. **New York, New York**

13. **Houston, Texas**

14. **Denver, Colorado**

15. **Los Angeles, California**

16. **Anchorage, Alaska**

17. **Honolulu, Hawaii**

18. Compare the time of sunrise in New York, New York, with that in Houston, Texas. Which is earlier and which is later? Are these cities in the same time zone?

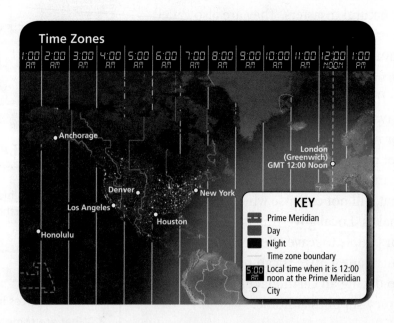

Time Zones

KEY
Prime Meridian
Day
Night
Time zone boundary
Local time when it is 12:00 noon at the Prime Meridian
City

Journal Activity

Fill in the graphic organizer in your Student Journal.

Demonstrate Understanding Complete the Sum-It-Up activity in your journal to demonstrate your understanding of Our Planet, Earth. After you complete the activity, discuss your diagram with your class. Be sure to support your diagram with information from the lessons.

21st Century Learning

Make a Difference

Think about earthquake or volcano safety in your community or a community like yours in an earthquake or volcano danger area. Develop ideas to raise community awareness of the dangers and the ways people can avoid them. Share your ideas on a Web page, poster, or handout.

Document-Based Questions

Success Tracker™
Online at myworldgeography.com

Use your knowledge of our planet Earth and Documents A and B to answer Questions 1–3.

Document A

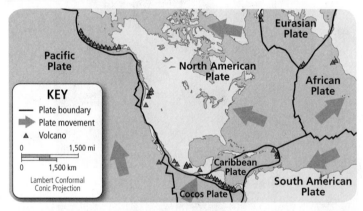

Document B

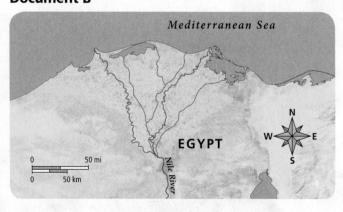

1. Why are there volcanoes where the North American Plate meets the Pacific Plate?

   A Erosion breaks down the land where plates meet.

   B Magma is forced through Earth's surface at plate boundaries.

   C Earth's rotation causes the sun to shine directly on this area.

   D Land in this area has been shaped by chemical weather.

2. How is the natural feature depicted on this map formed?

   A Tectonic plates push land upward.

   B A river flows into the ocean, depositing material on the seabed.

   C Wind and rain wear down mountains.

   D A river carves out a valley.

3. **Writing Task** Suppose a volcano forms on the ocean floor and grows thousands of feet upwards. Use that information and Document A to explain the many islands between Asia and Australia.

my worldgeography.com   Self-Test

Climates and Ecosystems

Hurricane Katrina spins toward New Orleans.

New Orleans residents trapped by floodwaters wave for help. ▲

Katrina caused severe destruction.

Airin McGhee

HURRICANE KATRINA STRIKES

Story by Miles Lemaire for myWorld Geography

Powerful tropical storms sweep across the southeastern United States and the Gulf Coast nearly every year. At first, teenager Airin McGhee thought that Hurricane Katrina would be just like any other storm. She was wrong. Instead, Katrina was so powerful that it flooded much of Airin's city, New Orleans, Louisiana.

When weather forecasters and government officials first started warning New Orleans residents about Hurricane Katrina in late August 2005, Airin was not worried. "Every year we would get the warning and up until that point it just never happened," she said. "Nobody expected Katrina to be like it was."

Fortunately, Airin and her mother and sister decided to leave New Orleans before the storm arrived. They drove through heavy traffic to Jackson, Mississippi, a city about 190 miles north of New Orleans. While they waited for the storm to pass, they feared the worst for their home, their city, and the friends and neighbors they had left behind.

Hurricane Katrina hit New Orleans on August 29. Its powerful winds ripped buildings apart and tore trees out of the ground. Worse, Katrina's winds and rain broke the levees, or raised flood barriers, that had protected much of the area. Millions of gallons of water poured through the broken levees into the city.

After Katrina ended, Airin's family tried to get news from friends in New Orleans. "I was really devastated for a while," Airin says, "because the cell phones were really bad and I just had all these thoughts of, 'Is this person okay? Is this person okay?' For weeks all … numbers had a busy signal and it was hard to get in touch with people."

When Airin's family was finally able to return to New Orleans, they saw the results of Katrina's destructive power in person. Years later, Airin's memories of what they saw are still strong. "We had six feet of water in our house," Airin said. "We lost everything. We lost my mom's car and my car, our entire house, including all the furniture and clothes … I pretty much lost everything."

It wasn't long before Airin's family was able to find another place to live, but they still feel the effects of the storm years later.

"I'll just never forget Katrina," Airin says. "It wiped away all my memories. I lost my high school diploma, all my pictures and things that you might take for granted. I collected things like my baby teeth and blanket. All those things are just gone."

When Airin thinks about how the storm affected her, she says, "It really taught me to value sentimental things. It changed how I do certain things, because now I want to capture every moment, and I find myself taking pictures of everything."

31

Climate and Weather

| **Key Ideas** | • Different areas of the world have different weather patterns. |
| | • Weather and climate are described using precipitation and temperature. |

Key Terms • weather • climate • precipitation • temperature

 **Visual Glossary**

The climate of Iquitos (ee KEE tohs), Peru, is hot and wet year-round. ▼

You have learned about the powerful forces that shape Earth, including global movements, water, and sunlight. These forces also shape Earth's weather patterns. Weather patterns can vary widely from one region to another.

Weather or Climate?

Do you look outside before you choose your clothing in the morning? If so, you are checking the weather. **Weather** is the condition of the air and sky at a certain time. Or do you choose your clothing based on the normal weather for the time of year in the place where you live? If so, you dress according to your local climate. **Climate** is the average weather of a place over many years.

How you feel about today's weather may depend on your local climate. If you live in a place with a wet climate, you may be unhappy to see rainy weather, because your climate means that you get rain frequently. On the other hand, if you live in a dry climate where water is scarce, you might be very happy to see rainy weather.

Rain is a form of **precipitation,** which is water that falls to the ground as rain, snow, sleet, or hail. **Temperature** is a measure of how hot or cold the air is. Precipitation and temperature are the main ways to describe both daily weather and long-term climate.

Comparing Climates

One way to understand and compare climates is to use climate graphs. Climate graphs show the average climate for a place for each month of a year. A climate graph has a curved line that shows average temperatures. It has bars that show average monthly precipitation. The next page has two examples of climate graphs.

Chicago, Illinois

This is a climate graph of Chicago, Illinois, a city in the north central United States. It shows that Chicago has cold winters, hot summers, and moderate precipitation year-round. Notice that the line for temperature is much higher in July than it is in January. However, the heights of the bars for precipitation do not change much.

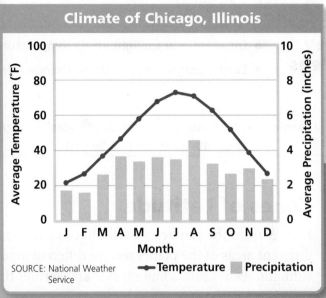

Climate of Chicago, Illinois

SOURCE: National Weather Service —— Temperature ▪ Precipitation

Bangalore, India

In some parts of the world, precipitation changes greatly from season to season. This is a climate graph of Bangalore, India. It shows that most of Bangalore's rain falls during a rainy season that lasts from May to October. Almost no precipitation falls from January to March.

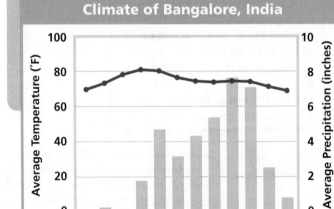

Climate of Bangalore, India

SOURCE: World Meteorological Organization —— Temperature ▪ Precipitation

Assessment

1. How is climate different from weather?

2. How would you describe your region's climate?

Core Concepts 3.2

Temperature

Key Ideas
- Differences in sunlight affect temperatures at different latitudes.
- Earth's temperature patterns change from season to season.

Key Terms
- polar zone
- temperate zone
- high latitudes
- middle latitudes
- tropics
- altitude
- low latitudes

→ Visual Glossary

Zones of Latitude

Energy from the sun heats Earth. Because of the tilt of Earth's axis, different areas of the planet receive different amounts of direct sunlight. As a result, some regions are warmer than others.

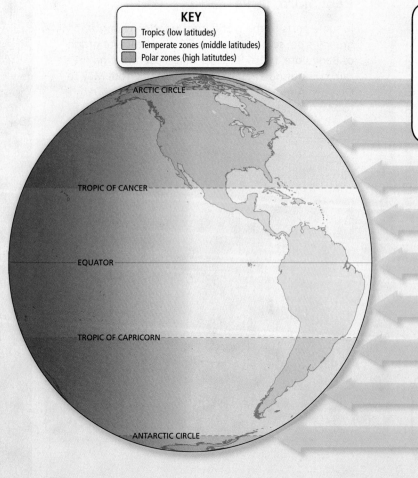

KEY
- Tropics (low latitudes)
- Temperate zones (middle latitudes)
- Polar zones (high latitutdes)

ARCTIC CIRCLE
TROPIC OF CANCER
EQUATOR
TROPIC OF CAPRICORN
ANTARCTIC CIRCLE

The **polar zones,** also known as the **high latitudes,** are the areas north of the Arctic Circle and south of the Antarctic Circle. In the polar zones, the sun is below the horizon for part of the year and near the horizon the rest of the year. Temperatures stay cool to bitterly cold.

The **tropics,** or the **low latitudes,** are the areas between the Tropic of Cancer and the Tropic of Capricorn. In the low latitudes, the sun is overhead or nearly overhead all year long. In this region, it is usually hot.

The **temperate zones,** or the **middle latitudes,** are the areas between the high and low latitudes. These areas lie between the Tropic of Cancer and the Arctic Circle in the Northern Hemisphere and between the Tropic of Capricorn and the Antarctic Circle in the Southern Hemisphere. They have a hot summer, a cold winter, and a moderate spring and fall.

34

Seasonal Changes in Temperature

Because of the tilt of Earth's axis, temperature patterns change from season to season. The maps below show the world's average monthly temperatures in January and July.

In January, it is winter in the Northern Hemisphere and summer in the Southern Hemisphere. In July, the seasons are reversed. Notice that temperatures are cooler year-round over western South America and other areas. The lower temperatures are due to the high altitude of these regions. **Altitude** is height above sea level. As altitude increases, temperature drops.

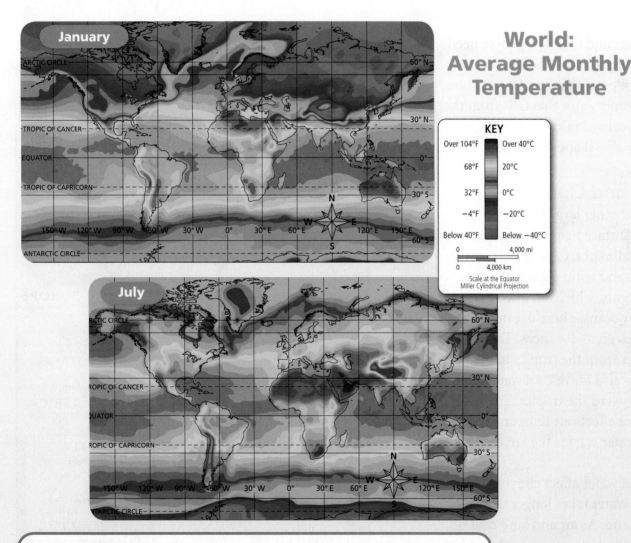

World: Average Monthly Temperature

KEY

Over 104°F	Over 40°C
68°F	20°C
32°F	0°C
−4°F	−20°C
Below 40°F	Below −40°C

0   4,000 mi
0   4,000 km

Scale at the Equator
Miller Cylindrical Projection

Assessment

1. Why are most of the tropics, or the low latitudes, warm all year?

2. How does the tilt of Earth's axis explain changes in temperature from one season to another in the temperate zones?

35

Water and Climate

Key Ideas
- Water affects climate and weather.
- Water is always moving in the process called the water cycle.

Key Terms • water cycle • evaporation

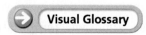
Visual Glossary

Like plants and animals, people need fresh water to live. All fresh water comes from precipitation. As you know, precipitation is water that falls from the sky in the form of rain, snow, sleet, or hail. Water also shapes climates.

Oceans and Climate

Oceans and other large bodies of water on Earth's surface help spread Earth's heat and shape climates. Global temperature differences and wind patterns create ocean currents, which act like large rivers within the oceans. These ocean currents move across great distances. They move warm water from the tropics toward the poles. They also move cool water from the poles toward the tropics. The water's temperature affects air temperature near it. Warm water warms the air; cool water chills it.

Bodies of water affect climate in other ways, too. Water takes longer to heat or cool than land. As air and land heat up in summer, water remains cooler. Wind blowing over the cool water helps cool land nearby. So in summer, areas near an ocean or lake will be cooler than inland

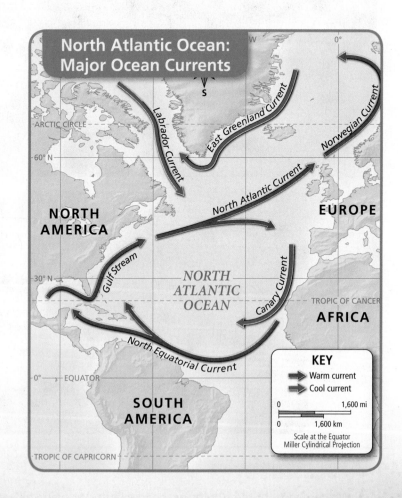

North Atlantic Ocean: Major Ocean Currents

NORTH AMERICA

EUROPE

AFRICA

SOUTH AMERICA

NORTH ATLANTIC OCEAN

Labrador Current
East Greenland Current
Norwegian Current
North Atlantic Current
Gulf Stream
Canary Current
North Equatorial Current

ARCTIC CIRCLE
60° N
30° N
0° — EQUATOR
TROPIC OF CANCER
TROPIC OF CAPRICORN

KEY
→ Warm current
→ Cool current

0 — 1,600 mi
0 — 1,600 km
Scale at the Equator
Miller Cylindrical Projection

36

areas at the same latitude and altitude. In the winter, on the other hand, water remains warmer than land. So in winter, areas near oceans or lakes are warmer than inland areas.

For example, in the Atlantic Ocean, the Gulf Stream, a warm current, travels northeast from the tropics. The Gulf Stream and the North Atlantic Current carry warm water all the way to Western Europe. That warm water helps give Western Europe a much milder climate than other regions at the same latitude.

The Water Cycle

Earth's water is always moving in a process called the water cycle, shown in the illustration below. The **water cycle** is the movement of water from Earth's surface into the atmosphere and back. As water heats up, it moves from rivers, oceans, and lakes up into the air. As it cools, it falls to Earth's surface and flows back to rivers, oceans and lakes. The water cycle includes precipitation and evaporation. **Evaporation** is the process in which a liquid changes to a gas.

The Water Cycle

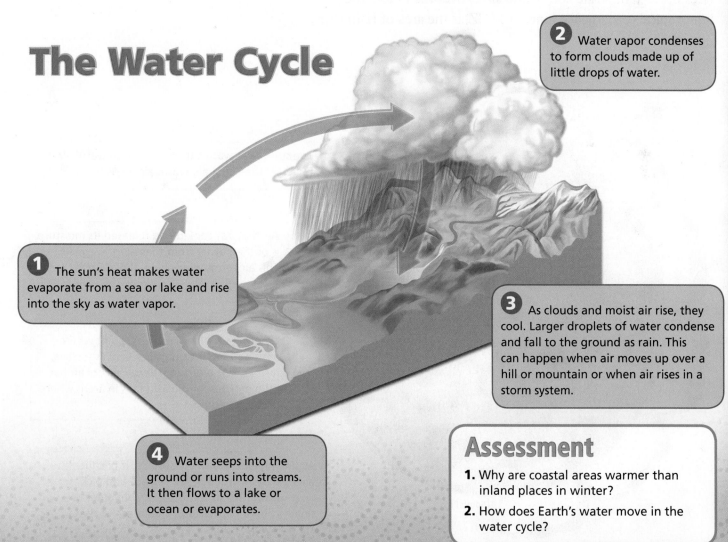

2 Water vapor condenses to form clouds made up of little drops of water.

1 The sun's heat makes water evaporate from a sea or lake and rise into the sky as water vapor.

3 As clouds and moist air rise, they cool. Larger droplets of water condense and fall to the ground as rain. This can happen when air moves up over a hill or mountain or when air rises in a storm system.

4 Water seeps into the ground or runs into streams. It then flows to a lake or ocean or evaporates.

Assessment

1. Why are coastal areas warmer than inland places in winter?
2. How does Earth's water move in the water cycle?

37

Air Circulation and Precipitation

Key Ideas
- Wind and air currents move heat and moisture between different parts of Earth.
- Air movement leads to precipitation and intense storms.

Key Terms • intertropical convergence zone • tropical cyclone • hurricane • tornado

 **Visual Glossary**

Belts of rising and sinking air form a pattern around Earth. Air rises near the Equator, sinks at the edge of the tropics, rises in the temperate zones, and sinks over the poles. The **intertropical convergence zone,** or ITCZ, is the area of rising air near the Equator.

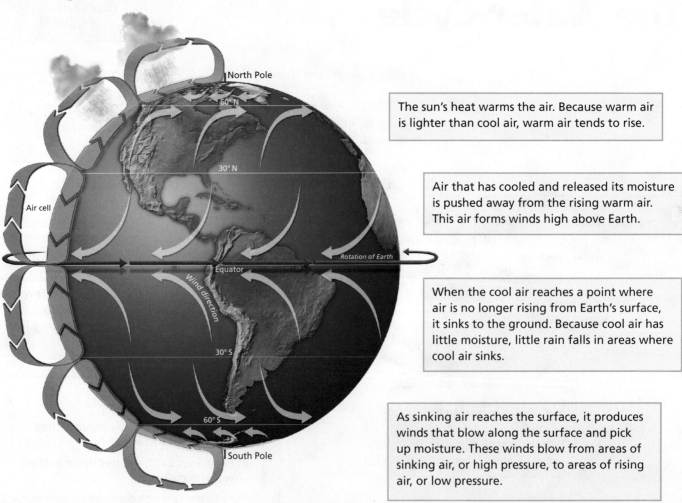

The sun's heat warms the air. Because warm air is lighter than cool air, warm air tends to rise.

Air that has cooled and released its moisture is pushed away from the rising warm air. This air forms winds high above Earth.

When the cool air reaches a point where air is no longer rising from Earth's surface, it sinks to the ground. Because cool air has little moisture, little rain falls in areas where cool air sinks.

As sinking air reaches the surface, it produces winds that blow along the surface and pick up moisture. These winds blow from areas of sinking air, or high pressure, to areas of rising air, or low pressure.

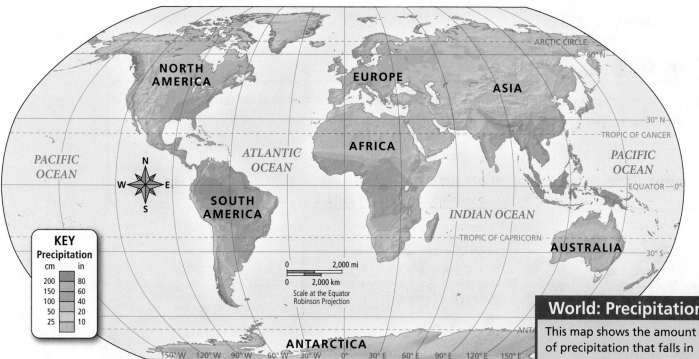

KEY
Precipitation

cm	in
200	80
150	60
100	40
50	20
25	10

0   2,000 mi
0   2,000 km
Scale at the Equator
Robinson Projection

World: Precipitation

This map shows the amount of precipitation that falls in an average year. Precipitation is heaviest near the Equator, where air usually rises. It is also heavy along coastlines, where moist air blows onshore and is forced to rise. Precipitation is lightest where cool air sinks near the poles and at the edges of the tropics, where deserts are normally found.

Raging Storms

Most storms occur when two air masses of different temperatures or moisture contents come together. Some storms bring small amounts of rain or snow, while others bring heavy wind and rain, causing great destruction.

A **tropical cyclone** is an intense rainstorm with strong winds that forms over oceans in the tropics. A **hurricane** is a cyclone that forms over the Atlantic Ocean. These storms can cause much damage. A **tornado** is a swirling funnel of wind that can reach 300 miles (500 km) per hour. Tornadoes can be more dangerous than hurricanes, but they affect smaller areas.

Most other storms are less dangerous. In winter, blizzards dump snow on parts of North America. Severe rainstorms and thunderstorms strike North America most often in spring and summer.

Assessment

1. Why is precipitation heaviest near the Equator?
2. How do physical processes such as air circulation and precipitation affect humans?

Tornadoes can cause severe damage.

39

Core Concepts 3.5

Types of Climate

Key Ideas
- Temperature, precipitation, and wind interact to form global patterns.
- Earth has a number of different climate regions.

Key Terms • tropical wet • tropical wet and dry • humid subtropical • maritime • subarctic • semiarid • arid • tundra

→ **Visual Glossary**

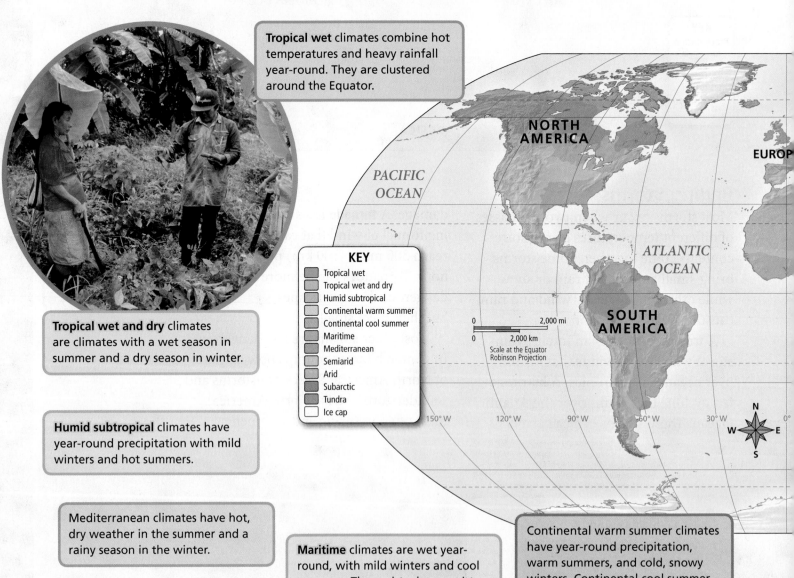

Tropical wet climates combine hot temperatures and heavy rainfall year-round. They are clustered around the Equator.

Tropical wet and dry climates are climates with a wet season in summer and a dry season in winter.

Humid subtropical climates have year-round precipitation with mild winters and hot summers.

Mediterranean climates have hot, dry weather in the summer and a rainy season in the winter.

Maritime climates are wet year-round, with mild winters and cool summers. They exist where moist winds blow onshore.

Continental warm summer climates have year-round precipitation, warm summers, and cold, snowy winters. Continental cool summer climates are similar, but they have generally lower temperatures.

KEY
- Tropical wet
- Tropical wet and dry
- Humid subtropical
- Continental warm summer
- Continental cool summer
- Maritime
- Mediterranean
- Semiarid
- Arid
- Subarctic
- Tundra
- Ice cap

NORTH AMERICA

EUROP

PACIFIC OCEAN

ATLANTIC OCEAN

SOUTH AMERICA

0 — 2,000 mi
0 — 2,000 km
Scale at the Equator
Robinson Projection

150° W 120° W 90° W 60° W 30° W 0°

40

You have already learned about the most important shapers of climate: temperature, precipitation, and wind. These factors form global patterns. For example, temperatures are warmest in and around the tropics and are coolest close to the poles. Precipitation is greatest near the Equator. These patterns of temperature and precipitation create world climate regions. Climate regions are areas that share a similar climate.

Subarctic climates have limited precipitation, cool summers, and very cold winters.

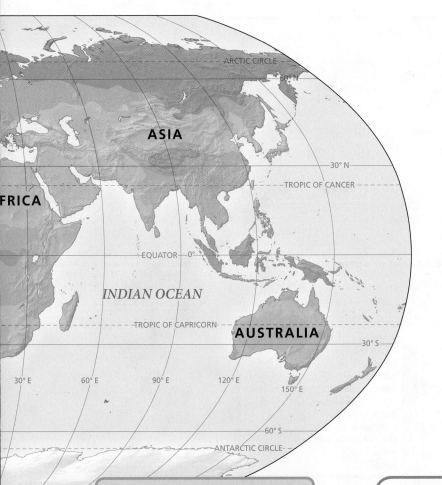

Semiarid, or dry, climates and **arid**, or very dry, desert climates occur where there is steadily sinking air.

Tundra climates have cool summers and bitterly cold, dry winters. Close to the poles, ice caps, or permanent sheets of ice covering land or sea, have bitter cold and dry climates year-round.

Assessment

1. In the winter, what kind of weather would you expect in a continental warm summer climate?
2. What factors explain the locations of Earth's tropical wet and tropical wet and dry climates?

41

Tropical or Subtropical Forest

Steady hot temperatures and moist air support the rich ecosystems known as tropical rain forests.

Temperate Forest

Moist temperate climates support thick forests of **deciduous trees,** or trees that lose their leaves in the fall. Some temperate forests include a mix of deciduous and ever-green trees.

Subarctic Forest

Coniferous trees are trees that produce cones to carry seeds. They also have needles. These features protect trees through the cold, dry winters of subarc-tic climates.

Tropical or Subtropical Grassland or Savanna

A **savanna** is a park-like land-scape of grasslands with scat-tered trees that can survive dry spells. Savannas are found in tropical areas with dry seasons.

Temperate Grassland and Brush

Vast grasslands cover regions that get more rain than deserts but too little to support forests.

42

Core Concepts 3.6

Ecosystems

Key Idea

- An ecosystem is a network of living things that depend on one another and their environment for survival.

Key Terms

- deciduous tree
- coniferous tree
- savanna
- ecosystem

→ **Visual Glossary**

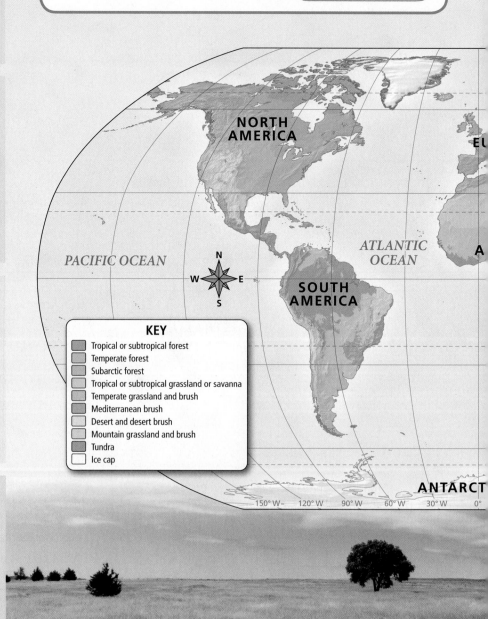

KEY

- Tropical or subtropical forest
- Temperate forest
- Subarctic forest
- Tropical or subtropical grassland or savanna
- Temperate grassland and brush
- Mediterranean brush
- Desert and desert brush
- Mountain grassland and brush
- Tundra
- Ice cap

The connections between living things and the environment form ecosystems. An **ecosystem** is a group of plants and animals that depend on each other and their environment for survival. Ecosystems can be small or large. The map below shows Earth's major types of ecosystems.

Ecosystems can change over time due to physical processes or human activities. For example, a lack of rain in a temperate forest ecosystem might kill off many plants and animals. The building of a city is an example of a human activity that changes an original ecosystem.

Mediterranean Brush

Shrubs and other low plants in Mediterranean climates have to hold water from winter rains to survive hot, dry summers.

Desert and Desert Brush

Dry semiarid areas and deserts with some rain support animals and low-lying desert plants. These plants need little water and can live in extreme temperatures. The driest desert areas have little or no plant life.

Mountain Grassland and Brush

In mountain grassland and brush regions, vegetation depends on elevation, since temperatures drop as altitude increases.

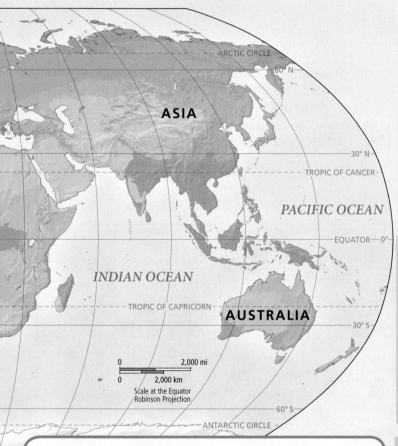

Tundra

The tundra is an area of cold climate and low-lying plants. Here, grasses grow and low shrubs bloom during brief, cool summers. Animals of the tundra are able to live with cold temperatures and scarce food.

Assessment

1. How do climate differences affect plant and animal life?
2. What features of the plants and animals in your own region let them live in your region's climate?

Ice Cap

Thick ice caps form around the poles, with their year-round climates of extreme cold. No plants can live on this ice.

43

Climates and Ecosystems

Part 3 Assessment

Key Terms and Ideas

1. **Summarize** What is a region's **weather**? What is a region's **climate**?

2. **Identify** What are the three most important factors of climate?

3. **Compare and Contrast** How do temperatures in the **low latitudes** differ from temperatures in the **middle latitudes**?

4. **Sequence** Rank these climates in terms of amount of precipitation, from most precipitation to least precipitation: **subarctic, arid, tropical wet.**

5. **Compare and Contrast** How are **deciduous trees** different from **coniferous trees**?

6. **Connect** What is the role of air temperature in the **water cycle**?

7. **Describe** How does the physical environment affect humans?

Think Critically

8. **Categorize** Explain in one sentence how today's weather is related to your region's climate.

9. **Predict** How would winter temperatures differ between two cities on the same continent at the same latitude, one on the coast and one inland?

10. **Draw Inferences** Use what you know about the amount of moisture in cool air to predict the level of precipitation in a tundra climate.

11. **Draw Conclusions** How does altitude affect temperature in different latitudes?

Identify

Answer the following questions based on the map.

12. What do the arrows on this map show?

13. In which zone of latitude is the West Wind Drift?

14. Is the North Atlantic Current warm or cool?

15. Is the California Current warm or cool?

16. Is the Brazil Current located in the Northern Hemisphere or the Southern Hemisphere?

17. Does the Benguela Current bring cool water to the polar zones or to the tropics?

18. What important parallel of latitude does the Kuroshio Current cross?

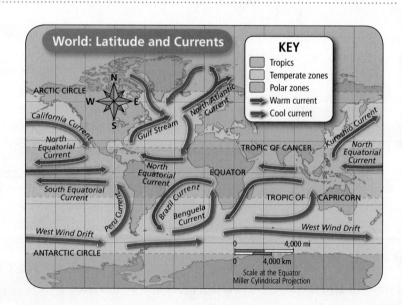

44

Journal Activity

Fill in the graphic organizer in your Student Journal.

Demonstrate Your Understanding Complete the Sum-It-Up activity in your journal to demonstrate your understanding of climates and ecosystems. After you complete the activity, discuss your predictions with a partner. Be sure to support your predictions with information from the lessons.

21st Century Learning

Give an Effective Presentation

Research and deliver an illustrated oral presentation on the features of one of the ecosystems described in Lesson 6. Be sure to address the following topics:
- Climate characteristics
- Effect of climate on animal and plant life
- Effect of climate on human life, including the economy

Document-Based Questions

Success ☆ Tracker™
Online at myworldgeography.com

Use your knowledge of climates and ecosystems and Documents A and B to answer Questions 1–3.

Document A

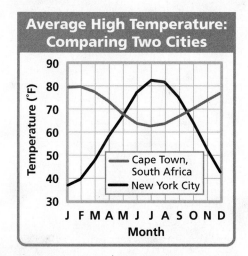

Document B

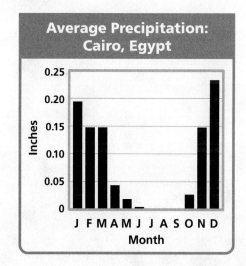

1. Examine Document A. Which of the following statements is true?

   A New York City and Cape Town are located in the same hemisphere.

   B New York City is in the Southern Hemisphere, while Cape Town is in the Northern Hemisphere.

   C New York City is in the Northern Hemisphere, while Cape Town is in the Southern Hemisphere.

   D none of the above

2. Examine Document B. Judging from the average precipitation Cairo receives, in which of the following climates is it most likely to be located?

   A tropical wet

   B maritime

   C arid

   D humid subtropical

3. **Writing Task** Using information from Document A as evidence, describe how a location's hemisphere affects its seasons.

my worldgeography.com   Self-Test

45

Human-Environment Interaction

Young people support clean energy sources.

Oil leaks from an abandoned oil barrel in Alaska. ▲

46

Environmental workers clean up an oil spill.

Lauren Hexilon

MAKING A DIFFERENCE

Story by Miles Lemaire for myWorld Geography

Lauren Hexilon wants to save the world.

Lauren has wanted to protect the environment for as long as she can remember. After she graduated from college recently, Lauren decided to go to work for the U.S. Environmental Protection Agency (EPA).

The EPA was an obvious choice for Lauren. After all, the organization's main focus is to protect human health and the environment. Today Lauren works with people who help protect public health and the environment in many ways. Some of their work deals with hazardous waste spills around the country. Hazardous waste includes chemicals, radioactive materials, and other waste dangerous to humans, wildlife, and the environment.

Cleaning up hazardous waste can be "a very long process," Lauren says. To dispose of waste safely, she explains, "you have to follow certain rules and procedures, so it takes a while to see a project from its beginning to its end."

Lauren doesn't clean up pollution and hazardous waste herself. Still, she helps protect the environment at her job each day. She spends much of her time working with young people to teach them about environmental issues. Raising public awareness is important, she says.

Right now Lauren is working with the University of North Texas on projects that help people understand threats to the environment. She is also helping to create an environmental video conference. This conference will connect young people from countries around the world. Lauren likes these projects because they teach people to protect the environment. Plus, she says, she gets to see the results of her work quickly.

But you don't have to work for the EPA to help prevent pollution and protect the environment. Lauren says that each of us makes choices every day that have an impact on the environment, whether we realize it or not. Take conserving energy, for example. "Flipping on a light switch, that's an environmental impact," says Lauren. "If you leave the light on, you're wasting electricity."

So what does Lauren think that young people should know about human interaction with the environment? Simply this: She would like each of us to think about how our actions affect the environment. Whenever possible, Lauren says, try to make good choices about your actions. For example, consider riding a bicycle or taking public transportation instead of driving in a car.

In fact, everyone can take small steps to improve the way they interact with the environment. We should think about "all the little things" we do each day, says Lauren. As she points out, "The little things add up."

47

Core Concepts 4.1

Environment and Resources

Key Ideas
- People depend on the environment for food, water, energy, and other natural resources.
- Some resources are replaced by Earth over time, but others are not.

Key Terms
- natural resource
- renewable resource
- nonrenewable resource
- fossil fuel

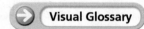 Visual Glossary

Humans depend on their natural environment to survive. We need the environment to provide energy, water, food, and other materials. In prehistoric times, people lived in areas where they could hunt, gather food, and find fresh water. Later, people settled where they found pasture for their livestock or fertile soils and sufficient water for farming. Today, rapid transportation and other technologies allow people to be less dependent on their immediate environment. However, people still need access to resources.

Natural Resources

Water is just one example of a **natural resource,** or a useful material found in the environment. People depend on many kinds of natural resources. These resources can be divided into two types: renewable and nonrenewable resources.

People use many natural resources in their daily lives. Above, a young woman in Chad uses soil to build a shelter. Below, German workers use metals to build an automobile.

48

Major Natural Resources			
Resource	Type	Formation	Major Uses
Soil	Renewable	Formed from rocks and organic material broken down by natural processes	Agriculture
Water	Renewable	Renewed through the water cycle	Drinking, agriculture, washing, transportation
Plants	Renewable	Usually grow from seeds; require water and sunlight	Food, lumber, clothing, paper
Animals	Renewable	Formed through natural reproduction; require water and food	Food, agricultural labor, transportation, clothing
Fossil fuels	Nonrenewable	Formed over millions of years from plant and animal material	Energy, plastics, chemicals
Minerals	Nonrenewable	Formed through a variety of natural geologic processes	Automobile parts, electronics, and many other human-made products

A **renewable resource** is a resource that Earth or people can replace. Examples of renewable resources include water, plants, and animals. All of these resources can be replaced over time if they are used wisely. For example, if you cut down a tree, another one can grow in its place. When dead plants decay, their nutrients increase soil fertility.

A **nonrenewable resource** is a resource that cannot be replaced in a relatively short period of time. Nonrenewable resources include nonliving things such as minerals, metal ores, and fossil fuels. **Fossil fuels** are nonrenewable resources formed over millions of years from the remains of plants and animals. Coal, natural gas, and petroleum are important fossil fuels. When nonrenewable resources such as fossil fuels are used up, they are gone.

Energy Resources

Sources of energy are important for human activity. Some sources, such as wind and sunlight, are renewable. Today, we mostly rely on nonrenewable energy resources such as coal and petroleum. Because these sources are nonrenewable, Earth will eventually run out of them.

Some countries have large supplies of petroleum and are able to export it, or sell it to other countries. Most countries, however, must buy petroleum and other energy resources from other countries.

Assessment

1. What do people need from the physical environment?
2. How are renewable and nonrenewable natural resources formed?

49

Land Use

Key Ideas
- People use land in different ways.
- Land use can change over time.

Key Terms • colonization • industrialization • suburb

→ **Visual Glossary**

The ways people use land are affected by both the natural environment and culture. In many regions, land use has changed over time.

Reasons for Land Use

How people use land depends partly on the environment. For example, people living in temperate climates with fertile soil may use land mainly for farming. People in arctic areas may use land mainly for hunting. Even in similar environments, however, people may use land differently because they have different customs and ways of life.

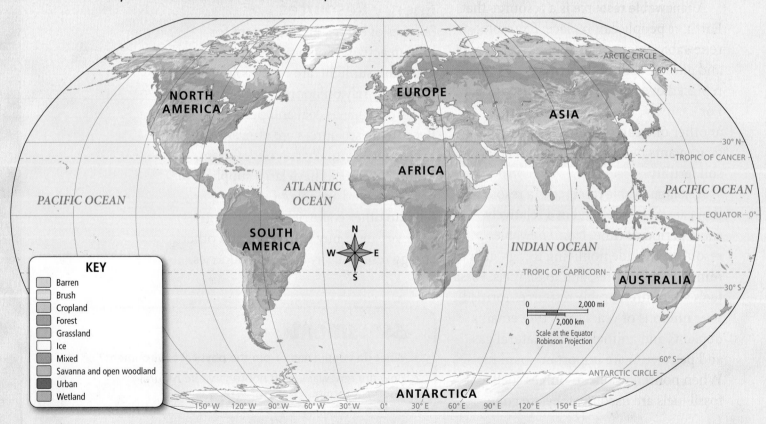

KEY
- Barren
- Brush
- Cropland
- Forest
- Grassland
- Ice
- Mixed
- Savanna and open woodland
- Urban
- Wetland

Scale at the Equator
Robinson Projection

Changes in Land Use

Land use can change over time. For example, colonization has led to many changes in land use. **Colonization** is a movement of new settlers and their culture to an area. Settlers may change a region's landscape. For example, European colonists brought new crops and new ways of farming to the Americas, Africa, and Australia. These new ways led to dramatic changes in land use as Europeans cleared large areas of land for cropland and livestock pasture.

Since the 1800s, industrialization has changed landscapes in many countries. **Industrialization** is the development of machine-powered production and manufacturing. Large cities have grown around factories. Technology such as machines for clearing land and building roads has made it easier for people to change their environment. This environmental change has allowed the growth of suburbs. A **suburb** is a residential area on the edge of a city or large town.

In the United States and some other countries, most people live in cities or suburban areas. Although cities and suburbs cover a relatively small area, they are an important use of land. Land uses covering large areas include cropland, forests, and grassland.

Land use varies around the world. Above, Tokyo, Japan, is a large city with millions of residents. Below, these people from the Dominican Republic use land for agriculture.

A large portion of Rio de Janeiro, Brazil, is built on steep hills along the Atlantic Ocean. ▼

Assessment

1. How does land use vary from place to place and over time?
2. How have people adapted to and changed the environment?

51

People's Impact on the Environment

Key Ideas
- People affect the environment in many ways.
- People try to decrease the negative effects of using resources.

Key Terms • deforestation • biodiversity • pollution • spillover

 Visual Glossary

All people need food, water, clothing, and shelter. To meet these needs, people have to use materials from their environment. As a result, people have impacts on the environment in their daily lives.

Extracting Resources

People extract, or remove, many kinds of natural resources from the environment. For example, to get wood for building houses, people cut down trees. Advances in technology have allowed people to extract some resources more easily. For example, to get petroleum for fuel, people drill deep wells, sometimes far into the ocean floor.

Extracting resources can harm ecosystems and the environment. For example, cutting down too many trees can cause deforestation. **Deforestation** is the loss of forest cover in a region. Animals that live in the forest may suffer as a result. Drilling oil wells and transporting oil can lead to oil spills, which harm the land and water. Deforestation and producing oil can also reduce biodiversity. **Biodiversity** is the variety of living things in a region or ecosystem.

A bird is covered in oil from an oil spill in Spain. Oil spills and other pollution can affect land, water, and animals. ▼

52

Other Impacts

People also affect the environment by growing food or producing other goods and services. For example, new technology has allowed farmers to plow more land for crops. But when land is cleared, soil is loosened and can erode, or wash away.

People's activities can also produce **pollution,** or waste that makes the air, soil, or water less clean. For example, many farmers use chemicals called fertilizers and pesticides to help plants grow and to kill pests. These chemicals can help farmers produce more food. They can also harm the environment by causing pollution.

Pollution is a **spillover,** which is an effect on someone or something not involved in an activity. For example, air pollution affects everyone who breathes the polluted air, even people who did not cause the pollution.

Finding the Best Solution

People try to increase the positive and decrease the negative effects of using resources. For example, using a resource might lead to economic growth but also create pollution that needs to be reduced. Working together, people, governments, and businesses can try to use resources wisely. In some cases, governments limit land use to preserve the environment.

▲ These wind turbines in Canada convert wind energy into electricity.

Advances in technology can also help protect resources and the environment. One way of protecting the environment is for people to use vehicles that burn less fuel, such as hybrid cars. Vehicles that burn less fuel create less air pollution. People can also use clean energy sources, such as solar power and wind power. They are considered clean energy sources because they do not pollute the air.

Assessment

1. How have new technologies affected people's ability to change the environment?
2. How might future uses of technology affect Earth?

53

Part 4 Assessment

Key Terms and Ideas

1. **Identify** List two **fossil fuels.**
2. **Recall** What is an example of a **natural resource**?
3. **Discuss** How might **colonization** affect a region?
4. **Paraphrase** In your own words, describe the causes and effects of **deforestation.**

5. **Sequence** Explain how **suburbs** develop.
6. **Summarize** How do people use natural resources?
7. **Cause and Effect** If a company pollutes a river, what is one possible **spillover**?

Think Critically

8. **Draw Inferences** Give two examples of ways technology has made people less dependent on the environment around them.
9. **Analyze Cause and Effect** Imagine that your state's supply of fossil fuels was suddenly cut in half. How might this affect daily life in your state?

10. **Solve Problems** Explain what the following statement means: *While trees are a renewable resource, it often takes human effort to make them renewable.*
11. **Synthesize** Imagine that a large factory is about to be constructed on the edge of a rain forest. How might this factory affect the region's biodiversity?

Identify

Answer the following questions based on the map.

12. India is a former British colony. Why do you think it was a valuable colony for Britain?
13. What natural resources are found in India?
14. What geographic features could also be natural resources?
15. How do you think land might be used in the Himalayas?
16. How do you think land might be used along the coast?
17. What environmental problems might use of India's natural resources cause?
18. How might altitude affect where people live in India?

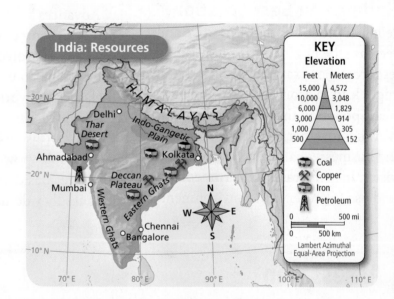

Journal Activity

Answer the questions in your Student Journal.

Demonstrate Your Understanding Complete the Sum-It-Up activity in your journal to demonstrate your understanding of human–environment interaction. After you complete the activity, discuss your answers in a small group. Be sure to support your answers with information from the lessons.

21st Century Learning

Search for Information on the Internet

Pollution can cause many harmful effects. Use online resources to research some of the effects of pollution and present your findings in a poster. When researching, remember the following:
- Use reputable Web sites, particularly those with addresses ending in *.gov* or *.edu*.
- Identify the site's author and check for bias.

Document-Based Questions

Success ⭐ Tracker™
Online at myworldgeography.com

Use your knowledge of human–environment interaction and Documents A and B to answer Questions 1–3.

Document A

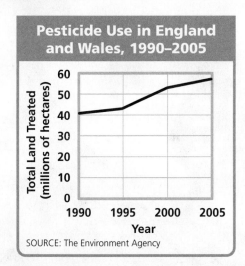

Pesticide Use in England and Wales, 1990–2005

SOURCE: The Environment Agency

Document B

1. **Examine** Document A. How has pesticide use changed in England and Wales in recent years?

   A It has increased.

   B It has decreased.

   C It has stopped completely.

   D It has not changed.

2. **Examine** Document B. Which of the following statements is true?

   A Major cities are spread out evenly across Massachusetts.

   B Most major cities are located far from Boston.

   C Most major cities are near Boston.

   D The location of Boston does not appear to have affected the locations of other cities.

3. **Writing Task** How might settlement and land use in Massachusetts be different if Boston were not its largest city? Explain your answer.

my worldgeography.com Self-Test

55

Economics and Geography

Surf shops are common in southern California.

Chris's childhood love of surfing helped inspire his first business.

56

Chris's business specializes in Web site design.

Chris Kerstner

An Extraordinary Entrepreneur

Story by Miles Lemaire for myWorld Geography

Chris Kerstner is still in his early twenties, but he has already created and successfully run four companies. In fact, Chris started his first business when he was still in middle school.

Chris is an entrepreneur, or a person who starts new businesses. "I surfed when I was a kid," Chris says, "so I'd repair surfboards for friends, and that kind of blossomed to the point where I was the main repair guy for all the local surf shops in Newport Beach [California]."

By the time he was old enough to drive, Chris had started a second business, this time on dry land: working on car stereos. This business grew quickly, Chris says. "It was like I had [an auto parts store] running out of my garage!"

Then, one night at a friend's party, Chris had an experience that led to his most successful company yet. "One of my friend's parents was talking to me about his small business and the Web designers that he had to deal with," Chris says. "He was telling me that they did great work but that they were never on time, and that he would pay anything for a Web designer who could get the work done on time. All I heard, as an entrepreneur, was 'I'll pay anything,' so immediately I turned around and said, 'Oh, yeah, I can do that. No problem!'"

The only problem was that Chris did not know anything about Web design. In fact, he did not even own a computer! But he did not let those obstacles stop him. Within a few weeks, Chris had taught himself how to design Web sites and had produced a Web site for his client.

It was this job that gave Chris the idea for his next company, which specializes in Web design and marketing. Chris created the company while attending business school at the University of Southern California. The company earned nearly $2 million during his first year of school alone. Today, Chris's business has offices in three countries. It has designed Web sites and marketing plans for many major companies.

Chris thinks that the business has been successful because of his belief in providing customers with fast, reliable service. That's the only way a company can survive in the fast-paced modern economy, he says.

So what advice would Chris give to someone else starting a business? Chris says that he loved his professors at business school, but that there was one thing he wished he had been taught in class: "Keep the customers happy. That's it! It's not complicated. … Just keep your customers happy, and that's it."

Economic Basics

Key Ideas
- People make choices about how to meet their wants and needs.
- Economies bring together people and businesses that make, sell, and buy goods and services.

Key Terms
- economics
- supply
- scarcity
- producer
- opportunity cost
- consumer
- demand
- incentive

Visual Glossary

Economics is the study of how people meet their wants and needs. People must answer three basic economic questions:

1. What goods and services should be produced?
2. How should goods and services be produced?
3. Who uses or consumes those goods and services?

The resources people use to make goods and services are called factors of production. The three main factors are land, labor, and capital. Geographers study where the factors of production are located.

Making Choices

There is no limit to the things that people want, but there are limits to what can be created. This difference between wants and reality creates **scarcity,** or having a limited quantity of resources to meet unlimited wants. Since people have limited money and time, they have to choose

Factors of Production

Entrepreneur
A person known as an entrepreneur combines resources to create new businesses.

Land, Labor, Capital
The three main factors of production are land and resources; human labor; and capital, or human-made goods like tools and buildings.

Goods and Services
Entrepreneurs use the factors of production to produce goods and services.

58

what they want most. Making a choice involves an **opportunity cost,** or the cost of what you have to give up.

Economics also involves demand and supply. **Demand** is the desire for a certain good or service. **Supply** is the amount of a good or service that is available for use. Demand and supply are connected to price. As the price of a product increases, people will buy less of it. That is, demand will decrease. If the price of the product decreases, demand will increase.

Supply functions in a similar way. If the price of a product increases, companies will make more of it. If the price of the product decreases, companies will make less of it. The price at which demand equals supply is the market price, or the market-clearing price.

Basic economic choices have influenced world events. For example, high demand for resources such as gold or oil has led to exploration and colonization.

Making Goods and Services

Economies bring together producers and consumers. **Producers** are people or businesses that make and sell products. **Consumers** are people or businesses that buy, or consume, products. Producers try to win consumers' business by offering better products for lower prices than other producers. If they sell more products, they

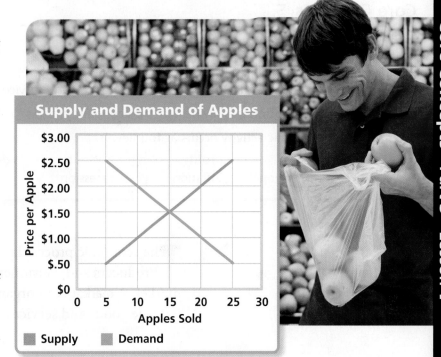

Supply and Demand of Apples

usually increase production. But producers will not make more products if the sale price is less than the marginal cost. Marginal cost is the cost of making one more unit of the product. Therefore, the marginal cost for the producer sets a minimum price for the product.

Businesses make products because of economic incentives. An **incentive** is a factor that encourages people to act in a certain way. Money is an incentive. The desire to earn money gives most producers an incentive to make and sell products. The incentive to save money leads most consumers to look for lower prices.

Assessment

1. On the line graph on this page, what is the market-clearing price?

2. How might a change in the price of one good or service lead to changes in prices of other goods or services?

59

Economic Process

Key Ideas
- Producers and consumers exchange goods and services in a market.
- Competition is a key part of the economic process.
- Economic activity occurs at four levels.

Key Terms
- market
- profit
- revenue
- specialization
- competition
- inflation
- recession

Visual Glossary

The economic process is complicated, but its basic idea is simple: Producers and consumers exchange goods and services in a market. A **market** is an organized way for producers and consumers to trade goods and services.

Exchanging Goods and Services

Throughout history, people have often engaged in barter, the trading of goods and services for other goods and services. Today, the means of exchange in a market is usually money. Modern governments issue money in the form of currency, or paper bills and metal coins. Different countries use different currencies. As a result, countries must establish the relative values of their currencies in order to trade. They must also establish a system for exchanging different currencies.

Businesses and the Economic Process

Businesses want to make a profit. **Profit** is the money a company has left after subtracting the costs of doing business. To make a profit, companies try to reduce expenses and increase revenue. **Revenue** is the money earned by selling goods and services. The price of resources affects revenue and profit. If resources become more expensive, the cost of making goods with them will also increase. Businesses' profits will drop.

Companies can increase profit and revenue through **specialization,** the act of concentrating on a limited number of goods or activities. Specialization allows people and companies to use resources more efficiently and to increase production and consumption.

Companies' profits are affected by **competition,** which is the struggle among producers for consumers' money. If one company raises the price of its products, another company may sell similar goods

Economists divide economic activity into four levels, as you can see in this table. ▼

Levels of Economic Activity	
Primary Industry	Collects resources from nature. Examples: farming, mining
Secondary Industry	Uses raw materials to create new products. Example: manufacturing
Tertiary Industry	Provides services to people and secondary industries. Examples: banking, restaurants
Quaternary Industry	Focuses on research and information. Example: education

Competition in the Market

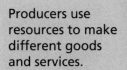
Producers use resources to make different goods and services.

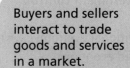
Buyers and sellers interact to trade goods and services in a market.

Competition between buyers and between sellers affects product price, quality, and marketing.

for a lower price to win more business. Companies use advertising to help increase demand for their products and to compete with other companies.

Nonprofit organizations are businesslike institutions that do not seek to make a profit. Nonprofit organizations can include churches, museums, hospitals, and other bodies.

A healthy economy grows as companies produce and sell more goods and services. In a growing economy, prices may increase over time. This general increase in prices is called **inflation.**

Economies do not keep growing forever. Eventually, economic activity falls as production slows and consumers buy fewer goods and services. This lack of demand for goods and services can lead to increased unemployment. A decline in economic growth for six or more months in a row is known as a **recession.**

Assessment

1. Does a person always need money to obtain goods or services?

2. How does competition affect producers and consumers?

61

Core Concepts 5.3

Economic Systems

Key Ideas
- Different societies have different types of economic systems.
- Most societies have economic systems with some element of government control.

Key Terms
- traditional economy
- market economy
- command economy
- mixed economy

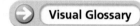 Visual Glossary

Every society has an economic system in which people make and distribute goods and services. There are four basic economic systems: traditional, market, command, and mixed. The roles of individuals, businesses, and government vary in each system. Economic goals, incentives, and government regulations can also vary.

Traditional Economies

A **traditional economy** is an economy in which people make economic decisions based on their customs and habits. They usually satisfy their needs and wants through hunting or farming, as their ancestors did. People in traditional economies usually do not want to change their basic way of life. Today, traditional economies are not common.

The Fulani people in Niger are livestock herders. ▶

Market Economies

A **market economy** is an economy in which individual consumers and producers make economic decisions. This type of economy is also called capitalism, or a free market. Market economies encourage entrepreneurs to establish new businesses by giving them economic freedom.

A consumer makes a purchase at a grocery store. ▶

62

Command Economies

A **command economy** is an economy in which the central government makes all economic decisions. This kind of system is also called a centrally planned economy. In a command economy, individual consumers and producers do not make basic economic decisions.

◀ In North Korea, government leaders make most economic decisions.

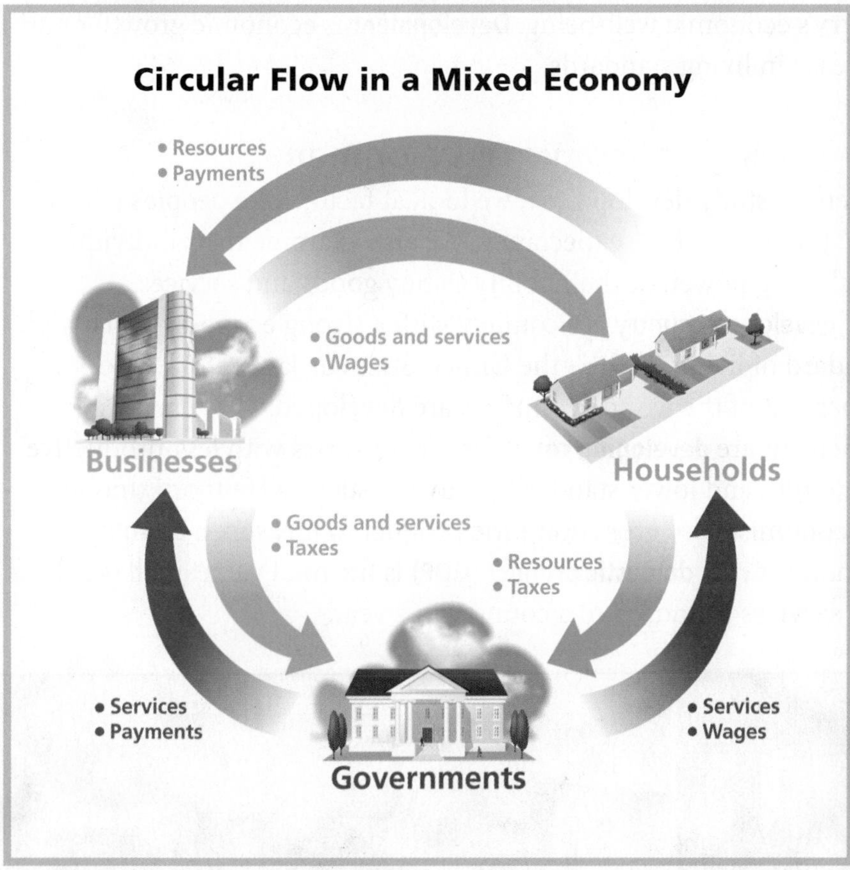

Circular Flow in a Mixed Economy

- Resources
- Payments

- Goods and services
- Wages

Businesses

Households

- Goods and services
- Taxes

- Resources
- Taxes

- Services
- Payments

- Services
- Wages

Governments

Mixed Economies

In reality, pure market or command economies do not exist. Most societies have mixed economies with varying levels of government control. A **mixed economy** is an economy that combines elements of traditional, market, and command economic systems. The diagram at left shows the circular flow of economic activity in a mixed economy.

Countries such as the United States and Australia have mixed economies that are close to pure market economies. In these countries, government makes some economic decisions. For example, government passes laws to protect consumers' rights. Government spending and taxation provide jobs and services and influence economic growth.

Countries such as North Korea and Cuba have mixed economies that are close to pure command economies. In these countries, government owns and controls most businesses.

Assessment

1. What are the differences among traditional, command, and market economies?

2. What are some possible advantages of the free-market system used in the United States and other countries?

63

Economic Development

Key Ideas
- The level of a country's development has direct effects on the lives of its people.
- There are many ways for a country to increase economic development.

Key Terms • development • developed country • developing country • gross domestic product (GDP) • productivity • technology

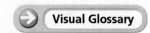 Visual Glossary

Economists use the concept of development to talk about a country's economic well-being. **Development** is economic growth or an increase in living standards.

Measuring Economic Development

When we study development, we look at factors like people's education, literacy, and life expectancy. We also examine their individual purchasing power, or their ability to buy goods and services.

A **developed country** is a country with a strong economy and a high standard of living, such as the United States or Japan. Only about 20 percent of the world's countries are developed. The remaining 80 percent are **developing countries,** or countries with less-productive economies and lower standards of living, such as Haiti or Ethiopia.

Economists use gross domestic product to measure a country's economy. **Gross domestic product (GDP)** is the total value of all goods and services produced in a country in a year.

World Population, 2008

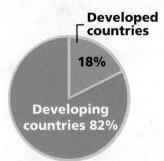

Developed countries

18%

Developing countries 82%

SOURCE: UN Population Division

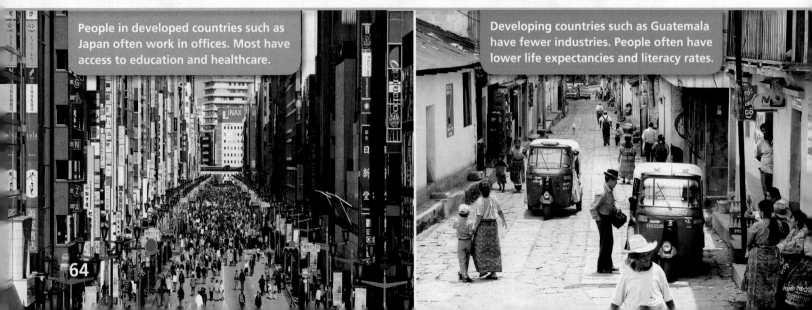

People in developed countries such as Japan often work in offices. Most have access to education and healthcare.

Developing countries such as Guatemala have fewer industries. People often have lower life expectancies and literacy rates.

64

World: Human Development

KEY
Human Development
High
Medium
Low
No data

Increasing Development

A country can increase economic development in many ways. It can find more resources to use in creating products. It can invest in capital goods such as factories and equipment. It can improve education and training to increase human capital. Human capital is workers' skill and knowledge.

Highly skilled workers usually earn higher wages, or money paid for work. Wages are also affected by supply and demand. If there is a high demand for workers and a limited supply of applicants, companies must pay higher wages to attract workers.

A country can improve development by increasing **productivity,** or the amount of goods and services produced given the amount of resources used. A business that increases productivity can produce goods and services more efficiently. More productive workers often earn higher wages.

Improved technology can lead to economic growth. **Technology** is the practical application of knowledge to accomplish a task. Technological advances can create new products, such as computers. They can make it easier for people to communicate and do business. However, it can be difficult for poor countries to afford new technology.

Assessment

1. What factors do economists use to study development?

2. How might economic factors affect the use of technology in various places, cultures, and societies?

65

Core Concepts 5.5

Trade

Key Ideas
- Individuals and countries trade with one another to get the things they need and want.
- Many countries are working toward the removal of trade barriers.

Key Terms • trade • export • import • tariff • trade barrier • free trade

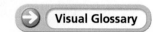
Visual Glossary

In the past, most people grew or hunted their own food. They made their own clothing. They built their own homes. In short, people did nearly everything for themselves. Today, however, most people depend on others to supply the goods and services they need. Our world is interdependent. That is, people and countries depend on one another for goods and services.

Trade and Geography

To get the products we need and want, we engage in trade. **Trade** is the exchange of goods and services in a market. When individuals engage in trade, they do so because they gain from that trade. In other words, trade benefits both the buyer and the seller.

Geographic location can give a country or region advantages in trade. For example, a region that is close to an ocean can more easily ship goods overseas. On the other hand, a manufacturing plant located far away from a market will need to add transportation costs to its products, making them higher in price.

Container ships, such as the ones in this photo, carry most of the world's goods from one port to another. ▼

66

Types of Trade

All of the buying and selling that takes place within a country is known as domestic trade. Domestic trade involves producers and consumers located inside the same country.

Domestic producers and consumers can also engage in international trade, or trade with foreign producers and consumers. International trade involves exports and imports. **Exports** are goods and services produced within a country and sold outside the country's borders. **Imports** are goods and services sold in a country that are produced in other countries. International trade requires a system for exchanging types of currency.

Trade Barriers and Free Trade

If imported goods are cheaper than domestic goods, consumers will usually buy more of them. These lower prices can harm domestic producers by reducing their sales. Governments sometimes try to protect domestic producers through tariffs. A **tariff** is a tax on imports or exports. Tariffs are an example of trade barriers. A **trade barrier** is a government policy or restriction that limits international trade.

Today, many countries are working toward **free trade,** or the removal of trade barriers. Free trade gives consumers lower prices and more choices. However, domestic producers can suffer if consumers prefer cheaper imported goods.

United States and China: Trade

Goods exported from China to the United States
- Household goods, $58.4 billion
- Computers, $53.7 billion
- Clothing and shoes, $51.5 billion

Goods exported from the United States to China
- Computers, $8.6 billion
- Aircraft, $7.5 billion
- Machinery, $7.2 billion

Assessment

1. How might geography affect the locations of economic activities?
2. How might scarcity encourage international trade and make countries interdependent?

67

Money Management

Key Ideas
- People must manage money to have enough for their needs and wants.
- Many people save and invest money.

Key Terms • budget • saving • interest • credit • investing • stock • bond  Visual Glossary

Money is anything that is generally accepted as payment for goods and services. Money is a scarce resource that people must manage to have enough for their needs and wants. Because people's needs, wants, and incomes can change, it is important to plan ahead.

Budgeting, Saving, and Lending

A key tool in money management is a budget. A **budget** is a plan that shows income and expenses over a period of time. A budget's income should be equal to or greater than its expenses. A budget should also include money reserved for saving. **Saving** is the act of setting aside money for future use. Many people save by using banks. A bank is a business that keeps money, makes loans, and offers other financial services. Credit unions are nonprofit banks owned by their members.

A man uses an automated teller machine (ATM) to access his bank account. ▼

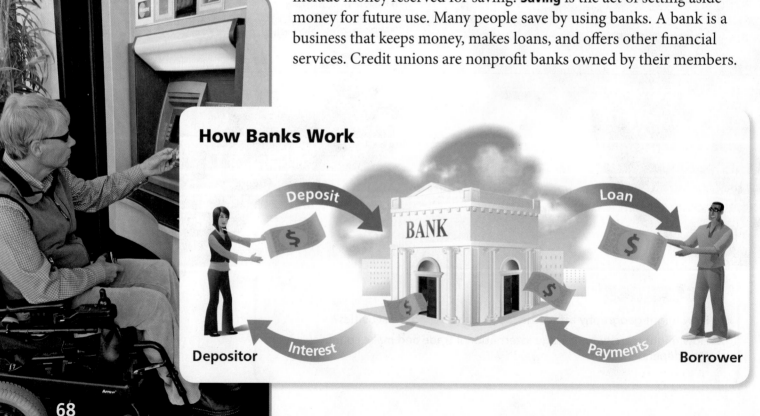

How Banks Work

Deposit · BANK · Loan · Depositor · Interest · Payments · Borrower

68

Many people who save money in banks do so using checking or savings accounts. Banks may pay interest on money deposited in these accounts. **Interest** is the price paid for borrowing money. Interest is an incentive for people to save money.

Banks use deposits to make loans to people and businesses around the world. These loans help people buy houses or make other large purchases. They help businesses get started or grow. As a result, banks are a big part of economic growth.

Loans are a form of credit. **Credit** is an arrangement in which a buyer can borrow to purchase something and pay for it over time, such as by using a credit card. Banks and other lending organizations charge borrowers interest on loans. As a result, it costs more for a borrower to purchase a good using credit than to pay cash for the good at the time of purchase.

Investing

Investing is the act of using money in the hope of making a future profit. Some people invest in stocks, bonds, or mutual funds. A **stock** is a share of ownership in a company. A **bond** is a certificate issued by a company or government promising to pay back borrowed money with interest. A mutual fund is a company that invests members' money in stocks, bonds, and other investments.

▲ Stockbrokers buy and sell stocks and bonds for investors at places such as the New York Stock Exchange.

Investments offer different levels of risk and return—the amount of money an investor might earn. In general, the safest investments offer the lowest rates of return. For example, a savings account is very safe, but it pays a relatively low rate of interest. Stocks are riskier but can earn a great deal of money for an investor if they increase in value. On the other hand, stocks can decline in value and become worth less than the stockholder paid. Bonds are less risky than stocks, but they usually offer a lower rate of return.

Assessment

1. How do banks function?
2. Why do people invest money in stocks, bonds, and mutual funds?

Part 5 Assessment

Key Terms and Ideas

1. **Recall** What is the most common type of economy today?

2. **Define** What is a **tariff** and why do governments sometimes use them?

3. **Paraphrase** Explain the relationship among **revenue, profit,** and the costs of doing business.

4. **Sequence** How does increased **productivity** affect business owners, employees, **consumers,** and entire nations?

5. **Explain** What is **opportunity cost**?

6. **Identify Cause and Effect** What role does risk play in investment?

7. **Identify** What level of economic activity includes mining? What level includes medical care?

Think Critically

8. **Draw Conclusions** What problems or issues might a company face if it has a shortage of one or more factors of production?

9. **Decision Making** How do societies organize and make decisions about the production of goods and services?

10. **Draw Inferences** How do factors such as location, physical features, and distribution of natural resources influence the economic development of societies?

11. **Summarize** How do government policies affect free market economies such as the U.S. economy?

Identify

Answer the following questions based on the map.

12. What kind of trade is shown on this map?

13. What is a major U.S. export?

14. What is a major U.S. import?

15. What are three goods that the United States produces?

16. What are three goods that Mexico produces?

17. What possible area of competition is shown on this map?

18. The United States and Mexico participate in free trade. What U.S. industries might free trade help or hurt?

United States and Mexico: Trade

Mexican exports to the United States:
Petroleum
Fruits and vegetables
Electronics
Computers
Automobiles

U.S. exports to Mexico:
Petroleum products
Plastics
Chemicals
Automobile parts
Electronics

Journal Activity

Fill in the graphic organizer in your Student Journal.

Demonstrate Your Understanding Complete the Sum-It-Up activity in your journal to demonstrate your understanding of economics and geography. After you complete the activity, discuss your answers with the class. Be sure to support your answers with information from the lessons.

21st Century Learning

Search for Information on the Internet

China had a command economy for many years, but since the 1970s the government has reduced its control over the economy. Use the Internet to research China's changing economy. Create a timeline to share your findings. Use a variety of online sources, including
- encyclopedias
- national and international newspapers
- magazines and journals

Document-Based Questions

Success ★ Tracker™
Online at myworldgeography.com

Use your knowledge of economics and geography and Documents A and B to answer Questions 1–3.

Document A

Supply and Demand of Product X

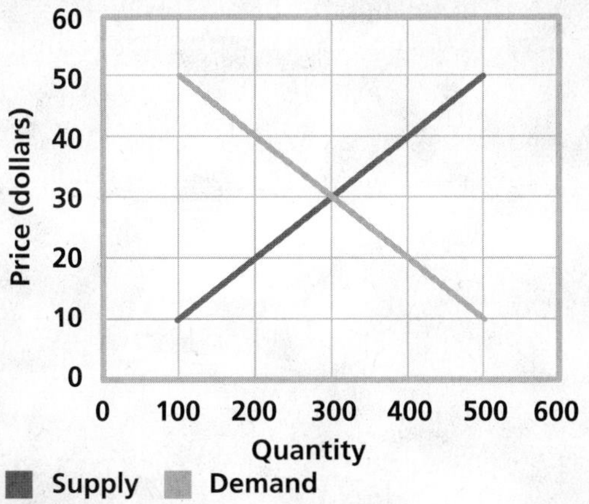

(Graph: Price (dollars) on y-axis from 0 to 60; Quantity on x-axis from 0 to 600. Supply and Demand lines intersecting.)

■ Supply   ■ Demand

1. Examine Document A. Which of the following statements is true?

   A As the price of Product X increases, demand for it decreases.

   B As the price of Product X decreases, its supply increases.

   C As the price of Product X increases, demand for it increases.

   D As the price of Product X decreases, its supply does not change.

Document B

UN Human Development Index (HDI) Values, 2005

Nation	HDI Value
Iceland	0.968
Samoa	0.785
Sierra Leone	0.336

SOURCE: *CIA World Factbook*

2. Examine Document B. The Human Development Index is a UN measure of levels of economic development and well-being in a country. Countries with higher HDI values have higher levels of development. Which of the following statements is true?

   A Samoa is less developed than Sierra Leone.

   B Samoa is more developed than Iceland.

   C Sierra Leone and Iceland are very different in terms of development level.

   D Sierra Leone is more developed than Iceland.

3. **Writing Task** A nation's rating in the UN Human Development Index is influenced by GDP per capita and people's education, literacy, and life expectancy. Why are these factors important to a country's development?

Population and Movement

U.S. and Mexican flags

Automobiles line up to cross the busy U.S.– Mexican border. ▲

72

U.S. students in a classroom

Ludwig Barragan

Searching for a New Home

Story by Miles Lemaire for myWorld Geography

Anyone who has ever moved to a new place knows that it can be hard to make friends and adjust to a new school. Moving to a different country can be even more challenging. You can ask Ludwig Barragan, who moved to the United States from Mexico a few years ago.

Like many other people, Ludwig and his mother decided to move in search of more opportunities and a better life. "My position in Mexico was fine economically," says Ludwig, "but I wanted to receive an education that I knew I wouldn't be able to get in Mexico. I love my country, yet the [school] system there was not what I wanted."

Ludwig and his mother moved to McAllen, Texas, a city on the U.S.–Mexican border. He looked forward to learning more about American culture and society.

Life in McAllen was an adjustment for Ludwig and his mother. "I would say that when you live so close to the border you live in a different world," Ludwig says. "You live in a place that is neither the U.S. nor Mexico."

Ludwig found that there were a number of different cultural groups in McAllen. "The number of immigrants [in] McAllen was huge," Ludwig says, "and there was a large community in my high school that spoke only Spanish. There was a second group there that were bilingual, and they were mainly people who were born in the U.S. but had parents that were from Mexico or spoke Spanish. It was hard to relate to them because … they didn't know the Mexican culture or values that I knew, yet they were not completely incorporated into the American culture."

At first, Ludwig felt that he didn't fit in. "I knew that I had to learn the language and the values even more. I tried to get in contact with the students that spoke mostly English. That's what I did and that's what helped me a lot."

Ludwig looked for ways that he could learn about the customs of his adopted country. He eventually joined the Junior Reserve Officers Training Corps (JROTC). The JROTC is a citizenship and military program supported by the U.S. armed forces. Ludwig says that the JROTC taught him much about life in the United States.

"My friends in Mexico made fun of me because here I was, a Mexican, carrying the U.S. flag with the JROTC," remembers Ludwig. "At first I said, 'Yeah, it's kind of weird,' but then later I realized that I don't have to feel bad about it. I chose this country because I love it and it doesn't mean that I love Mexico any less. I think … the beauty of immigration is that you can learn to love both cultures. I feel honored that I had a chance to carry the U.S. flag."

73

Population Growth

Key Ideas
- Earth's population has grown quickly in recent years.
- Population growth can affect economic development and the environment.

Key Terms • demographer   • birth rate   • death rate   • infant mortality rate

 Visual Glossary

Today, the world's population is around 7 billion. When people first began farming around 12,000 years ago, it was fewer than 10 million. Earth's population grew slowly, eventually reaching 1 billion by 1800. Since then, better food production and healthcare have caused a population boom.

Measuring Growth

Demographers are scientists who study human populations. They measure the rate at which a population is growing. To do this, demographers compare birth rates and death rates. The **birth rate** is the number of live births per 1,000 people in a year. The **death rate** is the number of deaths per 1,000 people in a year. When the birth rate is higher than the death rate, a population tends to grow. Population can also change when people move into or out of a region.

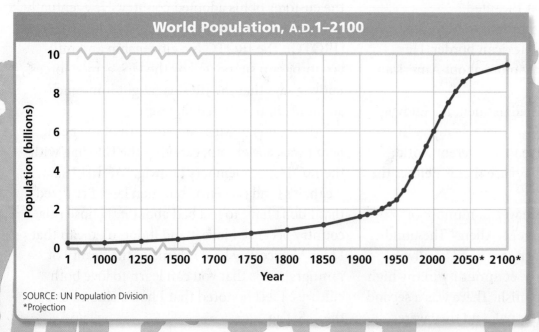

World Population, A.D. 1–2100

SOURCE: UN Population Division
*Projection

Causes and Effects of Population Growth

Causes of Growth

Until about two hundred years ago, the global birth rate was only slightly higher than the death rate. As a result, the population grew slowly. Then came the Industrial Revolution, which brought many changes.

Better medical care saved many lives. Improvements in food production increased the food supply and made food healthier. Living conditions improved. These and other changes led to a much lower death rate in most regions. By 1950, the world's population had begun to soar.

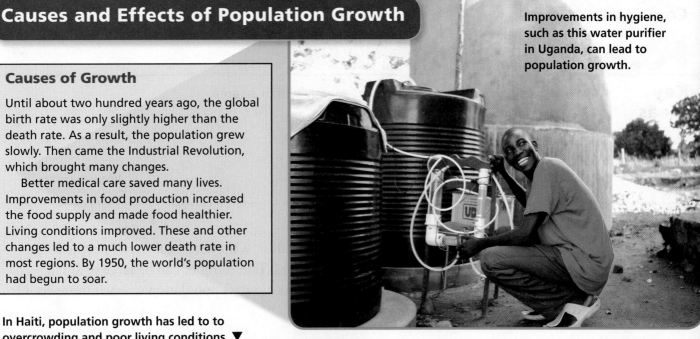

Improvements in hygiene, such as this water purifier in Uganda, can lead to population growth.

In Haiti, population growth has led to to overcrowding and poor living conditions. ▼

Effects of Growth

Population growth can have positive effects. For example, a growing population can produce and consume more goods and services. This can improve a country's standard of living. However, rapid population growth can also cause problems. The population can grow faster than the supply of food, water, medicine, and other resources.

The problems caused by rapid population growth are greatest in poor developing countries. A lack of clean food and water can lead to widespread starvation and disease. In these places, the **infant mortality rate**—the number of infant deaths per 1,000 births—is high.

The environment often suffers as well, as people use up resources to survive. Pollution is common. People cut down forests for firewood or clear land for farming. This can lead to desertification, or the spread of dry desert-like conditions. A lack of fertile soil makes it even harder to grow enough food.

Assessment

1. How are the birth rate and death rate used to measure population growth?

2. If the population of your town suddenly doubled, how might your daily life change?

75

Population Distribution

Key Ideas
- The distribution of a population can vary greatly within an area.
- Population density has important effects on an area.

Key Terms • population distribution • population density

 Visual Glossary

A country's population is the total number of people living within its borders. That number can be large or small. Geographers study a country's population to learn more about life in that country.

Population Distribution

Population distribution is the spreading of people over an area of land. The world's population is distributed unevenly on Earth's surface. Some places have many people. Other places are almost empty. What factors lead people to live where they do?

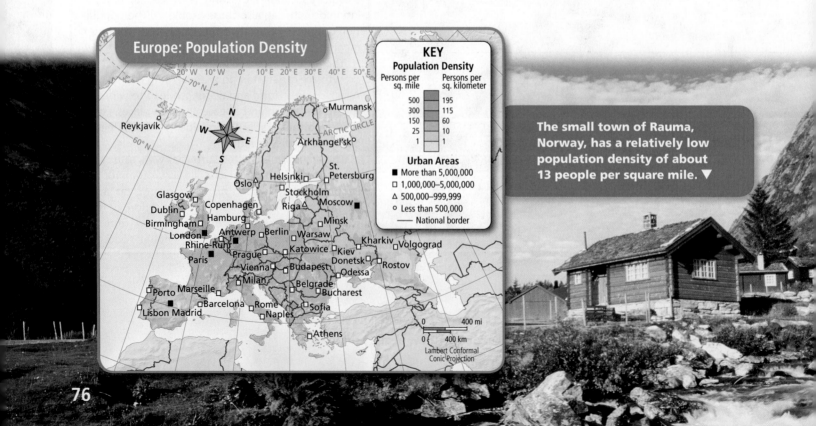

Europe: Population Density

KEY
Population Density

Persons per sq. mile	Persons per sq. kilometer
500	195
300	115
150	60
25	10
1	1

Urban Areas
- ■ More than 5,000,000
- □ 1,000,000–5,000,000
- △ 500,000–999,999
- ○ Less than 500,000
- — National border

Lambert Conformal Conic Projection

The small town of Rauma, Norway, has a relatively low population density of about 13 people per square mile. ▼

People try to live in places that meet their basic needs. Natural obstacles such as oceans, mountains, and extremely cold or hot weather limit the areas where people can live easily. Throughout human history, most people have lived in areas with fertile soil, fresh water, and mild climates. Regions with good soil and plenty of water became crowded. Places that were too cold or dry for farming never developed large populations.

After about 1800, improved transportation and new ways of making a living changed things. As factories and industries grew, the ability to farm became less important. Industrial centers and large cities could develop in regions that were less suited for farming. Today, population tends to be highest in areas that were centers of early farming, industry, or trade.

Population Density

Population density is the number of people per unit of land area. It is expressed as the number of people per square mile or square kilometer. Population density gives us a way to describe how thickly settled an area is. It also lets us compare places of different sizes and populations. The density figure for any country is an average. Population density can vary greatly from one part of a country to another.

Population density has some important effects on a region. The more people there are per square mile, the more crowded a place is. Cities with high population densities tend to have crowded roads and living conditions. These places require many resources to meet people's needs. Places with low population densities tend to have more undeveloped land.

London, in the United Kingdom, has a very high population density, about 13,000 people per square mile. ▼

Assessment

1. How are population distribution and population density different?
2. How might a rapid increase in a region's population density change the region?

Migration

Key Ideas
- People move from one place to another for a number of reasons.
- People may move within a country or from one country to another.

Key Terms • migration • emigrate • immigrate • push factor • pull factor

For thousands of years, people have migrated to new places. **Migration** is the movement of people from one place to another. Scientists believe that more than 50,000 years ago, a group of early humans migrated from Africa to Asia. Over many years, their descendants spread slowly across Asia and Europe. Some crossed from Asia to the Americas.

Forms of Migration

People often migrate within a country. In modern times, this internal migration has largely been movement to cities from the countryside. People generally migrate to cities to find jobs.

In the 1800s, many people migrated from Europe to the United States in search of a better life.

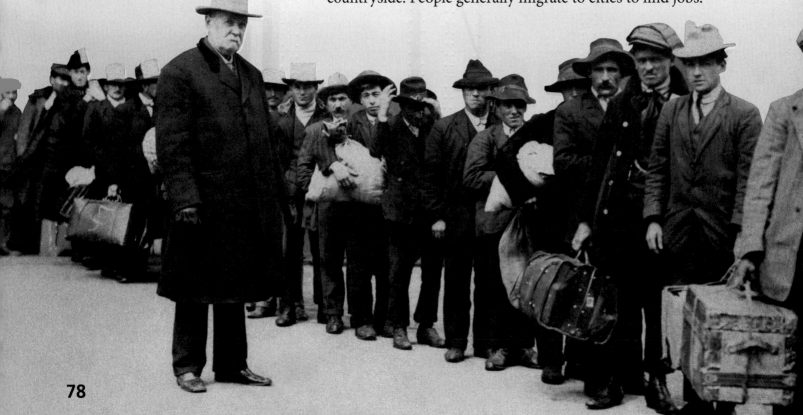

78

People also move from one country to another. When people leave their home country, they **emigrate,** which means to migrate out of a place. To enter a new country is to **immigrate,** or to migrate into a place. Moving to another country can lead to big changes in a person's life. For example, people moving to a new country may have to learn a new language and new customs. Mass migration can greatly change a region's culture and society. Migration can also affect a region's government, economy, and environment.

Reasons for Migration

People who migrate are often looking for a better life. They may move to escape poverty, a lack of jobs, or a harsh climate. In some countries, war or other conflict forces people to migrate. These reasons for migration are known as push factors. **Push factors** are causes of migration that push people to leave their home country.

Other reasons for migration are known as pull factors. **Pull factors** pull, or attract, people to new countries. One example of a pull factor is a supply of good jobs.

People generally migrate because they choose to do so. For example, millions of Europeans chose to migrate to the United States during the 1800s and early 1900s. Some of these people were Irish, fleeing a shortage of food. Others were Jews

These immigrants to the United States become U.S. citizens at a naturalization ceremony.

escaping persecution, or mistreatment. Millions more have come from Asia and Latin America since then.

History is also full of involuntary migrations. For the most part, these involved the forced movement of enslaved people. In the late 1400s European slave traders began buying and selling captured Africans. They shipped most of these enslaved people to the Americas. As many as 10 million enslaved Africans were forced to migrate to the Americas.

Assessment

1. Why did Europeans migrate to the United States in the 1800s and early 1900s?

2. Suppose your family migrated after a flood destroyed your home. Would the flood be considered a push factor or a pull factor? Explain.

79

Core Concepts 6.4

Urbanization

Key Ideas
- Cities around the world have grown quickly over the last two hundred years.
- The growth of cities has created many challenges.

Key Terms • urban • rural • urbanization • slum • suburban sprawl

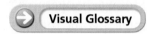
Visual Glossary

Panama City, Panama, had a population of 171,000 in 1950. By 2025, it is expected to grow to 2.4 million.

1950s

Panama City, Panama

Today

In many parts of the world, people are migrating to urban areas from rural areas. **Urban** areas are cities. **Rural** areas are settlements in the country. In China, for example, many new jobs have been created in cities in recent years. As a result, many rural Chinese workers have moved to cities in search of jobs. This process is known as urbanization. **Urbanization** is the movement of people from rural areas to urban areas.

The Shift from Rural to Urban

Over the last two hundred years or so, billions of people around the world have left rural agricultural areas to move to cities. In 2008, for the first time in history, more than half of the world's population lived in cities and towns.

In Europe and North America, urbanization began in the 1800s as modern industry developed. As a result, people moved to cities in search of jobs in factories and other businesses. Today, urbanization is happening most quickly in Asia and Africa. In those places, people move to cities in search of jobs, education, and better lives for their children.

80

Challenges of Urbanization

Rapid urbanization has created challenges for growing cities, especially those in poor countries. In some cases, cities simply have more people than they can handle. These cities cannot provide the housing, jobs, schools, hospitals, and other services that people need. One result is the spread of **slums,** or poor, overcrowded urban neighborhoods. Slums exist in cities around the world. Most people in slums live in run-down buildings or shacks. They are unable to meet their basic needs, such as enough food and clean water.

Urbanization can also create challenges in wealthy countries. Today, most large urban areas have a central core city. The core city has stores, office buildings, government buildings, and some housing. In wealthier countries, most people live in the suburbs surrounding the core city. As the population of a wealthy urban area grows, so does suburban sprawl. **Suburban sprawl** is the spread of suburbs away from the core city.

As suburbs spread, they replace farmland and other open spaces. New sewer lines, water lines, and roads must be built and maintained by the government. Because most people in suburbs use cars for transportation, suburban sprawl can increase pollution and energy use. Today, many towns and cities are working to limit sprawl.

Mumbai, India, had a population of 2.9 million in 1950. By 2025, it is expected to grow to 26.4 million.

1950s Mumbai, India

Today

World Urbanization

30% 70% — 1950
53% 47% — 2000
30% 70% — 2050*

Rural population | Urban population

SOURCE: UN Population Division
*Projected

Assessment

1. What are some causes of urbanization?

2. Think about living in a suburb versus living in the center of a city or town. List a few things you might like or dislike about each.

81

Part 6 Assessment

Key Terms and Ideas

1. **Identify** Define the terms **birth rate** and **death rate.**

2. **Summarize** Describe the process of **urbanization**.

3. **Recall** Name three negative effects of rapid population growth.

4. **Define** What is **migration**?

5. **Compare and Contrast** What is the difference between a **pull factor** and a **push factor**?

6. **Recall** What is **population density**?

7. **Explain** What factors affect **population distribution**?

Think Critically

8. **Draw Inferences** How do you think world population patterns might change in the future?

9. **Compare Viewpoints** What arguments could be made for living in an area that has a high population density or in one with a low population density? Explain your views.

10. **Synthesize** During the 1800s, millions of Europeans migrated to the United States. Identify at least one possible push factor and one possible pull factor behind this mass migration.

11. **Solve Problems** Imagine that you are a member of a city government that is trying to limit urban growth. What steps might you suggest?

Identify

Answer the following questions based on the map.

12. Describe London's population.

13. Which cities have populations between 500,000 and 1,000,000?

14. Which city is located at 0° longitude?

15. In general, where are the areas in the United Kingdom with the highest population density?

16. Describe Cardiff's population.

17. Which city is closest to 50° N latitude?

18. Which is the westernmost city shown on the map?

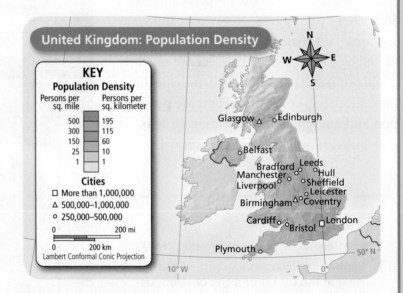

United Kingdom: Population Density

82

Journal Activity

Fill in the graphic organizer in your Student Journal.

Demonstrate Your Understanding Complete the Sum-It-Up activity in your journal to demonstrate your understanding of population and movement. After you complete the activity, discuss your predictions as a class. Be sure to support your predictions with information from the lessons.

21st Century Learning

Analyze Media Content

Find examples of recent articles about immigration to the United States. Then create a table to compare and contrast these articles. Ask yourself the following questions when reading:
- What is the main idea of each article?
- Does the author support every statement?
- Does the author show any bias?

Document-Based Questions

Success Tracker™
Online at myworldgeography.com

Use your knowledge of population and movement and Documents A and B to answer Questions 1–3.

Document A

Annual Birth & Death Rates in Selected Countries		
Country	Birth Rate (per 1,000 people)	Death Rate (per 1,000 people)
Austria	8.7	9.9
Chad	41.6	16.4
Pakistan	28.4	7.9
Sri Lanka	16.6	6.1
United States	14.2	8.3

SOURCE: *CIA World Factbook*

Document B

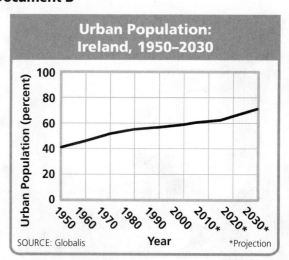

Urban Population: Ireland, 1950–2030

SOURCE: Globalis   Year   *Projection

1. Examine Document A. How does population growth in the United States most likely compare with that in Pakistan and Chad?

   A It is much faster.

   B It is much slower.

   C It is much faster than growth in Pakistan but slower than growth in Chad.

   D It is much faster than growth in Chad but slower than growth in Pakistan.

2. Examine Document B. What might be one cause for Ireland's changing rate of urbanization?

   A more dependence on agriculture

   B a higher death rate

   C growth in industry

   D housing shortages

3. **Writing Task** How do you think a graph showing urban population in Asia since 1950 might compare to Document B? Explain your answer.

83

Culture and Geography

Tepees at a Native American powwow

Native American dancers

84

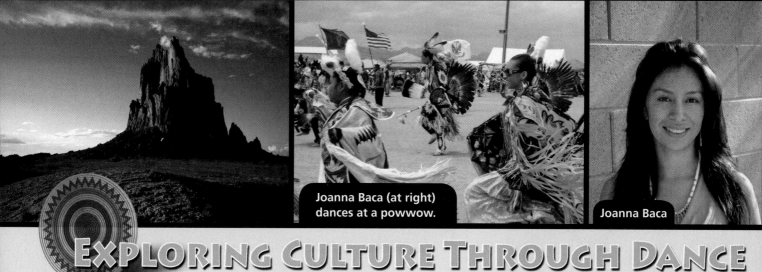

Joanna Baca (at right) dances at a powwow.

Joanna Baca

Exploring Culture Through Dance

Story by Miles Lemaire for myWorld Geography

When Joanna Baca and her family moved to Las Vegas, Nevada, from the Native American Navajo reservation in Shiprock, New Mexico, she looked for things that reminded her of home—and her Navajo culture.

"Most of our family stayed back home," Joanna says. "After we first moved here [Las Vegas], we didn't think there was anyone out here that was Native American, and it actually took us a while to find someone we knew."

In an effort to make their new city feel like home, Joanna and her family looked for community organizations that promoted Native American culture. Joanna eventually discovered the Las Vegas Indian Center. Among other things, this organization helps Native American high school students apply to and get accepted at colleges.

"[The Center helps] Native American kids find out what colleges are good for them," Joanna says. "They teach us that college is possible for Native American kids, not just for the kids that live on the reservation, but for kids who live in the city, too."

The more time Joanna spent with the organization, the closer she felt to her Navajo culture. She decided that she wanted to get involved in more aspects of Native American culture, especially traditional forms of dance.

Joanna had grown up going to powwows with her family. A powwow is a gathering where Native American people dance, sing, and honor Native American cultures. "I'd just see all the dancers there and how beautiful they were," Joanna remembers. She decided that she wanted to learn more about Native American dance. "I did ballet, jazz, and hip-hop before, and I thought they were fun," she says, "but I wanted to do something cultural, because dancing is a big part of my culture."

It has been several years since Joanna first started studying and performing Native American dances. She loves how these traditional forms of dance help her connect to her culture. But she also thinks dance is a wonderful way for non-Native American people to learn more about native culture.

"We go to events where they have dancers from all over the world, and they'll have a bit of everyone's culture in this one little get-together," Joanna says. "So we shared food, we were part of the dancing there, and a lot of people were like, 'Oh that's nice, I've never seen that type of dance before, what kind is that?' We'd tell them that it's Navajo, or native and … it got them very interested. Some of those people would come to the show again just to see our part of the performance and to see what it was all about."

85

What Is Culture?

Key Ideas
- Every culture has a distinctive set of cultural traits.
- Earth has thousands of different cultures.

Key Terms
- culture
- cultural trait
- norm
- culture region
- cultural landscape

→ **Visual Glossary**

All people have the same basic needs and wants, such as food, clothing, and shelter. But different cultures respond to those needs and wants in different ways. **Culture** is the beliefs, customs, practices, and behaviors of a particular nation or group of people.

Where Culture Comes From

The features that make up a culture are known as cultural traits. A **cultural trait** is an idea or way of doing things that is common in a certain culture. Cultural traits include language, laws, religion, values, food, clothing, and many other customs. Children learn cultural traits from their parents and other adults. People also learn cultural traits from the mass media and from organizations such as schools, social clubs, and religious groups. Common cultural traits are called norms. A **norm** is a behavior that is considered normal in a particular society.

French Quebec Culture Region

CANADA
Quebec
UNITED STATES
0 500 mi
0 500 km
Lambert Azimuthal Equal-Area Projection
120° W 110° W 100° W 90° W 80° W 70° W
50° N 40° N 30° N

Culture Regions

A **culture region** is an area in which a single culture or cultural trait is dominant. In Canada, French Canadian culture dominates much of the province of Quebec. The people of Quebec who have this culture identify themselves as French Canadian or Québécois (kay bek WAH).

Cultural Landscapes

Human activities create **cultural landscapes,** or geographic areas that have been shaped by people.

◀ Bolivia

Left, Egypt; below, Ukraine

86

Some cultural traits remain constant over many years. But culture can change over time as people adopt new cultural traits. For example, the way Americans dress today is very different from the way Americans dressed 100 years ago.

The environment can also affect culture. For example, the environment of a region influences how people live and how they earn their living. Humans can also shape their environment by creating cultural landscapes. The cultural landscape of a place reflects how its people meet their basic needs for food, clothing, and shelter. These landscapes differ from one culture to another.

Culture and Geography

Earth has thousands of different cultures and culture regions. In a specific culture region, people share cultural traits such as religion or language.

Culture regions are often different from political units. Occasionally, a culture region may cover an entire country. In Japan, for example, nearly everyone speaks the same language, eats the same food, and follows the same customs. A country may also include more than one culture region. For example, the French Canadian culture region of Quebec is one of several culture regions in Canada.

Culture regions can also extend beyond political boundaries. For example, many of the people who live in Southwest Asia and northern Africa are Arab Muslims. That is, they practice the religion of Islam. They also share other cultural traits, such as the Arabic language, foods, and other ways of life. This region of Arab Muslim culture covers several countries.

Clothing

Styles of clothing vary in different cultures.

A Spanish-born Swedish woman practices flamenco, a traditional Spanish dance. ▶

▲ A Saudi Arabian woman

Weddings in Japan (above) and Indonesia (left)

Assessment

1. Does every country form a single culture region? Explain.
2. What are some elements of the cultural landscape in the area where your school is located?

Food

People in different cultures eat different types of food.

◀ A man in Saudi Arabia sells vegetables.

Women in Ukraine selling potatoes and other produce

87

Families and Societies

Key Ideas
- The most basic unit of any society is the family.
- Family structures vary in different cultures, but every society has organized relationships among groups of people.

Key Terms • society • family • nuclear family • extended family • social structure • social class

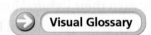
Visual Glossary

Culture, society, and family are all related. A **society** is a group of humans with a shared culture who have organized themselves to meet their basic needs. Societies can be large or small. A group of a few dozen hunter-gatherers is a society. So is a country of more than a billion people, such as India or China.

Kinds of Families

The most basic unit of any society is the family. A **family** is two or more people who are closely related by birth, marriage, or adoption. Traditionally, one person heads a family. A man has been the head of the family in many societies throughout history. Today, however, men and women often share this responsibility.

Family structures vary in different cultures. Two common family units are the nuclear family and the extended family. A **nuclear family** is a family that consists of parents and their children. An **extended family** is a family that includes parents, children, and other family members, such as grandparents, aunts, uncles, and cousins. Extended families are more common in developing countries. In some places, extended families work together on farms. In other places, relatives work separately but live together in order to share resources.

Nuclear and extended families are two kinds of family unit.

Nuclear Family

Extended Family

Kinds of Societies

Every society has a social structure. A **social structure** is a pattern of organized relationships among groups of people within a society. People interact with one another, with groups, and with institutions. For example, you have ties to friends and family members. You probably attend a school. You may also take part in a sports team or some other group. Adults have ties to coworkers and to economic institutions such as businesses and banks. Families may also have ties to religious institutions, such as a church, a synagogue, or a mosque.

Societies vary around the world and can change over time. All societies have some common institutions. These include government, religious, economic, and educational institutions.

Societies also have differences. One basic difference has to do with a society's economy. Some societies rely mainly on farming. Others depend on industry.

Industrial societies often organize members according to their social class. A **social class** is a group of people living in similar economic conditions. In modern societies, the main groupings are upper class, middle class, and lower (or working) class. The size of the world's middle class has increased greatly in recent years.

Assessment

1. What aspects of culture do all societies share?
2. What aspects of culture differ among societies?

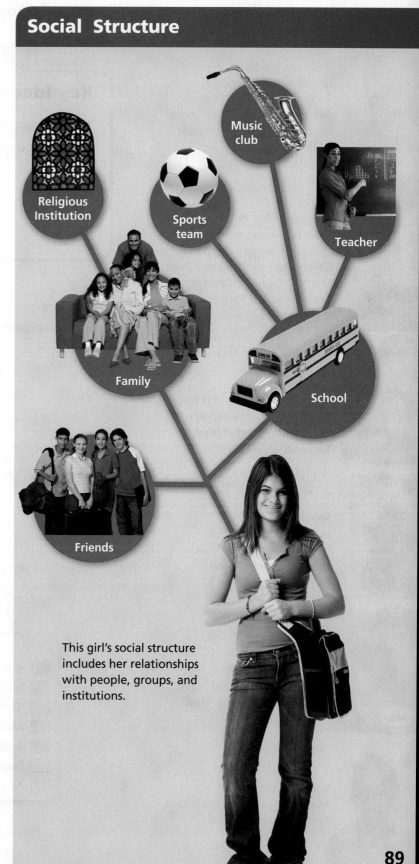

Social Structure

This girl's social structure includes her relationships with people, groups, and institutions.

Indo-European

Speakers 2.722 billion
Main languages English, German, Swedish, Afrikaans (South Africa), French, Spanish, Portuguese, Italian, Russian, Polish, Farsi (Iran), Hindi (northern India), Bengali (Bangladesh, India), Greek

Sino-Tibetan

Speakers 1.259 billion
Main languages Mandarin Chinese (northern China), Cantonese (southeastern China), Min Nan Chinese (Taiwan), Tibetan (Tibet), Burmese (Myanmar)

Niger-Congo

Speakers 382 million
Main languages Ibo and Yoruba (Nigeria), Xhosa (South Africa), Twi (Ghana), Swahili (Kenya, Tanzania, Uganda)

Afro-Asiatic

Speakers 359 million
Main languages Arabic (Southwest Asia, North Africa), Hebrew (Israel), Hausa (West Africa)

Austronesian

Speakers 354 million
Main languages Malay (Malaysia), Javanese (Indonesia), Tagalog (Philippines), Maori (New Zealand)

Dravidian

Speakers 223 million
Main languages Telugu (India), Tamil (India, Sri Lanka)

90

Core Concepts 7.3

Language

Key Ideas

- Language provides the basis for culture.
- Language can unify people or keep them apart.

Key Term
- language

 Visual Glossary

Cultures could not exist without language. **Language** is a set of spoken sounds, written symbols, or hand gestures that make it possible for people to communicate.

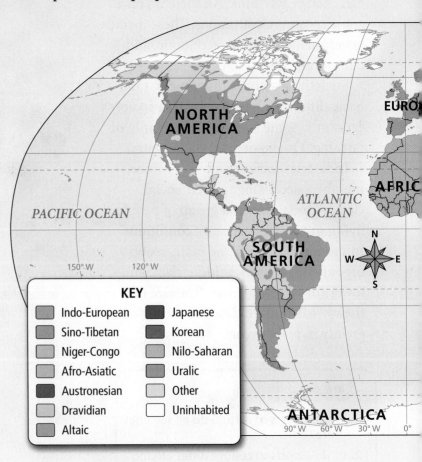

KEY

- Indo-European
- Sino-Tibetan
- Niger-Congo
- Afro-Asiatic
- Austronesian
- Dravidian
- Altaic
- Japanese
- Korean
- Nilo-Saharan
- Uralic
- Other
- Uninhabited

Without language, people would not be able to share information or ideas. They could not pass on cultural traits to their children.

Languages often vary from one culture to another. Within a country, differences in language can keep cultures apart and make it harder to unify the country. Language differences can also keep countries apart by preventing communication.

People who speak different languages sometimes turn to a third language in order to communicate with each other. In modern times, English has often served as the world's common language.

The map below shows the locations of the world's major language groups. Languages in each of these groups share a common ancestor. This ancestor was a language spoken so long ago that it gradually changed to become several related languages.

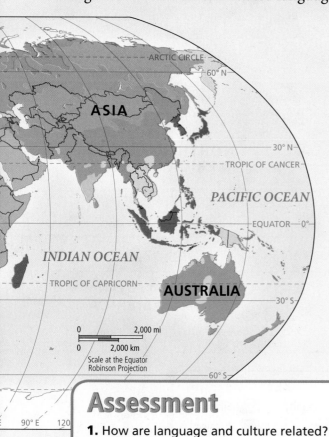

Assessment

1. How are language and culture related?

2. Which continent has the greatest number of language groups? Why might this be so?

Altaic

Speakers 140 million
Main languages Turkish, Kazakh (Kazakhstan), Bashkir (Russia), Tatar (Russia), Uighur (China), Mongolian (Mongolia)

Japanese

Speakers 123 million
Spoken mainly in Japan.

Korean

Speakers 66 million
Spoken mainly in North Korea and South Korea.

Nilo-Saharan

Speakers 38 million
Main languages Luo (Kenya), Maasai (Tanzania), Kanuri (Niger)

Uralic

Speakers 21 million
Main languages Hungarian, Finnish, Estonian, Sami (Norway, Sweden, Finland), Samoyed (Russia)

Other

Speakers 394 million
These include Native American languages (North and South America), Paleosiberian languages (eastern Russia), Aboriginal languages (Australia), and languages spoken in Southeast Asia.

Core Concepts 7.4

Religion

Key Ideas
- Religious beliefs play an important role in shaping cultures.
- The world has many different religions.

Key Terms • religion • ethics

Visual Glossary

An important part of every culture is religion. **Religion** is a system of worship and belief, including belief about the nature of a god or gods. Religion can help people answer questions about the meaning of life. It can also guide people in matters of **ethics**, or standards of acceptable behavior. Religious beliefs and values help shape cultures.

Judaism

Judaism is based on a belief in one God, whose spiritual and ethical teachings are recorded in the Hebrew Bible. It began in the Middle East around 2000 B.C. By A.D. 100, Jews lived in Europe, Southwest Asia, and North Africa. The Jewish state of Israel was established in 1948. There are about 14 million Jews.

Christianity

Christianity is based on the teachings of Jesus, who Christians believe was the son of God. The Christian Bible is their sacred text. Christianity began in Southwest Asia around A.D. 30 and spread to Europe and Africa. It later spread to the rest of the world. There are about 2.07 billion Christians.

Islam

Islam is based on the Quran, a sacred text. The Quran contains what Muslims believe is the word of God as revealed to Muhammad beginning in A.D. 610. Islam spread quickly across Southwest Asia and North Africa, then to the rest of the world. There are about 1.25 billion Muslims.

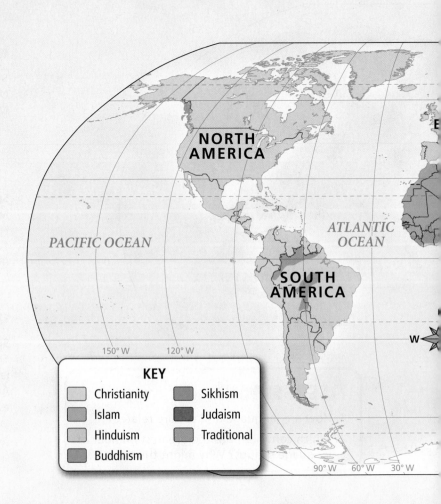

KEY
- Christianity
- Islam
- Hinduism
- Buddhism
- Sikhism
- Judaism
- Traditional

92

The world has many religions. Jews, Christians, and Muslims believe in one God. Members of other religions may believe in several gods.

All religions have prayers and rituals. Followers also observe religious holidays. For example, Jews celebrate the world's creation on Rosh Hashanah and their escape from slavery in Egypt on Passover. On Yom Kippur, Jews make up for their sins. Christians celebrate Jesus' birth on Christmas and his return to life on Easter. For Muslims, the holy month of Ramadan is a time to avoid food during daytime, to pray, and to read the Quran.

The world's major religions began in Asia. Hinduism, Buddhism, and Sikhism first developed in India. Judaism, Christianity, and Islam began in Southwest Asia before spreading throughout the world.

Hinduism

Hinduism evolved gradually over thousands of years in South Asia. It has several sacred texts. Hindus believe that everyone in the universe is part of a continuing cycle of birth, death, and rebirth. There are about 837 million Hindus.

Buddhism

Buddhism is based on the teachings of Siddhartha Gautama, known as the Buddha, who was born in India about 563 B.C. The Buddha's teachings include the search for enlightenment, or a true understanding of the nature of reality. There are about 373 million Buddhists.

Sikhism

Sikhism is based on the writings of several gurus, or prophets. Guru Nanak founded Sikhism about A.D. 1500 in South Asia. Sikhism's teachings include the cycle of rebirth and the search for enlightenment. There are about 24 million Sikhs.

Traditional Religions

Traditional religions include thousands of distinct religions. These religions tend to be passed down by word of mouth instead of through sacred texts. Each has its own set of beliefs. Examples include many African religions.

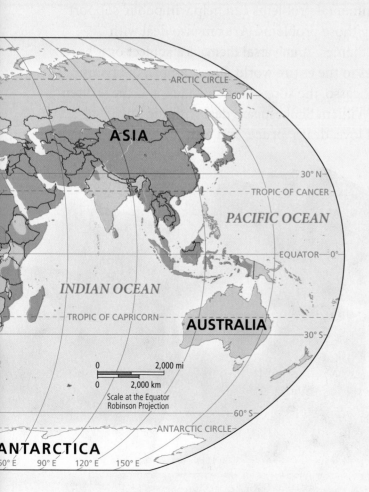

Assessment

1. How does religion help shape a culture?
2. What does the map tell you about the major religion where you live?

93

A print of a fish by Japanese artist Katsushika Taito, 1848

The Arts

Key Ideas
- Art is an important part of culture.
- Works of art can reveal much about society.

Key Terms
- universal theme
- visual arts
- architecture
- architect
- music
- literature

 Visual Glossary

The arts are an important aspect of culture. Works of art can reflect a society by dealing with topics or issues that are important to that society. Art can even shape society. For example, books that describe poverty or environmental problems can help win public support for solving those problems. Art can also deal with universal themes. A **universal theme** is a subject or idea that relates to the entire world. For example, the paintings of Pablo Picasso, the songs of the Beatles, and the written works of William Shakespeare deal with the universal themes of love, death, peace, and war.

Visual Arts

Art forms meant to be seen, such as painting, sculpture, and photography, are known as the **visual arts.** The visual arts can express emotions and spiritual ideas. They can also show us what life is like in other cultures and how people lived in the past. For example, a painting created in Italy in 1600 can show us how Italian people lived during this period.

Architecture

Architecture is the design and construction of buildings. A person who designs buildings is an **architect**. Architecture can show us what a society values and how it uses its resources. For example, are a society's most impressive buildings its religious buildings or its government buildings? Architectural works can be important cultural symbols.

This art museum in Bilbao, Spain, was designed by architect Frank Gehry.

94

Music

Music is an art form that uses sound, usually produced by instruments or voices. Music varies widely in different societies and cultures. It also changes over time as our tastes change. What one person considers beautiful music might be unpleasant noise to someone from a different place or time period. As a result, music can tell us about a society's tastes.

A Peruvian man plays a flute near the Inca ruins at Machu Picchu, Peru.

Literature

Literature is written work such as fiction, poetry, or drama. Literature can tell us what ideas a society considers important. By describing harmful things in society, literature can push for change.

A performance of Shakespeare's *A Midsummer Night's Dream*

Assessment

1. What are two ways in which the arts are related to society?

2. What might a painting of a main street in your area tell a stranger about your society?

95

Cultural Diffusion and Change

Key Ideas
- Cultures change over time.
- Cultural traits can spread from one culture to another.

Key Terms • cultural hearth • cultural diffusion • diversity

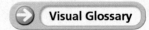 **Visual Glossary**

Chinese people in France celebrate the Chinese New Year.

All cultures change over time. That is, their cultural traits change. In general, for a new cultural trait to be adopted by a culture, it must offer some benefit or improvement over an existing trait.

How Cultural Traits Spread

A **cultural hearth** is a place where cultural traits develop. Traits from cultural hearths spread to surrounding cultures and regions. Customs and ideas can spread in many ways, including settlement, trade, migration, and communication. **Cultural diffusion** is the spread of cultural traits from one culture to another.

In the 1500s, Spanish explorers and settlers brought horses to the Americas. Many native peoples saw the advantages of using horses for moving quickly and for hunting. Horses soon became part of some Native American cultures.

Cultural traits can also spread through trade. Traders can move among different cultures. As they travel, they carry with them elements of their own culture, such as food or religious beliefs. Traders expose people to these new traits. If people find that an unfamiliar religion or other cultural trait improves their lives, they may make it a part of their own daily lives. For example, hundreds of years ago, Muslim traders helped spread Islam from Arabia to other cultures in Asia and Africa.

In a similar way, migrants spread cultural traits. Migrants bring cultural traditions with them to their new homelands. Over time, many migrants, or immigrants, have come to the United States. Immigrants have brought with them foods, languages, music, ideas, and other cultural traits. Some of these new ways of doing things have become part of American culture.

Technology and Culture

Technology also helps spread culture. The Internet, for example, has made instant communication common. Today, Americans can find out instantly what people in places such as Peru, India, or Japan are wearing, eating, or creating. If we like some of these traits, we may borrow them and make them a part of our culture.

Rapid transportation technologies, such as airplanes, make it easier for people to move all over the world. As they travel, people may bring new cultural traits to different regions.

Cultural change has both benefits and drawbacks. If customs change too quickly, people may feel that their culture is threatened. Some people worry that rapid communication is creating a new global culture that threatens diversity. **Diversity** is cultural variety. These people fear that the things that make people and cultures unique and interesting might disappear. They worry that we might end up with only a single worldwide culture.

Assessment

1. Why do cultures change?
2. What cultural traits have you borrowed in the last few years?

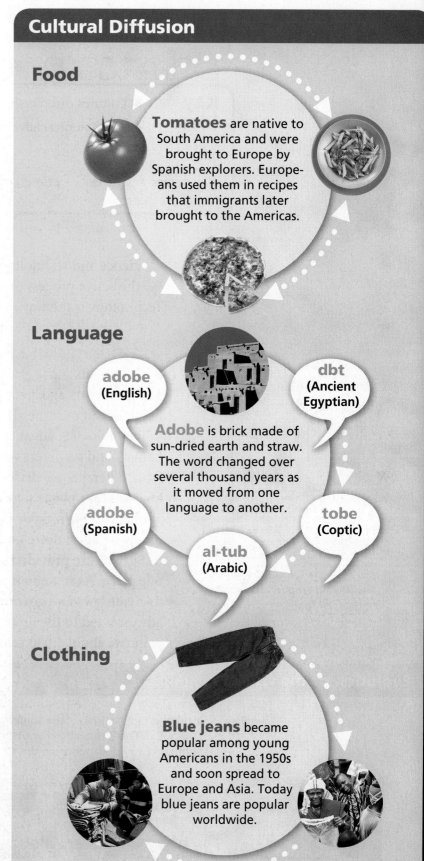

Cultural Diffusion

Food

Tomatoes are native to South America and were brought to Europe by Spanish explorers. Europeans used them in recipes that immigrants later brought to the Americas.

Language

adobe (English)

dbt (Ancient Egyptian)

Adobe is brick made of sun-dried earth and straw. The word changed over several thousand years as it moved from one language to another.

adobe (Spanish)

tobe (Coptic)

al-tub (Arabic)

Clothing

Blue jeans became popular among young Americans in the 1950s and soon spread to Europe and Asia. Today blue jeans are popular worldwide.

97

Science and Technology

Key Ideas
- Cultures often develop along with science and technology.
- Technological advances have greatly changed human life.

Key Terms • science • irrigate • standard of living

 Visual Glossary

Science and technology are important parts of culture. **Science** is the active process of acquiring knowledge of the natural world. Technology is the way in which people use tools and machines.

Technology and Progress

Early humans made gradual advances in technology. About 3 million years ago, people first learned how to make tools and weapons out of stone. They later discovered how to control fire.

Technological advances changed cultures. Early humans were hunters and gatherers who traveled from place to place to find food. Later, people discovered how to grow crops. They learned how to adapt plants to make them more useful. They tamed wild animals for farming or used them as food. Over time, people began to rely on agriculture for most of their food.

Agriculture provided a steady food supply and let people settle in one place. As settlements grew and turned into cities, people began to create laws and governments. They developed writing. These advances led to the first civilizations, or societies with complex cultures, about 5,000 years ago.

The Roman empire's thousands of miles of roads let armies and trade goods move easily.

Evolution of the Wheel

The wheel transformed culture. Below, the Sumerian Standard of Ur, about 2600 B.C., showing chariots pulled by donkeys; at right, a covered wagon from the 1800s

Early civilizations developed new technologies that allowed people to grow more crops. People invented tools such as the plow to help increase food production. They built canals and ditches to **irrigate,** or supply water to, crops. Cultures that lacked writing developed more slowly. Over time, agriculture and civilization spread across the world.

Modern Technology

Beginning around 1800, people developed new technologies that used power-driven machinery. This was the Industrial Revolution. It led to the growth of cities, science, and many new businesses. Eventually, people developed even more advanced technologies such as automobiles, airplanes, computers, and space travel.

All of these advances in science and technology have greatly changed people's lives and raised their standard of living. **Standard of living** is the level of comfort enjoyed by a person or a society. Modern technology also helps to connect people, products, and ideas.

Political decisions and belief systems can affect the use of technology. For example, the Chinese government has limited Chinese citizens' use of the Internet. This is an attempt to control discussion of government policies and other issues. Many religions have used technology as part of their practices. For example, religious groups have used the printing press to print the Hebrew Bible, the Christian Bible, the Quran, and other holy writings. Today, some religious organizations use radio, television, and the Internet to broadcast their beliefs.

Technology and Culture	
Technological Advances	Effects on Culture
Control of fire	Allowed humans to cook food, have light, protect themselves from animals
Irrigation	Increased food production; allowed people to do jobs other than farming; led to growth of cities
Wheel	Led to improved transportation in the form of carts and carriages; eventually led to trains, cars, and other vehicles
Printing press	Allowed the mass production of books; spread knowledge and ideas, increasing the number of educated people
Steam engine	Steam-powered machines performed work once done by hand; people moved to cities to find work in factories.
Refrigeration	Kept food fresh and safe longer; allowed food to be shipped over long distances from farms to cities

Assessment

1. What are science and technology?
2. How do you think technology might change culture in the future?

Over time, wheels led to better forms of transportation. At left, a French bicycle poster from 1925; below, a car from the 1950s

99

Culture and Geography

Part 7 Assessment

Key Terms and Ideas

1. **Define** What is **culture**?
2. **Recall** What is **religion**?
3. **Summarize** Does migration cause **cultural diffusion**? Explain why or why not.
4. **Connect** Are all **cultural traits** also **norms**? Explain.

5. **Draw Conclusions** How can **language** both unify and divide cultures?
6. **Compare and Contrast** What is the difference between a **nuclear family** and an **extended family**?
7. **Explain** Explain the relationship between technology and a **standard of living**.

Think Critically

8. **Draw Inferences** As technology makes it easier for people to travel to different countries, how might world culture regions change?
9. **Make Decisions** What other aspects of culture might link people in a country who speak different languages?

10. **Identify Evidence** Give two examples of ways in which today's cultures are influenced by past cultures.
11. **Draw Conclusions** How do you think ethics guide a country's laws?

Identify

Answer the following questions based on the map.

12. What does this map show?
13. What is the most widely spoken dialect in China?
14. What do the two purple and pink colors represent on the map?
15. What does the color orange represent on the map?
16. Across from which island do Chinese speakers of the Min dialect live?
17. Which dialect is spoken just to the north of the largest area of the Min dialect?
18. Not including the areas shown on the map as "other dialects or languages," in what part of China are most non-Mandarin dialects spoken?

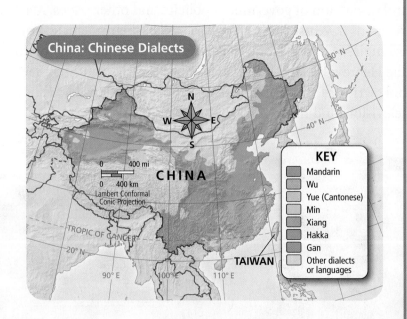

China: Chinese Dialects

KEY
- Mandarin
- Wu
- Yue (Cantonese)
- Min
- Xiang
- Hakka
- Gan
- Other dialects or languages

100

Journal Activity

Fill in the graphic organizer in your Student Journal.

Demonstrate Your Understanding Complete the Sum-It-Up activity in your journal to demonstrate your understanding of culture and geography. After you complete the activity, discuss your drawing with a partner. Be sure to support your answers to the questions with information from the lessons.

21st Century Learning

Work in Teams

Working with your partners, choose a country that is not familiar to anyone in your group. Then research and create an illustrated informational brochure about the country's culture. Be sure to

- provide examples of the country's art
- identify and describe the country's major religions and languages

Document-Based Questions

Success Tracker™
Online at myworldgeography.com

Use your knowledge of culture and geography and Documents A and B to answer Questions 1–3.

Document A

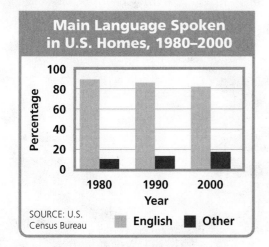

Main Language Spoken in U.S. Homes, 1980–2000

SOURCE: U.S. Census Bureau

■ English   ■ Other

Document B

" What a society [judges] important is [preserved] in its art."

—Harry Broudy

1. Examine Document A. Which of the following statements is probably true?

   A Migration to and cultural diffusion to the United States are likely decreasing.

   B Migration to and cultural diffusion to the United States are likely increasing.

   C Migration and cultural diffusion are unrelated to the changes shown in the graph.

   D Migration and cultural diffusion are no longer taking place in the United States.

2. Read Document B. Which of the following statements might Harry Broudy agree with?

   A Art does not reveal clues about past societies.

   B Art does not show the artist's beliefs.

   C Paintings reflect culture better than music does.

   D Looking at art is a good way to learn more about a society.

3. **Writing Task** Think of a favorite piece of art, such as a painting, a song, or a book. Then write one paragraph about what that piece of art reveals about your culture and beliefs.

Government and Citizenship

Supporters hold campaign signs.

A group of congressional interns

Voters in the 2008 presidential election

Anne Marie Sutherland

Serving Her Country

Story by Miles Lemaire for myWorld Geography

Anne Marie Sutherland has been trying to get people to vote since before she was old enough to join them at the polls.

Anne Marie is the daughter of a high school government teacher. She became interested in politics as a child. Her first experience with a political campaign was the U.S. presidential election in 1996, when she was just nine years old. "[M]y friends and I made some signs and walked up and down the street with them before the election," Anne Marie says. "We started talking to people, and we stayed up all night to see who would win."

As Anne Marie grew older, her interest in the political process increased. In 2000 and 2004, she worked as a volunteer on George W. Bush's presidential campaigns. In the 2008 presidential primaries, she helped manage candidate Mitt Romney's campaign in Atlanta, Georgia.

"We did lots of grassroots work," Anne Marie says about her work with the Romney campaign. "We were talking to different folks, getting signs out, working on some strategies for the area."

When Romney failed to win the Republican nomination for president, Anne Marie worked for 2008 Republican nominee John McCain. She looks back on her work with the Romney and McCain campaigns as a great learning experience. Most of all, she loved discussing political issues with people.

"What I took away from that opportunity was working directly with voters," Anne Marie says. "That's not something that you get to do for very long in politics [before] you move up and start taking on larger roles."

Anne Marie soon began taking on larger roles herself, winning an internship with U.S. Senator Saxby Chambliss. As part of her internship, Anne Marie helped other young people achieve their own goals. As she explains, "Every year a senator appoints a certain number of graduating [high school] seniors to the United States military academies. ... so I put most of my energy into working on that process.

"I love doing that," she says, "because what I'm able to do is [to help] prepare our future military leaders at such a young age. ... [S]ometimes when I'm working with them, I honestly think, 'This young student could really be our future president, or could be leading us in a major war, or could be the leader of any one of the branches of the military.' You never know."

Now 22 years old, Anne Marie is about to graduate from college with a degree in political science. She isn't content with helping other people achieve their dreams. "Maybe there is a campaign of my own in the future," she says. "I'd do anything I can to serve my country."

103

Foundations of Government

Key Ideas
- Governments are created to keep order in a society and provide for the people's common needs.
- A government's powers are either limited or unlimited.

Key Terms • government • constitution • limited government • unlimited government • tyranny

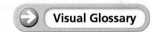

Hammurabi's Code is a set of laws created in ancient Babylon—now Iraq—around 1760 B.C. The code was carved onto a large stone slab, below. The photo at the bottom of the page shows the ruins of ancient Babylon. ▼

A **government** is a group of people who have the power to make and enforce laws for a country or area. The basic purpose of government is to keep order, to provide services, and to protect the common good, or the well-being of the people. Governments make and enforce laws to keep order. Protecting the common good can include building roads and schools or defending the country from attack. Governments also collect taxes, or required payments, from people and businesses. Governments use these taxes to pay for the goods and services they provide. The purpose of government has not changed much throughout history.

Origins of Government

Long before modern governments existed, people lived together in groups. These groups often had leaders who kept order and made decisions for the group. This was a simple form of government.

More complex governments first appeared in Southwest Asia more than 5,000 years ago. By that time, groups of people had begun to settle down. Villages grew into cities. People found that they needed an organized way to resolve problems and oversee tasks such as repairing irrigation canals and distributing food. They formed governments to manage those tasks.

Powers of Government

Today, most governments have a constitution. A **constitution** is a system of basic rules and principles by which a government is organized. A constitution also identifies the powers a government has. A government's powers are either limited or unlimited.

Limited Government

People gather in front of the U.S. Capitol.

Today, most constitutions call for limited government. **Limited government** is a government structure in which government actions are limited by law. Limited governments work to protect the common good and provide for people's needs.

In the United States, government actions are limited in order to protect people's individual freedoms. Generally, people in a limited government may gather freely to express their opinions and work to change government policies.

Unlimited Government

Chinese police arrest a protester.

Unlimited government is a government structure in which there are no effective limits on government actions. In an unlimited government such as China, a ruler or a small ruling group has the power to make all decisions for a country or society. This much power can lead to **tyranny,** which is the unjust use of power.

Unlimited governments often do not protect citizens' basic rights. They may censor, or restrict, citizens' access to the Internet and other forms of communication technology.

Assessment

1. How do constitutions limit the powers of government?
2. How do limited and unlimited governments differ?

Political Systems

Key Ideas
- Types of states have varied throughout history.
- There are many different kinds of government.

Key Terms • state • city-state • empire • democracy • nation-state • monarchy • authoritarian • communism

→ Visual Glossary

A **state** is a region that shares a common government. The first real states—called city-states—developed in Southwest Asia more than 5,000 years ago. A **city-state** is an independent state consisting of a city and its surrounding territory. Later, some military leaders conquered large areas and ruled them as empires. An **empire** is a state containing several countries. Geographic features such as rivers and mountains sometimes helped governments control territory by protecting against invasion.

A man votes in Kenya's 2007 presidential election.

Democracy

Examples Direct democracy: ancient Athens; representative democracy: United States

- **Democracy** is a form of government in which citizens hold political power; citizens are the ultimate source of government power and authority.

- In a direct democracy, citizens come together to pass laws and select leaders.

- In a representative democracy, citizens elect representatives to make government decisions.

- The powers of a democratic government are usually limited.

Queen Elizabeth II of the United Kingdom

Nation-States

Today, most states are nation-states. A **nation-state** is a state that is independent of other states. The United States is an example of a nation-state. We often use the general words *nation* or *country* to refer to nation-states.

All nation-states have some common features. For example, nation-states have specific territory with clearly defined borders. Nation-states have governments, laws, and authority over citizens. Most are divided into smaller states or provinces that contain cities and towns.

Forms of Government

Each state has a government, but there are many different kinds of government. Throughout history, most states were autocracies (ruled by a single person) or oligarchies (ruled by a small group of people). Today, however, many states have some form of democracy in which citizens hold political power.

A large statue of former leader Kim Il-Sung stands above people in communist North Korea.

Monarchy

Examples Absolute monarchy: Saudi Arabia; Constitutional monarchy: United Kingdom

- A monarchy is a form of government in which the state is ruled by a monarch.
- A monarch is usually a king or queen.
- Power is inherited by family members.
- Absolute monarchs have unlimited power.
- Monarchs in constitutional monarchies are limited by law and share power with other branches of government.
- The powers of a monarchy can be limited or unlimited.

Authoritarian Government

Examples Nazi Germany, Cuba, North Korea

- An authoritarian government is one in which all power is held by a single person or a small group.
- Government may control all aspects of life.
- One of the common forms of authoritarian government is communism, a political and economic system in which government owns all property and makes all economic decisions.
- The powers of an authoritarian government are unlimited.

Assessment

1. What are states, city-states, and nation-states?
2. Which form of government relies most on its citizens? Explain your answer.

107

Political Structures

Key Ideas
- Political structures help governments operate in an organized way.
- The U.S. government follows basic democratic principles.

Key Terms • unitary system • federal system

Visual Glossary

Central Government
Central governments are responsible for national affairs.

U.S. Capitol

Regional Government
Regional governments include state or provincial governments.

Texas State Capitol

Local Government
Local governments include county, city, and town governments.

Trumbull, Connecticut, town hall

Countries distribute power between the central government and smaller units of government. We can learn more about how a government functions by examining its structure and principles.

Systems of Government

Governments can distribute power in three basic ways: the unitary system, the federal system, and the confederal system. In a **unitary system,** a central government makes all laws for the entire country. In a **federal system,** power is divided among central, regional, and local governments. In a confederal system, a group of independent states join together and give limited powers to a common government. Most countries have a unitary system. The United States and some other countries have a federal system. The confederal system is rare.

Principles of Government

Every government has basic principles that affect the way it serves its people. Authoritarian governments may seek to control all aspects of society, even people's actions and beliefs. For example, some authoritarian governments limit citizens' use of communications technology such as the Internet. Most democratic governments act to protect individual rights and the common good.

In the United States, government follows basic democratic principles. For example, government follows the rule of law. That is, government powers are defined by laws that limit its actions. Also, government decides issues by majority rule. A law cannot pass unless the majority—most—representatives vote for it. At the same time, the majority may not take away the basic rights and freedoms of minority groups or individuals. In other words, government must balance majority rule with minority rights.

Branches of Government

Under the U.S. Constitution, power is divided among the three branches of government: the legislative, executive, and judicial branches. This division is called separation of powers. The Constitution also establishes a system of checks and balances that limits each branch's power. Each branch has some power to change or cancel the actions of the other branches.

Legislative Branch

U.S. Congress

The legislative branch establishes laws. In a representative democracy like the United States, citizens elect legislative representatives to make decisions for them. The legislative branch also imposes taxes, or required payments. Taxes are used to pay for government services and public goods such as roads, parks, fire departments, and national defense. Public goods are owned by everyone in the country.

Executive Branch

U.S. President Barack Obama

The executive branch carries out, or enforces, the laws. It also provides for the country's defense, conducts foreign policy, and manages day-to-day affairs. The United States and some other countries have a presidential system with an elected president as the head of the executive branch. Other democracies, such as the United Kingdom, have a parliamentary system. In this system, the parliament, or legislative branch, chooses a prime minister as chief executive.

Judicial Branch

U.S. Supreme Court

The judicial branch makes decisions about disputes. It does this through courts of law. These courts can range from local criminal courts to the highest court in the land. In the United States that court is called the Supreme Court. Among other things, the Supreme Court interprets the law. That is, it judges how a law should be applied and whether the law violates the Constitution.

Assessment

1. What are the three branches of government?

2. What are three key democratic principles?

Conflict and Cooperation

Key Ideas
- Governments and international organizations cooperate for many reasons, including avoiding war and improving trade.
- Conflict can have serious effects on countries.

Key Terms • sovereignty • foreign policy • treaty • diplomacy

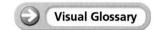 Visual Glossary

Every nation-state, or country, has clearly defined territory and sovereignty over that territory. **Sovereignty** is supreme authority, or power. Every country also has a central government. The central government takes care of matters that affect the whole country. This includes dealing with other countries' governments. Interactions between governments can take the form of conflict or cooperation.

Conflict

Most countries have a **foreign policy,** a set of goals describing how a country's government plans to interact with other countries' governments. A country's foreign policy reflects its values and intentions. Geographic factors such as location, physical features, and distribution of natural resources can influence foreign policy.

A country's foreign policy can lead to conflict with other countries. Wars and fighting begin for many reasons. Some wars begin as conflicts over control of land or resources. Others result from religious disagreements, political revolutions, or conflict between ethnic groups. Wars can lead to widespread death and destruction.

Food being distributed in Angola. ▼

Public Health Organizations

International Red Cross and Red Crescent Movement Provides medical aid, food, and other relief services to victims of war or natural disasters

World Health Organization Fights disease, especially among the world's poor, by providing health information, medical training, and medicine

10

Cooperation

Many people view the world as a global community in which people should cooperate to avoid conflict and help others. This cooperation may take the form of a **treaty,** a formal agreement between two or more countries. Some treaties are agreements to help defend other countries. Other treaties are agreements to limit the harmful effects of war. For example, the Geneva Conventions list rules for the proper treatment of wounded soldiers, prisoners, and civilians.

The United Nations (UN) is the largest international organization that works for peace. Nearly every country in the world belongs to the UN. Governments send representatives to the UN to engage in diplomacy. **Diplomacy** is managing communication and relationships between countries. The UN Declaration of Human Rights lists the rights that all people should have, including life, liberty, and security. The UN works to protect these rights around the world.

Governments also cooperate for reasons other than avoiding conflict. For example, governments often work with one another to improve their countries' economies through trade. International trade can provide new goods and markets. Trade agreements involving multiple countries have become common in recent years.

This water pump in South Africa was funded by the World Bank.

Economic Organizations

World Bank Provides loans for projects aimed at promoting economic development

International Monetary Fund (IMF) Seeks to prevent and resolve economic crises by offering advice, information, technical training, and loans

Humanitarian Organizations

United Nations (UN) Seeks to encourage international cooperation and achieve world peace but sometimes faces criticism

CARE International Seeks to end world poverty through development and self-help

◀ UN peacekeeping troops in Bosnia

Assessment

1. What are some of the functions of international organizations?
2. How do governments resolve conflict and cooperate?

111

Core Concepts 8.5

Citizenship

Key Ideas
- Citizens have basic rights, but those rights come with responsibilities.
- Rights and responsibilities can vary widely in different countries.

Key Terms • citizen • civic life • civic participation • political party • interest group

 Visual Glossary

The United States is a representative democracy. In a democracy, all political power comes from citizens. A **citizen** is a legal member of a country. In the United States, most people become citizens by being born on U.S. territory. Immigrants to the United States can become citizens through a legal process known as naturalization.

Rights and Responsibilities

Citizens' rights and responsibilities can come from a number of sources. These sources include constitutions, cultural traditions, and religious laws.

Americans' basic rights are protected by the Bill of Rights, a part of the U.S. Constitution. The Bill of Rights and other laws protect rights such as freedom of speech and freedom of religion. If the government violates these rights, citizens can fight the injustice in court. For the most part, these rights are also guaranteed to noncitizens.

Immigrants to the United States become citizens at a naturalization ceremony. ▼

112

Americans also have responsibilities. For example, we have the right to speak freely, but we also have the responsibility to allow others to say things we may not agree with. Our responsibilities include a duty to participate in government and **civic life,** or activities having to do with one's society and community. Voting is both a right and a responsibility for U.S. citizens.

Rights and responsibilities can vary widely in different countries and societies. Although most democratic governments protect basic human rights, nondemocratic governments often do not. Citizens who live in autocracies or oligarchies usually cannot take part in government or express their views openly.

Citizenship Worldwide

Ideas about rights and responsibilities can change over time. Many countries have become democracies over the past 200 years. These democracies now protect basic human rights such as freedom of expression and freedom from unfair imprisonment. Some of these countries did not protect these rights in the past or did not protect these rights for all people.

Today, international trade, transportation, and communication have linked the world's people. As a result, some people think that we should consider ourselves to be citizens of a global community. They believe that we are responsible for supporting human rights and equality for all people around the world.

Assessment

1. What is the main source of American citizens' basic rights?

2. How do the roles and responsibilities of citizens vary between democratic and nondemocratic countries?

Civic Participation

Voting is one type of **civic participation**, or taking part in government. Here are some others:

Keeping informed about local, state, and national issues

Contacting an elected representative, such as a state legislator or member of Congress

Voicing opinions at town meetings

Taking part in public gatherings, protests, or demonstrations

Signing a petition, a formal request for government to do something

Running for public office

Getting involved in a political party—a group that supports candidates for public offices

Joining an interest group—a group that seeks to influence public policy on certain issues

113

Part 8 Assessment

Key Terms and Ideas

1. **Recall** There are two types of democracy: direct and representative. Which kind of **democracy** is the United States?

2. **Identify** Describe the powers of an **unlimited government.**

3. **Connect** Why did **governments** first develop thousands of years ago?

4. **Describe** How does the U.S. government balance legislative, executive, and judicial power?

5. **Compare and Contrast** How are the **unitary system** and the **federal system** similar and different?

6. **Paraphrase** Explain **diplomacy** in your own words.

7. **Identify** Name two ways American **citizens** can participate in the political process.

Think Critically

8. **Draw Inferences** Consider that you can freely read about your government's actions and policies on the Internet. How might Internet access differ in a country with an authoritarian government?

9. **Make Decisions** Do you think that people who live in a democracy should be required to fulfill their civic responsibilities?

10. **Synthesize** Imagine that a country shares its borders with three others. How do you think its geography might relate to its foreign policy?

11. **Draw Conclusions** Who do you think is more likely to speak out against the government: a citizen in a limited government or a citizen in an unlimited government? Explain.

Identify

Answer the following questions based on the map.

12. Which country is the westernmost member of the European Union?

13. Which EU members border Latvia?

14. List the EU members with territory located to the north of 60° N latitude and to the east of 0° longitude.

15. Which EU members border Slovenia?

16. How many members made up the European Union in 2009?

17. What sea do Spain and Greece border?

18. How would you describe EU membership?

114

Journal Activity

Fill in the graphic organizer in your Student Journal.

Demonstrate Your Understanding Complete the Sum-It-Up activity in your journal to demonstrate your understanding of government and citizenship. After you complete the activity, discuss your If-Then statements with a small group. Be sure to support your statements with information from the lessons.

21st Century Learning

Analyze Media Content

Authoritarian governments usually allow little media freedom. Find political news articles from authoritarian and democratic countries. Then compare and contrast them in a short essay. Remember to
- include excerpts from a variety of articles
- discuss how the government might influence what is published

Document-Based Questions

Success Tracker™
Online at myworldgeography.com

Use your knowledge of government and citizenship and Documents A and B to answer Questions 1–3.

Document A

U.S. Presidential Elections: Eligible Voter Participation, 1980–2008

Year	Percentage of Eligible Voters
1980	54.2%
1984	55.2%
1988	52.8%
1992	58.1%
1996	51.7%
2000	54.2%
2004	60.1%
2008	61.7%

SOURCE: U.S. Election Project, George Mason University

1. Examine Document A. How has eligible voter participation changed in the time period shown?

   A It has declined steadily.

   B It has increased steadily.

   C It has declined since 1996.

   D It has increased since 1996.

Document B

" The accumulation of all powers, legislative, executive, and judiciary, in the same hands, whether of one, a few, or many … may justly be pronounced the very definition of tyranny."

—James Madison, *The Federalist,* No. 48

2. Read Document B. Which of the following statements would James Madison agree with?

   A Separate branches of government are unnecessary.

   B Unlimited government is not a form of tyranny.

   C Separate branches of government are essential.

   D A unitary system of government is ideal.

3. **Writing Task** Do you agree or disagree with James Madison? Write a short essay in which you respond to Madison's quotation. Be sure to explain your position clearly, supporting it with information from the lessons.

my worldgeography.com   Self-Test

115

Tools of History

Inca ruins in Peru

An archaeologist sketches a dig in Lima, Peru.

116

Archaeologists at a dig

Brian McCray

Digging for Clues

Story by Miles Lemaire for myWorld Geography

Brian McCray likes to dig in the dirt. But Brian isn't just playing around. He's an archaeologist who has traveled around the world to dig up objects from the past and learn more about the people who made them.

Carrying out an archaeological dig isn't as simple as picking a location, grabbing a shovel, and starting to dig, Brian says. He spends weeks or months researching the history of the dig's location before a shovel goes into the ground. Brian will study maps, look at photographs, and read written descriptions of the area. He wants to know as much as possible about the site before he begins to explore it.

Once an archaeological dig begins, archaeologists like Brian carefully examine all the objects found at the site. Then they record and save the objects for future research. Keeping good records is very important. All archaeological sites are drawn and mapped carefully, with detailed information about where each object was found. It can take months or years to fully examine all of the artifacts, or objects made by people, found at an archaeological site.

"The things that are deeper in the ground are, in most cases, older than the things closer to the surface," says Brian. "We keep track of every layer of soil and what we find there."

Brian's research has allowed him to travel throughout the Americas. He has studied sites in the northern United States, the Caribbean, and western South America. Brian has worked with the Digital Archaeological Archive of Contemporary Slavery. This research has helped historians learn more about the lives of enslaved Africans in North America and the Caribbean. But his most interesting discovery was in the Andes Mountains in South America. In the Andes, Brian studied something that researchers still don't fully understand.

"It was actually what appears to be a swimming pool," Brian says. "It was constructed by the Incas at the very end of the Incan Empire." That was almost 500 years ago.

What was the "pool" used for? "Who knows?" Brian says. "It was a big sunken court with really amazing cut-stone masonry and five or six canals bringing water down into it from up the hill … It's way too cold up there for anyone to want to swim all that often."

But although Brian and his fellow archaeologists don't yet know why the Incas built this pool, you can be sure that they'll keep digging to find out the answer. Who knows? Maybe Brian will be the one to finally uncover the truth.

117

Measuring Time

Key Ideas
- Throughout history, societies and cultures have organized time in different ways.
- People have used a number of different calendars to measure time.

Key Terms • historian • timeline • chronology • period • prehistory

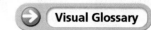 **Visual Glossary**

It can be hard to describe the concept of time. But **historians**—people who study events in the past—know that organizing time is important if we want to understand past events.

The timeline on this page shows watershed events—important points in history. The period 1940–1949 is an example of a decade, or a period of ten years. Below, a Sumerian writing tablet. ▼

Using a Timeline

Historians use timelines as a tool. A **timeline** is a line marked off with a series of events and dates. Historians use timelines to put events in a **chronology,** a list of events in the order in which they occurred.

A timeline is flexible. It can cover a day, a year, a decade (ten years), a century (one hundred years), a millennium (one thousand years), or any other period in history. A **period** is a length of time singled out because of a specific event or development that happened during that time. A period is also known as an era or an epoch. Historians use periods and eras to organize and describe human activities.

A.D. **1945** World War II ends.

| 1940 | 1941 | 1942 | 1943 | 1944 | 1945 | 1946 | 1947 | 1948 | 1949 |

3200 B.C. Sumerians develop the earliest known form of writing.

| 3000 B.C. | 2000 B.C. | 1000 B.C. | A.D. 1 | A.D. 1000 | A.D. 2000 |

1766 B.C. China's Shang dynasty begins.

A.D. 250 Maya Classic period begins in Mexico and Central America.

A.D. 1492 Christopher Columbus sails to the Americas.

118

Organizing Time

The past is often split into two parts, prehistory and history. **Prehistory** is the time before humans invented writing. *History* refers to written history, which began about 5,200 years ago.

We can also organize history by beginning with a key event from the past. Today much of the world uses the believed birthdate of Jesus as a key event. Years before that event are labeled B.C., for "before Christ," or B.C.E., for "before common era." Years after Jesus's birth are labeled A.D., meaning *anno Domini,* Latin for "in the year of our Lord." These years are also known as C.E., for "common era."

The Jewish calendar counts the years since the creation of the world, according to Jewish tradition. The Islamic calendar is dated from the year that the prophet Muhammad moved to the city of Medina.

Throughout history, societies have used different calendars. Maya and Aztec priests made calendars for farming and religious purposes. Today much of the world uses the Gregorian calendar, which has a 365- or 366-day year. It is based on the movement of Earth around the sun. The Jewish year, based on both sun and moon, varies from 353 to 385 days to adjust to the solar year. The Islamic year, however, is based on the cycles of the moon and lasts about 354 days.

Calendar Systems

Calendars are based on the movements of Earth, the moon, the stars, or a combination. Throughout history, people have used different methods to create calendars. The objects shown here were all different ways of measuring the passage of time.

Astrolabe This astrolabe was used by Muslim astronomers to calculate the positions of the sun, moon, planets, and stars. ▶

◀ **Aztec Calendar Stone** The Aztecs had two calendars: a 365-day agricultural calendar and a 260-day religious calendar.

Roman Calendar Early Roman calendars were based on the movements of the moon and had 10 months and 304 days. Later, the calendar had 12 months and 355 days. ▶

Assessment

1. How do people organize time?
2. If you created a timeline of everything you did yesterday, what would you choose to be the first event? What would be the last event? How would you decide which events are important enough to include on the timeline?

119

Historical Sources

Key Ideas
- Historical sources can provide important information.
- Historians must evaluate the accuracy and reliability of sources.

Key Terms • primary source • artifact • secondary source • bias

Visual Glossary

Historians try to accurately understand and describe the past. To understand past events, historians study historical sources.

Primary and Secondary Sources

A **primary source** is information that comes directly from a person who experienced an event. It consists of what the person writes, says, or creates about the event. Primary sources include letters, diaries, speeches, and photographs. Artifacts are also primary sources. An **artifact** is an object made by a human being, such as a tool or a weapon. We use primary sources to understand events from the points of view of people who lived at the time in which they happened.

Books, articles, movies, and other sources that describe or make sense of the past are secondary sources. A **secondary source** is information about an event that does not come from a person who experienced that event.

This U.S. poster created during World War II is an example of a primary source. ▼

We Can Do It!

Letters written by soldiers are primary sources.

Primary Sources

66 Yesterday, December 7, 1941—a date which will live in infamy—the United States of America was suddenly and deliberately attacked by naval and air forces of the empire of Japan . . . No matter how long it may take us to overcome this premeditated [planned] invasion, the American people in their righteous might will win through to absolute victory. 99

—President Franklin D. Roosevelt, December 8, 1941

Evaluating Historical Sources

Historical sources do not always give a true account of events. Even primary sources can be wrong or misleading. An author's personal opinions may have influenced what he or she recorded. Sometimes the author may not remember the event accurately. A historian must decide what, if anything, to trust in a primary source.

A historian must also be cautious when using secondary sources. Not all secondary sources are equally reliable. For example, the Internet includes millions of well-researched articles, books, and other reliable secondary sources. However, any Internet search will also find many inaccurate Web sites.

Historians and students of history—like you—must evaluate a source to determine its reliability. When you examine primary and secondary sources, ask yourself questions like these:

- Who created the source material? A witness to an event may be more trustworthy than someone looking back at the event from a later time. However, a scholar or publication with a good reputation is also a reliable source. For example, a college professor who specializes in Chinese history would be a reliable source on China.

- Is the information fact or opinion? A fact is something that can be proved true or false. An opinion is a personal belief. Opinions are valuable not as a source of facts but as a clue to the author's judgments or feelings.

- Does the material seem to have a bias? A **bias** is an unfair preference for or dislike of something. Biased material often leaves out facts that do not support the author's point of view.

The painting and article below are secondary sources. ▼

Secondary Sources

❝ Japanese planes attacked the U.S. naval base at Pearl Harbor, Hawaii, on December 7, 1941. . . . This disaster caused the American public to support an immediate American entry into the war. ❞

—*History of Our World*, Prentice Hall, 2008

Assessment

1. What is a primary source?
2. Which online source will likely be more accurate, an encyclopedia or a personal journal such as a blog? Explain.

121

Archaeology and Other Sources

Key Idea
- Archaeology and other historical sources offer clues to what life was like in the distant past.

Key Terms
- archaeology
- oral tradition
- anthropology

 Visual Glossary

Machu Picchu, Peru, is an Incan city abandoned in the 1500s and largely forgotten until the 1800s.

The Temple of Inscriptions in Palenque, Mexico, contains the tomb of the Maya ruler Pakal, who died in A.D. 683. ▼

Archaeologists Louis and Mary Leakey found many fossil remains of human ancestors in Africa's Olduvai Gorge.

Over time, much of the ancient world has disappeared. Large cities have collapsed into ruins. Buildings are buried under layers of soil and sand or covered by thick forests. The artifacts that show what life was like in ancient times are often buried or hidden. The science of archaeology aims to uncover this hidden history. **Archaeology** is the scientific study of ancient cultures through the examination of artifacts and other evidence.

Archaeologists and Anthropologists

Archaeologists are part treasure hunters and part detectives. They explore the places where people once lived and worked, searching for artifacts such as tools, weapons, and pottery. Archaeologists study the objects they find to learn more about the past.

Artifacts can help us identify the resources available to ancient people. They can help us understand how these people used technology and how they adapted to their environment.

Anthropology also helps historians understand the past. **Anthropology** is the study of humankind in all aspects, especially development and culture. Anthropologists seek to understand the origins of humans and the ways humans developed physically. This field often involves studying fossils—bones and other remains that have been preserved in rock.

Anthropologists also try to determine how human cultures formed and grew. Clues to the past can come from a culture's oral traditions. **Oral tradition** is a community's cultural and historical background, passed down in spoken stories and songs.

New Zealand's Maori people have passed down many aspects of their culture through oral tradition. ▼

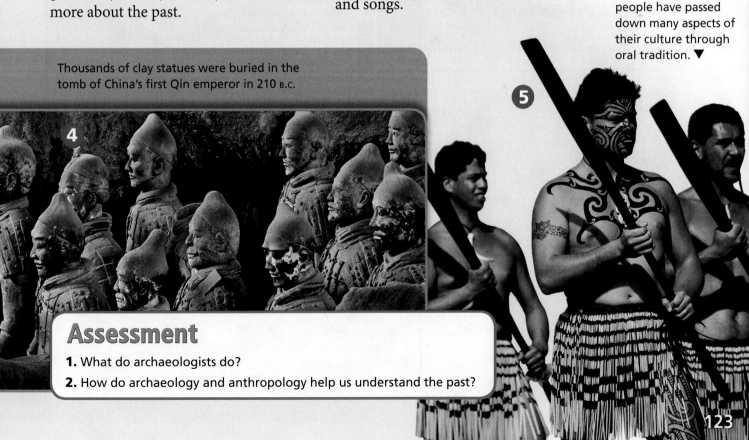

Thousands of clay statues were buried in the tomb of China's first Qin emperor in 210 B.C.

Assessment

1. What do archaeologists do?
2. How do archaeology and anthropology help us understand the past?

123

Core Concepts 9.4

Historical Maps

Key Ideas

- Historical maps offer visual representations of historical information.
- Historical maps show information about places at certain times.

Key Term • historical map

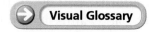

Visual Glossary

When you read about a historical event like an important battle, it can be hard to get a clear picture of what really happened. You may have to understand how landforms like rivers and hills affected the battle. Or perhaps the location of a nearby town, railroad, or road influenced the fighting. Sometimes the best way to learn about a historical event or period is by examining a historical map.

The title identifies the map's subject and time period.

The Roman Empire, about A.D. 117

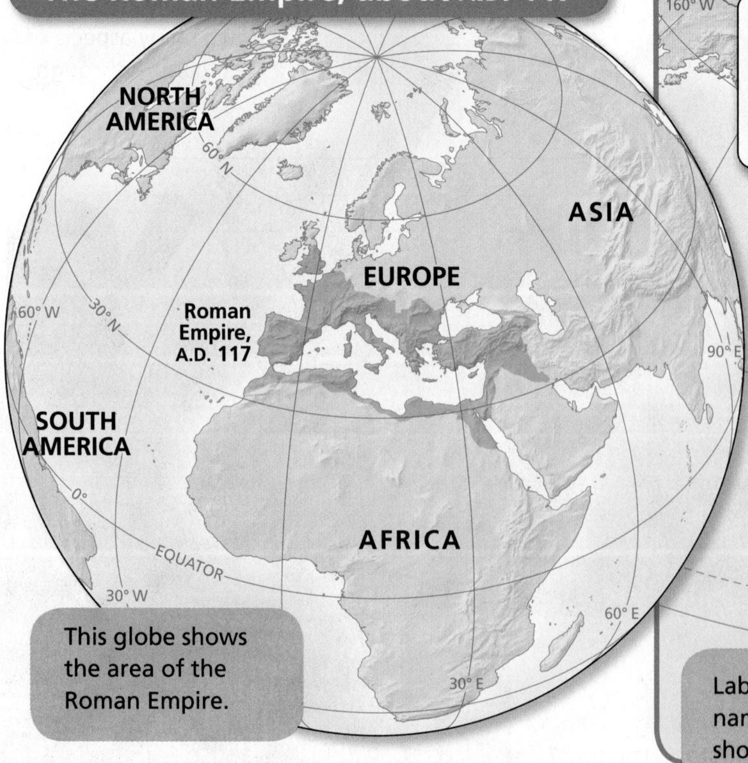

NORTH AMERICA
ASIA
EUROPE
Roman Empire, A.D. 117
SOUTH AMERICA
AFRICA
60° N
30° N
0°
EQUATOR
60° W
30° W
90° E
60° E
30° E

This globe shows the area of the Roman Empire.

North America, 1783

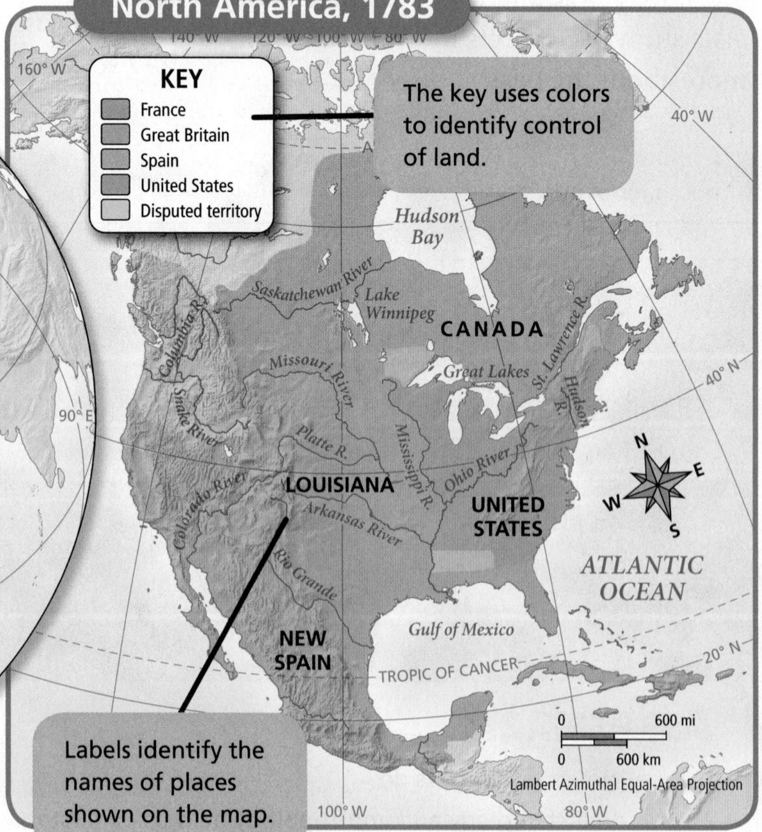

KEY
France
Great Britain
Spain
United States
Disputed territory
160° W
140° W
120° W
100° W
80° W
40° W
Hudson Bay
Saskatchewan River
Lake Winnipeg
CANADA
Columbia R.
Missouri River
Great Lakes
St. Lawrence R.
Hudson R.
Snake River
Platte R.
Mississippi R.
Ohio River
LOUISIANA
Colorado River
Arkansas River
UNITED STATES
Rio Grande
ATLANTIC OCEAN
Gulf of Mexico
NEW SPAIN
TROPIC OF CANCER
40° N
20° N
N
E
S
W
0
600 mi
0
600 km
Lambert Azimuthal Equal-Area Projection

The key uses colors to identify control of land.

Labels identify the names of places shown on the map.

A **historical map** is a special-purpose map that provides information about a place at a certain time in history. Historical maps can show information such as migration, trade patterns, or other facts.

Historical maps have similar features. Most have a title and a key. Most use colors and symbols to show resources, movement, locations of people, or other features. Use the following four steps to become familiar with historical maps.

1. Read the title. Note the date, the time span, or other information about the subject of the map. If the map includes a locator map, examine it to see what region is shown.

2. Study the map quickly to get a general idea of what it shows. Read any place names and other labels. Note any landforms.

3. Examine the map's key. Pick out the first symbol or other entry, read what it stands for, and find an example on the map. Repeat this process for the remaining key entries until you understand them all.

4. Study the map more thoroughly. Make sure you have a clear understanding of the picture the map presents. If you need help, reread the related section of your textbook or examine the map again.

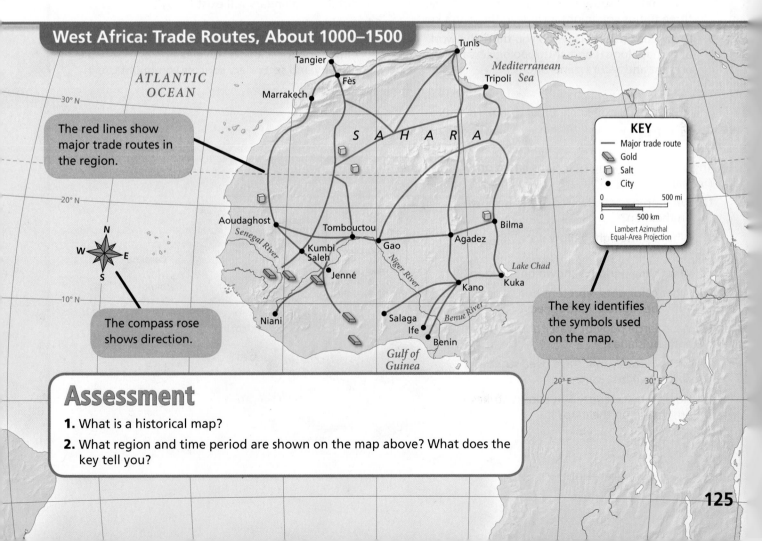

West Africa: Trade Routes, About 1000–1500

The red lines show major trade routes in the region.

The compass rose shows direction.

The key identifies the symbols used on the map.

KEY
- Major trade route
- Gold
- Salt
- City

0 — 500 mi
0 — 500 km
Lambert Azimuthal Equal-Area Projection

Assessment

1. What is a historical map?

2. What region and time period are shown on the map above? What does the key tell you?

125

Part 9 Assessment

Key Terms and Ideas

1. **Summarize** What is **archaeology**?

2. **Identify** When a person who did not experience an event describes the event, is the description a **primary source** or a **secondary source**?

3. **Compare and Contrast** Explain the difference between history and **prehistory.**

4. **Identify Cause and Effect** What do archaeologists do with **artifacts**?

5. **Synthesize** How do **timelines** show historical events or periods?

6. **Identify** What do **historical maps** show?

7. **Recall** What three questions should you ask when evaluating a source?

Think Critically

8. **Make Decisions** Imagine that you are creating a map that will show ancient trade routes. Name three things you might include in the map's key.

9. **Draw Conclusions** How do you think the work of archaeologists and anthropologists can help present and future generations?

10. **Draw Inferences** Why do you think so many different calendars still exist today?

11. **Analyze Primary and Secondary Sources** Imagine that you are writing a biographical profile of a famous political leader. Give examples of reliable primary and secondary sources you might use in your research.

Identify

Answer the following questions based on the map.

12. What area of the United States is shown on the map?

13. What do the light yellow dots represent?

14. What time period is shown on the map?

15. What color dots represent hurricanes with the highest wind speeds?

16. What large body of water borders Texas and Louisiana?

17. List two states that have been struck by category 4 hurricanes.

18. How many category 5 hurricane strikes are shown on the map?

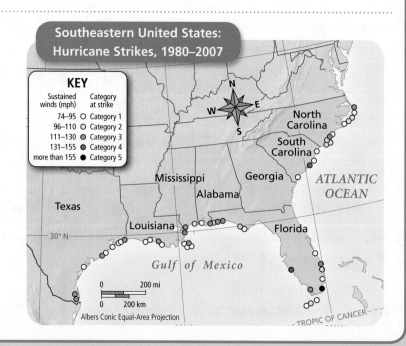

Southeastern United States: Hurricane Strikes, 1980–2007

KEY

Sustained winds (mph)		Category at strike
74–95	○	Category 1
96–110	○	Category 2
111–130	◉	Category 3
131–155	◉	Category 4
more than 155	●	Category 5

Journal Activity

Fill in the graphic organizer in your Student Journal.

Demonstrate Your Understanding Complete the Sum-It-Up activity in your journal to demonstrate your understanding of the tools of history. After you complete the activity, discuss your plan for using historical resources with a small group. Be sure to support your plan with information from the lessons.

21st Century Learning

Develop Cultural Awareness

Oral tradition remains an important part of many cultures. Research a song or story still passed on by oral tradition today, either in your own culture or in another. Then share the song or story with the class. Be sure to address the following topics:
- Origins of the song or story
- Cultural significance of the song or story

Document-Based Questions

Online at myworldgeography.com

Use your knowledge of the tools of history and Documents A and B to answer Questions 1–3.

Document A

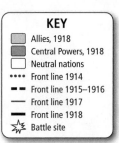

KEY
- Allies, 1918
- Central Powers, 1918
- Neutral nations
- •••• Front line 1914
- – – Front line 1915–1916
- — Front line 1917
- ▬ Front line 1918
- ⚔ Battle site

Document B

" [Alexander] was only twenty years old when he succeeded to the crown, and he found the kingdom torn into pieces by dangerous [groups of people]."

— Plutarch, *Life of Alexander,* about A.D. 100

1. Document A is a key to a historical map showing Europe during World War I. What information does this map not give you?

   A location of front line in 1917

   B locations of battles

   C members of the Central Powers in 1918

   D outcome of World War I

2. Document B is an excerpt about the ancient Greek leader Alexander the Great, written by a historian about 400 years after Alexander's death. Which of the following best describes this excerpt?

   A primary source

   B secondary source

   C artifact

   D prehistoric

3. **Writing Task** Using information from Documents A and B and your knowledge of the tools of history, describe how historians use sources to understand and explain historical events.

Regional Overview

Europe and Russia

The many countries of Europe plus Russia reach from the Atlantic Ocean to the Pacific Ocean. Russia spreads over two continents, Europe and Asia. More than 590 million people live in Europe with another 140 million in Russia. Most live in urban areas. More than 230 languages are spoken here, such as English, French, Spanish, Basque, Greek, Finnish, and Russian.

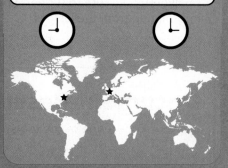

What time is it there?

Washington, D.C.	Paris, France
9 A.M. Monday	3 P.M. Monday

KEY
— National border
✪ Capital city
Orthographic Projection

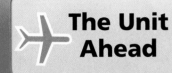

The Unit Ahead

➡ **Chapter 8** Ancient and Medieval Europe ➡ **Chapter 11** Eastern Europe

➡ **Chapter 9** Europe in Modern Times ➡ **Chapter 12** Russia

➡ **Chapter 10** Western Europe

my worldgeography.com

Plan your trip online by doing a Data Discovery Activity and watching the myStory Videos of the region's teens.

my Story

Yasmin

Age: 18

Home: Bjärred, Sweden

Chapter 10

my Story

Serhiy

Age: 16

Home: Bezpalche, Ukraine

Chapter 11

my Story

Boris

Age: 15

Home: Moscow, Russia

Chapter 12

A field of sunflowers and lavender in France

Regional Overview
Physical Geography

The Alps are rugged mountains that have their own snowy climate, perfect for winter sports like skiing.

Scandinavia is a long, narrow peninsula that extends from the northernmost part of Europe.

ARCTIC OCEAN

Ural Mountains

Northwestern Highlands

Scandinavia

Baltic Sea

North European Plain

ATLANTIC OCEAN

North Sea

Carpathian Mountains

Black Sea

Alps

Balkan Peninsula

Adriatic Sea

Mont Blanc
15,774 ft (4,808 m)

Mediterranean Sea

Iberian Peninsula

S i b e r i a

Caspian Sea

The West Siberian Plain borders the world's largest steppes region, an extensive area of cold and dry grasslands.

Regional Flyover

Suppose you fly in an airplane across Europe and Russia. If you began over the Atlantic Ocean, you would first notice that Europe is a giant peninsula stretching westward from a larger landmass. From it extend many smaller peninsulas, so that the whole continent of Europe is sometimes called the "peninsula of peninsulas."

Next, you might notice two important mountain ranges. The Alps stretch in an east-west arc through central Europe. Flying east, you would see a north–south mountain range called the Urals. These mountains form the traditional border between European Russia and Asiatic Russia.

The North European Plain sweeps east–west across Europe into European Russia. These lowlands have had both benefits and drawbacks for the region. The flat land is good for settlement and farming. It has also been a gateway for invading armies throughout history.

➡ In-flight Movie

Take flight over Europe and Russia and explore the region from the air.

my worldgeography.com | In-flight Movie

131

Regional Overview
Human Geography

Europe About 1890
Europe was composed of large empires at the end of the 1800s.

London about 1890

Europe Today
In the 1900s, large empires fell, leading to the creation of many smaller countries.

London today

Where People Live

Throughout history, the population density of Europe has been high because of its temperate climate, miles of coastline and rivers, and acres of good farmland.

Russia, on the other hand, is the largest nation on Earth, but about 80 percent of the population live in the smaller, European part of the country. This is because only about 7 percent of Russia's land is good for farming, and its harbors are blocked by ice for months. Russia is a land of extremes—harsh climate, rugged terrain, and great distances.

my World IN NUMBERS

Sweden
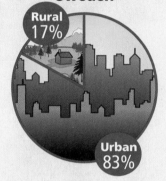
Rural 17%
Urban 83%

France
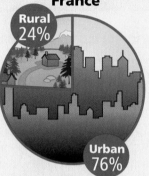
Rural 24%
Urban 76%

United Kingdom
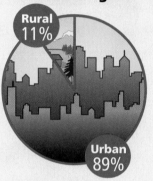
Rural 11%
Urban 89%

Italy

Rural 33%
Urban 67%

Ukraine
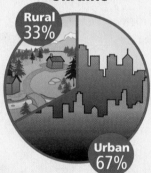
Rural 33%
Urban 67%

Russia
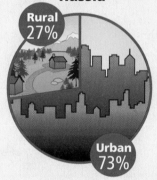
Rural 27%
Urban 73%

SOURCE: United Nations Secretariat, Population Division

Put It Together

1. Which mountain range separates European Russia from Asiatic Russia?

2. In what ways has the physical geography of Europe and Russia affected where people live and work?

3. True or false: According to the graphs above, Europe and Russia are mostly rural. Explain your answer.

 Data Discovery

Use your own data to make a regional data table.

Size Comparison

The land area of Europe and Russia is more than 150% larger than that of the United States.

my worldgeography.com Data Discovery

133

Chapter 1

Ancient and Medieval Europe

Essential Question

What are the challenges of diversity?

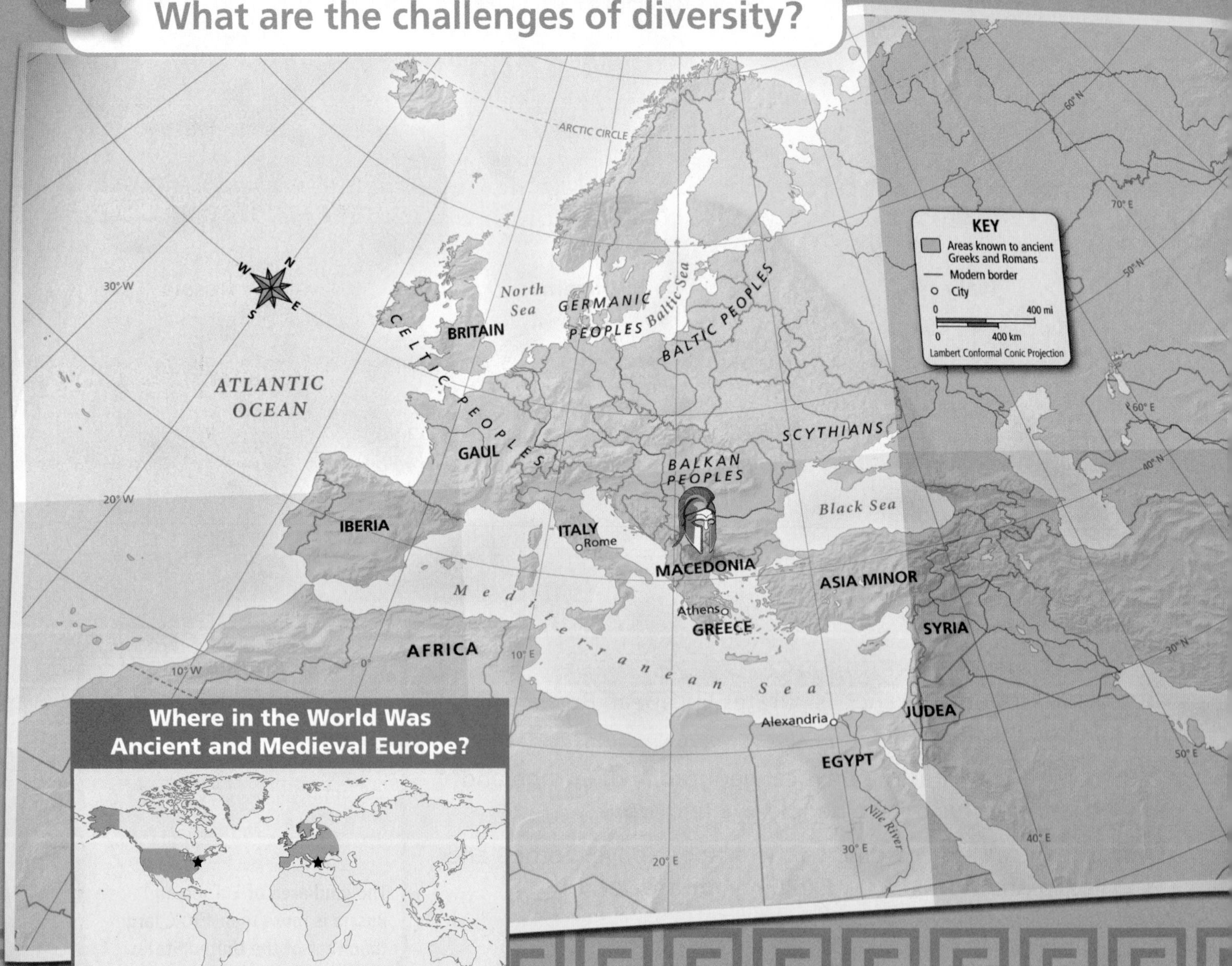

KEY
Areas known to ancient Greeks and Romans
Modern border
City
0 400 mi
0 400 km
Lambert Conformal Conic Projection
ARCTIC CIRCLE
ATLANTIC OCEAN
North Sea
Baltic Sea
Black Sea
Mediterranean Sea
BRITAIN
CELTIC PEOPLES
GERMANIC PEOPLES
BALTIC PEOPLES
GAUL
IBERIA
ITALY
Rome
BALKAN PEOPLES
SCYTHIANS
MACEDONIA
Athens
GREECE
ASIA MINOR
SYRIA
JUDEA
Alexandria
EGYPT
AFRICA
Nile River
N
S
E
W
60° N
50° N
40° N
30° N
70° E
60° E
50° E
40° E
30° E
20° E
10° E
0°
10° W
20° W
30° W

Where in the World Was Ancient and Medieval Europe?

Washington, D.C., to Macedonia: 4,960 miles

my Story

A Prophecy Fulfilled

In this section, you'll read about Alexander the Great, a Macedonian warrior who conquered much of the world known to the ancient Greeks. What does Alexander's story tell you about life in the ancient Greek world?

? Explore the Essential Question
- at **my worldgeography.com**
- using the **myWorld Chapter Activity**
- with the **Student Journal**

Story by Michael Chatlien for myWorld Online

In 334 B.C., Alexander the Great led his army from Europe into Asia. His troops came from Macedonia and Greece. Alexander wanted to defeat the Persian forces led by Darius III. The two armies met at the Granicus River in present-day Turkey. With 75,000 troops, Darius III seemed to have the advantage. Alexander had only 35,000 soldiers. Even so, he felt that he was destined to defeat Darius and conquer Asia. Indeed, his upbringing prepared him to become a great ruler.

Alexander's father was Philip II, the king of Macedonia. His mother was Olympias, a princess from western Greece. Olympias taught Alexander that he was descended from the great warrior Achilles. And Philip convinced his son that Macedonian kings were descended from the god Hercules.

At age 12, Alexander tamed Bucephalus. The name means "ox's head" and refers to the wild horse's massive head.

my worldgeography.com On Assignment

135

The Greeks perfected the phalanx, a wedge-shaped battle formation.

The Persian king Darius faced Alexander in battle three times.

"There is no part of my body remaining free of wounds. I have been wounded with the sword, shot with arrows, and hit with stones for the sake of your lives, your glory, and your wealth."

The respected philosopher Aristotle taught the young Alexander. From him, Alexander learned about science, the arts, and politics. While he studied, he also trained in sports and combat. When Alexander's father Philip conquered Greece, Alexander commanded a division in his father's army.

Philip then wanted to invade Asia, but his plans were cut short when a bodyguard murdered him. So at the age of 20, Alexander became king of Macedonia and Greece. Two years later, he invaded the Persian Empire, seeking to be ruler of Asia as well.

At the shores of the Granicus River, Alexander readied his troops for combat. It would be the first of three battles against the Persians. The Greek historian Arrian described how both armies waited at the edge of the river ready to attack. Alexander shouted for his men to show courage:

66 Alexander leaped upon his steed, ordering those about him to follow, and exhorting [urging] them to show themselves valiant men. 99

The cavalry attacked first, with warriors and horses moving in a phalanx formation. Archers and spear throwers then joined in to support the assault.

136

Alexander raises his sword to cut apart the Gordian knot.

Alexander is said to have wept when he looked out over his empire, sad because there were no more worlds to conquer.

Next the foot soldiers joined in and dealt the crushing blow. The modern historian Robin Lane Fox describes Alexander's army in combat:

66 Nobody who faced them ever forgot the sight; they kept time to their roaring of the Greeks' ancient war cry, Alalalalai; their scarlet cloaks billowed, and the measured swishing of their sarissas [long pikes], up and down, left and right, seemed to frightened observers like the quills of a metal porcupine. 99

The Greeks crushed the Persians. Darius and his troops retreated eastward. Alexander needed more troops, so he set off to find new recruits to join his army. On his march, Alexander came upon the legendary Gordian knot. This knot was tied to an ox cart. An ancient prophecy stated that the person who untied the knot would rule Asia. Alexander first tried to undo the huge knot and could not. Frustrated, he drew his sword and cut it with one stroke. This may not be a true story, but Alexander did go on to fulfill the prophecy.

Later, at the battle of Issus, the Greeks were again victorious. Darius escaped, but he offered Alexander a peace treaty. He said he would give Alexander a large sum of money and the Persian lands west of the Euphrates River. Alexander's general Parmenio advised his commander to accept the terms—but Alexander had greater ambitions.

He faced Darius again at Gaugamela. With a third victory here, Alexander took control of much of Southwest Asia. It was still not enough— Alexander wanted India.

After eight long years of marching and fighting, the army reached the western border of India. Alexander's troops had become homesick and wanted to turn back. Coenus, an old commander, gathered his courage as he spoke for his fellow soldiers,

66 Do not lead us now against our will. . . .But, rather, return of your own accord to your own land. . .and carry to the home of your fathers these victories great and small. 99

Alexander reluctantly agreed to return to Macedonia, but he would not make it home. He died of a mysterious illness at Babylon in 323 B.C.

Alexander's empire stretched from Macedonia and Greece in the west to the borders of India in the east. This region included much of the world that was known to the ancient Greeks. Indeed, the prophecy of the Gordian knot had come true.

 myStory Video

Join Alexander the Great as he conquers a vast empire.

Ancient Greece

Key Ideas
- Geography played a part in shaping Greek civilization.
- Through trade, conquest, and cultural exchange, ancient Greece prospered.
- Ancient Greece left a rich heritage in learning, philosophy, and the arts.
- Democratic government developed in ancient Greece.

Key Terms
- city-state
- direct democracy
- oligarchy
- philosophy
- cultural hearth

 Visual Glossary

 Reading Skill: Label an Outline Map Take notes using the outline map in your journal.

A Minoan ceremonial object in the shape of a bull's head ▼

The civilization of ancient Greece has had a great effect on today's world. Democratic government traces its roots back to this civilization. Modern science began with the ancient Greek thinkers. In the arts and architecture, ancient Greek ideas remain strong today.

The Aegean World

Greece is a peninsula and a group of islands that jut out from southern Europe into the Mediterranean Sea. The Aegean World also included the islands of Crete and Rhodes, and the lands of Ionia.

Physical Geography The Greek peninsula is a mountainous area with an irregular coastline. The land is rugged and mostly rocky. Only small valleys near the coast have fertile soil. In general, the climate in this region is warm and dry. Summers tend to be hot and dry and winters mild.

The seas around Greece are full of fish. Because they had so little farmland, the ancient Greeks depended on the sea for their food. The mountains contain large amounts of marble and limestone. The ancient Greeks used these resources to construct buildings.

Greek Settlements The ancient Greeks mostly settled in valleys with fertile soil near the coast. There they set up farms and fished. Mountains or bodies of water often separated these settled areas. As a result, each settled area tended to develop its own independent spirit.

Reading Check What were some of the natural resources found in ancient Greece?

138

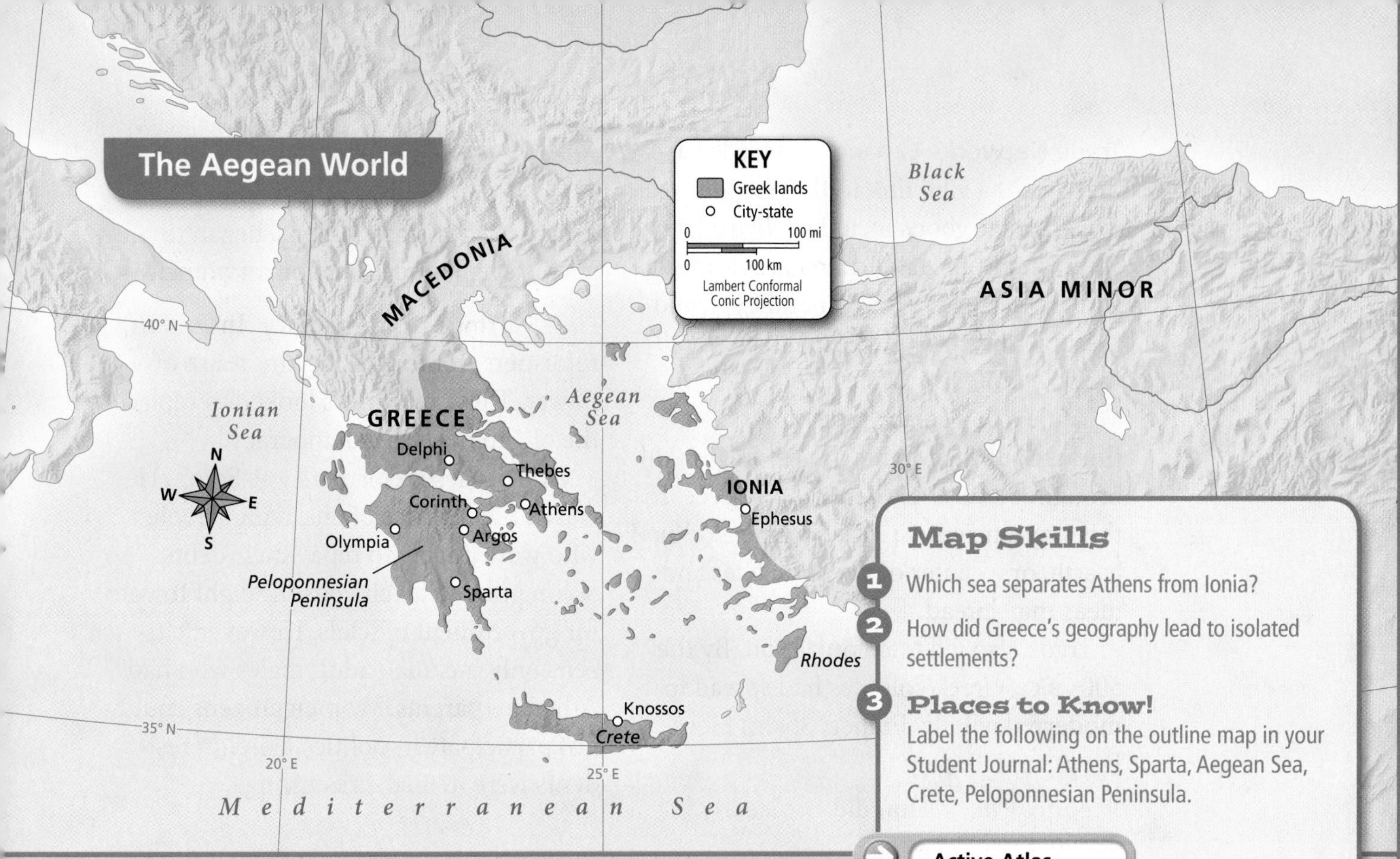
The Aegean World
KEY
Greek lands
City-state
0
100 mi
0
100 km
Lambert Conformal Conic Projection
MACEDONIA
GREECE
Ionian Sea
Aegean Sea
Black Sea
ASIA MINOR
IONIA
Delphi
Thebes
Corinth
Athens
Argos
Olympia
Sparta
Ephesus
Peloponnesian Peninsula
Rhodes
Knossos
Crete
Mediterranean Sea
40° N
35° N
20° E
25° E
30° E
N
S
E
W

Map Skills

1. Which sea separates Athens from Ionia?
2. How did Greece's geography lead to isolated settlements?
3. **Places to Know!** Label the following on the outline map in your Student Journal: Athens, Sparta, Aegean Sea, Crete, Peloponnesian Peninsula.

Active Atlas

The Rise of City-States

In prehistoric times, two civilizations developed in the Aegean region. The people called the Minoans lived on Crete and many other islands. The Mycenaeans (my suh nee uns) lived on the Greek mainland.

Minoans and Mycenaeans Around 3000 B.C., the Minoan civilization emerged on the island of Crete. The Minoans were skilled sailors who developed a writing system. They traded with mainland Greece, Egypt, and Sicily.

Around 1400 B.C., Mycenaeans from the mainland conquered the Minoans. They borrowed the Minoan system of writing and built fortified towns. Around 1200 B.C., the Mycenaean civilization collapsed for unknown reasons.

City-States Form The many fortified towns in Greece gradually developed into city-states. A **city-state** is a city or town that controls surrounding villages and farmland nearby.

Each city-state was independent and often fought frequently with other city-states. Many city-states were aristocracies run by wealthy landowners. The word *aristocracy* means "rule by the best people." Laws were based on tradition.

In many city-states, farmers and merchants rebelled against the aristocrats. To restore order, tyrants took control. A tyrant is a leader who gains total power by force. In some areas, the tyrants were replaced by an **oligarchy,** or government in which a small group of people rule.

fortified, *adj.,* strengthened by walls

myworldgeography.com Active Atlas

Trade Networks Expand Sea trade gave the Greeks a vital link to the outside world. Trade goods included olive oil, gold, silver, and iron. Greek merchants traded with people from Asia Minor, Egypt, and Mesopotamia. As trade expanded, so did the power of the city-states.

Trade also spread Greek culture throughout the Mediterranean region. It brought cultural influences to Greece. In this way, ancient Greece became a **cultural hearth,** or a center of new practices and ideas that spread.

Trade also led to colonization. By the 500s B.C., Greek colonies had spread to modern day Italy, France, Spain, Libya, Egypt, and Turkey.

Reading Check How did city-states develop?

Athenian Democracy

As Greek power and wealth spread, its largest city-state, Athens, began to encourage political freedom at home.

First Stirrings of Democracy In Athens, reformers wanted to stop the abuse of power. These reformers looked to replace the oligarchy with a democracy.

One of these reformers was Solon. He ended the practice of enslaving people who were unable to repay their debts. Solon granted all citizens the right to vote for government officials. However, citizens only included adult males who had Athenian parents. Women citizens could not participate in politics. Foreign residents were denied citizenship.

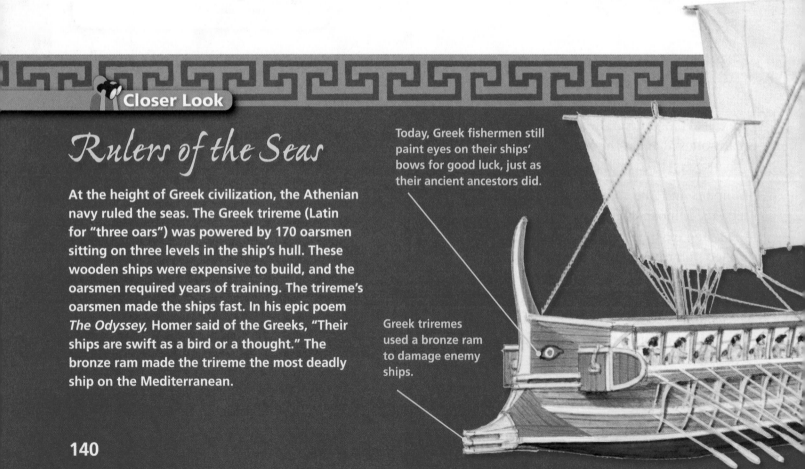

Closer Look

Rulers of the Seas

At the height of Greek civilization, the Athenian navy ruled the seas. The Greek trireme (Latin for "three oars") was powered by 170 oarsmen sitting on three levels in the ship's hull. These wooden ships were expensive to build, and the oarsmen required years of training. The trireme's oarsmen made the ships fast. In his epic poem *The Odyssey,* Homer said of the Greeks, "Their ships are swift as a bird or a thought." The bronze ram made the trireme the most deadly ship on the Mediterranean.

Today, Greek fishermen still paint eyes on their ships' bows for good luck, just as their ancient ancestors did.

Greek triremes used a bronze ram to damage enemy ships.

In the mid-400s B.C., the statesman Pericles made more democratic reforms in Athens. For example, he set up salaries for public officials so that poor people could serve in government. Pericles famously said,

66 Here each individual is interested not only in his own affairs but in the affairs of the state as well. 99

Athenian Direct Democracy Under Pericles, Athens became the world's first **direct democracy.** In direct democracy, citizens take part directly in the day-to-day affairs of government. Today, in most democratic countries, such as the United States, people instead participate in government through elected representatives.

However, there are some examples of direct democracy-style governments in the modern world. One of these is in Switzerland, where citizens have the ability to vote on federal laws. Another is the town hall style of city government used in many communities in the New England region of the United States.

Reading Check What reforms did Solon propose?

Life in Ancient Greece

The period between the end of the Persian Wars and the death of Alexander (about 500 B.C.–323 B.C.) is called the classical period. It was a time of great advances in learning and art. Athens, named for the goddess of wisdom, was the most important cultural center of classical Greece.

The Greeks were also skilled sea traders. Trade ships were usually powered by a single square sail. The wooden ships were durable, and some lasted as long as 80 years. Pirates and shipwrecks were constant threats. The Greeks most commonly traded olive oil, wine, and almonds.

THINK CRITICALLY **How was slavery connected to Greek naval power?**

The Greeks have cultivated olives for thousands of years. The ancient Greeks exported olive oil in clay vessels like the one below.

myWorldActivity
Let's Make a Trade

141

A New Form of Government and Justice

The kleroterion was used to select jurors at random. Random selection ensured fairness. ▼

The Athenians called their political system *demokratia,* which means "rule by the people." This political system affected law-making as well as the courts. There were no professional judges or lawyers in Athens. Every citizen had the right to bring another citizen to trial or to serve on a jury. Some of the most basic elements of modern democracy originated in Athens, including majority rule, civic debate, judgment by jury, and the rule of law.

THINK CRITICALLY **Why is civic debate important in a democracy?**

Bronze juror tickets with jurors' names were inserted into the slots of the kleroterion. ▶

Citizens of Athens
(Men of at least 18 years of age whose parents were Athenian)

Ecclesia
(Citizens' assembly; debated laws and important decisions)

Magistrates (9)
(Elected by the Ecclesia; applied the laws)

Boule (Council of 500)
(Chosen at random; debated important decisions and negotiated with foreign states)

People's Court (6,000 jurors)
(Selected at random; judged those who violated the laws)

142

Greek Religion The Greeks believed in many deities, or beings with supernatural powers. These gods and goddesses ruled over different areas of human life and the natural world. The chief god was Zeus, who ruled from his home on Mount Olympus. He was lord of the sky and rain.

The Greeks had no book or manuscripts to explain their religion. Rather, they used mythology, or a collection of stories told about history or gods. To honor the gods, the Greeks made beautiful statues in marble and built magnificent temples.

Love of Wisdom The Greeks also studied **philosophy,** or "love of wisdom." Greek scholars applied logic, or reason, to a study of knowledge and the world.

The Greek philosopher Plato wrote about government, ethics, and religion. Other important philosophers were Plato's teacher, Socrates, and Aristotle, Plato's student. In *Poetics,* Aristotle said,

> 66 Poetry, therefore, is a more philosophical and a higher thing than history: for poetry tends to express the universal, history the particular. 99

The ancient Greeks also investigated science and mathematics. People used to believe that the sun circled Earth. Using mathematics and careful observation, the astronomer Aristarchus (a ris TAHR kus) concluded that Earth circled the sun. Almost 2,000 years passed before scientists widely accepted this idea.

The Greeks also studied the past, but they did more than simply record events. The historian Herodotus is known as the father of history because he was the first to note events and analyze them. Two of ancient Greece's most important historians were also soldiers. Thucydides wrote the history of the Peloponnesian Wars, while Xenophon recorded Greek history as well as the sayings of Socrates.

Arts and Leisure The ancient Greeks developed a rich literary tradition, especially in poetry and drama. The playwrights Aeschylus, Sophocles, and Euripides wrote great tragedies, or serious works that have flawed heroes. Aristophanes' plays were comedies that often poked fun at Greek society.

The ancient Greeks made many advances in architecture. The most impressive type of public building in classical Greece was the temple. It consisted of a long chamber that housed a statue of a god or goddess. Columns surrounded the chamber. The most famous Greek temple is the Parthenon in Athens.

Greeks held public festivals to honor their gods. One such festival at Olympia was held every four years to honor Zeus. City-states would send their best athletes to compete in these festivals, which were known as the Olympic Games. Athletes from all over Greece competed in running, wrestling, and jumping.

Public and Private Life Though the public buildings in ancient Greece were impressive, most people lived in simple homes of mud bricks. They ate simple meals of bread, cheese, olives, and fish. Very few people ate meat since there was little space in which to raise <u>livestock</u>.

▲ On this ancient Greek vase, harvesters use sticks to knock olives from the trees.

livestock, *n.,* farm animals raised for food and profit

143

At the heart of the Greek city lay the agora, a public space that included the council-house, religious shrines, and the marketplace. Most of those who gathered in the agora were freemen, discussing politics or bargaining for goods and services.

These freemen were generally upper-class leaders of social and political life. The upper class included aristocrats, wealthy landowners, and, later, successful merchants. As free residents and citizens, they possessed more rights than anyone else.

For the most part, women ran the home. Women had few rights. They could not vote or own property. Some women served as priestesses in temples.

Slavery One third of the population of Athens were slaves. These people were owned by someone else and did not have the same rights as free people. Many slaves were captured during wartime or were children whose parents had been enslaved. Slaves did most of the hard labor in ancient Greece. A slave might be able to buy his or her freedom or obtain it from a grateful master.

Reading Check How did the Greeks influence the study of history?

Conflict and Decline

At sea, Athens' navy was superior. On land, Sparta's army challenged Athens.

Soldiers Rule Sparta The Spartans devoted themselves to military might from an early age. As adults, Spartan warriors were expected to put their military careers before wives and families.

A gold coin on which Alexander is portrayed as Ares, the god of war. ▼

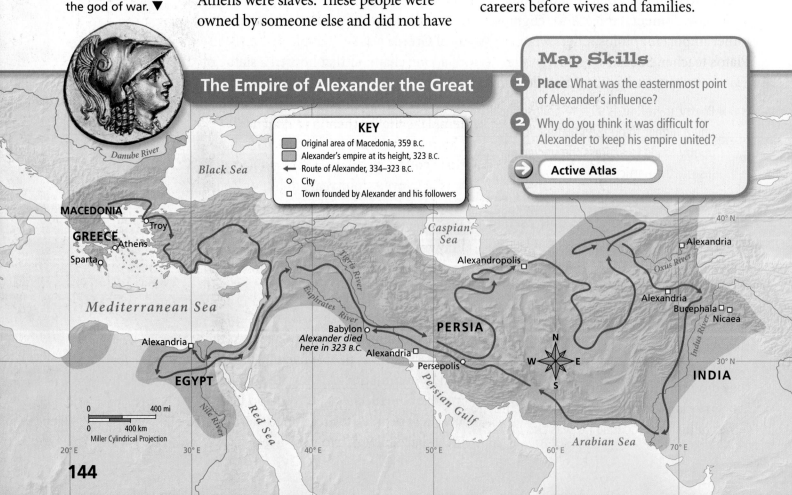

The Empire of Alexander the Great

KEY
- Original area of Macedonia, 359 B.C.
- Alexander's empire at its height, 323 B.C.
- ← Route of Alexander, 334–323 B.C.
- ○ City
- □ Town founded by Alexander and his followers

Map Skills

1 **Place** What was the easternmost point of Alexander's influence?

2 Why do you think it was difficult for Alexander to keep his empire united?

→ **Active Atlas**

144

Spartan women enjoyed more freedom than the women of Athens. They could own land and take part in business.

The city-state of Sparta was governed by an oligarchy led by the army. At the top of Spartan society were aristocrats who were also professional military men. Unlike the citizens of Athens, the people of Sparta played a much smaller part in government.

The Persian Wars War was frequent among the Greeks, but an outside threat united the city-states. That threat was the invading Persian army led by Darius, the king of Persia.

The Greek army met the Persians first at the Battle of Marathon. The Greeks surrounded the Persians, and the enemy fled to their ships in the Aegean Sea.

Darius's son Xerxes commanded the Persians in the second war with the Greeks. As allies, the Spartans joined the Greeks to stop the Persians at Thermopylae. Finally, Xerxes sailed for home after losing thousands of men and more than 200 ships in the Battle of Salamis.

Decline of the City-States In spite of their alliance, these two city-states remained enemies. War broke out between Athens and Sparta in 431 B.C. It was called the Peloponnesian War and continued off and on for 27 years. Athens was at last defeated, ending the golden age of this once-great city-state. The war also hurt other city-states around Greece, toppling governments and damaging trade. Greek culture did not end, but ongoing conflict kept it from reaching the unity or stability that had made it strong.

Spread of Greek Culture As you read at the beginning of this chapter, Alexander conquered most of the world known to the ancient Greeks. Greek culture eventually spread across southwest Asia, southern Europe, and North Africa. Today, the impact of Greek culture remains strong in democratic forms of government as well as in art and architecture.

Reading Check Which common enemy united Athens and Sparta?

As king, Alexander was popular and much loved. He died of an unknown illness at age 32. ▼

Section 1 Assessment

Key Terms

1. Use each of the following terms in a sentence: city-state, cultural hearth, direct democracy, philosophy.

Key Ideas

2. Where did most of the ancient Greeks settle?

3. Name some of the democratic reforms made during the golden age of Athens.

4. How did the Greeks defeat the Persians?

Think Critically

5. **Draw Conclusions** How were Sparta and Athens similar and different?

6. **Draw Inferences** Do you think Aristotle was influenced by Plato and Socrates? Explain why or why not.

Essential Question

What are the challenges of diversity?

7. How did the diversity of Alexander the Great's Empire affect Greek culture? Go to your Student Journal to record your answer.

Ancient Greek Literature

Key Idea
- The ancient Greeks left a legacy of many great works of literature, including moral fables and epic poems.

Ancient Greece produced a wealth of literature that influenced later cultures. Greek plays and works of philosophy are still read today. Storytelling also played a large role in Greek literature. *Aesop's Fables* is a collection of short tales that teach a moral by telling a story, usually about animals. Perhaps the most famous pieces of all Greek literature are the two epic poems by Homer—*The Iliad* and *The Odyssey*. An epic poem is a long poem that tells a story about heroes. In *The Odyssey*, the warrior Odysseus encounters many dangers as he tries to return home after the Trojan War.

▲ A portrait believed to be of the ancient Greek poet Sappho

Stop at each circled letter on the right to think about the text. Then answer the question with the same letter on the left.

A **Solve Problems** What problem is the dog making for the oxen?

B **Identify Evidence** What detail shows that the dog is being cruel, rather than trying to protect something he needs?

C **Synthesize** How does the moral at the end relate to the fable?

manger, *n.*, a box that holds food for cattle or horses

begrudge, *v.*, to give reluctantly

The Dog in the Manger

66 A Dog lay in a <u>manger</u>, and by his growling and snapping prevented
A the oxen from eating the hay which had been placed for them. 'What a selfish Dog!' said one of them to his
B companions; 'he cannot eat or sleep in the hay himself, and yet refuses to allow those to eat who can.' People often <u>begrudge</u> others what
C they cannot enjoy themselves. 99

—Aesop, *Aesop's Fables*, translated by George Fyler Townsend

Diego Velázquez's 1640 portrait of Aesop shows the ancient Greek author as a modest man holding a book of his fables. ▶

146

Stop at each circled letter on the right to think about the text. Then answer the question with the same letter on the left.

D Categorize Is the speaker giving Odysseus a warning or a recommendation? How do you dictionaryknow?

E Draw Conclusions What happens to men when they first hear the cry of the Sirens?

F Identify Evidence What happens to the men the Sirens bewitch? What evidence proves this?

Siren, *n.,* a mythical creature, part bird and part woman, who lures sailors to their death on the rocks

bewitch, *v.,* to cast a spell over

loll, *v.,* to relax in a leaning position

flay, *v.,* to strip off or to skin

The Sirens' Song

66 **Listen with care**

D to this, now, and a god will arm your mind.
Square in your ships' path are Sirens, crying
beauty to bewitch men coasting by;
woe to the innocent who hears that sound!
He will not see his lady nor his children
in joy, crowding about him, home from sea;

E the Sirens will sing his mind away
on their sweet meadow lolling.

F   There are bones
of dead men rotting in a pile beside them
and flayed skins shrivel around the spot. 99

—Homer, *The Odyssey*, translated by Robert Fitzgerald

An ancient Greek vase showing Odysseus resisting the call of the Sirens ▼

Analyze the Documents

1. **Synthesize** What do the dog in the fable and the Sirens have in common?
2. **Writing Task** Write your own fable to teach a lesson.

The ancient Greeks also enjoyed plays performed at outdoor theatres like this one in Taormina. ▼

147

Ancient Rome

Key Ideas
- The Roman empire expanded through trade and conquest.
- Roman ideas about law and government remain important today.
- Christianity arose during the Roman empire and spread throughout Europe.

Key Terms • patrician • plebeian • representative democracy • Pax Romana • aqueduct

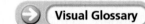

Reading Skill: Sequence Take notes using the graphic organizer in your journal.

◀ Livia, wife of the Roman emperor Augustus, shown as Ceres, the goddess of grains.

Historians are not sure about the origins of ancient Rome. One legend says it was founded by Aeneas, the Greek hero of Virgil's poem *The Aeneid.* Aeneas is said to have escaped after the Trojan War and traveled to Latium. There, he married a princess and founded the town that would become Rome.

We do know that by the 700s B.C., a shepherd people called the Latins lived in central Italy. From their simple villages came a great empire.

The Roman Republic

Around 1000 B.C., the Latins settled near the Tiber River in central Italy. This river gave them access to the sea. The region also had fertile soil and marble and limestone for building. The surrounding hills protected the settlement. The Latins named the village Rome.

Etruscan Influence To the north lived the Etruscans, an advanced group of artists, builders, and sailors. In their sea travels, the Etruscans had learned things from many other cultures, including the Greeks.

The Etruscans expanded into Latium, ruling with the consent of the Romans. The presence of the Etruscans added much to Roman society and its government. The Etruscans introduced a writing system that they adapted from the Greeks. This formed the basis of the Latin alphabet that we use today. In addition, the Etruscans brought a strong military tradition to Rome, including the use of the Greek phalanx formation. Roman cities were improved through Etruscan methods of paving streets and using stone arches to support heavy structures such as bridges.

From Kingdom to Republic In 509 B.C., the Romans overthrew the Etruscan kings and established a republic. A republic is a government without king or emperors.

The republic had a Senate and a citizens' assembly, which it adopted from the Etruscans. The assembly was divided into two groups: the **patricians** and the **plebeians.** The patricians were wealthy aristocrats. The plebeians were all the remaining citizens. A patrician's vote counted for more than a plebeian's vote. The assembly elected two consuls, who led the government. A group of 300 wealthy citizens were appointed to serve in the Senate, which passed the laws.

In the early 400s B.C., after many protests, the plebeians gained the right to have representatives called tribunes. A tribune could overturn the act of any public official that was unjust to any citizen. Then the plebeians were given their own assembly. Eventually, the plebeians' votes counted as much as the patricians' votes.

During a crisis, the power of government was given to a dictator. The Roman statesman Cicero describes the role of dictator.

> 66 [W]hen a serious war or civil [disagreements] arise, one man shall hold, for not longer than six months, the power which ordinarily belongs to the two consuls . . . he shall be 'master of the people.' 99

Roman Law The Romans wrote down their laws, the Twelve Tables, around 450 B.C. With written laws, people would know their rights and duties rather than rely on customs that could be ignored.

The Roman government was considered a **representative democracy,** meaning that elected representatives made the political decisions. This system prevented any one individual from gaining too much power. It differed from Athenian direct democracy. The republic of Rome influenced representative governments throughout the world, including, centuries later, that of the United States.

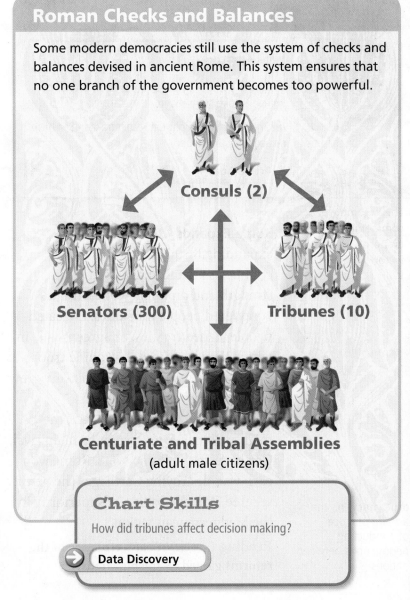

Roman Checks and Balances

Some modern democracies still use the system of checks and balances devised in ancient Rome. This system ensures that no one branch of the government becomes too powerful.

Consuls (2)

Senators (300)   **Tribunes (10)**

Centuriate and Tribal Assemblies
(adult male citizens)

Chart Skills

How did tribunes affect decision making?

→ **Data Discovery**

my worldgeography.com   Data Discovery

149

The Roman Empire

ATLANTIC OCEAN

BRITAIN
London

GAUL GERMANY
Lyon
Danube R.

SPAIN
Toledo

ITALY
Rome

DACIA

Black Sea

THRACE
Byzantium

ASIA MINOR

Cádiz

MAURETANIA Carthage
AFRICA

GREECE
Athens

MESOPOTAMIA

SYRIA

Mediterranean Sea

JUDEA

Alexandria

ARABIA

EGYPT

Red Sea

TROPIC OF CANCER

KEY
Roman Empire, A.D. 117
City
0   500 mi
0   500 km
Lambert Conformal Conic Projection

Map Skills

1 **Estimate** Using the scale bar, find how far the Roman Empire stretched from west to east.

2 **Interaction** How might the Mediterranean Sea have helped unify the empire?

→ Active Atlas

▲ This column commemorates the emperor Trajan's victories in the Dacian Wars (A.D. 100–106).

Rome Expands Rome set about expanding through alliances and conquests. The Romans used military strength and <u>diplomacy</u> to turn conquered people into allies. Defeated people signed treaties, or agreements, in which they promised to provide troops to Rome. In this way, the Roman army grew to be the largest force in Italy.

During the 200s and 100s B.C., the mighty Roman army fought its main rival, Carthage, in the Punic Wars. Rome won each war, destroying Carthage. The defeat secured Rome's position of superiority in the Mediterranean region.

Reading Check What were some of the reforms gained by the plebeians?

diplomacy, *n.,* the art and practice of conducting negotiations between nations

Rome Becomes an Empire

By 100 B.C., the republic was becoming unstable. After several revolts, the republic came under the control of dictators and military leaders.

Beginnings of Empire In the 50s B.C., Julius Caesar conquered Gaul, land that is much of present-day France and Belgium. He then invaded Italy and made himself the sole ruler of Rome and its territories. Hoping to restore the republic, aristocrats assassinated Caesar.

The result was chaos and the end of the republic. Caesar's nephew Octavian eventually emerged as the victor. He took the name Augustus and became the first Roman emperor in 27 B.C.

150

The Empire Unifies The rule of Augustus started a period of stability known as the **Pax Romana** (Roman Peace). This period lasted for about 200 years.

Rome set up colonies in conquered areas. Many Roman citizens migrated to these colonies. Some of the people conquered by the Romans became citizens. The spread of Roman law helped to unify the empire. The empire was also united by a network of roads that helped soldiers move and keep order.

Trade along Roman roads and across the seas also stabilized the empire. The use of coins made trade easier. The empire gained wealth from trade and tributes paid by provinces. Tributes were a type of taxation.

Gradually, wealthy Romans came to admire Greek culture. Greek books were copied and sold widely. Learned Romans read both Latin and Greek. Greco-Roman culture was spread throughout the empire with colonies in Gaul, Spain, and North Africa. In addition to cultural influences, Roman colonists received Roman citizenship and lived under Roman law.

Reading Check What was the result of Caesar's assassination?

Life in Ancient Rome

The basic social unit in ancient Rome was the family. The father had complete control over the family and the home.

Roman women worked in the home. They could not vote or participate in politics. Gradually, Roman women did gain more rights. Emperors' wives, such as Livia and Julia Agrippina, also influenced politics in Rome.

Slavery in Ancient Rome About one third of the people in Rome were slaves. The economy depended on their work.

Sometimes, a slave could buy his or her freedom. Freed slaves were allowed to become citizens. Household slaves sometimes became trusted companions. Other slaves led short, brutal lives. Some worked in copper or tin mines. Gladiator slaves faced death in arena matches in the Colosseum. Slaves also worked as farmers or as rowers on Roman warships.

myWorldActivity
What's the News in Rome?

province, *n.,* country or region under control of a larger government

One important Roman innovation was the **aqueduct,** a channel that moves water over great distances.

151

Roman Religion Romans worshiped many deities, some of whom were adopted from the Greeks and the Etruscans. In Rome, religion was tied closely to political life and emperors were sometimes worshiped as gods.

Roman Achievements Like the Greeks, Romans made statues in marble. Roman literature includes poetry by Virgil and Horace, and essays by Cicero. Architects perfected the arch and invented concrete to build temples and public buildings.

In Roman Egypt, Ptolemy (TAH luh mee) calculated the size and distance of the sun and the paths of the stars and planets across the sky. The Greek Galen discovered how parts of the body worked.

Reading Check What elements helped to unify the Roman empire?

Judaism and Christianity

The Jews of Judea lived in an area that came under direct Roman rule in A.D. 63. In the centuries before the Roman empire, the Jews had spread to Egypt and to other parts of southwest Asia. The Jews believed in one God. This belief is called monotheism. The Romans, who believed in many gods, did not force them to change their practices.

Jews Flee Harsh Rule Some Jews, however, resented foreign rule and rebelled against the Romans. The Romans struck back harshly and destroyed the Jewish Temple in Jerusalem in A.D. 70.

The Romans killed many thousands of Jews. Other Jews left the ruined province for other parts of the empire. Many moved to Italy and other parts of Europe.

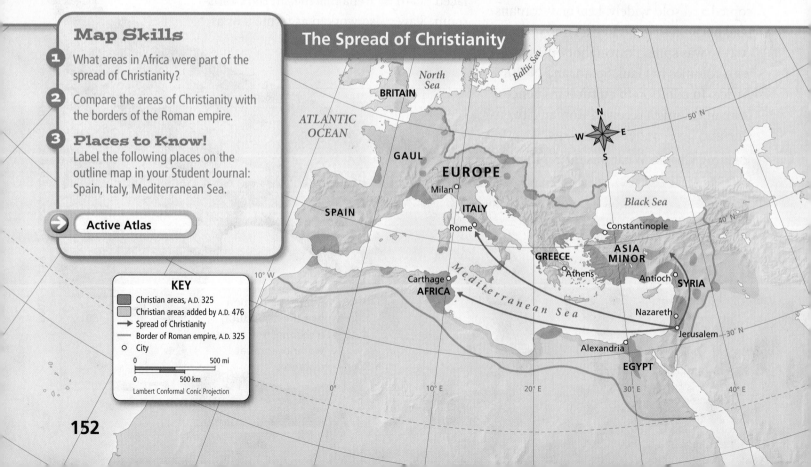

Map Skills

1. What areas in Africa were part of the spread of Christianity?

2. Compare the areas of Christianity with the borders of the Roman empire.

3. **Places to Know!** Label the following places on the outline map in your Student Journal: Spain, Italy, Mediterranean Sea.

→ **Active Atlas**

The Spread of Christianity

KEY
- Christian areas, A.D. 325
- Christian areas added by A.D. 476
- → Spread of Christianity
- — Border of Roman empire, A.D. 325
- ○ City

0 — 500 mi
0 — 500 km
Lambert Conformal Conic Projection

152

Birth and Spread of Christianity Around 4 B.C., a Jew named Jesus was born in Judea. He grew up in Nazareth and learned to be a carpenter.

When he was 30 years old, he became a religious teacher. Jesus preached that there was only one God. However, many of his followers believed that Jesus was the Messiah. Jews believed that a leader called the Messiah would bring them freedom. The name Christ comes from the Greek word for messiah. Jesus's followers later came to be known as Christians. Jesus's teachings formed the basis for a new religion, Christianity.

Christianity gradually spread across the Roman empire and into neighboring lands. For more than 200 years, Christians faced harsh treatment from the Roman government. Then, in A.D. 312, Roman emperor Constantine I became a Christian. Over the next 100 years, Christianity spread across much of Europe, and most Romans became Christians.

Reading Check Why did the Jews want to flee Roman rule?

The Western Empire Falls

Historians are not sure what caused the fall of the Roman empire. One theory proposes that the Romans used so many everyday objects made of lead that people may have sickened and died from lead poisoning. Most likely the collapse came from several factors.

Instability and Division From A.D. 235 to A.D. 284, there were 60 men who declared themselves emperor. Prices increased, taxes rose, and disease reduced the population. The Roman army weakened as it came to depend more on mercenaries, or soldiers who fought for money rather than for loyalty to a leader or nation.

Diocletian eventually divided the empire into eastern and western lands to make it easier to govern. Constantine moved the capital east, renaming it Constantinople. The Eastern Roman empire went on to thrive as the Byzantine empire, while the west fell to Germanic invaders.

Reading Check Identify one factor that led to the fall of the Roman empire.

Invaders!
- ▶ 378 Visigoths defeat the Roman army.
- ▶ 406 Vandals attack Gaul.
- ▶ 410 Visigoths sack Rome.
- ▶ 441 Attila (above) and the Huns begin to invade the empire.
- ▶ 450 Angles, Saxons, Jutes invade Britain (traditional date).
- ▶ 476 Rome falls to the Germanic leader Odoacer.

Timeline

Section 2 Assessment

Essential Question

Key Terms
1. Define each of these key terms with a complete sentence: patrician, plebeian, representative democracy, Pax Romana, aqueduct.

Key Ideas
2. Why was Julius Caesar assassinated?
3. How did the conversion of Constantine I affect religion in Europe?
4. Name three elements that led to the fall of the Roman empire.

Think Critically
5. **Compare and Contrast** How did Roman democracy differ from ancient Greek democracy?
6. **Problem Solving** If you were in charge of the Roman empire, how would you prevent it from collapsing? List at least three ways.

What are the challenges of diversity?
7. How did the Romans use citizenship to unify a diverse empire? Go to your Student Journal to record your answer.

153

The Fall of the Roman Empire

Key Idea
- Many different problems contributed to the fall of the Roman empire. Historians have investigated its causes for centuries.

For centuries, scholars have wondered why the powerful Roman empire collapsed. In its final years, the Roman empire was weakened by economic, military, political, and social problems. In the 1700s, the English historian Edward Gibbon wrote that Rome fell to stronger Germanic invaders. For generations, his ideas were unquestioned. Today, most historians agree that many factors led to the collapse of the empire. The topic remains popular with researchers and historians who continue to propose new ideas about what weakened the once-mighty empire.

▲ This Roman coin depicts Mars, the god of war.

Stop at each circled letter on the right to think about the text. Answer the question with the same letter on the left.

A Draw Conlusions How does Gibbon believe the Romans viewed their situation? Might he have been correct? Explain.

B Identify Bias What was Gibbon's view of the northern tribes? How can you tell?

C Draw Inferences What were the "fruits of industry," and why would the northern tribes want them?

voracious, *adj.,* extremely hungry

ravish, *v.,* to seize and carry away by force

barbarian, *adj.,* those considered uncivilized by the ancient Greeks and Romans

Numerous Enemies

A 66 **The Romans were ignorant of the extent of their danger, and the number of their enemies. Beyond the Rhine and Danube, the northern countries of Europe and Asia were filled with [a great many] tribes of hunters**

B and shepherds, poor, <u>voracious</u>, and turbulent [agitated]; bold in arms, and impatient to <u>ravish</u> the

C fruits of industry. The <u>Barbarian</u> world was agitated by the rapid impulse of war. 99

—Edward Gibbon,
The History of the Decline and Fall of the Roman Empire, 1776–1788

In this marble relief, a Germanic swordsman defends himself against a Roman warrior. ▼

154

Stop at each circled letter on the right to think about the text. Then answer the question with the same letter on the left.

D **Draw Conclusions** What does "the decay of their bodies and health" mean?

E **Draw Inferences** Why did the Romans use so much lead?

F **Synthesize** If most people in an empire accidentally ingested something that damaged their health, how might this have affected the empire as a whole?

chronic, *adj.,* occurring often and lasting a long time

metallurgist, *n.,* a person who works with metals

ingest, *v.,* to take food or chemicals into the body

Lead Poisoning

66 In 1983, Jerome O. Nriagu, an environmental scientist . . . theorized that the decline of the empire had its roots not in the decay of Roman ideals and morality, but in the **D** decay of their bodies and health. The cause of this decay, Nriagu wrote, was <u>chronic</u> lead poisoning. A soft gray metal that is **E** plentiful in nature, lead was used by the Romans to make many household items. Roman <u>metallurgists</u> blended lead with tin to make a silver-gray metal known as pewter. Craftsmen used the handsome metal to make cups, plates, spoons, cooking pots, **F** and wine vessels. . . . What the Romans did not know is that lead is one of the most poisonous metals a person can <u>ingest</u>. 99

—Bradley Steffens,
The Fall of the Roman Empire, 1994

▲ Lead keys from ancient Rome

Analyze the Documents

1. **Categorize** According to these documents, what was a danger within the empire and what was a danger outside the empire?

2. **Writing Task** Make an outline for a persuasive essay in which you try to convince people in the Roman empire to make changes to save themselves.

Early Middle Ages

Key Ideas
- The Byzantine empire influenced the religion and writing systems of Eastern Europe.
- Charlemagne united most of Western Europe.
- Feudalism and manorialism shaped relations among medieval Europeans.

Key Terms • schism • lord • vassal • feudalism • manorialism

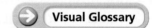 Visual Glossary

 Reading Skill: Summarize Take notes using the graphic organizer in your journal.

▼ The emperor Justinian ruled the Byzantine empire from 527 to 565.

After the fall of the Roman empire, a new age dawned in Europe. This age is often called the medieval period or Middle Ages. The word *medieval* comes from the Latin words for "middle" and "age." Historians use this term because the medieval period is beween the ancient and modern periods of European history.

The Byzantine Empire

As the Western Roman empire declined, power shifted east. The Eastern Roman empire remained strong. Its capital, Constantinople, grew rich on trade. Historians refer to the surviving eastern empire as the Byzantine empire.

Emperor Justinian's Rule Justinian ruled as an autocrat, or a single ruler with absolute power. He ruled both the empire and the Christian Church. Under Justinian, the empire expanded through conquest and trade. Justinian's wife Theodora served as his close advisor and, in effect, co-ruler. One of Justinian's greatest acts as emperor was to organize Roman laws into one code, called Justinian's Code. By the 1100s, these laws had reached Western Europe and helped monarchs unify their power. These laws remain part of many countries' laws.

Byzantine Christianity Since early Christian times, leaders called patriarchs had led the Christian churches in different regions. In the west, the head of the Church was the patriarch of Rome, known as the pope. The pope claimed the power to lead all Christians.

In the east, the highest official was the patriarch of Constantinople. This patriarch obeyed the Byzantine emperor. Unlike Christian priests in Western Europe, the Byzantine clergy had the right to marry. Greek, not Latin, was the language of the eastern Church.

A New Alphabet During Roman times, a people called the Slavs lived in what is now Poland, Belarus, and Ukraine. The Slavs had been farmers and traders for centuries. This commerce brought them in contact with the Byzantine empire.

In about 863, two Byzantine Greeks, the brothers Cyril and Methodius, traveled to Eastern Europe to bring Christianity to the Slavs. While there, they translated the Greek Bible into a Slavic language. This translation let people learn about Christianity in a language they understood. The brothers invented the Cyrillic alphabet. This alphabet combined Greek and Latin letters to express the sounds in the Slavic languages. In this way, writing and Christianity spread among the Slavic peoples. Today, people in Eastern Europe—as well as some in Russia and Mongolia—write in the Cyrillic alphabet.

Christianity Splits Gradually, the two branches of Christianity grew more divided. The Eastern church rejected the pope as leader of all Christians. Finally, the church went through an official **schism** (SIZ um), or split, called the Great Schism of 1054. The Byzantine church became the Eastern, or Greek, Orthodox church. The Western church became the Roman Catholic Church. These churches remain divided today.

The Byzantine Empire Falls By the time of the Great Schism, the Byzantine empire had begun to weaken. The emperors lost their lands to invaders such as the Arabs. Arabs conquered most of the Byzantine lands in North Africa and southwest Asia during the 600s. The Arabs were Muslims, or followers of Islam, a new religion. Like Judaism and Christianity, Islam was based on the worship of one god.

In addition, powerful merchants from the Italian city-state of Venice took control of important Byzantine trade routes. Then,

myWorldActivity
Write in Cyrillic

Cyril and Methodius, whom Christians revere as saints, hold religious documents writtten in Cyrillic. *How did this alphabet get its name?* ▼

157

in 1453, the Ottoman Turks captured Constantinople. This meant the end of the Byzantine empire. The Turks changed the city's name to Istanbul. They also introduced Islam and made Istanbul a center of Muslim culture.

Byzantine Achievements Building on Greco-Roman culture, the Byzantine empire lasted for almost 1,000 years. Its artists advanced art and architecture. Its scholars preserved ancient learning. One such scholar was Anna Comnena, the first important female historian in the west. The Byzantine <u>legacy</u> led to Europe's later cultural flowering, the Renaissance.

legacy, *n.,* something transmitted or received from a predecessor

Reading Check What did Cyril and Methodius achieve?

New Kingdoms in Europe

By around A.D. 450, Germanic tribes had taken control of most of the Western Roman empire.

Germanic Tribes Take Control Different tribes controlled the various parts of the region. A Germanic tribe called the Visigoths settled in Spain. The Angles, Jutes, and Saxons—later known as the Anglo-Saxons—took over most of Britain. And the Franks set up a kingdom in Gaul, in present-day France and Belgium.

Within each of these kingdoms, people were loyal only to their local leader. As a result, the idea of a central government disappeared.

Rise of the Franks A king of the Franks named Clovis defeated the last Roman commander in 486. He then established a kingdom that stretched from the Rhine region in the east to the Pyrenees Mountains in the west. Later, this area was named France after the Franks.

After Clovis's death, his kingdom was divided into smaller kingdoms. In the early 700s, however, the Frankish ruler Charles Martel united these kingdoms.

Charlemagne During the 770s, Charles Martel's grandson, Charlemagne (742–814), became king of the Franks. He conquered much of Western Europe and expanded the Frankish empire.

Charlemagne strongly supported the Catholic Church. He believed that by converting people to Christianity all across his growing empire, he could unite and strengthen it. Pope Leo III crowned Charlemagne Holy Roman Emperor in 800.

The Byzantine Empire

KEY

Byzantine Empire, about 1020

0 — 400 mi
0 — 400 km
Miller Cylindrical Projection

Map Skills

1 **Interaction** What cultures might have influenced Constantinople?

2 **Places to Know!** Label the following places on the outline map in your Student Journal: Asia Minor, Balkan Peninsula, Constantinople.

→ Active Atlas

This was important because a Christian pope had crowned a Germanic ruler as a successor to Roman emperors.

Charlemagne reestablished the rule of law, which had weakened after the fall of Rome. For example, he declared that judges should base their decisions on accepted laws. He also set up a school at his palace, though he himself could not write. This school attracted scholars from all of Europe.

After Charlemagne's death, the empire was divided among his sons. Some of these lands later became the modern countries of France and Germany.

Vikings and Magyars During the 800s and 900s, Viking invaders made terrifying raids along the coasts and rivers of Europe. The Vikings came from Scandinavia in northern Europe. They conquered parts of what are now England, Scotland, Ireland, France, and Ukraine. The Vikings who settled in France were called Normans. The Normans later conquered England.

Viking and Norman invaders also helped shape powerful kingdoms in England and in Ukraine. The kingdom in Ukraine, called Kievan Rus, adopted Eastern Christianity. The modern nations of Ukraine, Belarus, and Russia grew out of Kievan Rus.

During the 900s, a people called the Magyars conquered what is now Hungary. They made fearsome raids into Germany, Italy, and other parts of Western Europe. Around 1000, the Magyars converted to Christianity. The Magyars formed the kingdom of Hungary.

Christian Life The Christian church and its teachings were the center of medieval life. The church sent people across Europe to spread Christianity and gain new members. Gradually, most pagans in Europe converted to the Christian religion. A pagan was someone who worshiped more than one god. Although Western Europeans were divided politically, the Catholic Church united them through religion. Eastern Europeans were united through the Eastern Orthodox Church. *Orthodox* means following traditional or established beliefs.

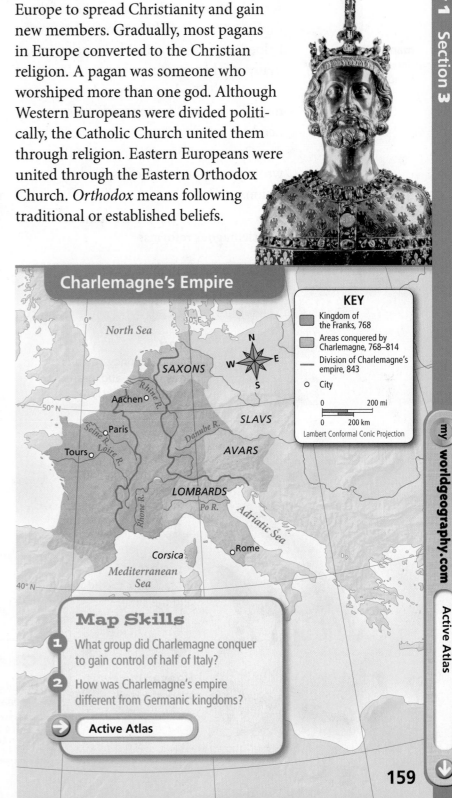

Statue of Charlemagne ▼

Charlemagne's Empire

KEY
- Kingdom of the Franks, 768
- Areas conquered by Charlemagne, 768–814
- Division of Charlemagne's empire, 843
- ○ City

0   200 mi
0   200 km
Lambert Conformal Conic Projection

Map Skills

1. What group did Charlemagne conquer to gain control of half of Italy?

2. How was Charlemagne's empire different from Germanic kingdoms?

→ **Active Atlas**

manuscript, *n.,* a document written by hand

Male Christian religious people called monks lived in monasteries, secluded communities focused on prayer and service. These monks made copies of the Bible and Greek and Roman works. They helped to preserve valuable <u>manuscripts</u>, many of which contained ancient learning.

Women joined religious orders as nuns. Some nuns became abbesses, or heads of female religious communities. The German abbess Hildegard of Bingen wrote poems and music inspired by her visions of God.

Reading Check What were some of Charlemagne's reforms?

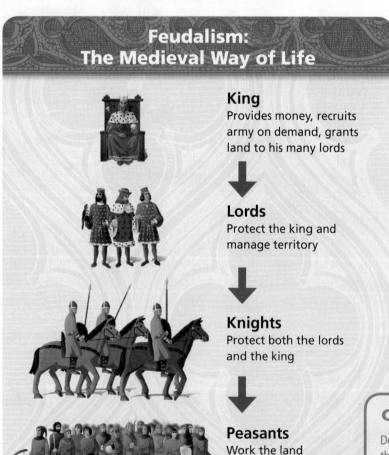

Feudalism: The Medieval Way of Life

King
Provides money, recruits army on demand, grants land to his many lords

Lords
Protect the king and manage territory

Knights
Protect both the lords and the king

Peasants
Work the land

Feudalism and Manorialism

As you have read, during the late Roman empire, people began to accept the protection and control of landowners from the nobility. In the Middle Ages, barbarians and other warriors took control of most of the land. They offered protection to the peasants, or small farmers, living on the land in return for service. Each landowning warrior pledged loyalty to a tribal leader called a **lord,** or to the king. A lord was a man who controlled large areas of land. In return for the warrior's service, the lord or king offered protection.

How Feudalism Worked As time went by, kings granted land to lords in return for service. Lords, in turn, granted land to noble soldiers called knights in return for military service. A noble who received the land was called a **vassal.** The system of rights and duties connecting lords and vassals was called **feudalism.**

The lord promised to protect his vassals. In return, the vassals provided military support and money or food for their lord. The peasants were subject to both lords and vassals. Lords and vassals also had trained warriors called knights to serve them.

Lords sometimes quarreled over territory. In these conflicts, a vassal and his knights would help their lord in battle.

Chart Skills

Describe the relationship between the king and the peasants in feudalism.

➔ Data Discovery

160

By the end of the early Middle Ages, feudalism had spread across both Western and Eastern Europe. Feudalism was supported by an economic system called manorialism.

How Manorialism Worked The economic relationship that existed between lords or knights and peasants was called **manorialism.** The center of the system was the manor, a huge estate that included the lord's house or castle, farmland, pastures, peasants, and possibly a village. Many of the peasants who lived on the manor were serfs, or people who belonged to the estate as laborers. They were not slaves, but they were not free to move, marry, or buy land without the lord's permission.

Each manor was self-sufficient, supplying all the food, clothing, and shelter needed by both the lord and peasants. Peasants and their lords were thus dependent on one another.

The wife of the lord was called a lady. She attended to domestic chores and managed the servants. Literacy was not common even among noblewomen. Ladies had few rights. Some lords chose a wife for her dowry, or a payment of money and land provided at the time of marriage. In most parts of Europe, women could own land. When a woman's parents died, however, their land passed to the oldest brother in many countries.

Peasants led hard lives working from sunup to sundown. Their diets seldom varied and disease was common.

Reading Check What was the knight's role in feudalism?

Culture Close-up

▲ Peasants farmed their own plots of land as well as those of the lord.

Section **3** Assessment

Essential Question

Key Terms

1. Write a short paragraph showing how these key terms are related: lord, vassal, feudalism.

Key Ideas

2. What was Justinian's Code?

3. How did medieval monks preserve ancient learning?

4. What was feudalism?

Think Critically

5. **Categorize** Draw a table of three rulers who tried to unify Western Europe after the fall of the Roman empire. Under each ruler, list his ethnic group, time of rule, and accomplishments.

6. **Draw Inferences** Do you think peasants often traveled far from the manor? Explain why or why not.

What are the challenges of diversity?

7. How did cultural differences between the East and the West affect the Christian church? Go to your Student Journal to record your answer.

Learned Women of the Middle Ages

Key Idea

- Most medieval women were expected to be obedient wives, mothers, and daughters, but a few women were educated, and some left fascinating written records of their lives and thoughts.

Most medieval women had limited roles. Peasant women worked in the fields or as servants. Noble women tended their husbands' manors. Women were not expected to become writers or teachers, but some did so anyway. Hildegard of Bingen was an educated noblewoman who became the abbess of a religious order. She had visions that she said were from God, and she wrote essays, poems, and songs. Christine de Pisan was a Venetian woman who lived in Paris. After her husband died, she made a living by copying manuscripts and by writing poems and books on women's behavior.

▲ A medieval woman uses scissors to cut cloth.

This medieval image shows Hildegard receiving divine visions in the form of flames. ▼

Stop at each circled letter on the right to think about the text. Then answer the question with the same letter on the left.

A **Categorize** What kind of story does the first sentence make you anticipate? Explain.

B **Draw Conclusions** Who or what affects the motion of the feather?

C **Draw Inferences** Who is the air and who is the feather? Explain what this reveals about Hildegard of Bingen.

adorn, *v.,* decorate

vestment, *n.,* ceremonial clothing

of its own accord, *adv. phrase,* on its own

borne, *v.,* carried

A Feather on the Breath of God

66 Listen now: a king sat on his
A throne, high pillars before him splendidly <u>adorned</u> . . . . They showed the king's <u>vestments</u> in great honor everywhere. Then the king chose to lift a small
B feather from the ground, and he commanded it to fly just as the king himself wished. But a feather does not fly <u>of its own accord</u>; it is <u>borne</u> up by the air. So too I am. . . . I depend entirely
C on God's help. 99

—Hildegard of Bingen, letter written in 1148

162

Stop at each circled letter on the right to think about the text. Then answer the question with the same letter on the left.

(D) Solve Problems What should a housewife do if she has more food than her family can eat?

(E) Draw Conclusions Why is it important not to give away anything that is stale or damaged?

(F) Synthesize According to Christine de Pisan, what is the best kind of charity?

indigent, *n.,* poor people

charity, *n.,* the giving of money or help to those in need

alms, *n.,* money and goods given to the poor

childbed, *n.,* the bed of a woman who is giving birth to a child

The Wise Housewife

66 This wise woman will take great care that no food goes bad around her house, that **(D)** nothing goes to waste that might help the poor and <u>indigent</u>. If she gives them to the **(E)** poor, she will ensure that the leftovers are not stale and that the clothes are not moth-eaten. [I]f she loves the welfare of her soul **(F)** and the virtue of <u>charity</u>, she will not give her <u>alms</u> only in this way, but with the wine from her own cellar and the meat from her table, to poor women in <u>childbed</u>, to the sick, and often to her poor neighbors. 99

—Christine de Pisan,
The Treasure of the City of Ladies,
translated by Sarah Lawson

Christine de Pisan instructing a young man ▶

Analyze the Documents

1. **Compare Viewpoints** Which of these writers was more concerned with practical matters and which was more concerned with spiritual matters?

2. **Writing Task** Decide what kind of an essay you would write about these two learned women. Then write the thesis statement you would use in the essay.

163

High and Late Middle Ages

Key Ideas
- The Crusades opened up medieval Europe to trade and new ideas.
- In the High Middle Ages, growth in trade routes led to the rise of cities.
- The Magna Carta limited the king's power and led to more democratic government.
- With the growth of cities, nation-building began in Europe.

Key Terms • Crusades • Reconquista • guild • Magna Carta

 Visual Glossary

Reading Skill: Analyze Cause and Effect Take notes using the graphic organizer in your journal.

◀ Knights wore suits of armor such as this one during the Middle Ages.

By 1000, feudalism had stabilized Europe and the population was growing. Universities formed, merchants gained power, and farming techniques improved. This period is called the High Middle Ages. It lasted until the early 1300s. During the Late Middle Ages, however, wars, disease, and famine hit Europe hard. As a result, the the feudal system weakened and collapsed.

The Crusades and the Wider World

By 1081, the Seljuk Turks had overrun much of the Byzantine empire. These people had migrated from Central Asia, and when they reached the Middle East, they converted to Islam. As they conquered new lands, they converted the defeated peoples to Islam.

The Turks also took control of Palestine. This region was sacred to Jews, Christians, and Muslims. It was known to Christians as the Holy Land. Many Christians in Europe objected to Muslim control of the Holy Land.

The Holy Wars Begin In 1095, Pope Urban II urged church leaders to organize the **Crusades,** a series of military expeditions to free the Holy Land from Muslim rule. At the Council of Clermont, named for the town in France where it was held, Pope Urban II urged people of all classes to unite to take back Jerusalem in a holy war,

❝ You common people who have been miserable sinners, become soldiers of Christ! You nobles, do not [quarrel] with one another. Use your arms in a just war! Labor for an everlasting reward. ❞

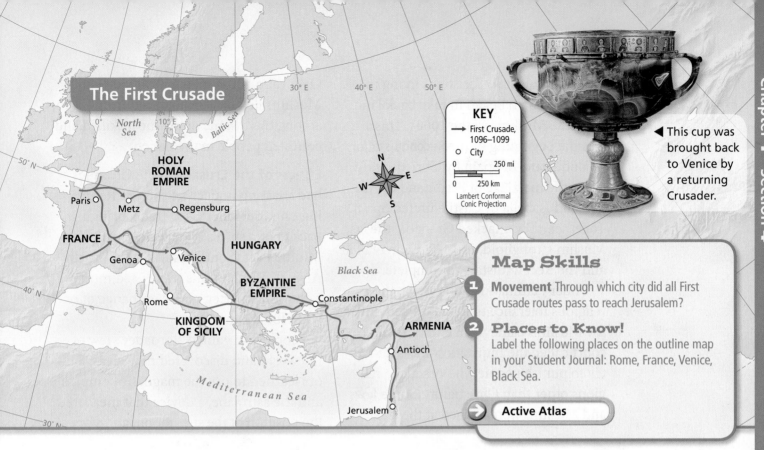

The First Crusade

KEY
→ First Crusade, 1096–1099
○ City

0 — 250 mi
0 — 250 km
Lambert Conformal Conic Projection

◀ This cup was brought back to Venice by a returning Crusader.

Map Skills

1. **Movement** Through which city did all First Crusade routes pass to reach Jerusalem?

2. **Places to Know!**
Label the following places on the outline map in your Student Journal: Rome, France, Venice, Black Sea.

→ Active Atlas

Europeans responded to the pope's call for different reasons. Some went to war for religious reasons. They believed that God wanted the Holy Land to be Christian. Others had more worldly reasons. Some knights wanted to win new possessions in the Holy Land. Others wanted the status that came from military success. Of course, Muslims in the Holy Land wanted it to remain Muslim. They did not want foreign Christian rulers.

By the summer of 1096, a large European army had formed and headed for the Holy Land. This force captured Jerusalem, and Christian leaders divided Palestine into four states. Many Muslims in the region faced brutal treatment. Then European leaders sent a second Crusade to the Holy Land. Internal quarrels weakened this force, and Muslims defeated them.

In 1187, the Muslim leader Saladin recaptured Jerusalem. Further Crusades were attempted but failed. These conflicts led to bitter feelings between Christians and Muslims that have lasted to this day.

Muslims in Spain By 718, Muslims had conquered most of Spain. Spanish Christians controlled only a small area in northern Spain. During Muslim rule, many Spanish people converted to Islam. Muslim leaders also tolerated the practice of Judaism and Christianity.

Muslims made important advances in mathematics and medicine. They studied the learning of the ancient Greeks and Romans. In addition, they built beautiful mosques and palaces. During the 900s, Córdoba became a center of Muslim culture. Muslim influence helped shape art and literature in Christian Spain.

my worldgeography.com Active Atlas

165

expel, *v.,* to force someone to leave a place

The Reconquista Christians living in northern Spain began to take back land from the Muslims in the 1000s. This was the beginning of the **Reconquista,** or reconquering of Spain by Christians. In 1469, the marriage of Ferdinand of Aragon and Isabella of Castile united Spain. Together, they attacked Granada, the last Muslim stronghold, in 1492. Granada fell and the Reconquista was complete.

Under Ferdinand and Isabella, the religious tolerance that had existed under the Muslims came to an end. A Church court called the Inquisition was set up to try to punish people who practiced religions other than Christianity. Some Jews and Muslims were burned at the stake.

Over time, more than 150,000 Jews and Muslims fled or were expelled from Spain, among them some of the most skilled and educated people in the nation.

Effects of the Crusades The Crusades had a lasting impact on society. Returning crusaders increased trade, bringing back exotic spices and fabrics from the Middle East (Southwest Asia and North Africa). Much of this trade used money rather than barter, or the exchange of one good for another.

People also gained a broader view of the world and discovered new ideas. Sailors learned to use the magnetic compass and the astrolabe, a device that measured the position of the sun, moon, and stars.

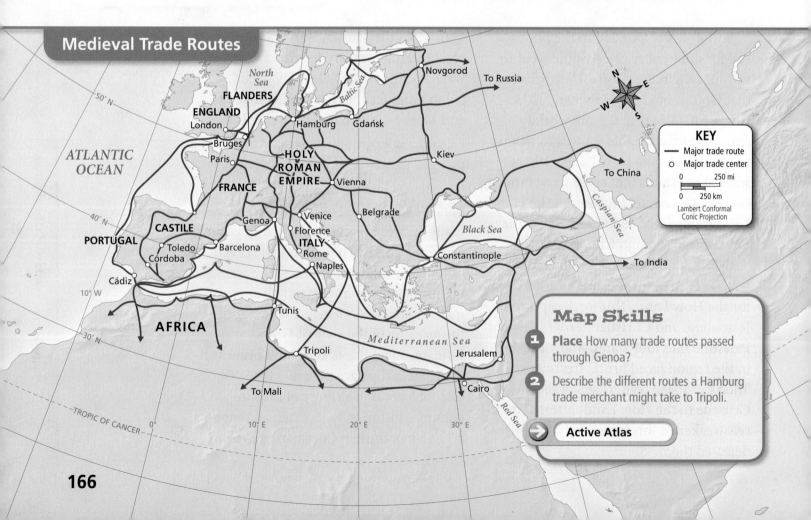

Medieval Trade Routes

KEY
— Major trade route
○ Major trade center
0 — 250 mi
0 — 250 km
Lambert Conformal Conic Projection

Map Skills

1 **Place** How many trade routes passed through Genoa?

2 Describe the different routes a Hamburg trade merchant might take to Tripoli.

→ **Active Atlas**

166

In this way, sailors could know their position on Earth's surface out of sight of land.

The compass and astrolabe were among the new ideas or technologies that Europe gained from contact with the Muslim world. Europeans also learned to make gunpowder and paper from Muslims, although these technologies first developed in China.

Muslims had preserved much of the learning of the ancient Greeks and Romans. Muslims also studied ancient Indian learning. Muslims drew on this ancient learning to make advances in science and mathematics. They passed this knowledge on to medieval Europeans.

Reading Check **How did the Crusades increase trade?**

The Rise of Cities

During the 1000s, more and more people moved from manors to cities. Many factors led to this migration.

Farming Improves During the Middle Ages, farmers found ways to improve agriculture. They gained more cropland by draining swamps and clearing forests. They also developed the horse collar and harness so horses instead of oxen could be used to plow fields. Horses plowed faster than oxen. In this way, they could plant more, harvest more, and even have surplus, or extra, crops.

As the food supply increased, people became healthier. Peasants were able to earn extra money by selling surplus crops. Some used this money to buy their freedom from their lord. Freed peasants sometimes moved to cities and towns.

Technology Develops While Europeans learned new technologies from the Muslims, they also developed new skills and products of their own. Among these were clocks, eyeglasses, and upright windmills. Military technologies like plate armor and cannons made the armies strong. Engineering advances let Europeans build soaring cathedral towers.

Commerce Begins In towns, many peasants learned special skills as craft workers. They specialized in leather goods or gold objects and sold these goods in their shops or at local markets or trade fairs.

Some merchants sold these goods along trade routes throughout Europe and Asia. They exchanged both goods and ideas. Some expanded commerce by setting up banks and issuing loans.

myWorldActivity
Trade Spices Up Life

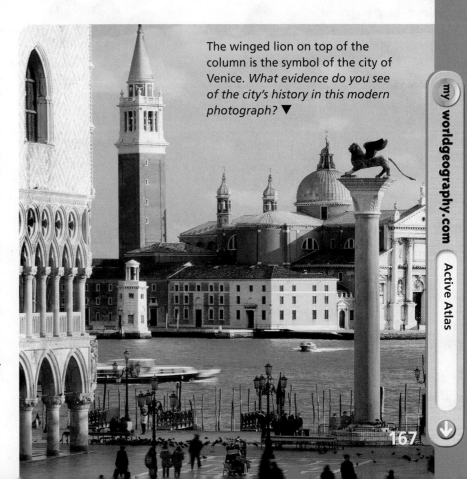

The winged lion on top of the column is the symbol of the city of Venice. *What evidence do you see of the city's history in this modern photograph?* ▼

167

The Italian Trade Centers The port of Venice was a busy place. Ships from Constantinople arrived loaded with gold, silks, and spices. Traders loaded these goods onto mules and began the trek to markets in Northern Europe.

The city-state of Venice was only one of the new commerce centers in present-day Italy. Cities such as Florence, Genoa, and Naples also served as hubs for goods coming into Europe.

The New Merchant Class As people moved to towns, many towns grew into cities. In urban areas, a person could earn a good living by working as a merchant, an artisan, or a craftsperson. As a result, the group of people who earned more than peasants grew.

This group became known as the middle class since they still ranked below the nobles. As their numbers increased, so did their political and economic power.

For protection, merchants and craftspeople formed **guilds.** A guild is an association of people who have a common livelihood. Guilds protected members from unfair business practices. They also set prices and wages. Women could sometimes become guild members. They often specialized in needlecraft and papermaking. Women were also active in the silk and wool trades.

City Life Develops As cities grew, they spread outward—and upward. People needed more living space and built homes with two or three stories. In the largest cities, a church called a cathedral formed the center of the city. These cathedrals became centers of learning and city life.

Weekly market stalls were replaced by permanent shops, though hawkers still rolled through the streets with their carts. There were no sewers or garbage collection, so medieval streets could be dirty as well as noisy and crowded.

Reading Check **Why were medieval city craftsmen known as a middle class?**

Limiting the King's Power

During the High Middle Ages, the power of kings was put to the test.

Normans Conquer England During the 1000s, England was fairly prosperous with good agricultural land. William, duke of Normandy in northern France, believed himself to be heir to the English throne.

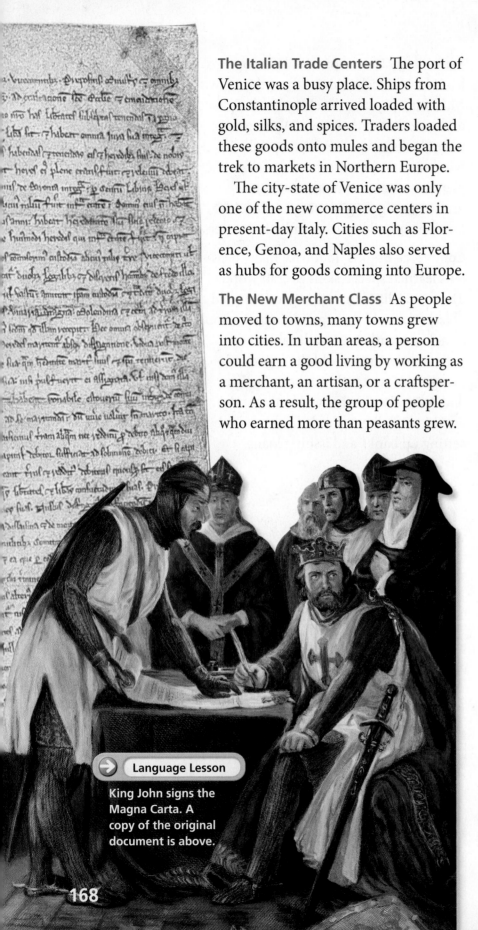

→ Language Lesson

King John signs the Magna Carta. A copy of the original document is above.

168

When it was given to an Anglo-Saxon noble named Harold, William invaded England with a huge army. He defeated Harold at the Battle of Hastings in 1066. William was crowned king of England and became known as William the Conqueror.

At the time, most of the people in England were Anglo-Saxon. The Normans treated them as inferiors. Many Anglo-Saxon lords tried to revolt, but after several years, William <u>subdued</u> them. Over time, the Normans and Anglo-Saxons intermarried, becoming one people.

Magna Carta After William's death, kings often struggled with lords for control of England. During the early 1200s, King John demanded large amounts of money without consulting the lords. He also set severe penalties for minor crimes.

Lords and church leaders rebelled. Soon, they forced King John to sign a charter called the **Magna Carta.** This was a document that limited the English king's power. The Magna Carta helped lead to more democratic government in England.

By the late 1200s, King Edward I expanded his meetings with lords and church leaders to include town representatives. These meetings came to be called the Model Parliament. They were the beginning of England's Parliament, its legislative or lawmaking assembly. Royal courts made rulings based on earlier cases. The courts created a body of common law, which was applied equally in any part of a country.

Hundred Years' War In the 1330s, the French attempted to take over an English-held province in southwest France. This conflict started a series of wars between France and England known as the Hundred Years' War (1337–1453).

By 1428, the English had taken over northern France. In Orleans, a peasant girl named Joan of Arc appeared. She claimed that she had been told by God to lead the French army into battle. In desperation, the French king agreed. The 17-year-old Joan led the army to victory. However, the next year, the English captured Joan and she was burned at the stake as a witch.

New weapons developed at this time changed warfare. The English longbow launched arrows that pierced the armor of French knights. In addition, gunpowder and cannons became common. Cannons could destroy castle walls. In this way, two of the major defenses of feudal lords—knights and castles—became much less effective.

subdue, *v.,* to bring under control

At the right, the English soldiers use longbows, while the French at the left use crossbows. *How might cannons be used in this scene?* ▼

Flea-ridden rats from ships reached land and transmitted the plague germs. ▼

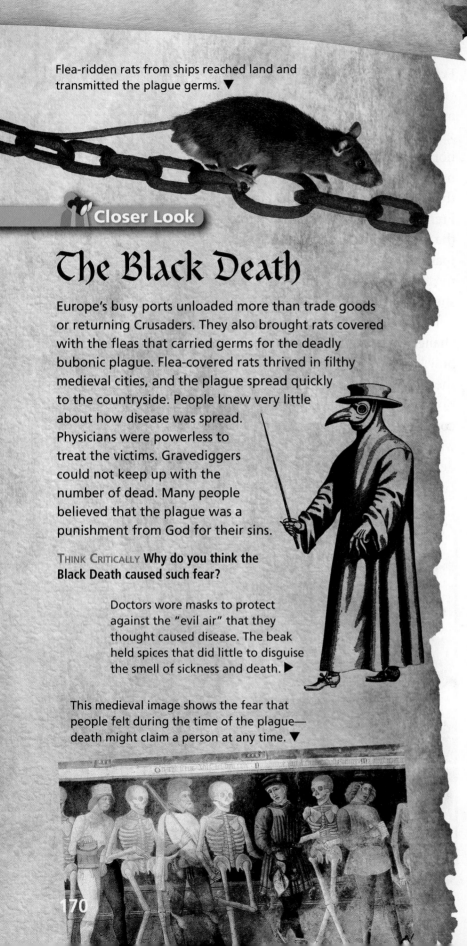

The Black Death

Europe's busy ports unloaded more than trade goods or returning Crusaders. They also brought rats covered with the fleas that carried germs for the deadly bubonic plague. Flea-covered rats thrived in filthy medieval cities, and the plague spread quickly to the countryside. People knew very little about how disease was spread. Physicians were powerless to treat the victims. Gravediggers could not keep up with the number of dead. Many people believed that the plague was a punishment from God for their sins.

THINK CRITICALLY **Why do you think the Black Death caused such fear?**

Doctors wore masks to protect against the "evil air" that they thought caused disease. The beak held spices that did little to disguise the smell of sickness and death. ▶

This medieval image shows the fear that people felt during the time of the plague—death might claim a person at any time. ▼

170

The French finally won the Hundred Years' War. The war led England and France down two different paths. The French increased the power of the monarchy. The English increased Parliament's "power of the purse," or its financial role in government.

Reading Check **What did the Magna Carta do?**

Medieval Society Weakens

Improvements in farming during the High Middle Ages caused Europe's population to grow. By the 1300s, the population had outgrown the food supply. When harvests, or crops gathered for food, were low, people experienced famines. Famines are times of hunger and starvation. Famines were just one of the hardships that increasingly weakened medieval society.

Famine Strikes In 1315, bad weather caused poor harvests in Europe. These conditions continued for two more years. By that time, many Europeans were starving. Historians estimate that about ten to fifteen percent of the population died during the winter of 1317.

The Black Death Arrives As the famines continued in later years, the constant hunger made people sickly. In 1347, Europe faced a terrible epidemic, or a widespread outbreak of disease. Because people were already weakened from poor nutrition, the epidemic was disastrous. The disease was bubonic plague, or the Black Death. Victims suffered swelling and extreme pain. Death came quickly, usually in a matter of days.

Michael Platiensis, an eyewitness, described the disease,

> Those infected felt themselves penetrated by a pain . . . Then there developed on the thighs or upper arms a boil. . . .This infected the whole body, . . . [three days later], there being no means of healing it, and then the patient expired.

Physicians had many theories about what caused the plague, all of them wrong. They tried several cures, but nothing worked. Some people falsely blamed the plague on Jews or beggars. These accusations spread, and, in some cites, thousands of Jews were tortured and killed.

By the time the Black Death ended in the early 1400s, the medieval world had begun to change. About 25 million Europeans died from the plague—from one quarter to one third of the population. The dead came from all levels of society, rich and poor. Suddenly, Europe faced a labor shortage. The disease also caused religious turmoil as many of the faithful began to have doubts.

Decline of Medieval Europe War, famine, and the Black Death changed medieval Europe profoundly. With millions of workers dead, production declined and food shortages were common. Economic uncertainty led to social upheaval. Important social structures such as manorialism and feudalism began to break down.

In manorialism, the labor of the peasant was vital. Following the plague, however, peasants began to leave the manors. In order to convince them to stay, lords offered for the first time to pay them wages. Some lords converted cropland to pastures for raising sheep. Some peasants still left the manors seeking higher wages or moving to cities.

Feudal lords found it harder to defend themselves against new weapons such as guns and cannons. In the cities, feudal influence weakened against wealthy merchants and powerful guilds. However, spurred by fresh ideas, a new age called the Renaissance was about to begin.

Reading Check How did the Black Death change Europe?

my**World**
IN NUMBERS
The Black Death killed **50,000** of **180,000** people in Paris.

Section 4 Assessment

 **Essential Question**

Key Terms

1. Use each of the following terms in a sentence: Crusades, Reconquista, guild, Magna Carta.

Key Ideas

2. Why did the middle class grow during the High Middle Ages?

3. What were some of the main results of the Crusades?

4. How did the Great Famine and the Black Death lead to the decline of feudalism?

Think Critically

5. **Draw Inferences** How do you think feudal lords felt about the growth of cities? Explain.

6. **Draw Conclusions** How might the Hundred Years' War affect nation-building in France and England?

What are the challenges of diversity?

7. How did diversity have both positive and negative effects on Spain? Go to your Student Journal to record your answer.

Ancient and Medieval Europe

Chapter Assessment

Key Terms and Ideas

1. **Compare and Contrast** How is an **oligarchy** different from a **direct democracy**?

2. **Recall** What was the job of a tribune in the ancient Roman Republic?

3. **Compare and Contrast** What are some similarities and differences between the government of ancient Athens and that of the Roman Republic?

4. **Discuss** Did **manorialism** encourage trade? Why or why not?

5. **Describe** How did Christianity spread during the early Middle Ages?

6. **Recall** How did William the Conqueror gain the English crown?

7. **Explain** How was the **Reconquista** connected to the Spanish Inquisition?

Think Critically

8. **Determine Relevance** How did the Pax Romana lead to stability across the Roman empire?

9. **Test Conclusions** Why do you think Sparta was able to take control of the Peloponnesian Peninsula and defeat Athens? Support your answer with evidence from the chapter.

10. **Analyze Information** About 25 million Europeans died from the Black Death. Name three factors that contributed to this huge death toll.

11. **Core Concepts: Economics** How did economics contribute to the decline of feudalism?

Places to Know

For each place, write the letter from the map that show its location.

12. Athens
13. Constantinople
14. Spain
15. Venice
16. Rome
17. Sparta
18. **Estimate** Using the scale, estimate how far Constantinople was from Rome.

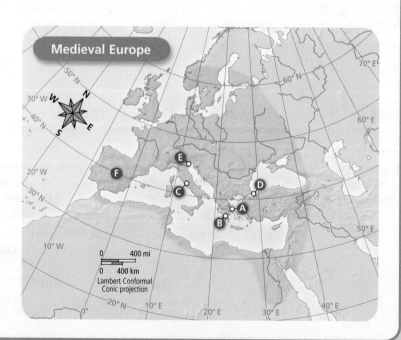

172

Essential Question

myWorld Chapter Activity

Piecing Together the Past Choose one image from the chapter activity cards. Follow your teacher's instructions and do your own field research to find similar objects in other European cultures. Then write a caption for each object you find, summarizing how it reflects diversity in European culture.

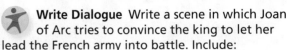

21st Century Learning

Generate New Ideas

Write Dialogue Write a scene in which Joan of Arc tries to convince the king to let her lead the French army into battle. Include:
- Joan's visions
- the king's desperation
- the city of Orleans
- the English army
- the French army

Document-Based Questions

Success Tracker™
Online at myworldgeography.com

Use your knowledge of the Middle Ages and Documents A and B to answer Questions 1–3.

Document A

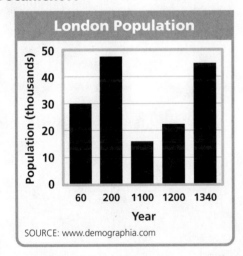

London Population

Population (thousands): 0, 10, 20, 30, 40, 50
Year: 60, 200, 1100, 1200, 1340

SOURCE: www.demographia.com

Document B

" Each trade occupied its own quarter—butchers and tanners around the Châtelet, money-changers, goldsmiths, and drapers on the Grand Pont, scribes, illuminators, and parchment- and ink-sellers on the left bank around the University [of Paris]."

— Historian Barbara Tuchman describing Paris during the High Middle Ages

1. Which of the following might explain the drop in London's population from A.D. 200 to A.D. 1100?

   A decline of Greece, rise of feudalism

   B decline of Greece, rise of trade

   C decline of Rome, rise of feudalism

   D decline of Rome, rise of trade

2. Based on Document B, which of the following best describes Paris during the High Middle Ages?

   A an economically busy city with few craft workers

   B an economically busy city with many craft workers

   C an economically quiet city with few craft workers

   D an economically quiet city with many craft workers

3. **Writing Task** Describe details in Document B that show prosperity in medieval Paris.

173

Chapter 2

Europe in Modern Times

Essential Question

What makes a nation?

KEY
- Austrian Habsburg territories
- Denmark and possessions
- England and possessions
- France
- Ottoman Empire
- Papal States
- Poland-Lithuania
- Portugal and possessions
- Russian Empire
- Spain and possessions
- Sweden
- United Provinces
- Venice and possessions
- — Holy Roman Empire, 1600
- — National border, 1600
- — Modern border
- ○ City

0 ____ 400 mi
0 ____ 400 km
Lambert Conformal Conic Projection

Where in the World Is London, England?

Washington, D.C., to London: 3,660 miles

my Story

The Battle of the Spanish Armada

In this section, you'll read about Queen Elizabeth I of England and the defeat of the great Spanish Armada. What does Elizabeth's story tell you about life in early modern Europe?

By Ruth Hull Chatlien for myWorld Online

In 1588, Europe's greatest power, Spain, prepared to attack the smaller kingdom of England. The Spanish army gathered supplies and horses for an invasion. The Spanish soldiers were to travel to England on barges. At the same time, a fleet of 130 Spanish ships, the Armada, gathered to protect the barges. The Spanish Armada used massive galleons, huge ships that rode high in the water and were clumsy to maneuver. The English captains manned "race ships." These were smaller, faster, and much easier to handle.

On the English shore, the troops gathered at Tilbury to hear their queen. This was a time when few women held power, but Elizabeth had earned her people's respect. The English people also loved their queen. At Tilbury, she knew that she had to prepare the troops to meet the Spanish, the best fighters of the day.

Explore the Essential Question ...
- at **my worldgeography.com**
- using the **myWorld Chapter Activity**
- with the **Student Journal**

> I know I have the body but of a weak and feeble woman, but I have the heart of a king, and of a king of England, too.

my worldgeography.com On Assignment

175

In 1587, Elizabeth's advisors convinced her to order the death of her cousin, Mary, Queen of Scotland. They saw Mary, a Catholic, as a threat to Elizabeth, a Protestant.

Elizabeth and trusted court advisors planned the strategy for the battle with the Spanish navy.

Spain's attack against England happened in a time of religious conflict between Catholics and Protestants. Catholicism had been the main religion of Western Europe until the early 1500s. At that time, some Christians left the Roman Catholic Church and started their own Protestant churches.

Spain's king, Philip II, was a very religious man who wanted to restore Catholicism to all of Europe. Elizabeth, who was a Protestant, urged Philip to let Protestants in the Netherlands practice their religion. At that time, the Netherlands was a Spanish possession.

Philip also believed that he should be king of England because he had been married to Mary I. Mary was Elizabeth's half-sister who ruled England before her death in 1558. Religious strife had shaken England ever since Henry VIII, father of Elizabeth and Mary, broke with the Catholic Church and started the Protestant Church of England.

As queen, one of Protestant Elizabeth's earliest acts was to order a compromise with Catholics. Unlike Philip, she did not want to force people to share her religion. "I have no desire to make windows into men's souls," she said. Her wise actions prevented civil war in England, although tension remained throughout her reign.

Spain and England were also rival empire-builders. England wanted an empire and colonies like those of Spain. Those colonies had brought fabulous wealth, such as gold and silver, to Spain. English ships had attacked Spanish ships and taken their gold and silver.

As the Spanish Armada set sail, the huge fleet appeared to be invincible, or unbeatable. Yet, the Spanish had several weaknesses. Besides sailing heavier ships, the Spanish captains had no maps of the coasts of Scotland or Ireland. The Spanish soldiers were brave fighters, but in the use of cannon, they lagged behind their rivals. In addition, food stores had been loaded too early and were rotting. Water barrels leaked, and cannon balls were poorly made or the wrong size. In addition, there were discipline problems on board the Spanish ships.

The Spanish were sure that they would win and saw the battle as a holy war. Philip even had the ships' sails painted with the cross of St. George, the symbol of the medieval Crusaders. In spite of the seeming advantage of the Spanish, Elizabeth predicted,

> Let tyrants fear. . . .We shall shortly have a famous victory over these enemies of my God, of my kingdom, and of my people.

The Spanish navy had helped make Spain a wealthy global empire. But the Spanish sailed old-fashioned, slower ships. Their loss to England changed sea warfare and the fortunes of Spain.

As the Spanish Armada neared the coast of England, the English fleet moved into position. For several days, the English managed to keep the Spanish ships at a distance.

At midnight, the English sent fireships loaded with explosives into the midst of the Spanish fleet. The Spanish commanders were forced to cut the ships' anchor cables and sail out to sea to avoid catching fire. The Spanish formation became disorganized, and the English took advantage of the confusion to attack at dawn. A decisive battle took place, and the losses to Spain far outweighed those of England. Spanish domination of the seas had ended.

The English felt this victory proved that God was on their side. English admirals received a medal that said, "God blew and they were scattered." This victory at sea was one of the greatest triumphs of Elizabeth's reign.

 myStory Online

Join Elizabeth and her advisors as they plan the battle against the Spanish Armada.

my worldgeography.com myStory Online

177

New Ways of Thinking

Key Ideas
- European Renaissance thinkers and artists took a new interest in humanity and the world around them.
- Critical thinking in Renaissance Europe led to the Reformation.

Key Terms • Renaissance • humanism • perspective • Reformation • Catholic Reformation

 Visual Glossary

 Reading Skill: Label an Outline Map Take notes using the graphic organizer in your journal.

Leon Battista Alberti drew on ancient models for his Renaissance church, Santa Maria Novella, in Florence, Italy.▼

The Late Middle Ages brought many changes to Europe. Feudalism came to an end. Farmers began producing more agricultural goods than they needed. Trade increased. These changes led to a new age in European history called the **Renaissance,** or "rebirth," a time of a renewed interest in art and learning.

The Italian Renaissance

Italy is a peninsula in southern Europe. Italy had been the center of the Roman Empire. This classical influence contributed to the Renaissance.

Trade Grows and Cities Compete Italian traders brought silks and spices back from Asia. They sold these in Italian cities such as Genoa, Venice, and Florence. These cities were major trade centers. In the markets, people exchanged coins of different lands. Merchants adopted a system to deposit money and write checks. These practices became the basis of modern banking.

Unlike the kingdoms of other parts of Europe, Italy was divided into city-states. These city-states were often ruled by one powerful family. In addition to ruling families, city-states were dominated by a wealthy merchant class. City-states fought often. They invented taxes on property and income and other ways to finance their wars.

Old and New Ideas Inspire Trade brought Europeans into contact with the learning of Asia and the Muslim world. For example, Muslim mathematician Al-Khwarizmi (al KWAHR iz mee) had used Hindu-Arabic numerals and developed algebra in the 700s. Muslim scholars had copied and preserved works from ancient Greece and Rome. Many of these had been lost in Europe. Europeans also learned Chinese techniques such as block printing and papermaking.

During the Renaissance, European scholars took an interest in ancient Greek and Roman ideas. This was the beginning of **humanism,** or the study of secular, or nonreligious, subjects such as history and philosophy. Humanists emphasized individual accomplishment and serving the people of this world instead of focusing on religion.

Art Copies Nature Medieval artists had focused on teaching spiritual lessons. As a result, their art was symbolic, not realistic. In contrast, the Greeks and Romans had honored nature and tried to make their art lifelike. Renaissance artists imitated the realism of classical art.

Art changed in two major ways during the Renaissance. First, artists studied the human body so that they could create lifelike statues and paintings. Second, Renaissance painters used **perspective,** a technique that allows artists to portray a three-dimensional space on a flat surface.

Artists Michelangelo and Leonardo da Vinci both created Renaissance masterpieces. Michelangelo carved sculptures, such as the statue *David*. He also painted scenes from the Bible on the ceiling of the Sistine Chapel in Rome. Leonardo painted the famous portrait *Mona Lisa*. He also drew thousands of diagrams of ideas for inventions. Architect Filippo Brunelleschi (fee LEEP po broo nel LES kee) used classical features such as domes, columns, and arches in his buildings.

Reading Check What did humanists emphasize?

A New Perspective

For *The Last Supper* (1495–1497), Leonardo used perspective to make the painting as realistic as possible. *How did Leonardo use perspective to focus on the figure of Jesus?*

Gutenberg's Press

Gutenberg and his pressmen examine a newly printed page (above). The page at the left was copied out by hand. The page at the right was printed using movable type. *How did Gutenberg's printing press change books?*

The Northern Renaissance

A network of land and sea trade routes linked the city-states of Italy with the kingdoms and small states of Northern Europe. These northern lands included England, Germany, and Flanders (a region now divided between France and Belgium). Like Italy, Germany and Flanders were divided into small, competitive states.

Northern Cities Grow Improved ships made traveling by sea faster than traveling overland. As a result of <u>rapid</u> sea travel, trade between northern and southern Europe increased. Trade also increased within northern Europe. Some northern towns decided to form trade associations so they could have more influence over trade. For example, the Hanseatic (han see AT ik) League was a group of more than 60 towns in Germany and other lands. They worked together to improve trade among members.

Cities and countries began to specialize in the production of certain goods. The countries of England, France, and Flanders produced cloth. Northeastern Europe produced grain. Germany, Hungary, and Austria mined copper, iron, gold, and silver. Trade helped northern cities such as London, Paris, Brugge (BROOG uh), and Lyon grow. A middle class of traders and craftsmen developed. Middle-class people were wealthier than peasants and could buy more goods. This encouraged trade.

Renaissance Ideas Spread Renaissance ideas spread to northern Europe in several ways. First, traders brought the new ideas with them. Second, rulers such as King Francis I of France invited Renaissance scholars and artists to visit their courts. Third, many northern nobles and wealthy members of the middle class traveled to Italy for their education. While in Italy, they learned about Renaissance ideas.

rapid, *adj.,* fast

myWorld Activity
A Life-Changing
Product

180

New technology helped spread knowledge. In the 1400s, German craftsman Johannes Gutenberg invented the printing press. Gutenberg made movable type, or pieces of metal formed into letters of the alphabet. He then printed pages by using a machine to squeeze paper against inked type. Before the printing press, the only way to reproduce writing was by hand. The press made it possible to create copies of books much faster than ever before. As more books became available, more people learned to read.

Renaissance ideas began to influence northern artists and writers. Flemish artist Pieter Bruegel (PEA tur BROO gel) the Elder painted lively scenes of peasant life. German artist Albrecht Dürer (AHL brekt DYOOR ur) used Italian techniques of realism and perspective to create life-like paintings.

The English playwright William Shakespeare wrote brilliant plays seen as key works of Renaissance humanism. In his play *Hamlet*, he expressed the Renaissance view of human potential:

66 What a piece of work is a man, how noble in reason, how infinite in faculties, in form and moving, how express and admirable in action, how like an angel in apprehension, how like a god! 99

Shakespeare's work remains popular today, both on stage and in movies.

Some northern writers, known as Christian humanists, combined classical and religious studies. The Dutch scholar Erasmus (ih RAZ mus) studied the New Testament in its original Greek language. He suggested the Catholic Church make

changes, such as teaching in modern languages instead of Latin. The English humanist Thomas More wrote about an ideal society in his book *Utopia*. Today, we use the word *utopia* to mean a place of perfection in laws and society.

Reading Check Who spread Renaissance ideas to Northern Europe?

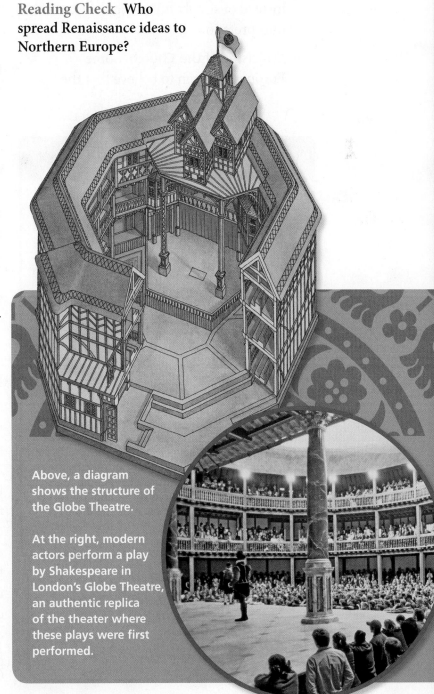

Above, a diagram shows the structure of the Globe Theatre.

At the right, modern actors perform a play by Shakespeare in London's Globe Theatre, an authentic replica of the theater where these plays were first performed.

181

The Protestant Reformation

During the Renaissance, humanism led Europeans like Erasmus to think critically about the Catholic Church. Some learned Europeans began to read the Bible and interpret it for themselves instead of simply following the Church's interpretation.

Criticisms of the Church Some Europeans began to believe that the Church did not uphold the Bible's teachings. Some felt that Church leaders were corrupt. Others thought that the Church had become too rich, or that it was too involved in politics.

The Inquisition also led to criticism. The Inquisition was a church court set up to try people accused of heresy, or religious belief contrary to established Church teachings. The Church gained wealth by taking property from people accused of heresy.

Early critics of the Church, such as John Wycliffe, Jan Hus (yahn hous), and Girolamo Savonarola (jee ROH lah moh sah voh nuh ROH lah), risked their lives by speaking out. Church leaders executed both Hus and Savonarola, yet the calls for reform did not end.

The printing press helped spread the desire for change. As books grew more common, more people were able to read the Bible and scholarly works. People formed their own ideas about religion. More people questioned Church teachings.

Luther Calls for Reform The Church made money by selling indulgences, or pardons for sin. A German monk named Martin Luther studied the Bible and came to believe that people could neither buy nor earn pardon for sin. In 1517, Luther drafted the 95 Theses, a list of arguments against indulgences. He sent the list to to a church official who called for an investigation of Luther's beliefs. Luther's call for reform started the **Reformation,** a religious movement in which calls for reform led to the emergence of non-Catholic, or Protestant, churches.

Comparing Catholicism and Lutheranism

	Catholicism	Lutheranism
Salvation	Faith and good works bring salvation.	Faith alone brings salvation.
Sacraments	Priests perform the seven sacraments, or rituals.	Accepts some sacraments, but rejects others because they lack Biblical grounding.
Head of the Church	The pope, together with the bishops	Elected councils
Importance of the Bible	Bible is one source of truth; Church tradition is another.	Bible alone is the source of truth.
Interpretation	Bible is interpreted by priests according to tradition and Church leadership.	People read and interpret the Bible for themselves.

Chart Skills

Note the differences in the heads of the two churches. Why was this difference important?

Data Discovery

182

Luther believed that religious salvation came only from faith. He also believed that the Bible—not the Church—was the only true authority for Christian life. He encouraged ordinary people to study the Bible. People began Lutheran churches based on Luther's teachings.

Other Protestants took the movement even further. In his book *Institutes of the Christian Religion*, John Calvin offered an explanation of Protestant beliefs. His main theme is the belief that God has complete control over the universe. Calvin also stressed morality and hard work.

The Reformation began a series of events in which churches continued to split up over various disagreements. One new group of Protestants, the Anabaptists, baptized only adults. Other new churches included the Baptists, the Mennonites, and the Quakers. In the 1700s, English clergyman John Wesley founded the Methodist Church.

The Reformation and Government
During this time period, many European rulers forced their people to follow the ruler's religion. Catholics and Protestants felt certain that their own beliefs were the only correct doctrines. Many people did not think other views should be allowed. Sometimes, state churches punished people of other faiths. Such abuses of religious power later led the authors of the U.S. Constitution to call for the separation of church and state.

doctrine, *n.,* teaching or principle

Protestant and Catholic Europe

Map Skills

1. **Place** Which country was Anglican?

2. **Movement** To which areas did Protestant (Anglican, Lutheran, or Calvinist) churches spread?

3. **Places to Know!** Label the following places on the outline map in your Student Journal: England, Wittenberg, Scotland, Sweden, Paris, Spain.

Active Atlas

KEY
- Mainly Roman Catholic
- Mainly Anglican
- Mainly Lutheran
- Mainly Calvinist
- Eastern Orthodox
- Eastern Orthodox with Muslim minorities
- Border as of 1600

0 — 400 mi
0 — 400 km
Lambert Conformal Conic Projection

myworldgeography.com Data Discovery

183

Each of the small states in Germany followed the religion of its ruler. Some German princes remained Catholic, while others became Lutheran. Religious conflict in Germany was a cause of the Thirty Years' War. The war raged in central Europe from 1618 to 1648. The fighting left Germany in ruins.

Religion in England Religion also played a major role in English politics. King Henry VIII wanted to have sons to rule after him, but he and his wife Catherine of Aragon had only one child who survived infancy—a daughter. Henry,

who was Catholic, asked the pope to allow him to end his marriage. The pope refused. In response, Henry declared that England was no longer under the authority of the pope. Instead, Henry formed a new church, the Church of England. This church is also called the Anglican church. As head of the Church of England, Henry ended his marriage.

Henry went on to have five more wives, one more daughter, and one son. Each of his three children later ruled England in turn. When power changed hands, England went from Protestant to Catholic, and finally, under the rule of Elizabeth I, to Protestant again.

Reading Check How did Martin Luther begin the Reformation?

The Catholic Reformation

Even after the Protestant Reformation, millions of Europeans remained Catholic. The Catholic Church was especially strong in Italy and Spain. In response to reformers' criticisms, the Church began to make changes. These changes, which helped keep Catholicism strong, are called the **Catholic Reformation.**

The Catholic Church Responds When Luther posted his 95 Theses, Pope Leo X did not take the event very seriously. He believed that the calls for change would soon end. However, the pope did excommunicate Luther—that is, he banned Luther from the Catholic Church.

In 1545, Pope Paul III took action against the Reformation. He called Church leaders to the Council of Trent where they rejected several key Protestant beliefs.

A New Church

CATHERINE of ARRAGON

Henry VIII broke with the pope to divorce Catherine of Aragon (above). Even though he was head of the Church of England, he never abandoned the Catholic faith.

184

First, it decided that only the Catholic Church and its leaders could interpret the Bible. Second, the council declared that Church tradition was just as important a guide for Christian life as the Bible. Third, the council decided that both faith and good deeds were needed for salvation.

The Church Renews Itself Over time, the Catholic Church ended many of the abuses that Protestants had criticized. This helped Catholics remain loyal to the faith. Also, Catholic mystics such as John of the Cross and Teresa of Avila wrote inspiring works about their faith. Mystics are people who aim to experience the presence of God. Many mystics have written about their experiences.

In addition, Ignatius (ig NAY shus) of Loyola helped the Church gain new strength. He was a Spanish soldier who became religious while recovering from war injuries. Loyola wrote a set of spiritual exercises that became the basis for the Jesuit order of priests. The Jesuits were disciplined and well trained. They became educators in Catholic schools. Many became missionaries. The Catholic Reformation and the work of Jesuits helped to spread Catholicism to European colonies around the world.

Reading Check How did Ignatius of Loyola help strengthen Catholicism?

myStory Online

Queen Elizabeth rallies the troops at Tilbury.

Section 1 Assessment

Key Terms

1. Explain how the following terms affected European life in the period covered in this section: Renaissance, Reformation, Catholic Reformation.

Key Ideas

2. What cultures helped to shape the Renaissance?

3. How did the Renaissance help cause the Reformation?

4. What were two Catholic responses to the Reformation?

Think Critically

5. **Compare and Contrast** How were Italy and Germany alike and different?

6. **Synthesize** How did the printing press affect the spread of Protestantism?

7. **Analyze Cause and Effect** How did trade expand knowledge?

Essential Question

What makes a nation?

8. How might a desire to build a stronger nation affect a ruler's decision to become a Protestant or a Catholic? Go to your Student Journal to record your answer.

185

Renaissance Views of Rulers

Key Idea
- With a new focus on social issues, Renaissance thinkers considered the use of power and the character of a good ruler.

The Renaissance brought an increased emphasis on secular, or non-religious matters, such as how to govern. Before the Renaissance, most thinkers had focused on religious matters. The Renaissance princes who ruled Italian city-states sought advice on the practical aspects of government. Niccolò Machiavelli's *The Prince* provided just such a guide for Renaissance rulers, though it had little say about what was good for society. In England, Thomas More wrote *Utopia* to express his ideas about the perfect society. These two Renaissance writers offered very different portraits of the ideal ruler.

▲ A medal with a portrait of Queen Elizabeth I

Portrait of Machiavelli ▼

Stop at each letter on the right to think about the text. Then answer the question with the same letter on the left.

A **Categorize** According to Machiavelli, what are the two possible ways for subjects to feel about their ruler?

B **Analyze Primary Sources** What emotion does Machiavelli think rulers should inspire, and why?

C **Identify Bias** How does Machiavelli's view of human nature shape his view of how to rule? Explain.

dispense with, *v.,* to get rid of
assert, *v.,* to argue, claim
fickle, *adj.,* not reliable or loyal
covetous, *adj.,* greedy

Feared Rulers

66 . . . [A] question arises:

A whether it be better to be loved than feared or feared than loved? It may be answered that one should wish to be both, but, because it is difficult to unite them in one person, it is much

B safer to be feared than loved, when, of the two, either must be dispensed with. Because this is

C to be asserted in general of men, that they are ungrateful, fickle, false, cowardly, covetous. . . . 99

—Niccolò Machiavelli, *The Prince*, 1513, translated by W. K. Marriott

186

Stop at each letter on the right to think about the text. Then answer the question with the same letter on the left.

D **Draw Conclusions** In More's ideal world, what kind of character do magistrates have?

E **Analyze Cause and Effect** How do the people respond to the rule of the magistrates?

F **Draw Inferences** What do you think the sheaf of grain stands for? Explain what it says about the role of the prince.

zealously, *adv.,* eagerly

magistracy, *n.,* the position of a magistrate, a powerful legal official

exact, *v.,* to get by force

diadem, *n.,* crown

sheaf, *n.,* bunch

Ideal Rulers

66 Any man who campaigns too <u>zealously</u> for a <u>magistracy</u> is sure to fail. They live together harmoniously

D and the magistrates are never proud or cruel. Instead they are called fathers, and deservedly. Because the magistrates do not <u>exact</u> honor from people against their will, the

E people honor them willingly, as they should. Not even the prince has the distinction of robe or <u>diadem</u>; he

F is known only by a <u>sheaf</u> of grain carried before him. In the same way the priest is known by a wax candle. 99

—Thomas More, *Utopia,* 1516, translated by H.V.S. Ogden

▲ Portrait of Thomas More by Hans Holbein

This statue of Grand Duke Ferdinando I de' Medici portrays the kind of Renaissance ruler that Machiavelli described. ▶

Analyze the Documents

1. **Compare Viewpoints** How are Machiavelli's and More's ideas about rulers similar and different?
2. **Writing Task** Write a letter to the U.S. president. Recommend that government officials be required to study either *The Prince* or *Utopia*, and explain why. Include a sentence stating why you decided against the other work.

Europe Expands

Key Ideas
- Renaissance ideals, competition among rulers, and the expansion of trade led to an age of exploration.
- Exploration and a search for wealth led European states to create colonial empires.

Key Terms • cartography • caravel • plantation • northwest passage • triangular trade • absolutism

 Reading Skill: Sequence Take notes using the graphic organizer in your journal.

A modern replica of English explorer Sir Francis Drake's ship *Golden Hind*

By 1300, innovations such as navigational charts, triangular sails, and magnetic compasses had made sailing easier. These new technologies also helped Renaissance mapmakers develop **cartography,** the science of making accurate maps and globes. A new age of exploration was about to begin.

The Age of Exploration

During the 1300s, Italian merchant Marco Polo published a book about his travels in China and India. His descriptions of the wealth and wonders of Asia increased European interest in the continent.

Portugal Sets Sail Portugal led the search for a sea route to Asia. The Portuguese sailed **caravels,** small, triangular-sailed oceangoing ships. Henry the Navigator, a Portuguese prince, paid for voyages to Asia and helped train explorers in navigation.

Throughout the 1400s, Portuguese ships explored the west coast of Africa by sailing farther and farther south. In 1488, Bartolomeu Dias became the first explorer to travel around the southern tip of Africa. In 1497, Vasco da Gama reached India. During the first half of the 1500s, the Portuguese established trading centers in India, Southeast Asia, and China. They enabled Portugal to end Italy's control over trade with Asia.

Closer Look

To the Far Horizon

New tools for navigation, better maps, and tales of riches sent European explorers out on the high seas. They sailed from Portugal, Spain, England, France, and the Netherlands looking for new trade routes and new lands to claim.

Modern replicas of Columbus's ships ▶

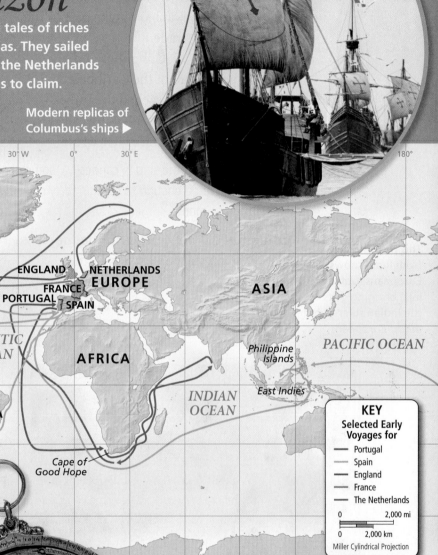

NORTH AMERICA

ENGLAND   NETHERLANDS
FRANCE   EUROPE
PORTUGAL
SPAIN

ASIA

West Indies
Caribbean Sea

ATLANTIC OCEAN

AFRICA

Philippine Islands

PACIFIC OCEAN

SOUTH AMERICA

INDIAN OCEAN

East Indies

PACIFIC OCEAN

Cape of Good Hope

KEY
Selected Early Voyages for
— Portugal
— Spain
— England
— France
— The Netherlands

0   2,000 mi
0   2,000 km
Miller Cylindrical Projection

Map Skills

1. **Movement** Which nation's explorers followed the coast of Africa to Asia?

2. **Movement** Which nation sent an explorer around the world?

3. **Region** Which nations' explorers sailed to eastern North America?

◀ Renaissance explorers used the astrolabe at left to determine their position and the compass below to find their direction.

THINK CRITICALLY **How did explorers use these tools to find their way across the oceans?**

189

finance, *v.,* to raise or provide funds

Reaching the Americas Italian explorer Christopher Columbus promised to reach Asia by sailing westward across the Atlantic. Spain's rulers agreed to <u>finance</u> his voyage. They wanted to take part in the rich Asian spice trade.

In October 1492, Columbus and his crew made landfall in the Caribbean. He believed he had reached the Indies—islands in Southeast Asia—so he called the native people Indians. He later wrote:

> 66 They came to the ship in canoes, … some of them large enough to contain forty or forty-five men. 99

Columbus did not reach Asia, but he helped Spain start an empire in the Americas.

Reading Check Why did Portugal and Spain look for water routes to Asia?

This painting from India shows Europeans (bottom left) bringing gifts to the Indian ruler. *Why might Europeans bring gifts?* ▼

An Age of Empires

The age of exploration was also an age of imperialism, or empire-building. European countries expanded their empires by taking over other lands as colonies. These colonies made European nations wealthy and powerful.

Spain Conquers the New World Many Spanish explorers followed Columbus to the Americas. In 1513, Vasco Nuñez de Balboa (VAHS koh NOO nyes deh bal BOH uh) became the first European to reach the Pacific Ocean from the Americas. This proved that he was not in Asia. The explorer Amerigo Vespucci (ah meh REE goh ves POOH chee) believed that explorers had found a "New World." A mapmaker at the time called the New World *America* after Vespucci.

Spain sent conquistadors, or conquerors, to the Americas to seize new lands. They used gunpowder, a Chinese invention, to help them conquer native peoples. On the Caribbean islands, the Spanish set up **plantations,** or large commercial farms.

In Mexico, Spanish troops under Hernán Cortés took control of the Aztec Empire. In Peru, troops under Francisco Pizarro conquered the Inca Empire. Spain took huge amounts of gold and silver from its American colonies. The Spanish empire covered much of the Americas.

Establishing New Colonies Explorers also searched for a **northwest passage,** a route between the Atlantic and Pacific Oceans along the northern coast of North America. They hoped to increase trade with Asia by finding a faster sea route.

190

The Columbian Exchange

Columbus's landing in America changed life around the world. European ships brought animals, food plants, and diseases that transformed life there. In turn, Europeans brought back new foods and other products.

Diagram Skills

Explain in your own words how this diagram shows the Columbian Exchange.

→ Data Discovery

Foods such as corn and cocoa were unknown in Europe. ▶

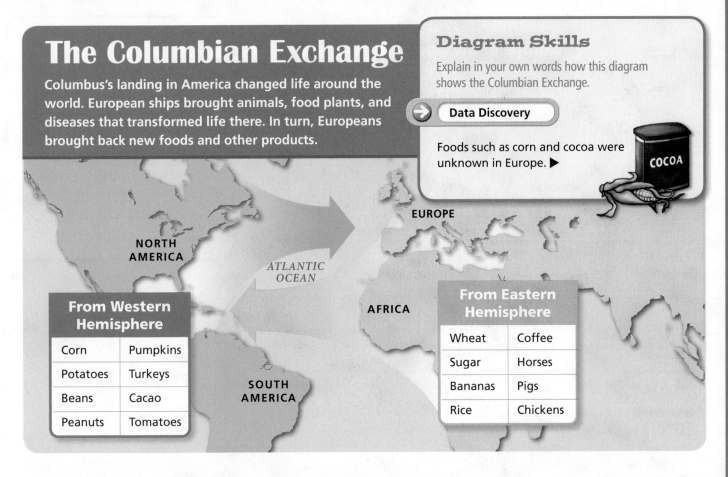

From Western Hemisphere

Corn	Pumpkins
Potatoes	Turkeys
Beans	Cacao
Peanuts	Tomatoes

From Eastern Hemisphere

Wheat	Coffee
Sugar	Horses
Bananas	Pigs
Rice	Chickens

NORTH AMERICA

ATLANTIC OCEAN

EUROPE

AFRICA

SOUTH AMERICA

Explorers never found a northwest passage, but others established new colonies in North America. Both England and France claimed lands in eastern North America. They also traded with Native Americans for furs to take back to Europe.

By the mid-1700s, England had a group of colonies stretching down the Atlantic coast of North America. Early settlements included Jamestown in Virginia and Plymouth Colony in New England. The Netherlands had also founded North American colonies, but the English took them over.

The Dutch, English, and French had colonies in other regions. The Dutch controlled land in the East Indies. England and France had additional colonies in India.

England also founded colonies in Australia during the early 1800s. Most of these colonies began as places to send people <u>convicted</u> of crimes. By the late 1800s, though, most colonists in Australia were not criminals. Those colonists went to Australia to make a living in agriculture, mining, or in Australia's growing cities.

Plantation Agriculture Plantations in the Caribbean and southeastern North America produced crops such as sugar and tobacco. Plantation agriculture required huge numbers of workers. At first, landowners used Native Americans, but they fell ill from European diseases. Europeans began to bring enslaved Africans to do this work.

convict, *v.,* to find or prove guilty

myworldgeography.com Data Discovery

myWorld Activity
Sailing for Riches

191

Europe in the Age of Absolutism

Map Skills

1 **Location** Which large country separated Spain's possessions?

2 **Place** Why might Spain have had trouble controlling its European empire?

3 **Places to Know!** Label the following places on the outline map in your Student Journal: Paris, Constantinople, London, Poland.

→ **Active Atlas**

KEY
— Border as of 1700
0 — 400 mi
0 — 400 km
Lambert Conformal Conic Projection

▲ A china vase made in the 1700s for King Augustus II the Strong, Elector of Saxony and King of Poland

In time, a system known as the triangular trade developed. The **triangular trade** was a three-stage pattern of Atlantic trade that carried goods and enslaved people between Europe, Africa, and the Americas. In the first stage, Europeans shipped manufactured goods from Europe to Africa. These goods were traded for slaves and gold. In the second stage, ships carried enslaved Africans to the Americas. In the third stage, ships carried sugar and other agricultural products back to Europe. Trade winds and ocean currents helped ships along this trade route.

Reading Check Why did European nations compete for colonies?

An Age of Absolutism

During this time, European nations grew in size and power to become nation-states. A nation-state is a region that shares a government and is independent from other states. Monarchs during this time felt that God had chosen them to rule, a belief called the divine right of kings. They also believed in absolutism. **Absolutism** is a political system of centralized and unlimited government power.

Absolute Power in Spain Perhaps the most powerful monarch in Europe was Spain's Philip II. Philip kept firm control over the Spanish empire. As he once said, "It is best to keep an eye on everything."

192

Philip was a Catholic, and he used his power to back Catholicism throughout Europe. Conflict between Catholics and Protestants led to fighting in the Spanish Netherlands.

Spain also came into conflict with England. King Philip wanted to end English attacks on Spanish ships carrying gold and silver from the Americas. He also wanted to force England, a Protestant country, to return to the Catholic Church. But, as you have read, in 1588, the English navy defeated a Spanish navy fleet, called the Armada.

The Sun King Just as the sun is the center of the solar system, Louis XIV was the center of the French government. Known as the Sun King, he centralized power around the throne. In fact, Louis believed he was so important that he said "L'état, c'est moi," meaning "I am the state."

Louis wanted to make France the greatest nation in Europe. He spent years building the biggest palace in Europe at Versailles. He encouraged the growth of industry and built canals and roads. He sent the French army to build colonies in Asia and the Americas. Under Louis, France was at war almost constantly.

Prussia and Austria In 1740, Prussia seized Austrian territory in what is now Poland. That same year, Austrian Empress Maria Theresa began her 40-year rule, making Vienna a cultural center.

Although both Austrian and Prussian rulers were absolutists, Prussia practiced religious tolerance. Both struggled for years to control Central Europe.

Reading Check How did European rulers use their power?

King Louis XIV wears robes decorated with golden fleurs-de-lis, a symbol of France.

Section 2 Assessment

Essential Question

Key Terms

1. Write complete sentences to define each of the following terms: cartography, plantation, northwest passage, triangular trade, absolutism

Key Ideas

2. Why did Spain support Columbus's voyages of exploration?

3. Which three European nations established colonies in eastern North America?

4. Why did European powers create colonies in the Americas?

Think Critically

5. **Identify Bias** What did the actions of Europeans reveal about their attitudes toward non-Europeans?

6. **Draw Inferences** How would Spain's discovery of huge quantities of silver and gold in the Americas affect relations with other European nations?

7. **Identify Evidence** How did absolutism help monarchs build power at home and abroad?

What makes a nation?

8. How might wars among European powers have helped build loyalty to the new nation-states? Go to your Student Journal to record your answer.

Section 3

An Age of Revolutions

Key Ideas

- The Scientific Revolution brought advances in knowledge and technology.
- The Enlightenment applied reason to human affairs and led to political revolutions in England, France, and other European countries.
- The Industrial Revolution transformed Europe's economy and landscape.

Key Terms • Scientific Revolution • Enlightenment • English Bill of Rights • French Revolution • Industrial Revolution

Reading Skill: Analyze Cause and Effect Take notes using the graphic organizer in your journal.

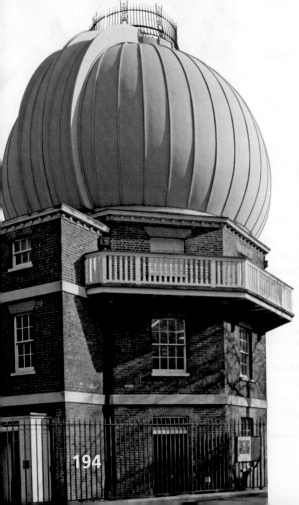

London's Royal Greenwich Observatory was established in the 1600s to study the stars and navigation. ▼

Medieval scholars had relied on religion and ancient writings to explain the world. But Renaissance thinkers questioned these old beliefs. Instead, they relied on logic, reason, and observation. Their ideas would transform science, government, and the economy.

A Scientific Revolution

During the Renaissance, scholars began studying the world around them. This led to the **Scientific Revolution,** a series of major advances in science during the 1500s and 1600s.

Science Changes Over time, scholars developed new ways to approach science. Francis Bacon taught that scientists should observe and interpret facts. René Descartes (ruh NAY day KAHRT) stressed the use of logic, or reason, to form scientific theories. Isaac Newton believed in testing theories using the scientific method, or controlled experiments.

Scientists Make Discoveries Medieval scientists believed that the sun, planets, and stars orbited, or circled, Earth. This theory was part of Catholic teachings. But in 1543, Polish astronomer Nicolaus Copernicus argued that the planets orbit the sun.

Italian astronomer Galileo Galilei (gal uh LAY oh gal uh LAY ee) agreed with Copernicus. Galileo published evidence that Earth circled the sun. In 1633, the Catholic Church put Galileo on trial for contradicting Church teaching. To save his life, Galileo signed a confession stating that his books were wrong.

194

Advances in Science

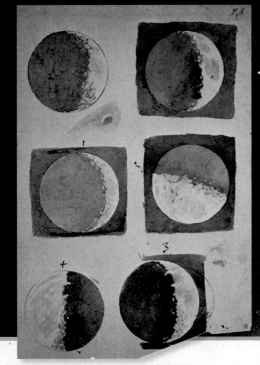

◀ Galileo sketched these phases of the moon that he saw through a telescope. In the background is a modern photograph of the moon.

The Scientific Method

Step One
State the problem.

Step Two
Gather information about the problem.

Step Three
Form a hypothesis, or educated guess.

Step Four
Experiment to test hypothesis.

Step Five
Record and analyze data.

Step Six
State a conclusion.

Step Seven
Share conclusions.

The English scientist Isaac Newton studied how the physical world worked. He described gravity and explained how objects moved in space.

Results of Discovery Scientific and technological advances improved life. Agricultural advances led to larger harvests. Inventors built instruments to measure longitude, latitude, and speed. The work of astronomers resulted in a more accurate calendar.

Thomas Newcomen and James Watt invented steam engines. Alessandro Volta and Michael Faraday conducted electrical experiments. Electricity and steam later became important energy sources.

Reading Check How did the scientific method change science?

The Enlightenment

The **Enlightenment** was a movement during the 1600s and 1700s to apply observation and reason to human affairs. The movement drew on the success of the Scientific Revolution.

Philosophers Study Society Enlightenment thinkers believed that nothing was beyond the human mind. Some studied the nature of reality. Many wrote about society and government. Thomas Hobbes believed that people were selfish and greedy and needed a strong ruler. Hobbes painted this picture of life without a strong ruler in his book *Leviathan*:

greedy, *adj.*, having a strong desire for wealth and possessions

66 There is … continual fear and danger of violent death, and the life of man [is] solitary, poor, nasty, brutish, and short. 99

195

myWorld Activity
Long Live the Revolution

consent, *n.*, agreement or approval

Other philosophers had political views that shaped modern democracy. John Locke wrote that people are born with the right to life, liberty, and property. Charles-Louis Montesquieu (MAHN tus kyoo) believed that the powers of government should be separated into branches. Jean-Jacques Rousseau (roo SOH) said that government depends on the people's <u>consent.</u> These ideas later shaped Americans' views of government.

Enlightened Rulers A few European rulers were influenced by Enlightenment ideas about government. Frederick II of Prussia improved education and outlawed torture. Joseph II of Austria ended serfdom, a system in which peasants were forced to work for a noble.

These reforms were limited. For example, Frederick II promoted religious tolerance but allowed discrimination against Jews. Frederick and other absolute monarchs kept firm control over their people. This would soon begin to change.

Reading Check How did Enlightenment thinkers shape democracy?

Democratic Revolutions

The political ideas of the Enlightenment helped shape modern government. They also led to a period of violent change.

Changes in England During the 1600s, the English Parliament gradually took power away from the monarchy. In 1628, Parliament forced King Charles I to sign the Petition of Right. This document ended illegal taxation and imprisonment.

Conflict between Parliament and the monarchy continued. A civil war began in 1642. In 1649, Parliamentary forces executed the king. England became a commonwealth, or a republic.

The English government went through many changes over the next 40 years. Charles I's sons regained the throne but had renewed conflicts with Parliament. Parliament then gave the throne to William and Mary in 1689, under the condition that they sign the English Bill of Rights. The **English Bill of Rights** was an act that limited the power of the monarch and listed the rights of Parliament and the English people. England's absolute monarchy had come to an end.

The Magna Carta Paves the Way

Magna Carta (1215)
The king and nobles must respect the law.

A Struggle for Democracy (1295–1641)
Representatives of the English people struggle with kings for power.

English Revolution and Restoration (1641–1688)
The monarchy is abolished and Parliament rules England as a republic. The monarchy is restored in 1660. Conflicts between the king and Parliament resume.

English Bill of Rights (1689)
King William and Queen Mary agree to the English Bill of Rights. The Bill of Rights ensures the superiority of Parliament over the monarchy.

American Declaration of Independence (1776)
The monarchy is abolished and replaced with a democratic government in the United States.

How does this flowchart show the changing relationship of government and the people?

196

Revolution in France In France, society was divided into three groups called estates: clergy (the First Estate), nobles (the Second Estate), and common people (the Third Estate). Most French people were in the Third Estate. They paid heavy taxes and had few rights.

Enlightenment ideas inspired some French people to demand a voice in government. However, King Louis XVI refused to give up any of his powers. On July 14, 1789, a mob stormed the Bastille, a Paris prison. This marked the start of the **French Revolution,** a political movement that removed the French king from power and formed a republic.

The Revolution took a brutal turn. During the Reign of Terror in 1793 and 1794, the republic's government killed thousands of its opponents.

Napoleon Takes Power Meanwhile, Napoleon Bonaparte rose quickly in the French army. In 1799, he took power in France as a dictator.

Napoleon wanted to create a mighty French empire. In the Napoleonic Wars, he conquered much of Europe. His invasion of Russia proved disastrous, however. The French army was weakened, and Napoleon was defeated in 1815.

Revolution Spreads French domination led to growing nationalism, or devotion to one's country. Many Europeans also wanted greater democracy. In 1848, revolutions broke out across Europe. By 1871, both Germany and Italy had become unified nations.

Reading Check What caused the French Revolution?

The Reign of Terror

The promise of the French Revolution quickly soured. What had been a revolution calling for brotherhood and liberty turned into a civil war. Respected leaders such as Robespierre became feared tyrants.

A French mob storms the Bastille. ▼

Robespierre, who sentenced hundreds to the guillotine, was executed himself in 1794. ▼

The French Republic's government used the falling blade of the guillotine (right) to silence opponents. ▶

Culture Close-up

my worldgeography.com Culture Close-up

197

Life in the Industrial Age

The Industrial Revolution has been chronicled in art, literature, and photography. It transformed life and society across Europe. Industrialization had both positive and negative aspects. Its innovations remain part of modern life.

- Widespread pollution from factories
- Long work hours, child labor common
- Overcrowded living conditions

The Industrial Revolution

Alongside these political revolutions, a different kind of revolution began. The **Industrial Revolution** was a shift from hand tools driven by animal or human power to large-scale machinery powered by fuels or natural forces. It led to a growth of cities and large organizations and to rapid changes in technology. The Industrial Revolution began in Britain but soon spread to the rest of Europe.

Technology Changes Industry Before the Industrial Revolution, most people were farmers. Others worked at home. There, they used hand tools to make cloth, leather goods, and other items.

In England in the mid-1700s, this process began to change. Fast, new machines in factories began to do much of the work once done by people in their homes. The textile industry was the first to change. Inventors developed machines for spinning thread and weaving cloth.

Transportation also changed. Coal and steampower made steamboats and locomotives possible. These ships and trains carried raw materials to factories. They brought finished goods to distant markets.

Industry Changes Landscapes
Entrepreneurs, or people who start businesses, built factories in areas that had a labor supply, resources such as coal, and good transportation. Towns without access to coal and iron or to transportation often did not industrialize.

Industrial towns grew quickly as workers moved there for jobs in factories. This rapid growth caused problems such as housing shortages. People had to live in crowded apartment buildings. Many people had no access to clean water.

Cities could not dispose adequately of waste, and coal-burning factories polluted the air. Diseases spread rapidly in these crowded, dirty conditions. Working conditions in factories were difficult. Factories and mines often hired young children to work dangerous jobs.

Trade Grows Workers in factories produced far more goods than individual workers ever had. Industrialized nations needed new places to sell these products. Many of the new markets were in European colonies in Africa and Asia. Colonies also provided raw materials for European manufacturers.

my World
IN NUMBERS

From 1770 to 1821, the British population grew from **8.3** million to **14.2** million.

198

- Better public education and social reforms
- Improvements in healthcare, public hygiene
- Advances in arts and sciences

Positive Effects The Industrial Age also brought improvements. During this period, doctors and scientists made advances in research and medicine. Louis Pasteur and Robert Koch discovered that germs caused disease. Researchers found ways to cure or prevent illness. Cities built sewer systems to dispose of waste and prevent disease. Inventors developed ways to use electric power.

Because production was more efficient, the cost of goods went down. With the number of jobs increasing and the price of products decreasing, people could afford to buy more goods. For example, people began to wear clothing made in factories instead of at home. Middle-class families purchased new labor-saving devices, such as sewing machines. As a result, the standard of living—or the level of comfort—rose for millions of people.

Another positive change was greater access to primary school education. Where once only some boys had attended school, now girls too could receive an education.

Reading Check How did life change during the Industrial Age?

Section 3 Assessment

Essential Question

What makes a nation?

Key Terms

1. Using full sentences, describe how each of the following terms relates to social and political change: Scientific Revolution, Enlightenment, English Bill of Rights, French Revolution, Industrial Revolution.

Key Ideas

2. How did the Industrial Revolution transform methods of manufacturing goods?

3. What did Isaac Newton contribute to the Scientific Revolution?

4. How did the Scientific Revolution influence Enlightenment thought?

5. How did the Enlightenment affect rulers' ideas?

Think Critically

6. **Categorize** Which of the events discussed in this section would you call political revolutions and which would you call cultural revolutions?

7. **Synthesize** How did the Enlightenment change governments in Europe?

8. How did the Napoleonic Wars encourage nationalistic feelings in Europe? Go to your Student Journal to record your answer.

Section 4

Wars and Hardship

Key Ideas
- World War I resulted in defeat for Europe's multinational empires and their division into new nations.
- The Great Depression brought hardship and political unrest to Europe.
- World War II brought catastrophe for Jews and other Europeans and led to the defeat of Germany and Italy by the Allied powers.

Key Terms • World War I • Great Depression • communism • fascism • World War II • Holocaust

(→) **Visual Glossary**

Reading Skill: Compare and Contrast Take notes using the graphic organizer in your journal.

Fighter pilots engage in a dramatic dogfight during World War I.

When the 1900s began, large multinational empires controlled central Europe. A series of alliances linked Europe's great powers into competing blocs.

The Great War: World War I

World War I (1914–1918), or the Great War, was the first modern global conflict. It involved most of Europe, the United States, Canada, and many parts of Africa and Asia.

Causes of War World War I had four main causes: nationalism, imperialism, militarism, and alliances.

- **Nationalism**—Nationalism, or devotion to one's nation or people, sometimes led to hostility toward other nations.
- **Imperialism**—European imperial powers competed to extend their empires by seizing territory to add to their colonies in Africa and Asia.
- **Militarism**—For decades, European countries had been building up military power and adopting warlike attitudes.
- **Alliances**—In a complex system of alliances, many European countries had agreed to defend one another from attack. These alliances pulled nations into the war.

200

War Breaks Out In June 1914, a Serbian nationalist killed the Austrian archduke. Austria-Hungary declared war on Serbia. One by one, the major European powers entered the war to support their allies. The fighting later spread overseas.

In Europe, armies fought on two fronts. On the Western Front, Germany battled the Allied Powers—France and Britain. Soldiers lived in a network of trenches dug into the earth. For years, they gained little ground. On the Eastern Front, Germany and Austria-Hungary fought Russia. But when the Russian Revolution began in 1917, Russia pulled out of the war.

In 1917, the United States entered the war on the side of the Allies. U.S. troops helped force the Germans out of France. Exhausted, Germany sought a truce, and the war ended on November 11, 1918.

Consequences of War The Allies forced Germany to sign the Treaty of Versailles. The treaty <u>humiliated</u> Germany. It made Germany give up territory and pay huge reparations, or sums for war damage.

Other treaties carved up Austria-Hungary into several new nations, ended the Ottoman Empire, and created new countries. For example, Yugoslavia was a federation of Slavic republics, including Serbia. Poland was shaped from parts of Germany, Austria-Hungary, and Russia. The maps below show these changes.

Reading Check What were the four main causes of World War I?

humiliate, *v.,* to embarrass or to reduce a person's feeling of self-worth

Map Skills

1 **Region** How did Europe change after World War I?

2 **Place** What areas of Europe changed the most? Why do you think this happened?

→ Active Atlas

Europe Before and After World War I

201

myWorld Activity
Runaway Prices

The Great Depression

Germany had lost land, people, and resources. At the same time, Germany owed billions of dollars in reparations. The government printed money to try to make these payments. As a result, German money lost value. The price of goods increased rapidly during a period of inflation. Many Germans lost their savings. This caused unrest and political instability in Germany.

A Global Financial Crisis Develops

During the 1920s, the American economy had grown dramatically. At same time, prices on the U.S. stock market rose.

Many Americans bought stocks, some with borrowed money, hoping to make a profit as the prices of stocks increased.

At first, stock prices soared. Then stocks leveled off and fell. Nervous lenders demanded repayment. Investors sold stocks to repay the loans. Heavy selling drove prices down quickly. In October 1929, the U.S. stock market collapsed.

Many investors lost fortunes selling their stocks for much less than they had paid. People and businesses who had borrowed money could not repay their debts. Soon, banks failed and businesses closed. As a result, millions of people were out of work. This was the beginning of the **Great Depression,** a deep, worldwide economic slump that lasted through the 1930s. It caused hardship around the world.

Europe Suffers Hard Times To protect its farmers, the United States put tariffs, or taxes, on imported farm products. These tariffs hurt European economies, so European countries imposed their own tariffs. Global trade slowed. The French and German governments lowered wages, hoping to help reduce the costs of goods. Instead, this only angered workers and increased hardship.

Banks around the world were linked by loans. As a result, U.S. banking problems spread to other nations. Some European banks failed. Most European countries had not yet recovered from World War I. These new financial troubles made hard times even harder.

Reading Check How did the Great Depression spread from the United States to Europe?

slump, *n.,*
a marked decline

A man uses German money as wallpaper. Inflation had made the money worthless. ▼

Unemployment in Europe, 1928–1938

Percentage Unemployed vs. Year (1928–1938)

Legend:
— Belgium
— Germany
— Norway
— Great Britain

SOURCE: *International Historical Statistics, Europe 1750–1993*

Chart Skills

In which years did each European nation on the graph experience the highest unemployment?

→ Data Discovery

A War of Ideas

After World War I, antidemocratic leaders took power in Italy, Germany, and other European countries. Those governments took control of daily life.

The Rise of Communism The 1917 Russian Revolution led to the formation of the communist government of the Soviet Union. **Communism** is an economic and political system in which the state, run by a Communist Party, takes over industry and farmland and controls most organizations.

Communism promised to share wealth among all workers. During the Great Depression, workers across Europe found this promise very appealing.

Fascism in Italy and Spain In Italy, nationalist pride led to fascism. **Fascism** is a political system that stresses national strength, military might, and the belief that the state is more important than individuals. Fascists use propaganda and violence to achieve goals and believe that a dictator—a leader with unlimited powers—should rule. In the 1920s, fascist Benito Mussolini took power in Italy. He promised to build a strong Italian empire. During the 1930s, fascists under Francisco Franco took control of Spain.

Nazis Take Power in Germany Many Germans resented the Treaty of Versailles and blamed it for their hardships. Some blamed Germany's democratic government for obeying the treaty.

Adolf Hitler had served in the German army during World War I. Like many other Germans, he felt that Germany had been treated unfairly after the war.

Hitler came to lead a small, fascist German political party, the Nazi Party. Hitler's ideas included extreme nationalism, racism, and anti-Semitism, or prejudice against Jews. Hitler unfairly blamed Jews for Germany's economic problems.

In 1923, the Nazis tried and failed to overthrow the government. Hitler was jailed, but worked after his release to rebuild the Nazi Party. Amid the Great Depression, the Nazis gained strength in the early 1930s. In 1932, the Nazis won more votes than any other party, but less than a majority of votes. Nonetheless, in 1933, Hitler became head of Germany's government.

Understanding Political Systems

	Democracy	Communism	Fascism
Individuals and the State	Individuals' rights are more important than government interests.	Government interests are more important than individuals' rights.	Government interests are more important than individuals' rights.
Values	Freedom, individuals' rights, justice	Obedience, discipline, economic security	Obedience, discipline, national pride, military power
Government	The people and their elected representatives make decisions; control of people's lives is minimal.	Communist party makes all decisions; extreme control of all aspects of life.	Fascist party controls all aspects of life; government is permanent and necessary for national progress.

Chart Skills

Compare the values associated with fascism to those of democracy and communism.

Data Discovery

▲ Flag of Italy under fascism

203

▲ The Nazis forced Jewish people to wear yellow stars for identification.

Once in power, Hitler ruled as a dictator. He controlled every aspect of German life, using secret police to spy on people. Hitler imprisoned or killed his opponents. Because Germany's economy improved under the Nazis, many Germans accepted Nazi rule.

The Nazi government passed a number of laws against Jews, eliminating their rights as citizens. In 1938, Nazis led anti-Jewish riots in Germany and Austria. For 48 hours, Nazis systematically destroyed Jewish synagogues and Jewish businesses. Nazi hatred toward Jews later led to the Nazi "Final Solution," or the attempted killing off of all Jews.

Reading Check Why were the German people attracted to the Nazi Party?

World War II

Under Adolf Hitler, Germany built a powerful army and formed an alliance with Italy and Japan. These countries were called the Axis Powers. Britain and France formed the Allied Powers, later joined by the United States and Soviet Union.

War Begins Hitler wanted to build a mighty German empire across Europe. In 1938, German troops occupied Austria and seized part of Czechoslovakia. Germany and the Soviet Union then secretly agreed to divide Poland between them. On September 1, 1939, Germany invaded Poland. Two days later, Britain and France declared war on Germany. **World War II,** the second major global conflict of the 1900s, had begun.

War in Europe By the end of 1940, Germany's powerful armies had conquered much of Europe. Italy attacked North Africa. At first, Britain fought on alone, with the help of some military aid from the United States.

The German air force repeatedly bombed British military targets and civilian areas, but the British did not give up.

Wartime Opponents, 1942

KEY
Allied territory, 1942
Axis territory, 1942
Neutral territory, 1942
— Borders as of 1938
0   400 mi
0   400 km
Lambert Conformal Conic Projection

North Sea
Baltic Sea
ATLANTIC OCEAN
Black Sea
Mediterranean Sea

Map Skills

Place Who controlled more of Europe in 1942, the Allies or the Axis Powers?

→ Active Atlas

204

British Prime Minister Winston Churchill inspired the people with stirring speeches:

66 We have before us many, many long months of struggle and of suffering. You ask, what is our policy? I will say: It is to wage war, by sea, land and air, with all our might and with all the strength that God can give us. 99

In June 1941, Germany broke its earlier agreement and invaded the Soviet Union. The Soviet Union joined the Allied Powers. Soviet resistance, brutal winter weather, and a lack of supplies finally forced Germany to retreat in 1943.

America Enters the War In late 1941, Japan bombed Pearl Harbor, a U.S. naval base in Hawaii. This pushed the United States into the war. American forces helped the Allies defeat Italy.

With U.S. help, the Allies pushed back into western Europe. On June 6, 1944, D-Day, more than 150,000 Allied troops invaded German-occupied France. The Allies slowly forced German troops back across France into Germany. At the same time, Soviet troops invaded Germany from the east. Germany surrendered on May 7, 1945. World War II ended later that year with Japan's surrender to the United States.

Effects of the War Approximately 17 million European soldiers died in World War II. Millions of civilians died as well. Many civilian deaths occurred in the **Holocaust,** the mass murder of Jews by the Nazis during World War II. The Nazis murdered 6 million Jews and another 5 million people from other groups.

After the war, Europe's cities, roads, and farms lay in ruins. Much of the continent needed to be rebuilt.

Reading Check How were the Allied forces able to win World War II?

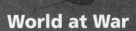

World at War

- 1914 World War I begins.
- 1918 World War I ends.
- 1919 The Treaty of Versailles
- 1939 Germany invades Poland; France and Britain declare war on Germany. World War II begins.
- 1941 The United States enters the war.
- 1945 Germany and Japan surrender. World War II ends.

[Timeline]

my worldgeography.com Timeline

Section 4 Assessment

? Essential Question
What makes a nation?

Key Terms
1. Define each of the following terms using a complete sentence: World War I, Great Depression, communism, fascism, World War II, Holocaust.

Key Ideas
2. Whom did the Nazis kill during the Holocaust?
3. How did competition among nations contribute to World War I?
4. How did the Great Depression affect Europe?
5. Which nations defeated the Axis Powers in World War II?

Think Critically
6. **Problem Solving** How did Germany's situation after World War I help cause the next world war?
7. **Compare Viewpoints** How might French citizens have felt about the Treaty of Versailles? Compare their viewpoint to that of German citizens.

8. Why did so many nations gain independence after World War I? Go to your Student Journal to record your answer.

The World Wars in Art

Key Idea
- Historical accounts of wars give us important information about conflicts and those involved in them.

▲ A poppy worn in remembrance of war veterans

Eyewitness accounts make the experience of battle frighteningly real. Ancient historians like Herodotus recorded the heroism of the Greeks against the Persians. In 1812, Philippe Paul de Ségur remembered Napoleon's "skeletons of soldiers" as the French army returned in defeat from Russia. But few accounts of war have been as powerful as those left by the poets, novelists, and artists who experienced World War I and World War II. Not only did they write about fighting the enemy on the battlefield, but these artists also recorded the horrors of the Holocaust.

Stop at each letter on the right to think about the text. Then answer the question with the same letter on the left.

A **Identify Evidence** What do the crosses indicate?

B **Synthesize** Who is the narrator and how did he come to be in Flanders?

C **Draw Inferences** Why does the poet use the image of a relay race here?

scarce, *adv.*, hardly or barely
quarrel, *n.*, disagreement, dispute
foe, *n.*, enemy

In Flanders Fields

66 In Flanders fields the poppies blow
A Between the crosses row on row,
That mark our place; and in the sky
The larks, still bravely singing, fly
<u>Scarce</u> heard amid the guns below.

B We are the Dead. Short days ago
We lived, felt dawn, saw sunset glow,
Loved and were loved, and now we lie
In Flanders fields.

Take up our <u>quarrel</u> with the <u>foe</u>:
C To you from failing hands we throw
The torch; be yours to hold it high.
If ye break faith with us who die
We shall not sleep, though poppies grow
In Flanders fields. 99
—Lieutenant Colonel John McCrae, M.D.,
after the Battle of Ypres, Belgium, 1915

British soldiers walk across the battlefield near Ypres during World War I.

206

Stop at each letter on the right to think about the text. Then answer the question with the same letter on the left.

D **Synthesize** How many times does the word "and" appear in the first sentence? How does this affect the way you read it?

E **Summarize** Why does mixing up the shoes seem so "crazy" to the narrator?

F **Draw Conclusions** Why does the German watch "with interest" how the men react to the cold?

heap, *n.,* pile

writhe, *v.,* to twist and turn

Heaps of Shoes

66 **Now another German comes and tells us to put the shoes in a certain corner,**
D **and we put them there, because now it is all over and we feel outside this world and the only thing is to obey.**

Someone comes with a broom and sweeps away all the shoes, outside
E **the door in a <u>heap</u>. He is crazy, he is mixing them all together, ninety-six pairs, they will be all unmatched.**

The outside door opens, a freezing wind enters and we are naked and cover ourselves up with our arms. The wind blows and slams the door; the German reopens it and stands
F **watching with interest how we <u>writhe</u> to hide from the wind, one behind the other.**

Then he leaves and closes it. 99
—Primo Levi, *Survival in Auschwitz,* 1958

Piles of shoes taken from prisoners sent to the concentration camp at Auschwitz ▼

Analyze the Documents

1. **Compare and Contrast** Both the poem and the text above show courage and bravery. Compare and contrast how each source does this.
2. **Writing Task** Write a short poem in reaction to either "In Flanders Fields" or to the excerpt from *Survival in Auschwitz.*

Rebuilding and New Challenges

Key Ideas
- After World War II, the Cold War divided Europe between the democratic West and the communist East.
- Western European nations joined together in the late 1900s to promote free trade and peaceful interaction.
- When communism collapsed in the Soviet Union, Eastern Europe adopted democracy and Germany reunified.

Key Terms • Cold War • Marshall Plan • Berlin Wall • European Union (EU)

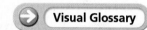 Visual Glossary

Reading Skill: Identify Main Ideas and Details Take notes using the graphic organizer in your journal.

When World War II ended, Soviet troops occupied most of Eastern Europe. The Soviet Union set up communist governments there. U.S. troops backed democratic governments in Western Europe.

Cold War and Division

The United States and Britain wanted to stop the Soviet Union from spreading communism. The result was the **Cold War,** a long period of hostility between the Soviet Union and the democratic West.

To encourage democracy and oppose communism, the United States created the **Marshall Plan,** a U.S. recovery plan that offered money to help European countries recover from the war. This money helped Western Europe rebuild.

A woman walks down a bombed-out street in Warsaw, Poland, in 1946. ▼

208

International Cooperation After World War II, many nations joined together to form the United Nations (UN). The UN's main task was to safeguard world peace. The UN later went on to help people cope with disasters and poverty.

The Berlin Wall Goes Up The Cold War divided Europe between Soviet-controlled, communist Eastern Europe and democratic Western Europe, mostly allied with the United States. This split ran roughly along the line where the troops of the Western Allies met the Soviet troops at the end of World War II.

This dividing line ran right through the center of Germany. The Soviets occupied East Germany, which became communist. West Germany, occupied by the Western Allies, became a democracy.

The Soviets and Western Allies also divided Germany's capital, Berlin, located within East Germany. In 1948, the Soviets blocked land and sea access to West Berlin. The United States and Britain flew supplies into Berlin for 11 months until the Soviets lifted the blockade.

About 2.5 million East Germans fled to the West by crossing into West Berlin. In 1961, East Germany built a wall around West Berlin to prevent escapes. The **Berlin Wall** symbolized Cold War divisions.

The Democratic West Unites Helped by American aid, Western Europe's economy recovered quickly. By 1951, factories were producing more than ever. Nations such as Italy adopted democracy. Meanwhile, European nations were forced to give up their colonies. For example, Britain made India and other colonies independent.

▲ This 1962 nuclear explosion at a U.S. testing site was part of a Cold War arms race with the Soviet Union.

In 1949, the United States and Western European countries formed a military alliance called the North Atlantic Treaty Organization (NATO). The United States was NATO's strongest member. After the war, the United States and the Soviet Union became the world's dominant nations, or superpowers.

Communists Control the East The Soviet Union viewed Eastern European countries as satellites, or dependent countries. In response to NATO, the Soviet Union and its satellites formed a military alliance called the Warsaw Pact in 1955. Eastern Europe had weak, state-controlled economies.

The Soviets often used force to control Eastern Europe. In 1956, Soviet forces invaded Hungary and blocked democratic change. In 1968, Soviet troops crushed a reform movement in Czechoslovakia.

Reading Check How did the Soviet Union gain and keep control of Eastern Europe?

symbolize, *v.,* to represent or express something

209

Closer Look

In 1946, Winston Churchill, former British prime minister, said "[A]n iron curtain has descended across the Continent." During the Cold War, the Iron Curtain was a fortified set of defenses between the democratic west and the communist east. East of the Iron Curtain, West Berlin was surrounded by the Berlin Wall, a concrete barrier that prevented East Germans from moving to democratic West Berlin.

THINK CRITICALLY **How might Germans have felt about the Iron Curtain?**

Map Skills

1. **Location** What nation was divided by the Iron Curtain?

2. **Places to Know!** Label these places on the outline map in your Student Journal: Romania, Belgium, Greece, Portugal, Italy.

Divided Europe

KEY
- NATO, 1957
- Warsaw Pact, 1957
- Iron Curtain

0 — 400 mi
0 — 400 km
Lambert Conformal Conic projection

ICELAND
NORWAY
SWEDEN
FINLAND
SOVIET UNION
UNITED KINGDOM
IRELAND
DENMARK
NETHERLANDS
BELGIUM
POLAND
EAST GERMANY
WEST GERMANY
LUXEMBOURG
CZECHOSLOVAKIA
FRANCE
AUSTRIA
HUNGARY
SWITZERLAND
ROMANIA
ITALY
YUGOSLAVIA
BULGARIA
ALBANIA
GREECE
TURKEY
PORTUGAL
SPAIN

North Sea
Baltic Sea
Black Sea
ATLANTIC OCEAN
Mediterranean Sea

Below, Greek children receive food supplied by the Marshall Plan. At right, construction of the Berlin Wall begins in 1961.

210

The European Union

Long-standing hostility between Germany and France played a role in fueling Europe's wars. After World War II, West German and French leaders searched for a way to exist in peace.

Forming a Community In 1951, France and West Germany agreed to coordinate their coal and steel production. This would tie the countries economically and help to prevent future wars. Italy, Belgium, Luxembourg, and the Netherlands also signed the agreement.

In 1957, those six countries formed the European Economic Community, or Common Market. This was a free trade zone. It let manufactured goods and services move freely among the countries. Trade increased dramatically.

Toward a Unified Europe Six more countries had joined the Common Market by 1986. The Common Market nations signed the Maastricht Treaty in 1992. This treaty created the **European Union (EU),** an economic and political partnership. Starting in 1995, an open-borders policy allowed people to move freely among many EU nations.

In 2002, most EU nations adopted a single currency called the euro. A currency is a unit of money, like the dollar. Sharing a common currency made trade easier. However, some countries rejected the euro so that they could keep control of their money. In 2003, a treaty let Eastern European countries join the EU. By 2008, the EU had grown to include 27 nations.

Reading Check Why did West Germany and France form a common market?

Democracy Spreads East

By the 1980s, communism was failing. Weak Soviet and Eastern European economies could not compete with Western market economies.

Communism Fails In Eastern Europe, government officials planned what farms should grow and what factories should produce. Officials made decisions based on the state's wishes rather than people's needs. For example, they made tanks instead of home appliances. Second, people had no motive to work hard because the government limited their pay. As a result of these two problems, communist countries often had shortages of food and consumer goods.

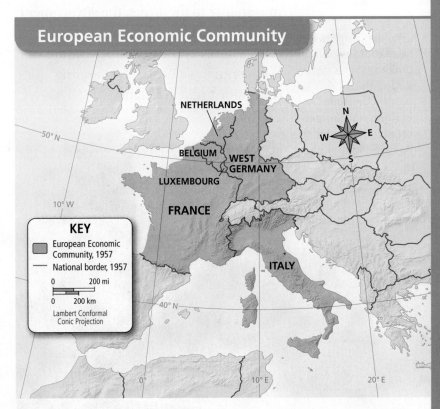

European Economic Community

KEY

European Economic Community, 1957

National border, 1957

0 — 200 mi
0 — 200 km

Lambert Conformal Conic Projection

211

In 1985, Mikhail Gorbachev became the new leader of the Soviet Union. Gorbachev was younger than other leaders and more open to change. In the late 1980s, Gorbachev began to loosen government control within the Soviet Union. He supported greater democracy, particularly in the Soviet satellites of Eastern Europe. Gorbachev also gave Eastern European countries more freedom to choose their own way.

A Democratic Revolution Spreads In 1980, a Polish shipyard workers' union called Solidarity went on strike. The Polish government granted some union demands and the union head, Lech Walesa (lek vah WEN suh), became a hero. Solidarity went on strike again in 1988. In response to the strike, the government agreed to hold free elections. Voters courageously chose Solidarity candidates over communist candidates, ending communist rule in Poland.

Poland's example inspired other countries. In Czechoslovakia, thousands of people protested the communist government in 1989. In response to the protests, the government agreed to give up power. This peaceful <u>transfer</u> of power is known as the Velvet Revolution. In free elections later that year, Czechoslovakians elected writer Vaclav Havel (VAHTS lahv HAH vul) president. Havel described his people's experience.

66 People have passed through a very dark tunnel at the end of which there was a light of freedom. 99
—Vaclav Havel, 1990

Romania overthrew its communist government in 1989, but its communist dictator killed many protesters before giving up power. Hungary's Communist Party went out of existence, and in 1990 the country elected a non-communist government. Bulgaria also held its first free elections in 1990.

Germany Reunifies During 1989, East Germans began protesting for democratic change. East Germany's communist government at first refused to make changes. The government then began to respond to some protester demands.

Finally, on November 9, 1989, East German border guards opened the gates of the Berlin Wall. East and West Germans rushed to greet each other.

Demands for reform led to free elections, which removed the communist government from power in 1989. A year later, on October 3, 1990, the two halves of Germany were reunified.

transfer, *n.,* a carrying over of something from one situation to another

myWorld Activity
Tear Down This Wall

Left, people pass the head of a Soviet ruler broken from a statue during the 1956 uprising in Hungary; at right, a volunteer collects money for the Polish Solidarity party.

212

The Soviet Union Falls Nationalism and the desire for reform rocked the Soviet Union. In 1990, the Soviet republic of Lithuania demanded independence. The Soviet army invaded Lithuania.

Soviet citizens took to the streets to protest the invasion. The army refused to fight the people. In 1991, the Soviet Union broke apart into 15 new nations, including Moldova, Ukraine, Belarus, Lithuania, Latvia, and Estonia in Eastern Europe. The largest post-Soviet nation was Russia.

Reading Check How did Eastern Europe gain freedom from communism?

▲ In this 1990 political cartoon, Soviet leader Mikhail Gorbachev is pictured as Humpty Dumpty sitting on a crumbling wall with the symbol of the Soviet Union. *What does this cartoon mean?*

THE WALL COMES DOWN

During the late 1980s, communist governments across Eastern Europe followed the lead of the Soviet Union. They began to allow their opponents to speak more freely. Some scheduled free elections. East Germany's government resisted these changes. In the fall of 1989, however, East German people began to hold peaceful protests. The protesters said they wanted democracy. East German leaders knew that the Soviet Union was no longer willing to put down peaceful protests. When border guards opened the Berlin Wall on November 9, 1989, Germans on both sides began to knock it down.

❝ **We are the people!** ❞
—Chant of East German democracy protesters, 1989

247

▲ In 2004, terrorists bombed this train in Spain. In the inset, a London man reads about the 2005 terrorist bombings in that city.

Europe Faces Challenges

After reunifying, Germany struggled economically. East German factories were outdated and inefficent, and many went out of business. Unemployment soared in eastern Germany. Some citizens failed to adapt to the market economy, which required initiative and hard work.

Integrating the East After the collapse of communism, Europe worked to rebuild ties between East and West. The EU opened membership to Eastern European nations who could show that they had democratic governments and strong market economies. Most eastern nations had to make reforms before joining the EU. Even so, their economies often remained weak due to problems similar to those in eastern Germany.

Communist rule had not prepared people for democracy either. Many people in formerly communist lands did not trust their leaders. Government corruption had been widespread under communist rule and remained a problem.

International Issues In the late 1900s, a global economy developed as foreign trade and multinational corporations grew. The EU began to consider issues such as free trade with nonmember nations.

Incidents of international terrorism also scarred Europe. In 2004, the terrorist group al-Qaeda exploded bombs on commuter trains in Madrid, Spain, killing nearly 200. Afterward, European countries worked together to fight terrorism.

Immigration was another challenge. When Eastern European countries joined the EU, thousands of Eastern Europeans moved to western European countries for work. Many Western Europeans resented the newcomers. In addition, immigrants from Africa and Asia, some of them illegal, poured into Europe. Some Europeans began to fear that immigrants would take their jobs. Europeans and their leaders had to find ways to accommodate growing populations with customs and languages from outside of Europe.

214

Wind farms such as this one off the coast of Denmark make Europe a world leader in alternative energy sources.

Energy and the Environment Because of its industry, Europe has long fought pollution. For example, it has tried to reduce the air pollution that causes acid rain, which kills forests. The EU also signed the Kyoto Protocol, an agreement to reduce the emission of greenhouse gases that contribute to climate change.

Europe also aims to reduce its dependence on foreign oil. The EU is trying to reduce energy consumption, switch to cleaner forms of transportation, and use renewable energy such as wind and bio-fuels.

Reading Check What economic challenges did Eastern Europe face after the collapse of communism?

Section 5 Assessment

Essential Question

Key Terms

1. Using complete sentences, describe how each of the following terms relates to consequences from World War II: Cold War, Marshall Plan, Berlin Wall, European Union.

Key Ideas

2. What kind of partnership is the European Union?

3. Why did the Soviet Union set up communist states in Eastern Europe?

4. Which two countries began the movement to create a European Union and why?

5. How did change in the Soviet Union clear the way for democracy in Eastern Europe?

Think Critically

6. **Draw Conclusions** Why did Western Europe develop stronger economies than Eastern Europe?

7. **Make Decisions** What decisions do you think the German government could make to improve the economy of the former East Germany?

What makes a nation?

8. Why do you think East and West Germans still felt that they belonged to a single nation even after more than 40 years apart? Go to your Student Journal to record your answer.

215

Democracy in Eastern Europe

Key Idea
- The people of Eastern Europe made great sacrifices to win independence and achieve freedom and democracy.

Democracy developed more slowly in Eastern Europe than in Western Europe. Large empires such as Russia and Austria controlled much of the region for centuries. The rulers of these empires did not allow the region's different peoples to form their own independent countries. In Hungary, the nationalist Lajos Kossuth (LAH yohsh KAW shoot) fought unsuccessfully to free his country from Austrian control during the revolutions of 1848. Vaclav Havel became president after Czechoslovakia threw off communist rule in 1989.

▲ Hungarian composer Béla Bartók fled the Nazi regime in 1940 to live in the United States.

Stop at each letter on the right to think about the text. Then answer the question with the same letter on the left.

A **Draw Conclusions** What was the Hungarian cause that Kossuth mentioned here?

B **Compare Viewpoints** How did some other people view Hungary's cause? Explain how that compared to Kossuth's view.

C **Identify Main Ideas and Details** What did Kossuth compare a salad to? Explain how the detail "leaf by leaf" relates to this idea.

consideration, *n.,* careful thought

despotism, *n.,* government by a ruler with absolute power

The Cause Of One Country

Hungarian revolutionary Lajos Kossuth ▼

❝ I first heard my humble claims contradicted, by telling me that the **A** cause of Hungary was not worthy of much <u>consideration</u>—because, **B** after all, it is only the cause of one country. . . . Let me tell those who don't care about the violation of the law of nations in Hungary . . . let me tell them that the freedom and independence of the world is **C** like the salad—not even the jaws of <u>despotism</u> can swallow at once—but only leaf by leaf. ❞

—Lajos Kossuth, "Speech at the Pittsburgh Banquet," 1852

Stop at each letter on the right to think about the text. Then answer the question with the same letter on the left.

D Categorize What were some of the sacrifices people made to gain freedom?

E Analyze Cause and Effect Why did the government persecute some people?

F Solve Problems What do you think Czechs and Slovaks today can do to make sure past sacrifices are not forgotten?

perish, *v.,* to die, especially a violent or early death

totalitarian, *adj.,* describing a government in which a dictator or one political party has complete control of the country

persecute, *v.,* to harass or subject to unfair treatment because of race, religion, ethnic origin, or political beliefs

The Price Of Freedom

66 We had to pay, however, for our present freedom. Many citizens **D perished** in jails in the 1950s, many were executed, thousands of human lives were destroyed, hundreds of thousands of talented people were forced to leave the country. Those who defended the honor of our nations during the Second **E** World War, those who rebelled against **totalitarian** rule and those who simply managed to remain themselves and think freely, were **F** all **persecuted**. We should not forget any of those who paid for our present freedom in one way or another. 99

—Vaclav Havel,
"New Year's Address to the Nation,"
January 1, 1990

Above, Czechoslovak president Vaclav Havel; below, demonstrators carry Czechoslovak flags in Prague during the Velvet Revolution in 1989.

Analyze the Documents

1. **Synthesize** According to Kossuth and Havel, what forces made it difficult to establish democracy in Eastern Europe?

2. **Writing Task** Write an opening paragraph on the topic *Eastern Europe's Fight for Democracy.* Include details from the two speeches in your paragraph. If you use a direct quote, be sure to format it correctly.

217

Chapter Assessment

Key Terms and Ideas

1. **Discuss** How did **humanism** help lead to the Reformation?

2. **Summarize** In what ways did art change during the **Renaissance**?

3. **Compare and Contrast** What different routes did Portugal and Spain take when trying to find a way to reach Asia during the Age of Exploration?

4. **Recall** What Renaissance attitudes helped bring about the Scientific Revolution?

5. **Explain** How did the **Industrial Revolution** change where people lived?

6. **Compare and Contrast** What did the English Civil War and the **French Revolution** have in common?

7. **Explain** How did **World War I** change the map of central and eastern Europe?

8. **Describe** What emotions did East Germans and West Germans experience when the **Berlin Wall** was opened? How do you know?

Think Critically

9. **Draw Conclusions** How did geography contribute to Italy's role in beginning the Renaissance?

10. **Distinguish Between Fact and Opinion** Thomas Hobbes described life without strong government as "poor, nasty, brutish, and short." Is that a fact or an opinion? Explain.

11. **Identify Evidence** Use evidence from the text to describe how World War I was a global war.

12. **Drawing Inferences** How was the Cold War like a war even though the United States and the Soviet Union never engaged in battle?

13. **Problem Solving** Turn again to the last red heading in Section 5. Which of the problems described in the blue headings should be Europe's first priority? Support your answer with examples from the text.

Places to Know

For each place, write the letter from the map that shows its location.

14. Berlin

15. London

16. Rome

17. Romania

18. Belgium

19. Constantinople

20. Portugal

21. **Estimate** Using the scale bar, estimate how far fighter pilots flew between Berlin and London during World War II.

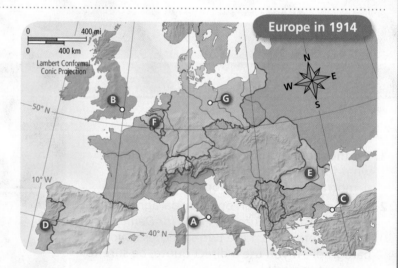

218

Essential Question

myWorld Chapter Activity

Technology Then and Now Follow your teacher's instructions to examine different kinds of technology that developed in early modern Europe. This technology may be related to advances in science or medicine, warfare, industry, or transportation. At the time, these inventions were cutting-edge technology. Make an illustrated poster linking these examples of past technology to current examples of technology.

21st Century Learning

Communication

Summarize Write an essay arguing for or against adding new Eastern European members to the European Union. Include
- the benefits of adding these members
- the drawbacks of adding these members
- the economic and political impact of adding these members
- your opinion
- two reasons in support of your opinion

Document-Based Questions

Success Tracker™
Online at myworldgeography.com

Use your knowledge of early modern Europe and Documents A and B to answer Questions 1–3.

Document A

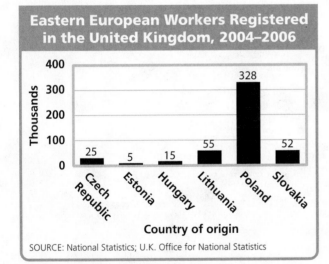

Eastern European Workers Registered in the United Kingdom, 2004–2006

SOURCE: National Statistics; U.K. Office for National Statistics

1. Which country shown here had the most workers registered in the United Kingdom?

   A Estonia

   B Latvia

   C Poland

   D Slovakia

Document B

" It's my dream to return to Poland, but not for 30 percent of my salary. So many have gone west [that] to return, they might not have to receive equal pay, but certainly more than now."

—Jacek Cukrowski,
"Where have all our migrants gone? Eastern Europe wants them back,"
Christian Science Monitor

2. What would convince Cukrowski to return to Poland?

   A more salary than he earns in the West

   B a better salary than Polish workers earn now

   C exactly the same salary that Polish workers earn

   D 30 percent of the salary that he earns in the West

3. **Writing Task** If Eastern Europeans keep moving to Western Europe for jobs, how might Eastern Europe's economy be affected? Explain.

219

Chapter 3

Western Europe

Essential Question

Is it better to be independent or interdependent?

KEY
- National border
- ★ Capital city
- ○ Other city

0 — 400 mi
0 — 400 km
Lambert Conformal Conic Projection

Where in the World Is Western Europe?

Washington, D.C., to Lund: 4,060 miles

220

my Story

Europe at Her Doorstep

Explore the Essential Question
- at **my worldgeography.com**
- using the **myWorld Chapter Activity**
- with the **Student Journal**

In this section, you'll read about Yasmin, a young woman living in Sweden who has family in Spain and Pakistan. What does Yasmin's story tell you about life in Western Europe today?

By Jake Johnson for myWorld Online

Yasmin straps on her dancing shoes. She glances in the mirror, adjusts her dress, and taps her way into the dance studio. With a rose in her hair and a colorful shawl stretched between her hands, Yasmin practices flamenco, a traditional Spanish dance. Inside the studio, the music makes Yasmin think of the warm Mediterranean while Sweden's winter winds blow outside.

Yasmin was born in Madrid, Spain, but she lives with her family in the coastal town of Bjärred in southern Sweden. Her father, Asif, is Pakistani and Spanish. Her mother, Monica, is Finnish and Swedish. Yasmin uses both of her parents' last names as a part of her heritage.

Yasmin's father Asif left Spain to work in Sweden in 1995. At that time, Sweden had just become a member of the European Union (EU). EU member countries allow people to move across borders without passports or complicated documents. Asif decided to try life in Sweden where more jobs were available. So, at age six Yasmin, along with her sister Sabina and brother Daniel, moved to frosty Sweden—a completely different world from Spain.

Yasmin remembers that she wasn't ready for the change in cultures. "At first, I was very different from the Swedish girls.

my worldgeography.com On Assignment

221

Yasmin stands in front of Lund's medieval cathedral.

Yasmin with her father and mother

In general, Swedes are much more quiet than Spaniards. I spoke very loud . . . I was a Spanish girl, and I yelled and ran around everywhere. I was more like the Swedish boys."

At home, Yasmin speaks Spanish with her father and Swedish with her mother. Everyone also speaks English. "The language that we speak is similar to the foods we eat. It is very mixed up," laughs Yasmin. She adds, "Sometimes we mix up our languages, even though our parents say we shouldn't. It's just easier to find the word you are looking for in another language. We even mix up languages within one sentence—but we all understand each other."

Even the family meal is a cultural medley. "We make it up as we go," explains Asif as he dices potatoes. He is making a Pakistani dish called alu gosht, a sort of a beef stew. Yasmin explains that this alu gosht includes Spanish olive oil, Swedish potatoes, and Chinese rice. The olive oil comes from the family's own olive trees in Spain!

Yasmin enjoys cooking and shopping at the farmers' market.

222

Yasmin attends classes in linguistics at Lund University.

The strait of Öresund separates Sweden from Denmark.

One of Yasmin's favorite possessions is her video camera. She has made several videos, including many that documented her trip to meet family in Pakistan. Music is also important to Yasmin, and she can play the piano, the flute, and the guitar.

Most days, Yasmin rides the bus to Lund to attend university classes. Lund is a medieval city full of gothic architecture and winding streets. Higher education is free in Sweden, so students from all over the world come to Lund University. Yasmin has many interests such as film and architecture, but she hasn't decided on a major.

One of Yasmin's new hobbies is tae kwon do, a form of martial arts that developed in Korea. At a dojo (a martial arts training school) near the university, she puts on a white uniform and her blue belt. Barefoot, Yasmin and a partner practice a complex routine designed for self-defense.

"Tae kwon do has a philosophy of peace," Yasmin says, "that teaches me to have the right mindset in order to be able to do the sport correctly."

Back in Bjärred, Yasmin walks along the beach. It's cold and windy, but beautiful. Bjärred is famous for its 500-meter pier into the strait of Öresund. It is the longest pier in the country. At the end of the pier is the Bjärred Kallbadhus (bath house). In the winter, people dive from the sauna there into the icy waters of the Öresund. Walking over the snow-covered dunes, Yasmin thinks about how much she cherishes the blazing sun of Spain. At the same time, she looks forward to ice-skating near her home in Sweden. Whether she's ice-skating, studying, or making a video, Yasmin has many choices, since Europe is at her doorstep.

Meet the Journalist

Name Jake Johnson
Favorite Moment Dinner with Yasmin's family

myStory Video

Join Yasmin as she shows you about life in her city.

my worldgeography.com myStory Video

223

Chapter Atlas

Key Ideas
- The landmass of Eurasia includes the continents of Europe and Asia.
- The climate of Western Europe is primarily temperate, although some areas are near the Arctic Circle.
- Western Europeans are mostly urban dwellers.

Key Terms • peninsula • plain • glacier • loess • tundra • taiga • pollution

→ **Visual Glossary**

Reading Skill: Label an Outline Map Take notes using the outline map in your journal.

A hillside village on the Greek island of Santorini; below, young women from Mykonos, Greece

Physical Features

The **peninsula** of Europe is attached to Asia, a continent that lies east of the Ural Mountains. A peninsula is land almost surrounded by water but still attached to the mainland. Geographers call this huge landmass composed of Europe and Asia *Eurasia*.

The three main landforms that cover Western Europe are **plains** (flat or gently rolling lands), uplands, and mountains. Most people live on plains. The North European Plain stretches from the Atlantic Ocean to the Urals, making it one of the largest level land areas on earth.

224

Western Europe: Physical

ARCTIC OCEAN
ARCTIC CIRCLE
Iceland
Norwegian Sea
Scandinavian Peninsula
ATLANTIC OCEAN
60° N
Baltic Sea
North Sea
Great Britain
Ireland
North European Plain
50° N
Central Uplands
Alps
Pyrenees
Italian Peninsula
Adriatic Sea
Balkan Peninsula
40° N
Iberian Peninsula
Sardinia
Mediterranean Sea
Sicily
Aegean Sea
10° W   0°   10° E   20° E   30° E

KEY
Elevation

Feet	Meters
6,000	1,829
3,000	914
1,000	305
500	152
Sea level	Sea level

— National border

0 — 400 mi
0 — 400 km
Lambert Conformal Conic Projection

Map Skills

1 **Region** Which part of Western Europe has the highest elevation?

2 **Interaction** Why might fishing be such a large industry in Scandinavia?

3 **Places to Know!** Label the following places on the outline map in your Student Journal: Iberian Peninsula, Ireland, Alps, Mediterranean Sea, North Sea.

→ **Active Atlas**

Most of northern Europe lies on the Scandinavian Peninsula, between the Arctic Ocean, the North Sea, and the Baltic Sea. The west coast of Norway features dramatic fiords, or long, narrow, deep inlets of the sea.

The Central Uplands in the center of southern Europe consist of mountains and plateaus, or raised areas of level land bordered by steep slopes.

The Alps stretch from France to Eastern Europe. Streams formed by **glaciers,** slow-moving masses of ice and snow, flow out of the Alps. These streams feed the Rhine River and the Danube River.

To the south is the warmer Mediterranean region. This region is named for the Mediterranean Sea nearby. Days are sunny and the climate is generally temperate. Here the land is mountainous peninsulas with narrow, <u>fertile</u> plains.

Active volcanoes may be found in Italy, Greece, and Iceland. At times, volcanic activity has led to earthquakes and tsunamis (tidal waves). Since ancient times, earthquakes have been widespread in the Mediterranean countries.

Reading Check What landform divides Europe from Asia?

fertile, *adj.,* rich in nutrients; able to grow many plants

225

Climate and Ecosystems

Most Western Europeans enjoy a mild climate because the Atlantic Ocean carries warm ocean water from the tropics to Europe's western coast. This water warms the air, bringing mild winters to places as far north as Scandinavia.

Most of Western Europe is located in the temperate zone, although its northern edges reach to the Arctic region. Land close to the Mediterranean Sea has wet winters and dry summers.

In ancient times, forests covered most of Western Europe. Today, people have replanted some forests, but most of the land has been cleared for cities, farms, and industry. One of north central Europe's natural resources is **loess,** a rich soil made of fine sediment deposited by glaciers and spread by centuries of wind.

Northern Scandinavia has few forests because of its Arctic climate. The Arctic **tundra** is a plant community made up of grasses, mosses, herbs, and low shrubs.

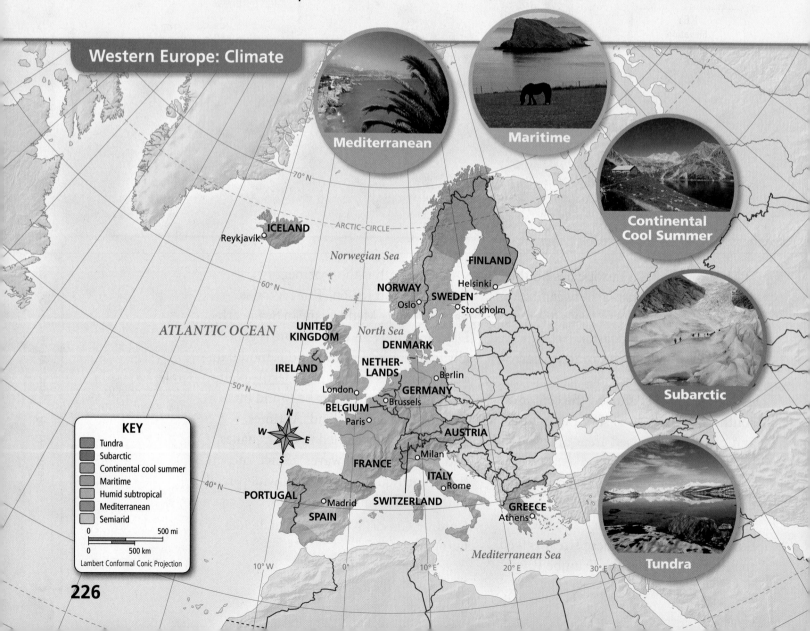

Western Europe: Climate

KEY
- Tundra
- Subarctic
- Continental cool summer
- Maritime
- Humid subtropical
- Mediterranean
- Semiarid

0   500 mi
0   500 km
Lambert Conformal Conic Projection

226

Trees are unable to grow here because it is too cold and dry. The **taiga,** a thick forest of coniferous trees, lies south of this zone. It extends from Scandinavia east across Eurasia for thousands of miles.

Mediterranean vegetation is a mix of small trees, forests, shrubs, and grasses. Trees and shrubs here must be hardy enough to survive the dry summer season.

Reading Check Contrast taiga vegetation with that of the Mediterranean region.

A Diverse Continent

In general, the nations of Western Europe have a high standard of living. Almost all Western Europeans can read and write. This region has strong education systems. There is a direct connection between good education and a high standard of living.

Across Western Europe, people speak a variety of different languages. About half of the people in Europe speak English and their native languages or <u>dialects.</u>

dialect, *n.,* a regional variety of a language

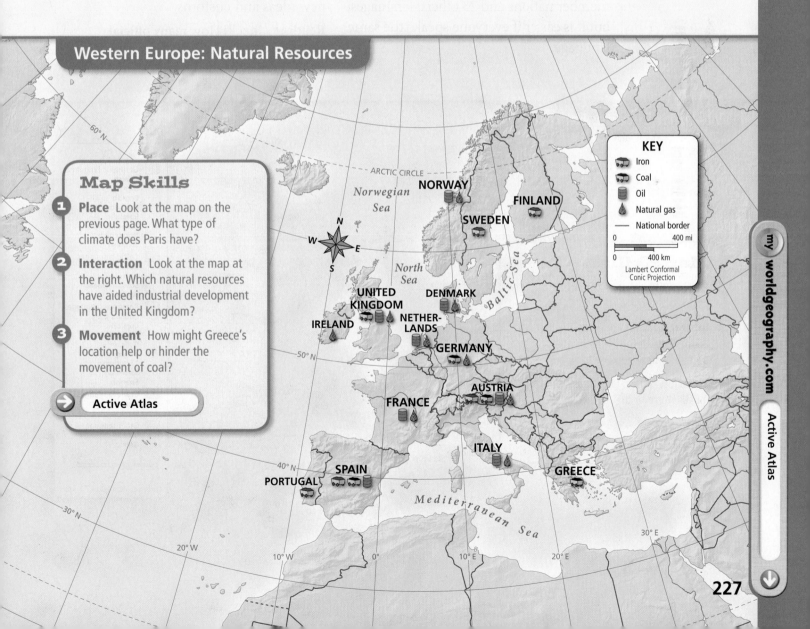

Western Europe: Natural Resources

Map Skills

1. **Place** Look at the map on the previous page. What type of climate does Paris have?
2. **Interaction** Look at the map at the right. Which natural resources have aided industrial development in the United Kingdom?
3. **Movement** How might Greece's location help or hinder the movement of coal?

Active Atlas

KEY
- Iron
- Coal
- Oil
- Natural gas
- National border

0 — 400 mi
0 — 400 km
Lambert Conformal Conic Projection

my worldgeography.com Active Atlas

227

Language is part of culture. Sometimes, language unites those from different cultures. For example, when North Africans move to France, they encounter a different culture. But many North Africans speak French. This makes the transition to a new life a little easier.

When European Union (EU) leaders meet to discuss economics or energy policy, they often conduct business in English. This helps make discussion and decision-making easier. The European Union has 27 member nations and 23 official languages, but it is easier if everyone speaks the same language.

Europe is a region of many different cultures. For 2,000 years, Christianity has been the dominant religion. A large Jewish population has also lived there continuously. Since World War II, people from around the world have moved to Europe for jobs and education. They brought different religions, languages, and customs. When people move to a new country, they often take on parts of its cultures. At the same time, newcomers have introduced Western Europeans to new ideas and customs.

Reading Check How many official languages are there in the European Union?

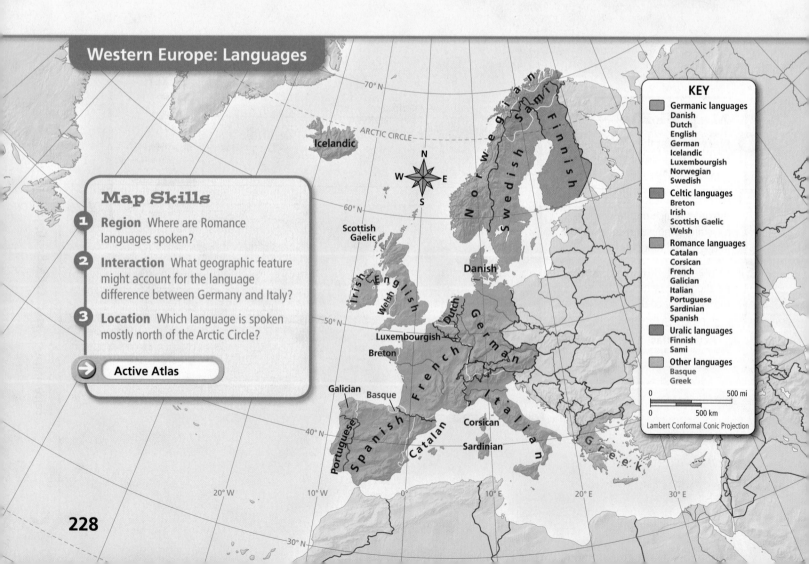

Western Europe: Languages

Map Skills

1. **Region** Where are Romance languages spoken?

2. **Interaction** What geographic feature might account for the language difference between Germany and Italy?

3. **Location** Which language is spoken mostly north of the Arctic Circle?

Active Atlas

KEY

Germanic languages
Danish
Dutch
English
German
Icelandic
Luxembourgish
Norwegian
Swedish

Celtic languages
Breton
Irish
Scottish Gaelic
Welsh

Romance languages
Catalan
Corsican
French
Galician
Italian
Portuguese
Sardinian
Spanish

Uralic languages
Finnish
Sami

Other languages
Basque
Greek

0 — 500 mi
0 — 500 km
Lambert Conformal Conic Projection

Where People Live and Work

Western Europe's geography shapes where and how people live. This region is largely urban and industrialized.

In Western Europe, most of the population lives within 100 miles of the coast. This is because being close to water offers many opportunities for trade. Europe's major rivers, the Danube and the Rhine, carry goods and people. They also carry large quantities of water. Western European highways often follow river routes to connect towns and cities that have grown along these rivers.

In northern Europe, people live near the coast. Even in Arctic climates, being near the ocean offers milder weather. Inland, <u>vast</u> empty areas separate towns and villages. Settlement is sparse because these areas are cold and dry.

In Southern and Central Europe, population is more evenly spaced. In the temperate climate of Italy, population is densest near the coast. People also live in large numbers inland as well.

In general, people do not choose to live in high mountains and marshy wetlands. Instead, they tend to settle in low, sunny, warm places close to water. Natural resources such as water, minerals, and rich farmland also attract people.

A recent report by the European Union addressed climate change trends. This report noted changes such as the melting of glaciers in the Arctic Ocean and drier conditions in the Mediterranean area of Southern Europe. Changes in climate may affect crop yields, water levels in rivers, and human health.

As a highly industrialized region, Western Europe has experienced air and water **pollution.** Pollution is harmful material released into the environment. One result of air pollution is acid rain. This occurs when exhaust from industries mixes with moisture in the air. This precipitation then falls as acid rain. It has damaged historic buildings, bridges, cathedrals, and monuments across Western Europe. Over the years, acid rain has also damaged forests and freshwater lakes.

Water pollution may result from chemical spills. A chemical spill is an accidental release of toxic or dangerous materials.

vast, *adj.,* very great in size, number, or quantity

myWorld Activity
Danube Cleanup

ENVIRONMENTAL CHALLENGES IN WALES

Over a period of 30 years, this forest has been destroyed by acid rain, due to the air pollution from nearby industrial plants.

Workers spread chemicals to clean up an oil spill on a Welsh beach. *What might be likely causes for the pollution shown in each photograph?*

One of Western Europe's busiest waterways, the Rhine River, was once one of the region's most polluted. From the 1950s to the 1970s, industrial waste flowed into the river. Fish disappeared from it and swimmers avoided it. A cleanup effort was launched, but in 1986, a chemical spill reversed years of effort. A chemical factory fire in Switzerland led to 30 tons of toxic chemicals being washed into the river as firefighters fought the blaze. Within 10 days, the pollution traveled the length of the Rhine to the North Sea. Today, the Rhine is much cleaner and fish are returning to swim in it again.

Reading Check How have Europe's coasts and waterways affected settlement?

The Urban Continent

Europe has been called the "urban continent" because so many people live in urban areas. An urban area may include a city and its surrounding suburbs. In the United Kingdom, for example, almost nine out of ten people live in cities.

Most countries in Western Europe have dense populations clustered in small land areas. To preserve land for growing food, for forests, and for recreation, most countries set strict limits on the expansion of cities and suburbs. This means that the region's cities tend to be tightly packed with people. Very few Europeans live in single-family houses with yards. Instead, most live in apartment buildings.

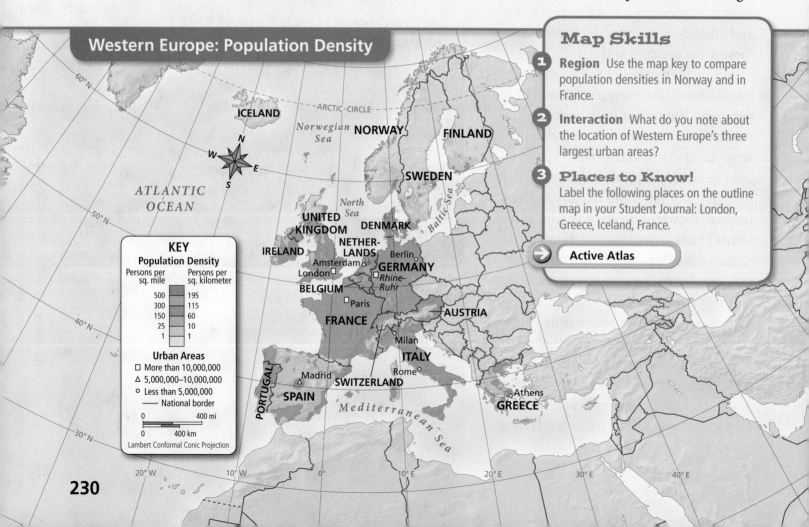

Western Europe: Population Density

Map Skills

1. **Region** Use the map key to compare population densities in Norway and in France.

2. **Interaction** What do you note about the location of Western Europe's three largest urban areas?

3. **Places to Know!** Label the following places on the outline map in your Student Journal: London, Greece, Iceland, France.

Active Atlas

KEY
Population Density

Persons per sq. mile	Persons per sq. kilometer
500	195
300	115
150	60
25	10
1	1

Urban Areas
☐ More than 10,000,000
△ 5,000,000–10,000,000
○ Less than 5,000,000
— National border

0   400 mi
0   400 km
Lambert Conformal Conic Projection

In order to reach their jobs, schools, and other activities, most Europeans use public transportation. Over time, urban areas have built up dense public transportation networks. Train, subway, trolley, and bus services connect neighborhoods and cities all over Europe.

Germany's Rhine-Ruhr region is one of Europe's largest urban areas. Five cities there have more than 500,000 inhabitants. Contrast that with Greenland, a territory of Denmark and the world's largest island. Greenland is six times as large as all of Germany, but has a population of only about 58,000 people.

European governments favor public transportation over driving by setting high taxes on gasoline. Gasoline in Europe can cost twice as much as gasoline in the United States. While most families in Western Europe have a car, they may use it only for occasional trips to the countryside or to a regional shopping center.

Reading Check Why are Europe's cities so crowded?

Germany's Rhine-Ruhr Region

KEY
- Urban area
- Autobahn
- Other highway
- Railway
- River
- ○ City

0   10 mi
0   10 km

Map Skills

The Rhine-Ruhr region is a transportation and industrial hub for the entire continent. What are the different forms of transportation available?

Active Atlas

Section 1 Assessment

Key Terms

1. Use each of the following terms in a sentence: peninsula, loess, tundra, pollution.

Key Ideas

2. What is Eurasia?

3. How does geography affect settlement patterns?

4. Why do some countries restrict urban growth?

Think Critically

5. **Compare and Contrast** Look at the physical map and the climate map in this section. Why is there more farming in France than in Scandinavia?

6. **Draw Conclusions** How does keeping a river like the Rhine clean benefit Western Europe?

Essential Question

Is it better to be independent or interdependent?

7. Look at the languages map in this section. Do you think the number of languages spoken by EU members helps or harms Western Europe? Go to your Student Journal to record your answer.

my**worldgeography**.com   Active Atlas

231

Energy for the Future

Key Ideas
- Renewable energy sources capture energy from nature using advanced technologies.
- An energy goal for the entire European Union must take into account differences in member nations' economic development.

Key Terms
- renewable energy
- biofuel
- nonrenewable energy
- wind turbine
- fossil fuel
- hydropower

In a region where 74 percent live in areas of high energy use such as cities, energy consumption is a hot topic. The European Union (EU) has promoted the use of **renewable energy,** or energy sources that can be replaced. Recently, EU member nations decided to boost their use of renewable energy sources by 20 percent by the year 2020.

In Italy, a man cooks using a solar reflector. ▼

Energy and Progress

While EU members might agree that it is important to conserve energy and find new sources of energy, changing energy policy raises concerns. The member nations of the EU do not all have the same economic and technological resources. Not every EU member can afford to invest in alternative energy sources.

In some cases, a nation's history affects its energy policy. Poland, for example, has long depended on heavy industry that burns coal as fuel. Changing to technologies that use renewable energy would be expensive for Poland and would take many years to develop. Other EU members such as Sweden and Denmark have long used "green energy" (clean, efficient, renewable energy) and can more easily meet the EU energy goal.

Concerns about energy consumption generally come as a society reaches a certain level of progress. During the Industrial Revolution, for example, Manchester, England, became a center for textile manufacturing. Once a rural market town, Manchester grew quickly as thousands of people moved there for jobs at coal-powered factories. Over the years, coal pollution left a coating of black smoke everywhere. People died from lung diseases after breathing coal smoke all their lives. Eventually, people became more aware of how using pollution-causing fuels affected human health and the environment.

Reading Check Why might some nations have trouble meeting the European Union's energy goal?

Power to the People

Everyday energy comes in many forms: gasoline for cars, natural gas for heating and cooking, or coal for the generation of electric power. Each of these forms of energy is made from fossil fuels and is **nonrenewable energy,** or energy that cannot be replaced. **Fossil fuels** come from carbon-based organic material that took millions of years to form. Nuclear energy, which comes from the metal uranium, is also considered nonrenewable.

Scientists have been able to find new ways to collect energy: wood, crops such as corn, and even weeds for **biofuels** (fuel from organic material), wind and water for electricity, or energy from the sun that solar cells can convert into electricity. These are all forms of renewable energy.

The EU Common Energy Policy seeks ways to bring more energy to its growing population without damaging the environment. Supporters of the policy also want the EU to become less dependent on energy from other parts of the world, such as Russia or Southwest Asia.

Reading Check Why are fossil fuels considered nonrenewable?

EU Energy Imports

Fuel: Coal, Oil, Gas, Nuclear

Percentage of Fuel Imported (0 25 50 75 100)

SOURCE: European Commission

Harnessing Energy

Whether renewable or nonrenewable, energy must be harnessed and processed before it reaches customers. Utility companies use different technologies to turn energy sources into forms of energy for homes, offices, and businesses.

This race-car driver uses biofuel made from crops grown on her family's farm in England. ▶

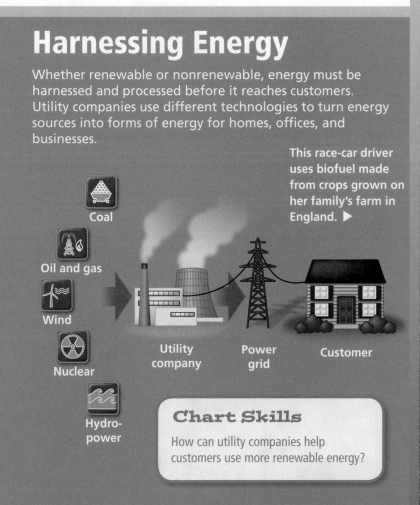

Coal

Oil and gas

Wind

Nuclear

Hydro-power

Utility company

Power grid

Customer

Chart Skills

How can utility companies help customers use more renewable energy?

Energy Choices

As EU members discuss how to reach their 2020 energy goal, they will learn more about the types of renewable energy sources available. They will also weigh the advantages and disadvantages of these alternative forms of energy. *Choose one form of energy below and make a case for its use.*

Sun Solar energy is collected by special panels and used for heating and electricity.

Wind Wind turbines, or giant windmills, use large blades to collect the wind's energy. A generator on the turbine turns the mechanical energy into electricity. A cable transfers the electricity to a transmission line.

Ocean Heat from the sun on the ocean can be harnessed for thermal energy, while tides and waves may provide mechanical energy.

Water Hydropower, or energy harnessed from flowing water, is converted into electricity.

Biofuel Biofuel is energy gathered by processing organic matter from food crops such as corn, sugar cane, or beets, or industrial waste from wood or paper mills.

Hydrogen Hydrogen is present in many compounds (water and biofuels) and can be used to store energy or to transfer it from place to place.

Earth Earth's internal heat, geothermal energy, can be tapped for heating and cooling buildings.

▲ Wind farms are a growing source of energy in Europe.

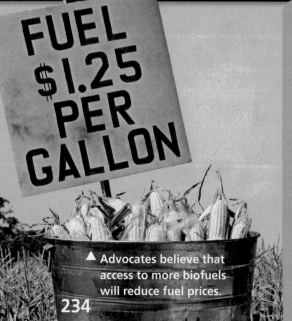

▲ Advocates believe that access to more biofuels will reduce fuel prices.

Food or Fuel?

People As populations grow, so does the need for food and fuel.

Farms Farmers receive subsidies to grow biofuel crops, but that means fewer crops for food.

Prices Biofuels might cost less to consumers, but production can lead to higher food prices and hunger in poorer countries.

Weather Poor harvests of biofuel crops can lead to increased use of fossil fuels, higher food prices, and food shortages.

In Spain, people dressed in corn costumes protest using food crops to produce fuel. ▶

234

Learning an Energy Lesson

In 2009, a dispute between Ukraine and Russia led to a three-week interruption of natural gas supplies to Europe. During one of the coldest winters in years, Europeans had to find other ways to stay warm. Schools closed and people used wood fires to heat their homes. Some people froze to death due to lack of heat.

The Russia-Ukraine pipeline supplies 80 percent of the EU's natural gas. Following the 2009 shortage, Europeans realized that they had become too dependent on a single energy source. This event also drew attention to the need to expand renewable energy sources.

Reading Check **What event highlighted Europe's energy dependence?**

Sharing the Burden

Members of groups like the EU share the benefits as well as the challenges of energy policy. Wealthier nations such as Germany, Denmark, France, and Spain use more renewable energy because they have invested in renewable technologies for many years. France, for example, leads the EU in biofuel production because it has many farms. Spain, with its windy hillsides and plains, is second in wind-energy production.

Some EU members have smaller economies and cannot contribute to the EU energy policy as much as wealthier nations. People in wealthier nations might see the expectation that they spend more on renewable energy as unfair. Some of the newer (and poorer) EU member nations have only recently been able to shift their attention from economic development to energy consumption.

Energy policy must also balance food and energy needs. If European farmers commit too much of their land to crops that will be used for biofuels, there will be less food for people to eat. These crops (corn, soybeans, wheat, and beets) could become scarce and prices could rise.

There is also a concern that land needed for housing or farms might instead be dedicated to energy production. In addition, there could be environmental damage as fossil fuel production expands to forested areas or to ocean drilling sites.

European individuals, companies, and governments are working to resolve these issues. Poorer nations want more economic growth. Europeans must balance that desire with the goals of energy independence and lower pollution.

Reading Check **What could happen if more European farmers grew corn for biofuel instead of food?**

Assessment

1. Name and define four kinds of renewable energy.

2. In what ways might energy investment differ among EU member nations?

3. How does Spain's geography allow it to be a leader in wind-energy production?

4. What is the primary goal of the EU Common Energy Policy?

5. Write a short paragraph outlining the advantages and disadvantages of growing crops such as corn for biofuel rather than food.

Northwestern Europe Today

Key Ideas
- The United Kingdom has a long history of democracy.
- Scandinavian nations offer a cradle-to-grave system of public services.
- Many people in Northwestern Europe favor limited ties with the European Union.

Key Terms
- constitutional monarchy
- Parliament
- cradle-to-grave system
- gross domestic product (GDP)
- cultural borrowing

Visual Glossary

Reading Skill: Sequence Take notes using the graphic organizer in your journal.

Beefeaters are ceremonial guards at the Tower of London. ▼

You might be surprised to learn that England has a queen, yet it also has a long history of democracy. During the summers in northern Scandinavia, there is sunshine at midnight. How can this be? The nations of Northwestern Europe are worth a closer look.

The United Kingdom and Ireland

The United Kingdom, or Britain, is an island nation made up of several regions. England, Wales, and Scotland are located on the largest island, Great Britain. Northern Ireland, on the nearby smaller island of Ireland, is also part of the United Kingdom. Most of this island is the independent nation of Ireland.

British Government You have read about King John signing the Magna Carta in 1215. This document limited the power of the king and gave rights to his people. It was the beginning of democratic government in England. Today, the British government is a **constitutional monarchy.** This means the monarch is the ceremonial leader, but Parliament makes the laws. Unlike the U.S. Constitution, the British constitution is not a single document, but a group of laws and court decisions. The symbolic head is Queen Elizabeth II, who symbolizes Britain's nationhood.

The British legislature, or **Parliament,** is located in London, England. It is made up of the House of Lords and the House of Commons. At one time, members of the House of Lords inherited their seats. Today, Parliament is moving toward a combination of elected and appointed members in both houses. These members are composed of high-ranking clergy, judges, and national leaders. The head of the majority party in the House of Commons is the prime minister, the true head of the British government.

Since the 1990s, some lawmaking power has moved from a national to a regional level. Scotland has its own Parliament and government that handles laws specific to that country. The Welsh National Assembly can pass laws that directly affect Wales. Northern Ireland also has a separate assembly with its own powers.

The official language of the United Kingdom is English. Some people also speak Welsh, Irish, or Scottish Gaelic. Thousands of immigrants come to Britain every year. Many come from countries that were once part of the British empire.

Prosperity and Partnerships Britain and Ireland both have a high standard of living and strong economies. In the past, Britain owed its wealth to iron and steel, textiles, and shipbuilding. Today, Britain is part of a global economy. The British work with international partners in finance and banking, high-technology fields, and service industries. Entrepreneurs, or people who start businesses, have had much success in Northwestern Europe.

One Nation, Four Countries

Known as the United Kingdom of Great Britain and Northern Ireland, these four countries act together on matters such as foreign policy. However, they act independently with regard to EU involvement and legal issues.

Map Skills

How might giving more power to regional governments strengthen the United Kingdom?

→ Active Atlas

SCOTLAND

NORTHERN IRELAND

WALES   ENGLAND

The United Kingdom and Ireland also benefit from being in the European Union. The European Union (EU) is an organization of European nations that promotes free movement of goods and people across borders. Ireland and Britain can trade with other member nations in an open market. There are no tariffs, or taxes, on goods imported from other member nations. Without tariffs, goods and services move freely. The EU has its own <u>currency,</u> the euro. Ireland uses the euro, but Britain does not. The British currency is the pound.

currency, *n.,* a system of money, especially the bills and coins, used in a country

heritage, *n.,* something possessed as a result of one's natural situation or birth

A Tourist Destination Britain is the world's sixth most popular travel destination. Many people visit Britain because of their <u>heritage</u>. Americans, for example, often travel to the United Kingdom to revisit the homes of their English, Irish, Scottish, or Welsh ancestors.

Tourists flock to famous places such as London's Buckingham Palace. They also visit ancient and historic sites such as Stonehenge and Shakespeare's home-town, Stratford-upon-Avon. Ireland draws visitors to its prosperous cities and green rural areas. Fishing is popular in Scotland's rivers. History lovers visit Welsh castles and villages.

Reading Check How has EU membership promoted economic development in Britain and Ireland?

The Scandinavian Countries

Denmark, Finland, Iceland, Norway, and Sweden make up the area known as Scandinavia. Life near the Arctic Circle is chilly, but full of variety.

Cradle-to-Grave Benefits Sweden, Norway, and Denmark are constitutional monarchies much like the United Kingdom. Each monarch is mainly a symbolic leader. Political decisions are made by an elected parliament. Finland is a democratic republic with a president. All are members of the EU except Norway. Norway has voted to remain outside the EU for several reasons. Some Norwegians feel that the EU's structure is not democratic. They also want to keep Norway's economic and political freedom.

The Cradle-to-Grave System

This system of social services originated after World War II in response to postwar hardships. Funding for the system comes from high taxes, such as payroll taxes and sales tax. These taxes fund benefits such as universal healthcare, education, and pensions.

Chart Skills

How does this diagram show advantages and disadvantages of the cradle-to-grave system?

→ **Data Discovery**

myWorld Activity
Cradle to Grave?

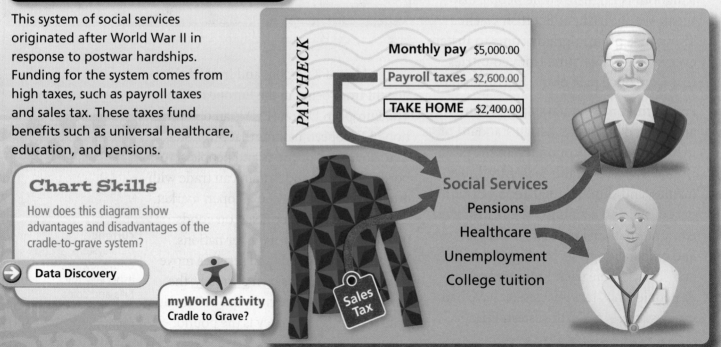

PAYCHECK

Monthly pay $5,000.00

Payroll taxes $2,600.00

TAKE HOME $2,400.00

Sales Tax

Social Services
Pensions
Healthcare
Unemployment
College tuition

238

The Scandinavian governments have a **cradle-to-grave system,** a system of basic services for citizens at every stage of life. It covers healthcare, education, and retirement. Benefits are funded through taxes. Because people believe this system is important, they are willing to pay high taxes for it. In Sweden, people pay on average almost 60 percent of their income in taxes. Clothing and food are also expensive due to taxes. On the other hand, healthcare costs and rents are low.

Fish, Forests, and Phones In the past, the Scandinavian countries depended on farming. Agriculture and dairy farming are still important in Denmark, where the climate is warmer. Today, the economies of these countries rely on multinational corporations, high-technology industries, and exports. Finland, for example, is a leading manufacturer of mobile telephones.

Scandinavia's geography also affects the economy. Miles of coastline and acres of forests supply the fishing and lumber industries. Oil production in the North Sea also helps this region maintain a high standard of living. Membership in the EU opens Denmark, Finland, and Sweden to free trade and global markets.

Located near the Arctic Circle, the northernmost Scandinavian cities have what are called white nights. From May to July, the sun appears on the horizon for almost 24 hours a day. This is because the northern hemisphere is tilted toward the sun at that time of year.

Reading Check Why do people in Sweden pay high taxes?

SCANDINAVIA: LAND OF THE VIKINGS

The gods, giants, and elves of ancient Scandinavian myths remain popular today. The adventures of the Norse warriors known as the Vikings left marks on territory from England to Russia. In modern times, Scandinavia has been known for its famous scientists and artists. These nations also have a long record of gender equality and human rights. *Why might people build replicas of ancient ships today?*

Danish carpenter Ole Kirk Christiansen invented one of the world's most popular children's toys. ▼

The dala horse was once a toy, but has become a symbol of Sweden. ▼

Modern-day replica of a Viking ship ▶

my worldgeography.com Data Discovery

Life in Northwestern Europe

Aspects of daily life in northwestern Europe are changing rapidly.

Living With Technology With almost universal access to the Internet, cellphones, and television, faraway places are much nearer. Life has become more fast-paced. Technology has changed how people work in surprising ways. Danish farmers use modern technology to produce healthier food. Scientists in Norway have discovered new ways to preserve water supplies.

Finland uses more than 3 percent of its **gross domestic product** for technology research and development. Gross domestic product (GDP) is the total value of all goods and services produced and sold in a country in a year.

In this region, finding ways to save energy is important. Due to its cold climate, Finland uses a great deal of energy for heating. One way to reduce energy use is driving cars with better gas mileage. Finland has passed a law raising taxes for cars with poor gas mileage. The owners of cars with higher gas mileage pay less in taxes.

Living in Cities Many of the large cities in this region are capital cities: London, Dublin, Copenhagen, Oslo, Stockholm, and Helsinki. These cities are centuries old and rich in history and culture.

London has museums and palaces, and Stockholm has historic city squares. In Dublin, people lunch at pubs, while in Helsinki they relax in saunas. Most people use public <u>transportation</u> rather than their cars for daily travels.

transportation, *n.,* a means of carrying people or goods from one place to another

A United Kingdom woman paints figures for a company that exports tableware and gifts. ▼

Chart Skills

Compare Norway's GDP with the world average.

→ (Data Discovery)

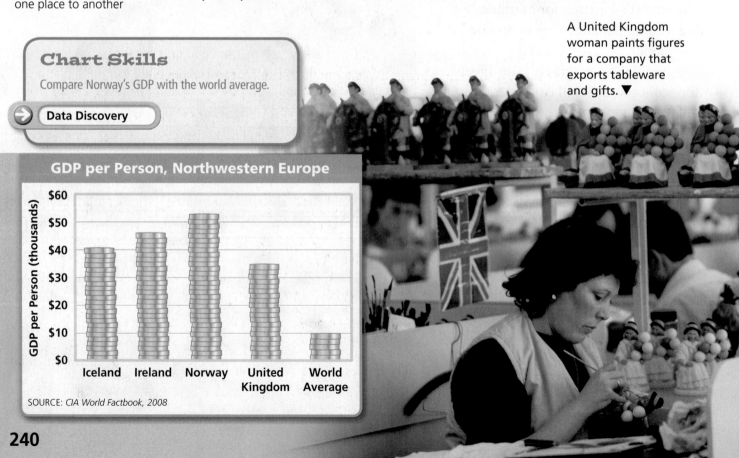

GDP per Person, Northwestern Europe

SOURCE: *CIA World Factbook, 2008*

240

Living Together Northwestern Europe is a region of many ethnic groups due to a large immigrant population. Some immigrants have lived there for generations. Others have come more recently.

The EU's open-border policy has also let people move between nations. In this chapter's myStory, you read about how the policy lets Yasmin move easily about Europe for family trips and education.

It is common to see people from the Caribbean, India, Pakistan, Turkey, or Somalia here. These newcomers face many challenges. To find jobs, they must learn how to get around. They may have to learn a language different from their parents' language.

Some immigrants have religious beliefs that <u>conflict</u> with local customs. For example, there is a significant Muslim population in Norway. Muslims have certain religious beliefs about food preparation. These beliefs can lead to higher prices in markets and restaurants—whether or not customers are Muslim.

▲ This London restaurant owner offers food from India, where he grew up.

conflict, *v.,* to clash or to be in opposition

Immigrants may also take part in **cultural borrowing,** an exchange that takes place when groups come into contact and share ideas, language, customs—and even food. Many Londoners enjoy eating at Indian or Ethiopian restaurants. In Copenhagen, people have grown to love Turkish coffee or food that mixes traditional Danish ingredients with those of France or Japan.

Reading Check What is one way that Finland tries to reduce energy use?

Section 2 Assessment

Key Terms
1. Use the following terms to describe Northwestern Europe today: constitutional monarchy, cradle-to-grave system, cultural borrowing.

Key Ideas
2. How has a long history of democracy affected Northwestern Europe?
3. Describe how technology has changed daily life for Northwestern Europe.
4. What sorts of challenges do immigrants face in a new country?

Think Critically
5. **Draw Conclusions** How does the EU open market benefit member nations?
6. **Categorize** Name three industries that developed because of Scandinavia's geography.

Essential Question
Is it better to be independent or interdependent?
7. What are the benefits of cultural borrowing? What might be some of the challenges? Go to your Student Journal to record your answer.

myworldgeography.com Data Discovery

241

West Central Europe Today

Key Ideas

- The countries of West Central Europe have strong international partnerships.

- The rich cultural heritage of West Central Europe makes tourism one of the region's largest industries.

- People in most of the countries in this region favor strong ties with the European Union.

Key Terms • privatization • gross national product (GNP) • polders • reunification    Visual Glossary

 Reading Skill: Identify Main Ideas and Details Take notes using the graphic organizer in your journal.

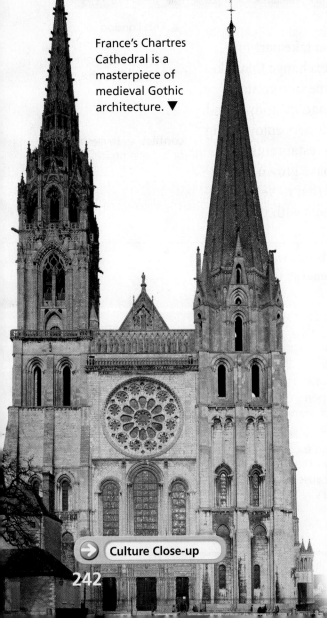

France's Chartres Cathedral is a masterpiece of medieval Gothic architecture. ▼

Culture Close-up

Rich in culture, the nations of West Central Europe include some of the largest and most prosperous on the continent. Most are members of the European Union, an organization that plays a major role in life in this region.

At the Center of the European Union

West Central Europe includes Austria, Belgium, France, Germany, Liechtenstein, Luxembourg, Monaco, the Netherlands, and Switzerland. All have joined the European Union (EU) except Switzerland, Liechtenstein, and Monaco. Why have some countries joined the EU while others have not?

EU membership is similar to playing on a school sports team. Each team member has different abilities or strengths, but the team works best when its members work together.

Just as not all students take part in sports, not every country in Europe is a member of the EU. Some countries do not meet certain guidelines. Some want to be members in certain ways, but not in others. Germany and France are the largest EU countries by population. They make up almost one third of the entire EU population. Some critics say that larger countries have more power in the EU government. If a country has more power, it can influence EU laws in its own favor. However, the EU has policies in place so that members work together.

Reading Check How might a larger nation influence laws in an alliance such as the European Union?

Closer Look

UNDERSTANDING THE EUROPEAN UNION

In the 1950s, European leaders wanted to ensure that world war would never happen again. In 1957, Belgium, Germany, France, Italy, Luxembourg, and the Netherlands formed the European Economic Community (EEC). Their main goal was economic unity through a single market.

The EEC later became the EU, which today consists of 27 member nations. The EU works to expand prosperity, to spread democracy, and to defend human rights and the rule of law. The EU single market system has removed trade barriers and raised standards of living. However, the EU has drawn criticism over powers given to unelected officials.

THINK CRITICALLY What are some advantages to having a single currency throughout several nations?

Council of Ministers
(represents national governments)

European Union

European Parliament
(represents the people)

European Commission
(represents collective EU interests)

◄ The euro is the EU currency.

The European Union, 2009

KEY
- European Union member states
- National border
- Disputed border

Finland
Sweden
Estonia
Latvia
Lithuania
United Kingdom
Denmark
Ireland
Netherlands
Germany
Poland
Czech Republic
Slovakia
Belgium
Luxembourg
Austria
Hungary
France
Romania
Slovenia
Bulgaria
Italy
Portugal
Spain
Greece
Cyprus
Malta

Main Aims of the EU
- To form a closer union among Europeans
- To remove trade barriers
- To improve the environment
- To fight terrorism, crime, and illegal immigration
- To give Europe a stronger voice in the world

Before France adopted the euro, signs showed prices in the national currency (French francs) as well as euro. ▶

myworldgeography.com   Culture Close-up

243

Algerian-born Zinédine Zidane (center) played for the French national soccer team, a team known for its ethnic diversity. ▼

France: History and Diversity

Known for its rich heritage, France has taken a leading role in the EU. The changing face of France presents many challenges.

The French Economy France has fertile soil, a mild climate, and large areas of level land. Its farms, dairies, and vineyards produce wines, cheeses, and grains. The EU ensures that these products reach people around the world.

However, France's largest industry is tourism. Around 75 million tourists a year come to see historic sites and scenic landscapes. French cities attract shoppers and art lovers. Some tourists come just to eat French cuisine!

France is a republic with a strong centralized government. In the past, the government owned many industries such as airlines, banks, and telecommunications. Much of that has changed due to **privatization,** or private ownership of businesses.

City of Light Paris, the capital of France, is known as the City of Light. It is the nation's cultural and economic center. Paris straddles the Seine River and is home to more than 2 million people. Its entire urban area covers around 890 square miles (2,300 square km) and is home to 12 million people.

Parisians live among Gothic churches, baroque palaces, elaborate gardens, and modern skyscrapers. Some Parisians work for the EU as their nation helps shape its policies.

The New Face of France In 2005, two North Africans youths were killed after a police chase in a Paris suburb. This event touched off riots all over France. In 2006, some French people held an anti-immigration protest, saying immigrants were changing French culture. Like the United States, France faces tough immigration issues.

More than 5 million immigrants live in France. An estimated 200,000 to 400,000 are living in the country illegally. Most immigrants come from Europe, and a large number come from North Africa and West Africa. Historically, most French practiced Catholicism. Today, 5 percent to 10 percent of the population is Muslim. Immigrants often face job discrimination and poor living conditions in France.

The French government recently added an immigration ministry. It offers immigrants money to return home. With this money, a family may be able to have a better life in its native country.

Reading Check How have immigrants changed religious life in France?

244

The Low Countries

Belgium, Luxembourg, and the Netherlands form the Low Countries. These countries are small in size, but they are politically and economically powerful.

Belgium: EU Headquarters Belgium serves as the political hub of Europe. Both the EU and NATO have their headquarters in the capital of Brussels. NATO is a military alliance that includes the United States, Canada, and many European nations.

Belgium is a constitutional monarchy. The country has few natural resources, so it relies on trade. It has a high standard of living and a high **gross national product (GNP),** which is the annual income of a nation's companies and residents. Almost 97 percent of Belgians live in cities.

Belgium is made up of three regions. In Flanders in the north, people speak a form of Dutch called Flemish. In Wallonia in the south, they speak French. In the third region around Brussels, people speak both French and Flemish. Periodically, some Flemish call for independence, but most Belgians prefer a united country.

Landlocked Luxembourg Luxembourg is a tiny landlocked country, one of Europe's oldest and smallest. It is a constitutional monarchy as well as a member of the EU and NATO.

Most of its citizens speak French, German, and Luxembourgish, a German dialect. Its key industries are banking and media. Because of its strict banking laws, people around the world use Luxembourg banks.

The Netherlands: A Fragile Balance The Netherlands is also known as Holland. Its people are Dutch. The Netherlands has a long history as a sea-trading nation.

More than half of the Netherlands is below sea level. For centuries, the Dutch have been working to hold back the sea. One way is to build dikes—levees or long dams—to keep out water. With dikes, the Dutch can live on **polders,** or areas of land reclaimed from lake bottoms or the seabeds. The famous Dutch windmills power pumps to drain water from land.

The Dutch live in a fragile balance with their environment. Industry and consumers produce air pollution. As the Dutch population has grown in urban areas, more rural land is needed for human use. Wildlife habitats may be threatened. Water pollution is also a concern because three of Europe's major rivers flow through the Netherlands.

Reading Check How do the Dutch use windmills?

myWorld Activity
Make a Travel Poster

fragile, *adj.,* easily broken or destroyed

The Dutch windmill aids in irrigation for farming. Some farmers also live in windmills. ▶

245

Germany: Industrial Giant

Germany has the largest population in the EU and Western Europe. Its economy is one of the world's largest.

A United Germany When the Berlin Wall came down in 1989, it marked the end of the split between East Germany and West Germany. **Reunification,** or the process of becoming unified again, brought many changes. Many East Germans "voted with their feet." They left the east and went west for a better life.

Germany is a member of international organizations such as the EU and NATO. Germany also joins other nations for international meetings about global economic issues. Through its membership in the Organization for Security and Co-operation in Europe (OSCE), Germany helps keep the region safe.

A Rich Culture German culture includes some of the world's finest music, art, poetry, films, and literature. Germans have also been leaders in the study of botany, mathematics, and military technology.

Modern German culture remains colored by the painful memories of World War II and the Holocaust, in which Nazis murdered six million European Jews and other innocent people. That troubled period partly resulted from excessive nationalism.

While many Germans feel proud of their nation, they want to avoid the mistakes of the past. They believe that one way to ensure a better future is through education. The country ranks high in the number of university professors, published book titles, and Nobel laureates.

Leading German Exports, 2005

Export	Percent of Total Exports	Value in Euros (billions)	Value in U.S. Dollars (billions)
1. Automobiles	17.4	155.12	183.72
2. Machinery	12.5	111.62	132.20
3. Chemicals	11.4	101.91	120.70
4. Metals	5.6	50.27	59.54
5. Electrical machinery	4.4	39.10	46.31

SOURCE: Federal Statistical Office, Federal Republic of Germany

Heat lamps are used to dry paint on a new car at a German automobile factory. ▼

Chart Skills

Data Discovery

Compare the value of Germany's top export with its third-largest export.

246

Building Tolerance Like the rest of Europe, West Germany <u>recruited</u> guest workers from nearby poorer countries to address the postwar labor shortages of the 1950s. Today, immigrants still come to Germany from these same regions: Turkey, the Middle East, and Eastern Europe. Other immigrants are of German descent and are returning to Germany after generations of living in Poland or Romania.

Because of its past and its diverse population, modern Germany encourages tolerance. However, conflict still occurs. Anti-immigrant and anti-Semitic groups such as the neo-Nazis have staged violent marches. Many Turks, Germany's largest immigrant group, claim that they often encounter racism and prejudice. Even popular Turkish soccer players say they have been taunted because they are not "real Germans." German leaders continue to encourage open-mindedness.

Reading Check What are some reasons that immigrants have moved to Germany?

Austria and Switzerland

Austria shares a language as well as economic and cultural ties with Germany. Austria was once the center of the Austro-Hungarian empire. Its size was dramatically reduced during the two world wars. When Soviet occupation ended in 1955, Austria has become a prosperous democracy. Tourism is a top industry in this country, famous for its Alpine scenery and ski resorts.

Switzerland is one of the world's oldest democracies. It has a long history of neutrality, or not taking sides in wars. This neutrality has led to Switzerland's uneasy relationship with international organizations such as the United Nations. Switzerland did not formally join the UN until 2002. Some people believe joining the UN will help the nation to grow. Other worry that membership will damage Switzerland's neutrality.

Reading Check What industry contributes to the economies of both Alpine nations?

recruit, *v.,* to increase or maintain the number of

Winter sports enthusiasts keep tourism a top industry in both Austria and Switzerland. ▼

Section **3** Assessment

Key Terms

1. Write a one-sentence definition of each of the following terms: gross national product, privatization, polders.

Key Ideas

2. Most of the immigrants in France and Germany come from which regions?

3. Give some examples of the cultural heritage in West Central Europe.

Think Critically

4. **Identify Evidence** What actions of the Dutch suggest that the country has a high population density?

5. **Draw Inferences** How might Switzerland's history of neutrality have affected its history?

Essential Question

Is it better to be independent or interdependent?

6. Why might EU membership appeal to smaller countries? Go to your Student Journal to record your answer.

A Sense of Identity

Key Idea

- The European Union promotes the idea of a common European identity, but deeply rooted nationalism causes many people to continue to identify with their nations more strongly.

▲ Yasmin is a European of Spanish, Pakistani, and Finnish heritage.

Nationalism has played a major role in European history. While national pride can be positive, it has also caused destructive wars that tore Europe apart. After World War II, European leaders founded the European Union (EU) to promote political and economic cooperation. Anyone who is a citizen of an EU nation also has European citizenship. But what is European citizenship? Will it ever replace national identity? In these passages, Nicole Fontaine, former President of the European Parliament, and Leszek Kolakowski, a Polish historian, express different views.

A girl draws the EU flag with chalk. ▶

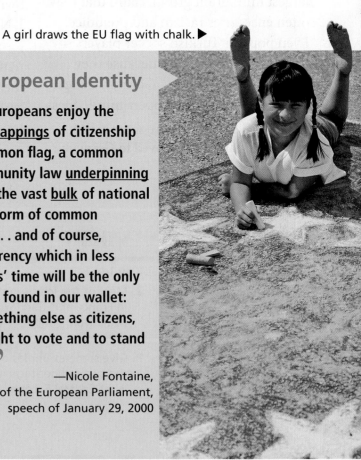

Stop at each letter on the right to think about the text. Then answer the question with the same letter on the left.

A Draw Conclusions What is the relationship between Community, or EU, law and the laws of the separate nations?

B Categorize Which of these trappings of citizenship are mostly symbolic?

C Summarize How does Fontaine define European citizenship?

institutional, *adj.,* related to institutions, or established organizations

trapping, *n.,* a thing usually associated with something

underpin, *v.,* to act as a foundation for

bulk, *n.,* a large part, or the largest part

Sharing a European Identity

❝ Not only do Europeans enjoy the <u>institutional</u> <u>trappings</u> of citizenship such as a common flag, a common anthem, Community law <u>underpinning</u>

A and directing the vast <u>bulk</u> of national legislation, a form of common government, . . . and of course,

B a common currency which in less than two years' time will be the only currency to be found in our wallet:

C we share something else as citizens, namely the right to vote and to stand for election. ❞

—Nicole Fontaine,
President of the European Parliament,
speech of January 29, 2000

248

Stop at each letter on the right to think about the text. Then answer the question with the same letter on the left.

D **Identify Main Ideas and Details** What two forces does Kolakowski think stand in the way of unification?

E **Analyze Cause and Effect** Why does he think many people distrust attempts to unify Europe?

F **Summarize** How does Kolakowski think that European identity could relate to national identity?

complex, *adj.*, having many different pieces
separatist, *adj.*, in favor of remaining apart
xenophobic, *adj.*, afraid of foreigners
wary, *adj.*, cautious, suspicious

Is a European Identity Possible?

❝ The question of national identity is endlessly <u>complex</u>. Given the extent to which progress towards unification has been accompanied by a rise in <u>separatist</u> and <u>xenophobic</u> tendencies,

D it is too soon to talk about the end of the nation state. And modern attempts—made by Napoleon, by Hitler, by Moscow—to unify Europe

E by force have made the various peoples of the continent <u>wary</u>. But assuming that national identities will persist, can a European identity be built alongside them or over

F them? Is there such an identity, and if not, is it desirable? Is there, or can there be, such a thing as European patriotism? ❞

—Leszek Kolakowski,
"Can Europe Happen?"
The New Criterion, May 2003

▲ Dairy farmers drove their tractors in the streets during a 2009 protest against EU milk pricing policies.

Analyze the Documents

1. **Identify Bias** Is Fontaine or Kolakowski more likely to have a biased view of European identity? Explain.

2. **Writing Task** Write your own definition of national identity. Name the qualities that define your own national identity.

◀ Flags at the European Parliament in Strasbourg, France

249

Southern Europe Today

Key Ideas
- An ancient and rich history lives on in Southern Europe today.
- The nations of Southern Europe have enjoyed strong growth as members of the European Union.
- Contemporary issues facing the region include immigration and globalization.

Key Terms
- Iberian Peninsula
- deportation
- cultural diffusion
- diversify

 Visual Glossary

Reading Skill: Analyze Cause and Effect Take notes using the graphic organizer in your journal.

◄ The Leaning Tower of Pisa, in Italy

The nations of Southern Europe have enjoyed especially strong growth as members of the European Union. Today, these nations face some of the region's greatest challenges.

A Region of Tradition

Spain, Portugal, Italy, and Greece have an ancient history of civilization. This rich past lives on in traditions that still shape the region today.

The Legacy of Empire Although the ancient Greeks and Romans lived thousands of years ago, their legacies remain. The idea of democracy—that citizens should have a voice in government—began in ancient Greece. The protection of people's rights regardless of wealth or class began in ancient Rome. Today, the European Union (EU) assures members of its commitment to these same ideas. The 12 stars on the EU flag and the EU motto, "United in diversity," tell of the goals of fairness and solidarity, or an attitude shared by a group.

Most of the languages spoken in Southern Europe originated in ancient Greek or Latin. The **Iberian Peninsula** (Spain, Andorra, and Portugal) remains a center of culture and commerce as it has since the Age of Exploration. Farmers and shepherds here live as they have for centuries. The cities of Southern Europe have cathedrals and palaces, many of which date back to the Middles Ages or the Renaissance.

Centuries of trade have influenced the artistic traditions of Southern Europe. Pablo Picasso, a famous Spanish artist, invented a new style of painting after he saw African art for the first time. Asian music influenced Italian opera composers in the 1800s. In Spain, the beautiful Alhambra Palace is a remnant of Islamic culture in Europe.

Religious Heritage Throughout history, armies, traders, and missionaries have passed through Southern Europe. This activity resulted in religious and cultural exchanges. Historians continue to study these events, as they still have a great effect on modern society.

In Rome, Italy, the tiny country of Vatican City serves as the worldwide center of the Roman Catholic Church. Saint Peter's Basilica, one of the holiest sites for Roman Catholics, was built near the site of an ancient Roman racetrack. Athens, Greece, a center of the Greek Orthodox Church, is also home to the Parthenon, an ancient Greek temple of the goddess Athena. Granada, Spain, blends Christian, Jewish, and Muslim influences. This is an example of **cultural diffusion,** or the spread of culture, and it is visible in Granada's colorful neighborhoods and restaurants and in local customs.

Artistic Richness Many famous artists, musicians, novelists, poets, and architects have come from the nations of Southern Europe. Italian architect Renzo Piano has designed buildings in cities around the world. Maria Callas, a famous soprano from Greece, sang many memorable roles for the opera stage.

Mediterranean Culture Mix

Along the Mediterranean, the nations of Southern Europe blend cultural influences that come from centuries of immigration, trade, art, and tradition. *What different cultural influences do you see below?*

For generations, Italians have celebrated religious holidays with city-wide processions that include holy statues. ▶

The Barcelos cockerel is a symbol of Portugal. ▶

◀ Dancing the flamenco, Yasmin keeps alive art from Spanish, Roma, Arabic, Jewish, and African cultures.

251

Southern Europe is rich in both classical and modern music. Spain's many classical composers include the pianist Isaac Albéniz who first performed at age four. Rock is popular everywhere, but world music has become a new favorite. Some of this music retains ethnic or folk traditions. Fado (FAH doo), sad songs about fate or destiny, is popular in Portugal, as is the music from African nations that were once Portuguese colonies. Flamenco, a Spanish dance, incorporates Arab music and African rhythms. The largest world music festival in the world is in Ariano Irpino, Italy.

Cheese-making is one of Italy's oldest industries. ▼

Reading Check How has cultural diffusion influenced life in Spain?

Modern, Prosperous Cities

Economic growth has been strong in this region, especially from 1980 to the early 2000s. Along with this growth, there has been a rise in living standards.

Economic Changes Many of the countries of Southern Europe lived under dictatorships until relatively recently. With the end of these regimes, these nations entered a new period of freedom and prosperity. In Spain, for example, the death of Francisco Franco in 1975 allowed a peaceful transition to democracy after decades of dictatorship.

As governments became more democratic, leaders liberalized, or made less strict, the laws for running businesses. This encouraged entrepreneurs to open new businesses. Jobs increased at both large and small companies. In addition, increasing privatization made businesses stronger and lowered prices.

Modernization has also boosted economic growth in the region. In Spain, for example, factories bought new, improved machinery. Modern factories can produce better goods for less money. Modern shipping companies then make sure that these goods reach buyers more quickly.

One challenge to Southern Europe's economy has been an increase in Asian imports. These imports are often some of the same goods made in Southern Europe. Because Asian manufacturers can make these goods in larger quantities and their workers earn less, their prices are lower. As a result, many countries in this region have had to work hard to compete.

Focus on Portugal Since joining the European Union in 1986, Portugal has experienced impressive economic growth. Much of this growth is due to Portugal's efforts to **diversify,** or add variety to, its types of industries. Many service-based industries, such as telecommunications, are now centered in Portugal.

Portugal's industries had once been limited to traditional products such as textiles, footwear, cork and wood products, and porcelain. Increasingly, a large service sector has developed. This sector includes telecommunications, financial services, healthcare, and tourism. Tourism is also a major industry for Portugal, bringing in almost $10 billion per year.

Privatization has also helped Portugal's economy. Moving businesses from government control to private control has helped business owners gain <u>confidence</u> in their nation's economy. This leads to growth in trade and and more jobs.

Portugal has also benefited from joining the EU single market. Soon after Portugal adopted the euro in 2002, the nation enjoyed a spike in economic growth that has since leveled off.

Still, Portugal has not escaped economic trouble. During the years of growth, debt increased. Repaying this debt will probably slow economic growth.

Effects of EU Membership Membership in the EU made this region better off. With access to open markets and funding from richer members, EU nations generally gain stronger economies and higher living standards.

GDP, Southern European Countries, 1976–2006

SOURCE: Organization for Economic Co-operation and Development

Chart Skills

How does the GDP trend for Italy and Spain compare to that of Greece and Portugal?

→ **Data Discovery**

Italy has long been an EU leader. Italy adopted the euro as its currency in 1999. Spain, Portugal, and Greece also experienced economic growth as EU members. This growth has slowed due to competition from Asia.

EU members sometimes find economic growth indirectly affected by the addition of new members. For example, Portugal has historically supplied Europe with low-cost labor. Recently, Portugal had its EU development funding cut by several billion euros. This happened with the entrance of new member nations such as Romania and Slovakia. Workers from these nations have begun to move to other EU countries like Portugal and are willing to work for lower wages.

Reading Check Describe one economic change in Southern Europe.

confidence, *n.,* the quality or state of being certain

my worldgeography.com Data Discovery

253

crisis, *n.,* an uncertain or difficult situation, possibly heading toward disaster

myWorld Activity
Southern Europe's Neighbors

Challenges for the Region

Although Southern Europe has experienced economic growth, it still faces many challenges.

Maintaining Growth Europe is now part of a larger, global economy. This has benefits and drawbacks.

In recent years, products from China have flooded European markets. Chinese workers earn lower wages, so the products they make sell for less. To help domestic companies survive, Southern European governments have increased tariffs, or taxes, on imported goods. Increasing tariffs raises the price of imported goods while domestic goods' prices remain low. Increasing government control of the market may, however, hurt economic growth.

The worldwide financial crisis of 2008 also posed serious economic challenges.

The economies of Spain, Portugal, Italy, and Greece have all experienced slowdowns. Industrial production fell, leading to a decrease in GDP. Some experts think that Southern Europe's years of rapid economic growth may be at an end.

Regional Newcomers Badolato, a village in Italy, had almost disappeared when a group of Turkish Kurds arrived. The Italians welcomed these refugees, who gave new life to the village. Because Italians are no longer having large families, the population is decreasing. With fewer people to fill open jobs, many employers now rely on immigrants such as those that have come to Badolato and other cities in Southern Europe.

However, Southern Europeans don't want so much immigration that it threatens their jobs or culture. Their governments have tried to control immigration.

Facing Regional Challenges
Muslim families in Rome (left) protest against anti-immigrant violence. At right, a woman enters an employment office in Spain, where unemployment has risen dramatically. *How does each photograph show challenges faced in Southern Europe?*

In Italy, the government uses fingerprinting to monitor immigrants. Some ethnic groups, such as the Roma (formerly known as Gypsies), believe these methods lead to discrimination.

The fear of **deportation,** or being sent back to one's home country, leads many immigrants to hide from officials in their new country. Any immigrant who does not follow a country's laws may be deported. As elsewhere in Europe, immigration shows the benefits and the challenges of living in an interconnected world.

Focus on Greece Since ancient times, Greek trading ships have brought back exotic goods from foreign lands. These same traders also introduced the world to Greek art and culture and important ideas such as democracy.

Shipping is still important in Greece, and China is a major trading partner. In 2007, Greek ships carried about 60 percent of China's imports of raw materials. These commodities included

coal, oil, and iron ore. In China, those products fueled the nation's explosive growth. This trade agreement benefited both Greece and China as well as other global trading partners. Yet, when global trade began to shrink in 2008, everyone involved in this trade experienced setbacks.

Reading Check What has caused Southern Europe's economic slowdown?

▲ Colorful shipping containers fill the busy port at Piraeus in Greece. *How does the geography of Greece contribute to its shipping industry?*

Section 4 Assessment

Essential Question

Key Terms

1. Use each of the following terms in a complete sentence: Iberian Peninsula, cultural diffusion, diversity, deportation.

Key Ideas

2. Describe three ways in which the past still affects Southern Europe.

3. What economic advantages did EU membership bring to Southern Europe?

4. What other cultures have spread ideas to Southern Europe through cultural diffusion?

Think Critically

5. **Identify Evidence** How has Southern Europe responded to immigration?

6. **Draw Inferences** Why are countries generally more open to immigrants during economic boom times?

Is it better to be independent or interdependent?

7. Has the European Union helped Southern Europe? Explain why or why not. Go to your Student Journal to record your answers.

255

Chapter Assessment

Key Terms and Ideas

1. **Discuss** Why does most of Western Europe have a mild climate?

2. **Describe** Where do most Western Europeans live, and why?

3. **Recall** What is a **constitutional monarchy,** and which nations have this form of government?

4. **Summarize** What does the **cradle-to-grave system** provide for citizens of Scandinavian countries?

5. **Explain** How does migration help cause **cultural borrowing** and **cultural diffusion**?

6. **Compare and Contrast** How are West Central Europe and Southern Europe similar? How are they different?

7. **Explain** What problems has Germany had to overcome since **reunification**?

8. **Recall** What cultures have influenced the artistic traditions of Southern Europe?

Think Critically

9. **Compare Viewpoints** How does the British viewpoint toward the EU compare to the viewpoint of France and Germany? Support your answer with details from the chapter.

10. **Draw Conclusions** How has immigration affected Western Europe? Explain.

11. **Predict** What long-term effect do you think EU membership will have on nationalism in Europe? Explain.

12. **Core Concepts: People's Impact on the Environment** What are some of the main causes of pollution? How has pollution affected Europe?

Places to Know

For each place, write the letter from the map that shows its location.

13. Scandinavian Peninsula
14. Italy
15. Iceland
16. France
17. Iberian Peninsula
18. Mediterranean Sea
19. Greece
20. **Estimate** Using the scale, estimate how far Iceland is from France.

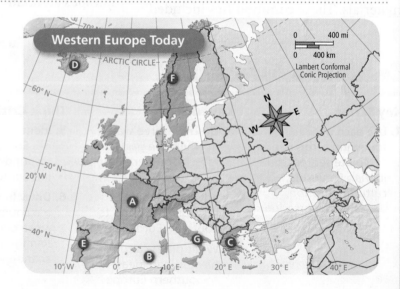

256

Essential Question

myWorld Chapter Activity

Norway and the European Union Follow your teacher's instructions to study data on whether or not Norway should join the European Union. Read and analyze graphs, photographs, and information about the advantages and disadvantages of EU membership for Norway. Take a stand based on your conclusions in support of your position on EU membership for Norway.

21st Century Learning

Develop Cultural Awareness

Western Europe's contact with other nations has added much to life on the continent. Make a small poster on each of the topics below to focus on cultural diffusion in Western Europe.
- Art and architecture
- Music
- Language
- Food

Document-Based Questions

Success Tracker™
Online at myworldgeography.com

Use your knowledge of Western Europe and Documents A and B to answer Questions 1–3.

Document A

Joining the Eurozone	
EU Member	**Year Euro Adopted**
Austria	1999
Belgium	1999
Finland	1999
France	1999
Germany	1999
Greece	2001
Ireland	1999
Netherlands	1999
Slovakia	2009
Spain	1999

Document B

" The people of Denmark have voted to reject membership of the single European currency. . . . The leader of the far-right, anti-Euro Danish People's Party, Pia Kjaersgaard, described the outcome as a great victory. 'This victory is a victory for Danes' wish to defend democracy, self-determination and the country's sovereignty,' she said."

—"Danes Say No to Euro,"
BBC News Online, September 28, 2000

1. Which Southern European country was last to adopt the euro?

   A Greece

   B Ireland

   C Slovakia

   D Spain

2. According to Kjaersgaard, why did the Danish people reject the euro?

   A They don't trust other EU members.

   B They are waiting to see if it succeeds.

   C They want to control their economy.

   D They have too much debt to switch.

3. **Writing Task** Explain why some Western European countries may want to have some independence from the EU.

Chapter 4

Eastern Europe

Essential Question

How can you measure success?

KEY
- National border
- ⊛ Capital city
- ○ Other city

0 — 200 mi
0 — 200 km
Lambert Conformal Conic Projection

Where in the World Is Eastern Europe?

Washington, D.C., to Bezpalche: 4,930 miles

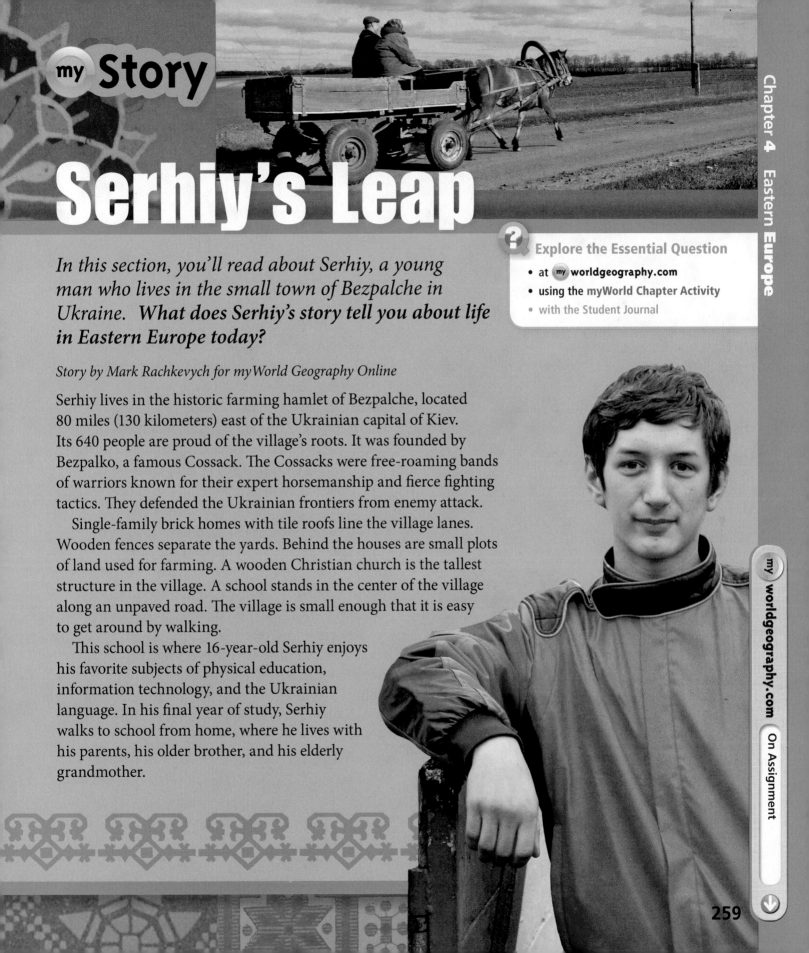

my Story

Serhiy's Leap

In this section, you'll read about Serhiy, a young man who lives in the small town of Bezpalche in Ukraine. What does Serhiy's story tell you about life in Eastern Europe today?

Explore the Essential Question
- at **my worldgeography.com**
- using the **myWorld Chapter Activity**
- with the Student Journal

Story by Mark Rachkevych for myWorld Geography Online

Serhiy lives in the historic farming hamlet of Bezpalche, located 80 miles (130 kilometers) east of the Ukrainian capital of Kiev. Its 640 people are proud of the village's roots. It was founded by Bezpalko, a famous Cossack. The Cossacks were free-roaming bands of warriors known for their expert horsemanship and fierce fighting tactics. They defended the Ukrainian frontiers from enemy attack.

Single-family brick homes with tile roofs line the village lanes. Wooden fences separate the yards. Behind the houses are small plots of land used for farming. A wooden Christian church is the tallest structure in the village. A school stands in the center of the village along an unpaved road. The village is small enough that it is easy to get around by walking.

This school is where 16-year-old Serhiy enjoys his favorite subjects of physical education, information technology, and the Ukrainian language. In his final year of study, Serhiy walks to school from home, where he lives with his parents, his older brother, and his elderly grandmother.

Scattering corn for the chickens is one of Serhiy's regular afternoon chores. He also must feed the family's pigs (below).

Serhiy buys bread at the only shop in Bezpalche.

His mother works a postal route three hours a day. On their small farm, his family grows beets, onions, cabbage, corn, and potatoes, and tends four pigs and three milking cows. Serhiy is personally responsible for caring for more than 40 rabbits. Small farms like this are common in Ukraine.

Ukraine used to be part of the Soviet Union. The Soviet government managed all the land in the country. Now Ukraine is an independent country. The new leadership broke up the large government farms, giving each family a small plot of land.

In villages like these, nature doesn't allow for breaks or long vacations. Serhiy rises at 6:00, feeds the livestock, and does other chores around the pens. Then he eats breakfast and heads to school for his first class, which begins at 8:30. He returns home at 2:30 and eats lunch. His favorite lunch is potatoes fried in lard and onions. His next chore is to take care of the rabbits. His grandmother pays him a small weekly allowance for this task. Then, at sunset, Serhiy starts his homework.

Short and broad-shouldered, Serhiy enjoys physical activity. He loves motorbikes and anything technical. "I even assembled a computer from scratch with a friend of mine," Serhiy says proudly, pointing at his PC, which he knows inside and out.

260

Serhiy plays games on a computer that he assembled himself, but he has no Internet connection.

The city of Kiev is about 80 miles from Serhiy's village.

But Serhiy can enjoy these hobbies only when time permits. On the weekends, his brother drives him 25 miles (40 kilometers) to the regional capital to take preparatory classes. Serhiy wants to go to the military academy in Kharkiv in eastern Ukraine. He hopes to become a pilot. But to do so, he will need to do well on the entrance exam. The prestigious and highly competitive academy accepts only one out of every four applicants.

Serhiy knows his small world and way of life will come to an end next summer when he graduates. Even if he is not accepted to the military academy, he will leave his village. The grocery store is the only real business in Bezpalche, so most young people must go elsewhere to make a living. Once his studies begin, he will not be able to take trips into the woods or drive his motorbike on country roads.

Still, Serhiy looks forward to military life. After all, could it be tougher than life in Bezpalche? Yet he worries, "Cities have wide boulevards, and I'll be a stranger among impersonal strangers."

He's willing to make the transition since he is drawn to the physical rigor of military exercises, the technical hardware and weaponry, and the challenges the regimen brings. "My family supports my decision, and my mother just worries like any other mother does," Serhiy says half-jokingly.

And if he doesn't get accepted when he applies in Kharkiv next summer, what is his backup plan? "Then I'll probably study computer programming in Cherkassy, the neighboring regional capital," Serhiy says.

How does he feel about leaving an environment where everything is familiar, where there are no surprises, and where everybody knows his name? "Well, I'm not just going to stay here," he says. "No one from my graduating class plans to remain in the village next summer, nobody."

Meet the Journalist

Name Mark Rachkevych
Favorite Moment Eating in a market and chatting with villagers in Bezpalche

➔ myStory Video

Join Serhiy as he shows you more about his life in Ukraine.

Chapter Atlas

Key Ideas
- Glaciers have shaped the physical features of this region.
- Climate varies from the south to the north of the region.
- Eastern European countries face many environmental challenges.
- Eastern Europe has a varied religious background.

Key Terms • ice age • mechanized farming • acid rain • emigrate

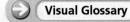 **Visual Glossary**

Reading Skill: Label an Outline Map Take notes using the outline map in your journal.

▲ The "Iron Gates" of the Danube River separate Romania from Serbia and the Carpathian Mountains from the Balkans.

◄ A young woman from Estonia

Physical Features

Eastern Europe is a region with both broad plains and high mountains. The most mountainous part of the region is the Balkan Peninsula, which juts into the Mediterranean Sea to the south. Two ranges, the Dinaric Alps and the Balkan Mountains, cover much of the peninsula.

Mountain ranges also stretch through the middle of Eastern Europe. The Carpathian Mountains begin close to the Danube River in Slovakia. They arch northeast and then bend back toward the Danube River, joining the Transylvanian Alps to the south.

262

Eastern Europe: Physical

Map Skills

1. **Region** What is the highest elevation in the North European Plain?

2. **Place** How does the landscape in the southwest differ from that in the northeast?

3. **Places to Know!** Label the following places on the outline map in your Student Journal: Balkan Mountains, North European Plain, Great Hungarian Plain, Danube River

21st Century Learning

KEY
Elevation

Feet	Meters
6,000	1,829
3,000	914
1,000	305
500	152
Sea level	Sea level

— National border

0 — 200 mi
0 — 200 km
Lambert Conformal Conic Projection

Between these two groups of mountains lies the Great Hungarian Plain. Another large plain, the North European Plain, stretches from the Baltic Sea to the Black Sea. Most of the farms and cities of this region are in these broad flatlands.

The physical features of the northern part of this region were shaped by an **ice age,** or time of lower temperatures when much of the land is covered in ice. Ice piled up as deep as two miles thick. Heavy sheets of ice, called glaciers, moved slowly across the land. Glaciers scraped up rocks and soil as they moved. They then dropped these materials when they melted. This process created ridges of hills that extend for hundreds of miles across the region.

Glaciers also formed lakes and rivers. The pressure of the glacier dug pits into the land. When the ice melted, pits became lakes. Most lakes in Europe are located in glaciated areas.

In the southern part of this region, deep valleys crisscross steep mountains. The Danube river flows through the Iron Gates, one of these deep valleys.

Reading Check What effects have glaciers had on the physical features of Eastern Europe?

263

Climate and Agriculture

The climate varies across Eastern Europe. In particular, the climate of the northern part of the region is very different from the climate of the southern part. As a result, farmers in the north face different challenges than farmers in the south. In the north, the winters can be very harsh. In the south, the mountains make cultivating the land difficult.

Latitude is the most important factor that influences climate in Eastern Europe. In the south, a band of Mediterranean and subtropical climate extends across much of the Balkan Peninsula. Summers here are dry, while winters are rainy. The rain and snow that <u>accumulate</u> in the mountains in wet winter months are very important for agriculture. During the hot, dry months

of spring and summer, melting snow flows downhill to the crops in the parched valleys below.

The continental cool summer climate covers much of the rest of Eastern Europe. In this area, winters are cold, and summers are generally mild.

Patterns of rainfall across the region vary from east to west. Each year, most of Eastern Europe receives between 20 and 40 inches of precipitation, or falling rain or snow. The amount of precipitation in the west is generally greater than the amount in the east.

Hills and mountains also have a major effect on the amount of precipitation an area receives. In general, warm air can hold more moisture than cool air. The higher air goes, the cooler it gets. When

accumulate, *v.,* to build up over time

Eastern Europe: Climate

Map Skills

1. **Place** Identify one country in Eastern Europe with a mostly Mediterranean climate.

2. **Region** What is the relationship between climate and latitude?

→ **Active Atlas**

KEY
- Continental cool summer
- Continental warm summer
- Humid subtropical
- Mediterranean
- National border

0 — 300 mi
0 — 300 km
Lambert Conformal Conic Projection

264

air cannot hold as much water, the water falls back to the earth as rain or as snow.

It is easy to see, then, how mountains affect precipitation. When wind blows against a range of mountains, the air rises and cools. Then it drops its moisture and continues over the mountains. Therefore, the side of the mountains facing the wind receives much more rain than the other side. The result is big differences in climate over small distances. Areas along the Adriatic coast, for example, receive as much as 200 inches of rainfall a year. The dry valleys on the other side of the Dinaric Alps may receive only 30 inches of rainfall during the same period of time.

The growing season on the North European Plain is shorter than the growing season farther south in the region.

Still, many people farm in this region. **Mechanized farming,** or farming with machines, is easy on the large expanses of flat land. Wheat and rye are common crops in this region. They are well suited to the cooler climate and easy to harvest with machines.

Because machines are important for agriculture here, many farms in northeastern Europe are large. Large farms are not as common in the southern part of this region. Because of the mountains, mechanized farming is more difficult. Also, more people are available to work the land. Many crops such as citrus fruits, olives, and grapes grow well in the warm climate.

Reading Check   How is agriculture in the north of Eastern Europe different from that in the south?

my World IN NUMBERS

In Albania, **58%** of the labor force work on farms. Most work on small family farms.

Harvesting Wheat in the North
Wheat grows best in areas without extremes of temperature. So wheat is a good crop for countries with cool summers and flat land.

Growing Olives in the South
Olive trees do well with warm, dry summers and cannot survive very cold winters. For that reason, olive growing is best suited to countries with a Mediterranean climate.

Coal or Nuclear:
Difficult Energy Choices

The search for energy to fuel economic growth is a major challenge in this region and across the world. Industry has developed near deposits of coal in Eastern Europe. These countries have struggled to deal with the air pollution caused by burning coal for energy. Would nuclear energy be a better choice for Eastern Europe?

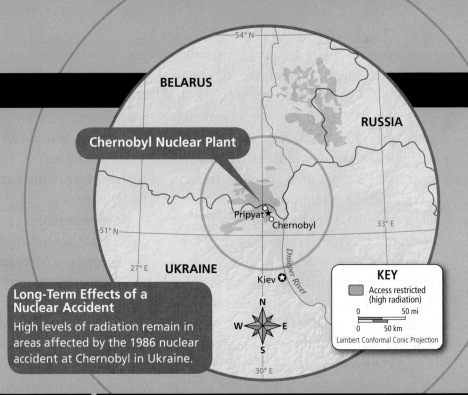

Chernobyl Nuclear Plant

BELARUS

RUSSIA

UKRAINE

Pripyat
Chernobyl

Kiev

Dnieper River

KEY

Access restricted (high radiation)

0   50 mi
0   50 km

Lambert Conformal Conic Projection

Long-Term Effects of a Nuclear Accident
High levels of radiation remain in areas affected by the 1986 nuclear accident at Chernobyl in Ukraine.

Coal Energy

 Pros

Large reserves of coal are readily available in parts of Eastern Europe.

Technology to reduce coal pollution has been developed.

 Cons

Mining coal is dangerous and damages the environment.

Burning coal creates pollution that causes acid rain and may contribute to climate change.

These smokestacks emit smoke from burning coal.

266

Nuclear Energy

Pros

One power station creates a lot of power.

Under normal conditions, nuclear energy produces less air pollution than coal.

Cons

A serious accident can spread radioactive pollution over a large area. People must move, and health problems continue for years.

Nuclear waste is very dangerous and must be stored for a long time.

This meter shows high radiation in the area near Chernobyl.

Natural Resources and the Environment

Physical geography influences industry as well as agriculture. The location of Eastern Europe's factories depends on the location of natural resources. For example, industry has grown in areas of Poland where coal is available. Both iron ore and coal are found in one region of Ukraine. As a result, steel is an important industrial product there.

Oil and gas are in very short supply in Eastern Europe. Many countries must import the oil and gas they need to develop industry. For example, countries such as Ukraine, Moldova, and Belarus have become dependent on oil and gas imports from Russia.

The need for energy to fuel industry has created serious environmental problems. In 1986, an explosion occurred at one of the towers at the Chernobyl nuclear power plant in Ukraine. Winds spread radioactive pollution over a huge area in Europe. Many people became sick and died from the radiation. Farmland was contaminated, so that the food grown there was no longer safe to eat. More than 20 years later, the area around the power plant was still contaminated. A reporter described one city in Ukraine that had been evacuated shortly after the accident:

> 66 A dead city. Homes, schoolrooms, playgrounds, and other places are crumbling as wild nature reclaims the land. Pripyat once had some 50,000 residents. Now they are gone, perhaps forever. Only the artifacts of their lives remain behind, rotting to dust. 99
>
> —Jeffrey Young, Voice of America, June 10, 2009

Other Eastern European countries have drawn on their coal reserves. Burning coal and other fossil fuels sends chemicals into the air that cause **acid rain,** that is, precipitation that is acidic. Forests have been damaged by acid rain and other pollution. In parts of Poland and the Czech Republic, forests have been destroyed by acid rain, and soils are too contaminated for crops. Worse, polluted water and soil have caused higher rates of birth defects, cancer, and other diseases.

Today, many countries have begun to address environmental problems. To join the European Union, countries must install equipment to make power plants cleaner. Now the problem of acid rain is much less serious in Eastern Europe, and the forests are starting to recover.

Reading Check What has caused damage to the forests of Eastern Europe?

In 1994, nearly 55 percent of the forest land in Poland was damaged by acid rain. Since then, however, much of the damage has been reversed.

267

Eastern Europe: Traditional Religions

Map Skills

1. **Regions** Identify one country that is mostly Catholic and one that is mostly Orthodox.

2. **Place** Where is Islam found? Why do you think Islam spread to those areas?

3. **Places to Know!**
Poland, Ukraine, Black Sea, Baltic Sea, Bosnia and Herzegovina

Active Atlas

KEY
- Roman Catholicism
- Eastern Orthodoxy
- Islam
- Protestant Christianity
- ✡ Large Jewish communities, 2008

0   300 mi
0   300 km
Lambert Conformal Conic Projection

Religious Diversity in Eastern Europe

dominant, adj., having the most power or influence

Eastern Europe is a region with a diverse religious history. Christianity is the <u>dominant</u> religion. In addition, many Jewish people and Muslims call this region home.

The first major division in the Christian religion occurred with the split between the Catholic Church and the Eastern Orthodox Church in the year 1054. The pope in Rome led the Catholic Church, while the patriarch of Constantinople was the leading figure for Eastern Orthodoxy. Constantinople is now Istanbul, in Turkey. From these centers, both churches sent missionaries into Eastern Europe. Eastern Orthodoxy became dominant in much of the Balkan Peninsula, as well as in Ukraine and Belarus.

With the Reformation in the 1500s, Protestant groups broke off from the Catholic Church. The Reformation began in Germany, and Protestantism spread to countries in northeastern Europe, including Estonia and Latvia. The Roman Catholic Church remained stronger in most of Central Europe, including Poland, the Czech Republic, Slovakia, and Hungary.

Christianity is not the only religion in Europe. Today, Muslims are the largest group of non-Christians. Many Muslims live in Bosnia, Albania, Kosovo, and the Crimean Peninsula in Ukraine. In fact, the southern part of Eastern Europe has long been a borderland where the Christian and Muslim worlds meet. This boundary has shifted over time as control of the region passed between Christian and Islamic states.

268

A Catholic bishop from the Czech Republic

A Muslim imam from Bosnia

An Eastern Orthodox priest from Ukraine

A Jewish rabbi from Poland

Judaism also has a long history in Eastern Europe. Europe was once home to most of the world's Jewish people. But during the Holocaust of the 1940s, two thirds of the Jews in Europe were murdered. Many others later left the region. Since then, there has been a revival of Jewish communities in some areas. In others, Jewish people continue to **emigrate,** or leave one area to move to another. About 30,000 Jews leave Ukraine each year for the United States, Israel, and other places.

The laws of the Soviet Union restricted religion. For many years, Eastern European governments discouraged religion.

Today, many people in Eastern Europe do not belong to any religion. More than half of the people in the Czech Republic and 40 percent of those in Estonia claim no religious faith.

Still, religious life has become more active since the end of communism. Now people have more opportunities to start and join religious organizations. With the fall of communist governments, people in this region have had the chance not only to return to traditional religious practices, but also to live more freely in other areas of their lives.

Reading Check Where are many Muslims found in this region?

myWorld Activity
Hailstorm

Section 1 Assessment

Key Terms

1. What causes acid rain?

2. Use the term *mechanized farming* to describe agriculture in Eastern Europe.

Key Ideas

3. Where are the major groups of mountains located in Eastern Europe?

4. How does the climate of Eastern Europe change from the north to the south?

5. What are some of the important resources of Eastern Europe?

Think Critically

6. **Identify Cause and Effect** Why are crops grown in the north different from those grown in the south of this region?

7. **Draw Inferences** What might influence whether people in a region practice one religion or another?

Essential Question

How can you measure success?

8. To join the European Union, countries must meet certain environmental standards. Do you think protecting the environment should be one measure of a country's success? Explain why or why not. Go to your Student Journal to record your answer.

Influence of Religion on Cultures of Eastern Europe

Key Ideas
- Christianity, Islam, and Judaism have all influenced the cultures of countries in Eastern Europe.
- The role of religion is different in each country in Eastern Europe.

Key Terms
- secular
- nationalism
- pilgrimage
- fasting

Religion has shaped the traditions and cultures of the countries in Eastern Europe. Most of the region is Christian, but different forms of Christianity dominate in different countries. In other areas, Islam is the majority religion. And, while Judaism has never been the dominant religion in any country in Europe, Jewish communities have also influenced Eastern European culture. The examples below show some ways that religion has shaped the countries of this region.

St. Olaf's Church is located in Tallinn, the capital of Estonia. The first Protestant sermons in Estonia were delivered at this church.

Protestants in Estonia

Protestant Christianity is the main faith in Estonia. Roman Catholicism was long ago the chief religion. But after the Protestant Reformation, the country turned to Lutheranism, a form of Protestant Christianity.

Lutheranism brought many changes to Estonian culture. Previously, religious services had been held in Latin, the language of the Catholic Church. The Bible was in Latin, too. But Lutherans performed church services in the Estonian language. They translated the Bible into Estonian. As a result, many Estonians learned to read and write. Estonian literature began to develop. Pastors and teachers wrote children's stories based on traditional folk tales. These stories helped spread cultural and religious values.

The Estonian people today are mostly **secular,** that is, they are not very religious. But Lutheran beliefs still lie at the heart of Estonian culture.

Reading Check What is the main religion in Estonia?

Catholicism in Poland

The Roman Catholic Church plays a major role in a number of Eastern Europe countries. It is especially important in Poland. Most Poles belong to the Catholic Church. Catholicism is integral to Polish life. It is a key part of Poland's national identity.

For centuries Poland was occupied by its powerful neighbors, Russia and Germany. The Catholic Church in Poland opposed foreign rule. It helped unify Poles and promote Polish **nationalism**. Nationalism is a strong devotion to one's nation. The role of the Church as defender of Polish culture continued even under communist rule. The communists tried to stamp out religion. But they could not end Polish loyalty to the Catholic Church.

Today Catholicism continues to influence daily life in Poland. Most Poles go to church. They take part in religious holidays and parades. They also make **pilgrimages,** or religious journeys, to Catholic shrines. In many ways, Catholic values still guide Polish culture.

Reading Check How did the Catholic Church help unify Poland?

Pope John Paul II, below, was the first Polish pope. He supported Polish efforts to shake off communist rule. ▼

Map of the Jewish quarter of Kraków, Poland.

The Jewish Heritage of Eastern Europe

During the 1900s, the Jewish population of Eastern Europe endured great suffering. Millions were killed during the Holocaust. When the region was under communist control, many of the remaining Jews left the region because of prejudice and restrictions on practicing their religion. The Jewish population remains small, but many people now celebrate the contribution of Jews to the culture of Eastern Europe.

A band performing at the Jewish Culture Festival in Kraków

271

Orthodox Religion in Serbia

Eastern Orthodox Christianity is the main religion in Serbia and many other Balkan states. Orthodox Christianity shares ancient roots with Catholicism. In the Middle Ages, however, disagreements over beliefs and practices led Christians to split into separate Catholic and Orthodox churches.

Instead of a single authority, the Orthodox church has nine patriarchs, or high-ranking bishops. The Serbian Orthodox Church has its own partriach.

In Serbia, Christian holidays are celebrated according to the Orthodox calendar. For example, Christmas is celebrated on January 7 rather than December 25. The Christmas feast includes roast pork and special bread with a coin baked inside. Whoever gets the piece with the coin is said to have good luck for the coming year. Orthodox families in Serbia also have a patron saint whom they honor on a particular day.

Serbia is home to other religions, too, including Islam. But many Serbians believe that Orthodox Christianity is a key part of their national identity.

Reading Check **What is the main religion in Serbia?**

An Orthodox priest leads a religious procession in Serbia.

272

Muslim Culture in Bosnia

Islam is the chief religion in Bosnia. Muslim influence there dates to the Ottoman conquest of the Balkans in the late 1300s. The Ottoman Turks ruled the region for 500 years. Many Bosnians converted to Islam during this time.

Bosnian Muslims tend to be less strict in their religious practices than Muslims in Southwest Asia. Some consume alcohol, pork, and other foods seen as forbidden by Islam. More women work outside the home. In addition, Bosnian Muslim women do not generally cover their heads, as do many Muslim women in Southwest Asia.

Still, Islam is important in the lives of many Bosnians. They read the Quran, the Muslim holy book. They celebrate the key Muslim holidays, known as the Eids. They also observe Ramadan, a month of **fasting**, or limits on eating. During this period, Muslims avoid eating between sunrise and sunset every day.

Bosnia has a long history of religious tolerance. The Ottomans allowed non-Muslims to practice their own faiths. Bosnia has suffered ethnic conflict in recent years. But most Bosnians continue to maintain a tradition of tolerance.

Reading Check **How did Islam enter Bosnia?**

Like all Muslims, these Bosnian men are expected to pray five times each day.

Assessment

1. How did Lutheranism promote literacy in Estonia?

2. How are religion and national identity linked in Poland and Serbia?

3. How is Bosnia different from many Muslim countries?

4. Why do you think Eastern Europe became home to many religions?

5. How does religion in Eastern Europe reflect divisions within Christianity?

Eastern Europe Today

Key Ideas

- Some countries of this region have had great success building new governments and economies.
- Other countries have broken apart or have failed to form strong, democratic governments.
- Ethnic conflict has troubled some countries.

Key Terms • entrepreneur • capital • cuisine • secede • ethnic cleansing

 **Visual Glossary**

 Reading Skill: Compare and Contrast Take notes using the graphic organizer in your journal.

This skyscraper was built in Warsaw while Poland was under communist rule. Today, it stands at the heart of Poland's financial district.

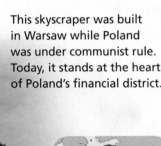

Each country in Eastern Europe has taken a different path since the end of communism. Some countries have built strong economies. Some countries are successful democracies. Other countries have broken apart, divided by ethnic conflict.

Poland and the Baltic Nations

Poland and the Baltic nations of Lithuania, Latvia, and Estonia have been among the most economically successful countries in Eastern Europe. They have also created democratic governments. Still, this change has not been easy. The people of these countries faced challenges and uncertainty after the fall of the Soviet Union.

Poland's Quick Reforms Poland was the first nation in Eastern Europe to make the transition to democracy at the end of the communist era. In the 1980s, a Polish labor union called Solidarity opposed the communist party, which controlled the government. After the fall of communism, the popular leader of Solidarity, Lech Walesa (lek vah WEH suh), was elected president.

Poland's leaders then took on the challenge of creating a market economy. In the communist system, the government controlled prices and planned production for the economy. In the early 1990s, the government stopped controlling prices, cut support for old state-owned factories, and encouraged new private businesses. After a slow start, the Polish economy recovered and grew throughout the 1990s.

Many citizens became **entrepreneurs**, people who organize and manage their own businesses. This Polish entrepreneur comments on starting a new business:

> 66 I truly never would have thought my idea of opening a high-end art supply store would work out when my country became independent from the Soviet Union. But because the arts are so important here in Poland, and the government helped me all along the way, it's been a very exciting time. 99
>
> —Entrepreneur from Bialystok, Poland

The Transition in the Baltic States The Baltic nations of Lithuania, Latvia, and Estonia were once republics of the Soviet Union. All three nations left behind the communist economic system and moved to a market economy during the 1990s. They now have democratic governments.

Estonia's economy has been especially successful. Industries in Estonia have **capital**, money or wealth used to invest in a business. Capital allows businesses to obtain more modern equipment to make high-quality goods. They can export these goods to other countries. Today, Estonia's main trading partners are Finland, Germany, and Sweden. Latvia and Lithuania have also experienced growth. Although Russia is still Lithuania's main trading partner, Lithuania now trades with Germany and Poland as well.

All of the Baltic nations as well as Poland have been accepted into the European Union. Membership in the EU has helped these nations to find new trading partners and improve their economies.

Cultural Life in Poland and the Baltic States Poland and the Baltic nations are well known for their rich cultural heritage. Poles have worked hard to preserve their history and culture. Many Polish cities have art and history museums. Poles also celebrate their cultural heritage at festivals. For example, music festivals highlighting the music of the famous Polish composer Frederic Chopin are popular.

In recent years, people in the Baltic States have revived traditions and religious practices that the Soviets banned. For example, Latvians now celebrate the summer festival of Jani (YAH nee) with traditional songs and dances.

Reading Check What is one reason Estonia has had economic success in recent years?

Each June, Latvians celebrate the Jani festival. Women and men—even cattle—wear wreaths of flowers or leaves.

275

Central Europe

The countries of Central Europe include the Czech Republic, Slovakia, Hungary, and Slovenia. Like other countries of Eastern Europe, these nations needed to build new governments and strengthen their economies.

Slovakia and the Czech Republic In 1989, communism gave way to democracy in Czechoslovakia. Soon, representatives of the Czechs and Slovaks disagreed about how to run the country. They divided peacefully in 1993 into two nations: the Czech Republic and Slovakia. Most people in the Czech Republic are of the Czech <u>ethnic</u> group. The majority of people in Slovakia are ethnic Slovaks.

Both nations have built democratic governments and experienced economic growth. The change to a market economy was easier for the Czech Republic. This nation had a strong economy with many different industries. It was able to modernize many of its factories fairly quickly.

Under Soviet control, Slovakia's economy was less diverse. Because building new industries takes time, economic growth was slow at first. However, Slovakia's government took action. In 1998, it lowered taxes for any foreign companies that created new businesses and jobs. Foreign investment increased rapidly, bringing more money to help improve Slovakia's economy. Both Slovakia and the Czech Republic have joined the European Union and expanded trade with the nations of Western Europe.

ethnic, *adj.,* defined by a shared nationality, identity, or heritage

Chart Skills

To figure out each nation's growth rate as a percentage, subtract the 1993 number from the 2008 number. Then, divide this number by the 1993 number. Which nation had a higher growth rate during this time period, Slovakia or the Czech Republic?

→ Data Discovery

Industrial Growth in the Former Czechoslovakia

Since they separated in 1993, both Slovakia and the Czech Republic have enjoyed economic growth. These figures represent economic output per person in each nation.

Czech Republic
1993
$12,774
2008
$26,000

Slovakia
1993
$8,371
2008
$21,900

SOURCE: *CIA World Factbook*

Workers in a Czech car factory ▼

276

Hungary Hungary has had some economic and political success since the fall of communism. It now has a stable, democratic government and a market economy. Debt has been a challenge, however. Hungary borrowed from other countries to modernize its economy. The resulting heavy debt has slowed economic growth. The government must deal with this problem for Hungary's economy to develop successfully.

Hungarians have also been returning to many traditions since the end of communism. Most Hungarians are Roman Catholic. Traditional Christian holidays are celebrated again as national holidays. The Hungarian language is different from other languages spoken in Europe. Hungarians also cook a unique **cuisine**, that is, style of food. Many Hungarian dishes use

the spice paprika, which is made from bell or chili peppers. Hungarians take great pride in their distinct cultural heritage.

Slovenia In 1918, Slovenia became part of the new country of Yugoslavia. There was tension between the different republics of Yugoslavia. Many Slovenians came to believe that their homeland would be better off if they split from Yugoslavia. The leaders of Slovenia had managed their economy more successfully than some other republics in Yugoslavia.

In 1990, fully 90 percent of Slovenia's citizens voted for independence. Slovenia fought the short Ten-Day War to separate from the rest of Yugoslavia. Slovenia then began to build a democratic government and a free market economy. Despite many challenges, Slovenia has improved its economy. It became the first Balkan country to join the EU and the North Atlantic Treaty Organization (NATO) in 2004.

Reading Check How has Hungary changed since the end of communism?

my **World** IN NUMBERS

If there were **100** people in the world, about **34** would live in a democracy.

The Danube River flows through Budapest, the capital of Hungary. Budapest is a major center of business, transportation, and culture. ▼

Culture Close-Up

my worldgeography.com Culture Close-Up

277

The Balkan Nations

All the former communist nations of the Balkan Peninsula have gone through major political changes since 1990. At times, these changes involved warfare and the breakup of nations along ethnic or religious lines. Conflicts and political problems have disrupted the economies of the region.

Yugoslavia Splits After World War I, the country of Yugoslavia was created from six different territories—Serbia, Croatia, Slovenia, Macedonia, Montenegro, and Bosnia (formally known as Bosnia and Herzegovina). Each of these territories formed a republic within Yugoslavia. In each republic, a different ethnic group formed the majority.

After World War II, Yugoslavia's strong leader, Josip Broz Tito, kept the country united. But after Tito died in 1980, the union began to weaken.

Serbia was the largest republic and dominated the national government. Other republics resented Serbia's power. They began to **secede**, or break away, from the union. In 1991, Slovenia and Croatia declared independence. Macedonia broke away later that year, followed by Bosnia a year later.

The new countries combined different ethnic groups. For example, most people in Croatia are Croats, but many Serbs also live there. Conflicts broke out among the different ethnic groups. Some groups tried to gain complete control of an area by attacking and forcing out the other ethnic groups. This policy is called **ethnic cleansing**. Serbs in some areas of Bosnia, for example, killed Muslims or forced them from their homes. Serbs then took control of those areas. Ethnic cleansing is a violation of international law.

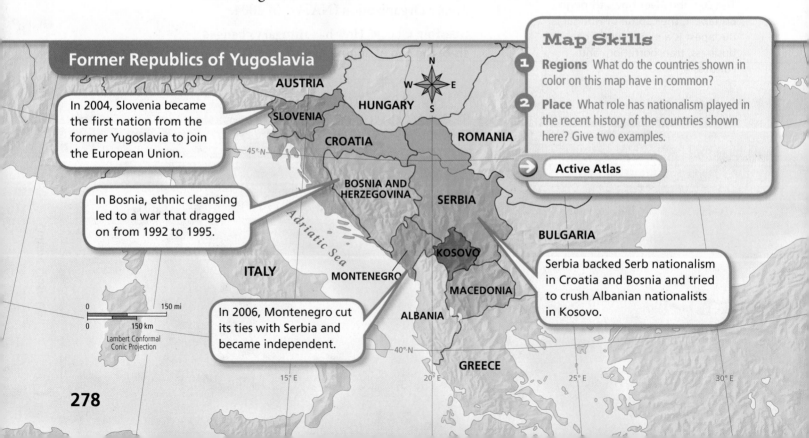

Former Republics of Yugoslavia

In 2004, Slovenia became the first nation from the former Yugoslavia to join the European Union.

In Bosnia, ethnic cleansing led to a war that dragged on from 1992 to 1995.

In 2006, Montenegro cut its ties with Serbia and became independent.

Serbia backed Serb nationalism in Croatia and Bosnia and tried to crush Albanian nationalists in Kosovo.

0   150 mi
0   150 km
Lambert Conformal Conic Projection

Map Skills

1. **Regions** What do the countries shown in color on this map have in common?

2. **Place** What role has nationalism played in the recent history of the countries shown here? Give two examples.

Active Atlas

278

Ethnic Conflict Continues As conflicts arose in the 1990s, the United Nations, the United States, and other European countries worked to negotiate peace between warring groups. The United Nations and NATO sent troops to enforce peace treaties. These efforts have brought an end to large-scale warfare in the region. Still, ethnic violence continues in some areas.

These conflicts disrupted economies in the region. Unstable conditions made trade difficult. In addition, many people were forced from their homes and had to start new lives in different countries.

Some governments in this region are trying to make reforms in order to join the European Union. In general, the governments of the former Yugoslavia have been slow to shift from government control to private enterprise. The standard of living in these countries is low compared to that of many other nations of Eastern Europe.

Other Balkan Nations Yugoslavia was not the only communist nation on the Balkan Peninsula. Romania, Albania, and Bulgaria also became communist after World War II. Unlike Yugoslavia, Romania and Bulgaria were dominated by the Soviet Union. When communism ended in the late 1980s, these countries also shifted to market economies.

Political corruption was a problem in all three countries. Bulgaria and Romania have been accepted as members of the European Union after dealing with many political and economic problems. Albania, by contrast, has not been accepted into the European Union. This country remains poorer and less developed. Still, Albanians continue to work to improve their economy and control crime. Albania also hopes to be accepted into the European Union.

Reading Check Why did some republics secede from Yugoslavia?

Albania was the last country in Eastern Europe to give up communism. It is still one of the poorest nations in Europe.

Ukraine, Belarus, and Moldova

Ukraine, Moldova, and Belarus all gained independence from the Soviet Union in 1991. Since then, all have changed in different ways. Ukraine is a democracy. Belarus is the only example of a dictatorship in Europe today. Moldova is a small country with a very weak government that cannot control all of its territory or provide many basic services.

Ukraine has become a working democracy. Traveling ballot boxes allow people in remote villages, like this woman, to vote in their own homes.

potential, *n.,* ability, possibility

Ukraine Ukraine is the second-largest country in Europe in land area and the sixth largest in population. Since gaining independence, Ukraine has created a democratic system of government. Freedom of the press has increased since independence. Ukraine still faces serious political problems such as corruption. However, Ukraine's democracy has also survived some serious conflicts. For example, disputes over the results of the 2004 presidential elections led to widespread protests, but the different parties worked out a peaceful resolution.

Still, Ukraine's economy has not grown rapidly. Corruption and complicated business laws have discouraged foreign companies from investing. Russia is still the largest trading partner for Ukraine.

In addition, efforts to expand agriculture have been difficult. The Soviets had set up collective farms, where land and equipment were shared among many farmers. The Ukrainian government divided this land among the families who lived on each farm. However, small farms without advanced equipment are not profitable. Many people, like Serhiy, are leaving rural areas because they cannot make a living on their small family farm. Still, Ukraine has rich soil. Many believe that this country has the <u>potential</u> to improve its agriculture and achieve more economic success.

Belarus Since 1994, Belarus has been ruled by President Lukashenko. The country's constitution lists many freedoms. In reality, the government limits liberties such as freedom of the press and freedom of religion. People who have opposed Lukashenko have been punished.

Belarus must import many of the raw materials and energy resources that it needs from other countries. The country's main trading partner has been Russia. These close ties create another risk. When Russia's economy has difficulties, the economy of Belarus also suffers. Economic growth has been slow. Almost half of the population lives in poverty.

Moldova Moldova is a tiny country with ties to its neighbor Romania and also to Russia. Many of its people speak Romanian, but there are also large numbers of Ukrainians and Russians.

280

This protest sign compares President Alexander Lukashenko of Belarus to two notorious dictators of the past: Joseph Stalin of the Soviet Union and Adolf Hitler of Nazi Germany.

About 80 percent of the people of Moldova live below the poverty line. Many poor peasants in rural villages, like this boy, have barely enough to survive.

Moldova continues to face political turmoil, economic challenges, and corruption.

Most of the Russians and Ukrainians live in a region called Transdniestria. This region declared its independence in 1990. Moldova fought a war to keep the region from seceding. The leaders of Transdniestria and Moldova agreed to stop fighting, but they could not find a solution. Moldova still claims the territory, but it does not control the area. Transdniestria still claims independence. Other governments have accused Transdniestria of being a center for smuggling, or illegal trade.

Moldova has also had slow economic growth. Thousands of people have left the country to look for jobs in Romania. Many Moldovans must live on the money that their relatives abroad send back to them. Like Belarus, Moldova is one of the poorest countries in Europe. The government faces many serious political and economic challenges.

Reading Check What is one challenge faced by Moldova?

myWorld Activity
Press Conference

Section 2 Assessment

Essential Question
How can you measure success?

Key Terms

1. Use the terms *secede* and *ethnic cleansing* to describe the breakup of Yugoslavia.

2. What is capital?

Key Ideas

3. What political and economic changes have taken place in Poland and the Baltic nations since the end of communism?

4. What is one reason that conflict broke out in the Balkans in the 1990s?

5. Which country is more democratic, Ukraine or Belarus? Explain your answer.

Think Critically

6. **Identify Cause and Effect** How could joining the European Union improve a country's economy?

7. **Draw Inferences** Why were many Polish citizens able to become entrepreneurs in the 1990s?

8. Give an example of one country in Eastern Europe that has been successful in recent years. Why do you think this country has been successful? Go to your Student Journal to record your answer.

Ethnic Conflict in Bosnia

Key Idea
- Although Bosnia has long been home to diverse ethnic groups, some Serbians in the 1990s attacked Bosnian Muslims, hoping to establish a purely Serbian state.

Bosnian Muslims, Serbs, and Croats had lived in peace for years. But when Bosnia declared independence in 1992, many Bosnian Serbs felt threatened. They did not want to live in a Muslim-led country. In fact, some Serbs had long resented their Muslim neighbors. This distrust went back to Muslim Turks' conquest of Serbia in the late 1300s. Determined to create a unified Serbian nation, Bosnian Serbs went to war. In the following sources, the former president of Serbia calls for ethnic unity, and a Bosnian Muslim soldier explains his views on Bosnia and why he chose to fight.

▲ This newspaper was found in the streets of war-torn Bosnia.

Slobodan Milosevic (mee LOH sheh vich), leader of Serbia, 1989–1997, and leader of Yugoslavia, 1997–2000 ▼

Stop at each circled letter on the right to think about the text. Then answer the question with the same letter on the left.

Ⓐ Identify Main Ideas What "greatest evil" is Milosevic talking about?

Ⓑ Draw Inferences Who might Milosevic be referring to here as "those who would take away our dignity"?

Ⓒ Draw Conclusions What do you think Milosevic wanted Serbs to do?

sap, *v.,* to drain, reduce

coalition, *n.,* alliance, groups working together

For a Unified Serbian People

66 Serbia and the Serbian people are faced with one of the
Ⓐ greatest evils of their history: the challenge of disunity and internal conflict. This evil, which has more than once caused so much damage and claimed so many victims, more than once <u>sapped</u> our strength, has always come hand in hand with
Ⓑ those who would take away our dignity. . . . All who love Serbia
Ⓒ dare not ignore this fact, especially at a time when we are confronted by the . . . forces in the anti-Serbian <u>coalition</u> which threaten the people's rights and freedoms. 99

Slobodan Milosevic, quoted in "The Fall of Yugoslavia"

Stop at each circled letter on the right to think about the text. Then answer the question with the same letter on the left.

(D) Identify Evidence Why did Tica (TEE tsuh) think there was a "terrible misunderstanding"?

(E) Summarize Why did Tica decide to fight?

(F) Compare and Contrast How does Tica compare Serbian plans for Bosnia with life in the United States?

shell, *v.,* to bomb, fire upon

canton, *n.,* small territory

For a Diverse Bosnia

66 Bosnia is a mixed country. There has always been some kind of tolerance, in this town anyway. In the first days of this war, I thought there was some **(D)** terrible misunderstanding. When they started <u>shelling</u> my city, I understood only one thing: someone wants to destroy my life, take my job, kill my parents, wreck my apartment. When I started **(E)** fighting, it was just to defend my family. . . . My country is Bosnia, with all three peoples in it. I call myself a Bosnian, and I know what that means. But the Serbs and Croats want ethnic <u>cantons</u>, racially pure. Who . . . wants to live in an ethnic canton? **(F)** I don't. It would be like having California for the whites and Chicago for the blacks, instead of America. It's completely mad. 99

Emir Tica, quoted in *Seasons in Hell: Understanding Bosnia's War*

During the ethnic conflict in Bosnia, heavy shelling left many people homeless. ▼

Analyze the Documents

1. **Compare Viewpoints** How are the views of Milosevic and Tica in direct conflict?
2. **Writing Task** Nationalism can be a positive or negative force. Which role did it play in Bosnia? Write a paragraph explaining your thinking.

283

Chapter Assessment

Key Terms and Ideas

1. **Recall** Why is **mechanized farming** common on the North European Plain?

2. **Compare and Contrast** Why can the climate differ on different sides of a mountain range?

3. **Explain** How have resources influenced industry in Eastern Europe?

4. **Recall** What are the main traditional religions in Eastern Europe?

5. **Explain** How has Poland's economy been successful since the breakup of the Soviet Union?

6. **Compare and Contrast** Did the Czech Republic or Slovakia have faster economic growth after the breakup of the Soviet Union and the end of communism? Why?

7. **Explain** Why did many Balkan states **secede** from Yugoslavia?

Think Critically

8. **Make Inferences** Why might agriculture on the Hungarian Plain and the North European Plain be similar? Use the maps in this section to answer the question.

9. **Draw Conclusions** What long-term effect might the end of communist policies toward religion have on religious practices in Eastern Europe?

10. **Solve Problems** What action did the government of Slovakia take to improve its economy?

11. **Core Concepts: People's Impact on the Environment** What is one economic activity that has resulted in damage to the environment in this region?

Places to Know

For each place, write the letter from the map that shows its location.

12. **Bosnia and Herzegovina**

13. **Poland**

14. **Ukraine**

15. **Balkan Mountains**

16. **Baltic Sea**

17. **Black Sea**

18. **Estimate** Using the scale bar, estimate the distance from the Black Sea to the Baltic Sea.

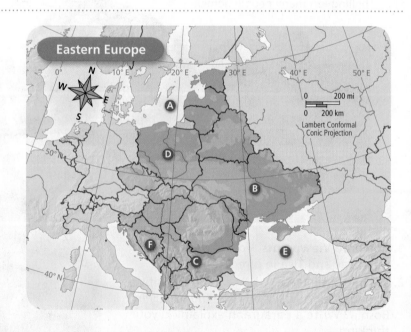

284

Essential Question
myWorld Chapter Activity

Open for Business You work at a business that is hoping to open a new branch in Eastern Europe. Evaluate information about different countries, and choose the country that would offer the best location for your business.

21st Century Learning
Evaluating Web Sites

Search for three different Web sites that provide information on nuclear energy. What benefits and drawbacks does each site give for nuclear energy? Find the name of the organization that created each site. Can you find the goals of this organization? Do the goals of the organization influence the information that is presented on the site?

Document-Based Questions

Success Tracker™
Online at myworldgeography.com

Use your knowledge of Eastern Europe and Documents A and B to answer Questions 1–3 below.

Document A

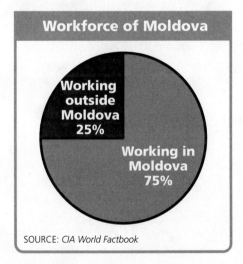

Workforce of Moldova

Working outside Moldova 25%

Working in Moldova 75%

SOURCE: *CIA World Factbook*

1. According to the graph, what percentage of Moldovan workers had jobs in other countries?

A 15 percent

B 20 percent

C 25 percent

D 30 percent

Document B

" Many specialists, doctors, go to work abroad. They go where they are paid better, but for the country, this is not a solution."

—Grigore, a student in Moldova

2. According to Document B, why do some people go abroad to work?

A They do not like Moldova's government.

B They cannot find jobs in Moldova.

C They think the weather in Moldova is too cold.

D They earn more money if they work abroad.

3. **Writing Task** What do you think the speaker in Document B meant when he said "for the country, this is not a solution"? Write a paragraph explaining both the benefits and drawbacks to Moldova of so many people leaving the country to find jobs.

my worldgeography.com Self-Test

Chapter 5

Russia

Essential Question

What should governments do?

KEY
- National border
- ★ Capital city
- ○ Other city

0 — 500 mi
0 — 500 km
Lambert Azimuthal Equal-Area Projection

Where in the World Is Russia?

Washington, D.C., to Moscow: 4,860 miles

my Story

Boris's Bigspin

In this section, you'll read about Boris, a young skateboarder living in Moscow. What does Boris's story tell you about life in Russia today?

? Explore the Essential Question
- at **my worldgeography.com**
- using the **myWorld Chapter Activity**
- with the **Student Journal**

Story by Dmitry Saltykovskiy for myWorld Online

It's a sunny day in Moscow, and people hurry past a huge monument to the German philosopher Karl Marx. The 200-ton block of stone bears the inscription "Workers of the world, unite," a quote from Marx that became famous among communist workers. When the statue was unveiled in 1961, Russia was a communist nation, and Marx was an honored figure. Today, Russia is a very different place, and the monument to Marx is better known as a fun place for skateboarders to try tricks like the ollie or the bigspin.

Boris, a 15-year-old Russian skateboarder, loves to try jumps off of the step at the base of the monument. When the Soviet Union collapsed in 1991, Boris had not yet been born. He has never lived under communism, but he still has clear memories of hard times in Russia.

"I was born in troubled times," Boris says. "After the Soviet Union fell, people were trying to make money. It was a dangerous period with lots of crime and fighting between businesses. My father disappeared around that time. I was just four years old. He owned his own business, and he was kidnapped. We never saw him again. I am sad that I can't really remember what he looked like now."

my worldgeography.com On Assignment

287

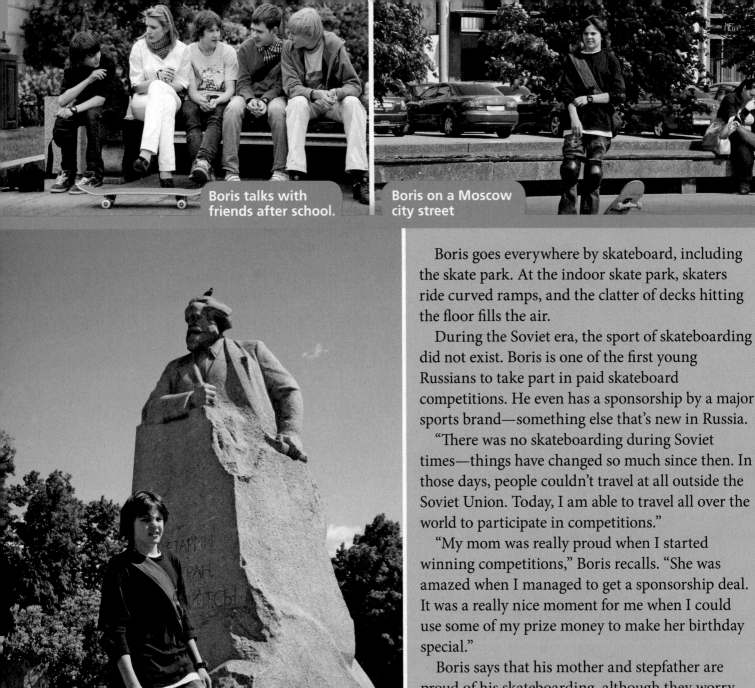

Boris talks with friends after school.

Boris on a Moscow city street

Boris in front of a monument to Karl Marx

Boris goes everywhere by skateboard, including the skate park. At the indoor skate park, skaters ride curved ramps, and the clatter of decks hitting the floor fills the air.

During the Soviet era, the sport of skateboarding did not exist. Boris is one of the first young Russians to take part in paid skateboard competitions. He even has a sponsorship by a major sports brand—something else that's new in Russia.

"There was no skateboarding during Soviet times—things have changed so much since then. In those days, people couldn't travel at all outside the Soviet Union. Today, I am able to travel all over the world to participate in competitions."

"My mom was really proud when I started winning competitions," Boris recalls. "She was amazed when I managed to get a sponsorship deal. It was a really nice moment for me when I could use some of my prize money to make her birthday special."

Boris says that his mother and stepfather are proud of his skateboarding, although they worry about him being injured. They also hope that he will consider a professional career someday. "Moscow is growing so quickly that I've become interested in real estate!" Boris laughs.

Boris at the skate park in Moscow

Boris shoots basketball at the park.

Working on the computer at home

Following the 2008 Russian invasion of Georgia, Boris decided to change his last name. Georgia had once been part of the Soviet Union, but it declared its independence in 1991. Since then, relations have been tense between Russia and Georgia.

"My father was half Georgian, and he had a very un-Russian sounding last name. With all the problems between our two countries, my mom decided that we should change our name. I was really sad because I felt like I was giving away a piece of my father, but really we had no choice. Russians have become quite anti-Georgian and my name marked me as different."

The tension between Russia and Georgia also means that Boris has been unable to visit family in Georgia. "I used to go there every summer. It was really nice to get out of Moscow when the weather was hot. Now there are no airplane flights."

The wheels of Boris's deck leave the ground, and then he rolls off to the park for a game of basketball. For Boris, his skateboard is not only the best way to get around Moscow, but also a ticket to a promising future in the new Russia.

Meet the Journalist

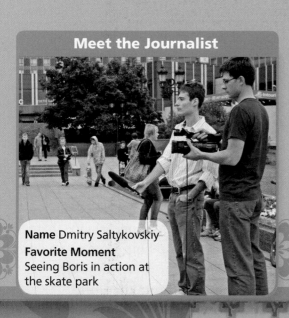

Name Dmitry Saltykovskiy
Favorite Moment Seeing Boris in action at the skate park

myStory Online

Skateboard along with Boris as he shows you life in his city.

my worldgeography.com myStory Online

289

Chapter Atlas

Key Ideas

- Russia is the world's largest country in area, reaching from Europe to the eastern edge of Asia.
- Russia has rich mineral, energy, and other resources, located mostly in Siberia.
- Most of Russia has a low population density.

Key Terms • Siberia • Ural Mountains • Lake Baikal • steppes • Kamchatka Peninsula • permafrost

 **Visual Glossary**

Reading Skill: Label an Outline Map Take notes using the outline map in your journal.

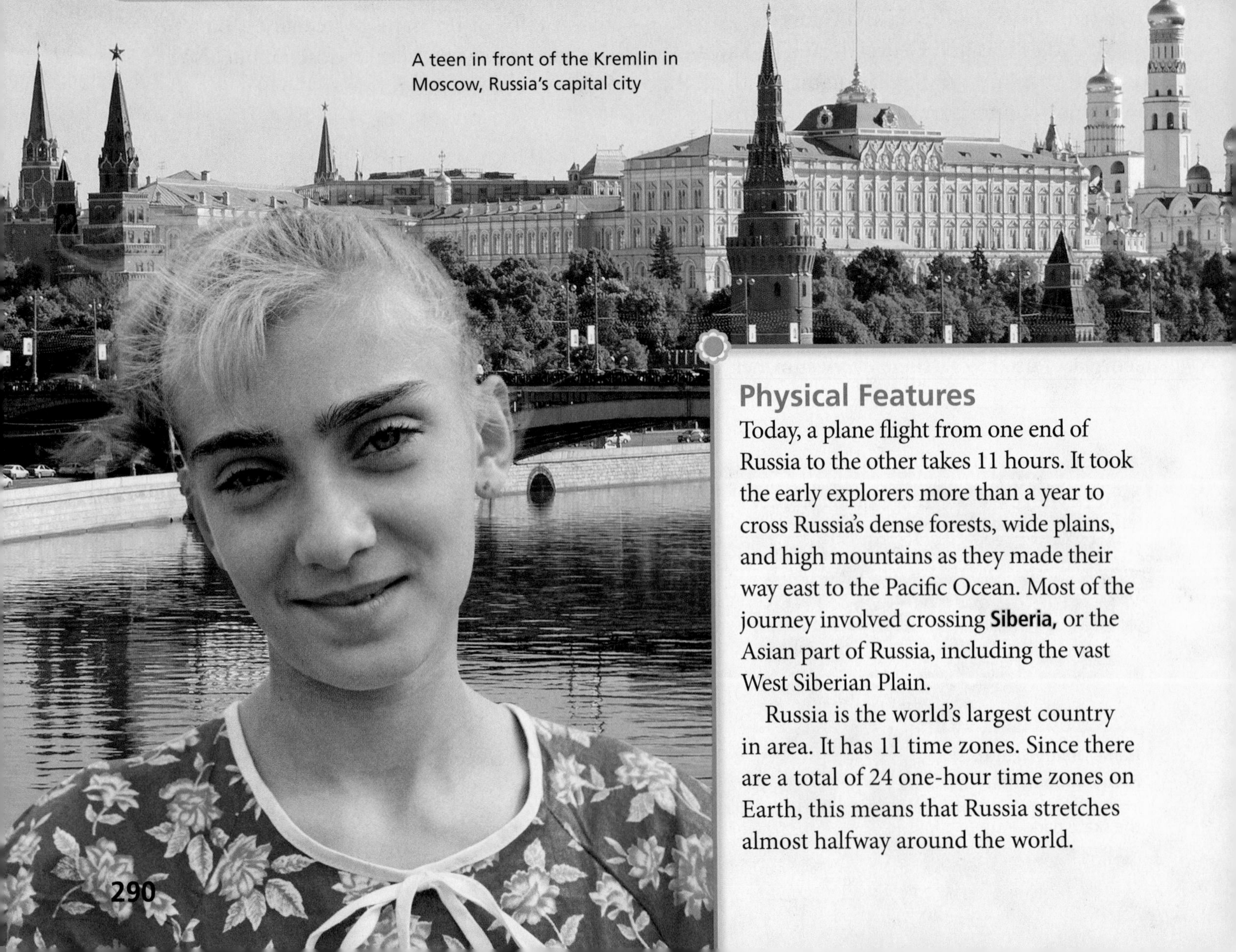

A teen in front of the Kremlin in Moscow, Russia's capital city

Physical Features

Today, a plane flight from one end of Russia to the other takes 11 hours. It took the early explorers more than a year to cross Russia's dense forests, wide plains, and high mountains as they made their way east to the Pacific Ocean. Most of the journey involved crossing **Siberia,** or the Asian part of Russia, including the vast West Siberian Plain.

Russia is the world's largest country in area. It has 11 time zones. Since there are a total of 24 one-hour time zones on Earth, this means that Russia stretches almost halfway around the world.

Russia: Physical

KEY
Elevation

Feet	Meters
6,000	1,829
3,000	914
1,000	305
500	152
Sea level	Sea level

0   600 mi
0   600 km
Lambert Conformal Conic Projection

Map Skills

1 **Place** In which mountain range is Mount Elbrus?

2 **Region** Which ocean lies north of Russia?

3 **Places to Know!**
Label the following places on the outline map in your Student Journal: Siberia, Kamchatka Peninsula, Ural Mountains, Kuril Islands, Lake Baikal.

Active Atlas

Russia spreads across two continents, Europe and Asia. The dividing line runs along the low peaks of the **Ural Mountains**, a range that separates European Russia from Asian Russia. European Russia is located east of Latvia, Lithuania, Estonia, Belarus, and Ukraine. Asian Russia lies immediately north of China, Mongolia, and Kazakhstan.

A Vast Land

Russia has many different kinds of landforms and waterways. The Russian Plain covers much of European Russia.

It stretches east to the Ural Mountains. South of the Russian Plain are the Caucasus Mountains. These mountains run east-west between the Caspian Sea and the Black Sea. They form the southern border between European Russia and Asia.

East of the Urals is the broad West Siberian Plain. Farther east are central and eastern Siberia. This huge area consists of rugged plateaus framed by high mountains on the east and south.

291

spectacular, *adj.,* striking or excellent

Many of these <u>spectacular</u> mountains are volcanic in origin. Some are covered by glaciers year-round.

European Russia's longest river, the Volga, flows into the Caspian Sea. This river is famous in the songs and stories of the Russian people. Russia's European rivers also include the Don, which flows into the Black Sea, and the Dvina, which flows north to an arm of the Arctic Ocean.

In Siberia, there are many other large rivers that flow north to the Arctic Ocean. These include Russia's longest, the Yenisey, as well as the Ob and Lena. Another important Siberian river is called the Ankara. Far to the east is the mighty Amur River, which forms the border between Russia and China.

Despite its many rivers, canals, and long coastlines, Russia lacks many good harbors and ports. In European Russia, usable ports include St. Petersburg, Kaliningrad, Novorossiysk, and Sochi. In addition, there are ports in Murmansk in the far north on the Arctic Ocean and Vladivostok on the Pacific coast.

Russia: Climate

KEY
- Tundra
- Subarctic
- Continental cool summer
- Continental warm summer
- Humid subtropical
- Semiarid

0 — 600 mi
0 — 600 km
Lambert Conformal Conic Projection

Semiarid

Continental, cool summer

Subarctic

Map Skills

1. **Location** Along which body of water does Russia's southernmost semiarid region lie?

2. **Region** How much of Russia's land is subarctic?

→ Active Atlas

Russia, however, does have many large lakes and seas. Perhaps the most famous is **Lake Baikal** in the heart of Siberia. More than one mile deep, Lake Baikal holds about 20 percent of Earth's fresh water—more than all of the North American Great Lakes combined. Baikal is also home to plants and animals found nowhere else. Due to the threat of pollution from factories located along its shores, Lake Baikal was the birthplace of Russia's environmental movement.

Reading Check **Which landform separates European Russia from Asian Russia?**

Climate and Vegetation

Vast stretches of Russian lands have a subarctic climate because they lie near the Arctic Circle. North of this area is the tundra climate region, a cold, dry, treeless area covered in snow for most of the year. European Russia in the southwest has a continental climate. In cities such as Moscow and St. Petersburg, people experience long, cold winters and warm summers. Parts of southern Russia have a semiarid, or moderately dry, climate.

Russia's natural vegetation is closely tied to its climate. In the cool continental climate north of Moscow, thick coniferous forests grow. South of Moscow are temperate forests. To the east, vast areas of grasslands called **steppes** cover the land. Here, mild, moist summers and rich soils make good farmland.

In Siberia, weather and climate are more extreme than in European Russia. Here, winters are long and cold. Cold, dry conditions in parts of Siberia account for a type of low-lying vegetation called tundra. Tundra covers about one tenth of Russia and stretches all the way from the Finnish border east to the **Kamchatka Peninsula.** This peninsula in the Russian Far East is famous for its 160 volcanoes, 29 of which are active.

Near Yakutsk, Siberia, a family hauls water that they took from a hole in the ice on a local lake.

South of the tundra is the Russian taiga, a land of dense coniferous forests. The Russian taiga covers more than four million square miles (10 million square kilometers). One of the many challenges for human settlement in northern Russia is **permafrost.** This is permanently frozen soil that often lies beneath the tundra and the taiga. It makes construction of roads, railroads, and housing difficult.

Vegetation in Russia's Far East region differs from that of the rest of the country. Because this area is close to the ocean and is located farther to the south, it is warmer and has vegetation similar to the nearby Koreas. Its animals include the Amur tiger, the world's largest cat. The eastern edge of Russia features the Kuril Islands and the Kamchatka Peninsula.

myWorld Activity
Roam Across Russia

Reading Check Where in Russia are there active volcanoes?

Russia's Resources

Russia has rich mineral and energy resources, especially in Siberia. Its resources include timber, fish, and hydroelectric power. About one third of all of Earth's coal is located in Siberia. In spite of extremes of climate and the country's massive size, vast reserves of oil and gas in West Siberia have made Russia wealthy in recent years.

Russia also has metal ores such as iron, gold, cobalt, nickel, and platinum ore. It sells these valuable minerals to many different buyers around the world for industrial use.

It can be difficult to mine Russia's rich natural resources because they are so hard to reach. Long distances and harsh climates separate resources from processing plants and markets.

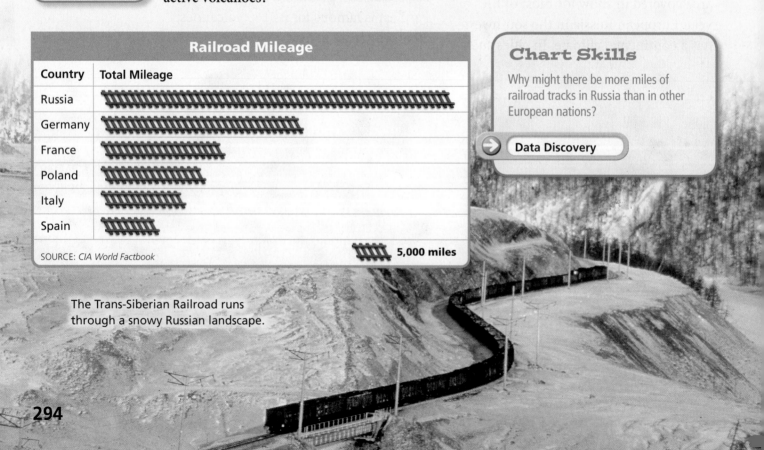

Railroad Mileage	
Country	Total Mileage
Russia	
Germany	
France	
Poland	
Italy	
Spain	

SOURCE: *CIA World Factbook*

5,000 miles

Chart Skills

Why might there be more miles of railroad tracks in Russia than in other European nations?

Data Discovery

The Trans-Siberian Railroad runs through a snowy Russian landscape.

294

This makes it important for Russia to build and <u>maintain</u> an extensive transportation system to move products to markets. The poor quality of roads can make transport difficult. Truck drivers often find it easier to drive on frozen rivers and lakes than on Russian roads.

Many of Russia's great rivers are navigable, or passable, for only a few months of the year because they are usually blocked by ice. Underground pipelines generally transport Russia's huge reserves of oil and natural gas. An extensive railroad network moves goods to consumers.

Large-scale economic development in Siberia began only after the Trans-Siberian Railroad was completed in 1905. This famous railroad connects the city of Moscow in the west with Vladivostok on the Pacific. It also connects with rail lines running to Mongolia and China. It was built to help Russians settle the open lands of Siberia, to develop industrial centers, and to transport troops to the Pacific to protect Russia against threats of invasion by Japan and China.

Reading Check Name two challenges Russia faces in developing its economy.

maintain, *v.,* to keep in good condition

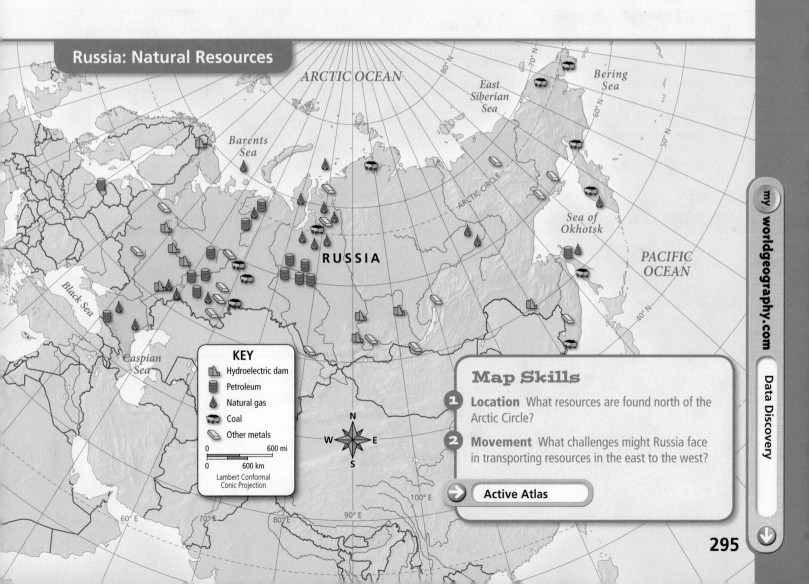

Russia: Natural Resources

KEY
- Hydroelectric dam
- Petroleum
- Natural gas
- Coal
- Other metals

0 — 600 mi
0 — 600 km
Lambert Conformal Conic Projection

Map Skills

1 **Location** What resources are found north of the Arctic Circle?

2 **Movement** What challenges might Russia face in transporting resources in the east to the west?

Active Atlas

my **worldgeography.com** Data Discovery

295

The People of Russia

Russia has a population of about 140 million people. Most live in the European part of the country. Russia's most densely settled areas also have the best climates and soils for agriculture. In contrast, the huge landmass of Siberia is sparsely populated, with around 20 people per square mile.

The largest cities are also located in the west, in European Russia. Moscow, the capital, is the largest metropolitan area in Russia, with more than 10 million people.

St. Petersburg, Russia's second largest city, is located on the Baltic Sea. It was called Leningrad during the Soviet era. St. Petersburg was founded by Russia's tsar, or emperor, Peter the Great, to rival the capitals of Europe.

Russia's huge population consists of many diverse ethnic groups with many languages and customs. The first Russians were East Slavs, who migrated into the area from east-central Europe. Today, about 80 percent of the population are Russian-speaking Slavs.

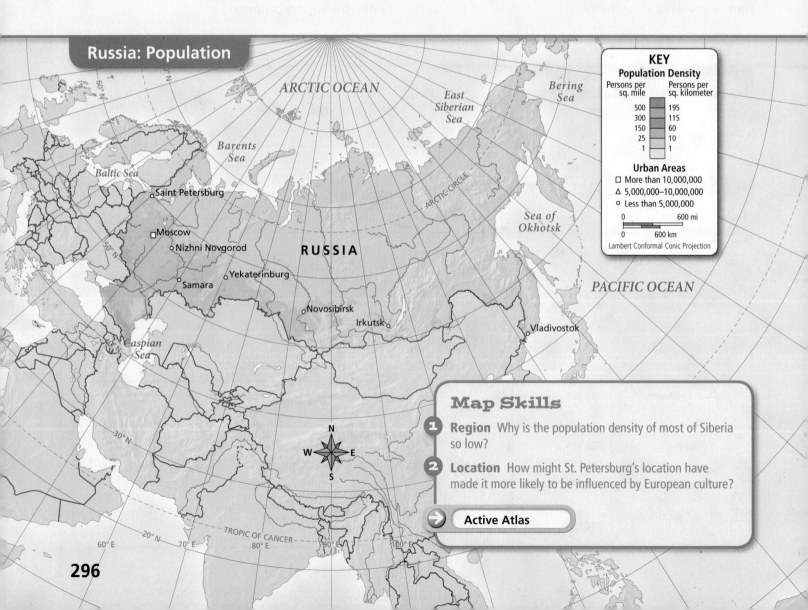

Russia: Population

KEY

Population Density

Persons per sq. mile	Persons per sq. kilometer
500	195
300	115
150	60
25	10
1	1

Urban Areas
- □ More than 10,000,000
- △ 5,000,000–10,000,000
- ○ Less than 5,000,000

Lambert Conformal Conic Projection

Map Skills

1. **Region** Why is the population density of most of Siberia so low?

2. **Location** How might St. Petersburg's location have made it more likely to be influenced by European culture?

Active Atlas

296

In Moscow, Boris (right) joins his friends to talk about sports and school. Boris participates in skateboarding competitions all over the world.

Language Lesson

This family lives in a village near Siberia's Lake Baikal. They belong to the minority Buryat nationality but also speak Russian.

Traditionally, the Slavic people who form most of the population were Russian Orthodox Christians. However, the communist rulers of the Soviet Union pursued a policy of discouraging religion. Today, after the collapse of the Soviet Union, more and more Russians attend Orthodox churches. Religious observance has also increased for Russia's many Muslims, Protestants, Jews, and Buddhists.

Along with Slavic Russians, there are at least 100 other ethnic and nationality groups in Russia. Each has a distinctive culture, language, and religion. Since Russian-speaking Slavs have dominated the nation for such a long time, many of these minority groups struggle to maintain their unique identities.

pursue, *v.,* to follow

Reading Check Who were the first Russians?

Section 1 Assessment

Essential Question

What should governments do?

Key Terms

1. Use each of the following key terms in a complete sentence: Siberia, Ural Mountains, Lake Baikal, steppes, Kamchatka Peninsula, permafrost

Key Ideas

2. What challenges does climate present for human settlement in Russia?

3. Where are most of Russia's mineral resources found?

4. Why does the Far East region of Russia have a milder climate than most of the rest of the country?

Think Critically

5. **Identify Evidence** What facts could you use to explain why Siberia has a low population density?

6. **Solve Problems** What might minority groups do to preserve their identity in a country whose population is mostly ethnic Russian?

7. Look at the railroad mileage chart in this section. The Russian government paid the cost of building the Trans-Siberian Railroad. Why might governments invest in transportation systems? Go to your Student Journal to record your answer.

History of Russia

Key Ideas

- Following centuries of invasion, Russia became an empire under the tsars.

- The Russian Revolution introduced communism and led to the establishment of the Soviet Union.

- Communism's flaws caused the Soviet Union to collapse, leading to its breakup into Russia and other republics.

Key Terms • tsar • Kremlin • serf • Bolsheviks • soviet • collectivization

 **Visual Glossary**

Reading Skill: Cause and Effect Take notes using the graphic organizer in your journal.

Russia's history spans many centuries. It is a rich story of invaders, ruthless leaders, and dramatic change that continues today.

Russia Emerges

Modern Russians are descended from East Slavs who migrated from Poland and Ukraine into western Russia in the 400s and 500s. They encountered invading Goths from Germany, along with Huns, Avars, Magyars, and Khazars from Asia.

The East Slavs The East Slavs were energetic traders. They founded trading posts along rivers that became the cities of Kiev and Novgorod. By the 800s, Scandinavian raiders and merchants, called Vikings, dominated Novgorod, Kiev, and other trading centers. They soon merged with the Slavic population.

Early Russia The Scythians, who arrived on the steppes before the East Slavs, were skilled goldsmiths. ▼

Kievan Rus Period The Viking prince Rurik and his allies invade Kiev in this medieval Russian drawing. ▶

East Slav

| 200 | 300 | 400 | 500 | 600 | 700 | 800 |

The role of Vikings in Russian history remains uncertain. Russia's *Primary Chronicle* claims that Slav and Finnish tribes invited a Viking of the Rus tribe to rule them. Some later scholars claimed that "Rus" refers to a Slav, not Viking, tribe. In any case, it was the Rus who gave their name to the first known East Slavic state: the Kievan Rus.

The Kievan Rus Forms Located in present-day Ukraine, Kiev became the region's economic and cultural center. Kiev's early rulers grew rich from trade and united the Slavic tribes. Under Vladimir, the Kievan Rus formed close ties with the Byzantine empire around the year 1000.

Vladimir adopted the Byzantines' Eastern Orthodox Christianity. He converted all of Kiev in a mass ceremony. Byzantine culture influenced Russian language, art, and music as well as the architectural style of Russian churches.

Gradually, many tribal leaders became princes. Princes were granted large areas of land, or appanages. They ruled these appanages and passed them on to family members. Competition between princes in the Kievan Rus was fierce. Some historians believe this rivalry weakened the state and invited a Mongol invasion.

In 1240, Mongol armies from Central Asia, known as the Golden Horde, took Kiev. The Kievan Rus collapsed. Russian princes now had to accept the authority of Mongol khans, or rulers.

As Kiev declined, the city of Moscow began to grow in importance. Its princes ruled an area known as Muscovy. It was a key trading center, and the Mongol khans favored its rulers. In 1328, the head of the Eastern Orthodox Church moved to Moscow, making the city even more important.

Reading Check **What caused the fall of the Kievan Rus?**

Mongol Period Tamerlane, a Turkic chief, challenged Mongol rule in Russia in the 1300s. ▼

Muscovy Period Ivan IV, or Ivan the Terrible, was the first Russian ruler to be crowned tsar. ▶

1156 Building begins at the Kremlin.

Kievan Rus				Mongol Rule			Muscovy
900	1000	1100	1200	1300	1400	1500	

988 Prince Vladimir converts to Christianity.

1147 Moscow is founded.

Timeline

my **worldgeography.com** Timeline

Imperial Russia

Prince Ivan III of Muscovy overthrew the Golden Horde by 1480. He set about establishing a Russian state to rival those of Europe. He began by calling himself **tsar,** or emperor, a term derived from *Caesar,* the title of the Roman emperors.

The Rise of the Tsars Ivan III was eager to show Russia's greatness to the world. He invited European architects to design the **Kremlin,** a grand complex of palaces, state offices, and churches in Moscow.

The reign of tsar Boris Godunov was a time of political unrest and lawlessness. People left the farms for cities. Food shortages resulted. Godunov forced people to work the land by beginning the practice of serfdom. A **serf** is a peasant who is legally bound to live and work on land owned by his or her lord.

The Romanov Dynasty In 1613, an assembly elected a new tsar, Michael Romanov, the 16-year-old son of an influential noble. The Romanovs ruled Russia for the next 300 years.

The first great Romanov tsar, Peter the Great, dreamed of a Russia to rival European nations. As an absolute monarch, he modernized and westernized Russia, importing western ideas and technologies.

Catherine II, known as Catherine the Great, took power in 1762. She ruled as an "enlightened despot," or wise ruler. Catherine transformed the new capital, St. Petersburg, into a cultural center. By the end of her rule in 1796, Catherine had greatly expanded Russia. She added some 200,000 square miles through wars, including much of Ukraine and parts of Poland.

Closer Look *Westernization of Russia*

Peter the Great used force in his efforts to westernize Russia. His reforms called for changes to very old customs. Many Russians resented the tsar's autocratic, or unlimited, power. Still, his reforms improved life in Russia greatly. Peter set up academies of science, mathematics, and engineering. He also increased trade with Europe. This brought new technologies to Russia.

THINK CRITICALLY **Why might Russians have resented westernization by force?**

Peter the Great (1682–1725)

Peter insisted that Russian nobles shave their beards to follow the European custom of being clean-shaven. ▶

300

In spite of their reforms, neither Peter the Great nor Catherine the Great helped the serfs, who made up most of the population. To maintain power, the tsars needed the support of nobles. Nobles lived off of the work of the serfs, so they preferred to keep them in <u>servitude.</u>

The Imperial Age Ends In spite of westernization, Russia lagged behind Western Europe in many ways. While many European nations moved toward democracy in the 1800s, Russia's tsars clung to absolute monarchy. Where much of Europe began to industrialize, Russia's economy remained dependent on agriculture and serf labor.

Russia lost the Crimean War to Britain, Turkey, and France in 1856. This loss shocked the nation. In addition to the loss of life and land, the war revealed the poor state of the Russian army. Soldiers used outdated equipment, and most marched in their own ragged clothing. Many were escaped serfs who had joined the army hoping for liberty.

Russia's leaders aimed to modernize. Support grew for emancipation, or freeing, of the serfs. Tsar Alexander II freed them in 1861, but made them pay nobles for land. Peasants did not gain economic freedom and remained desperately poor.

Some Russian reformers pushed for greater democracy. Meanwhile, in 1905, violent worker unrest scared Russia's leaders. Tsar Nicholas II responded with the October Manifesto. This charter granted civil rights and limited democracy. Russian troops crushed the worker revolts, but the peace was short-lived.

Reading Check **Why didn't early Russian tsars free the serfs?**

servitude, *n.,* a legal requirement to work for another

Peter hired Italian architects to design his new capital, St. Petersburg, in a European style. ▼

Catherine the Great (1762–1796)

Russian artists used European techniques to make fine decorative objects such as this china vase. ▼

301

myWorld Activity
Making a Living
Timeline

Communist Russia

Russia's monarchy collapsed during World War I. The war put a huge burden on Russia. Because peasants had to leave farms to fight in the army, food production fell dangerously. Inflation pushed prices out of reach of workers. Nicholas II increased his powers and tried to prevent unrest.

However, Russia's parliament forced Nicholas II to give up the throne in March, 1917. In October of 1917, Vladimir Lenin and the Bolsheviks took power. The **Bolsheviks** were a Russian political group that called for worker control. The Bolsheviks killed Nicholas and his family in 1918. After 300 years, the Romanov dynasty had come to an end.

The Bolshevik takeover is known as the Russian Revolution. The Bolksheviks put in place a new political and social system called communism.

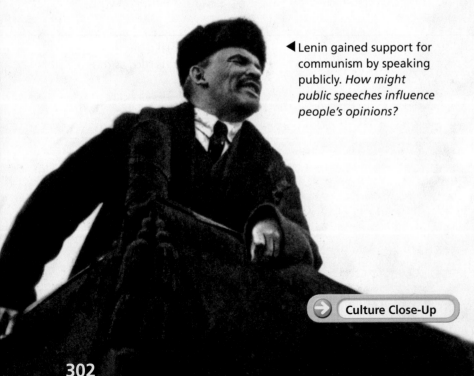

◀ Lenin gained support for communism by speaking publicly. *How might public speeches influence people's opinions?*

Culture Close-Up

What Is Communism? Lenin based the Bolshevik government on his understanding of the works of Karl Marx, a German philosopher from the 1800s. Marx wrote during the Industrial Revolution. He wanted to ease the widespread poverty that had developed among workers.

Marx thought that the people as a whole, not individuals, should own workplaces. In this way, everyone would share the goods and services produced. Marx believed that the working class, or people who work for a living, should control both the government and the economy as a group. The working class would in time no longer be a group separate from the owners. Instead, a classless, or communist, society would develop.

Lenin and the Bolsheviks used Marx's arguments before the revolution to try to gain support in **soviets,** or workers' councils. Lenin claimed that the Bolsheviks spoke for the working class.

After the revolution, the Bolsheviks renamed themselves the Communist Party. Lenin put the government and the economy under Communist Party control. The Communists fought a civil war in Russia. They crushed their opponents.

Repression and Domination In 1922, Russia united with other parts of the former Russian Empire to form the Soviet Union.

After Lenin died in 1924, Josef Stalin took control of the party and government. He issued Five-Year Plans pushing for the development of heavy industry and rapid collectivization of agriculture.

Collectivization is a shift of control from an individual or company to a group called a collective.

These policies forced many peasants to become tenants on their land, with the state acting as landlord. Stalin used brutal tactics to enforce his policies and maintain power. He crushed all opposition and sent millions into prisons and labor camps. Millions died there.

The horrible famine of 1932–1933 showed how disastrous collectivization could be. Collectives in Ukraine and the Caucasus region were forced to send all their grain to Russia. This left none for the Ukrainians. More than six million people died. Still, one of Stalin's officers called the famine a great success. He said it showed the peasants "who is the master. It cost millions of lives, but the collective farm system is here to stay."

Cold War Russia The Soviet Union worked with Western powers to defeat Germany during World War II. After the war, however, relations with the West, particularly the United States, chilled.

Soviet troops had occupied Eastern Europe. They opposed democracy and set up pro-Soviet communist governments. This brought tension with the United States and other Western nations.

The West aimed for containment, an effort to contain, or to stop the spread of, communism throughout the world. The United States and the Soviet Union vied for economic, political, and cultural power around the world. This rivalry, which stopped short of direct, armed conflict, was called the Cold War.

Reading Check How did Stalin deal with opposition?

Understanding Communism

The two basic elements of communism are a centralized, one-party government and government economic control. The government made all decisions about where people should live and work. People had to obey the government completely. *Does government control ensure the loyalty of the people? Explain why or why not.*

The figures in this Soviet monument carry a hammer and a sickle, the symbols of the Soviet Union. ▶

SOVIET GOVERNMENT

- Controlled by the Communist Party
- Centrally-planned economy
- The state owns all land, businesses, and housing.
- The state provides healthcare, childcare, and education.

COMMUNIST PARTY

Central Committee
Top members of the Communist Party who elect the Politburo and general secretary

Politburo
The "Political Bureau" of the Communist Party, it set government policies.

General Secretary
The leader of the Communist Party and Politburo and head of the government

myworldgeography.com Culture Close-up

303

denounce, *v.,* to reject publicly

Communism to Nationalism

Stalin's successor, Nikita Khrushchev, denounced Stalin's brutal tactics. Still, the Communist Party kept tight control.

The Communist System Weakens The communist system slowly weakened. To compete in the Cold War, the government focused on building weapons and military vehicles. The government failed to invest in new technologies.

Meanwhile, state ownership gave farmers little reason to grow more food. As a result, the Soviet Union went into debt to import food and high-technology goods. The Soviet economy could not meet its people's wish for better living standards.

During the 1980s, the Soviet Union fought a failed war to support a communist government in Afghanistan. As with the Crimean War, the lost war in Afghanistan brought calls for reform.

Openness and Restructuring Real reform in the Soviet Union began with Mikhail Gorbachev. After he came to power in 1985, he introduced two new policies, glasnost and perestroika. Glasnost, or "openness," meant greater freedom of speech and media freedom.

Glasnost destroyed the myth that people were living well under communism. It highlighted failures in the country's long war in Afghanistan. Glasnost also forced the government to reveal details about the 1986 Chernobyl nuclear accident. This accident caused serious health problems and environmental damage.

Perestroika, or "restructuring," reduced government control over the economy and created freer markets. Also, for the first time, the government allowed non-communist parties to form.

The Collapse Comes The Soviet Union eased its control over Eastern Europe. People in non-Russian parts of the Soviet Union began to seek independence.

Some top Communist Party officials resisted these changes. In August 1991, Soviet security officials seized power.

Hardline communists disliked Mikhail Gorbachev. They saw him as a leader who wanted to reduce the power of the Soviet government.

Boris Yeltsin raises his fist in triumph after the 1991 coup. Yeltsin's actions broke the power of the Communists and led to the fall of the Soviet Union.

Within three days, supporters of democracy forced the Soviet officials to back down. At the end of 1991, the Soviet Union officially broke apart, and the Cold War came to an end. All of the former Soviet republics gained independence. The largest of these was Russia.

The Russian Federation As the first president of a new Russia, Boris Yeltsin was head of a nation on the verge of economic collapse. The sudden shift to a free-market economy brought great hardship. Inflation and unemployment soared. A very few individuals gained control of state-owned property. These well-connected individuals, known as oligarchs, held great influence over the politics and economy of Russia.

The Russian Federation, as the country was now called, also had to deal with unrest in its non-Russian regions. From 1994 to 2005, Russia fought a war against rebels in Chechnya who wanted independence. Both sides brutally mistreated

The Soviet Union and Present-Day Russia

KEY
Soviet Union, 1991
Russia, 1992

people. The region was left in ruins by the time Russia regained control.

Yeltsin resigned in 1999, naming Vladimir Putin as acting president. Putin then won an election in 2000. Putin reduced the power of the oligarchy and increased the power of the government.

Reading Check What new policies did Gorbachev set?

Section 2 Assessment

? Essential Question

Key Terms

1. Explain how the following key terms describe power relations in Russian history: tsar, serf, Bolshevik

Key Ideas

2. What changes did Peter the Great make to Russia?

3. What changes did Lenin make to the economy and government of Russia?

4. What were some results of collectivizing agriculture?

Think Critically

5. **Compare Viewpoints** How were Stalin's and Gorbachev's ideas about government different?

6. **Synthesize** What caused the Soviet Union to collapse?

What should governments do?

7. Think about the famines that have occurred throughout Russian history. What actions might a government take during disasters such as famines? Go to your Student Journal to record your answer.

305

The Russian Revolution

Key Idea

- During the Russian Revolution, Bolsheviks promised the people a better life, but soon turned to brutal methods to keep power.

For centuries, tsars ruled Russia with absolute power. Under their rule, a huge gap existed between wealthy landowners and poor workers. In 1905, a revolution led to the creation of a parliament, but it was ineffective. The suffering caused by World War I caused even more discontent among Russians. In early 1917, starving people rioted in the capital, St. Petersburg. The tsar was forced to give up his throne. In October 1917, revolutionary Bolsheviks, led by Vladimir Lenin, overthrew the government. Civil war broke out, and the Bolsheviks used increasingly harsh measures to maintain control.

▲ A Russian serf weaves cloth on a loom, about 1910.

Lenin addresses a political meeting in 1917. ▼

Stop at each letter on the right to think about the text. Then answer the question with the same letter on the left.

Ⓐ **Analyze Cause and Effect** What have the revolutionaries already done, and why does that make it important to act quickly?

Ⓑ **Identify Evidence** How does Lenin try to cover up his intention to take power? Explain.

Ⓒ **Identify Main Ideas and Details** For whom does Lenin claim the revolutionaries are acting?

disarm, *v.*, to force a person or country to give up a supply of weapons

cadet, *n.*, a person who is training to become a military officer

relinquish, *v.*, to give up or surrender

A Call to Power

❝ We must at all costs, this very evening, this very night, arrest the
Ⓐ government, having first <u>disarmed</u> the officer <u>cadets</u>, and so on. We must not wait! We may lose everything! Who must take power?
Ⓑ That is not important at present. Let the Revolutionary Military Committee do it, or "some other institution" which will declare that it will <u>relinquish</u> power only to the
Ⓒ true representatives of the interests of the people, the interests of the army, the interests of the peasants, the interests of the starving. ❞

—Vladimir Lenin,
"A Call to Power," October 24, 1917

306

Stop at each letter on the right to think about the text. Then answer the question with the same letter on the left.

D **Identify Bias** What attitude toward Lenin is conveyed by the words "bloodthirsty beast"?

E **Draw Conclusions** In the beginning, how did ordinary people feel about the revolution?

F **Compare and Contrast** According to the Russian Red Army soldier, what did the revolution bring about? Is that similar to or different from what he expected?

intrude, *v.,* to force oneself into a situation where one isn't wanted

ranks, *n.,* a body of people grouped together as members of an organization

Constituent Assembly, *n.,* an elected legislature that the Bolsheviks disbanded

existence, *n.,* standard of living

Letter to Lenin

D " My words to you, you bloodthirsty beast. You <u>intruded</u> into the <u>ranks</u> of the revolution and did not allow the <u>Constituent Assembly</u> to meet. You said: 'Down with prisons, Down with shootings, Down with soldiering. Let wage workers be secure.' In a word you promised heaps of gold and a heavenly <u>existence</u>. The people

E felt the revolution, began to breathe easily. We were allowed to meet, to say what we liked, fearing nothing. And then you, Bloodsucker, appeared and took

F away freedom from the people. . . . You've organized a terror and thousands of the people are shot mercilessly every day; . . . workers are starving, the people are without shoes or clothes. "

—a Red Army soldier, "Letter to Lenin," December 25, 1918

▲ This military cap and the seal above it bear the hammer and sickle, symbols of the Soviet Union.

Red Army soldiers, 1932 ▼

Analyze the Documents

1. **Draw Inferences** What do you think happened to the soldier who wrote the letter to Lenin? Explain.
2. **Writing Task** Write your own letter to Lenin in which you tell him what, if anything, you think he should have done differently.

Russia Today

Key Ideas

- Russia had a strong economic recovery in the early 2000s.
- Many of Russia's democratic reforms have disappeared as government control has grown.
- Russia uses its energy resources as a source of international power.

Key Terms • KGB • disposable income • censor • superpower

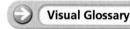 **Visual Glossary**

 Reading Skill: Identify Main Ideas and Details Take notes using the graphic organizer in your journal.

Shoppers walk through a new public plaza in Moscow. ▼

Few nations have experienced as much upheaval as Russia did in the 1900s. Since 2000, the country has continued to change at a remarkable pace.

Russia Recovers

Gorbachev's policies of glasnost and perestroika opened a new era of social and political change in Russia. One of the biggest changes has been Russia's increasing self-confidence.

Finding a New Identity At the end of the Soviet period, Russians discovered that communism was more than a political system—it was also a cultural identity. If Russia was no longer a communist nation, then what should it be? In 1990, historian James Billington said:

66 It boils down to whether [Russians] can find an…identity for themselves as a way of feeling good about themselves without feeling hostile to others. 99

The hardships that occurred in the shift to a market economy brought a rise in depression and alcoholism. The country also faced violence, crime, and corruption. Although there had been corruption during the Soviet era, it increased greatly in the years that followed.

Restoring Confidence Elected president in 2000, Vladimir Putin acted quickly to rebuild the country. He did this through strong leadership and by increasing government control. Since then, some have charged that Putin's policies undermine human rights, democracy, and peaceful relations with Russia's neighbors and the United States.

Some scholars point to Putin's background as a member of the **KGB,** the Soviet secret police. His past may have led him to favor strong government control. Supporters argue that his policies reduced political corruption, crime, and terrorism. His reforms to banking, private property, and labor law helped Russia's economy grow. Under Putin, some Russians began to believe that state-controlled capitalism might work better than a free-market economy.

However, many Russians preferred the Soviet era, when the government was in charge of pensions, healthcare, and wages. Many feel that under communism they faced less uncertainty.

Putin strengthened the Russian military. He <u>demonstrated</u> Russia's renewed military might by crushing unrest in regions on Russia's borders, such as Chechnya, where rebels had fought Russian control since 1994.

Putin's two terms as president also brought real improvements in daily life. His economic reforms reduced poverty and led to the emergence of a new middle class. Many in this new middle class are professionals who work in fields related to the global economy. The middle class now makes up about one fifth to one third of the population. Since 1999, Russians on average have doubled their **disposable income,** or the amount of money left after taxes are paid. By the end of 2007, fewer than 15 percent of all Russians lived below the poverty level. Just ten years earlier, 38 percent lived in poverty.

Putin also oversaw dramatic growth in Russia's energy industry. This industry took advantage of Russia's vast oil and natural gas reserves. Russia became one of the world's leading producers of oil and gas.

Reading Check How did Putin change the role of Russia's government?

demonstrate, *v.,* to show the workings of

Contrasting Systems

Under the communist Soviet Union, Russians, such as the woman at the left, faced empty shelves in stores. American shoppers, such as the woman at the right, seldom encounter such shortages. *How might communism affect the supply of items such as food and clothing?*

Communism
- The Communist Party makes all political decisions.
- Command economy (The government makes most economic decisions and owns most property.)
- The political leadership values obedience, discipline, and economic security.

Democratic Capitalism
- The people and their elected representatives make decisions.
- Market economy (Private consumers and producers make most economic decisions and own most property.)
- The political leadership values freedom and prosperity.

Comparing Standards of Living

Life Expectancy

	United States	Russia
Overall	78.1 years	65.9 years
Male	75.3 years	59.1 years
Female	81.1 years	73.1 years

Infant Mortality (per 1,000 births)

	United States	Russia
Total	6.3 deaths	10.8 deaths
Male	7.0 deaths	12.3 deaths
Female	5.6 deaths	9.2 deaths

SOURCE: *CIA World Factbook*

Chart Skills

How does life expectancy for men in Russia compare with that for men in the United States? How does it compare for women in these two nations?

→ **Data Discovery**

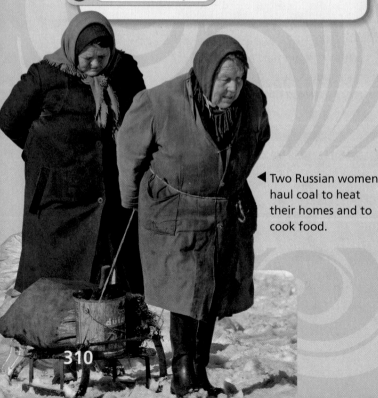

◀ Two Russian women haul coal to heat their homes and to cook food.

310

Russia Faces Challenges

Russia's new wealth and stability brought newfound confidence. However, Russians have also been facing some serious challenges.

Social and Economic Woes With change came new health concerns. Russia's birth rates and life expectancy are low. Life expectancy is the number of years a person can expect to live. Male life expectancy is the lowest of all industrialized nations in the world. Alcoholism is a major problem in Russia. Half of working-age men die due to excessive drinking. Rates of infectious disease are also high. These include HIV/AIDS and tuberculosis, a lung disease.

Social and economic changes since the 1990s have led to an increase in migration. After the fall of the Soviet Union, civil unrest and unemployment forced thousands of people to leave their homes. Many left polluted cities with high unemployment. Some returned to former lives in the countryside. There, they could raise some of their own food. At the same time, others migrated from rural areas to more thriving cities to try to find work. Large numbers of Russians, many of them skilled workers, have left their homeland to seek better lives in North America, Israel, and Western Europe.

Putin Draws Criticism Putin's efforts to solve some of Russia's major problems have had mixed results. He remains popular among Russians, but criticism continues in spite of the government's efforts to silence it.

The Russian constitution calls for freedom of speech and of the press. However, the government continues to control the media. The government owns most of the large radio and television stations. This means that if the government doesn't want the general public to know about a news story, they can **censor** it, or keep it from being reported.

One of Putin's most controversial actions was to put Russia's energy industry under government control. Private energy companies suddenly lost all that they owned to the government. Putin argued Russia needed control of its energy industry to regain its status as a global superpower. A **superpower** is an extremely powerful nation.

Human Rights and the Law Russia's record on human rights remains uneven. Ethnic and religious tensions continue, especially with Muslims and others from the Caucasus region. A few Russian journalists who have criticized the government have died under suspicious circumstances. Some have accused the Russian government of killing them.

Corruption in business practices and politics is common in Russia. In 2008, Dmitry Medvedev won election to follow Putin as president. Medvedev promised to fight corruption, although critics questioned his commitment. Medvedev said,

> 66 [Corruption] must receive our sustained attention because this problem is a profound and important one. 99

Reading Check How does the Russian government control the media?

Russia and the World

Russia remains one of the world's leading powers. It has the world's largest stockpile of nuclear weapons. It is also one of the world's top energy producers.

A World Partner Russia is a member of the Group of 8 industrialized nations, or G-8. As a member of the G-8, Russia joined the United States in 2006 to announce shared anti-terror initiatives. Russia has worked with the G-8 on other issues. These include climate change, energy, and economic development.

Russia has also taken part in other international efforts. One of these was the North Korean Six-Party Talks, aimed at convincing North Korea to give up nuclear weapons.

Russia has strongly opposed efforts by the former Soviet republics of Ukraine and Georgia to join NATO. Both countries border on Russia.

my**World**
IN NUMBERS

In 2008, the economic output per person for Russia was **$15,800**. For the United States, it was **$47,000**.

◀ A protester holds a photograph of Russian journalist Anastasia Baburova, who was killed in 2009.

**myWorld Activity
Russia Trivia Game**

Russia has supported independence movements in the Georgian regions of Abkhazia and South Ossetia. Georgian troops entered South Ossetia in 2008 to try to regain control of the region. Russian troops responded by driving Georgian troops out of South Ossetia. Russian forces also bombed and invaded other parts of Georgia. Russia's invasion of Georgia damaged its relations with the United States and other Western nations.

Russian Energy Russia has also flexed its muscles in global energy markets. Russia is the second largest oil-exporting nation in the world. Russia is also the world's largest exporter of natural gas. Oil and gas pipelines from Russia reach far into Europe and Asia. In the past, Russia has halted the flow of natural gas to Western Europe through Ukraine. It has done this in response to disagreements with the government of Ukraine. Russia has signed exclusive agreements to supply gas to Germany and other European nations to try to win their backing for Russian policies. Western Europeans have criticized Russia for using energy to increase its power.

Cooperation and Conflict Russia controls much of the energy supply for the European Union (EU). Russia has opposed the EU membership of former Soviet republics such as Estonia, Latvia, and Lithuania.

Transporting Russian Energy

Map Skills

1. **Region** According to the map, Russian oil pipelines extend to which European nations to the west?

2. **Movement** Through which nations must Russian gas travel to reach Italy?

→ **Active Atlas**

KEY
— Oil pipeline
— Gas pipeline

0 — 500 mi
0 — 500 km
Lambert Azimuthal Equal-Area Projection

However, Russia has <u>cooperated</u> with the EU on matters such as energy and climate change. These agreements include other former Soviet republics such as Ukraine, Belarus, and Kazakhstan.

Russia is a trading partner with Iran, which has poor relations with the United States. Russia has also loaned money to Iran to build nuclear reactors.

The United States has objected to this project. It is concerned that Iran will use the reactors to develop nuclear weapons. Russia's relationship with the United States has remained calm but cool.

Another foreign policy issue is Russia's relationship with China, the world's largest country in population. The Soviet Union and China had been competitors and enemies. This changed when Russia and China formed the Shanghai Cooperation Organization with several Central Asian countries in 2001. This organization has become a loose alliance. Joint military practices between Russia and China have worried Western nations.

The Future of Russia Strong post-Soviet leadership has reshaped Russia's politics and economy. Rich natural resources and continued superpower status make Russia an important player on the global stage. Whether it works together with the United States and other Western powers or takes a more hostile attitude, Russia has the world's full attention.

Reading Check What is the Shanghai Cooperation Organization?

cooperate, *v.*, to work together toward an agreed goal

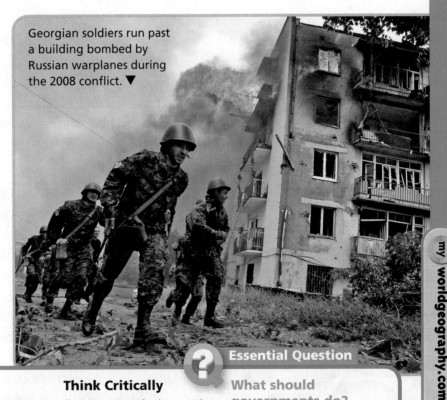
Georgian soldiers run past a building bombed by Russian warplanes during the 2008 conflict. ▼

Section 3 Assessment

Essential Question

What should governments do?

Key Terms
1. Define each key term using a complete sentence: KGB, disposable income, censor, superpower.

Key Ideas
2. In what ways did the Russian government under Vladimir Putin halt democratic reform?
3. How did Russia's petroleum industry change under Putin?
4. What are some of the major health problems in Russia?

Think Critically
5. **Draw Conclusions** Why do you think Russia has opposed membership in the European Union for former Soviet republics?
6. **Draw Inferences** Why might Russia want closer relations with China?

7. Think about the life expectancy and infant mortality graphs in this section. What do you think the government can do about the health problems in Russia? Go to your Student Journal to record your answer.

The Soviet Industrial Legacy

Key Ideas
- Stalin's Five-Year Plans boosted the development of industry in the Soviet Union.
- Stalin used force to increase the pace of industrial development.
- Free-market reforms have reduced government control of the modern Russian economy.

Key Terms
- Five-Year Plan
- industrialization
- command economy
- heavy industry
- gulag

These days, most adults in the village of Muslumovo on the Techa River have health problems. "What can we do?" says a local man. "We need water. Cows drink it, birds drink it, we drink it. And by the time we're forty, we're all ill." Recently, scientists discovered the cause of this widespread sickness. In 1957, there was an explosion at the nearby Mayak nuclear plant. The radiation that is making everyone ill dates back even further to the Soviet industrial push of the 1930s.

Build for the Motherland

Following Lenin's unexpected death in 1924, a new Soviet leader emerged. Josef Stalin wanted to transform the Soviet Union with a series of **Five-Year Plans.** These were government plans for the economy that made basic decisions and set priorities for five years. Each Five-Year Plan pushed for the collectivization of farms and rapid **industrialization,** or development of industry. These government plans concentrated on building **heavy industry,** or the manufacture of steel, equipment, or weapons. Stalin's plans indeed transformed the Soviet Union, but at a terrible cost.

Stalin believed that for communism to survive, the Soviet Union would have to become a world industrial leader. He imposed a full-scale **command economy,** or one in which the government makes all basic economic decisions. He expected citizens to accept all economic hardships as honorable sacrifices for the Soviet motherland.

By the 1930s, millions of workers were working on the nation's construction projects as inmates of forced-labor camps. Later known as **gulags,** these camps housed political prisoners charged with crimes such as private ownership of land or criticism of the government.

Both men and women worked on Soviet industrialization projects. ▼

Industrialization and the Gulags

Millions of gulag prisoners built Stalin's factories, dams, and canals. Perhaps as many as 20 million people passed through the gulags from 1928 to 1939. Conditions in the camps were horrible. Prisoners lived in fear and exhaustion. Food was poor and medical care almost nonexistent. Millions died as a result.

THINK CRITICALLY How did Stalin use the gulags for industrialization?

▲ Gulag laborers were treated like beasts of burden.

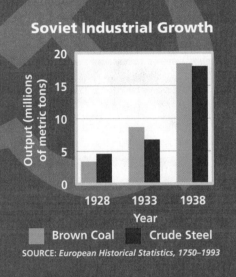

Soviet Industrial Growth

Output (millions of metric tons) vs Year

Legend: Brown Coal, Crude Steel

SOURCE: European Historical Statistics, 1750–1993

Soviet Industrial Centers

KEY
— 1939 border
○ Industrial center

ARCTIC OCEAN

Lambert Conformal Conic Projection

SOVIET UNION

Leningrad, Moscow, Donbas, Perm, Sverdlovsk, Chelyabinsk, Kuzbas

ARCTIC CIRCLE

Stalin believed that the success of the Five-Year Plans depended on education. Before the Revolution, 65 percent of the population was illiterate. The government taught millions to read and write. Worker training programs also prepared men and women for Five-Year-Plan projects.

Stalin expanded universities so that students could learn math, science and engineering. Even there, Stalin attempted to dictate the behavior and thinking of professors and students.

At first, people were eager to work on Stalin's projects. They believed that if they worked hard, they would live well. However, workers soon discovered that they were expected to produce a great deal for low wages. In addition, they paid heavy fines if they were late or absent.

Many Soviets expected that the Five-Year Plans would raise standards of living, but Stalin pushed only heavy industry. This led to widespread shortages in clothing, housing, and food.

Reading Check Why did Stalin want to transform the Soviet economy?

Stalin's Industrial Legacy

Industrialization left its mark on all of modern Russia. Factories, mines and industrial cities cover what had been Siberian wilderness. Universities expanded by Stalin educate today's scientists and business people.

The rush to industrialize also meant that the Soviet government ignored pollution, health issues, and environmental concerns in favor of economic progress.

Acid rain has damaged thousands of acres of woodlands. Vast areas of what was once good farmland are now unusable due to soil contamination. Waterways and habitats remain damaged from dams built to generate hydroelectric power. Perhaps the most serious threat is radioactive pollution such as that found in Muslumovo.

Reading Check What have been some of the negative effects of industrialization?

The Legacy Remains

Muslumovo

In the 1930s, the region around Muslumovo supplied copper for industry and the military. People began to become ill in the 1950s, but they kept quiet. They feared the government's reaction if they complained. The modern Russian government has been more sympathetic, offering villagers new homes in another town.

▲ A sign in Muslumovo forbids villagers from fishing in the area due to high levels of radiation.

Kuzbass

Kuzbass, or the Kuznetsk Basin, holds some of the largest coal deposits in the world. This coal fueled new factories in the basin and elsewhere along the Trans-Siberian Railroad. The basin also supplied iron, steel, zinc, and aluminum. Today, the Kuznetsk Basin remains an important industrial center in Russia.

▲ A woman walks through snow covered with soot released by the factories in the Kuzbass region.

Norilsk

During the Soviet era, foreigners were not allowed to visit Norilsk. The Soviets did not want outsiders to know about the missiles kept there. This secrecy also hid the city's pollution. Norilsk processes nickel, copper, platinum, gold, and silver, and almost half of the world's supply of palladium, a metal used in automobile exhaust systems.

▲ A copper worker in Norilsk breathes through a filter to keep contaminants out of his lungs.

The New Russian Economy

After the fall of the Soviet Union, the Russian economy collapsed. The recovery and boom of the early 2000s came mainly from earnings from Russia's massive energy resources. Wages rose, and Russians could afford to purchase consumer goods they had never before owned.

Russia: Average Monthly Wage, 2001–2008

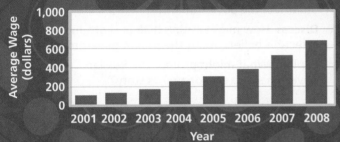

SOURCE: Goskomstat

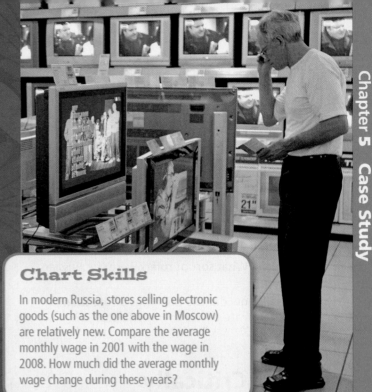

Chart Skills

In modern Russia, stores selling electronic goods (such as the one above in Moscow) are relatively new. Compare the average monthly wage in 2001 with the wage in 2008. How much did the average monthly wage change during these years?

The New Russian Economy

Industrialization left another kind of legacy in Russia. A recent survey showed that many Russians have a favorable view of Stalin's dictatorship. They believe that Stalin did much for Russia. They, too, see themselves working to make Russia great.

Many of the more successful Russians in today's economy are under age 35. One young company executive recently exclaimed, "Is there anything better that can be offered to me than creating the new Russian economy?"

This younger generation has grown up since the collapse of communism, and many accept the uncertainties of a market economy. They use computers, cellphones, and the Internet—all of which are fairly new to Russia. Many are optimistic about being able to earn good wages and about starting new businesses.

The push to industrialize had both positive and negative results for Russia. Stalin's vision for Russia continues to influence life today.

Reading Check Why might modern Russians have a positive view of Stalin?

Assessment

1. Summarize the main purpose of Stalin's Five-Year Plans.

2. How did Stalin use education to promote industrialization?

3. State one way in which each city on the previous page shows evidence of the Soviet push to industrialize.

4. How might more economic freedom change Russia?

5. What types of technology can modern Russians use that were not available during the Soviet period?

317

Chapter Assessment

Key Terms and Ideas

1. **Recall** In what ways does **Siberia** present Russia with great advantages and great challenges?

2. **Compare and Contrast** Describe the climate and vegetation on the tundra and the **steppes.**

3. **Explain** What sort of rulers were the Russian **tsars?**

4. **Recall** How did the buildings of the **Kremlin** demonstrate power in imperial Russia?

5. **Discuss** How did communism shape the Soviet government and economy?

6. **Summarize** What was **collectivization** and how did affect the Soviet Union?

7. **Discuss** How might Putin's **KGB** background affect his beliefs about the role of government?

8. **Explain** What might prompt the Russian government to **censor** a news story?

Think Critically

9. **Draw Conclusions** Why do you think Josef Stalin took actions such as collectivization and the jailing of opponents? Explain.

10. **Compare Viewpoints** One of Stalin's officers said the Great Famine would show the peasants "who is the master. It cost millions of lives, but the collective farm system is here to stay." Do you think Stalin agreed with him? Why?

11. **Identify Evidence** What historical evidence would support the statement "Russia has a long history of autocratic government"?

12. **Drawing Inferences** Why do you think many Russians want the government to be in control of wages, pensions, and healthcare?

Places to Know

For each place, write the letter from the map that shows its location.

13. **Kamchatka Peninsula**

14. **Yakutsk**

15. **Lake Baikal**

16. **Moscow**

17. **St. Petersburg**

18. **Ural Mountains**

19. **Estimate** Using the scale, estimate the distance from Moscow to Lake Baikal.

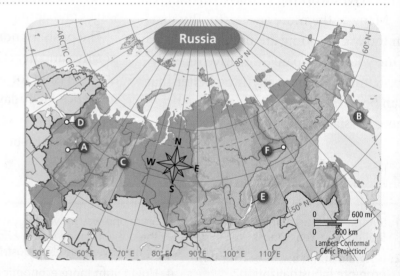

Essential Question

myWorld Chapter Activity

Memo to Russia Follow your teacher's instructions to examine information on some of the challenges facing Russia today. Consider environmental data, Russian health and crime figures, as well as the nation's international partnerships and other information as you set priorities. After your review, prepare an official government memo detailing which problem Russia should address first and why.

21st Century Learning

Search for Information on the Internet

Search for three different Web sites for additional information about the political, economic, and social challenges facing Russia. The following types of Web sites might prove helpful:
- encyclopedias or museums
- international organizations, such as the UN or World Trade Organization
- U.S. sites such as *CIA World Factbook*

Document-Based Questions

Success Tracker™
Online at myworldgeography.com

Use your knowledge of Russia and Documents A and B to answer questions 1–3.

Document A

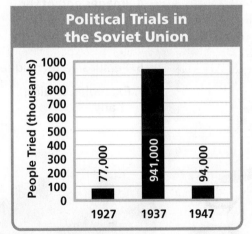

Political Trials in the Soviet Union

People Tried (thousands)

Year	People Tried
1927	77,000
1937	941,000
1947	94,000

SOURCE: Open Society Archives

1. How did the number of people brought to trial change from 1927 to 1937?

   A It decreased.

   B It increased by half.

   C It increased by more than 10 times.

   D It increased by 100 times.

Document B

" You might well ask why a prisoner worked so hard for ten years in a camp. . . . In the camps they had these gangs to make the prisoners keep each other on their toes. . . . It was like this—either you all got something extra or you all starved."

—Alexander Solzhenitsyn, *One Day in the Life of Ivan Denisovich* (a book about life in a Soviet prison camp)

2. What would be the punishment if a prisoner stopped working hard?

   A The guards would whip him in front of his gang.

   B The guards would take food away from his gang.

   C He would be put into a new labor camp.

   D He would have to give his food to his gang.

3. **Writing Task** What do you think the gang would say to a prisoner who stopped working hard? Write a dialogue.

my worldgeography.com Self-Test

Media Watchdog

Your Mission Use the Media Analysis Checklist to study the poster on the facing page. Examine how the poster conveys its message. Then go online and evaluate an article or opinion piece.

Media messages are everywhere in modern society. Can you believe everything you see, hear, and read on television, in print, or on the Internet? Who keeps track of the media's honesty and objectivity? When a member of the media is accused of bias, how can you know who is right?

By understanding how to analyze media content, you can spot bias and persuasive messages. Practicing this skill will help you to evaluate whether or not public officials and news sources are telling you the truth. You can also apply these techniques to advertising, which will help you decide how to spend your money more wisely.

Media Analysis Checklist

1. Author
2. Intended audience
3. Words or phrases
4. Images and other design elements
5. Overall message
6. Persuasive techniques
7. Examples of bias, if any

STEP 1

Determine the Message.

Copy the Media Analysis Checklist at the left onto your own paper. Use it to record your observations about the poster at the right. Who published the poster, and who is its intended audience? (Hint: Look at the flag at the bottom of the poster.) Read the poster and study its visual elements, such as the use of colors or photographs. Considering the words and visuals together, what is the poster's message?

STEP 2

Check for Bias.

Next, evaluate how the poster uses persuasive techniques such as bright colors or a photograph with children. Note how the poster uses words that are short, simple, and to the point. Do these words encourage you to feel a certain way? Consider whether or not your reaction is based on facts or on opinions and feelings. Record your observations on your Media Analysis Checklist.

STEP 3

Analyze Online Media.

Make a second, blank copy of the Media Analysis Checklist. Now go online to sources suggested by your teacher. Find an article or opinion piece about Europe or Russia, and analyze it as you did the poster. Once you have completed your Media Analysis Checklist, use your findings in a class discussion.

It's not them and us, it's you and me

2008 European Year of Intercultural Dialogue

www.dialogue2008.eu

European Union

9 May – Europe Day

my worldgeography.com 21st Century Learning

321

Africa

The continent of Africa is home to a wide range of climates and ecosystems, from rain forests to savannas and deserts. More than 900 million Africans live in 53 countries. They speak more than 2,000 different languages and belong to several thousand ethnic groups. Some of the countries with the largest populations are Nigeria, Democratic Republic of the Congo, South Africa, Ethiopia, Morocco, and Egypt.

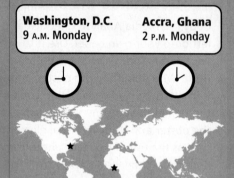

What time is it there?

Washington, D.C.	Accra, Ghana
9 A.M. Monday	2 P.M. Monday

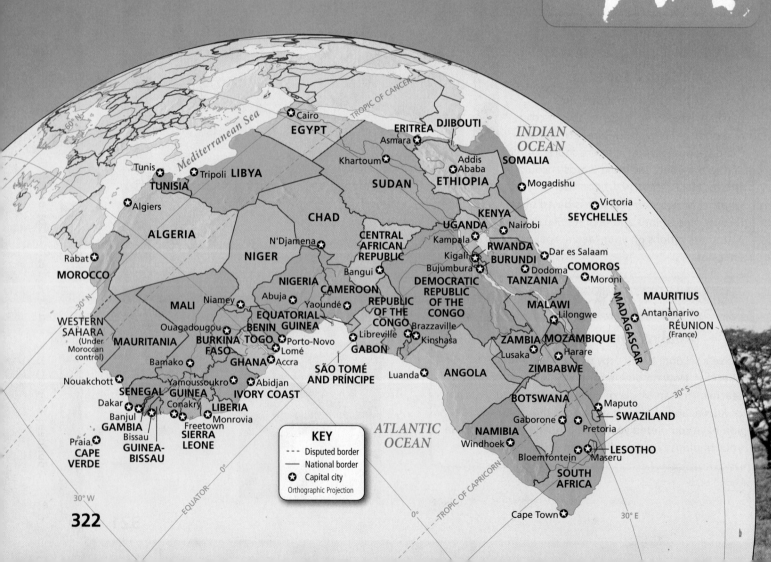

KEY

- - - Disputed border
- —— National border
- ✪ Capital city

Orthographic Projection

The Unit Ahead

→ **Chapter 6** West and Central Africa

→ **Chapter 7** Southern and Eastern Africa

→ **Chapter 8** North Africa

my worldgeography.com

Plan your trip online by doing a Data Discovery Activity and watching the myStory Videos of the region's teens.

my Story

Evelyn
Age: 15
Home: Kpong, Ghana
Chapter 6

my Story

Khulekani
Age: 19
Home: Port St. Johns, South Africa
Chapter 7

my Story

Shaimaa
Age: 18
Home: Cairo, Egypt
Chapter 8

Giraffes on the savanna in Tanzania

Regional Overview
Physical Geography

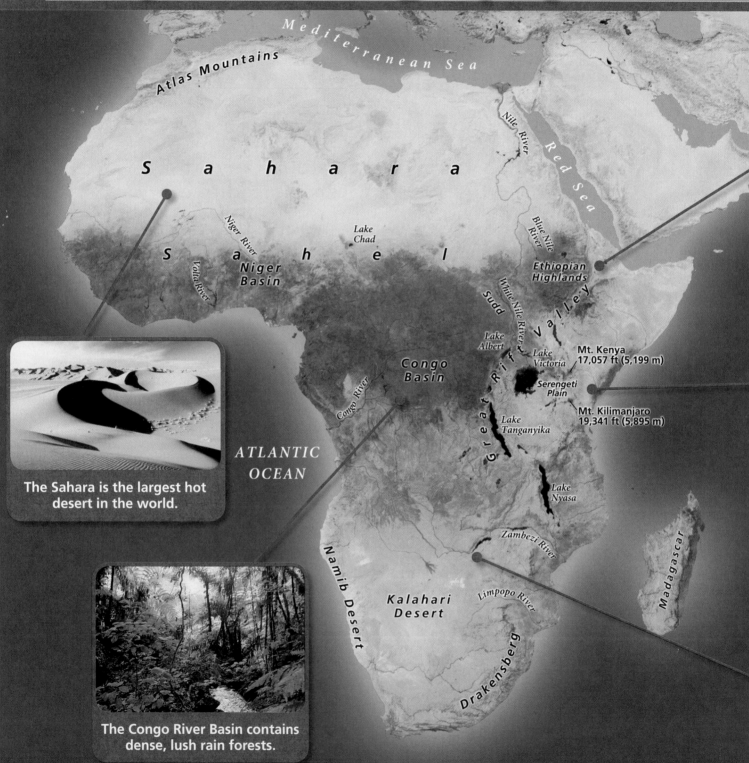

Mediterranean Sea

Atlas Mountains

Nile River

Red Sea

Sahara

Niger River

Lake Chad

Blue Nile River

Sahel

Volta River

Niger Basin

Ethiopian Highlands

White Nile River

Sudd

Lake Albert

Great Rift Valley

Lake Victoria

Mt. Kenya 17,057 ft (5,199 m)

Congo Basin

Serengeti Plain

Congo River

Mt. Kilimanjaro 19,341 ft (5,895 m)

Lake Tanganyika

ATLANTIC OCEAN

Lake Nyasa

Zambezi River

Namib Desert

Kalahari Desert

Limpopo River

Madagascar

Drakensberg

The Sahara is the largest hot desert in the world.

The Congo River Basin contains dense, lush rain forests.

The Ethiopian Highlands have a higher elevation than most of Africa.

The Serengeti plain is home to many different kinds of animals.

INDIAN OCEAN

Victoria Falls is one of Africa's most stunning natural features.

Regional Flyover

Take a trip by plane over Africa. You take off from South Africa and head north. The first thing you see is a strip of green land, and then suddenly a tall mountain range. Those mountains are the start of the high plateau on which most of Africa is located. Past the mountains, you see the Kalahari Desert.

Continuing north, the land slowly gets wetter and greener. It turns from desert into grasslands, and then dips down into the lush rain forests of the Congo River Basin. You pass the Equator. Then, the land below you slowly starts to get drier. The rain forest gives way to grassland, and then eventually to the semiarid Sahel region as you pass over Lake Chad.

Finally you cross over the Sahara, a huge desert. As your plane lands, the Mediterranean Sea is in front of you. To your east is the Nile River and to your west the Atlas Mountains. You have flown 4,600 miles and passed over 8 countries, and still you have only seen a small sample of the continent of Africa.

➔ **In-Flight Movie**

Take flight over Africa and explore the region from the air.

my worldgeography.com In-Flight Movie

325

Human Geography

Water

Rainfall and access to water are so important in Africa that they largely determine where its people live. Few people live in the dry deserts, but huge cities can spring up where rivers cut through them. Dense populations thrive in wetter areas. In between the deserts and rain forests, smaller groups of people live on grasslands and semiarid plains. Some countries in Africa are packed with natural resources such as gold or oil, while others are less fortunate. Although Africa contains 22 percent of Earth's land, it is home to only 14 percent of Earth's people. Each region of the continent presents a different set of challenges to its people. Africans have adapted to these challenges in different ways, giving rise to a wide variety of cultures and ways of living.

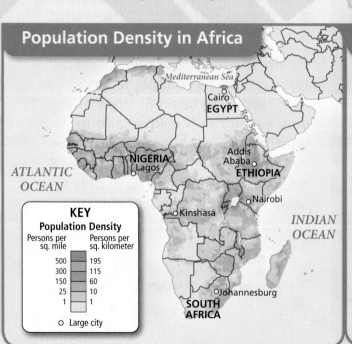

Population Density in Africa

KEY
Population Density

Persons per sq. mile	Persons per sq. kilometer
500	195
300	115
150	60
25	10
1	1

o Large city

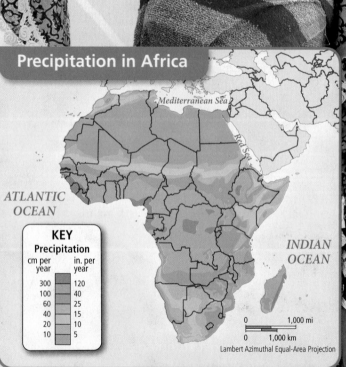

Precipitation in Africa

KEY
Precipitation

cm per year	in. per year
300	120
100	40
60	25
40	15
20	10
10	5

0   1,000 mi
0   1,000 km
Lambert Azimuthal Equal-Area Projection

	Egypt	Ethiopia	South Africa	Nigeria	United States
Food per day per person (kcal)*	3,320	1,810	2,900	2,600	3,830
Oil production per day (barrels)	664,000	0	199,100	2,352,000	8,457,000
Gross domestic product per capita	$5,000	$700	$9,700	$2,100	$45,800
Population	82 million	83 million	49 million	146 million	304 million

SOURCE: CIA World Factbook Online, 2009
* SOURCE: UN Food and Agriculture Organization (2003)

Put It Together

1. What physical feature covers most of northern Africa?

2. Is Nigeria densely or sparsely populated?

3. How are rainfall and population density related? Why do you think this is the case?

Data Discovery

Find your own data to make a regional data table.

Size Comparison

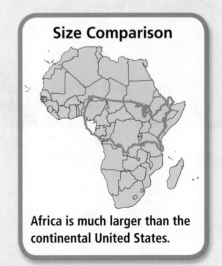

Africa is much larger than the continental United States.

my worldgeography.com

Data Discovery

327

Chapter 6

West and Central Africa

Essential Question

Who should benefit from a country's resources?

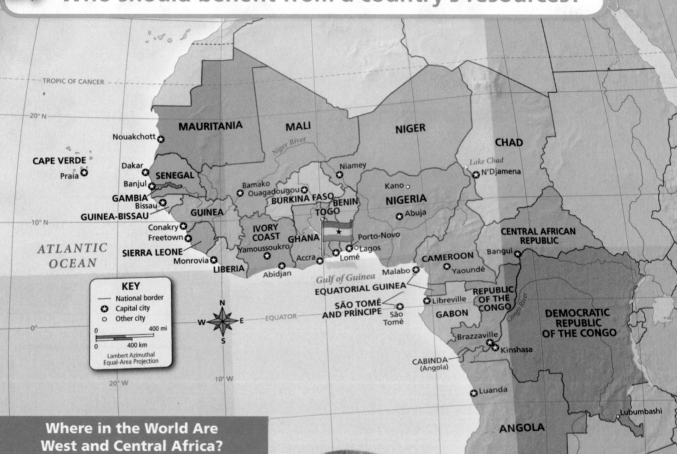

KEY
— National border
☆ Capital city
○ Other city

0 — 400 mi
0 — 400 km
Lambert Azimuthal
Equal-Area Projection

Where in the World Are West and Central Africa?

Washington, D.C., to Kpong: 5,250 miles

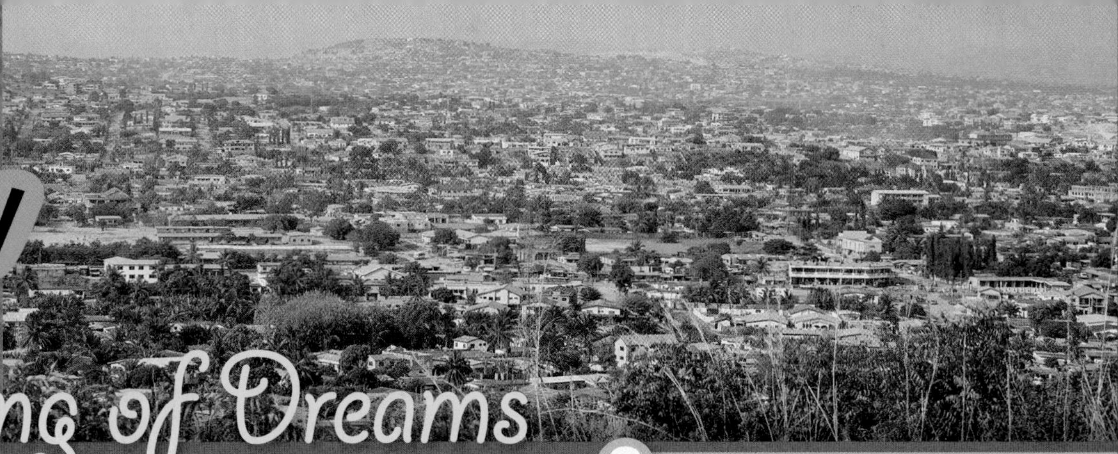

my Story

A String of Dreams

In this section, you'll read about a girl from Ghana named Evelyn who works in her grandmother's bead-making business. What does Evelyn's story tell you about life in West and Central Africa?

Explore the Essential Question
- at **my worldgeography.com**
- using the **myWorld Chapter Activity**
- with the **Student Journal**

Story by Chrispat Okutu for myWorld Geography Online

The Kenashie Market in Accra, Ghana, is full of vendors selling everything from coconuts and chickens to textiles and furniture. Men, women, and children of all ages hustle to sell the goods balanced atop their heads or heaped in their heavy carts.

In West Africa, where Ghana is located, there is a long tradition of women trading in the marketplace. In some countries, women organize and dominate many local markets. Overall, though, women earn less than men. In Ghana, only 70 percent of women can read and write, in contrast to 84 percent of men.

Evelyn, a 15-year-old Ghanaian girl, takes part in her region's tradition of women selling goods in the marketplace. She helps her grandmother make and sell their authentic Ghanaian beads at different markets near their home village of Kpong. Kpong lies about 30 miles away from the bustling

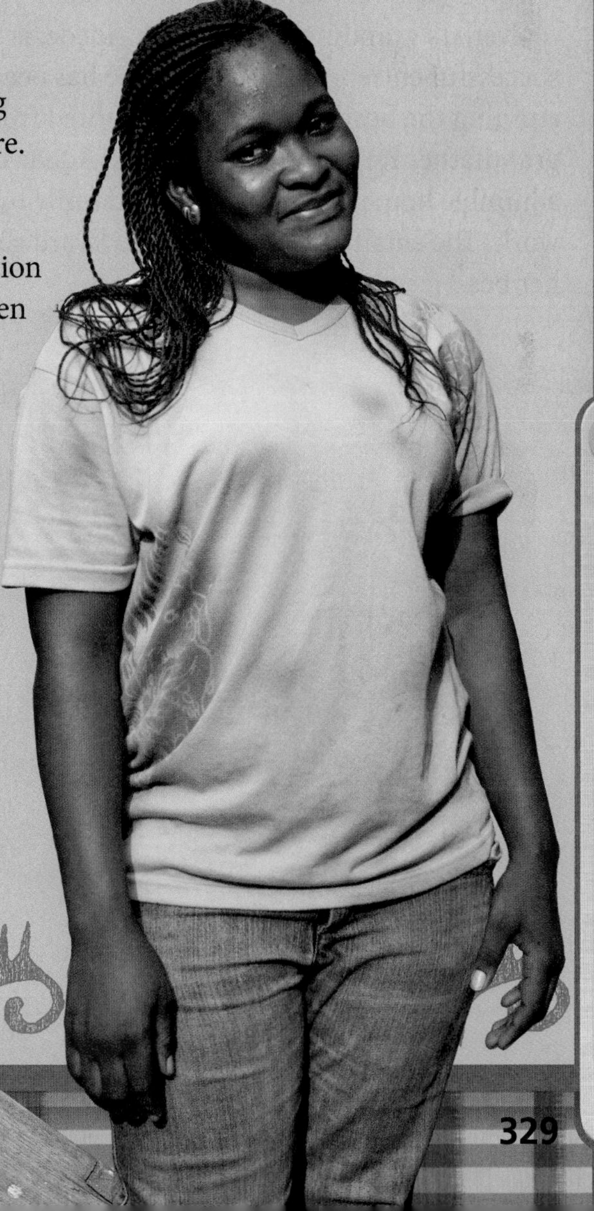

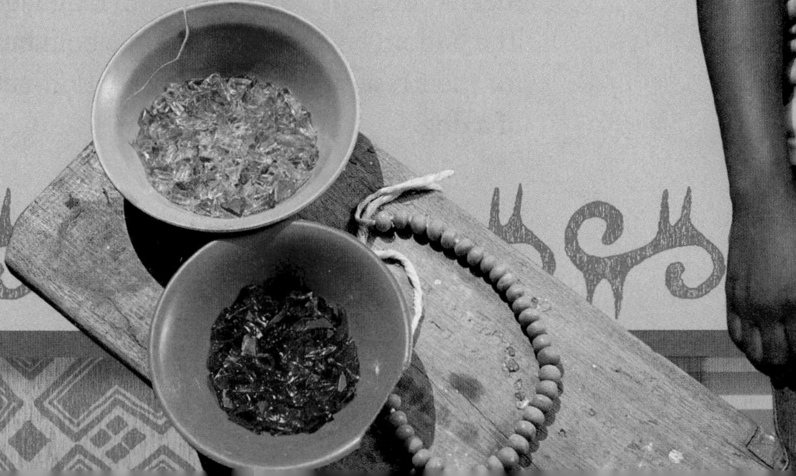

329

Bottles are crushed on a stone. The glass is poured into molds that are baked in a kiln.

Members of Evelyn's family string finished beads.

markets of Accra. Kpong is Evelyn's home and where her grandmother's bead business, Adede Beads Enterprises, is located. The plantain farms and thick greenery that surround the small village of Kpong are very different from Accra.

Evelyn's grandmother, Madam Adede, is a successful entrepreneur herself. She has been running the bead business she inherited from her grandfather for more than 31 years. Adede owns a humble home where she and her family live and work. The small building in the backyard serves as her bead factory.

Evelyn crushes bottle glass to make beads. The pail blocks the glass from flying up into her eyes or spilling onto the ground.

Adede specializes in the ancient craft of bead making practiced by the Krobo people of eastern Ghana. Adede taught this craft to two daughters and six grandchildren. She expects the business to continue for many generations. Adede has chosen Evelyn to take over her business someday. Evelyn has just graduated from high school. She hopes to study accounting at a university. But the cost won't be easy for her family to afford.

Evelyn already plays an important role in the family business. It is her job to crush glass in preparation for making the beads. Today she is making transparent glass beads, which are formed from a very fine glass powder. Evelyn begins by breaking glass bottles they have collected. It is hard work, but Evelyn is accustomed to the heavy labor and stifling heat that comes with everyday life at the bead factory in Kpong.

Crushing the glass is the first of many steps necessary to produce a finished piece of clear beaded jewelry. Adede explains that they also make glazed beads and *bodom* beads. The word *bodom* means "dog" in Twi, a common language in Ghana. The bodom beads are very large, bold beads, named for their resemblance to the attention-getting bark of a dog.

330

The busy marketplace features many kinds of goods.

The sign for the family business

The family beads on sale at the Krobo Odumase Market

Beads, such as those made by Evelyn, are worn not only for adornment, but also to identify the various ethnic cultures of Ghana. Beads are often worn at parties, weddings, and church services.

Today the family is taking its beads to sell at the Krobo Odumase Market a few miles from Kpong. Adede's bead stand in the marketplace displays their colorful jewelry to the buyers in the market. Everyone works hard to sell as much as possible. They need money not only to support the family but also to send Evelyn to university.

For her part, Evelyn plans to pay back this kindness. Evelyn says, "After university, I'll get a job outside and help my grandma, too, because I have my siblings to take care of. It's important to have two jobs. So if one fails, you have the other one." The road ahead of Evelyn is difficult, but her family's bead business has paved the way.

Meet the Journalist

Name Travis Hamilton
Favorite Moment Seeing children play and laugh

myStory Video

Join Evelyn as she explores the Krobo Odumase Market.

my worldgeography.com myStory Video

331

Chapter Atlas

Key Ideas
- Location together with wind and rainfall patterns creates a wide variety of environments in West and Central Africa.
- Climate zones vary from very dry to wet and tropical.
- Climate zones influence where and how people live in West and Central Africa.
- People have both adapted to and changed the environments of this region.

Key Terms • Sahel • savanna • arable land • desertification • deforestation • malaria

→ **Visual Glossary**

Reading Skill: Label an Outline Map Take notes using the outline map in your journal.

A group of people travels by boat on the Niger River in Niger. ▼

Physical Features

The physical features of West and Central Africa are rich and varied. They range from vast deserts to dense rain forests. The world's largest hot desert, the Sahara, reaches down into West and Central Africa from the north. Other dry areas also occur in the far south. Between the dry areas, grasslands blend into the lush tropical rainforest at the region's center.

In contrast, the region's landforms do not have great variety. Much of the continent of Africa as a whole is a plateau. Although highland areas exist, no major mountain chains interrupt the plateau.

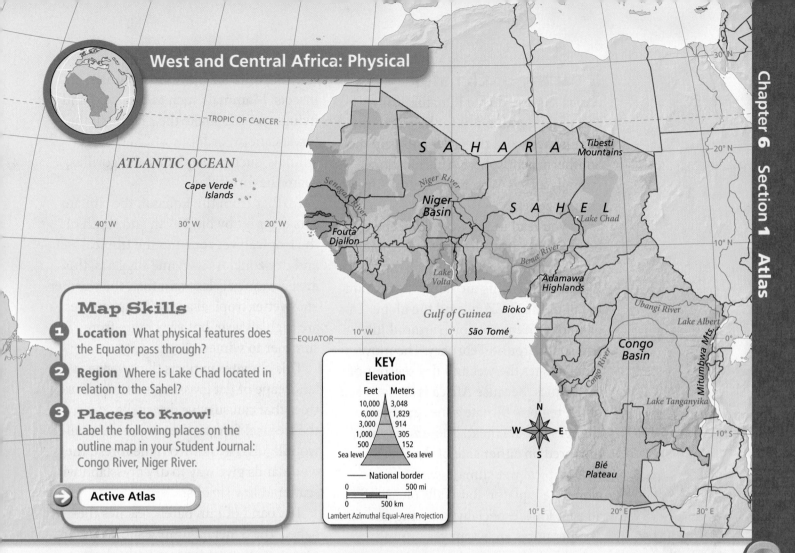

West and Central Africa: Physical

Map Skills

1. **Location** What physical features does the Equator pass through?

2. **Region** Where is Lake Chad located in relation to the Sahel?

3. **Places to Know!** Label the following places on the outline map in your Student Journal: Congo River, Niger River.

Active Atlas

KEY

Elevation

Feet	Meters
10,000	3,048
6,000	1,829
3,000	914
1,000	305
500	152
Sea level	Sea level

— National border

Lambert Azimuthal Equal-Area Projection

The plateau has been ground down by millions of years of weathering and erosion. Low elevations in the northwest build to higher elevations in the southeast.

West and Central Africa boasts some of the largest drainage basins in the world. A drainage basin is the entire area of land from which rainfall flows into a river or lake. The Chad basin drains a huge area. At its center lies the large but shallow Lake Chad. Lake Chad is the largest body of water in the Sahel. The **Sahel** is a semiarid, fairly dry area that lies between the Sahara and regions to the south that receive more rainfall.

The Niger River basin is the largest in western Africa. More rain falls in some parts of the basin than in others. Heavy rain causes flooding at times in parts of the basin.

The huge Congo River drains most of central Africa. Heavy rainfall feeds the Congo through most of the year. In fact, the Congo basin hosts Africa's largest network of navigable rivers, or rivers that ships can pass through. However, waterfalls and rapids can make passage difficult and dangerous.

Reading Check What are two important rivers in the region?

A Variety of Climates

Africa sits astride the Equator. Roughly half of the continent is in the Northern Hemisphere, and the other half is in the Southern Hemisphere. This location strongly affects West and Central Africa's climate zones.

As you read in the Core Concepts, a belt of rising air called the intertropical convergence zone, or ITCZ, circles the Equator. The rising air causes heavy rain to fall in the ITCZ around the globe. This band of rain moves north around July and south around February. The movement creates the wet and dry seasons of the tropics. Because Africa is so flat, each of the region's climate zones gradually changes into the next. These zones are mirrored on either side of the Equator.

A tropical wet climate can be found along the Equator. Rain falls plentifully all year long, especially in spring and fall. Temperatures are warm year-round.

In West and Central Africa, dense rain forests grow in the tropical wet zone.

The forests teem with birds, reptiles, and insects. Mammals such as monkeys and flying squirrels make their home in the forest canopy, or topmost layer. Large animals, such as elephants and gorillas, roam the forest floor.

Farther from the Equator, the climate gets drier bit by bit. North and south of the tropical wet zone lies the tropical wet and dry zone. As its name suggests, this area always gets less rain than the warmer and wetter tropical areas. Temperatures are high all year, but vary more from summer to winter.

This climate supports the **savanna,** a landscape of flat grasslands with scattered trees that can survive dry spells. Near the tropical forests, the savanna has tall woodlands. Farther from the forest, the woodlands give way to dry grassland with scattered low shrubs.

The band of rain barely reaches the Sahel. The Sahel has only a short rainy season of at most three months. Less rain falls than on the savanna. Daily temperatures are high. As in a desert, evening temperatures can dip very low.

Beyond the bands of precipitation lie the arid zones. These desert regions get little rainfall. Brutally hot days contrast with very cold nights. Not surprisingly, fewer animal species live in the drier regions, especially in the desert, where vegetation is sparse. Small mammals, such as rats and hares, are found along with gazelles, hyenas, and ostriches.

Reading Check How is a tropical wet climate different from a tropical wet and dry climate?

A man herds cattle in the semiarid Sahel.▼

myWorld Activity
Compare Climates

334

West and Central Africa: Climate

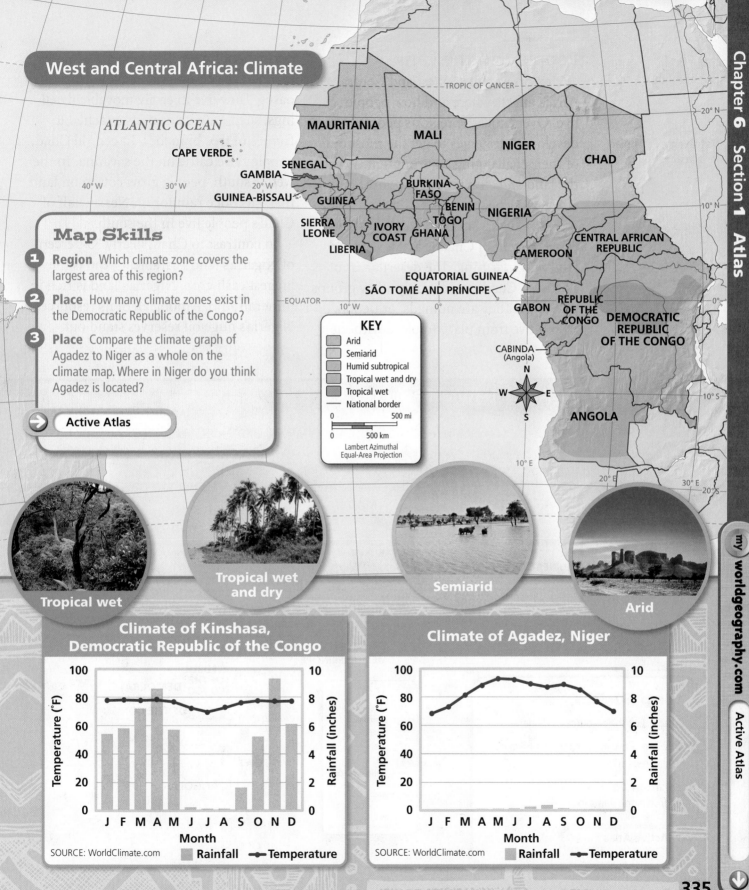

ATLANTIC OCEAN

TROPIC OF CANCER

MAURITANIA
CAPE VERDE
SENEGAL
GAMBIA
GUINEA-BISSAU
GUINEA
SIERRA LEONE
LIBERIA
IVORY COAST
GHANA
MALI
BURKINA FASO
BENIN
TOGO
NIGER
NIGERIA
CHAD
CAMEROON
CENTRAL AFRICAN REPUBLIC
EQUATORIAL GUINEA
SÃO TOMÉ AND PRÍNCIPE
GABON
REPUBLIC OF THE CONGO
DEMOCRATIC REPUBLIC OF THE CONGO
CABINDA (Angola)
ANGOLA

EQUATOR

Map Skills

1 **Region** Which climate zone covers the largest area of this region?

2 **Place** How many climate zones exist in the Democratic Republic of the Congo?

3 **Place** Compare the climate graph of Agadez to Niger as a whole on the climate map. Where in Niger do you think Agadez is located?

→ Active Atlas

KEY
- Arid
- Semiarid
- Humid subtropical
- Tropical wet and dry
- Tropical wet
- — National border

0   500 mi
0   500 km
Lambert Azimuthal Equal-Area Projection

Tropical wet

Tropical wet and dry

Semiarid

Arid

Climate of Kinshasa, Democratic Republic of the Congo

SOURCE: WorldClimate.com   Rainfall   — Temperature

Climate of Agadez, Niger

SOURCE: WorldClimate.com   Rainfall   — Temperature

my worldgeography.com   Active Atlas

335

People and the Land

The environment of West and Central Africa affects where and how people live. Over time, the region's people have developed <u>strategies</u> to get the most out of their challenging environment. What the land and climate will support often affects how people make a living.

Take Chad as an example. Less than three percent of Chad is **arable land,** or land fit for farming. The desert areas of northern Chad support only a few groups of people. They are nomads, or people who move from place to place without a permanent home. The nomads who live in Chad raise camels and a few crops in oases. They live in easily movable dwellings, such as tents or mats attached to frames of tree branches. In central Chad, people raise cattle on the savanna. In the wetter south, people grow cotton on land that was once rain forest. Nearly half of Chad's people live in the south.

In contrast to Chad, nearly 33 percent of Nigeria's land is arable. Cacao is the biggest cash crop. Nigeria's land is rich in minerals, too. Among all of its resources, Nigeria's huge oil reserves stand out.

strategy, *n.,* a plan for reaching a goal

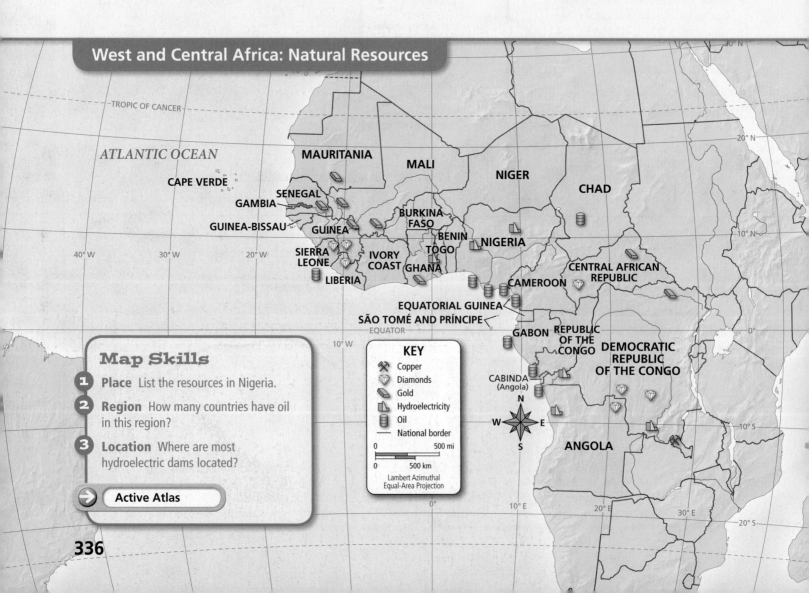

West and Central Africa: Natural Resources

Map Skills

1. **Place** List the resources in Nigeria.
2. **Region** How many countries have oil in this region?
3. **Location** Where are most hydroelectric dams located?

→ **Active Atlas**

KEY
- Copper
- Diamonds
- Gold
- Hydroelectricity
- Oil
- National border

0 — 500 mi
0 — 500 km
Lambert Azimuthal Equal-Area Projection

336

Tapping this resource, however, hurts Nigeria's environment. An estimated 1.5 million tons of oil have dripped from leaky pipelines into the Niger Delta over the past 50 years. Oil seeps into wetlands, forests, and farmlands. It pollutes air and water and causes fires.

Many countries in this region have rich natural resources. Like Nigeria, Angola, Cameroon, Chad, and other countries also have oil reserves. The Democratic Republic of the Congo has deposits of copper, diamonds, uranium, and other minerals. Liberia and Sierra Leone have diamond fields. These natural resources have the potential to bring great wealth to the region. As you will read, they have also often caused conflict.

Many people in the region use land to farm and graze animals. Although not always harmful, this use of land can hurt the environment. During dry periods in the Sahel, herders allow too many of their animals to graze. In addition, people also chop down trees for firewood or to sell.

These uses, combined with drought, have caused parts of the Sahel to dry out and become desert. This change from arable land to desert is called **desertification.** Chad and other Sahel nations are working on ways to stop desertification.

The Ivory Coast (also called Côte d'Ivoire) gets plentiful rain. Even so, desertification threatens this nation as well. The main culprit is deforestation. **Deforestation** is the loss of forest cover that occurs when the trees in a forest are removed faster than they can grow back. The soil dries out without the shade of trees to protect it from the hot sun.

The Ivory Coast has a very high rate of deforestation. More than 90 percent of its forests have been cleared by the timber industry in the past few <u>decades.</u> Foreign-owned companies have done much of the harvesting of this raw material for their industries. Deforestation is also a problem in the Democratic Republic of the Congo.

decade, *n.,* a period of ten years

Reading Check What causes desertification?

Deforestation

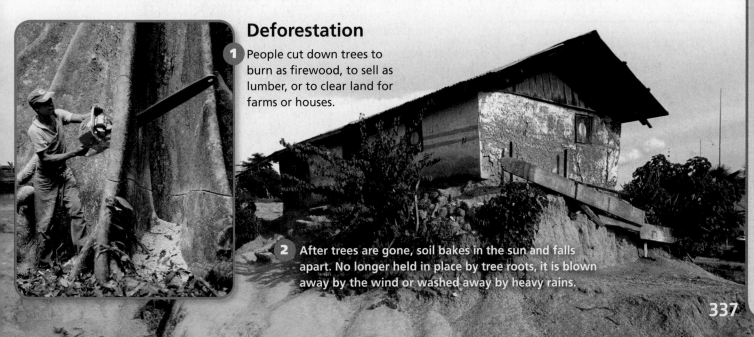

1 People cut down trees to burn as firewood, to sell as lumber, or to clear land for farms or houses.

2 After trees are gone, soil bakes in the sun and falls apart. No longer held in place by tree roots, it is blown away by the wind or washed away by heavy rains.

Population

Just as the environment affects what people do for a living, it also affects where they live. As you have read, Nigeria has plenty of land that is good for farming. Not surprisingly, it also has the largest population in the region. In fact, it is the most populous nation in all of Africa, with 148 million people. In contrast, fewer people live in countries that are in desert regions. For instance, Mauritania is home to only about 3.3 million people.

People often think of Africans as rural farmers. In this region of Africa, many people do still farm or raise livestock. However, more and more people are moving to cities such as Lagos in Nigeria or Accra in Ghana.

People may move to cities to look for work because a season's crops have failed. Conflict forces others from their homes. Some move away from the Sahel because of desertification. The desert spreads to where they raise animals or crops.

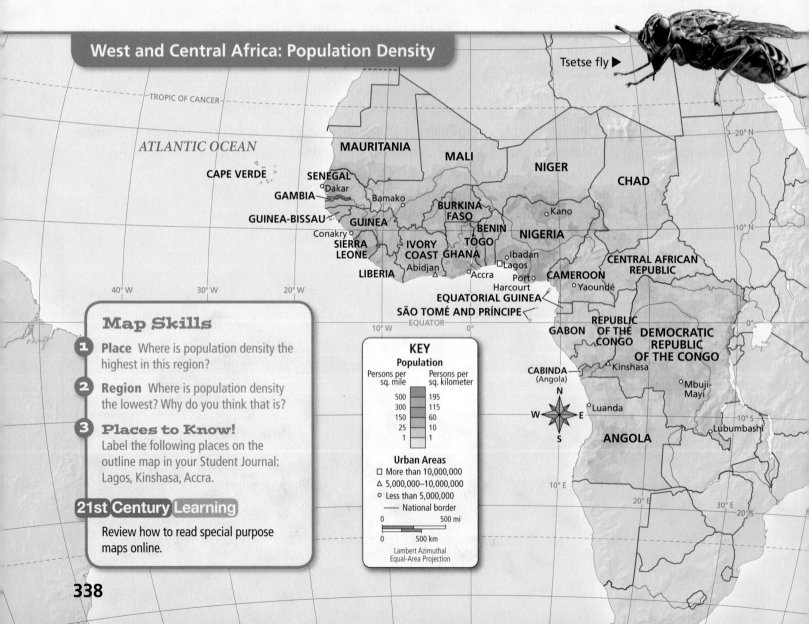

West and Central Africa: Population Density

Tsetse fly ▶

Map Skills

1 **Place** Where is population density the highest in this region?

2 **Region** Where is population density the lowest? Why do you think that is?

3 **Places to Know!** Label the following places on the outline map in your Student Journal: Lagos, Kinshasa, Accra.

21st Century Learning

Review how to read special purpose maps online.

KEY

Population

Persons per sq. mile	Persons per sq. kilometer
500	195
300	115
150	60
25	10
1	1

Urban Areas
- □ More than 10,000,000
- △ 5,000,000–10,000,000
- ○ Less than 5,000,000
- — National border

0 — 500 mi
0 — 500 km

Lambert Azimuthal Equal-Area Projection

338

Unfortunately, the city doesn't always hold a better life for them. Because the cities are growing so quickly, they are overcrowded. There are shortages of good housing and good jobs.

Reading Check How are West and Central Africa's populations changing?

The Problem of Disease

Some big environmental challenges in West and Central Africa come in very small packages: insects. Insects carry parasites, or small organisms that live off of a larger organism. The tsetse (TEE tsee) fly spreads a parasite that causes a disease known as sleeping sickness. It is fatal to both humans and cattle. The disease is widespread. The presence of the tsetse fly limits where cattle can be raised, and where people can live.

Mosquitoes spread **malaria**, another life-threatening disease caused by parasites. Mosquitoes thrive in environments that are hot and wet. Therefore, malaria is common throughout the tropical and subtropical regions of Africa. Ninety percent of deaths from malaria occur in these regions.

Some diseases are both treatable and preventable. Sadly, many people in this region cannot afford to take even the simplest measures to protect themselves.

Nigerian doctor Emmanuel Miri visits rural villages to educate communities on disease prevention and treatment.

66 Most people in rural areas are farmers, and when you have a disease like Guinea worm [a parasite], you are incapacitated, unable to continue with your work. By preventing the hundreds of thousands of cases that we do each year, we are freeing up that many more people to farm so that they will have food and be able to take care of their families. 99

—Emmanuel Miri

Local education programs like Miri's are helping to combat many diseases.

Reading Check How does malaria spread?

my World
IN NUMBERS
Mosquito nets treated with insecticide help prevent malaria. Yet, in 2007, only **6%** of households in the Ivory Coast owned one.

Section 1 Assessment

Key Terms
1. Use the following terms to describe the challenging environment of West and Central Africa: deforestation, desertification, malaria.

Key Ideas
2. What are some ways in which the Sahel is different from the tropical wet zone?

3. Why do so few of Chad's people live in the north of the country and so many in the south?

4. What is one problem oil production causes in Nigeria?

Think Critically
5. Summarize Why are people in West and Central Africa moving from the countryside to the city?

6. Draw Inferences Use what you have learned in this section to explain why Ghana has a higher percentage of arable land than Mali.

? Essential Question
Who should benefit from a country's resources?

7. How might not having abundant farmland or natural resources affect a country? Go to your Student Journal to record your answer.

339

History of West and Central Africa

Key Ideas

- The people of West Africa traded with each other from an early date, leading to well-developed trading kingdoms.

- The Atlantic slave trade, beginning in the 1500s, followed by European colonization in the 1800s, disrupted life in the region.

- Most West and Central African countries gained independence in the 1960s, but deeply rooted problems remain.

Key Terms • salt trade • Atlantic slave trade • middle passage • colonialism • imperialism • Pan-Africanism

⊙ **Visual Glossary**

Reading Skill: Sequence Take notes using the graphic organizer in your journal.

Geography shaped life in early West and Central Africa in many ways. The people turned to trade to cope with a challenging environment. The natural resources and location of the area encouraged trade.

Trade in Early West and Central Africa

During ancient times in the savannas and forests of West Africa, people grew crops and raised animals. Sometimes, a community produced more food than it needed. In this case, the farmers or herders eagerly traded their products at local markets. In time, small kingdoms arose to guide and direct this local trade.

Empire of Ghana
Arab traders traded salt like this for gold. Gold had little value south of the Sahara but was prized by Arab traders.

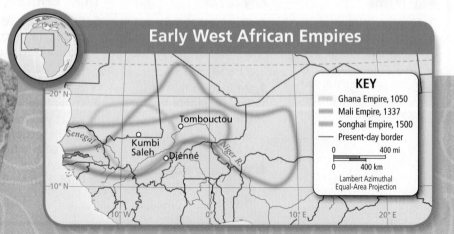

Early West African Empires

KEY
- Ghana Empire, 1050
- Mali Empire, 1337
- Songhai Empire, 1500
- Present-day border

0   400 mi
0   400 km
Lambert Azimuthal Equal-Area Projection

Tombouctou
Kumbi Saleh
Djénné
Senegal R.
Niger R.

20° N
10° N
10° W
0°
10° E
20° E

Salt for Gold Beginning around A.D. 750, these kingdoms began to develop a long-distance trade with Arab traders who lived in North Africa. They exchanged all sorts of goods with their neighbors. The bestsellers were gold and salt. Unlike today, salt was rare and expensive. West Africans traded gold for the Arabs' salt in what was called the **salt trade.**

Arab trading partners brought more than salt to the region. They also carried scholarship, law, and the religion of Islam to West Africa. The trade networks gave birth to new cities. Rulers gained power by collecting taxes and tribute.

Three great trading empires arose in West Africa between 600 and the mid-1600s. Each had its days of glory. Each fell due to a combination of factors.

Ghana Leads the Way Ghana, the first of the great empires, flourished between 600 and 1200. The modern country of Ghana took its name from this empire. However, the empire of Ghana ruled over much of present-day Mali and Mauritania. It did not include present-day Ghana.

Success led to a larger population, which strained resources. Then, around 1050, power struggles with peoples to the north weakened Ghana. In 1240, the leader of a newer empire called Mali attacked Ghana's last strongholds. Soon Mali swallowed up the old empire.

Mali Makes an Impression Mali's greatest emperor, Mansa Musa, ruled from about 1312 to 1337. He practiced Islam. He made a spectacular pilgrimage, or religious journey, to the Arabian city of Mecca in 1324. The trip strengthened Mali's ties with North Africa. It drew the world's attention to the empire. However, Mali, too, weakened and <u>declined.</u>

decline, *v.,* to get weaker

Songhai's Glory In the mid-1400s, the empire of Songhai took over from Mali. It became the largest empire in African history. Songhai took over the great trading cities of Tombouctou (also spelled Timbuktu) and Djenné. Tombouctou flourished as the center of the salt trade and of Islamic learning and culture in West Africa. But by the early 1600s, the empire had split into smaller states.

Reading Check What was the effect of Mansa Musa's pilgrimage to Mecca?

Empire of Mali

A Spanish map from the late 1300s shows Mansa Musa. Mansa Musa's pilgrimage to Mecca in 1324 drew the world's attention.

Songhai Empire

At its height, Songhai controlled a region roughly the size of the United States. The Great Mosque at Djenné (right) was rebuilt in the 1900s.

my worldgeography.com Timeline

Timeline

341

Europeans in the Region

In the late 1400s, West and Central Africans began trading with new partners, Europeans. Like Arab traders, gold drew Europeans to West and Central Africa. Soon, they became involved in the slave trade.

Trading in enslaved people was not new in Africa. Various forms of slavery existed before European contact. Slaves were part of the trans-Saharan trade. However, the Europeans' slave trade affected many more people. It had more serious effects on African society.

The Atlantic Slave Trade Begins In the 1500s, Europeans began to colonize the Americas. They brought enslaved Africans across the Atlantic Ocean to work on colonial plantations. This trade is called the **Atlantic slave trade**. It was part of the triangular trade between Europe, its American colonies, and Africa. African traders sold slaves for manufactured goods from Europe, such as cloth and guns. Thousands of the captives died during the grueling **middle passage,** the voyage across the Atlantic that formed the middle leg of the triangle.

Effects of the Trade The Atlantic slave trade was the largest forced migration in history. Perhaps 13 million people left Africa in slave ships. This migration had several effects.

Some scholars believe that the slave trade changed the relationship between African states in the region. Stronger states attacked weaker ones to get slaves to trade. These wars hurt governance and economies in the region.

Africans who went to North America, the Caribbean, and South America brought their cultures with them. Their traditions influenced religion, music, and other ways of life in the Americas.

Colonialism Slavery was outlawed in the United States and Europe in the early 1800s. But European interference was far from over. In the late 1800s, European countries looked to Africa for more colonies. **Colonialism** is a policy by which one country seeks to rule other areas. The policy of creating an empire by taking over other areas is also often called **imperialism**. European countries had colonized nearly all of Africa by 1900.

Reading Check What was the triangular trade?

This model of a slave ship from 1790 shows the cruel way slave traders packed their ships with as much human cargo as possible. The captives were locked in these positions for six weeks or more. ▼

Closer Look

EUROPEAN COLONIZATION IN AFRICA

In the 1880s, European powers made a mad dash for territory in Africa. This rush is known as the "Scramble for Africa." Africans resisted the start of European rule. But they couldn't stand against the Europeans' powerful new weapons, such as the Maxim machine gun. From the 1880s until the 1960s, European powers ruled almost every part of Africa. Some of colonization's damaging effects are still being felt today.

Poster showing Africa as a market for British goods ▲

THINK CRITICALLY   What did European powers want from the colonies?

CAUSES European nations wanted colonies
- to win prestige.
- to get natural resources needed to produce industrial goods in Europe.
- as markets for goods made in factories.

EVENT Europeans got colonies

In 1884, European leaders met and divided up Africa among themselves. No African leaders took part. Before long, Europe controlled nearly the entire continent.

EFFECTS Colonial powers hurt Africa
- by ignoring the location of ethnic groups when drawing borders.
- by not developing colonial economies beyond their own aims.
- by forcing Africans to extract resources or grow cash crops.

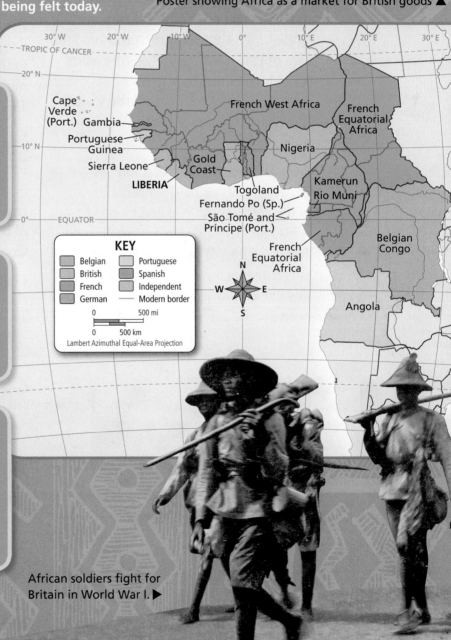

African soldiers fight for Britain in World War I. ▶

343

myWorld Activity
The Promise of
Independence

Independence and Beyond

Most Africans did not take part in colonial government. Some colonies, however, did ask a small number of Africans to help run their governments. As these Africans became educated, leaders emerged. They grew frustrated with the unfair rule of colonial powers. After World War II, a political leader in Ghana named Kwame Nkrumah (KWAH mee n KROO muh), promoted the idea of Pan-Africanism. **Pan-Africanism** was a political and social movement to unite black Africans around the world. Throughout Africa, Africans called for independence.

Early Dreams and Harsh Realities

Between 1960 and 1975, nearly all of the colonies in West and Central Africa became independent nations. The <u>transition</u> of power to African governments was mostly peaceful. But in some countries, the people had not been involved in government for decades.

transition, *n.,* movement from one condition to another

Also, Europeans still controlled many economic structures. The borders of the countries were drawn without regard to ethnic and language groups.

Despite bright hopes, the new nations soon ran into problems. Groups within countries fought one another. Governments banned opposition parties. Military dictators often led these governments.

Trouble in the Congo For example, Belgium abruptly granted independence to the Belgian Congo in 1960. Within months, the new nation was in chaos. In 1965, army leader Joseph Mobutu seized power. Mobutu renamed the country Zaire (zah EER) after a traditional name for the Congo River. He claimed to want to restore the nation's cultural identity. Instead, he ruled as a dictator for 32 years of incredible corruption. Meanwhile, Congo's people suffered.

Civil War in Nigeria In the 1940s, Nigerian leaders united more than 40 ethnic groups to oppose British rule.

A happy crowd greets the news of independence in the Belgian Congo in 1960.

By 1965, the dictator Joseph Mobutu (middle left) controlled the Congo, using violence to maintain power.

Everyone from soldiers to market women joined the call for freedom. Nigeria became independent in 1960.

However, ethnic unity did not last long. In 1967, three eastern states that were controlled by the Igbo (ig boh, also called Ibo) ethnic group attempted to leave Nigeria. They wanted to secede, or formally break away, and form their own country. The new country would be called the Republic of Biafra. One reason behind the move was that Igbos had been the victims of ethnic fighting in northern Nigeria.

Another reason was that Biafra was rich in oil. A bloody civil war followed. An estimated 500,000 to several million people died before Biafra rejoined Nigeria.

Economic Dependence and Dictatorship The new nations often continued relationships with their former colonial rulers. They stayed loyal to their former rulers in return for technical advice and loans. This arrangement tended to keep their economies focused on exporting cash crops and natural resources that mainly benefited European nations. As a result, homegrown manufacturing and businesses grew slowly. Taking on foreign loans created huge debts.

From 1945 until 1989, the United States and the Soviet Union carried on a rivalry called the Cold War. African nations were caught in the middle. To further their ends, both sides often supported dictators that were friendly to their point of view.

When the Cold War ended, so too did some of the support from Cold War powers. This paved the way for a new push for democracy throughout the region. By the early 1990s, most nations in the region had reestablished some form of elected government. Some of these democracies have been successful. Others have remained unstable.

Reading Check What happened after Nigeria gained independence?

▲ In 1960, Nigeria's first president, Nnamdi Azikiwe (NUM dee ah ZEE kway) said, "The past is gone with all its bitterness." But soon Nigeria plunged into conflict.

Section 2 Assessment

Key Terms

1. Use the following words to explain how outsiders have affected West and Central Africa throughout history: salt trade, Atlantic slave trade, middle passage, colonialism, imperialism, Pan-Africanism.

Key Ideas

2. How were the West African trading empires able to grow and become wealthy?

3. Describe the effects of the Atlantic slave trade.

4. What are some reasons why European powers created African colonies?

Think Critically

5. **Compare Viewpoints** How might Nnamdi Azikiwe's view of the future in 1960 be different from that of someone who fought in Nigeria's civil war in later years?

6. **Summarize** How did Cold War rivalries affect West and Central Africa?

Essential Question

Who should benefit from a country's resources?

7. What role did natural resources play in the history of West and Central Africa? Go to your Student Journal to record your answer.

Famous Cities and Kingdoms of West Africa

Key Ideas
- A variety of cities and kingdoms rose in West Africa before the arrival of Europeans in the region.
- Each city or kingdom contributed to the region's culture and history.

Key Terms • Tombouctou • Yoruba • oni • Benin

As you have read, large, wealthy kingdoms such as Ghana, Mali, and Songhai flourished in West Africa before the colonial period. Tombouctou became an important city and cultural center during the Mali and Songhai eras. But these kingdoms were not the only kingdoms in the region. Many other states and cities also contributed to West and Central Africa's rich cultural legacy, including Ife, Oyo, and Benin.

Tombouctou: Center of Trade and Learning

You have already read about the city of **Tombouctou** (also spelled Timbuktu). It was founded around A.D. 1100 in modern-day Mali. For many centuries, it was one of the most important cities in West Africa.

Tombouctou was part of the Mali and Songhai empires. It became important because of its location at the edge of the Sahara. Caravans, or groups of traders, carrying gold came up from the south. Most did

▲ A sign in Arabic and French points to Tombouctou.

A modern-day camel caravan makes its way across the Sahara. ▼

not travel past Tombouctou across the dry Sahara. Desert caravans loaded with salt came from the north to Tombouctou. There they traded salt for gold. The city grew rich from the trade. Its wealth made it famous as far away as Europe.

But Tombouctou was more than just a marketplace. It was a college town—a center of Islamic learning and law. The University of Sankore (SAN kohr) was founded in a mosque in Tombouctou. It attracted the best minds from all over West Africa. Tombouctou was a large town, and one quarter of its people were scholars. They left behind thousands of manuscripts that help modern historians learn about African history.

Around 1600, the city began to decline. However, people around the world, and especially in West Africa, remembered its wealth and wisdom. A proverb from the region shows the city's fame:

> 66 Salt comes from the North, gold comes from the South, but the word of God and the treasures of wisdom come from Timbuktu [Tombouctou]. 99

—Proverb from West Africa

Reading Check Which empires claimed Tombouctou?

The Yoruba Cities

The **Yoruba** ethnic group lives mainly in modern Nigeria, southeast of Tombouctou. Yorubas have a common language, culture, and history in western Nigeria. The traditional Yoruba homeland included both forests and savanna. This homeland was to the southeast of the empire of Ghana. It did not come under the control of the empires of Ghana, Mali, or even Songhai.

The various groups of Yoruba people of the region never united into one kingdom. They did found many city-states, ruled by kings. Sometimes one city was the most powerful, sometimes another. But as far back as historians can tell, every Yoruba state recognized Ife (EE fay) as the most important city of all.

According to Yoruba stories, Ife was the place where life itself was created. It was the oldest city in the area, dating back to around 1000. It was also the most important religious and cultural center of the Yoruba people.

A manuscript written in Sankore during Tombouctou's glory days ▼

347

Artists in Ife produced beautiful bronze statues. The rulers of the city were called **onis** (OH neez). They were the religious leaders of the Yoruba people. The Yoruba believed that the first oni of Ife was Oduduwa and that he was the first to bring iron to the area.

Ife did not build a large kingdom. The Yoruba city-state of Oyo did. The people of Oyo used iron and a strong cavalry, or soldiers fighting on horseback, to dominate the grassy savanna. In 1730, Oyo defeated the neighboring kingdom called Dahomey and began to expand to the south. Although Oyo became more powerful than its neighbor Ife, its kings always recognized Ife's special position.

Eventually the Oyo empire reached the coast. There Oyo traders acted as middlemen for traders from Europe.

The Oyo sold the European traders slaves from farther inland. The empire fell quickly after it lost control of trade routes on the coast. Outsiders conquered it.

Reading Check **Where did the Yoruba believe life was created?**

▼ A bronze sculpture from Ife

The Oyo and Benin Empires, 1625

KEY
- Benin empire
- Oyo empire
- ○ City

0 — 100 mi
0 — 100 km
Mercator Projection

OYO EMPIRE

Niger River

○ Ife

BENIN EMPIRE

ATLANTIC OCEAN

Map Skills

1. **Location** Where is the city of Ife in relation to the Oyo empire?

2. **Interaction** How did being near the Atlantic coast affect both Oyo and Benin?

Benin, an Empire in the Forest

To the south of Oyo and Ife, the city of **Benin** began to expand in the rain forest along the coast in present-day southern Nigeria. By around 1300, Benin City was the most powerful city in its area. Its neighbors had to send it tribute, or regular payments sent to an overlord. Over time it grew into an empire.

Like the people of Oyo, the people of Benin recognized the spiritual and cultural importance of Ife. They asked a prince from Ife to be their king. Benin became an artistic center in its own right. Its artisans produced famous woodcarvings and brass work.

The Benin empire was well organized and strong before Europeans arrived on the scene. When the Europeans did come, Benin was one of the first and most important African states they had to deal with. Long before Oyo fought its way to the coast, the Benin empire was trading with Europeans.

Traders from Benin, like those from Oyo, served as middlemen for the slave trade. The empire came to depend on this trade. When the British abolished the slave trade in the 1800s, Benin became weak and politically unstable. The British were able to conquer it.

Reading Check **What geographic area was Benin's home?**

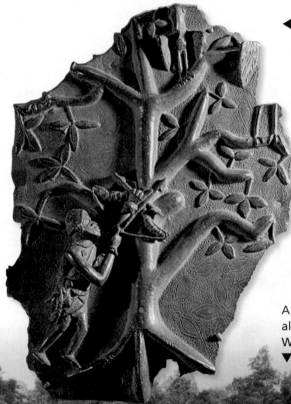

◀ Artisans in the forest kingdom of Benin produced beautiful bronze reliefs.

A forested area along the coast of West Africa today ▼

Assessment

1. How did Tombouctou's geography help make it rich?

2. What do Tombouctou's manuscripts show about the city?

3. Why was Ife so important even though it was not powerful?

4. Why was access to the coast so important for Oyo and Benin?

5. What was one factor that caused Benin to fall?

Section 3

West and Central Africa Today

Key Ideas
- Many West and Central African countries have struggled to build their economies.
- Some of the nations in the region still experience violent upheaval.
- The people of the region enjoy rich, varied cultures.
- West and Central Africans search for solutions to economic problems, disease, and violence.

Key Terms • infrastructure • corruption • griot • African Union • microcredit

 Visual Glossary

Reading Skill: Identify Main Ideas and Details Take notes using the graphic organizer in your journal.

Traffic moves slowly along a rough road in Lagos, Nigeria.

After independence, many countries in West and Central Africa struggled to establish strong economies and stable governments. Today, West and Central Africans still struggle with poverty and unrest. They seek ways to solve continuing problems.

Economic Challenges

The nations of West and Central Africa are among the poorest in the world. Even nations with rich natural resources have struggled to build and maintain healthy economies.

Legacies of Colonialism Colonial powers did little to foster the economies of their colonies. When they gained independence, the new nations of West and Central Africa did not have strong infrastructures. **Infrastructure** is the body of public works, such as roads, bridges, and hospitals, that a country needs to support a modern economy. To build infrastructure, nations borrowed money from other countries. Many now owe huge debts.

Some of the nations in this region still depend on exporting one or two products. This dependence is risky because the price of products can go up and down drastically. In return for raw materials, West and Central Africans import manufactured goods. They often spend more on imports than they earn with exports. This situation is called a negative balance of trade.

Corruption **Corruption,** or the use of power for personal gain, is common in this region. International observers consider Nigeria to be one of the most corrupt nations in the world. The country is in the top ten of the world's largest oil exporters. Yet, around 70 percent of Nigerians live on less than one dollar per day. Corruption and poor management of money by the government both play a role in keeping most Nigerians poor.

Oil is a very capital-intensive business. In other words, it requires a large investment of money to buy machinery. Often, businesses from other countries have made this investment and, in turn, gained huge profits. Nigerians living near the oil fields resent the fact that oil profits often benefit only foreigners and corrupt officials. This resentment has led to violence that has hurt the country as a whole.

Subsistence Farming Another challenge in this region is that the majority of people are subsistence farmers. For example, about 80 percent of people in Mali survive by growing food to eat. Many parts of West and Central Africa lack good farmland, so farming is a difficult way of life. Since they don't make money by selling goods, many farmers cannot afford equipment that would make their farms more profitable.

Children often work on the family farm. Sending them to school is a sacrifice for the family. Many parents make the sacrifice because they know education will improve the lives of their children.

Reading Check How have many nations in the region paid for infrastructure?

Political Challenges

When the colonies of West and Central Africa became independent, they faced many political problems. As you have read, the borders that new nations inherited cut across ethnic groups. Also, poverty and weak economies meant that vital goods were scarce, or hard to find. Competition over scarce necessities and rich natural resources caused tension.

In many nations, violence between ethnic groups raged in civil wars. Years of warfare damaged economies and hurt the formation of strong democratic governments. Some countries still struggle with poor economies and bad leadership, leading to more violence.

A Country in Turmoil: The Democratic Republic of the Congo As you have read, the greedy dictator Joseph Mobutu ruled the Democratic Republic of the Congo (which he called Zaire) for more than 30 years. In 1997, rebels led by Laurent Kabila caused Mobutu to fall from power.

myWorld Activity
Two Economies

A farmer in Nigeria uses a hand tool to tend to his field. ▼

351

In the Democratic Republic of the Congo, rebel forces have recruited children in their teens, sometimes by force, to fight.

In Ghana, citizens vote to elect their president and legislative representatives, as do citizens in the United States.

ceasefire, *n.,* an agreement to stop fighting temporarily

Kabila renamed the country the Democratic Republic of the Congo. But he did little to restore democracy. Former Mobutu supporters, with the aid of Uganda and Rwanda, rebelled in 1998. Uganda and Rwanda supported the rebels to continue their own ethnic conflicts. Angola, Namibia, and Zimbabwe joined the war on the side of the Kabila government. The conflict continued despite a <u>ceasefire</u> in 1999.

In 2001, Joseph Kabila came to power when his father was assassinated. With help from the United Nations, his government and the rebels reached a peace agreement in 2002. However, real peace has been slow in coming. Rebel forces still fight in the eastern part of the country. The fighting goes on in part because various groups want to control the rich mineral resources of that area.

The fighting has left the nation in shambles. Since 1998, an estimated 5 million people have died because of the war or the poor conditions brought about by the war.

Ghana, Back From the Brink Compared to other nations in the region, Ghana, where Evelyn lives, was in good shape upon independence. Still, it has had its problems. Ghana's first president was the independence movement leader Kwame Nkrumah. As he worked to build Ghana's economy, he also became a dictator. He fell from power in a coup, or sudden overthrow, in 1966.

Ghana then suffered several coups until air force officer Jerry Rawlings seized power in 1981. He restored constitutional democracy and won election as Ghana's president in 1992. Since that time, Ghana has been fairly stable.

Rawlings introduced several economic reforms. By the 1990s, Ghana had one of the fastest-growing economies in Africa. Its greatest income comes from gold and cacao production. In the future, Ghana plans to diversify exports and improve the status of women. It also aims to promote good governance.

Reading Check How did Ghana come to achieve stability?

352

The Cultures of the Region

There are many rich and varied cultures in West and Central Africa. Traditional and modern ways exist side by side, often blending to form new traditions.

Religion Before contact with the outside world, ethnic groups throughout the region developed their own religions. Then new religions were introduced through trading networks. Islam spread south from the Sahara. Mali, for example, has an overwhelmingly Muslim population. Next, Europeans brought Christianity to the region. For example, in Angola, many ethnic groups practiced religions based on ancestor worship and local deities. After the arrival of the Portuguese in the 1400s, many people adopted Christianity.

The Arts In West and Central Africa today, people enjoy both traditional dance and modern ballet. Modern music reflects traditional rhythms and styles. Even when it comes to sports, fans flock to both traditional and newer games. In Senegal, for example, the two most popular sports are soccer and traditional wrestling.

Stories are told through both oral tradition and literature. In West Africa, musician-storytellers called **griots** use music to track their heritage and record history as well as to entertain. Many see hip-hop artists as modern griots. Writers and filmmakers use literature and the cinema to explore Africa's cultural heritage as well as issues facing Africa today.

Reading Check How do griots preserve traditions in West Africa?

A Nigerian girl reads from the Quran. ▼

▲ West and Central Africans have created ceremonial masks for centuries.

Culture Close-up

In Senegal, a griot plays the kora, a traditional instrument. ▼

▲ A dancer wears a traditional mask and costume in Central Africa.

myworldgeography.com Culture Close-up

353

Hope for Change in the Future

Violence, poverty, and disease threaten daily existence for many in this region. Many countries are searching for <u>innovative</u> solutions to their problems. They seek to create better opportunities for the next generation of West and Central Africans.

innovative, *adj.,* fresh, new, or original

The Cost of Warfare Political instability and ethnic conflict threaten the safety of young people in this region. In some places, children are the victims of violence. For example, an estimated 10,000 child soldiers fought in Sierra Leone's ten-year civil war. In addition, thousands of people are forced to flee their homes to escape violence. In the Democratic Republic of the Congo alone, nearly 1.5 million people were internally displaced in 2007.

Poverty and Disease Poverty is another challenge faced by people in this region. Most people do not get to enjoy the benefits of the region's rich natural resources. Conflict, bad government, weak economies, and other factors lead to people being undernourished. A person who is undernourished does not have enough food to make a healthy diet. In West Africa, around 15 percent of the population is undernourished. In Central Africa, more than 50 percent of the population is undernourished.

Undernourishment makes people more vulnerable to diseases. Malaria and sleeping sickness affect millions of people every year. Another disease, acquired immunodeficiency syndrome (AIDS) is an epidemic in the continent of Africa south of the Sahara. Southern Africa has been hit the hardest. Still, many people in West and Central Africa suffer from this illness or know someone who does.

The African Union In 2002, an organization called the **African Union** was formed to promote unity among African states and to foster development and end poverty. The African Union continues the work of an earlier group called the Organization of African Unity, which was established in 1963. In recent years, the African Union has sent peacekeepers to several countries. It also works with international organizations to develop economic programs.

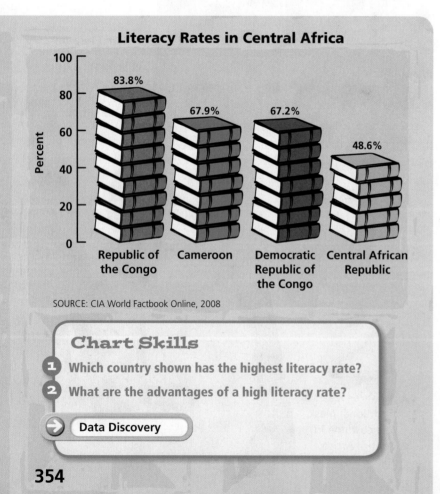

Literacy Rates in Central Africa

SOURCE: CIA World Factbook Online, 2008

Chart Skills

1. Which country shown has the highest literacy rate?
2. What are the advantages of a high literacy rate?

→ Data Discovery

354

An Eye Toward the Future The African Union, along with many foreign aid agencies, has identified these key factors in getting rid of poverty and promoting development in Africa:

- democracy
- women's rights
- development of infrastructure
- development of social services (such as education and healthcare)

The people of the region are working toward these goals by investing locally. Giving **microcredit,** or small loans usually less than $200, to individuals to fund their own businesses is a growing practice. Women use microcredit to start and run small businesses similar to Adede's bead business. The region is also investing in people by building new universities.

On a larger scale, others are developing new ways to meet people's needs. New technologies aim to improve lives without harming the environment. For example, many nations in the region have a huge potential for generating hydroelectricity.

Angola gets around 75 percent of its electricity from water power.

In all these ways, West and Central Africans are working to meet the challenges of their daily lives. The filmmaker Ousmane Sembene of Senegal sums up the hope for the future this way:

> 66 Forty years ago, we had nothing—no doctors, no engineers, no writers. We had no university. We thought a flag and a national anthem were enough for independence. . . .That is now a thing of the past. One has to count on the people. And despite all the problems, success for us is a certainty. Every day we're working hard, because we're dreaming of a better quality of life. 99
>
> —Ousmane Sembene

Reading Check How are West and Central Africans working to make their lives better?

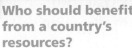

Evelyn looks forward to going to a university. ▶

Section **3** Assessment

Key Terms

1. Use the following terms to describe the obstacles standing in the way of progress in West and Central Africa, and how they might be overcome: infrastructure, microcredit, corruption.

Key Ideas

2. Describe how subsistence farming weakens economies.

3. How have neighboring countries made the Democratic Republic of the Congo's problems worse?

4. What health problems does undernourishment lead to?

Think Critically

5. **Analyze Cause and Effect** How do corruption and undemocratic governments contribute to poverty in West and Central Africa?

6. **Draw Inferences** How might other nations learn from the progress Ghana has made?

Essential Question

Who should benefit from a country's resources?

7. How does unequal access to oil wealth affect the lives of Nigeria's people? Go to your Student Journal to record your answer.

355

Things Fall Apart

Key Idea
- In his famous book *Things Fall Apart,* Chinua Achebe tells the story of Okonkwo, an Igbo leader whose traditions are hurt by European colonization.

The Nigerian author Chinua Achebe is considered by some to be the father of African literature. His most famous novel is *Things Fall Apart*. In the novel, Chinua Achebe tells the story of the meeting between Igbo and European colonizers in the late 1800s. He tells the story from the point of view of the Igbo. Achebe has said that he wrote *Things Fall Apart* to show his readers "that we in Africa did not hear of culture for the first time from Europeans." Below are two excerpts from the novel.

Read the text on the right. Stop at each circled letter. Then answer the question with the same letter on the left.

A **Analyze** How important are clans in Igbo society?

B **Infer** What do you think the "male" type of Okonkwo's crime might be?

C **Draw Conclusions** Why do you think Okonkwo will be able to return after seven years?

inadvertent, *adj.,* by accident

Okonkwo is exiled after accidentally killing a clansman.

❝ The only course open to Okonkwo was to flee from the clan. It was a crime against the earth goddess to kill a clansman and a man who committed it **A** must flee from the land.

The crime was of two kinds, **B** male and female. Okonkwo had committed the female, because it had been <u>inadvertent.</u> He could return to the clan after **C** seven years. ❞
—Chinua Achebe, *Things Fall Apart*

▲ A traditional Igbo mask

Read the text on the right. Stop at each circled letter. Then answer the question with the same letter on the left.

(D) Summarize Why does the elder think Europeans cannot possibly understand Igbo customs?

(E) Develop Cultural Awareness How have European attitudes affected Igbo who converted to Christianity?

(F) Analyze Cause and Effect Why does the elder believe Europeans have caused things to fall apart?

tongue, *n.,* language

Okonkwo discusses the white man with an elder.

66 'Does the white man understand our custom about land?'

'How can he when he does not

(D) even speak our <u>tongue</u>? But he says that our customs are bad; and our own brothers who have taken up his religion also say that our customs are bad. How do you think we can fight when our own brothers have turned against us? The white man is very clever. He came quietly and peaceably with his religion. . . . Now

(E) he has won our brothers, and our clan can no longer act like one. He has put a knife on the things that

(F) held us together and we have fallen apart.' 99

—Chinua Achebe, *Things Fall Apart*

▲ An Igbo town today

Analyze the Documents

1. **Draw Conclusions** How does the first document show that the Igbo "did not hear of culture for the first time from Europeans?"

2. **Writing Task** These excerpts are taken from a work of fiction, based on real events. What do you think the author is trying to say about how the Igbo view their experience under colonial rule? Write a paragraph explaining your answer.

Chinua Achebe in his younger days ▶

357

Chapter Assessment

Key Terms and Ideas

1. **Summarize** What produces the different climate zones of West and Central Africa?

2. **Compare and Contrast** How are the **Sahel** and **savanna** different from each other?

3. **Sequence** How does **deforestation** lead to **desertification**?

4. **Describe** In what ways did **imperialism** affect West and Central African countries?

5. **Explain** What do subsistence farmers do to make a living?

6. **Identify** What is a **griot**?

7. **Describe** What are some effects of disease on West and Central African people?

Think Critically

8. **Draw Inferences** Why has the Democratic Republic of the Congo been so unstable since independence?

9. **Draw Conclusions** What are some of the lasting effects of European colonialism?

10. **Categorize** Which religions were brought to West and Central Africa from other regions?

11. **Core Concepts: Five Themes of Geography** What are the five themes of geography? How would geographers use these themes to describe West and Central Africa?

Places to Know

For each place, write the letter from the map that shows its location.

Identify the following:

12. **Niger River**

13. **Congo River**

14. **Accra**

15. **Lagos**

16. **Kinshasa**

17. **Estimate** Using the scale, estimate the distance between Accra and Lagos.

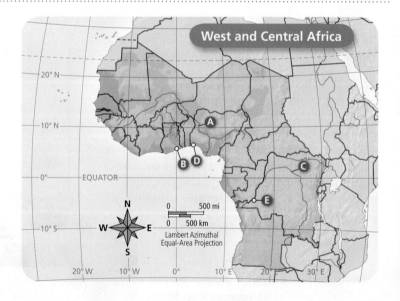

West and Central Africa

358

Essential Question

myWorld Chapter Activity

To Drill or Not To Drill? Follow your teacher's instructions to prepare advice for the president of a fictional African country that has just discovered oil deposits within its borders. Review evidence to see if you think developing the resource is a good idea or not. Prepare a report for the president recommending or advising against developing oil resources in your country.

21st Century Learning

Make a Difference

Research an aid organization in your community that helps people in West and Central Africa. Find out three things that you could do to help that organization. Present your findings to the class.

Document-Based Questions

Success Tracker™
Online at myworldgeography.com

Use your knowledge of West and Central Africa and Documents A and B to answer Questions 1–3.

Document A

Infant Mortality in Selected Countries

A bar graph titled "Infant Mortality in Selected Countries." The y-axis reads "Average Deaths per 1,000 Live Births" from 0 to 100. Democratic Republic of the Congo ≈ 84, Ghana ≈ 52, United States ≈ 6.

SOURCE: CIA World Factbook Online, 2008

Document B

" We spent three days running from the rebels. We went 60 km [kilometers], walking in the day and sleeping in the bush at night. We ran with nothing. I saw so many people being killed that I just left without collecting my things. Even children are being killed."

—Woman in the Democratic Republic of the Congo

1. What did you learn in this chapter that explains the difference in infant mortality in the Democratic Republic of the Congo, Ghana, and the United States as shown in Document A?

A Ghana has been very unstable in recent years.

B The Democratic Republic of the Congo has an efficient healthcare system.

C The United States is very diverse.

D Conflict in the Democratic Republic of the Congo makes good healthcare impossible.

2. Who do you think the woman quoted in Document B is most afraid of?

A the government of the Democratic Republic of the Congo

B the rebel army

C African Union peacekeepers

D Belgian colonists

3. **Writing Task** How does civil violence affect a country and its people? Explain your answer.

Chapter 7

Southern and Eastern Africa

Essential Question

Is conflict unavoidable?

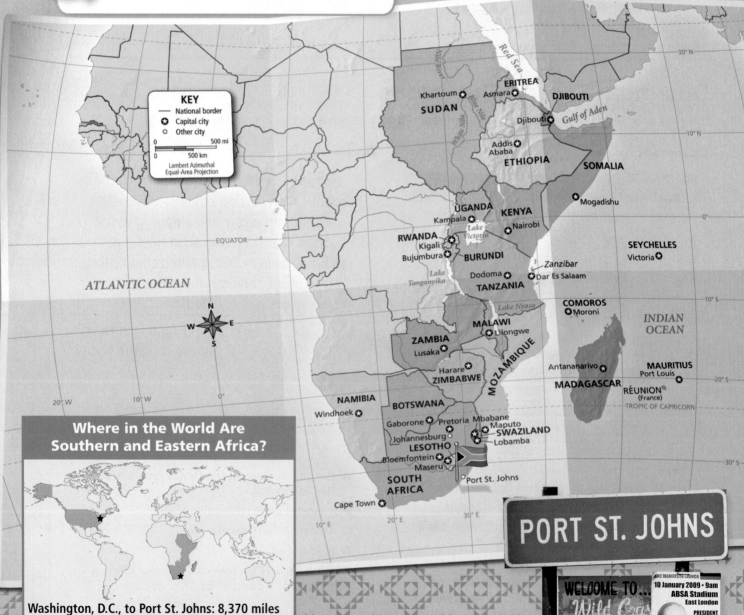

KEY
— National border
⊕ Capital city
○ Other city

0 ————— 500 mi
0 ————— 500 km
Lambert Azimuthal Equal-Area Projection

Where in the World Are Southern and Eastern Africa?

Washington, D.C., to Port St. Johns: 8,370 miles

PORT ST. JOHNS

WELCOME TO... Wild Coast GUEST HOUSE

ANC MANIFESTO LAUNCH
10 January 2009 • 9am
ABSA Stadium
East London
PRESIDENT JACOB ZUMA SPEAKS

my Story

A Hopeful Song

In this section, you'll read about Khulekani, a young South African man who lives in Port Saint Johns. What does Khulekani's story tell you about life in Southern and Eastern Africa today?

Explore the Essential Question
- at **my worldgeography.com**
- using the **myWorld Chapter Activity**
- with the **Student Journal**

Story by Greg Fell for myWorld Geography Online

At 19, Khulekani is a young man with strong principles and big dreams. Khulekani is a member of the Xhosa (KOH sah) people, the second-largest ethnic group in South Africa. His parents passed away ten years ago. Now he lives with his aunt and his sister.

Khulekani lives in a settlement called Nonyevu, on a hill that overlooks the town of Port Saint Johns, in the Transkei region of South Africa. Behind the town is the mighty Umzimvubu River. From Khulekani's home, the view of the lush, tropical landscape is spectacular. Still, life can be difficult for Khulekani and his family.

"We have no water or electricity in Nonyevu. This is a problem for me because I often get homework that requires me to watch television. Without electricity I cannot watch television. When my school shirt gets dirty and there is no rainwater I have to use water from the tap in town, and this water is not clean enough for washing."

Along with water and electricity, healthcare is also lacking in parts of Transkei. The HIV/AIDS epidemic has taken a heavy toll in this area.

361

Khulekani doing the laundry

Filling a water jug to bring home

Cooking breakfast

Until 1994, the apartheid system oppressed black South Africans. Under apartheid, white South Africans controlled the country, even though black South Africans are a majority. Since the fall of apartheid, South Africans of all races have shared power. The racial divide is slowly healing. Like most young South Africans today, Khulekani has moved past the racial divisions of the past.

"You see, now everything is right," he says, "because we are equal. White people can help black people if they are suffering. Black men have also oppressed other black men, so all in all, it just depends on how good or nice you are, rather than your skin color. Either way you are equal."

Still, like all South Africans, Khulekani is aware of the huge gap between developed and undeveloped areas in his country. He and his family struggle to get by, but many South Africans, mostly white, live more comfortable lives.

On a typical morning, Khulekani wakes up at 6 A.M. and boils water on his gas stove for a bath. He makes his breakfast, usually bread and tea. Then it's time to go to school. Khulekani walks to school, where he is in 11th grade. When he finishes school next year, he hopes to study at a nearby university. His goal is to graduate and become an accountant.

362

An assembly at school

Khulekani meets his friends in town.

Having breakfast and rushing off to school are things teenagers do all over the world. But because Khulekani's family is so poor, everyday routines can be challenging. For example, just to have enough water for drinking, cooking, and washing, Khulekani must carry six-gallon jugs of water more than a half a mile. He is responsible for carrying all the water his family needs.

"You must not waste things like water and just throw them away. I don't have the means to get new things so I must look after what I have. The things we have must only be used in the right way in order to survive."

Despite the challenges he faces, Khulekani remains positive, "Yes, things like carrying water from town and doing homework without electricity can affect my schoolwork but I can work past those things."

Today, being involved at school helps Khulekani enjoy his life. He runs a local youth leadership group, for example. "I like to be involved with the youth group. I like to do positive things."

Khulekani is also a part of the school choir. He is optimistic about the choir. He tells us it is the highlight of his day, "The reason why I want to sing in the choir is because I want to take advantage of my opportunities. I want to learn how to do everything in life."

They sing mostly Xhosa hymns, and Khulekani finds joy when he is singing with the choir.

"I like to be happy, and singing with other kids makes me happy. It's very nice. It takes away the worries."

Khulekani believes in his future and the future of South Africa. He believes that once he has made his own way in the world, he can come back and help fix the problems in his town.

Meet the Journalist

Name Greg Fell

Favorite Moment Choir practice: everything that Khulekani had said to us about the joy singing brought him was true.

myStory Online

Join Khulekani as he shows you more about his life in South Africa.

Choir practice

myworldgeography.com

myStory Video

363

Chapter Atlas

Key Ideas

- Southern and Eastern Africa have a variety of physical features including the Great Rift Valley, highland plateaus, and Africa's great lakes.

- The region's ecosystems vary greatly, and include tropical areas, savannas, highlands and arid zones.

- Some parts of the region are rich in natural resources, but feeding the population has proved difficult.

Key Terms • Great Rift Valley • Serengeti Plain • poaching • ecotourism

 Visual Glossary

 Reading Skill: Label an Outline Map Take notes using the outline map in your journal.

◄ Mount Kilimanjaro, Africa's highest mountain

◄ A woman from Tanzania

Remarkable Land and Water

Southern and Eastern Africa, where Khulekani lives, are home to diverse and impressive physical features. From the huge desert of the Sahara to Africa's great lakes, this region has some of Earth's most breathtaking landscapes and wildlife.

One of Southern and Eastern Africa's unique features is the **Great Rift Valley.** This is a long, unusually flat area of land between areas of higher ground in Eastern Africa. It was formed when two of Earth's plates moved away from each other. This movement caused the land in between them to sink and form a valley.

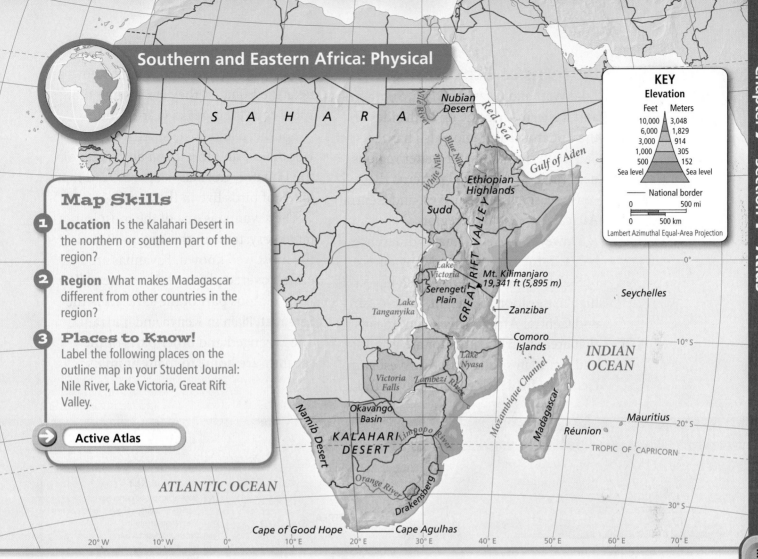

Southern and Eastern Africa: Physical

Map Skills

1 **Location** Is the Kalahari Desert in the northern or southern part of the region?

2 **Region** What makes Madagascar different from other countries in the region?

3 **Places to Know!** Label the following places on the outline map in your Student Journal: Nile River, Lake Victoria, Great Rift Valley.

Active Atlas

KEY
Elevation

Feet	Meters
10,000	3,048
6,000	1,829
3,000	914
1,000	305
500	152
Sea level	Sea level

National border

0 — 500 mi
0 — 500 km

Lambert Azimuthal Equal-Area Projection

The valley's sides rise steeply into mountains and high plateaus. Africa's highest point, Mount Kilimanjaro, sits along the Great Rift Valley. There are also large plains between mountain ranges.

Near the Great Rift Valley lie a group of large and beautiful lakes. One of these, Lake Victoria, is the largest lake in Africa. Africa's great lakes support plant, animal, and human life in areas around them. So do the large rivers that originate, or start, in this region. The Nile, the Zambezi, the Orange, and the Limpopo are the largest. A spectacular waterfall called Victoria Falls is on the Zambezi River.

Rivers serve as a transportation network. But the Sudd swamps block movement between East Africa and Egypt, in North Africa. In the Sudd, floating mats of vegetation and tall papyrus reeds make it difficult for ships to pass.

Parts of Southern and Eastern Africa are very dry. Deserts ring the region: the Sahara, Nubian, Kalahari, and Namib. The Namib Desert, along the coast of Namibia, has some of the world's tallest sand dunes.

Reading Check How do lakes and rivers affect plant, animal, and human life in Southern and Eastern Africa?

transportation, *n.,* system used to move people or things

my worldgeography.com

Active Atlas

365

Patterns of Ecosystems

Like West and Central Africa, Southern and Eastern Africa lie on both sides of the Equator. This region also has the Sahara in the north and wetter regions near the Equator. Wind patterns that cause seasonal rains in West and Central Africa also affect this region.

However, there is a major difference between the two regions. Many parts of Southern and Eastern Africa have a higher elevation, or height, than West and Central Africa. This height means that areas near the Equator are less hot and wet than similar areas in West and Central Africa. For example, even though Mount Kilimanjaro and Mount Kenya are near the Equator, they are so high that snow caps their peaks year-round.

Southern and Eastern Africa have woodlands and forests on both sides of the Equator. Gorillas, leopards, and many kinds of birds live in these areas.

The savanna is one of the most important ecosystems in this region. It is also the most well known. Savannas are flat, grass-covered plains with few trees. The most famous part of the savanna is the **Serengeti Plain** in Kenya and Tanzania. The Serengeti and other parts of the savanna are home to many animals.

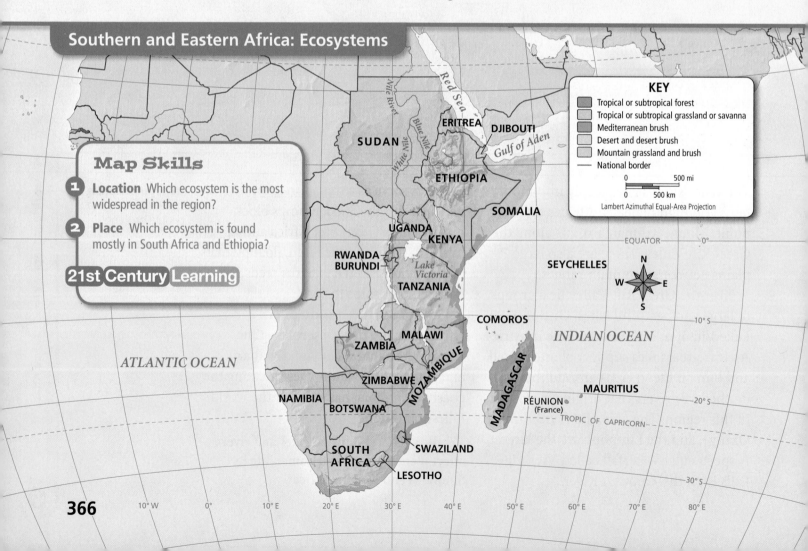

Southern and Eastern Africa: Ecosystems

Map Skills

1. **Location** Which ecosystem is the most widespread in the region?
2. **Place** Which ecosystem is found mostly in South Africa and Ethiopia?

21st Century Learning

KEY
- Tropical or subtropical forest
- Tropical or subtropical grassland or savanna
- Mediterranean brush
- Desert and desert brush
- Mountain grassland and brush
- National border

0 — 500 mi
0 — 500 km
Lambert Azimuthal Equal-Area Projection

366

Large herds of elephants, lions, wilde-beests, zebras, giraffes, gazelles, and other animals live on the plains. This wildlife shapes the way people see the region. Still, many Africans live in towns and cities and may never see one of these animals in the wild.

Many African animals have become endangered. This can happen because they are hunted too much or because people move into places they live. Governments have tried to protect the animals. However, **poaching,** or illegal hunting, is still a problem. Kenya, South Africa, and other countries have set up national parks to protect animals. At the same time, these countries promote **ecotourism**. This is a kind of tourism in which people learn about conservation and try to do little or no harm to the environment.

As in West and Central Africa, the trees in many forested areas in Southern and Eastern Africa have been cut down. Cleared land is used for farmland or min-ing. South Africa, Madagascar, Kenya, and other countries in the region are trying to grow new forests in some areas.

Reading Check What type of ecosystem supports zebras and lions?

my World IN NUMBERS

150,000 gazelles and **3,000** lions live in Tanzania's Serengeti National Park.

Mountain gorillas live in high tropical woodlands in Rwanda, Uganda, and neighboring countries.

Gazelles, lions, elephants, zebras, and many other animals thrive on the wide-open plains of the savanna.

Culture Close-up

myworldgeography.com Culture Close-up

367

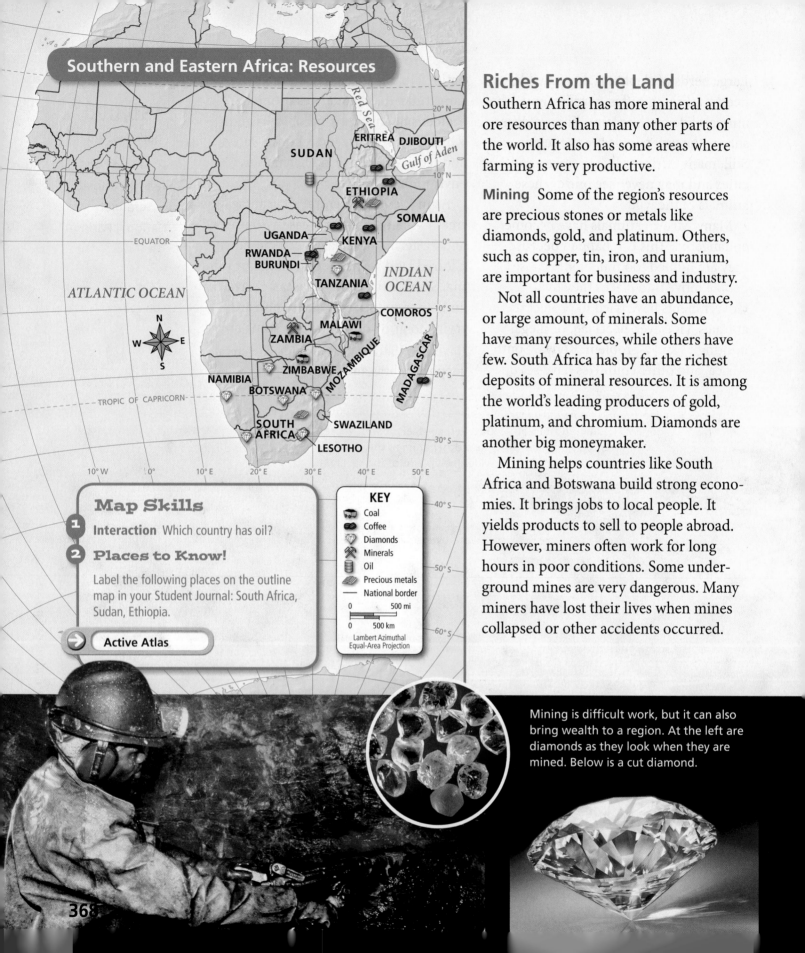

Southern and Eastern Africa: Resources

(Map showing Southern and Eastern Africa with resource symbols for countries including SUDAN, ERITREA, DJIBOUTI, ETHIOPIA, SOMALIA, UGANDA, KENYA, RWANDA, BURUNDI, TANZANIA, COMOROS, MALAWI, ZAMBIA, ZIMBABWE, MOZAMBIQUE, MADAGASCAR, NAMIBIA, BOTSWANA, SOUTH AFRICA, SWAZILAND, LESOTHO. Oceans: ATLANTIC OCEAN, INDIAN OCEAN, Red Sea, Gulf of Aden. Lines: EQUATOR, TROPIC OF CAPRICORN.)

Map Skills

1. **Interaction** Which country has oil?

2. **Places to Know!**

Label the following places on the outline map in your Student Journal: South Africa, Sudan, Ethiopia.

→ Active Atlas

KEY

- Coal
- Coffee
- Diamonds
- Minerals
- Oil
- Precious metals
- — National border

0   500 mi
0   500 km

Lambert Azimuthal
Equal-Area Projection

Riches From the Land

Southern Africa has more mineral and ore resources than many other parts of the world. It also has some areas where farming is very productive.

Mining Some of the region's resources are precious stones or metals like diamonds, gold, and platinum. Others, such as copper, tin, iron, and uranium, are important for business and industry.

Not all countries have an abundance, or large amount, of minerals. Some have many resources, while others have few. South Africa has by far the richest deposits of mineral resources. It is among the world's leading producers of gold, platinum, and chromium. Diamonds are another big moneymaker.

Mining helps countries like South Africa and Botswana build strong economies. It brings jobs to local people. It yields products to sell to people abroad. However, miners often work for long hours in poor conditions. Some underground mines are very dangerous. Many miners have lost their lives when mines collapsed or other accidents occurred.

Mining is difficult work, but it can also bring wealth to a region. At the left are diamonds as they look when they are mined. Below is a cut diamond.

368

Mining can also hurt the environment. Some types of mining leave large scars on the land. Mining can cause pollution. Air and water can be polluted when minerals are processed and when fuel is burned to run drills.

Farming People also use the land in this region to farm and raise animals. Farmlands can be found in most of the countries in the region. But there are many areas that are very dry. These places cannot rely on regular rainfall for crops. Sudan, Ethiopia, Somalia, and Namibia struggle to find enough water to grow their crops.

Because so much of the region is dry, many farmers irrigate their land. Cotton, tobacco, and tea are grown in irrigated areas. People also raise cattle and other livestock in drier parts of the region. In some of these areas, wild animals are a threat to the herds. Herders must defend their animals at night.

Some of the region has very fertile land. In South Africa and other countries, people grow many crops. They run large commercial farms or plantations. These farms grow crops such as sugar cane, cotton, avocados, and tropical fruits. They often export their crops.

Coffee is Ethiopia's most important export. In fact, the plant was probably first grown in Ethiopia's highlands. The word *coffee* may even come from the Kaffa region of Ethiopia, where the crop is grown.

Reading Check **What are the advantages and disadvantages of diamond mining?**

irrigate, *v.,* to bring water to an area

Coffee is Ethiopia's largest export. Red coffee berries are grown on plantations like this one. Ethiopian coffee is enjoyed around the world. *Can you think of some other products from Africa that you might be able to find in your hometown?*

369

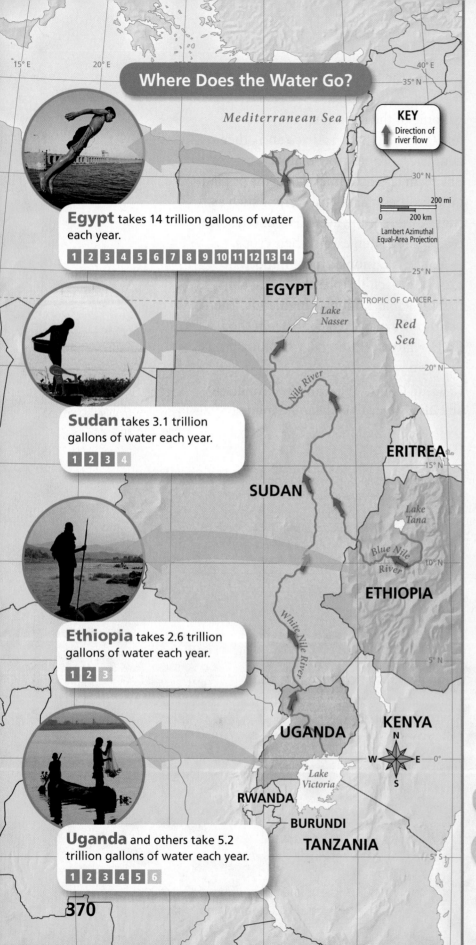

Where Does the Water Go?

Egypt takes 14 trillion gallons of water each year.

`1 2 3 4 5 6 7 8 9 10 11 12 13 14`

Sudan takes 3.1 trillion gallons of water each year.

`1 2 3 4`

Ethiopia takes 2.6 trillion gallons of water each year.

`1 2 3`

Uganda and others take 5.2 trillion gallons of water each year.

`1 2 3 4 5 6`

KEY
↑ Direction of river flow

370

Challenges of the Environment

Water—who has it and who doesn't—is a huge challenge for countries in this region. Countries that have enough water resources have a better chance of feeding their populations. Countries that do not have enough water struggle to support their populations. Lack of water and good farmland leads to famine, or a shortage of food. Sudan and Ethiopia receive more food aid than many other countries in the world for this reason.

The region's many rivers provide a valuable benefit to some countries. Dams have been built along major rivers to generate hydroelectricity. They also provide water for nearby farms.

But these dams can cause conflict. For example, the Nile flows through Sudan and other countries before reaching Egypt. Dams built in Uganda take water away from Sudan. Who gets to decide how much water each country can take?

Reading Check What are the advantages and disadvantages of building dams?

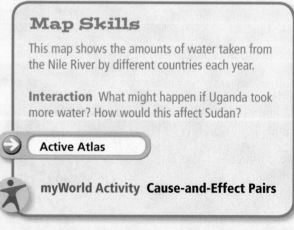

Map Skills

This map shows the amounts of water taken from the Nile River by different countries each year.

Interaction What might happen if Uganda took more water? How would this affect Sudan?

→ **Active Atlas**

myWorld Activity **Cause-and-Effect Pairs**

Disease

As in West and Central Africa, disease causes many problems in Southern and Eastern Africa. Some diseases stem from the environment. Just as mosquitoes carry malaria, tsetse flies carry sleeping sickness. The flies live in many areas between the Sahara and the Kalahari Desert. These areas are known as the tsetse belt.

Sleeping sickness can be deadly to both people and the cattle they raise. The disease makes it impossible to raise cattle in the tsetse belt.

Many people in Southern and Eastern Africa do not have access to clean water, and so they contract diseases carried by water. For example, cholera and river blindness have crippled and killed many Southern and Eastern Africans.

AIDS, which does not stem from the environment, has reached epidemic proportions in this region. You will read more about AIDS later.

Reading Check What harm does the tsetse fly cause?

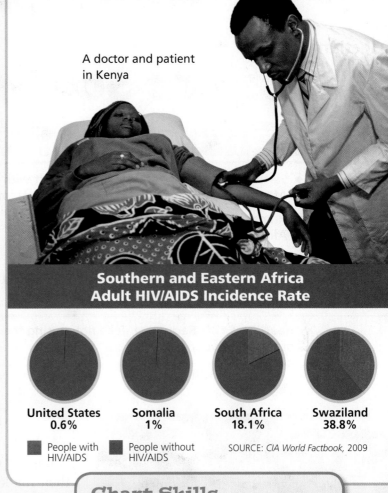

A doctor and patient in Kenya

Southern and Eastern Africa Adult HIV/AIDS Incidence Rate

| United States 0.6% | Somalia 1% | South Africa 18.1% | Swaziland 38.8% |

■ People with HIV/AIDS ■ People without HIV/AIDS

SOURCE: *CIA World Factbook*, 2009

Chart Skills

The United States population is 307,000,000. Swaziland has 1,123,000 people. Which country has more people living with HIV/AIDS?

➜ **Data Discovery**

Section 1 Assessment

Key Terms

1. How was the Great Rift Valley formed?

2. How do ecotourism and poaching affect the environment?

3. In which nations is the Serengeti Plain located?

Key Ideas

4. What are some animals that live on the savanna?

5. What resources help make countries like South Africa more prosperous than others?

6. Why might a dam in Uganda cause trouble in Sudan?

Think Critically

7. **Compare Viewpoints** Why do some people believe mining helps people in the region while others say it is harmful? Give evidence.

8. **Compare and Contrast** Somalia and Botswana have different resources. How might this difference affect the lives of their people?

Essential Question

Is conflict unavoidable?

9. How do you think the lack of resources in some countries might cause conflict? How might the abundance of resources in other countries cause conflict? Go to your Student Journal to record your answers.

371

Section 2

History of Southern and Eastern Africa

Key Ideas
- Earth's first people lived in Africa.
- Humans settled throughout Africa, creating societies, states, and trade networks.
- Contact with Arabs and Europeans influenced the culture, religions, and ethnic makeup of the region.
- In the 1800s, Europeans colonized and settled in the region, but African nations gained independence in the 1900s.

Key Terms • fossil • Boers • ethnocentrism • Mau Mau • apartheid
• African National Congress

 Visual Glossary

Reading Skill: Sequence Take notes using the graphic organizer in your journal.

Southern and Eastern Africa may have been home to the earliest humans. From ancient times to the present, many different cultures and civilizations have left their mark on the region.

Early Humans and Great Civilizations

The first humans may have lived in Africa two million years ago. In particular, the remains of early humans have been found in countries such as Ethiopia and Tanzania.

Earth's First People Scientists have found fossils of early human beings in Eastern Africa. **Fossils** are the remains of ancient humans or animals. Most early humans lived in warm places. They moved around in search of food. One kind of early human called *Homo erectus* lived in Africa between 1 and 2 million years ago. Early humans spread out from Africa to other continents.

▲ Scientists searching for fossils
◀ The skull of an early ancestor of human beings who lived in South Africa 2.5 million years ago

372

Nubia and Aksum The first civilization in this part of Africa was in Nubia. Nubia is a region in modern-day Sudan. It was home to the states of Kush and Meroë. Civilization in Nubia grew from around 2000 B.C. Nubia became a center of trade. It traded with its neighbor, Egypt. Skills and technologies from Egypt were introduced into Nubia. Nubians passed these on to other parts of Africa. The most important technology was iron-making.

The kingdom of Aksum was located in what is today Ethiopia. Aksum had a port on the Red Sea. This location helped make Aksum a center for trade in and beyond Africa. Aksum's traders sold gold, ivory, and other goods. They traded with Rome and India. Roman traders may have brought Christianity to Aksum. It became a Christian kingdom. Ethiopia still is mostly Christian today.

The Bantu Migrations Around A.D. 500 the population of the Bantu people in western Africa grew until their land could not accommodate them. They left their homeland and migrated across Southern Africa. This migration spread the Bantu language. The Bantu brought with them their farming methods, including the raising of cattle. They also spread their knowledge of iron tools. Many groups the Bantu met adopted their language. They began raise to cattle and make iron.

Great Zimbabwe In Southern Africa, Great Zimbabwe thrived in the 1400s. It was a large trading city founded by Bantu speakers. Great Zimbabwe's traders took gold and ivory to Africa's east coast ports. There they traded for goods from China, India, and Southeast Asia.

Arab Influence Traders who spoke Arabic came to Eastern Africa by sea and across the Sahara. They practiced Islam. Some settled in the region, mostly along the eastern coast and on the island of Zanzibar. Zanzibar and coastal areas were tied into a large trading network. It included the Mediterranean, India, and Southeast Asia. Arab traders widened East Africa's slave trade. They brought their language, religion, and cultural influence to the region. Arab merchants also founded cities, including Mogadishu in modern-day Somalia.

Reading Check How did early civilizations spread ideas in Africa?

This doorway from Zanzibar shows the artistic influence of Arab merchants who lived and traded in the region.

▼ This large enclosure is one of the most impressive remains of the city of Great Zimbabwe. *What can you infer about the culture that built it?*

373

Europeans in Southern and Eastern Africa

In the 1400s, Europeans began to come to Southern and Eastern Africa. They came first to trade and later to set up colonies.

First Meetings and the Slave Trade

Portugal began to trade with Eastern Africa in the 1400s. Around 1500, the Portuguese took control of parts of Eastern Africa. They wanted to control trade along the Eastern African coast. They expanded the slave trade.

Southern and Eastern Africans, like the West and Central Africans, suffered from the effects of the trans-Atlantic slave trade. Constant warfare and loss of population weakened their societies. They became vulnerable to European empires.

constant, *adj.,* continuing; not stopping

European Rule

Many European nations spread their empires into Africa in the late 1800s. As in West and Central Africa, Europeans traded and conquered territory in Southern and Eastern Africa. They also founded colonies of settlers there. By around 1900, European nations ruled most of Africa.

Some European colonies were founded by trading companies. These companies needed to send supplies to traders traveling to Asia. They sent settlers to build supply posts. For example, the Dutch East India Company started a settlement in South Africa. It was called Cape Town. Over many years, Dutch settlers spread out to create the Cape Colony. Many farmers from the Netherlands, France, and other European countries settled there. They became known as **Boers,** which is Dutch for "farmers." More European settlers came, especially when gold and diamonds were discovered. Great Britain took the colony from the Dutch in 1795. British settlers also moved to modern-day Kenya and Zimbabwe.

Colonial Impact

Many Southern and Eastern Africans hated colonial rule. Europeans often took Africans' lands. They forced Africans to work for little or no pay. Europeans held high positions.

European Rule in Southern and Eastern Africa

KEY
- British
- British and Egyptian
- French
- German
- Italian
- Portuguese
- Independent
- (1963) Date of Independence

SUDAN (1956), ERITREA (1993), DJIBOUTI (1977), ETHIOPIA, SOMALIA (1960), UGANDA (1962), KENYA (1963), RWANDA (1962), BURUNDI (1962), TANZANIA (1961), SEYCHELLES (1976), COMOROS (1975), MALAWI (1964), ZAMBIA (1964), MOZAMBIQUE (1975), ZIMBABWE (1980), MADAGASCAR (1960), NAMIBIA (1990), BOTSWANA (1966), RÉUNION, MAURITIUS (1968), SWAZILAND (1968), SOUTH AFRICA (1910), LESOTHO (1966)

0 600 mi / 0 600 km
Lambert Azimuthal Equal-Area Projection

Map Skills

1 **Location** Which was the only Portuguese colony in the region?

2 **Place** What is different about Sudan?

Active Atlas

374

Colonialism: Positive and Negative

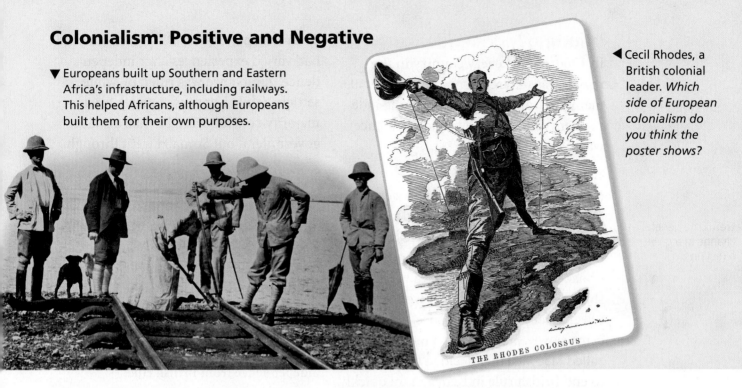

▼ Europeans built up Southern and Eastern Africa's infrastructure, including railways. This helped Africans, although Europeans built them for their own purposes.

THE RHODES COLOSSUS

◄ Cecil Rhodes, a British colonial leader. *Which side of European colonialism do you think the poster shows?*

But Africans had little political power. Many Europeans also looked down on African cultures. They believed their own cultures were superior, an attitude called **ethnocentrism.** For example, colonial leader Cecil Rhodes believed that British people were better than others.

> 66 I contend that we are the first race in the world, and that the more of the world we inhabit the better it is for the human race. 99
>
> —Cecil Rhodes

However, not everything European colonialists did was negative. Though the British had held African slaves for centuries, they outlawed slavery in 1833. They then helped fight the slave trade across Africa. Europeans brought modern healthcare to Southern and Eastern Africa. They built up infrastructure to access resources.

This infrastructure also helped Africans. Europeans built schools. More Africans had access to education. With that education, Africans felt ready to take charge of the governments of their own countries.

Reading Check How was the first colony in South Africa founded?

◄ Haile Selassie, the Emperor of Ethiopia from 1930 to 1974, resisted European aggression. He fought the Italian army, which invaded his country in the 1930s. Ethiopia was never colonized by Europeans.

my**worldgeography.com** Active Atlas

375

Winning Independence

In 1900, almost every country in the region was under colonial rule. By 1960, many African nations had become independent. But the road to independence was very bumpy.

Trouble in Kenya The Kikuyu (kee KOO yoo) people of Kenya were one group that opposed colonial rule. The British had taken much of their land, and British ethnocentrism made good relations difficult. In the 1940s, the Kikuyu started a political party that worked toward Kenya's independence. Change came slowly. Some began a movement called **Mau Mau** that decided to use force to end British rule in Kenya more quickly. The British and the Mau Mau fought for four years. Finally, Kenya gained independence in 1963. Kikuyu leader Jomo Kenyatta led the new nation.

trend, *n.,* general change in a given direction

British soldiers guard Kenyan villagers while looking for Mau Mau fighters.

After Independence Different countries had varied experiences after independence. Zimbabwe was ruled by white settlers, while Kenya was under black majority control. Namibia had a stable government, but Somalia went through great conflict.

In Kenya, as in other countries such as South Africa, urbanization and industrialization were important <u>trends</u> after independence. Factories were built in major cities. Rural people left farms behind to find work in factories. These trends made Kenya and South Africa richer but hurt traditional rural life.

Reading Check Why did the Kikuyu want independence from British rule?

The Rise and Fall of Apartheid

South Africa gained independence from Britain in 1910. However, the white minority kept political and economic power for themselves.

South Africa Under Apartheid In 1948, the white minority in South Africa adopted **apartheid,** an official government policy of keeping white and black South Africans apart. It was similar to American segregation in many ways. Apartheid laws secured power for white South Africans. Black people could only live and work in certain places, and harsh laws made travel difficult. Schools and hospitals were segregated. Black people could not vote. The Prohibition of Mixed Marriages Act made marriage between people of different races illegal.

Mandela and the End of Apartheid Many people inside and beyond South Africa believed apartheid was wrong. Black South Africans organized and protested. White police all too often responded with violence. The government banned groups like the **African National Congress** (ANC), a political party that worked for black civil rights. Many ANC leaders were jailed. Other nations criticized South Africa sharply. Some refused to trade with South Africa. That hurt its economy.

One man who played a key role in ending apartheid was Nelson Mandela. He was an ANC leader who was jailed in 1962. He continued to protest from his prison on Robben Island. Another man who played a role was F. W. de Klerk, South Africa's president from 1989 to 1994. Although he was white, de Klerk realized that apartheid was destroying South Africa. In 1990, he released Nelson Mandela from prison. Together, Mandela

myWorld Activity
Where I'm From

◀ Nelson Rolihlahla Mandela led the struggle against apartheid and became South Africa's president. He shared a Nobel Peace Prize with F. W. de Klerk in 1993.

and de Klerk worked to end apartheid. In 1994, South Africans of all races voted together. Mandela became president. South Africa was truly independent.

Reading Check Who were two people who helped end apartheid?

Section 2 Assessment

Essential Question

Is conflict unavoidable?

Key Terms
1. What is ethnocentrism?
2. Who were the Boers? What does the word *boer* mean and what language does it come from?
3. What system did the African National Congress fight?

Key Ideas
4. Where do scientists believe the first human beings came from?
5. What were some effects of the Bantu migrations?
6. How did contact with Arabs influence Southern and Eastern Africa?
7. How did apartheid hurt black South Africans?

Think Critically
8. **Analyze Cause and Effect** What caused Kenyans to fight British rule?
9. **Compare and Contrast** How was Kenya's path to independence different from South Africa's?

10. Apartheid in South Africa ended without civil war or large-scale ethnic conflict. What do you think made this possible? Go to your Student Journal to record your answer.

Literature of Southern and Eastern Africa

Key Idea
- Stories from Southern and Eastern Africa show the varied cultures and traditions of this large region.

▲ A page from an Ethiopian religious book

The cultures of Southern and Eastern Africa have a long tradition of storytelling. Some parts of the region, such as Ethiopia, have used writing to record their history for centuries. In other parts of the region, such as South Africa, stories were passed down orally from one generation to another. In Ethiopia, Christian themes influenced the literature. Ethiopian monks wrote about the lives of their kings, often comparing them to kings from the Bible. One of these stories tells about King Galawdewos, who ruled in the 1500s. In Southern Africa, people like the 'Msuto were cattle herders. They passed down stories about the lives of their chiefs and important people. A beautiful princess is the main character in one of these stories.

Stop at each circled letter on the right to think about the text. Then answer the question with the same letter on the left.

A **Identify Details** Who is Galawdewos compared to?

B **Identify Evidence** What are some signs of this kingdom's wealth?

C **Make Inferences** How can you tell that the king and his people were religious?

Mar, *n.,* a local term meaning "Lord"

reign, *v.,* to rule

surmounted, *v.,* topped; covered

Galawdewos

66 God made <u>Mar</u> Galawdewos <u>reign</u> over the beautiful country of Ethiopia and placed him on the throne of his father, giving him wisdom . . . like that of Solomon the son

A of David. . . .

He built in [his capital] a beautiful tower the corners of which were <u>surmounted</u> with . . . precious marble and the interior engraved with figures of gold and silver. He also constructed a palace which was decorated and adorned

B inside and outside with gold and precious stones. . . .

C In the town a building belonging to the church was also constructed. 99

—*The Ethiopian Royal Chronicles*

378

Stop at each circled letter on the right to think about the text. Then answer the question with the same letter on the left.

(D) Identify Details What is the countryside like?

(E) Analyze Primary Sources What details make this household seem prosperous?

(F) Identify Main Ideas Why was Maholia called the Shining Princess?

kraal, *n.,* a traditional dwelling encircled by a fence; a livestock pen

calabash, *n.,* gourd used for holding liquid

beheld, *v.,* saw

The Story of the Shining Princess

66 Far up in the mountains, nestling in a cool green valley,

(D) stood a most beautiful <u>kraal</u>. The hut was a bright green, for it was finely thatched with grass, and the floor within was of the firmest and most brilliantly polished red earth.

(E) Around the inner walls stood the cooking pots made of red clay, and along with these were shining green <u>calabashes</u> overflowing with the richest milk and cream. . . . This was the home of a great Chief's wife. The Chief, who had been dead for many years, had left his Queen alone in the world with only one little daughter named Maholia. . . .

As [Maholia] grew up, she became more and more celebrated for her beauty and charm; in fact she was so lovely that she dazzled the eyes of all who <u>beheld</u> her, and she became known among her people as the Shining

(F) Princess. 99

—Traditional 'Msuto tale
from *Black Fairy Tales,* by Terry Berger

A traditional kraal in Southern Africa ▼

Analyze the Documents

1. **Compare and Contrast** How do these sources describe kingdoms that are both alike and different?

2. **Writing Task** Write another paragraph to add to one of these documents. Try to make your writing match the style and content of the existing story.

379

Section 3

Southern and Eastern Africa Today

Key Ideas
- This region's many different historic influences and ethnic groups have produced vibrant and varied cultures.
- Many nations in the region struggle with ethnic conflict and corrupt or underperforming governments.
- Despite the many challenges facing the region, there are reasons to hope that it will overcome its obstacles.

Key Terms • indigenous • Swahili • genocide • AIDS
• nongovernmental organization (NGO)

Visual Glossary

Reading Skill: Compare and Contrast Take notes using the graphic organizer in your journal.

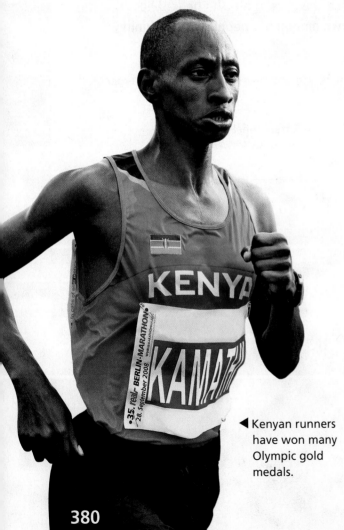

◀ Kenyan runners have won many Olympic gold medals.

Southern and Eastern Africa have a wealth of natural resources. But the region also faces unique and serious challenges. Some of its nations have had more success than others in building peace and prosperity.

A Variety of Ethnic Groups and Religions

Most people in Southern and Eastern Africa are **indigenous,** or native, to the region. There are many different groups of people in the region. They belong to hundreds of different ethnic groups, speak different languages, and practice different religions.

Ethnic Groups Some ethnic groups live in a single country. Others stretch across borders. Few countries are made up of a single ethnic group. Some of the largest groups are the Zulu and Xhosa, who live in South Africa; the Kikuyu in Kenya; and the Hutu and Tutsi in Rwanda. In the past, different ethnic groups lived different lifestyles. For example, the Maasai, in Kenya and Tanzania, herded cattle. The Baganda in Uganda farmed and lived in large villages. However, today many people in the region live in cities. They no longer make a living in the ways that their ancestors did.

380

Religions Practiced in Southern and Eastern Africa

2%
14%
24%
60%

- Christianity
- Indigenous religions
- Islam
- Other

SOURCE: Association of Religion Data Archives (ARDA)

A procession of Ethiopian Christians

Chart Skills

1. Which two religions are most widely practiced in this area?
2. What percentage of people practice Islam?

→ Data Discovery

Languages The diverse people of Southern and Eastern Africa speak many different languages. Most belong to the Bantu language family. This fact is a legacy of the Bantu migrations. Languages from outside the region have also made inroads. English is spoken as a second language in countries that were once part of the British Empire. In South Africa, Afrikaans (af rih KAHNZ) is widely spoken. It comes from the Dutch spoken by early colonists.

Arab influence is widespread throughout the region. Arabic is spoken in Sudan. It also helped create the Swahili language. **Swahili** is a Bantu language. It is unique because it has many Arabic elements and words from other languages. For example, when you count from one to ten in Swahili, three of the numbers come from Arabic, while seven are Bantu. Swahili developed because of trade between Eastern Africa and Arab countries. It is now used as a common language throughout much of Eastern Africa.

Religions Many people in Southern and Eastern Africa practice indigenous African religions. Others practice Islam or Christianity. Some mix their indigenous religions with one or the other. Christianity is strongest in the southern part of the region. Islam is mostly practiced in northern parts of the region. Although Islamic countries surround Ethiopia, it has been a center of Christianity for many centuries.

Reading Check What are three indigenous groups in Southern and Eastern Africa?

Ndebele (un duh BEE lee) people from South Africa paint their homes in bright colors. ▶

381

Conflict in Southern and Eastern Africa Today

As Europeans carved up Africa and then left their colonies, they created many new countries. They often drew borders without regard to where different ethnic groups lived. Sometimes one ethnic group was divided between two different countries. In other places, opposing ethnic groups were included in the same country. These ethnic groups fought for power after Europeans left. Some of these conflicts are still going on. Two of the most deadly conflicts in recent years have taken place in Sudan and Rwanda.

ethnic, *adj.*, group of people with the same nationality, language, or religion

myWorld Activity
Analyze Conflicts

Conflicts in Sudan Sudan is divided among many different ethnic groups. In the north, most people are Arabs and practice Islam. In the south, most people belong to other ethnic groups and are not Muslims. After independence, northerners dominated the country. Southerners rebelled twice. This led to two civil wars between north and south. The wars continued until 2005 and killed several million people.

Since 2003, Darfur has been the scene of another bloody conflict. Darfur is a region in the west of Sudan. Black farmers have fought Arab herders over scarce water resources. The herders support the Sudanese government, while the farmers oppose it. Militias of herders with government backing have attacked civilian farmers. Hundreds of thousands of people, mostly black farmers, have been killed. Many more have been forced to flee their homes. Many people call the Darfur conflict a **genocide,** or an attempt to destroy a whole people.

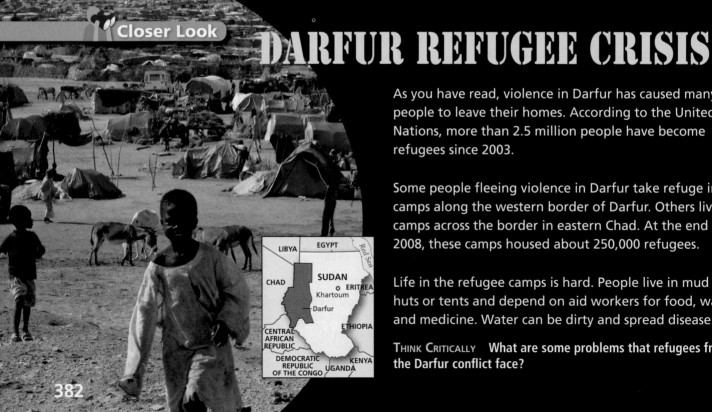

Closer Look

DARFUR REFUGEE CRISIS

As you have read, violence in Darfur has caused many people to leave their homes. According to the United Nations, more than 2.5 million people have become refugees since 2003.

Some people fleeing violence in Darfur take refuge in camps along the western border of Darfur. Others live in camps across the border in eastern Chad. At the end of 2008, these camps housed about 250,000 refugees.

Life in the refugee camps is hard. People live in mud huts or tents and depend on aid workers for food, water, and medicine. Water can be dirty and spread disease.

THINK CRITICALLY   What are some problems that refugees from the Darfur conflict face?

382

Genocide in Rwanda Rwanda has had a troubled history since the colonial period. The country is divided between two ethnic groups, the majority Hutu and the minority Tutsi. Before Belgium colonized the region, the Tutsi formed an elite class that ruled the Hutu. The Belgians favored the Tutsis and used them to keep control of the Hutus. After independence, violence flared up against the Tutsi and the Hutu took control. Further fighting and struggles for power between the groups continued.

Eventually the situation exploded into a horrible genocide. During a few months in 1994, Hutu military and militia groups killed an estimated 800,000 to 1 million Tutsis. The United Nations sent French, Canadian, and other troops to Rwanda to stop the killings. However, they were not effective. The murders stopped when the Tutsi once again came to power. Millions of Hutus fled the country to neighboring Zaire, today called the Democratic Republic of the Congo. Fighting between the two groups continues in that country.

Many people abroad regret that foreign countries could not or did not do more to stop the killing. Kofi Annan, former Secretary General of the UN and a high UN official during the genocide, believes more should have been done to stop it.

> 66 The international community failed Rwanda and that must leave us always with a sense of bitter regret. 99
> —Kofi Annan

Reading Check How did colonialism lead to conflicts in Southern and Eastern Africa?

Governing the Region

Southern and Eastern African countries have many different forms of government. Some are democratic, while others are ruled by dictators.

Democracy Today, one of the most democratic governments in the region is South Africa. Since the end of apartheid, fair and free elections have produced a stable government. Citizens participate in their government and can freely join voluntary organizations. But the new multiracial democracy has experienced growing pains as it tries to <u>integrate</u> and improve South African society. The lingering legacy of apartheid is that black South Africans are still, on average, much poorer than white South Africans. Inequalities remain in areas such as healthcare, unemployment, education, and landownership.

Dictatorship Unlike South Africa, Sudan is a dictatorship. Though the country calls itself a republic, President Omar al-Bashir rules by force. People cannot participate in the government or choose their leaders.

Zimbabwe has also been a dictatorship. A single political party has held on to power for more than 28 years. Even though there is a constitution, President Robert Mugabe has ruled like a dictator. Corruption and oppression have become common. Failed policies have led to economic collapse. Millions of people from Zimbabwe have fled to South Africa.

Reading Check What is a major social problem in South Africa after apartheid?

integrate, *v.,* bring together, particularly people from different groups

Problems and Potential

Serious obstacles stand in the way of economic development in the region. Political violence hurts economic growth. Poor transportation systems and low literacy rates also hold back development. On the other hand, the region possesses rich natural resources. It could one day use them to build up economies. Countries like Kenya and South Africa have proved that progress is possible in Southern and Eastern Africa.

Barriers to Development One major obstacle to development is the lack of stable governments in some countries. Somalia, for example is ruled by competing militias and warlords. Without a government, theft and violence are common. Piracy has become a serious problem. Gunmen off the Somali coast have attacked ships, seizing cargoes and holding crews for ransom.

Another obstacle to development is the lack of resources in some countries. For example, frequent droughts have helped keep Ethiopia among the world's poorest

African Union Peacekeepers
Former South African President Thabo Mbeki reviews African Union peacekeeping troops.

countries. Corruption also hurts development, because corrupt countries are unreliable places to do business. Corrupt leaders also steal foreign aid. Lack of education is another serious obstacle. Many families in the region cannot afford to send their children to school. Boys often have more access to education than girls. This makes it difficult for women to get better jobs and improve their situation.

Another problem is disease. Of all the regions in the world, Southern and Eastern Africa have been hit hardest by HIV and AIDS. **AIDS** is an often-deadly disease caused by the HIV virus. It attacks the immune system. It kills about 1.5 million people in this region each year, and that number is rising. Many countries are too poor to properly treat the sick. Also, when so many people get sick or die, work that is necessary to the economy does not get done. This holds back development and hurts everybody.

Hope for the Future While Southern and Eastern Africa have difficult obstacles to overcome, there are positive signs for the future. Governments are

Piracy in Somalia
Pirates in small, fast boats attack larger, slower cargo ships.

384

making serious efforts to fight AIDS. For example, the Ugandan government sends text messages on mobile phones to educate people about the epidemic. Globalization makes international trade faster and easier. It lets countries like Kenya and South Africa ship more export goods and improve their economies.

Foreign governments and **nongovernmental organizations (NGOs),** groups that operate with private funding, are helping to deal with environmental problems, poverty, disease, and conflict. They also help provide more opportunities for education, especially for women. Nations in the region have formed different organizations to cooperate in solving common problems. The African Union (AU) is the most important. Recently, it has sent peacekeeping troops to Sudan and Somalia.

Reading Check What are some barriers to development in this region?

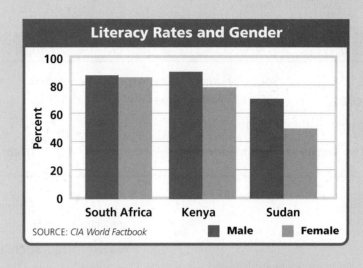

Literacy Rates and Gender

SOURCE: *CIA World Factbook*   ■ **Male**   ■ **Female**

Chart Skills

1. In which country are literacy rates most similar for men and women?

2. Do you think boys and girls have equal access to education in all of these countries? Explain.

→ **Data Discovery**

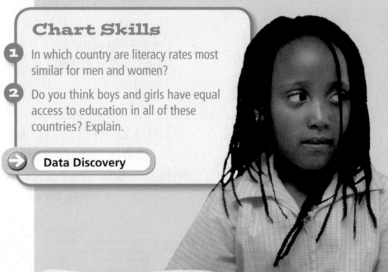

Section 3 Assessment

Key Terms

1. Name one example of a genocide from this region.

2. What part of the body does the HIV virus attack?

3. How do NGOs (nongovernmental organizations) help improve life in Southern and Eastern Africa?

Key Ideas

4. How does HIV/AIDS hold back development?

5. Which groups are fighting in Darfur, and what are they fighting about?

6. Describe some of the successes and failures of South Africa since the fall of apartheid.

Think Critically

7. **Compare and Contrast** How are the recent histories of Rwanda and South Africa similar? How are they different?

8. **Solve Problems** What do you think are the most effective ways Southern and Eastern Africans are improving their region? Why do you think these are the most effective?

? **Essential Question**

Is conflict unavoidable?

9. In the countries of Sudan, Rwanda, Kenya, and South Africa, what has caused ethnic violence? Go to your Student Journal to record your answer.

The Effects of Colonialism

Key Idea
- Southern and Eastern African peoples had varying experiences under European rule.
- Each modern society shows the effects of its colonial past.

Key Terms
- Scramble for Africa
- abolish
- Great Trek

Colonialism had a major effect on Southern and Eastern Africa. Countries such as Tanzania, Sudan, and South Africa were deeply changed by colonial rule. During the late 1800s, European powers raced to seize giant pieces of territory before their rivals arrived in the region. This race was called the **scramble for Africa.** At the Berlin Conference in 1884, European countries met and divided up Africa. The effects of the division and colonization of Africa can still be seen.

Tanzania

In what is now Tanzania, the first Europeans to arrive were the Portuguese. They came to trade with local Africans and Arab merchants. They set up forts along the coast in the early 1500s.

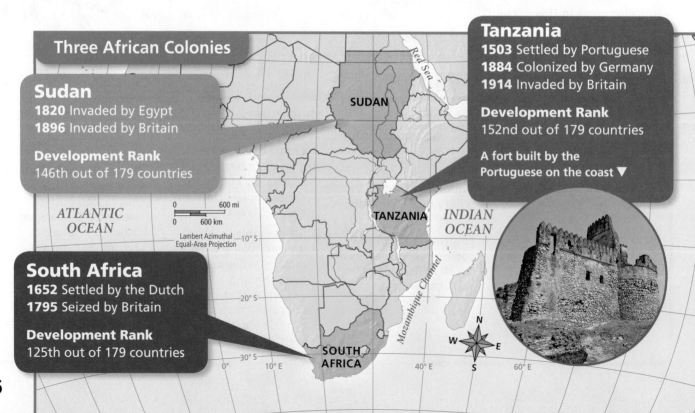

Three African Colonies

Sudan
1820 Invaded by Egypt
1896 Invaded by Britain

Development Rank
146th out of 179 countries

Tanzania
1503 Settled by Portuguese
1884 Colonized by Germany
1914 Invaded by Britain

Development Rank
152nd out of 179 countries

A fort built by the Portuguese on the coast ▼

South Africa
1652 Settled by the Dutch
1795 Seized by Britain

Development Rank
125th out of 179 countries

ATLANTIC OCEAN
INDIAN OCEAN
Red Sea
SUDAN
TANZANIA
SOUTH AFRICA
Mozambique Channel

0   600 mi
0   600 km
Lambert Azimuthal Equal-Area Projection

The Portuguese traded gold, ivory, and slaves. Their presence caused resentment. In 1698, Arabs and local Africans forced them out.

In 1884, Germany colonized the area. Germans set up plantations to grow crops such as cotton and rubber for export. They also built railroads and schools. But German rule was harsh. In 1905 Tanzanians rebelled. The Germans brutally put down the rebellion.

Britain seized the German colony in modern-day Tanzania after World War I. The British ruled with a lighter hand. They governed through local leaders. In the process, however, they created tribal organizations, groupings, and divisions that had not existed before. In this way, they changed local society.

Tanzania became a united and independent nation in 1961. But the British left it with a weak economy that relied on export crops. The country remained poor.

Reading Check Which three European powers colonized modern-day Tanzania?

Sudan

Sudan was ruled by both Egypt and Britain. Egypt invaded Sudan in 1820. It wanted to control the upper Nile River and to have access to resources in Sudan. Egypt ruled Sudan harshly.

In the late 1800s, the British invaded Egypt and then Sudan. They wanted to protect the Suez Canal, the route by sea from Britain to its colony of India.

For the next six decades, Britain and Egypt ruled Sudan together, although the British held the real power. The British tried to modernize Sudan. They put an end to, or **abolished,** the slave trade. They built rail and telegraph lines. They built schools and educated new leaders.

Despite these benefits, colonial rule also harmed Sudan. You have read that Sudan is divided between a largely Arab Muslim north and a black non-Muslim south. This division developed before the colonial period. However, Britain worked to keep the two regions separate. It wanted to limit Muslim influence in the south. This policy helped divide Sudan and keep the south less developed.

Sudan gained independence in 1956, but the country has remained divided. Power rests mainly with Arab Muslims in the north. Southern rebels fought two civil wars for independence but failed. As you read, conflict today is especially severe in the western region of Darfur.

Reading Check What is the most important division in Sudanese society?

Sudan
Troops from the British colony of India helped conquer Sudan for Britain.

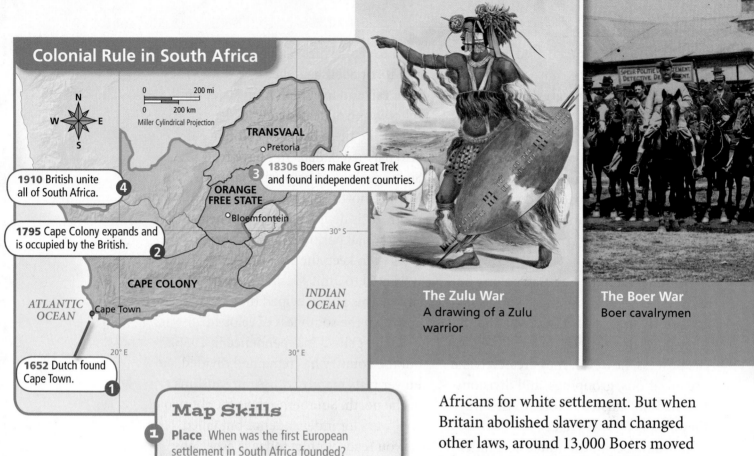

Colonial Rule in South Africa

0 — 200 mi
0 — 200 km
Miller Cylindrical Projection

TRANSVAAL
Pretoria

1910 British unite all of South Africa. **4**

1830s Boers make Great Trek and found independent countries. **3**

ORANGE FREE STATE
Bloemfontein

1795 Cape Colony expands and is occupied by the British. **2**

CAPE COLONY

ATLANTIC OCEAN
Cape Town

INDIAN OCEAN

30° S

1652 Dutch found Cape Town. **1**

20° E   30° E

The Zulu War
A drawing of a Zulu warrior

The Boer War
Boer cavalrymen

Map Skills

1 **Place** When was the first European settlement in South Africa founded?

2 **Place** What happened in 1795?

South Africa

The Dutch were the first Europeans to settle in South Africa. They founded Cape Town near the southern tip of Africa. The settlement grew into the Cape Colony.

Dutch and British Rule Dutch and other non-British Europeans who settled in Cape Colony are called Boers or Afrikaners. As the Boers moved inland, they set up large farms. They pushed Africans off the land. They killed or enslaved Africans who resisted.

In 1795, Britain took over the Cape Colony. At first the British continued Boer policies. They seized lands from Africans for white settlement. But when Britain abolished slavery and changed other laws, around 13,000 Boers moved inland to escape British rule. This migration was called the **Great Trek.** Boer migrants formed several small, independent countries known as Boer republics. They maintained white rule.

After the discovery of diamonds and gold inland from the Cape Colony, the British moved to expand their rule. In 1879, they attacked the Zulu Kingdom, a powerful African state. Although the Zulus fought back fiercely, the British were able to defeat them.

In 1899, the British went to war against the Boer republics. The fight dragged on for four brutal years. The British imprisoned tens of thousands of Boer and African civilians before winning the war.

In 1910, a united South Africa gained independence. Afrikaners and English-speaking whites shared power. The black

388

Apartheid
◄ A sign marking a segregated beach in South Africa

▲ Soldiers in the all-white military of the apartheid era

Today
A multiracial crowd in modern South Africa

majority remained powerless. As you read, the apartheid system of white rule lasted until 1994.

New Migrants While the British ruled South Africa, many non-Europeans migrated there. Some came from other British colonies like India and Malaysia. Most worked as contract laborers on large farms. They were treated poorly by the white-ruled government.

Apartheid's Aftermath Racial inequality is still a major problem in South Africa. It is a legacy of the colonial rule and apartheid. Black South Africans are more likely than white South Africans to live in poverty, to have HIV or AIDS, and to go without basic services such as clean water. Khulekani, for example, lacks running water. Many black South Africans also live in dangerous urban slums.

However, the widespread violence and oppression that plagued South Africa during the apartheid period are a thing of the past. South Africans from different races and ethnic groups are working to overcome the divisions left by the difficult history of their country.

Reading Check What did the Boers and the Zulu have in common?

Assessment

1. How did Germany govern Tanzania?

2. How did colonial British rule affect the society of Sudan?

3. Which European power united South Africa?

4. What was similar about the colonial experiences of these three countries?

5. How does the legacy of apartheid affect South Africa today?

389

Chapter Assessment

Key Terms and Ideas

1. **Discuss** Why do Southern and Eastern Africans clear forests for mining?

2. **Summarize** Why is the location of water resources so important in Southern and Eastern Africa?

3. **Recall** Where did the Bantu come from and where did they migrate to?

4. **Categorize** Give three examples of early civilizations in the region and name a feature of each.

5. **Analyze Cause and Effect** How did European control change Southern and Eastern Africa?

6. **Summarize** What have been some of the main consequences of **apartheid** in South Africa?

7. **Synthesize** Given the challenges that the region's people and governments face, why are **nongovernmental organizations (NGOs)** important in Southern and Eastern Africa?

Think Critically

8. **Solve Problems** Economic progress has been slow for the nations of this region. What geographic and human factors contribute to the problem? What factors allow or contribute to progress?

9. **Compare and Contrast** How is the role of citizens in Sudan today different from their role in the United States?

10. **Compare Viewpoints** During the apartheid era in South Africa, what main views were held and by whom?

11. **Core Concepts: Cultural Diffusion and Change** How has the movement of people influenced religion, culture, and language in Southern and Eastern Africa?

Places to Know

For each place, write the letter from the map that shows its location.

12. **South Africa**

13. **Madagascar**

14. **Kenya**

15. **Lake Victoria**

16. **Khartoum**

17. **Kalahari Desert**

18. **Draw Inferences** What might be some geographic reasons for South Africa being the region's economic superpower?

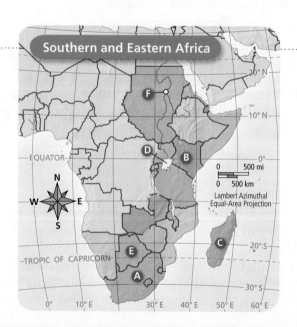

390

Essential Question

myWorld Chapter Activity

Agents of Change Follow your teacher's instructions to participate in a community group meeting attended by important individuals involved in the fall of apartheid in South Africa. Learn how different individuals helped take down apartheid. Think about ways that different groups of people can live together peacefully, and about what causes conflicts to occur.

21st Century Learning

Analyze Media Content

Using reliable sources in the library or online, research an ethnic conflict in the region. Find three examples and create a report card for each.
- type of media (print, online, TV, or radio)
- accuracy in describing conflict and participant views
- reliability (Is the source objective?)

Document-Based Questions

Success Tracker™
Online at myworldgeography.com

Use your knowledge of Southern and Eastern Africa, as well as Documents A and B, to answer Questions 1–3.

Document A

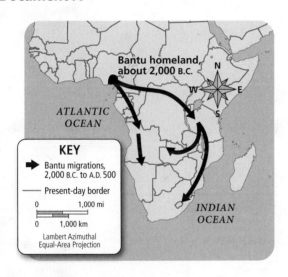

Bantu homeland, about 2,000 B.C.

ATLANTIC OCEAN

INDIAN OCEAN

KEY
→ Bantu migrations, 2,000 B.C. to A.D. 500
— Present-day border
0   1,000 mi
0   1,000 km
Lambert Azimuthal Equal-Area Projection

Document B

Bantu Genes		
Country or Region	Number of People Tested for Gene Type	Number of People With Bantu Gene Type
Kenya	227	223
Tanzania	41	41
Mozambique	4	2
Southern Africa	23	20

SOURCE: *Genetics and Molecular Biology,* volume 24 (1998), no. 4

1. Where was the Bantu people's original homeland?
A Europe
B North Africa
C West Africa
D Southern Africa

2. Which of the following can you conclude from Document B?
A Very few Tanzanians are of Bantu heritage.
B Most Kenyans are of Bantu heritage.
C Most Mozambicans are of European heritage.
D Most people in the world are of Bantu heritage.

3. **Writing Task** Based on what you have learned from the chapter and the documents above, explain the information presented in Document B.

391

Chapter 8

North Africa

Essential Question

How much does geography shape a country?

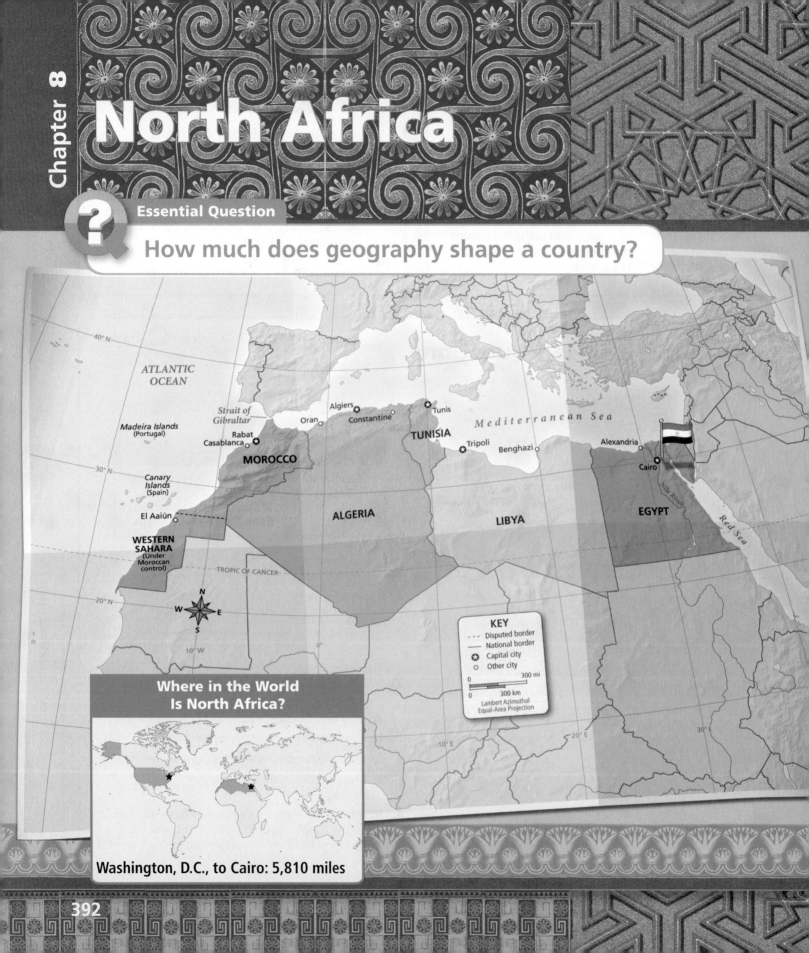

ATLANTIC OCEAN

Strait of Gibraltar

Madeira Islands (Portugal)

Oran · Algiers · Constantine

Tunis

Mediterranean Sea

Rabat · Casablanca

TUNISIA

Tripoli · Benghazi

Alexandria

MOROCCO

Canary Islands (Spain)

Cairo

El Aaiún

ALGERIA

LIBYA

EGYPT

Nile River

Red Sea

WESTERN SAHARA (Under Moroccan control)

TROPIC OF CANCER

KEY
- - - Disputed border
— National border
✪ Capital city
○ Other city

0   300 mi
0   300 km
Lambert Azimuthal Equal-Area Projection

Where in the World Is North Africa?

Washington, D.C., to Cairo: 5,810 miles

my Story

SHAIMAA'S NEIGHBORHOOD

Explore the Essential Question
- at **my worldgeography.com**
- using the **myWorld Chapter Activity**
- with the **Student Journal**

In this section, you'll read about Shaimaa, a young Egyptian woman who lives in Cairo. What does Shaimaa's story tell you about life in North Africa today?

Story by Oliver Wilkins for myWorld Geography Online

Sitting on the top of Cairo's medieval city wall, 18-year-old Shaimaa is focused on her sketchbook. Pencil in hand, she traces the domes and towers that make up the skyline of Darb al-Ahmar, the neighborhood where she was born and raised. Her spot overlooks a large park, and the sound of birds fills the air. For Shaimaa, it seems a million miles away from the hustle and bustle of the crowded neighborhood below where she lives with her family.

"I have four sisters. We all sleep in the same room. My older sister Asmaa got married. They had to leave the area because they couldn't afford an apartment."

Shaimaa's parents, like many in the neighborhood, moved here from the countryside. They originally came from a village in southern Egypt. They moved to Cairo to find a new life.

Shaimaa's apartment is located in one of the hundreds of small alleys that make up Darb al-Ahmar. The neighborhood lies in the shadow of the citadel, or fortress. The citadel was once home to Cairo's rulers and its wealthiest families lived in Darb al-Ahmar.

Shaimaa at a market

Laundry drying in Darb al-Ahmar

The neighborhood was very prosperous. Its wealthy residents built beautiful mosques.

But later, the area fell on hard times. For many years the beautiful buildings crumbled. As the population mushroomed, the area became overcrowded. Like many parts of Cairo today, Shaimaa's neighborhood is struggling to support a growing population.

Every weekday Shaimaa leaves her house at 9 A.M. and makes her way through the bustling market to catch a bus to school in downtown Cairo. She is studying computer science and hopes to continue at a university at the end of the year.

However, Shaimaa's real passion is to help restore her neighborhood. Most days after school she volunteers at a community center to do her part.

With hammer in hand, Shaimaa nails together a wooden backdrop, painted with the minarets and domes of Darb al-Ahmar's distinctive skyline. Today she is helping a group of children

Two puppets and a backdrop showing the skyline of Darb al-Ahmar

394

The puppet show

Shaimaa on the city wall

to prepare a puppet show on the history of their neighborhood. Puppet shows are a traditional form of entertainment. Shaimaa hopes that by bringing these old stories to life, she may be able to encourage a sense of pride in the neighborhood.

"We are trying to tell the people about this neighborhood through the program. We are trying to make people proud of Darb al-Ahmar by reminding them about their history, trying to revive the heritage and the folklore of the neighborhood."

In the courtyard of the school, the children rehearse the puppet show. In two weeks they will be performing it in the park by the city wall. It's hard to believe now, but the park was a garbage dump until a few years ago. After centuries of people throwing their trash over the wall, the dump grew into a hill, Shaima recalls.

"I remember before it was a park, it was a dusty hill. We were frightened to go in there because the wild dogs would chase us."

Sketching on the top of the wall, Shaimaa gazes down on her neighborhood. She points out the buildings that are undergoing restoration.

"Here, each house is like a piece of art from the past. After being restored, each house regains its sense of history. "

Shaimaa is optimistic about the future of her neighborhood. "I hope that I'll have more chances to represent the habits and traditions of my neighborhood and to let other people know more about Darb al-Ahmar."

myStory Video

Join Shaimaa as she shows you more about her life in North Africa.

Meet the Journalist

Name Oliver Wilkins
Favorite Moment Watching Shaimaa teach her mother to write.

my worldgeography.com myStory Video

395

Chapter Atlas

Key Ideas

- North Africa is very dry, especially in the vast desert called the Sahara.

- People settle where rivers or rainfall provide water.

- More and more North Africans are moving to cities.

- People in the region have altered their environment with both positive and negative consequences.

Key Terms • oasis • delta • nomad • urbanization

 Visual Glossary

 Reading Skill: Label an Outline Map Take notes using the outline map in your journal.

▲ The Atlas Mountains in Morocco.

◀ A Tunisian woman ▶

Physical Features

The five countries of North Africa lie along the Mediterranean coast from Morocco in the west to Egypt, Shaimaa's home, in the east. The region is very dry. In fact, most of North Africa is desert.

The world's largest hot desert, the Sahara, covers much of North Africa. Conditions in the Sahara are harsh. In some places it does not rain for years at a time. Sandstorms are common. Temperatures can be extremely high during the day but cool or even cold at night. Life in the Sahara centers around oases. An **oasis**

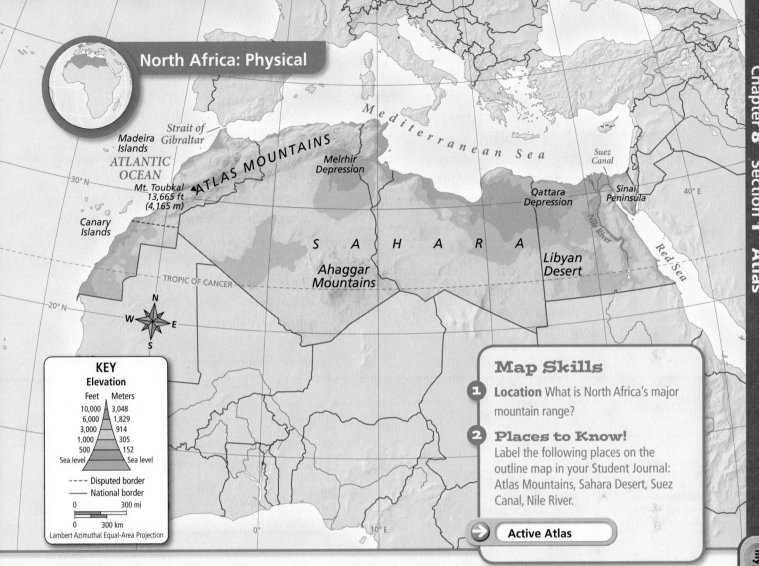

North Africa: Physical

Madeira Islands
Strait of Gibraltar
ATLANTIC OCEAN
Mt. Toubkal 13,665 ft (4,165 m)
Canary Islands
ATLAS MOUNTAINS
Melrhir Depression
Mediterranean Sea
Qattara Depression
Suez Canal
Sinai Peninsula
Nile River
Red Sea
SAHARA
Ahaggar Mountains
Libyan Desert
TROPIC OF CANCER
30° N
20° N
40° E
0°
10° E

KEY
Elevation
Feet	Meters
10,000	3,048
6,000	1,829
3,000	914
1,000	305
500	152
Sea level	Sea level

- - - - Disputed border
——— National border
0   300 mi
0   300 km
Lambert Azimuthal Equal-Area Projection

Map Skills

1 Location What is North Africa's major mountain range?

2 Places to Know! Label the following places on the outline map in your Student Journal: Atlas Mountains, Sahara Desert, Suez Canal, Nile River.

→ **Active Atlas**

is a place in a desert where water can be found.

The Atlas Mountains run through Morocco, Algeria, and Tunisia. They sit between the desert and the sea. Clouds move in from the west and drop their rain as they rise over the mountains. That gives more rainfall to the slopes of the mountains facing the coast and to areas north of the mountains.

The country of Egypt gets almost no rain. It is about 96 <u>percent</u> desert. But the remaining land is green and lush thanks to the Nile River. The Nile travels through its valley north from eastern Africa and Sudan to the Mediterranean Sea, splitting Egypt in two. It brings water to a strip of land along its banks and to its triangle-shaped delta. A **delta** is a flat plain formed on the seabed where a river deposits material over many years. Until a dam was built on the Nile, the river flooded every year, coating its banks in rich soil.

One part of this region, Egypt's Sinai Peninsula, sits between Asia and Africa. The peninsula is a mountainous desert separated from Africa by the Suez Canal.

Reading Check **What is an oasis, and why would people live near one?**

percent, *n.,* one part out of one hundred

Living in a Dry Place

North Africa's population is increasing rapidly. Cities are large and expanding. But people still live in areas where water is <u>available</u>, mostly along the coasts or near rivers. Away from these areas, the land is too dry to support more than a handful of people.

Settlement Patterns Almost all Egyptians live near the Nile River, where water makes agriculture possible. Few live in the deserts that make up the rest of the country. Egypt has the largest population in the region. In fact, almost half of all North Africans are Egyptians.

Most people in western North Africa live near the coast or in the mountains. Rain supports farming in these areas.

A small population lives in the Sahara. Many of these people live and farm in oases. Others are **nomads,** people who move from place to place without a permanent home. Away from oases it is too dry for agriculture, so people who live in the desert make a living by herding animals such as sheep and goats.

available, *adj.,* present, ready to be used

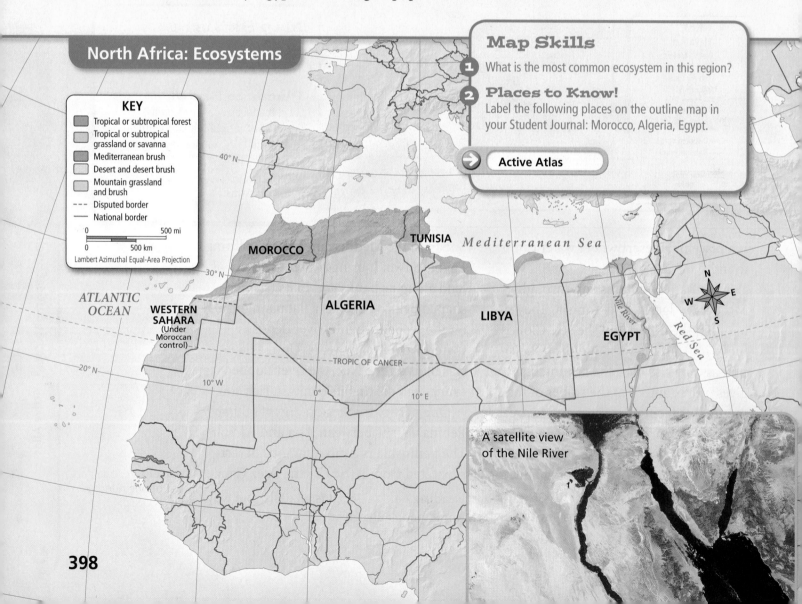

North Africa: Ecosystems

KEY
- Tropical or subtropical forest
- Tropical or subtropical grassland or savanna
- Mediterranean brush
- Desert and desert brush
- Mountain grassland and brush
- - - Disputed border
- — National border

0 ——— 500 mi
0 ——— 500 km
Lambert Azimuthal Equal-Area Projection

ATLANTIC OCEAN
WESTERN SAHARA (Under Moroccan control)
MOROCCO
TUNISIA
Mediterranean Sea
ALGERIA
LIBYA
EGYPT
Nile River
Red Sea
TROPIC OF CANCER

Map Skills

1. What is the most common ecosystem in this region?

2. **Places to Know!** Label the following places on the outline map in your Student Journal: Morocco, Algeria, Egypt.

Active Atlas

A satellite view of the Nile River

398

Cities Slightly more than half of all North Africans live in cities. Over the past century, farmers across the region have left their villages and migrated to urban areas in search of jobs and a higher standard of living. North Africa is experiencing urbanization. **Urbanization** happens when people in an area move into cities and those cities grow larger.

Cairo, the capital of Egypt, is the largest city in Africa and home to more than one in five Egyptians. It is Egypt's economic, political, and educational center. That makes it a magnet for poor people from the countryside, like Shaimaa's parents, who have moved there in large numbers.

The trend of urbanization is even stronger in the western part of the region. More than half of all Moroccans, Tunisians, and Algerians live in cities, as do more than three quarters of Libyans.

Rapidly growing urban populations can cause problems. Cities have trouble providing services like drinking water to so many people. Many cities are severely overcrowded. Still, people keep moving to the cities to find new opportunities.

Reading Check **Why do people in North Africa move to cities?**

myWorld Activity
On the Move

The Nile River, Egypt. Many of Egypt's people live in rural areas near the Nile.

Marrakech, Morocco. Urban North Africans visit cafes and souqs, or markets.

my worldgeography.com   Active Atlas

399

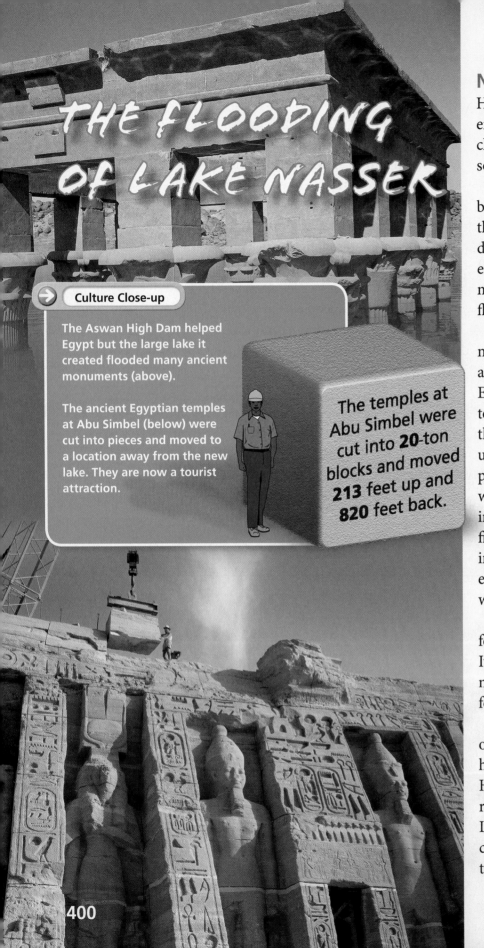

THE FLOODING OF LAKE NASSER

Culture Close-up

The Aswan High Dam helped Egypt but the large lake it created flooded many ancient monuments (above).

The ancient Egyptian temples at Abu Simbel (below) were cut into pieces and moved to a location away from the new lake. They are now a tourist attraction.

The temples at Abu Simbel were cut into **20**-ton blocks and moved **213** feet up and **820** feet back.

North Africa's Environment

Human beings have changed the environment of North Africa. These changes have made life easier, but they sometimes have had negative side effects.

In 1964, the Egyptian government built a dam across the Nile River called the Aswan High Dam. Building the dam allowed people to use water more efficiently, irrigate more land, and grow more crops. It also stopped dangerous flooding, and it produces electricity.

Unfortunately, the dam has also had negative effects on Egypt's environment and people. Before the dam was built, Egyptian farmers relied on annual floods to bring fertile soil to their fields. Since the river no longer floods, farmers must use chemical fertilizers to keep their land productive. These fertilizers eventually wash back into the river and through it into the sea. That pollutes water, killing fish and hurting people who fish for a living. Fortunately, fish stocks have recovered in recent years to near what they were before the dam was built.

As water collected behind the dam, it formed a giant lake called Lake Nasser. It is now a habitat for malaria-carrying mosquitoes. The creation of Lake Nasser forced 100,000 people out of their homes.

Like Egypt, Libya has also made serious changes to its environment. As you have read, Libya gets very little rain. However, there are large underground reserves of water deep in the Sahara. The Libyan government has built pipelines to carry water to the coast. The water is used to irrigate farmland and support growing coastal cities, where four out of every five Libyans now live.

Across this region and other parts of Africa, desertification is a major environmental problem. You learned already that this can happen when people cut down forests. It can also happen in regions such as North Africa that have few forests to begin with.

One way desertification happens is through overgrazing. Herders allow their goats to eat the grass in an area down to the roots. Without those roots, there is nothing left to hold the soil in place. Wind then blows top away, leaving barren desert behind. So much of North Africa is desert already that the region cannot afford to create more.

However, desertification can be slowed or even <u>reversed</u>. When land that is at risk is set aside and herds of sheep or goats are kept away from it, desertification can be reversed and plant life can return. People can also prevent the spread of deserts by planting a "green wall." This is a belt of trees and other vegetation planted along the edges of the desert. The trees and other plants hold soil in place and protect the land.

Algeria pioneered this technique in the 1970s. Since then, belts of forest have been planted along the edges of deserts in other parts of Africa and in different countries around the world.

Reading Check What are two environmental issues in North Africa?

reverse, *v.,* turn back, turn in the opposite direction

A landscape in Morocco that shows the effects of desertification. Overgrazing can cause desertification.

Resources and Trade

Water and oil are the most important natural resources in North Africa. The Nile River flows through several countries before it reaches Egypt. As you read in Southern and Eastern Africa, deciding who gets to use that water is a difficult issue. If other countries take too much water, Egypt could face shortages.

The Nile River in Egypt, and rainfall in the western part of the region, allow farming. Cotton, olives, citrus fruits, and other crops are important exports.

Oil Although North Africa does not produce as much oil as parts of Southwest Asia, every nation in the region has enough to satisfy its own needs and to export, or sell abroad. Algeria and Libya have the largest reserves by far.

Most of North Africa's oil and natural gas reserves are found inland, in the heart of the Sahara. Governments and international companies have built pipelines. They transport oil and gas to the coast, where they are shipped around the world.

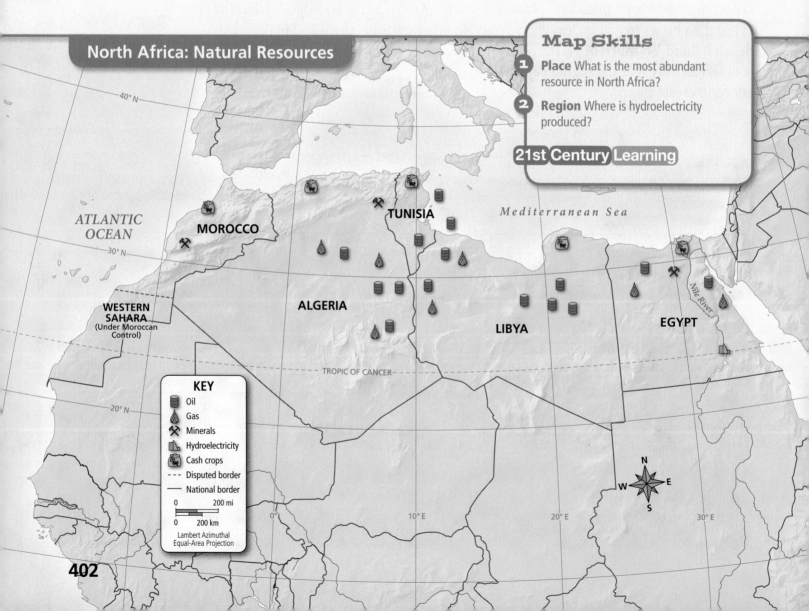

North Africa: Natural Resources

Map Skills

1 **Place** What is the most abundant resource in North Africa?

2 **Region** Where is hydroelectricity produced?

21st Century Learning

KEY
- Oil
- Gas
- Minerals
- Hydroelectricity
- Cash crops
- Disputed border
- National border

0   200 mi
0   200 km
Lambert Azimuthal
Equal-Area Projection

The Suez Canal The canal was built in Egypt in 1869. It allows large ships to pass from the Mediterranean to the Red Sea. The canal makes traveling by sea between Asia and Europe shorter by thousands of miles. Ships do not have to go around the entire continent of Africa. That makes the cost of transportation cheaper. Businesses can pass the money they save on transportation on to consumers in the form of lower prices.

One of the most important goods that passes through the Suez Canal today is oil. More than 3,000 oil tankers use the canal every year.

Because of its role in world trade, the Suez Canal affects people around the world. The canal is good for Egypt, too, since it collects a fee from each ship that passes through.

Reading Check Which two North African countries have the largest oil reserves?

Crossroads of Continents

North Africa's closeness to Europe, Asia, and Africa south of the Sahara has helped shape life there for thousands of years.

The Sahara made travel between North Africa and other parts of Africa difficult in the past. However, it was not an impassable barrier. People, ideas, and goods have long moved across it.

North Africa and Southern Europe have had connections across the Mediterranean for thousands of years. Today European languages, especially French, are often spoken as second languages in parts of the region. Millions of North African immigrants also live in Europe.

The country of Israel, in Southwest Asia, shares a land border with Egypt. North Africa's majority religion and language both came from Southwest Asia.

Reading Check How did Southwest Asia change North Africa?

my World IN NUMBERS

In 2007, **20,384** ships passed through the Suez Canal. They carried **710** million tons of cargo.

Section 1 Assessment

Essential Question

Key Terms

1. Use the following words to describe life in the Sahara: nomad, oasis.

2. How are deltas formed?

3. What is urbanization?

Key Ideas

4. What single factor most affects where people in North Africa live?

5. What have been the positive and negative changes caused by the Aswan High Dam?

6. How has urbanization affected North Africa?

7. How does the Suez Canal affect world trade?

Think Critically

8. **Compare and Contrast** Compare the Egyptian desert to the Nile River Valley. Which of these areas occupies more space? Which is home to more Egyptians?

9. **Identify Main Ideas** What do you think is the most important environmental problem facing North Africa?

How much does geography shape a country?

10. How does water shape human settlement patterns in North Africa? Go to your student journal to record your answers.

myworldgeography.com 21st Century Learning

History of North Africa

Key Ideas

- Ancient Egypt was among the world's first complex civilizations.
- The Arab-Islamic conquest made lasting changes to the region's culture.
- Europeans colonized North Africa in the 1800s, but its nations achieved independence in the 1900s.

Key Terms
- pharaoh
- mummy
- theocracy
- Berbers
- hieroglyphics
- Pan-Arabism

Visual Glossary

Reading Skill: Analyze Cause and Effect Take notes using the graphic organizer in your journal.

The Great Sphinx in Egypt ▼

North Africa produced one of the world's first civilizations. The ancient Egyptians took advantage of their country's fertile river valley and built a wealthy and sophisticated society. Ancient Egypt's achievements influenced other cultures. In fact, ancient Egypt is considered a cultural hearth, or one of the places where human civilization began.

Ancient Egypt

About 5,000 years ago the civilization of ancient Egypt developed in the Nile River Valley. It endured for almost 3,000 years.

Ancient Egypt Develops An ancient Greek writer called Egypt "the gift of the river." The Nile River made Egyptian civilization possible. The river was like an oasis surrounded by desert. Every summer it brought great floods. They left behind deposits of silt, a rich soil, along the river's banks. Plants and animals thrived in this environment. In ancient times, nomads lived around the river. They survived by hunting, gathering, and fishing.

Fertile soil made the river valley a perfect place for agriculture, which spread into Egypt from Southwest Asia. Societies that farm are different from fishing and hunting-gathering societies. Farming produces more food than hunting and gathering or fishing. It allows the population to expand. Small villages grow into towns and then cities.

By about 3,000 B.C., as many as one million people may have lived along the Nile. They shared a language, a culture, and religious beliefs.

Early on, Egypt developed a powerful government ruled by a **pharaoh,** or king of ancient Egypt. The Nile River and the need to use it for irrigation encouraged powerful central government in Egypt. A single ruler could direct the people's labor to build irrigation canals. Canals changed Egypt's environment. They brought water to fields far from the river. They also helped control floods. Pharaohs taxed the people to pay for building the canals or forced people to work part of the year for no pay. Pharaohs also used these methods to build temples and tombs.

The pharaoh was not just a political leader. Egyptians also believed he was like a god and worshipped him after his death. That belief made Egypt a **theocracy,** a government based on religion.

Egypt's strong central government made it different from ancient civilizations in Iraq and India. They were often politically divided. Egypt was more like China, which unified at an early date.

Egyptian Culture The Egyptians were among the first people to study mathematics, astronomy, engineering, and other scientific fields. They built trade networks into Eastern Africa and other regions. Egyptian culture influenced other parts of the world.

The Egyptians invented **hieroglyphics,** a system of writing using pictures and other symbols. Hieroglyphics were used to help the government keep records and to write about history and religion. Egyptians also invented papyrus, the first paper, which they made from reeds that grew along the banks of the Nile River.

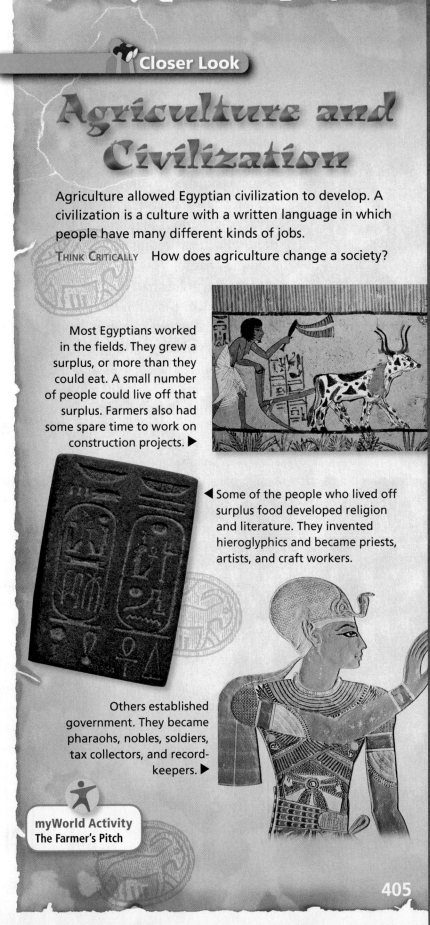

Closer Look

Agriculture and Civilization

Agriculture allowed Egyptian civilization to develop. A civilization is a culture with a written language in which people have many different kinds of jobs.

THINK CRITICALLY How does agriculture change a society?

Most Egyptians worked in the fields. They grew a surplus, or more than they could eat. A small number of people could live off that surplus. Farmers also had some spare time to work on construction projects. ▶

◀ Some of the people who lived off surplus food developed religion and literature. They invented hieroglyphics and became priests, artists, and craft workers.

Others established government. They became pharaohs, nobles, soldiers, tax collectors, and record-keepers. ▶

myWorld Activity
The Farmer's Pitch

405

Egyptian Religion Ancient Egyptians believed in hundreds of gods that controlled all places and things. They also believed in an afterlife, life after death. Pharaohs and the very rich were buried with valuables, favorite pets, food, and even boats to take them to the afterlife.

Many pharaohs built elaborate tombs. In fact, the famous pyramids of Giza are tombs. Each has rooms on the inside to hold the pharaoh's body and possessions.

Some Egyptians had their bodies mummified, or turned into mummies after death. A **mummy** is a body that has been preserved so it will not decompose. The corpse's internal organs were removed and the brain pulled through the nose with a hook.

◀ An ancient Egyptian mummy

Then the body was dried and wrapped in sheets of linen to preserve it. Much of what we know about ancient Egypt comes from its tombs.

Greek and Roman North Africa After more than 2,000 years of rule by pharaohs, Egypt was conquered by Persians and then Greeks. Greeks ruled Egypt for 302 years. The famous Queen Cleopatra VII was the last Greek ruler of Egypt. Around 800 B.C, Phoenicians from modern-day Lebanon built the powerful city of Carthage in what is now Tunisia. Eventually the whole region fell under Roman rule. By the A.D. 400s most North Africans had converted to Christianity.

Reading Check Why was Ancient Egypt

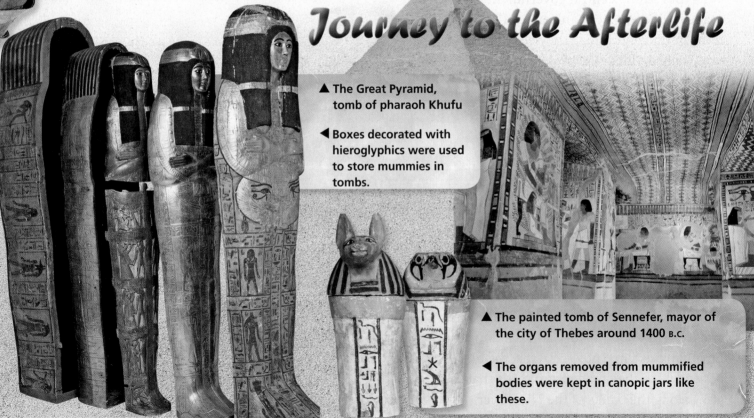

Journey to the Afterlife

▲ The Great Pyramid, tomb of pharaoh Khufu

◀ Boxes decorated with hieroglyphics were used to store mummies in tombs.

▲ The painted tomb of Sennefer, mayor of the city of Thebes around 1400 B.C.

◀ The organs removed from mummified bodies were kept in canopic jars like these.

406

called the "gift of the Nile"?

Arab North Africa

With the arrival of Arab Muslims from Southwest Asia, North Africa's religion, language, and culture were transformed.

The Arab Conquest In the A.D. 600s, the religion of Islam was first preached in Arabia. Followers of Islam are called Muslims. The first Muslims were Arabs. Arab Muslim armies built an empire that stretched from Spain to Iran. North Africa was part of this empire.

Religious leaders and merchants followed the army, building trading centers and mosques, or Islamic houses of worship. Then many Arab migrants came. They spread Islam to Egyptians and **Berbers,** the indigenous people of western North Africa. These migrants also helped spread the Arabic language throughout the region. Most North Africans converted to Islam, although many Jews and Christians continued to live in the region.

North Africa became one of the most culturally productive parts of the Islamic world. Arab rulers founded cities such as Kairouan in Tunisia and Cairo in Egypt. Both grew into major centers of religion and learning. Cairo became one of the largest cities in the world. Art and literature flourished under Arab rule.

Trade in Arab North Africa While earlier conquerors saw the Sahara as a barrier, the Arabs saw it as an opportunity. They quickly came to control the trans-Saharan caravan routes that linked Africa south of the Sahara with North Africa. Merchants spread Arabic and Islam to peoples they traded with in the Sahara and beyond.

transform, *v.,* change into a new form or appearance

Painted tiles are often used to make decorative geometric shapes in Arab architecture. ▼

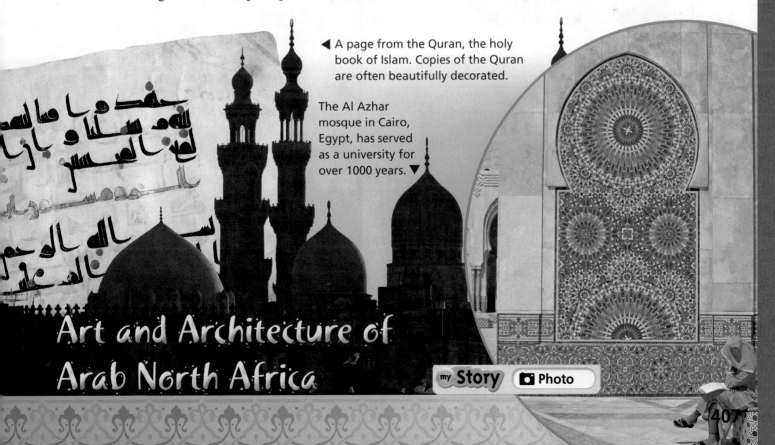

◀ A page from the Quran, the holy book of Islam. Copies of the Quran are often beautifully decorated.

The Al Azhar mosque in Cairo, Egypt, has served as a university for over 1000 years. ▼

Art and Architecture of Arab North Africa

my Story   📷 Photo

407

Reading Check How did the Arabs change North Africa?

European Rule and Independence

The united Arab empire did not last long. Various states gained and lost power in the region over time.

European Colonization During the 1800s, European powers came to rule North Africa. They wanted to control the region's resources, to guard important trade routes, or to force local rulers to pay debts they owed to European lenders. Britain took control of Egypt, while

majority, *n.*, a group with more than half of a population

France ruled most of western North Africa. Spain and Italy governed other parts of this region.

The Struggle for Independence
Resistance to European rule began immediately and grew into nationalism. North Africans resented that they did not get a say in their own government. Many protested European rule. Most of the region gained independence in the 1950s.

Algeria had a longer road to travel. Around one million Europeans had settled in Algeria. Many argued that Algeria was a part of France. Some Algerians agreed and wanted to be

The leader of France visits Algiers in 1958. At this time around 15 percent of the city's people were Europeans. ▶

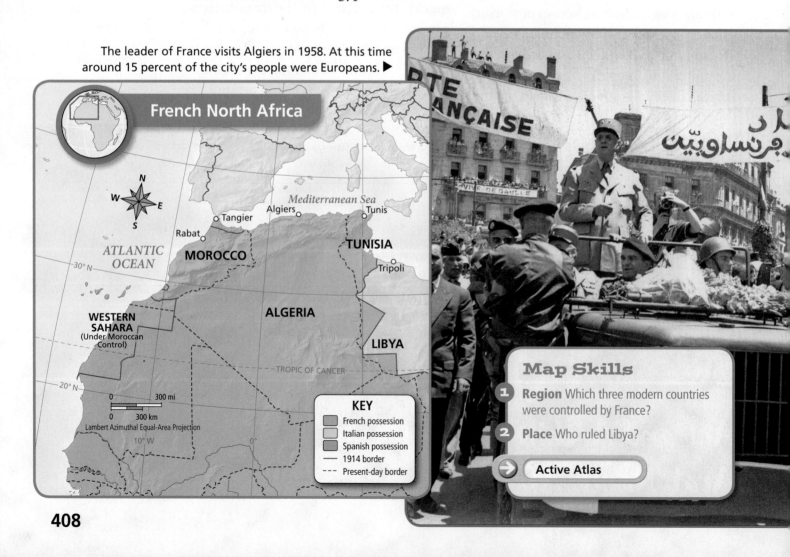

French North Africa

KEY
- French possession
- Italian possession
- Spanish possession
- —— 1914 border
- - - - Present-day border

Map Skills

1. **Region** Which three modern countries were controlled by France?
2. **Place** Who ruled Libya?

→ **Active Atlas**

more like the French. But the <u>majority</u> disagreed. They argued that Algeria had a different culture, language, and religion from France. According to a nationalist,

66 Islam is our religion, Arabic our language, Algeria our fatherland. 99

—Ben Badis

It took eight years of bloody war for the country to win independence. In 1962, French troops left. Most Europeans in Algeria fled the country.

Egypt Since Independence Egypt gained its formal independence in 1922, but Britain continued to quietly control the country for many years. In 1952, a group of military officers led by Gamal Abdel Nasser overthrew the government and seized control of Egypt. Nasser ruled like a dictator.

Nasser tried to modernize and strengthen Egypt. In 1956, he seized control of the Suez Canal from its British and French owners. Britain, France, and Israel responded by attacking Egypt, but the United States and the United Nations forced them to withdraw. As a result, Egypt gained control of the canal.

This event, the Suez Crisis, was seen as a major success of Nasser's rule. Arabs in other countries admired him for standing up to European powers and for building the Aswan High Dam. He was a leader of the Pan-Arab movement. **Pan-Arabism** is the idea that all Arabic-speaking peoples should unite into one country.

In another area, Nasser was less successful. He opposed the existence of the country of Israel and tried to fight it. In 1967, Israel defeated Egypt and its allies Jordan and Syria. Israel took the Sinai Peninsula from Egypt. Nasser's successor, Anwar Sadat, failed to take the Sinai back when he went to war with Israel in 1973. Egypt only regained the Sinai when it signed a peace agreement with Israel in 1979.

Reading Check What happened to the Sinai Peninsula in 1967 and 1979?

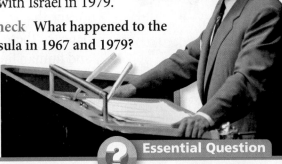
Gamal Abdel Nasser, Egypt's president from 1956 to 1970 ▼

Section 2 Assessment

Key Terms

1. Use the following words to describe ancient Egyptian religion and government: pharaoh, theocracy, mummy, hieroglyphics.

2. Who are the Berbers?

3. What do people who support Pan-Arabism believe?

Key Ideas

4. How did the Arab-Islamic conquest of North Africa change the region?

5. What were two of Gamal Abdel Nasser's major achievements?

Think Critically

6. **Analyze Cause and Effect** Why was the development of agriculture important for ancient Egypt? What did agriculture allow?

7. **Compare and Contrast** How were independence struggles in Algeria and Egypt different?

? Essential Question

How much does geography shape a country?

8. How did physical geography shape the development of ancient Egypt? Go to your student journal to record your answers.

Ancient Egyptian Culture

Key Ideas
- Ancient Egypt produced a rich culture including religion, art, and literature.
- Religion was an important theme in ancient Egyptian art and literature.

Key Terms • polytheist • pictogram • scribe • Book of the Dead

In the previous section, you read about the development of ancient Egypt and its pharaohs. In addition to creating a government, the ancient Egyptians produced one of the longest-lasting and richest cultures in world history. Their religion, and especially their belief in the afterlife, influenced many aspects of their culture. Most of what we know today about ancient Egypt comes from surviving tombs and the paintings, objects, and documents they contain.

Egyptian Religion

Unlike modern Jews, Christians, and Muslims, ancient Egyptians did not worship a single god. Ancient Egyptians were **polytheists,** which means that they believed in many different gods and goddesses. They believed these gods and goddesses controlled different parts of nature and human life.

Gods and Goddesses Ra was one of the most important Egyptian gods. He was god of the sun, as well as the chief of all the other gods. Isis was a goddess of nature and fertility, while Horus ruled the sky.

Each god had familiar symbols. Sometimes these were animals reflecting the god's personality, such as Horus' high-flying falcon. Sometimes symbols related to the god's area of influence. Osiris often appeared with a Pharaoh's crown and mummy wrappings, showing that he was king of the dead. Gods and goddesses were often represented as having the heads of animals or as animals themselves. The goddess Bastet appeared as a cat while Isis was often shown as a cow.

The Egyptians worshipped their gods and goddesses in temples. An image of the god was kept in a temple and treated like royalty. It was dressed, fed, and praised. Egyptians believed it was important to keep the gods happy. If they did, the gods would reward them.

The Egyptian god Horus, shown as a falcon wearing a crown ▶

For example, a god might provide a good harvest or keep disease away. The priests and priestesses who tended to the gods were wealthy and powerful landowners. Common people were not allowed into the temples.

Isis, Osiris, and Set Like other ancient cultures, the Egyptians had many stories about their gods. One story was the myth of Isis, Osiris, and Set. Osiris and his wife Isis ruled Egypt until Osiris' brother Set grew jealous. Set planned to trick Osiris and steal his throne. Set hired craftsmen to build a beautiful box. It was designed so that only Osiris would fit inside it. The sneaky Set offered the box to the person it fit best. Of course, that person was Osiris. As soon as Osiris got into the box,

Set shut him in. He threw the box, with Osiris inside, into the Nile River. The box became Osiris' coffin.

Isis searched the world for her husband. Eventually she found Osiris' body and brought it back to Egypt. Set tried to take the body from her and they fought, but Isis won. She wrapped Osiris in bandages, like a mummy, and brought him back to life. She and Osiris went to live in the underworld where Osiris became god of the dead.

Egyptians believed that after death, they would travel through the underworld to Osiris. He would judge who could pass to live among the gods.

Reading Check According to ancient Egyptian religion, who were Ra and Horus?

ISIS AND OSIRIS

Isis and her husband Osiris

Osiris judges the dead.

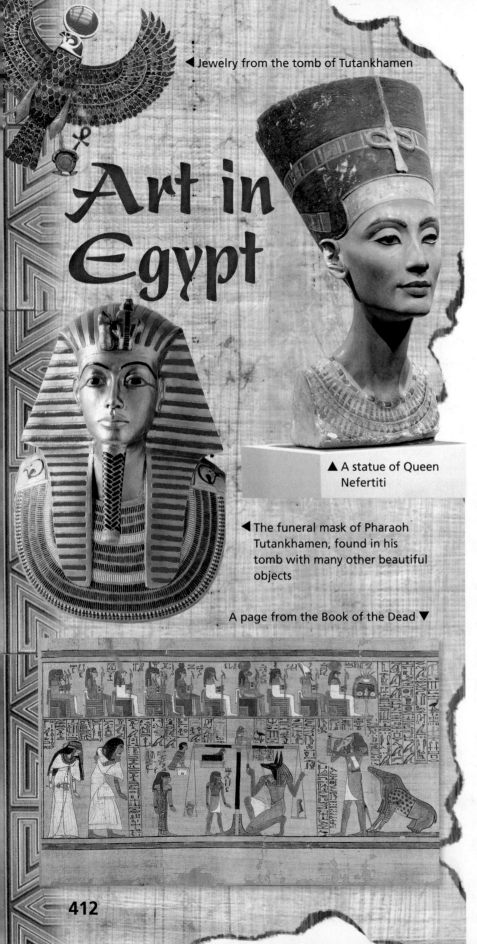

◄ Jewelry from the tomb of Tutankhamen

Art in Egypt

▲ A statue of Queen Nefertiti

◄ The funeral mask of Pharaoh Tutankhamen, found in his tomb with many other beautiful objects

A page from the Book of the Dead ▼

Art in Ancient Egypt

The Egyptians' beliefs and myths affected the art they created and the buildings they built. Ancient Egyptians worked hard to prepare for the afterlife. Pharaohs and other wealthy Egyptians built tombs with many rooms, stocking them with precious objects and useful goods. Thieves robbed most of these tombs in ancient times, but they missed the tomb of Pharaoh Tutankhamen. This tomb was discovered by archaeologists in 1922.

The walls of tombs were often richly painted. These paintings sometimes showed scenes from the life of the person buried in the tomb, such as hunting trips, military expeditions, or religious festivals. The paintings could also depict scenes from mythological stories.

Reading Check **What did Egyptians paint on the walls of their tombs?**

Writing and Literature

As you read, ancient Egyptians invented their own system of writing called hieroglyphics. Different forms of hieroglyphics were invented elsewhere in the world, but Egyptian hieroglyphics were used only in Egypt.

Egyptian hieroglyphics included three kinds of symbols. The first kind was called a **pictogram,** or picture symbol. A picture of a cow meant "cow." Next, there were sound symbols, or phonograms. These were similar to our letters. Last, there were guide symbols. These told readers what topic or idea a nearby symbol referred to. For example, an eye symbol might appear after a symbol with

Egypt has the largest population of any Arabic-speaking country. It produces many of the most popular books, films, and television shows in Arabic. An Egyptian writer says of Egypt's film industry,

66 With a scale of production unequalled anywhere else in the Arab world, and with its Egyptian-Arab cultural appeal, it became the commercial cinema for all Arab countries. 99

—Samir Farid

Raï (rah EE) music is originally from Algeria, but it appeals to Arabic-speaking people from many different countries. Raï blends traditional and modern styles and deals with current issues.

Minority Groups Ethnic and religious minorities also live in North Africa. The Berbers are the largest ethnic minority. They speak their own language, Tamazight, and live in the western part of the region. Berbers have worked to preserve their culture. Today, Tamazight is an official language in two countries.

The **Copts** are a minority group in Egypt. They practice Christianity. Coptic Christianity has been practiced in Egypt since ancient times. Copts are generally tolerated by the Muslim majority but are sometimes treated as second-class citizens. The Copts are the largest Christian population in the Middle East.

Large Jewish populations lived in the region from ancient times until the 1900s. Most now live in Israel, but small numbers remain, particularly in Morocco.

Reading Check **What regions are often considered part of the Middle East?**

North African Life

A woman prepares couscous, a common dish in western North Africa. ▶

◀ Berber men in Algeria enjoy a cup of tea.

◀ Algerian raï singer Rachid Taha gives a performance.

415

Economy and Development

North Africa is the wealthiest and most developed region in Africa. It benefits from large oil reserves, trade with Europe, good educational systems, and relatively <u>stable</u> governments.

Living Conditions The standard of living in North Africa is generally higher than in other parts of Africa. But, it is not as high as in Europe or North America. Many North Africans live in poverty. Water shortages and urban problems such as overcrowding are serious issues.

One way to compare living conditions from place to place is to compare life expectancy, or how long an average person lives. High life expectancy is a sign that a country has a good healthcare system and enough food. Libya has the highest life expectancy in Africa.

You can also compare different countries by their **gross domestic product (GDP).** Gross domestic product is the total value of all goods and services produced in a country over a single year. Bigger countries often have bigger GDPs. For example, Algeria has more people than Libya, and it has a higher GDP.

But GDP does not show how real Algerians or Libyans live. In a big country, all those goods and services are shared among more people. The **gross domestic product (GDP) per capita** gives a better picture of conditions. It is a country's GDP divided by the number of people in the country. Libya has a higher GDP per capita than Algeria. That means that on average, a Libyan

GDP of Libya and Algeria, 2008

Libya
$88.86 billion

Algeria
$235.5 billion

10 billion dollars

SOURCE: CIA World Factbook

Chart Skills

1. What is Algeria's gross domestic product?

2. Does this graph show that, on average, an Algerian earns more than a Libyan? Explain your answer.

→ **Data Discovery**

416

has a higher income than an Algerian. On average, a Libyan has more purchasing power, meaning he or she can afford more things, than an Algerian. The problem with this measure is that it does not show inequality. Some people earn more than others but the GDP per capita does not reflect this difference.

The **human development index,** or HDI, takes more into account. An HDI is a number that reflects a country's average life expectancy, education, income, and other factors. HDI values are shown as decimals. For example, Egypt's HDI is 0.7. The closer a country's HDI is to one, the higher its standard of living.

Looking at the literacy rate, or the percentage of adults who can read, is also helpful. A high literacy rate suggests that country has a good education system. Tunisia's literacy rate is 74.3 percent. The United States' is 99.9 percent. Educated workers are more productive, so education can improve a country's economy.

North Africa's Economies Oil production is the most important primary industry in North Africa. A primary industry extracts natural resources. Agriculture is also an important primary industry. Secondary industries make finished products from raw materials. Food processing, textile production, and crafts such as making leather goods or jewelry are important secondary industries in North Africa.

Oil, food, and manufactured goods are all exported from North Africa to Europe. In this trade, Europeans buy needed products, and North Africans receive the money they need. Voluntary trade like this can benefit both sides.

Tourism brings a great deal of business into the region. Tourists flock to North Africa for its historic sites and warm winters. Tourists spend money at hotels and restaurants. These services are called tertiary, or third-level, industries. Fourth-level or quaternary industries, such as scientific research, produce knowledge. They are less important in North Africa than in more developed regions.

Despite its advantages, the region still suffers from economic problems. For example, corruption and unemployment are serious issues.

Reading Check What are three factors that the human development index measures?

myWorld Activity
Human Bar Graph

extract, *v.,* to get, take out, remove

A silversmith's shop in a market in Tunisia ▼

my worldgeography.com Data Discovery

417

▲ Muslim Brotherhood members protest against the Egyptian government.

Different Forms of Government

Each nation in North Africa has its own form of government. All are different from the American system of government, with different methods of selecting leaders and making laws. For example, many political parties compete for office in Morocco, while political parties are banned in Libya.

Egypt: Secularism and Islamism Egypt is not a democracy, but its people have some say in their government. A single party has ruled Egypt since the 1950s. It controls the newspapers, television, and radio. The government of long time president Hosni Mubarak imprisons many of its opponents. Corruption is common, and the police regularly abuse people they arrest. Egyptians elect members of parliament, but the largest

opposition party is not allowed to run for office. The government has not been able to greatly improve Egyptians' standard of living. Rapid population growth makes this problem even more difficult.

Because of these problems, many Egyptians oppose the government. But it is the issue of religion and politics that most divides Egyptians. The government is based on **secularism,** the idea that religion and government should be separate. However, many Egyptians are Islamists. They believe that the government should be run according to Islamic law.

The **Muslim Brotherhood** is an Islamist party. It is the largest group that opposes the Egyptian government. It also opposes the policies of the United States, and the country Israel. In addition to supporting Islamism, the brotherhood pushes for a more democratic Egypt and against corruption. The party generally does not use violence to achieve its goals. However, small groups of Islamic extremists in Egypt have comitted terrorist attacks that target foreign tourists.

Algeria: An Unstable Government As a republic, Algeria has a constitution. However, the country is politically unstable, and elections have been manipulated or rigged.

As in Egypt, Algeria's rulers are secular, and there is a moderate Islamist opposition. However, violent Islamic extremists are more powerful in Algeria than elsewhere in the region. They fought a civil war with the government from 1991 to 2002. Even after the end of the civil war, terrorism remains a problem.

Morocco: A Constitutional Monarchy Morocco is the only nation in North Africa still ruled by a king, Mohammed VI. The king is very powerful but does not completely control the government. A written constitution limits his power. An elected parliament plays a role in government.

In recent years, Morocco has taken steps to increase women's equality. People have more rights than ever before, but the government restricts some civil liberties such as complete freedom of speech.

Morocco has also been criticized for its decades-long occupation of neighboring Western Sahara. This occupation has complicated relations with neighboring countries and with the African Union. Still, Morocco has made greater strides towards full democracy than most other North African nations.

Reading Check How is secularism different from Islamism?

Members attend a meeting of the Moroccan parliament. After the 2007 election, control of parliament changed peacefully from one political party to another. An opposition party won the election, and the head of that party became the prime minister. *How does this fact show that Morocco is different from Egypt?*

Section 3 Assessment

Key Terms

1. Use the following terms to describe Egypt's government and its interaction with religion: secularism, Muslim Brotherhood.

2. How are the gross domestic product and the gross domestic product per capita different?

Key Ideas

3. What is a culture region, and which culture regions is North Africa a part of?

4. What are some ways to measure and describe North Africa's standard of living?

5. What religion do the Copts practice, and where do they live?

Think Critically

6. **Compare and Contrast** How is Morocco's system of government similar to Egypt's? How is it different?

7. **Compare and Contrast** What aspects of culture link North Africa and Southwest Asia? What aspects might divide societies?

Essential Question

How much does geography shape a country?

8. How has oil affected life in North Africa today? How has geography affected standards of living in different North African countries? Go to your Student Journal to record your answers.

419

Reform in Morocco

Key Idea
- Morocco's king believes his government is democratic, but some Moroccans say that recent reforms have not gone far enough.

▲ The flag of Morocco

Morocco is a constitutional monarchy. That means there are written limits to the king's power. Still, Morocco's king is a very powerful figure. Mohammed VI came to office promising great reforms, such as a freer press and more openness for political opposition. Many Moroccans love their leader and appreciate his reforms. But other Moroccans such as Khadija Riyadi argue that human rights are not fully respected. They complain that journalists are mistreated, especially if they say anything negative about the King. Study these selections to learn about Morocco's struggle to define its democracy.

Stop at each letter on the right to think about the text. Then answer the question with the same letter on the left.

A **Summarize** According to the King, who chose the monarchy?

B **Synthesize** How does the King justify his rule?

C **Draw Inferences** If the king has a "permanent symbiosis" with his people, will he ever step down and end the monarchy?

quadruple, *adj.,* having four parts

sovereignty, *n.,* independence, self-government

symbiosis, *n.,* relationship in which both members benefit and cannot live without each other

The King in His Own Words

66 This is the truly authentic Moroccan monarchy we have chosen for **A** ourselves, whose effectiveness I have reinforced through the citizens' commitment to development. It is a system based on strong attachment to a <u>quadruple</u> legitimacy: religious, historical, **B** constitutional, and democratic; it is also based on deep respect for the nation's struggle and the sacrifices made for the country's <u>sovereignty</u>, unity, and progress, as well as on **C** the permanent <u>symbiosis</u> between the people and the Throne. 99

—King Mohammed VI of Morocco, speech marking his 8th year as king, July 30, 2007

King Mohammed

420

Stop at each letter on the right to think about the text. Then answer the question with the same letter on the left.

D **Summarize** According to the author, what is the state of freedom of the press in Morocco?

E **Draw Inferences** Why might the government crack down on the news media?

F **Analyze Cause and Effect** What may journalists do if they are punished when they anger the government?

mete, *v.,* distribute, usually justice or punishment

taboos, *n.,* customs that forbid people from doing or talking about certain things

The Other Side

D 66 Freedom of the press is going through a real crisis in Morocco. Moroccan courts are used as a

E mechanism to clamp down on the press and <u>mete</u> out severe punishment to journalists who are known for their courage in breaking

F <u>taboos</u>. 99

—Khadija Riyadi, president of the Moroccan Human Rights Association, interview with Al-Jazeera, September 2007

Khadija *Riyadi*

▼ King Mohammed VI

Analyze the Documents

1. **Identify Bias** Does the king have a bias in evaluating how democratic his government is? Explain.
2. **Writing Task** Write a letter from Khadija Riyadi to King Mohammed explaining your point of view about freedom of the press in Morocco.

421

North Africa

Chapter Assessment

Key Terms and Ideas

1. **Describe** How was ancient Egyptian religion related to government?

2. **Summarize** What is **secularism,** and how is it different from Islamism?

3. **Recall** What effect do the Atlas Mountains have on rainfall?

4. **Categorize** How do North Africa and much of Southwest Asia form a culture region?

5. **Analyze Cause and Effect** What is a major cause of desertification in North Africa?

6. **Summarize** How was ancient Egypt different from other ancient civilizations?

7. **Synthesize** How do countries in North Africa treat minority groups? Compare the situations of the **Berbers** and the **Copts**.

Think Critically

8. **Analyze Primary and Secondary Sources** What does Ben Badis's statement in Section 2 tell you about Algerian nationalism?

9. **Problem Solving** What are some steps that governments can take to slow down or reverse desertification?

10. **Identify Evidence** What aspects of modern North African culture demonstrate that Arab Muslims conquered the region in the A.D. 600s?

11. **Core Concepts: Economic Development** What are three different ways to measure a country's level of economic development?

Places to Know

For each place, write the letter from the map that shows its location.

12. **Algiers**

13. **Rabat**

14. **Nile River**

15. **Sinai Peninsula**

16. **Cairo**

17. **Atlas Mountains**

18. **Estimate** Using the scale, estimate the distance between Cairo and Algiers.

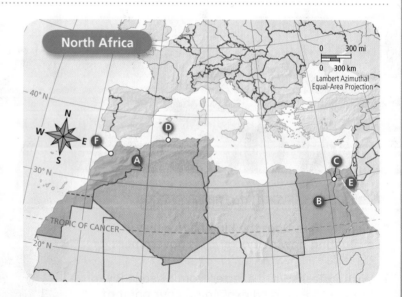

422

Essential Question

myWorld Chapter Activity

National Crest Follow your teacher's instructions to draw a national crest for a North African country that represents its physical geography, history, government, and economy. Consider how the physical geography of your country affects everything else about it.

21st Century Learning

Search for Information on the Internet

Using reliable online sources, research a pharaoh of your choosing. Using at least two sources, find and record the following information:
- name
- dates of reign
- major accomplishments

For each of your sources, write a sentence explaining why you believe it is trustworthy.

Document-Based Questions

Success Tracker™
Online at myworldgeography.com

Use your knowledge of North Africa, as well as Documents A and B, to answer Questions 1–3.

Document A

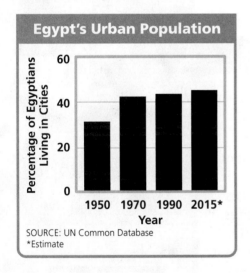

Egypt's Urban Population

SOURCE: UN Common Database
*Estimate

Document B

" In a city where the streets were designed to accommodate half a million cars more than three million daily cross the capital. Cairo is now home to 20 percent of Egypt's population. The streets are packed. . . . Pollution levels have soared."

—Dena Rashed, "To Salvage a City"

1. Which of the following describes the change seen in Document A?

   A corruption

   B desertification

   C urbanization

   D Islamization

2. Which of the following does Document B suggest?

   A Cairo is well governed.

   B Cairo is overcrowded.

   C Cairo is a medium-sized city.

   D Cairo is Egypt's cultural capital.

3. **Writing Task** Why do you think so much of Egypt's population lives in Cairo?

Come to Africa

PLAN A TOURISM CAMPAIGN

Your Mission Your group has just been asked to investigate tourism for the African Union. Your job is to increase the number of people who come to the continent, visiting landmarks, going on tours, staying in hotels, and eating in restaurants.

If you had a chance to travel to Africa, what would you do on your trip? Would you want to see the monuments of past civilizations, visit the habitat of wild animals, or explore the vegetation of the rain forest? Would you want to learn about African music and arts? Whatever your interests, you would probably begin by researching places in Africa, reading tour books, or visiting tourism Web sites.

Your impressions of Africa would probably be influenced by tourism books or Web sites. You would find that the best tourism campaign finds a way to combine the uniqueness of a place with the expectations that visitors have for travel there. A trip that is called "the vacation of a lifetime" makes you want to travel! To reach visitors and persuade them to travel, a good tourism campaign should also be innovative. It should generate interest by conveying its message in an exciting and intriguing way.

STEP 1

Research Your Country.

Decide with your teacher whether your group will design a tourism campaign for Botswana, Egypt, Ethiopia, Ghana, Kenya, Mali, Republic of the Congo, Uganda, or Tanzania. Research the geography, economy, history, and culture of your country. Study photographs and tourism information to learn what makes these countries appealing to tourists.

STEP 2

Choose Your Specialty.

Based on your country's strengths, determine the special focus of your tourism campaign. You might choose to appeal to people interested in historic sites, eco-tourism, wildlife habitats, photo safaris, culture, or sports. Decide what kind of marketing campaign (print or multimedia) will attract the attention of tourists interested in one of those areas.

STEP 3

Plan Your Marketing Campaign.

Develop a proposal for your marketing campaign. Explain who your target audience is, how you will portray the country, and what persuasive techniques you will use. Your campaign may take the form of a Web site, an illustrated brochure, a television commercial, or a video. Write a memo to the head of the tourism ministry that describes your proposal in detail.

Southwest Asia

Southwest Asia is a region of towering mountains in the north and vast deserts in the south. It is a continental crossroads that connects Asia to Europe and Africa. The region includes the world's most important oil producer, Saudi Arabia, and several other oil-rich nations. Southwest Asia is also the birthplace of three great world religions: Judaism, Christianity, and Islam.

What time is it there?

Washington, D.C.	Jidda, Saudi Arabia
9 A.M. Monday	5 P.M. Monday

KEY
— National border
✪ Capital city
Orthographic Projection

The Unit Ahead

➡ **Chapter 16** Arabia and Iraq

➡ **Chapter 17** Israel and Its Neighbors

➡ **Chapter 18** Iran, Turkey, and Cyprus

my worldgeography.com

Plan your trip online with a Data Discovery Activity and the myStory Videos of the region's young people.

Hanan
Age: 20
Home: Jidda, Saudi Arabia
Chapter 16

Maayan
Age: 18
Home: Adi, Israel
Chapter 17

Muhammad
Age: 15
Home: Jerusalem, Israel
Chapter 17

Bilal
Age: 18
Home: Urfa, Turkey
Chapter 18

Dry mountains rise above fertile plains in eastern Turkey.

427

Regional Overview
Physical Geography

Black Sea

Caspian Sea

Anatolia

Taurus Mountains

Elburz Mountains

Zagros Mountains

Tigris River

Mesopotamia

Euphrates River

Iranian Plateau

Mediterranean Sea

Syrian Desert

Persian Gulf

Hejaz

Red Sea

Arabian Peninsula

Asir

Rub' al-Khali

Green mountains and fertile valleys run through Turkey, Syria, Lebanon, Israel, Jordan, northern Iraq, and western Iran.

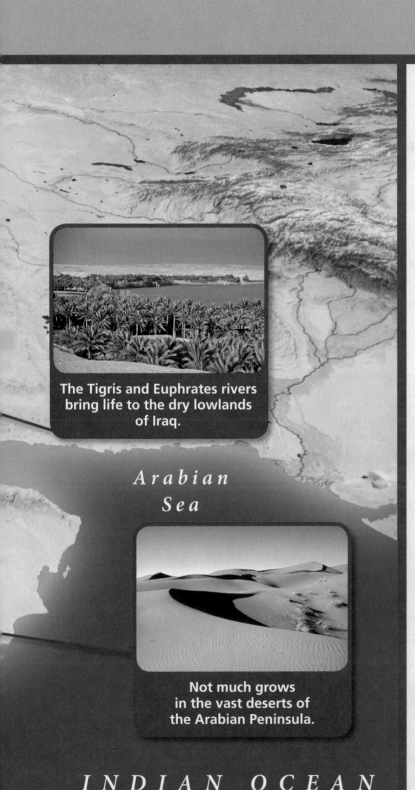

The Tigris and Euphrates rivers bring life to the dry lowlands of Iraq.

Arabian Sea

Not much grows in the vast deserts of the Arabian Peninsula.

INDIAN OCEAN

Regional Flyover

Suppose that you are in an airplane flying toward Southwest Asia. Flying east from Europe, you come to Turkey, whose mountains and plains lie between the Black Sea and the Mediterranean Sea. To its south is the Mediterranean island country of Cyprus.

Along the eastern shore of the Mediterranean lies a range of hills that runs through Syria, Lebanon, Jordan, and Israel. Next, you come to the flat valley of the Tigris and Euphrates rivers in Iraq. Farther east, you come to the high plateaus and mountains of Iran.

Turning south from Iran, you fly across the Persian Gulf, surrounded by oil wells and refineries. Across the Persian Gulf lies the Arabian Peninsula. Vast deserts stretch across this peninsula. Small countries line the coast of the peninsula. These are Kuwait, Bahrain, Qatar, the United Arab Emirates, Oman, and Yemen. You fly across Saudi Arabia, which covers most of the peninsula. In Saudi Arabia, your plane lands in Jidda.

➡ **In-Flight Movie**

Take flight over Southwest Asia and explore the region from the air.

my **worldgeography.com** In-Flight Movie

429

Regional Geography
Human Geography

A Diverse Region

Southwest Asia is home to different peoples and religions. Arabs are the main ethnic group in most countries. However, Turks are the dominant group in Turkey, Persians are the dominant group in Iran, and Jews are the dominant group in Israel. A people called the Kurds are spread across several countries. Most people in the region are Muslims, or people who follow the religion of Islam. However, the region's Muslims belong to different branches of Islam. Most follow either Sunni or Shia Islam. There are also Christians and other religious minorities and a Jewish majority in Israel.

Judaism
This Jewish man is worshiping at the Western Wall in Jerusalem.

Christianity
This Christian man is worshiping at a shrine in Lebanon.

Islam
This Muslim man is reading from the Quran, Islam's holy book.

 **my World IN NUMBERS**

Southwest Asia has a rich variety of ethnic groups and religions. Arab Muslims dominate most countries in the region, but they follow different branches of Islam. Turkish Muslims dominate Turkey, Persian Muslims dominate Iran, and Israeli Jews dominate Israel. Each country has many minority groups.

Southwest Asia: Religion

KEY
- Christianity
- Druze
- Ibadism
- Judaism
- Shiism
- Sunnism
- Yezidi
- Zoroastrianism
- Sparsely populated

0 400 mi
0 400 km
Lambert Conformal Conic Projection

Southwest Asia: Ethnicity

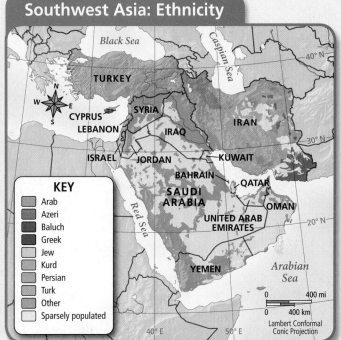

KEY
- Arab
- Azeri
- Baluch
- Greek
- Jew
- Kurd
- Persian
- Turk
- Other
- Sparsely populated

0 400 mi
0 400 km
Lambert Conformal Conic Projection

Put It Together

1. What physical features cause parts of this region to be sparsely populated?

2. In which country do most of the region's Jewish people live?

3. In which countries do the Kurds live?

→ **Data Discovery**

Find your own data to make a regional data table.

Size Comparison

Southwest Asia is slightly smaller in area than the United States.

431

Chapter 9

Arabia and Iraq

Essential Question

How much does geography shape a country?

KEY
— National border
★ Capital city
○ Other city

Lambert Conformal Conic Projection

Where In the World Are Arabia and Iraq?

Washington, D.C., to Jidda: 6,570 miles

my Story

Hanan's Call to Care

Explore the Essential Question
- at my worldgeography.com
- using the my World Chapter Activity
- with the **Student Journal**

In this section, you'll read about Hanan, a young Saudi woman who has become a professional in a country where women face many difficulties. What does Hanan's story tell you about life in Arabia and Iraq today?

Story by Danya M. Alhamrani for myWorld Geography Online

In the darkness of the early morning, Hanan awakes to the sound of adhan. This is the Islamic call to prayer, sung out by a muezzin, often from the minaret, or high tower, of an Islamic house of worship called a mosque. The adhan call tells the faithful that it is time to begin their daily prayer rituals. They will perform these rituals five times over the course of the day.

As the muezzin's voice drifts through the warm stillness remaining from the night, it is joined by another, then another, and yet another voice calling out the prayer, in Arabic: "Allahu akbar. Hayya alal sala. Hayya alal falah." That is Arabic for "God is most great. Come to prayer. Come to success."

The calling continues as Hanan walks to the bathroom to make her wudu, her ritual washing before beginning prayer. She covers herself from head to toe with her sharshaf, a long, traditional robe, and joins her mother for the first prayer of the day.

433

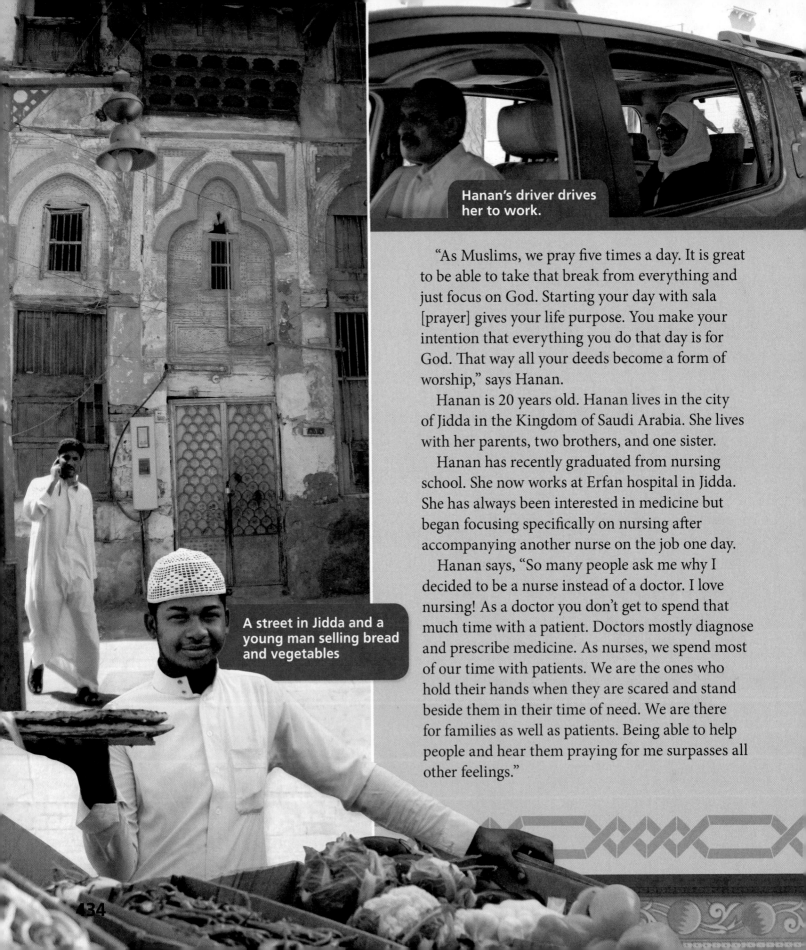

Hanan's driver drives her to work.

A street in Jidda and a young man selling bread and vegetables

"As Muslims, we pray five times a day. It is great to be able to take that break from everything and just focus on God. Starting your day with sala [prayer] gives your life purpose. You make your intention that everything you do that day is for God. That way all your deeds become a form of worship," says Hanan.

Hanan is 20 years old. Hanan lives in the city of Jidda in the Kingdom of Saudi Arabia. She lives with her parents, two brothers, and one sister.

Hanan has recently graduated from nursing school. She now works at Erfan hospital in Jidda. She has always been interested in medicine but began focusing specifically on nursing after accompanying another nurse on the job one day.

Hanan says, "So many people ask me why I decided to be a nurse instead of a doctor. I love nursing! As a doctor you don't get to spend that much time with a patient. Doctors mostly diagnose and prescribe medicine. As nurses, we spend most of our time with patients. We are the ones who hold their hands when they are scared and stand beside them in their time of need. We are there for families as well as patients. Being able to help people and hear them praying for me surpasses all other feelings."

434

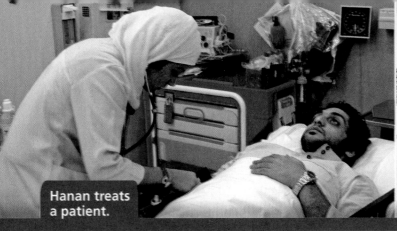

Hanan treats a patient.

Hanan's family in their living room

Many nurses in Saudi Arabia come from other countries, but the number of Saudi nurses is growing. Nursing, however, is not a typical profession for Saudi women.

In fact, few Saudi women work outside the home. Saudi law and culture place many restrictions on the lives of women. For example, Saudi women are not legally allowed to drive cars. They may not travel abroad without the permission of their husband or a male relative.

Saudi culture strongly encourages women to stay home and take care of their families rather than work. Because of these cultural and legal restrictions it is difficult for them to hold jobs. Still, 20 percent of Saudi women work outside their homes.

Restrictions aside, Hanan's biggest headache is her hectic schedule. The necessity of working around-the-clock in shifts takes a toll on family life.

"Nursing is a tough profession," Hanan says. "People who want to go into this line of work need to have patience and endurance. I end up missing a lot of family gatherings due to long working hours. I sometimes stay at home on my days off just to get some rest."

Despite the hardships she sometimes faces, Hanan loves her job and looks forward to a long career in her chosen field of nursing.

 myStory Video

Join Hanan as she shows you more about life in her city.

Meet the Journalist

Name Camilo Moreno
Favorite Moment Watching families pray together at the beach

Hanan and her mother praying together

my worldgeography.com myStory Video

435

Chapter Atlas

Key Ideas

- Physical geography has made much of this region rich in oil and natural gas.
- The climate of Arabia and Iraq makes water scarce.
- The region is home to different ethnic and religious groups.

Key Terms
- plate
- fossil fuel
- desalination
- urbanized
- majority

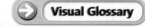
Visual Glossary

Reading Skill: Label an Outline Map Take notes using the outline map in your journal.

◀ A Yemeni woman. Her hands are painted with henna.
Behind her is the Rub' al-Khali desert in Oman. Its name means "the empty quarter" in Arabic.

Physical Features

Arabia, or the Arabian Peninsula, is surrounded on three sides by water. To the west, the Red Sea separates the peninsula from Africa. To the south are the Gulf of Aden and the Arabian Sea. The Persian Gulf and the Gulf of Oman to the east separate the peninsula from the rest of Asia. All of these bodies of water are arms of the Indian Ocean.

North of the Arabian Peninsula are the nation of Iraq and other parts of Southwest Asia. Arabia and Iraq are part of the continent of Asia.

436

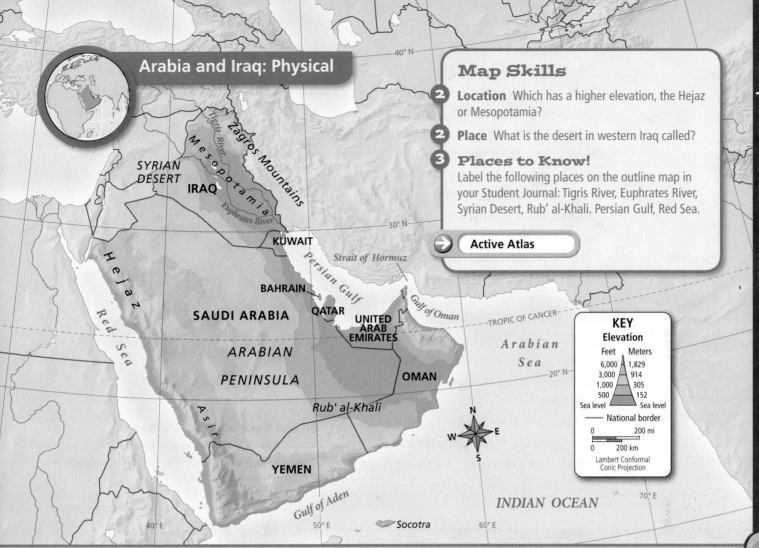

Arabia and Iraq: Physical

Map Skills

2 **Location** Which has a higher elevation, the Hejaz or Mesopotamia?

2 **Place** What is the desert in western Iraq called?

3 **Places to Know!**
Label the following places on the outline map in your Student Journal: Tigris River, Euphrates River, Syrian Desert, Rub' al-Khali. Persian Gulf, Red Sea.

→ **Active Atlas**

KEY
Elevation

Feet		Meters
6,000		1,829
3,000		914
1,000		305
500		152
Sea level		Sea level

— National border

0 — 200 mi
0 — 200 km

Lambert Conformal Conic Projection

As you read in the Core Concepts Handbook, Earth's crust consists of separate **plates,** or blocks of rock and soil. Most of Arabia and Iraq are on the Arabian Plate. Mountains rise sharply from the Red Sea and Gulf of Aden to form the plate's southeastern and western edges. The Arabian Plate is, in effect, a plateau, or raised flat area, that slopes gradually toward the east.

Near the eastern edge of the Arabian Plate, the plate's rocks bend downward to form a long, broad depression, or dip. In the south, the Persian Gulf also lies within this depression.

The Tigris (TY gris) and Euphrates (you FRAY teez) river valleys also lie within this depression. These rivers provide fresh water to a region that is mostly desert. They are the only major rivers in the region.

The eastern edge of the Arabian Plate presses against the Eurasian Plate. The pressure has pushed up rocks to form mountains in northeastern Iraq and in the southeastern corner of the Arabian Peninsula, in the nation of Oman.

Reading Check Which major rivers flow through Iraq?

my worldgeography.com Active Atlas

437

Oil and Gas Riches

There was once a shallow sea between what is now the Arabian Peninsula and the rest of Asia. When living things in the sea died, their decayed bodies formed a thick layer of muck on the sea floor. Forces within Earth slowly pushed the Arabian Plate against the Eurasian Plate and bent it downward into folds.

These pockets are known as fold traps because the undersea layer of muck became trapped in them. Heat and pressure from inside Earth transformed the muck over millions of years into oil and natural gas. Because oil and gas are the remains of living things, they are called **fossil fuels.**

Many fold traps formed in the rock of the Arabian Plate. They lie mainly beneath the Persian Gulf and the Tigris and Euphrates river valleys.

These fold traps have given Saudi Arabia the world's largest oil reserves and output. Iraq, Kuwait, Qatar, Oman, and the United Arab Emirates have also grown rich by selling their oil and gas.

Reading Check **Where are the largest oil reserves?**

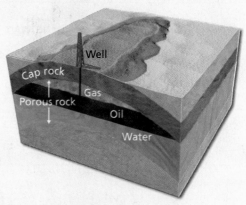

Oil and Gas Field in a Fold Trap
A hard cap rock traps gas and oil in a fold trap. Wells are drilled through the cap rock to reach the gas and oil beneath it.

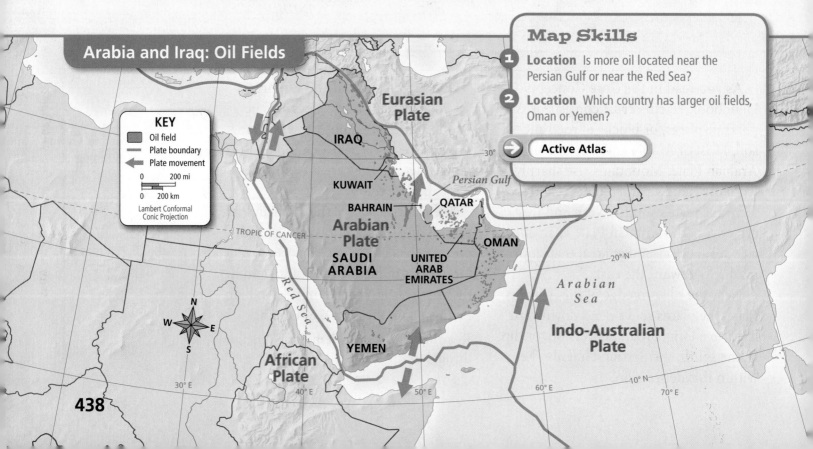

Arabia and Iraq: Oil Fields

KEY
- Oil field
- Plate boundary
- Plate movement

0   200 mi
0   200 km
Lambert Conformal Conic Projection

Map Skills

1. **Location** Is more oil located near the Persian Gulf or near the Red Sea?

2. **Location** Which country has larger oil fields, Oman or Yemen?

→ **Active Atlas**

438

Living on Oil

Iraq and most countries in Arabia rely on oil and natural gas to pay for nearly all of their needs.

The Importance of Oil Because these countries lack water, they use money from oil and gas sales to build water facilities. Even so, most countries in the region do not have enough water to grow their own food. They use money from oil and gas sales to pay for food grown in other regions.

The countries of Arabia also rely on millions of foreign workers, paid with oil money, to keep their economies running.

Arabia and Iraq produce more than one fourth of the world's oil. People in other parts of the world use oil to power their cars, to heat their homes, and for other purposes. As a result, the rest of the world is very dependent on this region's oil supplies. Any disruption of oil exports from this region creates shortages of oil and sends oil prices soaring.

In the long run, prospects are uncertain for the nations rich in oil and gas. These nations are slowly using up their oil and gas reserves, and it will take millions of years for more oil and gas to form.

Oil and the Environment Oil production has sometimes harmed the region's environment. Oil spills in the Persian Gulf have killed sea life and polluted shorelines. Oil production and processing create toxic chemicals that have polluted the soil, and the rivers of Iraq.

Reading Check Why is oil so important to Arabia and Iraq?

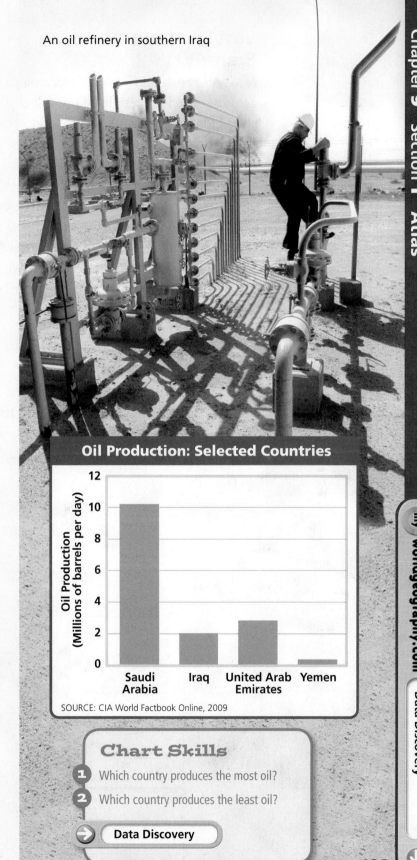

An oil refinery in southern Iraq

Oil Production: Selected Countries

Oil Production (Millions of barrels per day) by country: Saudi Arabia about 10.2, Iraq about 2, United Arab Emirates about 2.8, Yemen about 0.3

SOURCE: CIA World Factbook Online, 2009

Chart Skills

1 Which country produces the most oil?

2 Which country produces the least oil?

→ Data Discovery

my worldgeography.com Data Discovery

439

Vast Deserts and Scarce Water

Most of Arabia and Iraq is desert, or an area that receives very little rainfall or snowfall. You read in the Core Concepts Handbook that a belt of deserts circles the subtropical latitudes. Most of the region lies in this subtropical desert belt.

The main ecosystems across the region are desert and desert scrub. Deserts have few plants and animals. Desert scrub has some plants. Camels, which can live without much water, live in the desert and were used by people to cross it.

The region's deserts are dry, but the hills and mountains of northern and eastern Iraq are slightly moister. They get some rainfall. Moist air comes from the Mediterranean Sea in the west. In the summer, moist air from the Indian Ocean drops rain in the mountains of Yemen.

moist, *adj.,* slightly wet

Farming is possible only where there is enough water. The mountains of Yemen and Iraq receive enough rainfall to support some farming. Elsewhere, farming depends on water taken from rivers or oases in the desert. The most important rivers in the region are the Tigris and the Euphrates in Iraq. The water from these rivers nurtured one of the world's first civilizations thousands of years ago. Most people in Iraq live in the valleys around these rivers. Their water is crucial to the country. It supports Iraq's population, which is by far the largest in the region.

The driest countries in the region, such as Saudi Arabia, Kuwait, and the United Arab Emirates, depend on **desalination,** or the removal of salt from seawater. These countries have large desalination plants.

Reading Check Which parts of Arabia and Iraq get seasonal precipitation?

Arabia and Iraq: Water Resources

A marsh in Iraq

Desalination plant

KEY
- Arid
- Semiarid
- Humid
- Wet
- National border
- Water pipeline
- ○ City
- ● Desalination plant

0 — 400 mi
0 — 400 km
Lambert Conformal Conic Projection

myWorld Activity
Water Caucus

440

Population Patterns

People cannot live without water. Because water is very scarce in most of the region, its people cluster where there is water for drinking and cleaning.

As a result, the region's population has clustered for centuries in the places with the most water. These places include the mountains of Iraq and Yemen, near the Tigris and Euphrates rivers of Iraq, and desert oases on the Arabian Peninsula.

As you just read, some nations in the region have used money from oil and gas sales to to build desalination plants. These plants provide fresh water for growing populations. As a result, people in these countries depend on water from desalination. Countries usually build desalination plants near their cities.

Except for Yemen, the countries of the region are heavily **urbanized.** This means that most of their people live in cities.

Money from oil and natural gas sales has helped these countries develop jobs in construction and services. These kinds of jobs are usually found in cities. Many people from outside the region have also moved to oil-producing areas in search of jobs. They generally settle in the cities.

Arabia and Iraq have some of the highest rates of population growth in the world. These high rates of growth result from both migration and high birth rates. Local customs and religious traditions practiced in many parts of the region favor large families. When most women have many children, populations grow quickly. This high rate of population growth poses challenges for the region. The growing population will need more jobs, water, education, and other services.

Reading Check Why are populations growing in this region?

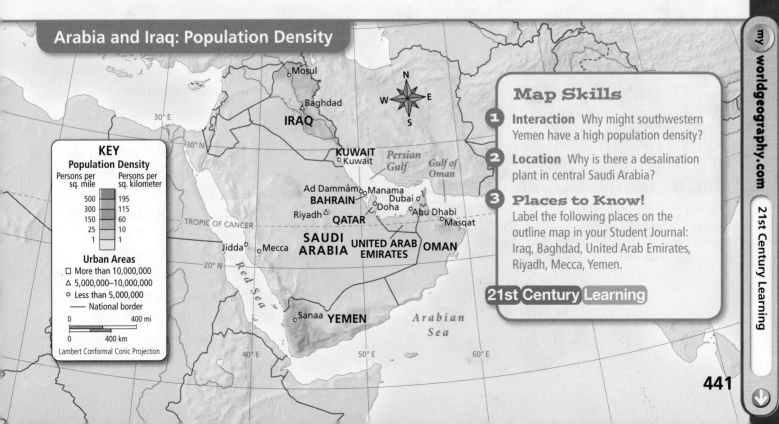

Arabia and Iraq: Population Density

KEY
Population Density

Persons per sq. mile	Persons per sq. kilometer
500	195
300	115
150	60
25	10
1	1

Urban Areas
□ More than 10,000,000
△ 5,000,000–10,000,000
○ Less than 5,000,000
— National border

0 — 400 mi
0 — 400 km
Lambert Conformal Conic Projection

Map Skills

1. **Interaction** Why might southwestern Yemen have a high population density?

2. **Location** Why is there a desalination plant in central Saudi Arabia?

3. **Places to Know!** Label the following places on the outline map in your Student Journal: Iraq, Baghdad, United Arab Emirates, Riyadh, Mecca, Yemen.

21st Century Learning

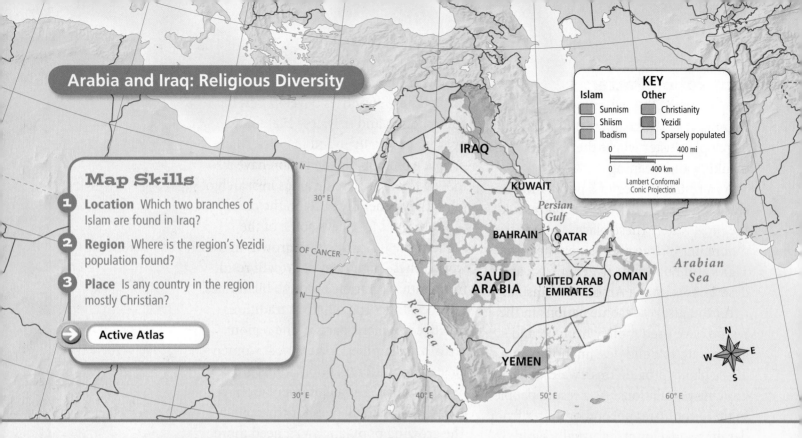

Arabia and Iraq: Religious Diversity

Map Skills

1 **Location** Which two branches of Islam are found in Iraq?

2 **Region** Where is the region's Yezidi population found?

3 **Place** Is any country in the region mostly Christian?

→ Active Atlas

KEY

Islam
- Sunnism
- Shiism
- Ibadism

Other
- Christianity
- Yezidi
- Sparsely populated

0 — 400 mi
0 — 400 km
Lambert Conformal Conic Projection

Above: a crowded market in Baghdad, Iraq
Right: Shia Muslims
Below: Sunni Muslims

A Diverse Region

In most countries of Arabia and Iraq, Arab Muslims form a **majority,** or more than half, of the population. In every country, Arabs dominate politics. However, most countries in Arabia and Iraq have large non-Arab minorities. Even among Arab Muslims, there are important religious differences.

In Kuwait, Qatar, and the United Arab Emirates, a majority of the people are not Arabs. These people are not citizens, but as foreigners they make up most of the population. These people come from countries such as India, Sri Lanka, Pakistan, Bangladesh, and the Philippines.

Iraq has a large minority of Kurds, who are not Arabs. Most Kurds are Sunni Muslims. Iraq's Kurds live mainly in the north. Many Kurds also live in neighboring Iran, Turkey, and Syria.

442

Iraqi Kurds suffered brutal treatment under Saddam Hussein. In recent years, they have <u>created</u> a self-governing area in northern Iraq.

The vast majority of the people of Arabia and Iraq follow Islam. However, there are important differences within Islam. Long ago, the religion split into two main groups—the Sunnis and the Shias. Most people in Oman follow a third branch of Islam, called Ibadism.

The majority of the region's people are Sunnis, even though Shias are the majority in some places. Most Iraqis are Shia Arabs. Since the elections of 2005, Shias took power in Iraq for the first time.

Most of the citizens of Bahrain are Shia, but their ruler is a Sunni. Sunnis rule Kuwait, Saudi Arabia, and Yemen. However, large Shia minorities live in all three of these countries.

In Iraq, a three-way civil conflict developed among Sunni Arabs, Shia Arabs, and Kurds after U.S.-led forces overthrew Iraq's secular, Sunni-led dictatorship in 2003. Tensions among these groups could lead to conflict in the future.

The region also has small non-Muslim religious minorities. Iraq's Christians are an ancient community. Most practice eastern forms of Christianity that are different from Eastern Orthodox, Roman Catholic, or Protestant Christianity.

From ancient times to the recent past, Iraq and Yemen had important Jewish communities. However, 180,000 Jews fled, mostly to Israel, because of discrimination in the mid-1900s. Only a few hundred Jewish people remain in the region today.

Iraq's Yezidis are Kurdish speakers who practice a religion that combines Islam with more ancient religions. Finally, while most foreign workers in the Persian Gulf countries are Muslims, there are also Christians, Hindus, and Buddhists.

create, *v.,* form, cause to exist

Reading Check **What are some differences among Muslims in this region?**

Section 1 Assessment

Key Terms

1. What are fossil fuels?

2. Use the word desalination in a sentence.

Key Ideas

3. Describe the fossil fuel resources of Arabia and Iraq.

4. What are some natural sources of water in Arabia and Iraq, and where are they located?

5. Describe the region's religious diversity.

Think Critically

6. **Draw Conclusions** What might happen to Arabia and Iraq if they began to use up their oil reserves?

7. **Compare and Contrast** In what ways has the urban population in the region changed in recent years? Give reasons for the changes.

Essential Question

How much does geography shape a country?

8. What features of Arabia and Iraq depend on the region's geography? What features do not depend on its geography? Go to your Student Journal to record your answers.

History of Arabia and Iraq

Key Ideas

- Civilization developed along the rivers of Mesopotamia.
- Islam arose in Arabia and spread to other regions in the early Middle Ages.
- Britain controlled parts of the region and redrew borders in the early 1900s.
- The region gained independence and oil wealth, but some countries faced dictatorship and war.

Key Terms • civilization • monotheism • Quran • caliph • mosque • minority • dictator

 Visual Glossary

Reading Skill: Summarize Take notes using the graphic organizer in your journal.

Reconstructed gates of the ancient city of Babylon ▼

Arabia and Iraq have played a key role in world history. This region was one of the places where **civilization** began. A civilization is a culture that has a written language and in which people have many different kinds of jobs. Writing first developed in this region. The world's first known empires also developed in what is now Iraq. Later, Arabia was the birthplace of Islam, one of the world's major religions. Over the centuries, foreign powers controlled much of this region. In modern times, Arabia and Iraq became the world's most important source of oil, a fuel that every country in the world needs.

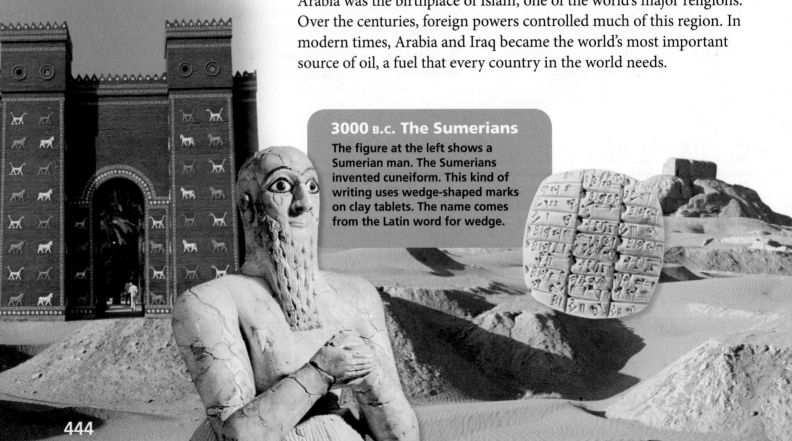

3000 B.C. The Sumerians

The figure at the left shows a Sumerian man. The Sumerians invented cuneiform. This kind of writing uses wedge-shaped marks on clay tablets. The name comes from the Latin word for wedge.

444

Early Civilizations and Empires

Mesopotamia means "between the rivers" in Greek. It refers to the valley of the Tigris and Euphrates rivers. This region is mainly in present-day Iraq.

In Mesopotamia, people developed a new way of life. For thousands of years, people lived by hunting, fishing, and gathering wild plants. About 10,000 years ago, people in Southwest Asia began to plant crops and raise animals. These farmers produced plenty of food for everyone. Some people were now free to do other work. They became potters and weavers and merchants.

Farmers and others had to pay taxes. These taxes supported priests and government officials. Populations grew. By 4000 B.C., the first cities appeared.

A Birthplace of Civilization Sumer was a region in southern Mesopotamia. Sumerians developed a civilization. Around 3000 B.C. they created the world's first writing system, which is called cuneiform (kyoo NEE uh form). They built irrigation canals and invented mathematics and the potter's wheel.

331–129 B.C. Greek Rule

After Alexander conquered Mesopotamia in 331 B.C., Greeks ruled the region for 200 years. Later, Romans and Persians fought over the region.

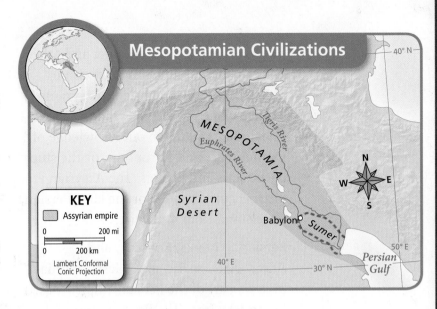

Mesopotamian Civilizations

KEY
Assyrian empire
0   200 mi
0   200 km
Lambert Conformal Conic Projection

MESOPOTAMIA
Tigris River
Euphrates River
Syrian Desert
Babylon
Sumer
Persian Gulf

We can learn about the Sumerians from the Epic of Gilgamesh. This is one of the world's oldest written stories. The story is based on a real Sumerian king, Gilgamesh, who lived around 2700 B.C.

> 66 Surpassing all kings, powerful and tall beyond all others, violent, splendid, a wild bull of a man . . . huge, handsome, radiant, perfect. 99
> —The Epic of Gilgamesh

The most complete version of this story appears on cuneiform tablets.

The First Empires Sumerian cities grew into the first city-states. Each was a small country, focused on a single city. Around 2270 B.C., King Sargon from the city of Akkad conquered Sumer and other parts of Mesopotamia to found the first known empire. Later, around 1700 B.C., the city-state of Babylon built an empire that included all of Mesopotamia.

The Assyrian people built an even larger empire. Assyria was an area in northern Mesopotamia. By around 900 B.C., Assyria had defeated Babylon.

445

Assyria brought Mesopotamia and other areas, including Egypt, into its empire.

Both the Babylonians and Assyrians contributed to world civilization. The Babylonians added to our knowledge of mathematics and astronomy, or the study of the stars and planets. The Assyrian empire became a model for the later Persian, Greek, and Roman empires.

Persians, Greeks, Romans, and Arabs Around 550 B.C., Mesopotamia became part of the Persian empire, based in modern Iran. The Persian empire stretched from North Africa to India.

Alexander the Great defeated the Persian Empire in 331 B.C. When he died, his Greek empire split apart. But Alexander's influence <u>persisted.</u> He had founded dozens of new cities and spread Greek culture far and wide. Mesopotamia remained under Greek rule for 200 years.

The Roman Empire eventually took over the western parts of Alexander's empire. After 235 B.C., Persians regained power in the east. Persians fought with the Roman Empire for control of the fertile lands of Mesopotamia. For several centuries they continued to fight with the Eastern Roman empire, which was also called the Byzantine empire.

Through trade, Greeks, Romans, and Persians met the Arab tribes of the Arabian Peninsula. Many Arabs were nomads. They had no permanent homes. They herded sheep, goats, and camels. Nomads visited oases for food and water. Oases were centers for trade.

Reading Check Which civilization first developed writing?

persist, *v.,* to continue, often in spite of setbacks

▲ A copy of the Quran, the holy book of Islam

A New Religion

One important oasis was the city of Mecca. It was a trading and religious center. People throughout the Arabian Peninsula traveled to Mecca. They went to worship at a shrine called the Kaaba. Many worshiped more than one god. In the A.D. 600s, however, this changed.

A man named Muhammad made Mecca a center for the new religion of Islam. Its believers are called Muslims. Like Jews and Christians, Muslims worship only one god, whom they consider the Creator, or God. Worshiping only one god is called **monotheism.**

The Birth of Islam Muhammad was born in Mecca. One day, he was meditating in a cave. There, Muslims believe, he saw the angel Gabriel, who brought him a message from God. Muhammad later received more messages.

Muhammad shared these messages with the people of Mecca. Some people began to follow the ideas Muhammad spread. They believed that Muhammad was bringing messages from the God recognized by Jews and Christians. These messages were collected and preserved in the **Quran,** the holy book of Islam.

The wealthy people of Mecca wanted visitors to keep coming to the Kaaba. They knew that most of these visitors worshiped many gods. They opposed Muhammad's teachings. Muhammad and his followers had to leave Mecca.

In A.D. 622 they moved to the city of Medina. When Mecca attacked the Muslims in Medina, the Muslims won.

446

Muhammad returned to Mecca in 632. He made the Kaaba a place of worship for Islam before dying later that year.

Muhammad's followers argued over how to choose leaders to follow him. One group believed that Muhammad had chosen his son-in-law, Ali, and his heirs, as leaders. This group became known as the Shia. Another group, known as the Sunnis, wanted Muhammad's father-in-law, Abu Bakr, as the next leader.

Muhammad's Sunni followers chose Abu Bakr to be the new leader. He became their first **caliph**. The caliph was the Muslims' political and religious leader.

Over time, differences in belief grew between Sunni and Shia Muslims. Today, about 15 percent of all Muslims are Shia. In some parts of Arabia and Iraq, however, most Muslims are Shia.

The Beliefs of Islam The word *Islam* means "submission" in Arabic. This term comes from the idea of submitting one's will to God. Muslims believe that the will of God lies in the words of the Quran.

Like Judaism and Christianity, Islam stresses the importance of family, community, and social justice. Many Muslims turn to the Quran and Muhammad's teachings to help them make good choices. The Quran, Muhammad's teachings, and the traditions of the Muslim community form the basis for Islamic law.

Reading Check Why did Sunni and Shia Muslims split?

myWorld Activity
Comparing Religions

Muslims circle around the Kaaba, in Mecca, as part of their pilgrimage to that city. ▶

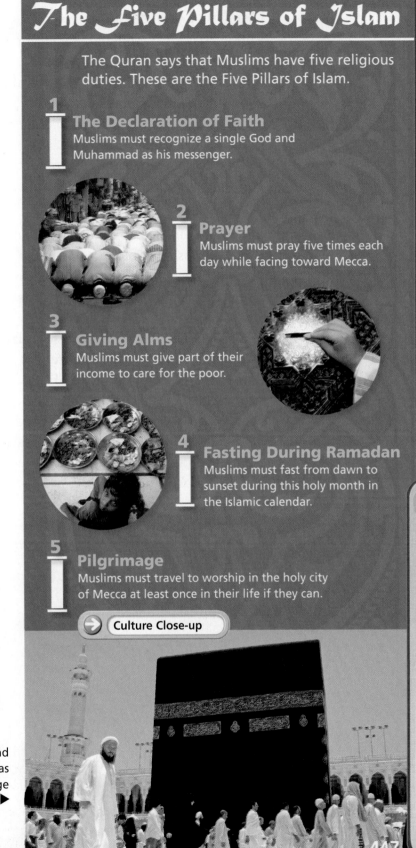

The Five Pillars of Islam

The Quran says that Muslims have five religious duties. These are the Five Pillars of Islam.

1 The Declaration of Faith
Muslims must recognize a single God and Muhammad as his messenger.

2 Prayer
Muslims must pray five times each day while facing toward Mecca.

3 Giving Alms
Muslims must give part of their income to care for the poor.

4 Fasting During Ramadan
Muslims must fast from dawn to sunset during this holy month in the Islamic calendar.

5 Pilgrimage
Muslims must travel to worship in the holy city of Mecca at least once in their life if they can.

Culture Close-up

my worldgeography.com Culture Close-up

447

Muslim Civilization

Within 10 years of Muhammad's death, Muslims under the first caliphs had conquered all of Arabia and Iraq. Within 100 years of Muhammad's death, the caliphs ruled a vast empire, stretching from India to Spain. Arabia and Iraq were at the center of a rich civilization. Muslim civilization made great advances in science, mathematics, and the arts.

A Muslim Empire During the 600s and 700s, the Muslims conquered all of the Persian Empire, much of the Byzantine Empire, North Africa, Spain, and parts of India and Central Asia. In 762, the caliphs founded Baghdad, in present-day Iraq, as the capital of their empire.

The Muslim Empire controlled key trade routes between Asia, Africa, and Europe. One of these was the Silk Road to China. Sea routes from Eastern Africa brought goods, as well as many enslaved Africans, to Arabia and Iraq.

The caliph's control allowed merchants to travel more safely. The empire grew prosperous from trade. Cities grew along busy trade routes. Baghdad became the largest and one of the richest cities in the world. In the empire's cities, people from distant lands came together to trade.

A Center of Learning Travel and trade brought the Muslim Empire into contact with ideas from around the world. Muslim scholars learned about Greek science and philosophy through contact with the Byzantine Empire. They learned about advances in mathematics and astronomy made in India.

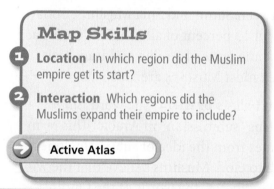

Map Skills

1 **Location** In which region did the Muslim empire get its start?

2 **Interaction** Which regions did the Muslims expand their empire to include?

→ Active Atlas

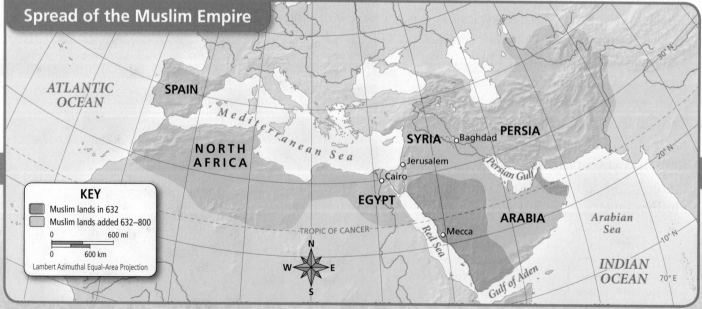

Spread of the Muslim Empire

KEY
- Muslim lands in 632
- Muslim lands added 632–800

0 — 600 mi
0 — 600 km
Lambert Azimuthal Equal-Area Projection

448

Baghdad became more than a center of Muslim culture and trade. It became a center of learning. Literature and other arts blossomed. Muslim architects built beautiful **mosques,** or Islamic houses of worship. Muslim scientists and mathematicians built on the work of the Greeks and Indians. Their work formed a basis for modern chemistry, physics, and medicine. They also developed algebra. Our own system of numerals came to us from India by way of Arab Muslims.

The Ottoman Empire   After the 900s, the Muslim Empire fell apart into several states. These states were partly independent. The last caliph in Baghdad was defeated by Mongol invaders in 1258. In the 1500s, Ottoman Turks conquered much of the region. The Ottoman Empire, centered in Turkey, included Iraq and much of the Arabian Peninsula. At its height it included most of Southwest Asia outside of Persia. The Ottomans remained in control until World War I ended in 1918.

Reading Check **How did trade advance Muslim learning?**

The Persian Gulf in Modern Times

World War I brought much of the region under European control. The region's countries gained independence later in the 1900s. Still, foreign powers continued to play a role.

British Domination   By World War I, the British dominated several countries on the Arabian Peninsula. These countries were Bahrain, the United Arab Emirates, Oman, Qatar, Kuwait, and part of Yemen.

Britain defeated the Ottoman Empire in World War I. After the war, Britain and the League of Nations created Iraq from part of the Ottoman empire, ignoring divisions in the new country.

Within Iraq's borders were Shia Arabs in the south, Sunni Arabs in the west, and non-Arab Kurds in the north. There were also Turks, Assyrian Christians, and Jews. Until 2003, the Sunni Arab **minority**—a group with less than half of the population—dominated the country. Their rule led to conflicts with the other groups.

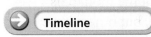
Timeline

622 Muhammad and his followers establish the first Islamic community in Medina.

1258 Mongol invaders conquer Iraq and destroy Baghdad.

1918 Britain defeats Ottoman Turks and occupies Iraq and parts of Arabia.

500	750	1000	1250	1500	1750	2000

762 Caliphs make Baghdad the center of a vast Muslim Empire.

1500s Ottoman Turks make Iraq and much of Arabia part of their empire.

my **worldgeography.com** Timeline

449

vital, *adj.*, extremely important, needed for survival

Oil was discovered in Iraq in 1927 and in Saudi Arabia and Kuwait in 1938. The region became a <u>vital</u> source of fuel for the world's growing energy needs.

In 1930, Saudi Arabia, Oman, and northern Yemen were the only independent countries in the region. Saudi Arabia controlled much of the Arabian Peninsula, including Mecca. Saudi Arabia is an absolute monarchy. This means that its king has total control over the country. There is no elected government.

Independent Iraq Britain controlled Iraq and Kuwait. However, Iraqis fought to end British rule. In 1921, Britain put King Faisal, an Arab, into power. Iraq gained independence in 1932. Still, King Faisal kept close ties with Britain. He let a British company take control of Iraq's oil.

In 1958, Iraqi army officers forced King Faisal out of power. This caused a period of disorder during which Iraq's Kurds rebelled. In 1963, the Baath Party took power. It took over the oil industry. It used oil income to improve people's lives, but became oppressive. Baath leader Saddam Hussein took control in 1979.

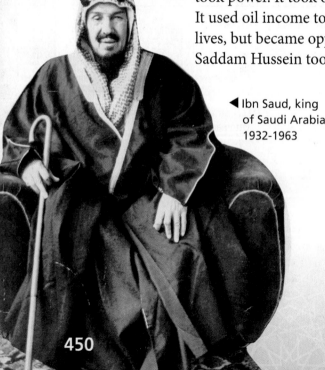

◄ Ibn Saud, king of Saudi Arabia 1932-1963

Under Baath rule, Iraq became a one-party government. When elections were held, Iraqis had no choice of parties. The Baath leader had total control over the country. Under Saddam Hussein, Iraq became a dictatorship, a country under the control of a dictator. A **dictator** is a leader who seizes power undemocratically and has complete control over a country.

The Gulf Monarchies The smaller Persian Gulf states—Kuwait, Bahrain, Qatar, the United Arab Emirates, and Oman—are all monarchies like Saudi Arabia. These smaller countries gained full independence from Britain only in the 1960s and 1970s. Some monarchs have complete control, but others have more limited power.

In 1960, Saudi Arabia, Iraq, and Kuwait joined Iran and Venezuela to form OPEC, the Organization of the Petroleum Exporting Countries. Qatar and the United Arab Emirates joined OPEC later. This organization helps members agree on a shared oil policy. Often members agree to limit oil production. This keeps the price of oil high and increases their income.

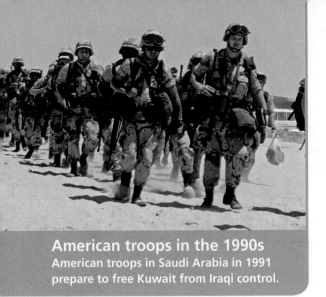

American troops in the 1990s
American troops in Saudi Arabia in 1991 prepare to free Kuwait from Iraqi control.

Persian Gulf Conflicts In 1980, under Saddam Hussein, Iraq invaded Iran's oil-rich lands. Iraq had the open support of Saudi Arabia, Kuwait, and other Arab states. The United States also quietly supported Iraq. The Iran–Iraq War dragged on for eight years at a high cost. It ended without a clear winner in 1988.

Then Iraq invaded Kuwait in 1990. The United States and other nations went to war with Iraq. The United States and its allies wanted to defend Kuwait's independence. They also wanted to protect the world's oil supplies. These countries quickly defeated Iraq in 1991. They drove Iraqi troops out of Kuwait.

In 2003, U.S. President George W. Bush claimed that Iraq was a threat to the region and the world. He claimed that Iraq had weapons of mass destruction.

Later that year, the United States and some allies again went to war with Iraq. U.S.-led forces quickly removed Saddam Hussein from power. No weapons of mass destruction were found.

Some Iraqis resisted U.S.-led forces. Fighting also broke out among Iraq's Kurds, Sunni Arabs, and Shia Arabs. The United States and its allies supported the creation of a democratic Iraqi government in 2005. Additional US troops were sent to Iraq in 2007 to support the Iraqi government. US and other foreign troops were still in Iraq in 2009.

Reading Check What form of government does Saudi Arabia have?

Section 2 Assessment

Key Terms

1. Use the following terms to describe religion in Arabia and Iraq: monotheism, Quran, mosque, caliph.

Key Ideas

2. Describe the importance of the Sumerians to world history.

3. What are the main beliefs of Muslims?

4. What role did the United States play in the history of Arabia and Iraq?

Think Critically

5. **Draw Conclusions** Use what you know about history in Arabia and Iraq to explain how trade contributed to the region's rich cultural heritage. Give examples.

6. **Categorize** Identify different groups within Islam and explain their role in modern Iraq.

Essential Question

How much does geography shape a country?

7. How has geography shaped the history of Arabia and Iraq? Are there parts of its history that did not depend on its geography? Go to your Student Journal to record your answers.

451

The Roles of Men and Women in Islam

Key Idea
- There are different views within Islam on the proper roles of men and women.

▲ A copy of the Quran

Traditionally, Muslim men and women have had different roles. Men were supposed to protect and provide for their families and lead them in religious matters. Women were supposed to take care of their homes and children. Today, many Muslims argue that men and women are equal under Islam. You have already read about the roles of men and women in Saudi Arabia in "Hanan's Call to Care." You will read more about this issue in the next section.

Stop at each circled letter on the right to think about the text. Then answer the question with the same letter on the left.

A **Synthesize** How does Seyyed Hossein Nasr see the roles of men and women in Islamic tradition?

B **Draw Conclusions** In what ways is a man the leader of the household? In what ways is a woman the leader?

C **Draw Inferences** Seyyed Hossein Nasr quotes the Prophet Muhammad. What does the quote he gives suggest about the role of women in Islam?

quantitative, *adj.,* measured in numbers

complementarity, *n.,* a state of adding qualities that the other lacks

imam, *n.,* Islamic religious leader

mistress, *n.,* woman in charge

Men and Women in Islamic Tradition

❝ The traditional structure of Islamic society is based not on <u>quantitative</u> equality, but on the reality **A** of <u>complementarity</u>. . .
In this complementarity of functions, the man is seen as the protector and provider of his family and its <u>imam</u>, religiously speaking. The woman is the real <u>mistress</u> of the household, in which the **B** husband is like a guest. . . .
Islam has honored the work of the homemaker and mother as being of the highest value, to the extent that the Prophet said, 'Heaven lies under **C** the feet of mothers.'❞

—Seyyed Hossein Nasr,
The Heart of Islam

Stop at each circled letter on the right to think about the text. Then answer the question with the same letter on the left.

D Distinguish Between Fact and Opinion What words does Asma Barlas use that tell you that she is giving her opinion here?

E Synthesize According to Asma Barlas, does the Quran say men are more powerful than women?

F Identify Evidence Does Asma Barlas see men and women as equals? Give reasons for your answer.

authorize, *v.,* to give permission for

appoint, *v.,* to choose

contrary, *adj.,* opposite, different

imply, *v.,* suggest, point to

Men and Women as Equals in Islam

66 The Qur'an . . . does not <u>authorize</u> male rule over women

D . . . Indeed, my own reading is that it does not even <u>appoint</u> men

E as heads of the household . . . To the <u>contrary</u>, it says that women and men are each other's friends and guides …

It is true that the Qur'an treats women and men differently with respect to some issues, but this doesn't mean that it treats them unequally or establishes them

F as unequal. . . . [D]ifferences in themselves do not <u>imply</u> inequality . . . 99

—Asma Barlas,
"Women's Rights and Role in Islam"

Analyze the Documents

1. **Compare Viewpoints** Identify similarities and differences in these two authors' views of the roles of men and women in Islam.

2. **Writing Task** Review these two documents. Next, review material from the chapter or other sources on the lives of women in Arabia and Iraq. Then write a paragraph discussing how women's place in the region compares to the ideals these authors present.

Muslim women wearing different kinds of clothing ▼

453

Arabia and Iraq Today

Key Ideas
- Regional traditions and modern global culture have shaped the region's culture.
- Many oil-rich countries in the region have worked to make their economies less dependent on oil.

Key Terms • fundamentalism • Islamism • jihad • terrorism • entrepreneurship • hijab

Visual Glossary

Reading Skill: Analyze Cause and Effect Take notes using the graphic organizer in your journal.

▼ A luxury hotel in Dubai, United Arab Emirates

Islam and other traditions have shaped the cultures of Arabia and Iraq. So have the rich oil and natural gas reserves that come with the region's geography. Oil has brought wealth and contact with outside cultures. The region's people have worked to balance tradition and modern culture.

Religious Traditions

The people of Arabia and Iraq value their cultural traditions. Islam is a very important source of tradition. Most people in the region are Muslims who follow the five pillars of Islam. Islam shapes many parts of daily life.

Although most people in the region share a religion, they have different ideas about politics and cultural activities. For example, some Muslims believe that women should not mix with men in public. Others believe that Islam allows unrelated men and women to work together. There are many cultural traditions as well. Some traditions concern the foods that people like to eat, or the importance of tribal membership. Others concern how to welcome guests, treat elders with respect, or give gifts.

Fundamentalism One powerful <u>tradition</u> in the region is a branch of Sunni Islam called Wahhabism, which was founded in the 1700s. Wahhabis believe in returning to the original teachings of Islam, interpreting the Quran literally, and rejecting all modern interpretations of Islamic scripture. Wahhabism is a form of **fundamentalism,** or the belief that holy books should be taken literally, or word for word. Fundamentalist Muslims believe the Quran provides clear meanings that do not need to be debated.

Wahhabis also believe that government should be based on the original teachings of Islam. It is a form of **Islamism,** or the belief that politics and society should follow Islamic teachings. The rulers of Saudi Arabia are Wahhabis. Wahhabism determines much of the kingdom's politics. Most Muslims in the region are neither Wahhabis nor Islamists.

While Wahhabis are both fundamentalist and Islamist, the two beliefs do not always coincide. Many fundamentalists are Islamists, because they believe that Islamic scripture calls for Islamic government. However, not all Islamists are fundamentalists. Some Islamists, like other Muslims, accept less literal interpretations of Islam.

Islamism and Jihad A small number of Muslims in the region see European and American influence as a threat. They have adopted a form of Islamism that draws on the tradition of **jihad.** The word *jihad* in Arabic simply means "struggle." It can refer to the struggle to be a better person.

However, some groups use the word to mean violent struggle. Some of the region's Islamists believe in violent jihad. This small minority supports the use of violence to attack Westerners or Muslims with different approaches to Islam. Those calling for violence include groups such as al Qaeda. Al Qaeda is a group of radical Islamists led by Osama bin Laden, who came from Saudi Arabia. Al Qaeda practices **terrorism.** Terrorism is the use of violence against innocent civilians to create fear for political reasons. In fact, the holy writings of Islam call on Muslims to avoid violence toward innocent people. Most Muslims reject violent jihad and terrorism.

Reading Check **Are all Islamists fundamentalists?**

tradition, *n.,* practices handed down from one generation to the next

Students study the Quran at an Islamic school in Medina, Saudi Arabia. ▶

455

my World
IN NUMBERS

Arabia and Iraq have a little more than **1%** of the world's population but nearly **50%** of the world's oil.

A Region Built on Oil

The world today depends on oil to power cars, trucks, and other vehicles; as a fuel for industries; for heating homes; and as a raw material for plastics and other products. Oil is one of the world's most important products. It is also a vital source of income for this oil-rich region.

One-Track Economies Oil and natural gas were found in the region in the 1920s and 1930s. Every country in the region but oil-poor Yemen had an oil boom, or rapid growth in jobs, construction, and income due to oil production. From then on, the economies of the oil-rich countries specialized in oil production. Specialization led to trade. The region sold oil to other countries. It bought many basic goods, such as food, from other countries. Income from oil allows the region to buy goods that it cannot grow or make.

Oil sales have made some governments in the region wealthy. Many give cash or free services directly to citizens, even if they do not work. As a result, the region's businesses can hire millions of foreign workers. These workers do jobs that citizens are unwilling or unable to do.

Economic growth depends on four conditions: natural resources, educated workers, investment in local businesses, and **entrepreneurship** (ahn truh pruh NUR ship). Entrepreneurship is the willingness to take the risks of starting a business.

The region's oil and gas are great natural resources. However, money from oil sales lets the region get by without meeting the other three conditions for economic growth. Until recently, education in the region has failed to prepare its people—especially its women—for many available jobs. There has been little investment outside the oil industry. There has also been little entrepreneurship. As a result, the region has depended largely on oil sales.

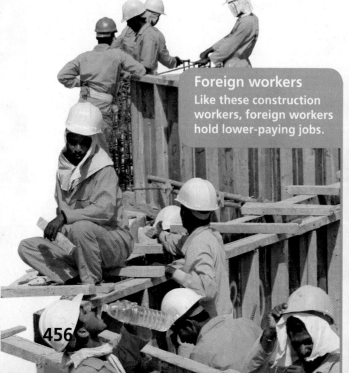

Foreign workers
Like these construction workers, foreign workers hold lower-paying jobs.

Saudi workers
Like these investment bankers, Saudis usually hold higher-paying jobs.

456

Trying to Diversify In recent years, leaders in the region have seen the need to diversify their economies. To diversify is to go from just one or two sources of income, such as oil and gas, to many sources. To help diversify, many countries in the region have improved education for the whole population, including women. They have encouraged investment and entrepreneurship.

Two parts of the region have built economies that depend less on oil. Bahrain, and Dubai, a state in the United Arab Emirates, have become regional financial centers. Their economies have diversified away from reliance on oil. They now rely more on services.

Banks from Bahrain, Dubai, and elsewhere have provided finance to other parts of the region. The region's banks keep the savings of people in the region who have made money from oil. The banks invest this money in new businesses that help diversify the region's economy. The countries' governments have also used government money saved from oil earnings. They have invested these savings in construction projects. Some of these have strengthened the region's economy.

These projects include desalination plants that provide water to many parts of the region. According to a Saudi prince,

> 66 Currently, Saudi Arabia is the largest producer of desalinated water in the world, and the kingdom continues to invest in research and development to make access to fresh water more affordable. 99
> —Prince Dr. Turki Al Saud Al Faisal, from ibm.com

Governments have also invested in education, so that their people can compete in the global economy in areas other than the oil industry.

Reading Check Why are there so many foreign workers in Arabia?

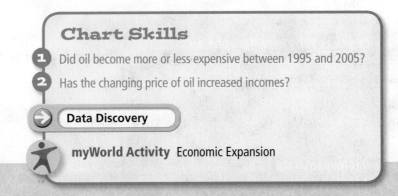

Chart Skills

1. Did oil become more or less expensive between 1995 and 2005?
2. Has the changing price of oil increased incomes?

→ **Data Discovery**

myWorld Activity Economic Expansion

Oil, Population, and Income

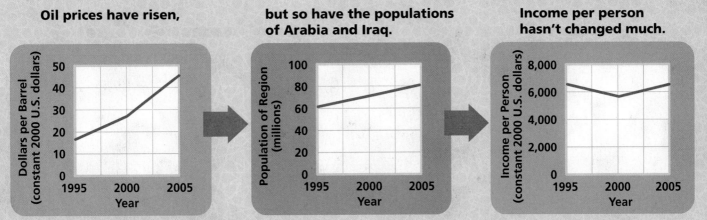

Oil prices have risen, but so have the populations of Arabia and Iraq. Income per person hasn't changed much.

SOURCE: *CIA World FactBook, BP Statistical Review*

Closer Look

Arab Culture, Old and New

Culture in Arabia and Iraq today is a mix of modern and traditional elements. One traditional art form is Arabic calligraphy, or decorative writing. Most Muslims believe that depicting humans or animals in art is forbidden by Islam. Because of this, art forms that show letters and geometric designs are highly developed in the Islamic world.

Contemporary music of the region uses more modern elements as well as traditional styles. Arabia has long been famous for its poetry. Many modern Arabic songs use traditional poems, but back them up with synthesizers instead of the instruments that would have been used in the past.

THINK CRITICALLY *Why is calligraphy an important art form in Islamic societies?*

Tradition These artists are decorating the covering that will go over the Kaaba in Mecca. They are using Arabic calligraphy.

Cultural Change A piece of calligraphy used as a background for modern dance. ▼

Below is modern Iraqi singer Shatha Hassoun.

458

Arabia and Iraq in the Modern World

Income from oil changed society in the region. From the mid-1900s, elite people in the region met Westerners working in the oil industry. They bought televisions and computers. They traveled to foreign countries and sent their children to study there. They were <u>exposed</u> to Western and global culture.

The Pull of Global Culture Modern, foreign culture appealed to many people in the region. They have adopted some aspects of modern global culture. Some of the region's people work for Western firms. Others work for local firms using Western business practices. The region has become part of the modern world. However, not all people in the region are comfortable with this change.

The Place of Women Traditionally, women in the Arab world have had to obey men. In much of Arabia, they cannot travel without the permission of a father, husband, or other male relative.

In most of the region, women are expected to cover their faces and hair. They are expected to wear concealing, baggy garments known as **hijab.**

Despite the pull of global culture, tradition still shapes the lives of men and especially women in this region. In most countries, women face more restrictions than in the United States or other Western countries. The most restricted country is Saudi Arabia, where women are forbidden to drive cars or ride bicycles. They cannot legally meet with unrelated men in public. Many Saudi women cannot pursue certain careers, since that would mean working with unrelated men.

However, attitudes are changing. In some countries, such as Iraq, women are free to work outside the home. Some can dress as they wish. Even in Saudi Arabia, women like Hanan are finding ways to pursue careers.

Reading Check How is life changing for women in Arabia and Iraq?

expose, *v.,* to show, make aware of, uncover

▲ Hanan at work

Section 3 Assessment

Key Terms

1. Explain the different meanings of the word jihad.
2. What is entrepreneurship, and why is it important?

Key Ideas

3. How are some Islamic traditions regarding women different from those in modern Western culture?
4. Why do leaders in Arabia and Iraq want to diversify their countries' economies?

Think Critically

5. **Analyze Cause and Effect** How have Islamic traditions shaped lives in this region?
6. **Categorize** What benefits and problems have resulted from Western involvement in Arabia and Iraq?

Essential Question

How much does geography shape a country?

7. What are some challenges the region's nations could face if oil and gas reserves run out? Go to your Student Journal to record your answer.

Patterns of Government in Arabia and Iraq

Key Ideas
- The most common form of government in Arabia and Iraq over the years has been monarchy.
- Some countries in the region have become more democratic.

Key Terms
- consensus
- constitutional monarchy
- bureaucracy
- absolute monarchy
- Baath Party

Arabia and Iraq have had different types of government over the centuries. Kings ruled city-states and empires in ancient Mesopotamia. After the spread of Islam in the A.D. 600s, Muslim Caliphs ruled a vast empire. A dictator controlled Iraq from 1979 to 2003. Today, monarchs rule most of the region. Some have total power, while others rule according to constitutions and share power. Democracy is also growing in the region.

Tribal Government

From ancient times to the present day, tribal governments have existed in Arabia and Iraq, especially among nomads. These tribes are often made up of families that claim to share a common ancestor.

Male elders, usually called sheikhs, govern the tribes. They usually rule through **consensus,** or agreement. That means they do not use force. Instead they consult with different people to arrive at a decision that the whole tribe can live with.

Reading Check What is government by consensus?

◀ Tribal elders in Saudi Arabia

460

Monarchy

Monarchy has been Arabia and Iraq's most common form of government from ancient times to the present.

Kings in Ancient Mesopotamia Some of the world's first known kings ruled the city-states of ancient Mesopotamia. They gained power during times of war, when the cities needed a strong leader. The king was said to rule on behalf of the gods. He used his religious authority to command the loyalty of his subjects.

The Mesopotamian city of Babylon built a large kingdom. Babylon's greatest king was Hammurabi, who gained the throne around 1800 B.C. He wrote one of the earliest known codes of law.

The Caliphs Even after the spread of Islam, monarchy remained the main form of government in the region. Rulers called caliphs governed the Muslim empire. Though caliphs were religious figures, they ruled like kings.

The caliphs built up a large bureaucracy to handle most of the details of government. A **bureaucracy** is a group of hired government officials.

Monarchy Today Monarchs govern most of Arabia today. Some are called kings, while others have a title of emir or sultan. Saudi Arabia and some other states are **absolute monarchies,** or states in which the ruler controls the government alone. The people have no say in politics. There are no limits to the ruler's power.

Other countries have written constitutions that limit the king's power. These countries are **constitutional monarchies.**

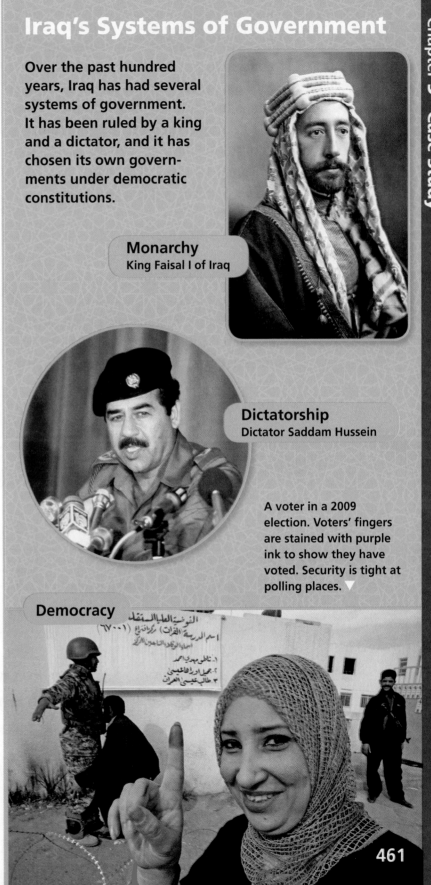

Iraq's Systems of Government

Over the past hundred years, Iraq has had several systems of government. It has been ruled by a king and a dictator, and it has chosen its own governments under democratic constitutions.

Monarchy
King Faisal I of Iraq

Dictatorship
Dictator Saddam Hussein

A voter in a 2009 election. Voters' fingers are stained with purple ink to show they have voted. Security is tight at polling places. ▼

Democracy

461

In some kingdoms, government is based on Islamic principles. Religion helps support those governments. Citizens are expected to remain loyal to their king and faithful to the teachings of Islam. Connections between the ruling family and important tribal leaders also help support the government.

Reading Check **What is an absolute monarchy?**

Dictatorship in Iraq

Dictatorship has been less common in Arabia and Iraq. In fact, the only true dictator in the region was Iraq's Saddam Hussein. Saddam took power in 1979 as the leader of Iraq's **Baath Party.** This party formed after the country's independence from Britain. It was a nonreligious party.

It promised to end the legacy of colonial rule by gaining control over the nation's resources, particularly oil.

As dictator, however, Saddam served his own interests. Under his rule, the state controlled all major industries, the school system, and the news media. Saddam appointed loyal friends and family members to top positions in government. He started wars with two of his neighbors, Kuwait and Iran.

Saddam was a brutal ruler. He created a powerful secret police to stamp out opposition. Political opponents were often jailed or killed. When the Kurds of northern Iraq opposed him, he sent the army against them and used chemical weapons to kill them. He held elections, but the results were always rigged to keep him in power. Average citizens had few rights.

Saddam Hussein ruled Iraq for more than twenty years. In the end, it took a U.S.-led invasion in 2003 to remove him from power. The new government elected after the invasion tried and executed the former dictator in 2006.

Reading Check **What kind of ruler was Saddam Hussein?**

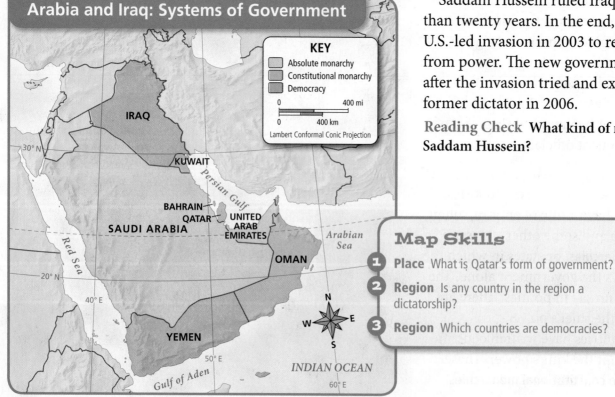

Arabia and Iraq: Systems of Government

KEY
Absolute monarchy
Constitutional monarchy
Democracy

0 — 400 mi
0 — 400 km
Lambert Conformal Conic Projection

IRAQ, KUWAIT, BAHRAIN, QATAR, UNITED ARAB EMIRATES, SAUDI ARABIA, OMAN, YEMEN, Persian Gulf, Red Sea, Arabian Sea, Gulf of Aden, INDIAN OCEAN

Map Skills

1 **Place** What is Qatar's form of government?

2 **Region** Is any country in the region a dictatorship?

3 **Region** Which countries are democracies?

▲ Yemen's parliament

Steps Toward Democracy

Various countries in the region have now taken steps toward democracy. Iraq is one of these. Since the American invasion of Iraq, Iraqis have formed a democratic government. A new constitution, passed in 2005, set up a parliamentary system. The government is led by a president, a prime minister, and a national assembly. The court system is based on Islamic and European law. Citizens have the right to vote and participate in politics. Continuing violence in Iraq has not been able to stop elections from taking place.

Yemen is another example of a new democracy. Since becoming a republic in 1990, Yemen has opened up its political system. It now has an elected president and a two-house legislature. Elections are said to be free and fair.

Some Arabian kingdoms are also becoming more democratic. Kuwait, for example, has a national assembly that is elected entirely by popular vote. It is known for its lively political debates. In 2005, the assembly granted women the right to vote and run for office. In 2009, four women won seats in parliament.

Reading Check Of Iraq, Yemen, and Kuwait, which is ruled by a monarch?

Assessment

1. How have government and religion often been linked in Arabia and Iraq?

2. What two kinds of monarchies exist in the region?

3. How has Iraq's government changed since 2003?

4. What obstacles might limit the growth of democracy in this region?

5. What does a bureaucracy do?

Chapter Assessment

Key Terms and Ideas

1. **Draw Conclusions** How do the physical features of Arabia and Iraq, such as desert oases, affect where people live in the region?

2. **Summarize** Why are **fossil fuels** important to Arabia and Iraq?

3. **Recall** What are some important accomplishments of early **civilizations** in Arabia and Iraq?

4. **Categorize** What are some features of the religion of Islam? Make sure you include the Five Pillars of Islam.

5. **Analyze Cause and Effect** How did British control change Arabia and Iraq after World War I?

6. **Compare and Contrast** Compare and contrast **Islamism** and **fundamentalism** in their beliefs and their influence on modern society in Arabia and Iraq. Is there any overlap between the two? Give examples in your explanation.

7. **Synthesize** Why do many countries in Arabia and Iraq want to boost **entrepreneurship** to lessen their dependence on oil?

Think Critically

8. **Problem Solving** Water and oil are both important to Arabia and Iraq. How are the region's supplies of these two resources related? How can the region use a wealth of one resource to take care of a shortage of the other?

9. **Make Inferences** Since World War I, Iraq has overthrown its king and fought several wars. What role did oil play in these conflicts? How might oil and instability be linked? Explain.

10. **Compare Viewpoints** How do traditional Islamic cultures in the region view the role of women in society? How do these views differ from those held in most Western nations?

11. **Core Concepts: Culture and Geography** What role has religion, especially religious differences, played in the history of Arabia and Iraq?

Places to Know

For each place, write the letter from the map that shows the place's location.

12. Persian Gulf

13. Mecca

14. Euphrates River

15. United Arab Emirates

16. Yemen

17. Iraq

18. **Draw Inferences** Which of these countries does not have a coastline on the Persian Gulf?

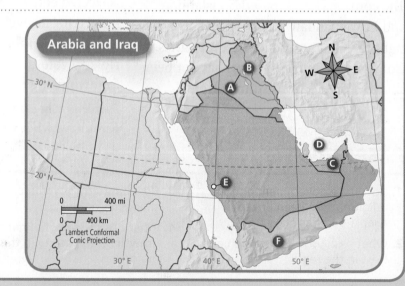

464

Essential Question

How much does geography shape a country?

Water for Arabia and Iraq Follow your teacher's instructions to participate in a regional meeting on water scarcity and oil dependency in Arabia and Iraq. Remember to consider how one nation's needs interact with the needs of other nations in the region.

21st Century Learning

Develop Cultural Awareness

Using reliable sources in the library or online, research an ethnic group in the region. Create a Venn diagram that includes the regional ethnic group's culture and your own culture. List information such as the following:
- main religious views
- foods
- language

Document-Based Questions

Success Tracker™
Online at myworldgeography.com

Use your knowledge of Arabia and Iraq, as well as Documents A and B, to answer Questions 1–3.

Document A

" Brother Osama: How much blood has been spilled? How many innocent children, women, and old people have been killed, maimed, and expelled from their homes in the name of "al-Qaeda"? …
This religion of ours comes to defense of the life of a sparrow. It can never accept the murder of innocent people, regardless of what supposed justification is given for it."

—Sheikh Salman al-Oadah,
Islamic religious leader from Saudi Arabia

Document B

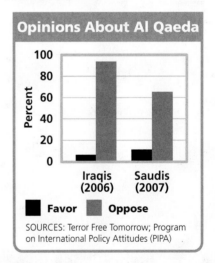

Opinions About Al Qaeda

SOURCES: Terror Free Tomorrow; Program on International Policy Attitudes (PIPA)

1. Which of the following sums up the main idea of Document A?

A Islam calls for violent jihad.

B Al Qaeda's killings are justified

C Islam opposes the killing of innocent people.

D This leader sees Osama bin Laden as his brother.

2. Which of the following can you conclude from Document B?

A Saudis support only 10% of al Qaeda's actions.

B Large majorities in Iraq and Saudi Arabia oppose al Qaeda.

C Only 10% of Iraqis support al Qaeda.

D Al Qaeda is most popular in Iraq.

3. **Writing Task** Based on what you have learned from the chapter and the documents above, explain the information presented in Document B.

Chapter 10

Israel and Its Neighbors

Essential Question

Is conflict unavoidable?

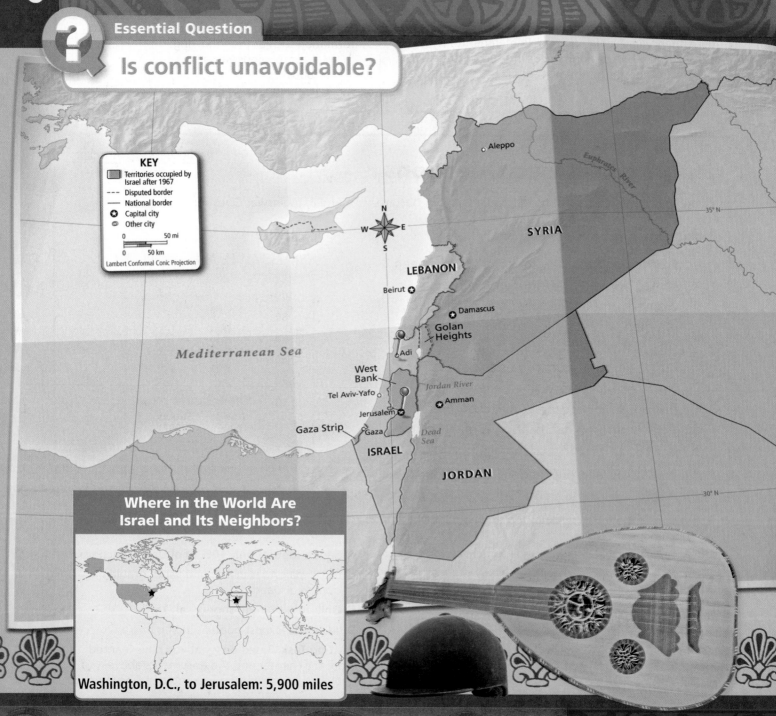

KEY
- Territories occupied by Israel after 1967
- --- Disputed border
- — National border
- ✪ Capital city
- ◉ Other city

0 — 50 mi
0 — 50 km
Lambert Conformal Conic Projection

Mediterranean Sea

SYRIA

Aleppo

Euphrates River

35° N

LEBANON

Beirut ✪

Damascus ●

Golan Heights

Adi

West Bank

Jordan River

Tel Aviv-Yafo

Amman ✪

Jerusalem ✪

Gaza Strip

Gaza

Dead Sea

ISRAEL

JORDAN

30° N

Where in the World Are Israel and Its Neighbors?

Washington, D.C., to Jerusalem: 5,900 miles

466

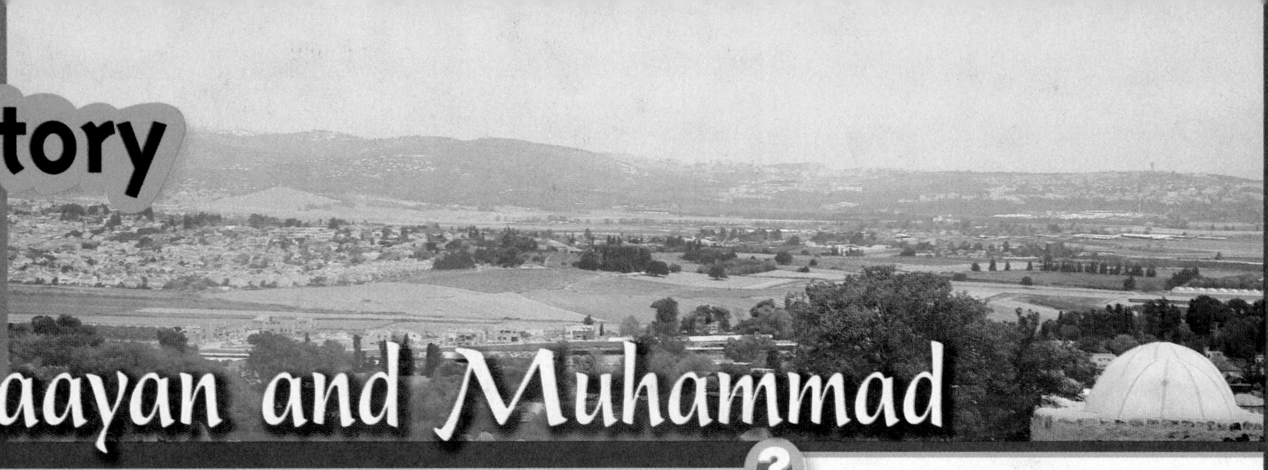

my Story

Maayan and Muhammad

In this section, you'll read about Maayan, a young Jewish Israeli woman, and Muhammad, an Israeli Arab boy. What do Maayan's and Muhammad's stories tell you about life in this region today?

Story by Hila Baroz for myWorld Geography Online

Explore the Essential Question

- at my worldgeography.com
- using the **myWorld Chapter Activity**
- with the **Student Journal**

Maayan is an 18-year-old Israeli woman from Adi, a small community in northern Israel. She decided to put off her required military service in order to volunteer in Magen David Adom (MDA). MDA is Israel's equivalent to the Red Cross. Maayan is a paramedic giving first-aid treatment to injured and sick patients.

Maayan studied in an agricultural school near her home. The school has a dairy barn and a horse ranch. Maayan completed the school's horse care program and she enjoys riding horses. She loves the landscapes of her childhood, and does not think she would like to live in the city. Still, not everything is peaceful and quiet in the region where she grew up. Israel faces the threat of terrorist attacks.

"MDA is a reflection of the country we live in. At any given moment, something might happen, and you must always be prepared. I've learned to save lives in a place where life is not taken for granted."

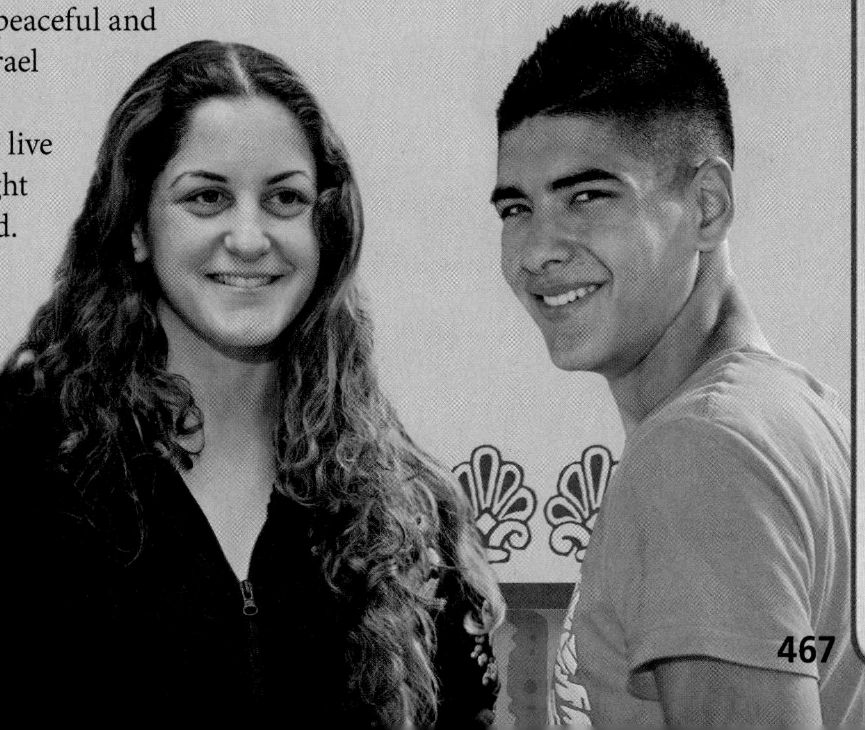

467

Maayan practices first aid at MDA.

Maayan's family eating together

Talking about her first-aid work, Maayan says, "The first few seconds are the most critical. Whatever mistake you make during those seconds, even the most sophisticated hospital equipment could not put right. It gives you a sense of mission."

"I remember how we once [revived] a 48-year-old woman. It took us an hour and a half. Eventually, we managed to bring her back to life. . . . After this case, I felt tremendous pride and satisfaction."

When Maayan returns home from MDA, she drives past Arab villages. "My ignorance is so great. I see these houses, but I don't know anything about the people who live in them. There's this huge cultural gap, and there's also fear. Sometimes when I take the bus and I see an Arab sitting inside I'm afraid the bus might blow up. I wish we didn't live in a conflict, but you have to learn a lot about the other side and get to know it."

Fifteen-year-old Muhammad likes to walk the narrow streets of the Old City of Jerusalem where he was born. Muhammad lives in a Jerusalem neighborhood called Beit Safafa. His family has been living here for many generations. It was built by two large families, or clans, and Muhammad's is one of them. Like Maayan, Muhammad enjoys horseback riding. "I particularly like to ride my cousins' horses. . . . I am sure I'd like to spend the rest of my life in Beit Safafa."

Muhammad is a Muslim living in Israel as part of its Arab minority. Both he and his family have many Arab Palestinian friends and acquaintances living in the Israeli-controlled West Bank.

Seven years ago, Israel built a wall near Muhammad's home—part of the West Bank security barrier—to try to prevent terrorist attacks on Israel.

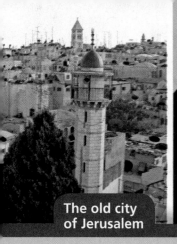
The old city of Jerusalem

Muhammad practices playing the oud.

Muhammad's father prepares coffee.

Muhammad doesn't like the barrier, because security restrictions make it difficult or impossible to cross. Those who do cross may have difficulty returning. Muhammad says, "I still remember how we used to walk to Bethlehem, which is only two miles away. . . . Some people in my neighborhood are Israeli Arabs whose partners are Palestinian. Because of the barrier, they cannot meet now."

Muhammad is learning to play the oud (ood), a traditional pear-shaped wooden stringed instrument, in a music school not far from the Old City. Both Arabs and Jews attend this school. Muhammad plays traditional Arab music. In the school, he joined a Jewish-Arab youth orchestra, with 25 musicians. They play original adaptations of traditional Arab music and combinations of eastern and western musical styles.

"I don't really care about the conflict. Only human beings are important to me. In music, there are no Arabs or Jews, only people playing together and getting to know each other. In our music school, there are both Jewish and Arab teachers. This orchestra is proof we can coexist."

→ myStory Video

Join Maayan and Muhammad as they show you more about life in their hometowns.

Meet the Journalist

Name Hila Baroz
Favorite moment Interacting with a video crew made up of a Jew, a Christian, and a Muslim

my worldgeography.com myStory Video

469

Chapter Atlas

Key Ideas
- Israel and its neighbors are a continental crossroads, near the points where Europe, Asia, and Africa meet.
- Water is a scarce but vital resource for Israel and its neighbors.
- The region has a complex pattern of ethnic and religious differences.

Key Terms
- Fertile Crescent
- Druze
- rain shadow
- Alawite
- aquifer

 Visual Glossary

 Reading Skill: Label an Outline Map Take notes using the outline map in your journal.

Mountains along the coast of Lebanon ▼

▲ A boy from coastal Lebanon

A Continental Junction

Israel and its neighbors—Lebanon, Syria, Jordan, the Golan Heights, West Bank, and Gaza Strip—are in Southwest Asia. The West Bank and Gaza Strip together are sometimes called the Palestinian Territories.

These countries and territories lie on or near the coast of the Mediterranean Sea where the continents of Asia and Africa meet. This region is a continental crossroads, and it also borders Turkey, where Asia and Europe meet.

Four geographic zones make up this region. On its western edge, a narrow

470

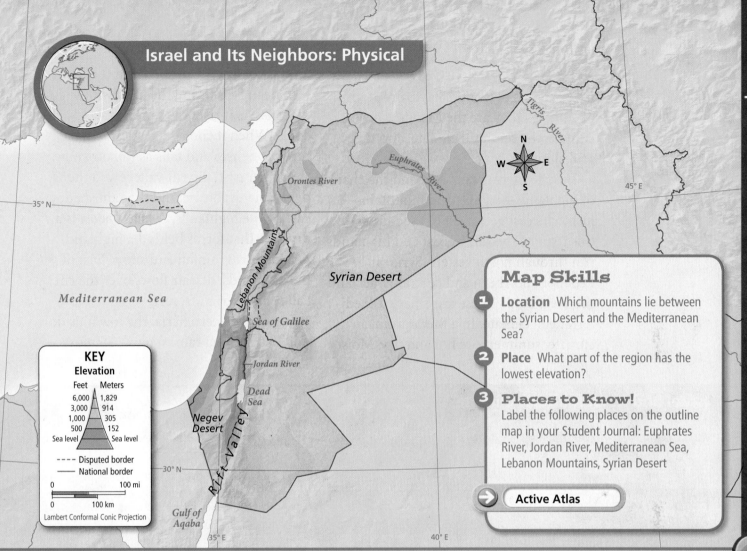

Israel and Its Neighbors: Physical

Map Skills

1 Location Which mountains lie between the Syrian Desert and the Mediterranean Sea?

2 Place What part of the region has the lowest elevation?

3 Places to Know!
Label the following places on the outline map in your Student Journal: Euphrates River, Jordan River, Mediterranean Sea, Lebanon Mountains, Syrian Desert

→ Active Atlas

KEY
Elevation

Feet	Meters
6,000	1,829
3,000	914
1,000	305
500	152
Sea level	Sea level

- - - - Disputed border
——— National border

0   100 mi
0   100 km
Lambert Conformal Conic Projection

coastal plain runs along the Mediterranean Sea. Just east of this plain is a chain of hills and mountains. Farther east is a branch of the Great African Rift Valleys. This chain of valleys runs from Africa through the Red Sea into Israel and its neighbors. Above these valleys to the east is a vast desert plateau. The Syrian Desert covers much of this plateau.

Flowing through one of the rift valleys is the Jordan River. Its water flows from Syria and Lebanon into the freshwater Sea of Galilee. It then flows south from this lake to the Dead Sea, also in this rift valley. The Dead Sea shoreline is the lowest land on Earth, at 1,378 feet (420 meters) below sea level.

The Euphrates River flows from the rainy mountains of Turkey, through eastern Syria, and across the Syrian Desert into Iraq. These river valleys and the relatively rainy Mediterranean coast and highlands are part of the Fertile Crescent. The **Fertile Crescent** is a region that stretches from the Mediterranean coast east through Mesopotamia (modern Iraq) to the Persian Gulf. It has good conditions for growing crops.

Reading Check Which three continents meet in or near this region?

my worldgeography.com   Active Atlas

471

Wet and Dry Climates

Israel and its neighbors have three types of climate. They are the Mediterranean climate, the semiarid climate, and the arid climate.

The Mediterranean coast and the chain of highlands—or hills and mountains—just to its east gets most of the rainfall in this region. The rainy coast and highlands run through northwestern Syria, all of Lebanon, northern and central Israel, and the West Bank. These areas have a Mediterranean climate. In a Mediterranean climate, summers are hot and dry. Moist air flows over this region from the Mediterranean Sea during the mild winter months. As it rises over the highlands, it cools. When it cools, most of the moisture <u>condenses</u> and falls as rain or snow.

Farther east, the rift valleys and the desert plateau lie behind the rain shadow cast by the highlands. A **rain shadow** is a dry area that forms behind a highland that captures rainfall and snow. East of the highlands, dry air flows over the rift valley and Syrian Desert.

In northwestern Syria, the low hills do not cast a strong rain shadow. So most

condense, *v.,* to become denser, change from a gas to a liquid

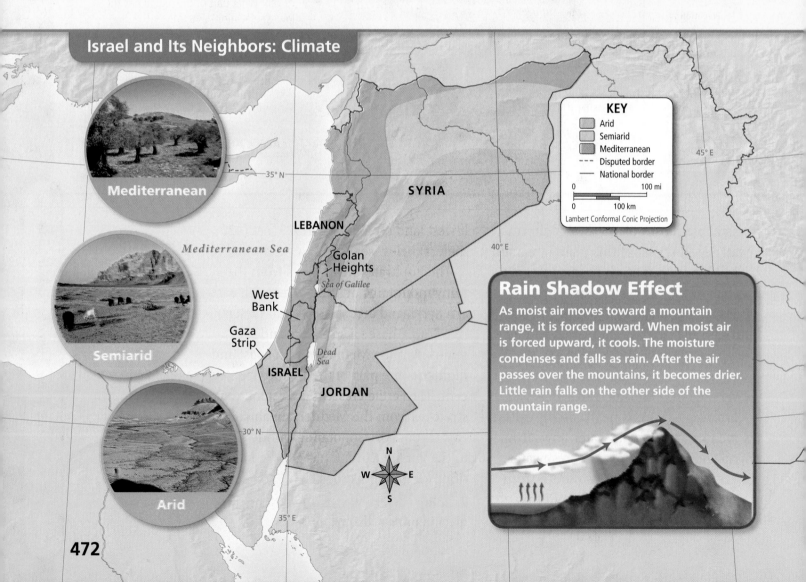

Israel and Its Neighbors: Climate

KEY
- Arid
- Semiarid
- Mediterranean
- --- Disputed border
- — National border

0   100 mi
0   100 km
Lambert Conformal Conic Projection

Rain Shadow Effect

As moist air moves toward a mountain range, it is forced upward. When moist air is forced upward, it cools. The moisture condenses and falls as rain. After the air passes over the mountains, it becomes drier. Little rain falls on the other side of the mountain range.

472

of northern Syria has a semiarid climate. This is a dry climate, but with enough rainfall for some animals and plants, such as wheat. The semiarid climate stretches through central Syria to western Jordan.

Southeastern Syria and eastern Jordan have an arid, or desert, climate. This area is behind the rain shadow cast by the hills around the rift valleys. Very little moisture reaches the plateau. Few plants or animals can live in the desert.

Southern Israel and Jordan also have an arid climate, with a belt of semiarid climate just to its north. In the semiarid zone, low hills cause the air to lose some moisture during winter.

The desert to the south is part of the belt of subtropical deserts that stretches around the world. These deserts include the Sahara and the deserts of Arabia. As you learned in the Core Concepts Handbook, cool, dry air tends to sink over this belt of deserts. This sinking air keeps moist air from flowing in from the Mediterranean Sea. It also keeps air from rising and dropping rain or snow.

Reading Check Why is the climate of eastern Jordan so dry?

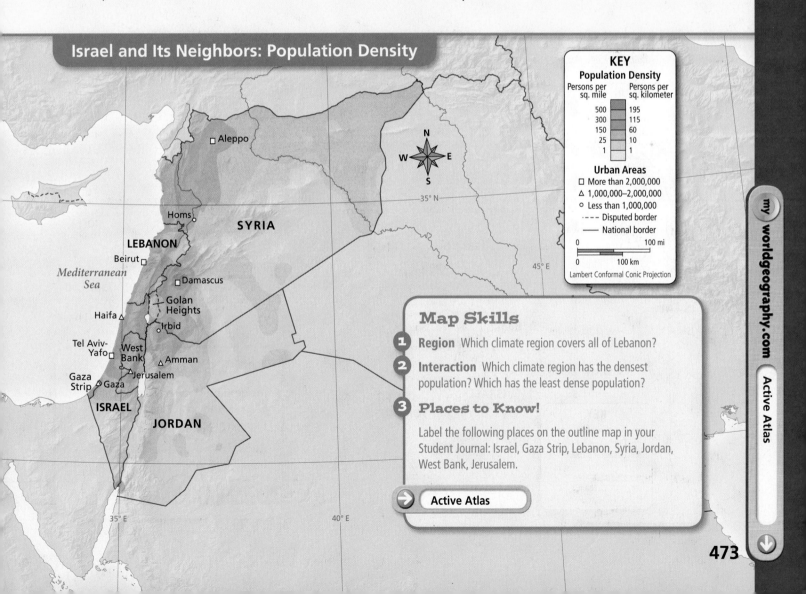

Israel and Its Neighbors: Population Density

KEY
Population Density

Persons per sq. mile	Persons per sq. kilometer
500	195
300	115
150	60
25	10
1	1

Urban Areas
□ More than 2,000,000
△ 1,000,000–2,000,000
○ Less than 1,000,000
---- Disputed border
— National border

Lambert Conformal Conic Projection

Map Skills

1 **Region** Which climate region covers all of Lebanon?

2 **Interaction** Which climate region has the densest population? Which has the least dense population?

3 **Places to Know!**

Label the following places on the outline map in your Student Journal: Israel, Gaza Strip, Lebanon, Syria, Jordan, West Bank, Jerusalem.

Active Atlas

my worldgeography.com Active Atlas

Water for a Thirsty Region

Israel and its neighbors get little rain outside the winter rainy season. Fresh water is a scarce resource here.

Many of the region's streams run only during the rainy winter or shrink to a trickle in the summer. People need year-round sources of fresh water.

Main Water Sources Some of the most important sources of water for Israel and its neighbors are their aquifers. **Aquifers** are underground layers of rock where water collects. Wells and pumps can bring this water to the surface for use. However, the region's population and water use have grown faster than these aquifers can refill. Some are slowly running out of water. This makes wells run dry. Desalination plants are another possible source of fresh water for this region. However, they are expensive.

Lebanon is the only country in the region with plenty of fresh water. Syria, on the other hand, has a water shortage. Few rivers run year-round. An exception is the Euphrates River, which flows across eastern Syria. The Euphrates is a major

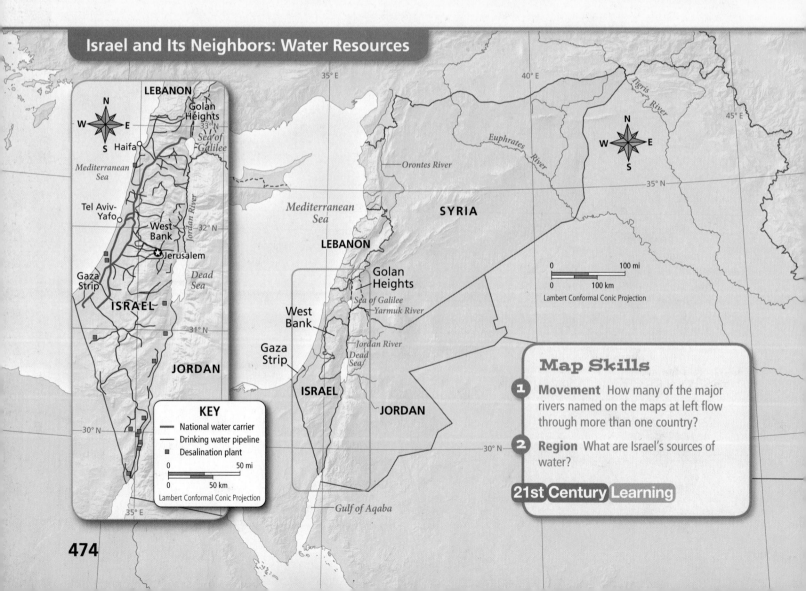

Israel and Its Neighbors: Water Resources

KEY
— National water carrier
— Drinking water pipeline
■ Desalination plant

Lambert Conformal Conic Projection

Map Skills

1 Movement How many of the major rivers named on the maps at left flow through more than one country?

2 Region What are Israel's sources of water?

21st Century Learning

474

source of water for Syria. Syria also uses water from aquifers, but some wells have run dry.

Conflicts Over Water Competition over the Euphrates has brought tensions. The river flows from Turkey through Syria to Iraq. Turkey takes water from the Euphrates. This reduces the supply for Syria and Iraq.

Jordan has the region's most serious shortage of water. It shares the Jordan and Yarmuk rivers with Israel and Syria. Jordan has had disagreements with its neighbors over these rivers.

Israel depends on two main water sources. It gets surface water from the Jordan River and the Sea of Galilee. The Sea of Galilee is the largest body of fresh water in the region. Israel also takes water from underground aquifers.

Israel also has had tensions with its neighbors over water. The Jordan River flows from the Golan Heights, an area that Syria claims and that Israel has occupied since 1967. Water also flows into the Jordan River from southern Lebanon and from the country of Jordan.

Israel also uses aquifers that lie partly under the West Bank, which is home to many Palestinians. Some Palestinians complain about Israel's use of these aquifers. Because the aquifers are limited, both sides fear a loss of their water. However, Israel has made agreements with Jordan and with the Palestinians over water use.

An Israeli water expert has warned that disagreements over water with other countries in the region could lead to war:

> 66 I can promise that if there is not sufficient water in our region, if there is scarcity of water, if people remain thirsty for water, then we shall doubtless face war. 99

—Meir Ben Meir,
Israel's former Water Commissioner

Reading Check What river does Israel share with three other countries?

occupy, *v.*, to take or hold, especially by military force

myWorld Activity
Water Rules

An Israeli farmer watering crops

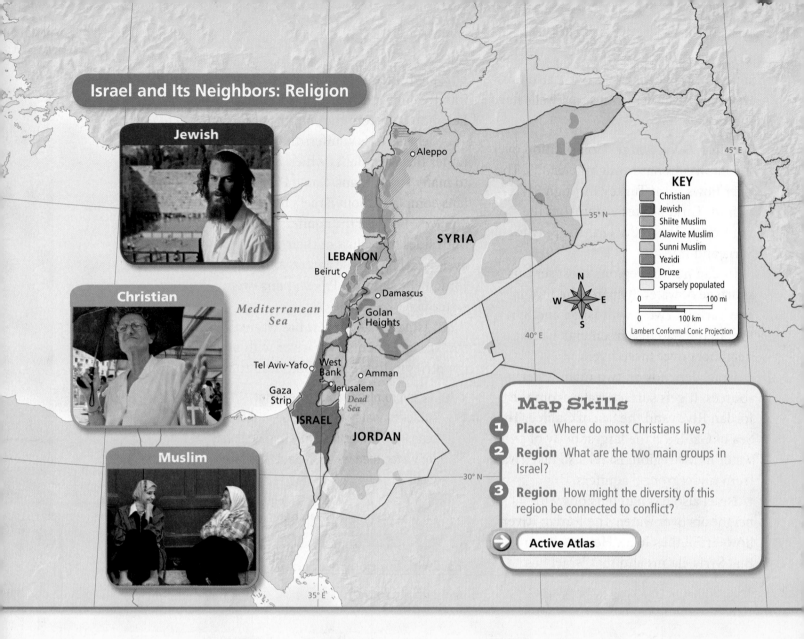

Israel and Its Neighbors: Religion

Jewish

Christian

Muslim

KEY
- Christian
- Jewish
- Shiite Muslim
- Alawite Muslim
- Sunni Muslim
- Yezidi
- Druze
- Sparsely populated

0 — 100 mi
0 — 100 km
Lambert Conformal Conic Projection

SYRIA

Aleppo

LEBANON
Beirut

Damascus

Golan Heights

Mediterranean Sea

Tel Aviv-Yafo
West Bank
Amman
Gaza Strip
Jerusalem
Dead Sea
ISRAEL
JORDAN

Map Skills

1 **Place** Where do most Christians live?

2 **Region** What are the two main groups in Israel?

3 **Region** How might the diversity of this region be connected to conflict?

→ **Active Atlas**

A Region of Many Peoples and Religions

Most of the people of Israel and its neighbors fall into two broad ethnic groups, or groups sharing a language and an identity. These groups are the Jews and the Arabs. Most of Israel's people are Jews. Most Israeli Jews speak Hebrew.

Arabs speak Arabic. Arabs make up a large majority of the people in the Palestinian Territories, Jordan, Lebanon, and Syria. Arabs also make up a minority of the population of Israel. Syria has an important Kurdish minority in the northeast. Syria also has much smaller Turkish and Armenian minorities.

Differences Among Jews Most people in Israel are Jewish. Some Israeli Jews strictly follow the rules of Judaism, while others are less strict. Most Israeli Jews, even if they are not religious, identify with the culture and history of Judaism. This is a cornerstone of their identity.

476

Israel's Jews have ancestors from many parts of the world. Some families have lived in the area for thousands of years. Other families immigrated from neighboring countries or other areas in Southwest Asia and North Africa. Still others came from Europe, Russia, North America, Ethiopia, and elsewhere. These immigrants have brought different customs from their former homes.

Differences Among Arabs The Arabs of the region share an ethnic identity, but they follow several different religions. Most Arabs here are Sunni Muslims, but some are Shia Muslim, Alawite Muslim, Christian, or Druze. The **Druze** follow a religion that combines Islam with other teachings. The **Alawites** follow a form of Islam similar to Shia Islam.

Most Arabs of Israel, the West Bank, and the Gaza Strip are Sunni Muslim. Some are Christian. Many Israeli Arabs consider themselves Palestinian, like the Arabs of the West Bank and Gaza Strip.

In Lebanon, almost all of the people are Arabs, but no one religious group has a majority. The two largest groups of Lebanese are the Shia Muslims and Christians. There are also Sunni Muslims and Druze in Lebanon.

Most Syrians, including Syria's Kurds, are Sunni Muslims. However, some are Christians. Others are Shia or Alawite Muslims. Smaller numbers are Druze. Syria's rulers for the past 40 years belong to a family of Alawites.

A large majority of Jordanians are Sunni Muslim Arabs. Jordan has a small Christian population and smaller groups of Shia Muslims and Druze.

Tensions among ethnic and religious groups in this region have led to conflicts within and between its countries. For example, Israel and its Arab neighbors have fought several wars. Lebanon suffered through years of war among its Christian, Druze, and Muslim groups.

Reading Check Which ethnic group lives in every country of this region?

my World IN NUMBERS

This region's population is **13%** Jewish, **10%** Christian, **73%** Muslim, and **4%** Druze or another religion.

Section 1 Assessment

Key Terms

1. Use the terms *rain shadow* and *aquifers* to describe where water can be found in Israel and its neighbors.

2. What is the Fertile Crescent?

Key Ideas

3. How does the climate change from the coast to inland areas?

4. What is the most important resource for Israel and its neighbors? Explain.

5. How would you describe ethnic and religious patterns in this region?

Think Critically

6. **Draw Inferences** How might religious patterns in the region contribute to conflict?

7. **Analyze Cause and Effect** How has water affected the relationships among Israel and its neighbors?

? Essential Question

Is conflict unavoidable?

8. Describe steps that Israel and its neighbors have taken to reduce conflict over water resources. Go to your Student Journal to record your answer.

477

History of Israel and Its Neighbors

Key Ideas
- Judaism is the oldest monotheistic religion, and its idea of justice remains important around the world.
- Nearly 2,000 years ago, the religion of Christianity developed in this region.
- During the Middle Ages, the region became mainly Muslim and Arabic-speaking.
- Seeking safety from persecution, Jews founded the state of Israel in 1948, but conflict between Jews and Arabs continues.

Key Terms
- agriculture
- Trinity
- prophet
- Crusades
- ethics
- anti-Semitism
- messiah
- Zionism

 Visual Glossary

Reading Skill: Compare and Contrast Take notes using the graphic organizer in your journal.

A jar made in Canaan around 1500 B.C. ▼

Israel and its neighbors are part of the Fertile Crescent. The first people in the Fertile Crescent were hunters and gatherers. Then, about 10,000 years ago, they began to practice **agriculture,** or the raising of plants and animals. These early farmers built permanent villages. They developed new tools for farming, such as plows.

A Cradle of Civilization

Villages grew into towns. One of the world's oldest towns, Jericho, still exists today in what is now the West Bank. It was settled about 9,000 years ago.

Present-day Israel and the Palestinian Territories were once called Canaan. North of Canaan, in modern Lebanon and Syria, was a region called Phoenicia. The Phoenicians invented an alphabet. Through trade, the Phoenicians spread their alphabet, which is the basis for our own. The Canaanites—the people of Canaan—and the Phoenicians were pagan. That is, they worshiped more than one god.

After 2000 B.C., a people known as Israelites moved into the region. Unlike the Canaanites, the Israelites worshiped only one God. Their religion came to be known as Judaism.

Reading Check When was Jericho settled?

The Origins of Judaism

The Israelites practiced monotheism, the belief in a single God. They rejected the gods of the Canaanites.

Abraham's Covenant According to the Hebrew, or Jewish, Bible, Abraham was the father of the Jewish people. According to the Bible, God promised that Abraham would found a great nation in Canaan. In return, Abraham and his people had to obey God. God's agreement with Abraham is called a covenant. Abraham's grandson Jacob, later called Israel, had twelve sons. Their families grew to form the people known as the Israelites.

Escape From Slavery Famine drove the Israelites to Egypt, where the Egyptians enslaved them. According to the Bible, God chose an Israelite named Moses to lead his people out of Egypt. Moses was later known as a **prophet,** a messenger of God. The pharaoh, or Egyptian king, refused to let the Israelites go. God then caused Egypt to suffer until the pharaoh freed the Israelites. Moses then led his people out of Egypt to the edge of Canaan. The Jewish holiday of Passover commemorates this event.

During this time, according to the Bible, God gave Moses a law code including the Ten Commandments. The Ten Commandments are ten rules for good behavior. The Israelites took control in Canaan and established first the kingdom of Israel and later the kingdom of Judah. In 587 B.C., however, the Babylonian empire conquered the Israelite kingdom of Judah.

Captivity, Return, and Diaspora The Babylonians destroyed the great Temple of Jerusalem and carried away many people from Judah as captives. However, the people of Judah preserved their religion. They came to be known as Jews, a name derived from *Judah*. Captivity in Babylonia was the start of the Jewish Diaspora, or scattering. After the Persians conquered Babylonia, the Persian king allowed Jews to return to Judah. The Jews rebuilt their Temple in Jerusalem.

The region eventually came under Roman rule as the province of Judea. The Romans demanded heavy taxes and outlawed parts of the Jewish religion. Jews rebelled against Rome twice. The Romans destroyed the Temple in A.D. 70 and later killed thousands of Jews. Many Jews fled the region, and the Romans banned Jews from Jerusalem.

Reading Check What was the Diaspora?

Moses leading his people out of Egypt in a scene from the Hebrew Bible ▼

479

The Beliefs of Judaism

Judaism developed a system of **ethics**—or beliefs about what is right and wrong. Judaism also developed a tradition of acting responsibly within a community. These traditions are guidelines for living a just and righteous life.

Faith in One God At the core of Judaism lies the belief that there is a single God who created the universe and has always existed. This God does not take a physical form. Most Jews refer to God as *He*. However, for Jews, God is neither male nor female. God knows the thoughts and actions of people. He rewards the good and punishes the evil. Jews believe that they carry on the Israelites' covenant with God. They believe that God chose them to bear the responsibility of upholding his laws and serving as an example of justice to other peoples.

The Holy Scriptures The scriptures, or religious writings, of Judaism include the Hebrew Bible, known as the Tanakh. The Tanakh has three parts: the Torah, the Nevi'im, and the Ketuvim. The Torah, or Law, tells the story of the Israelites from God's creation of the world until the death of Moses. It provides the basis for Jewish ethics and religious practice. The Nevi'im, or Prophets, contains the teachings of the many prophets of Judaism. The Ketuvim, or Writings, includes psalms (sacred poems or songs) and proverbs (writings of wisdom). Another Jewish religious text, not part of the Tanakh, is the Talmud. This text explains and interprets the Torah.

The Ten Commandments and Justice Jews' covenant with God includes rules that form a system of ethics. According to the Bible, God gave rules to Moses on the journey from Egypt to Canaan. They include the Ten Commandments. These are guidelines for acting justly and fairly that are meant to create a stable and peaceful society. Judaism calls on people to follow the righteous example of God. Jewish ideas of justice form a basis for democracies, legal systems, and ethics in many parts of the modern world.

Reading Check Why is justice important to Jews?

▼ A jeweled Torah cover, with wrapped Torah scrolls below and to the right

▲ Israeli Jewish worshipers

480

The Birth of Christianity

Around A.D. 35, a new religion arose in the Roman province of Judea. This religion, based on Jewish traditions, was Christianity.

Jewish Roots Judaism included a belief in a **messiah**—a leader chosen by God. This messiah would restore the Jewish nation and help create God's kingdom in the world. For Christians, this messiah was Jesus.

As with Abraham, what we know of Jesus comes mainly from scripture. According to the Christian Bible, Jesus was a Jew born in Judea. He grew up in the town of Nazareth. As an adult, Jesus began to preach about Jewish beliefs and ethics. He preached forgiveness, compassion for the poor, and trust in God. He attracted many followers.

According to scripture, the Roman governor of Judea put Jesus to death by crucifixion, or nailing to a cross. The cross became an important Christian symbol.

The Story of the Resurrection According to the Christian Bible, two days after Jesus' death, some of his followers went to his tomb and found it empty. Jesus then appeared to many followers. God, they believed, had raised Jesus from the dead, or resurrected him.

Unlike other Jews, Jesus' followers believed that his resurrection proved that he was the messiah. Jesus' followers called him "Christ," which was a Greek translation of the word *messiah*. His followers became known as Christians.

The Early Church and Its Spread At first, most Christians came from a Jewish background. However, one of Jesus' followers, Paul—known to Christians as Saint Paul—began preaching Christian beliefs to non-Jews. Gradually, non-Jewish Christians began to outnumber Christians with a Jewish background. For hundreds of years, Christians faced harsh treatment in the Roman Empire.

In 312, however, Roman Emperor Constantine became a Christian, and the religion spread throughout the Roman world. Today it is the most practiced religion in the world. There are more than 2 billion Christians today.

Reading Check **Why is the resurrection important to Christians?**

▼ An early Christian painting of Jesus

481

Beliefs of Christianity

The beliefs of Christianity are based on the life and teachings of Jesus, as described in the Christian Bible. Christians believe that Jesus was more than a wise man, like Abraham or Moses. They believe that he was God in human form. They see Jesus' death as proof of his humanity and his resurrection as proof that he is the son of God.

For Christians, the resurrection is also God's promise of eternal life. The resurrection shows that God controls life and death. For Christians, belief in Jesus can lead to a rewarding life after death. Christians believe that Jesus died on the cross because of people's sins, or evil actions. They believe that Jesus' resurrection, with its promise of eternal life, is proof of God's forgiveness.

concept, *n.,* an idea about how something is or should be

The Christian Bible The Tanakh, or Hebrew Bible, makes up most of the Christian Bible. Christians refer to the writings from the Tanakh as the Old Testament. In addition to the Old Testament, the Christian Bible contains the New Testament. The New Testament contains writings about the life and teachings of Jesus and the writings of early Christian leaders.

The Trinity The **Trinity** is one of the most complex <u>concepts</u> of Christianity. Most Christians believe that God exists in three forms, or persons. Together, these three persons form the Trinity. These three persons are God the Father, the creator; God the Son, or Jesus; and the Holy Spirit. The Holy Spirit (also known as the Holy Ghost) is sometimes described as the power of God as experienced on Earth. The idea of the Trinity separates Christianity from the other two monotheistic religions. Judaism and Islam do not recognize the Trinity.

Reading Check What are the two main parts of the Christian Bible?

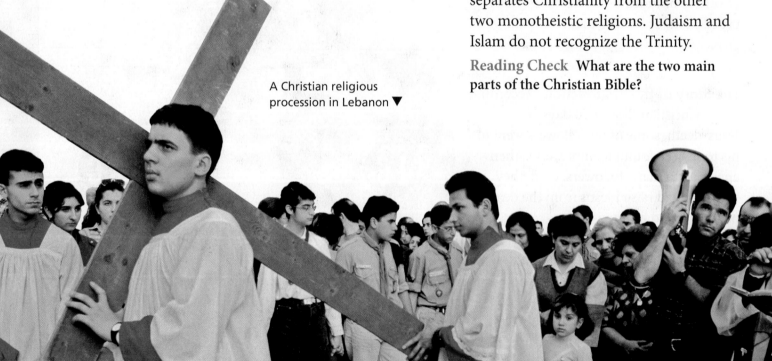

A Christian religious procession in Lebanon ▼

482

A Crossroads of Empires and New Religions

Over the centuries, armies from different empires conquered the region that is now Israel and its neighbors. Some of these conquests brought new religions to the region or re-established old religions.

Life Under the Romans and Byzantines After the Jewish revolt of A.D. 135, the Romans changed the name of the region from Judea (or land of the Jews) to Palestine as punishment for the revolt.

After his conversion in 312, Roman Emperor Constantine made the region a center of Christian worship. Palestine and Syria were part of the Eastern Roman, or Byzantine, empire. In Byzantine times, most people in the region were Christian.

Arab Conquest and Islam Between 614 and 629, the Byzantine empire lost control of Syria and Palestine to the Persian empire. The weakened Byzantine empire recovered the province in 629. However, Muslim Arabs attacked the region just five years later. The Byzantines were too weak to hold back the Arabs.

By 640, the Arabs had conquered the entire region. In 661, Damascus became the capital of a Muslim empire. Muslims recognize Abraham and Jesus as prophets. However, they believe that Muhammad was God's last and most important prophet. Muslims believe that Muhammad traveled to heaven from Jerusalem.

Because of its importance to Muhammad and earlier prophets, Muslims consider Jerusalem a holy city. There they built an important mosque in 705.

Islamic law favored Muslims but tolerated Christians and Jews. By the 800s, most people in the region had converted to Islam, and Arabic was the main language.

Crusaders and Muslim Rule Beginning in the late 1000s, Christian soldiers from western Europe attacked Palestine in religious wars called the **Crusades.** They aimed to stop the spread of Islam and to take control of Palestine from the Muslims.

Around 1100, Crusaders established Christian kingdoms in Palestine. Muslims and Jews suffered brutal treatment under the Crusaders. In 1187, however, Muslim forces reconquered Jerusalem.

In 1517, the Muslim Ottoman Turks conquered the entire region. The Ottoman Turks ruled until the early 1900s.

Reading Check Why is Jerusalem a holy city for Muslims?

myWorld Activity
Diversity Mosaic

The Dome of the Rock, a Muslim shrine built in Jerusalem in 691 ▼

Culture Close-up

483

Independence and Conflict

Britain, France, and other European nations defeated the Ottoman empire in 1918, at the end of World War I. This defeat ended Ottoman rule.

European Mandates After World War I, most of the world's nations joined to form the League of Nations. The League of Nations created mandates for areas conquered during the war. Mandates were territories placed under the control of powerful nations with a promise of future independence. Syria (including modern Lebanon) became a French mandate. Palestine (modern Israel and Jordan) became a British mandate.

Zionism and Jewish Settlement In Europe, Jews faced cruel and sometimes violent anti-Semitism. **Anti-Semitism** is discrimination against Jews. In the late 1800s, Jews in Europe formed a movement called Zionism. **Zionism** aimed to create a Jewish state in Palestine because of Jews' historic connection to the region. A Jewish state would allow Jews to create a safe homeland. Jews from the Diaspora began to move to Palestine, where an ancient Jewish community already existed.

discrimination, *n.,* unfair treatment of a person or group

Independence Anti-Semitism in Europe grew and led to the Holocaust during World War II. This pushed more Jews to migrate to the Palestine Mandate.

Meanwhile, the mandates gained independence: Lebanon in 1943 and Syria and Jordan in 1946. Thousands of Jews migrated from Europe to Palestine after the end of World War II in 1945. Tensions mounted between the Arab majority and Jews over the future of Palestine.

In 1947, the United Nations created a plan to partition, or divide, Palestine into two separate states—an Arab state and a Jewish state. Arabs rejected the UN plan, which Jews accepted. Israel declared independence as a Jewish state in 1948.

Arab-Israeli Conflicts Tensions erupted into violence. Neighboring Arab states attacked Israel. During the Arab-Israeli War of 1948, half of the Arab people in the land that came under Israeli control fled as refugees. Israel gained more territory than under the UN plan. Arab states took control of the West Bank and Gaza Strip. Many Jewish refugees from Arab countries came to Israel. Israel and Egypt fought a second war in 1956.

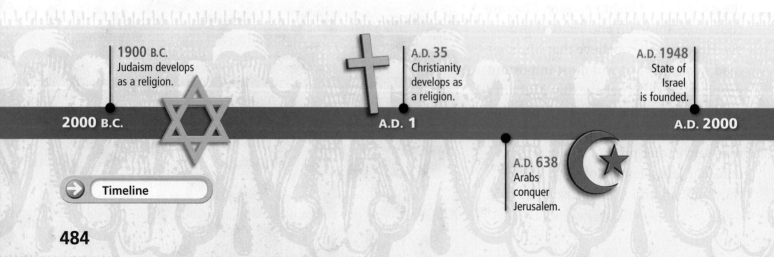

1900 B.C.
Judaism develops as a religion.

2000 B.C.

A.D. 35
Christianity develops as a religion.

A.D. 1

A.D. 1948
State of Israel is founded.

A.D. 2000

A.D. 638
Arabs conquer Jerusalem.

Timeline

484

In 1967, Syria, Jordan and Egypt massed troops on Israel's border and threatened to attack. Israel then attacked Syrian, Jordanian, and Egyptian territory. After six days, Israel controlled the West Bank of the Jordan River and East Jerusalem—both of which Jordan had controlled. Israel also gained control of the Sinai Peninsula and the Gaza Strip from Egypt and the Golan Heights from Syria. Egypt and Syria attacked Israel in 1973, hoping to regain their lost territories. However, Israel defeated them.

In 1979, the United States helped Egypt and Israel reach a peace agreement. Under this agreement, Israel returned the Sinai Peninsula to Egypt. Israel and Jordan signed a peace treaty in 1994.

War in Lebanon When Lebanon gained independence, Christians were the largest group and held the most power. After Palestinian Arabs fled Palestine, Muslims

▲ Israeli artillery in the Syrian Desert in 1973

became the largest group and demanded more power. In 1975, civil war broke out between Muslims and Christians. Syrian troops invaded Lebanon in response. In 1982, Israel invaded to stop terrorist attacks from Lebanon. War continued until 1990. Peace during the 1990s allowed Lebanon to rebuild. Israeli and Syrian troops had left by 2005. However, tensions among Lebanese groups remained.

Reading Check What are some reasons for the conflict between Jews and Arabs?

Section 2 Assessment

Key Terms

1. Use the term *ethics* to describe Jewish beliefs.

2. Explain the meaning of the term *Trinity* in Christianity.

3. Describe how anti-Semitism and Zionism affected the founding of Israel.

Key Ideas

4. In what historical order did religions influence the region of Israel and its neighbors?

5. How do the scriptures of Judaism and Christianity show that these religions have common roots?

6. What conflict between Arabs and Jews followed the United Nations plan to divide the Palestine Mandate?

Think Critically

7. **Compare Viewpoints** Why are ethics so important to Judaism and Christianity?

8. **Analyze Cause and Effect** How did conquest bring a new religion and culture to the region of Israel and its neighbors?

Essential Question

Is conflict unavoidable?

9. Give an example of a conflict in the region. Could it be avoided? If so, explain how. Go to your Student Journal to record your answers.

Religious Traditions and Art

Key Ideas
- The region of Israel and its neighbors is sacred to Judaism, Christianity, and Islam.
- The art of each religion reflects that religion's beliefs.

Key Terms
- ritual object
- illumination
- icon
- calligraphy

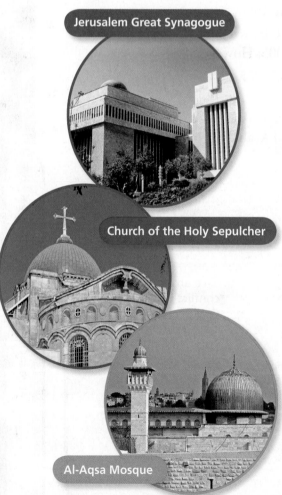

Jerusalem Great Synagogue

Church of the Holy Sepulcher

Al-Aqsa Mosque

The region around present-day Israel was important to Judaism, Christianity, and Islam from their earliest days. This was the region where Judaism developed some 4,000 years ago. Christianity was born here 2,000 years ago. Jerusalem is sacred to Muslims, who have also lived in the region for hundreds of years. Therefore, some of the artistic traditions of all three religions took shape in this region. These traditions remain important here today.

Jerusalem's Sacred Architecture

Jerusalem is sacred to all three religions. Jerusalem was the capital of the ancient kingdom of Judah.

It was once the site of the Holy Temple of Jerusalem, the most sacred building of Judaism. The Romans destroyed the Temple in A.D. 70. The Western Wall of the Temple, which still stands today, is one of the holiest sites of Judaism. After the Temple was destroyed, Jewish people built many synagogues in Jerusalem. Several modern synagogues, such as the Jerusalem Great Synagogue, have striking forms.

Jerusalem also has many places sacred to Christians. In some of these places, Christians have built churches and other religious buildings. The Church of the Holy Sepulcher in Jerusalem stands on the site where some Christians believe Jesus's body was laid after his death on the cross and where he was resurrected. This is one of the holiest sites in the world for these Christians.

The site of the former Jewish Temple is also the most sacred place in Jerusalem to Muslims. Muslims call this site the Noble Sanctuary. Here they believe that the prophet Muhammad rose to heaven one night and returned after meeting God. On this site stand two sacred Islamic buildings: Al-Aqsa Mosque and the Dome of the Rock.

Reading Check Which site in Jerusalem is sacred to both Jews and Muslims?

486

Jewish Art

Much of Jewish religious art takes the form of **ritual objects,** or objects used in religious practice. The Torah urges Jews to glorify God by using beautiful ritual objects. Synagogues are often beautifully decorated and house many ritual objects. These include Torah scrolls, which may be hand-decorated and carried in beautifully carved cases.

Jews have also illuminated texts. **Illumination** is the art of decorating books with elaborate designs and sometimes pictures in gold, silver, and bright colors. Bibles, prayer books, and other religious texts have been illuminated. The art of illumination peaked in the late 1400s. Illumination continued, however. Jewish marriage contracts, or ketubbot, were elaborately decorated. Today, ketubbot are still made, but tend to be preprinted rather than hand-decorated.

A new tradition of Jewish painters and sculptors has emerged in modern times. Jewish painters, such as Marc Chagall, have created art based on religious themes. Chagall's works include *The Bible*

Series. In these paintings, he uses the experience of Jews in Europe in the 1900s to illustrate Bible stories.

Reading Check Why are Jewish ritual objects often works of art?

Christian Art

Early Christian art was kept hidden from Roman eyes. Christians mainly used symbols, such as the cross, that only other Christians would recognize and understand.

Christian art forms developed more fully after Christianity became the religion of the Roman empire in the A.D. 300s. Christians adopted many art forms to express their faith. In fact, for hundreds of years, artists created works exclusively for Christian religious purposes.

An illuminated page from the Mishne Torah, a book of Jewish religious law ▼

Hanukah menorah ▼

487

Paintings, statues, stained glass, and illuminated manuscripts all formed a part of the Christian artistic tradition.

Works of art themselves, churches were richly decorated with religious art. Churches had paintings, sculptures, mosaics, and stained glass showing biblical figures and themes.

Christian illuminated books date back before A.D. 100. They reached their artistic height in the Middle Ages. Monks in monasteries adorned texts such as Bibles and prayer books by hand until the invention of printing in the mid-1400s.

Under the Byzantine empire, Christians created beautiful religious icons. **Icons** are images venerated, or admired and held sacred, by believers. Icons show important Christian figures, such as Jesus, his mother, Mary, and various saints and biblical events.

Icons still play an important role in the Eastern Orthodox Church. Icons are painted in a unique style. Painting as well as admiring, praying in front of the icons are considered acts of worship. One of the finest examples is a Russian icon of Mary, Our Lady of Vladimir, from the 1100s. The icon, originally of Greek origin, became a model for all Russian icons of Mary.

Reading Check Which branch of Christianity still uses icons?

Islamic Art

Islam took the ban on idols to mean that all images of animals and people were prohibited. Islamic art focuses on patterns rather than objects. Geometric patterns, flowers, and bright colors are common in Islamic art styles.

Mosaic religious figures inside the Church of the Dormition in Jerusalem ▼

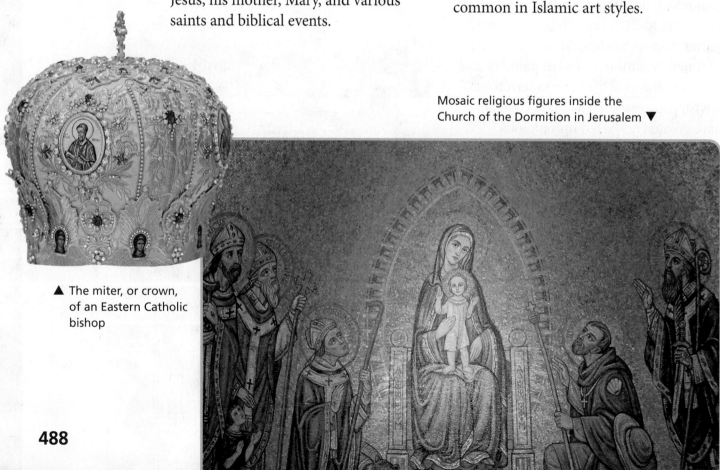

▲ The miter, or crown, of an Eastern Catholic bishop

488

Wood carvings, plaster, brickwork, mosaics and ceramic tile beautify mosques and other Islamic buildings. The architecture of mosques is an important art form in and of itself.

Although Islamic artists could not use images of people or animals, they found ways to decorate mosques. Often they created complex geometric patterns of stars, angles, squares, and more complex shapes. They used brightly colored tiles or stone grillwork to create these patterns.

For Muslims, the beauty of the written words and the book itself are very important. **Calligraphy,** or artistic lettering, is the highest Islamic art form. Muslim artists are among the world's finest calligraphers. Like Jews and Christians, Muslims illuminated their sacred manuscripts. They often combined calligraphy with illumination. Copies of the Quran have especially rich decorations.

As Islam spread throughout the world, new Islamic art styles emerged. Local styles of art were blended into the greater Islamic tradition. Islamic art has a remarkable uniformity throughout the Muslim world.

Reading Check Why is calligraphy highly valued by Muslims?

A silver and turquoise carrying case for a Quran ▶

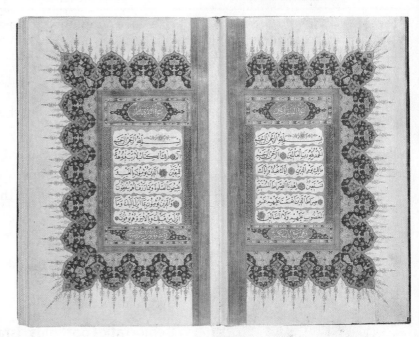

▲ This richly decorated Quran features beautiful Arabic calligraphy.

Assessment

1. How did Byzantine Christians use icons?

2. How has Jewish art changed over time?

3. What kinds of figures does Christian art usually show?

4. Why aren't paintings of people very important to Islamic art?

5. How do you think these three artistic traditions affected one another?

489

Israel and Its Neighbors Today

Key Ideas
- Political systems in the region include democracy, autocracy, and monarchy.

- Standards of living vary widely across the region.
- Israelis and Palestinian Arabs have been fighting over land and security.

- The region is important to the world because it is sacred to Judaism, Christianity, and Islam and is located at a crossroads for trade.

Key Terms
- parliamentary democracy
- capital
- hereditary monarch
- Israeli settlement
- autocracy
- Intifada

 Visual Glossary

 Reading Skill: Summarize Take notes using the graphic organizer in your journal.

This Israeli man is voting in an election, a key feature of a democracy. ▼

As you have learned, the region of Israel and its neighbors contains sites sacred to three great religions: Judaism, Christianity, and Islam. Followers of each of these religions live in the region. Tensions among religious groups have led to conflict here. However, there are many differences among the region's countries besides religion.

Different Political Systems

There are great differences among the political systems of Israel and its neighbors. These systems range from Israel's strong democracy to Syria's autocracy.

Democratic Footholds Israel has a **parliamentary democracy,** or a democracy in which parliament chooses the government. Its parliament is called the Knesset. The Knesset elects the prime minister, who runs the government. Like Britain, the nation has no written constitution. Instead, its basic laws and practices function as an unwritten constitution. All citizens 18 and older—including both Jews and Arabs—may vote in elections to choose Knesset members.

The Palestinian Authority (PA) was established to govern the Gaza Strip and West Bank, which remain subject to Israeli control. According to its constitution, the PA is also a democracy. Since 2006, however, a conflict between the two main Palestinian parties—Hamas and Fatah—has divided the PA. In 2007, armed fighters from Hamas seized control of the Gaza Strip. At the same time, Fatah took control in the parts of the West Bank governed by the PA.

Lebanon also has a democracy. However, its constitution requires that its leaders belong to specific religious groups. For example, the president must be a Christian and the prime minister must be a Sunni Muslim.

Seats in Lebanon's parliament are reserved for religious groups in a way that no longer reflects their populations. Tensions among the religious groups have made it hard for them to govern together.

A Constitutional Monarchy Jordan's King Abdullah II is a **hereditary monarch,** a ruler who is the son or younger relative of the previous ruler. The king is more powerful than most presidents, but a constitution limits his power somewhat. A two-chamber legislature passes laws. The king appoints members of one chamber. Citizens freely elect members of the other.

A Family Autocracy Syria has an autocracy. An **autocracy** is a government controlled by one person who has not won a free election. In Syria, that person is President Bashar al-Assad. He took office when his father died, so power stayed in the family. His family controls the only legal party, the Ba'ath Party. Syria has been under a state of emergency since 1963. The state of emergency <u>suspends</u> protections for Syria's people and most of the powers of parliament.

suspend, *n.,* to call off, cancel, or remove

Reading Check What is the Knesset?

Political Systems

Parliamentary Democracy
Lebanon's elected parliament, shown below, makes laws for the country.

Monarchy
The king of Jordan and his sister, shown below, are both members of the royal family.

Autocracy
Bashar al-Assad is the president of Syria, an autocracy. He relies on the support of the army to hold power.

491

Different Standards of Living

Standards of living vary throughout the region. Israel has a higher standard of living than its neighbors. Israel's neighbors are poor by comparison.

A Land of Opportunity Israelis enjoy a high standard of living, even though Israel has few resources and faces ongoing conflict. Most Israelis are employed in the service sector. Israel also has a large industrial sector.

Israel's success is partly due to its strong schools and universities. Israel offers its citizens more educational opportunities than its neighbors. As a result, it has highly skilled workers. These skilled workers produce valuable products that allow them to earn high incomes.

Israel's skilled workforce has also attracted capital from other countries. **Capital** is money or goods that are used to make products. Israel's large supply of capital has created a strong economy. Foreign aid from the United States also helps boost Israel's economy.

Because Israel has few natural resources of its own, it benefits from trade. Israel trades its people's skill for resources by selling its goods and services and buying natural resources.

Barriers to Success Israel's neighbors lack these strengths. Some earn money from limited supplies of mineral resources. However, most have relatively poor schools and universities. In many Arab countries, women have fewer opportunities for education. Ongoing tension and conflict in Lebanon and the Palestinian Territories have also discouraged the creation of capital and jobs. Corruption has also weakened the economies of some Arab countries.

Different Outcomes Because Israel's Arab neighbors have weak economies, most people in these countries are relatively poor. The middle class is small compared to Israel's. However, a small number are rich. In Lebanon, the rich often belong to families that have been wealthy for many years. In other Arab countries, wealthy people often have government connections and benefit from corruption. In these economies, the poor earn little.

Reading Check How has education helped Israel?

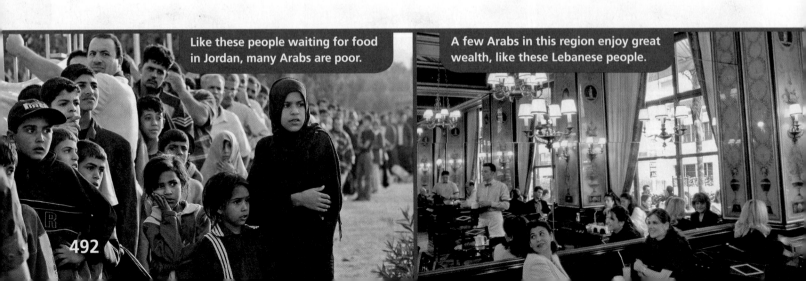

Like these people waiting for food in Jordan, many Arabs are poor.

A few Arabs in this region enjoy great wealth, like these Lebanese people.

492

Closer Look

THE ECONOMIES
of Israel and Its Neighbors

Israel's economy is different from those of its neighbors. Israel's workers make products that require advanced skills and technology. Neighboring economies depend mainly on activities that require less skill and technology. As a result, Israelis tend to have higher incomes than their neighbors.

THINK CRITICALLY If education improved in countries neighboring Israel, how might that affect their economies?

Workers preparing medicines in Israel

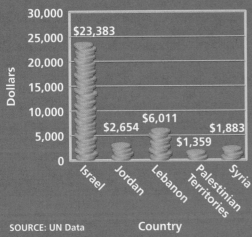

Per Capita GDP, 2007

Dollars — Country

- Israel: $23,383
- Jordan: $2,654
- Lebanon: $6,011
- Palestinian Territories: $1,359
- Syria: $1,883

SOURCE: UN Data

Farmers delivering wheat in Syria

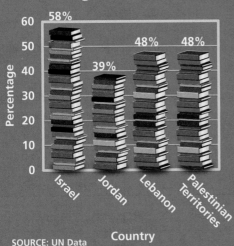

College Enrollment

Percentage — Country

- Israel: 58%
- Jordan: 39%
- Lebanon: 48%
- Palestinian Territories: 48%

SOURCE: UN Data

Shoppers at an outdoor market in Jordan

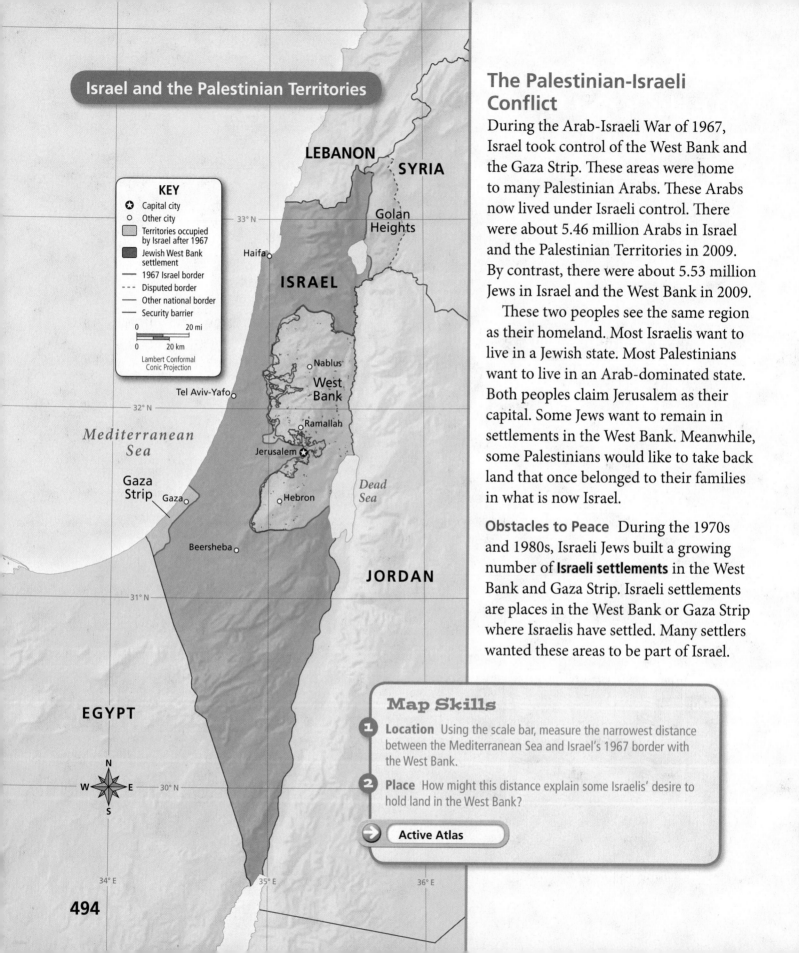

Israel and the Palestinian Territories

KEY
- ★ Capital city
- ○ Other city
- Territories occupied by Israel after 1967
- Jewish West Bank settlement
- 1967 Israel border
- Disputed border
- Other national border
- Security barrier

0 — 20 mi
0 — 20 km
Lambert Conformal Conic Projection

LEBANON
SYRIA
Golan Heights
Haifa
ISRAEL
Nablus
West Bank
Tel Aviv-Yafo
Ramallah
Jerusalem ★
Mediterranean Sea
Gaza Strip
Gaza
Hebron
Dead Sea
Beersheba
JORDAN
EGYPT

33° N
32° N
31° N
30° N
34° E
35° E
36° E

The Palestinian-Israeli Conflict

During the Arab-Israeli War of 1967, Israel took control of the West Bank and the Gaza Strip. These areas were home to many Palestinian Arabs. These Arabs now lived under Israeli control. There were about 5.46 million Arabs in Israel and the Palestinian Territories in 2009. By contrast, there were about 5.53 million Jews in Israel and the West Bank in 2009.

These two peoples see the same region as their homeland. Most Israelis want to live in a Jewish state. Most Palestinians want to live in an Arab-dominated state. Both peoples claim Jerusalem as their capital. Some Jews want to remain in settlements in the West Bank. Meanwhile, some Palestinians would like to take back land that once belonged to their families in what is now Israel.

Obstacles to Peace During the 1970s and 1980s, Israeli Jews built a growing number of **Israeli settlements** in the West Bank and Gaza Strip. Israeli settlements are places in the West Bank or Gaza Strip where Israelis have settled. Many settlers wanted these areas to be part of Israel.

Map Skills

1 **Location** Using the scale bar, measure the narrowest distance between the Mediterranean Sea and Israel's 1967 border with the West Bank.

2 **Place** How might this distance explain some Israelis' desire to hold land in the West Bank?

→ Active Atlas

494

By 1988, Israel controlled more than half of the land in the West Bank, although Israelis made up less than one tenth of the West Bank's population. Some Israelis think it was wrong to build the Israeli settlements. Most other nations have opposed the settlements.

During this time, Palestinians living in Arab countries had launched repeated terrorist attacks against Israel. Many attacks <u>targeted</u> Israeli civilians. Civilians are people other than soldiers.

In the late 1980s, some Palestinians began the Intifada. The **Intifada** was a campaign of violent resistance against Israeli control. Israeli troops fought the Intifada. More than 1,000 people died, mainly young Palestinians.

A Peace Plan Frustrated In 1994, Israel agreed to a peace plan with the Palestine Liberation Organization, or PLO, which represented Palestinians. This plan created the Palestinian Authority to rule the parts of the West Bank and Gaza Strip not controlled by Israel. Israel agreed to remove settlers from the Gaza Strip and parts of the West Bank. The PLO recognized Israel's right to exist and agreed to end terrorist attacks on Israel.

However, each side accused the other of violating the peace plan, and the plan failed. In 2000, Palestinians launched a second Intifada. Terrorists also attacked civilians inside Israel. These attacks brought the peace process to a halt, and Israel again fought back. The fighting died down around 2005 when Israel removed its settlers from the Gaza Strip.

Israel built security barriers around the Gaza Strip and the West Bank in the 1990s and 2000s. The West Bank barrier separated Arab from Jewish areas to prevent attacks on Israel. It also separated some Palestinian villages from each other and blocked some Palestinians' access to their farmland. The barriers succeeded in reducing attacks on Israel but made life more difficult for Palestinians.

target, *v.,* to aim for, make a target

Palestinians at a checkpoint along Israel's security barrier ▼

myWorld Activity
Peace Conference

Ongoing Conflict and Hopes for Peace
In 2006, a Palestinian political party called Hamas won the most seats in the Palestinian parliament. Hamas has stated that it wants to eliminate the state of Israel. Hamas fighters took control of the Gaza Strip in 2007. Israel then imposed a blockade on the Gaza Strip, blocking all traffic by air, sea, or land. Hamas began shooting rockets into Israel. These rockets killed more than a dozen Israeli civilians.

In response, Israel bombed the Gaza Strip in 2008 and 2009 and sent troops to kill or capture Hamas fighters. Hundreds of Palestinian civilians were killed, as were hundreds of Hamas fighters.

Most Palestinians and Israelis want peace. Many support creating an independent Palestinian state in the Palestinian Territories alongside Israel. However, violence from both sides will need to end for this solution to work.

Reading Check Which city do both Israelis and Palestinians claim as their capital?

A Region of Worldwide Importance

Israel contains sites holy to three major world religions. The region lies along key trade routes linking three continents.

A Region Sacred to Three Religions
Jews, Christians, and Muslims all believe that they worship the God who made a covenant with Abraham. This region is the Jewish Holy Land and the land where Jesus lived and died. According to Islamic tradition, Jerusalem is the place where the prophet Muhammad rose to heaven. Jews, Christians, and Muslims retain an intense interest in this region.

At the Intersection of Three Continents Israel and its neighbors sit at a continental crossroads. Throughout history, many peoples passed through the region. Ancient trade routes through the region connect Africa, Europe, and Asia.

Bombing in Israel
A bus in Israel blown up by Palestinian suicide bombers

Bombing in the Palestinian Territories
A neighborhood in the Gaza Strip damaged by Israeli bombing

A Gateway to Vital Oil Supplies

Southwest Asia has the world's largest oil reserves. Most of these reserves surround the Persian Gulf to the east of Israel and its neighbors. Israel, Jordan, and Lebanon have almost no oil reserves, while Syria has only small reserves.

Still, Europe and other parts of the world depend on oil that must pass through or past Israel and its neighbors. It is difficult to reach the Persian Gulf by air from the United States or Europe without flying over this region.

For this reason, Israel and its neighbors have great economic and military importance. Regional conflicts could disrupt the flow of oil from the Persian Gulf. Thus, tensions within the region can drive up oil prices. For military as well as cultural reasons, the United States and other nations have a strong interest in Israel and its neighbors.

Reading Check Why is this region so important for trade?

my **Story** ⬛ Photo

Jerusalem is a city sacred to three religions: Judaism, Christianity, and Islam. In this photograph, Jews worship at Jerusalem's Western Wall, a sacred Jewish site and a remnant of the Jewish Temple. Both Christian and Muslim holy sites lie close by.

Section 3 Assessment

Key Terms

1. Use the terms *parliamentary democracy* and *autocracy* to describe governments in the region.

2. Define the terms *Intifada* and *Israeli settlement*.

3. Describe the role of capital in Israel's economy.

Key Ideas

4. Describe differences in standards of living in the region.

5. What are the main reasons for the conflict beween the Israelis and the Palestinians?

6. How does the location of oil make Israel and its neighbors important to the rest of the world?

Think Critically

7. **Draw Inferences** Israelis and Palestinians agreed to a peace plan in 1994. Why do you think both sides accused the other of breaking its promises?

8. **Compare and Contrast** How are the democracies in the region the same and different?

? Essential Question

Is conflict unavoidable?

9. What evidence from this chapter—including the myStory in the chapter opener—shows how Arabs and Jews might avoid conflict? Go to your Student Journal to record your answers.

Voices of Fear and Hope

Key Idea
- Both Israelis and Palestinians have experienced fear, pain, and loss during their conflict, but many remain hopeful for peace in the future.

In late 2008, low-level conflict between Israelis and Palestinians led to an all-out war that continued into 2009. Palestinian fighters from Hamas fired missiles from the Gaza Strip into Israel. Israel responded by bombing Gaza. Still, there are many on both sides who hold out hope for peace. Below are the words of one Palestinian and one Israeli. An Israeli airstrike killed Saber Abu Reesh's brother. A missile from Hamas killed Tziona Peleg's niece.

▲ Palestinians participate in a candlelight vigil.

Stop at each circled letter on the right to think about the text. Then answer the question with the same letter on the left.

A **Analyze** How does his brother's death affect Saber Abu Reesh's attitude toward peace?

B **Summarize** What conditions does this Palestinian require for peace?

C **Infer** Why does Saber Abu Reesh see his brother as an innocent victim?

dignity, *n.,* state of being worthy of honor and respect

mobile, *n.,* cellphone

A Palestinian Brother

" I can't forget the death of my brother, but in order to stop more **(A)** killing . . . I would agree to reach a fair and lasting peace. . . . [B]ut this **(B)** peace must achieve our goals to live in <u>dignity</u> and respect. . . . I heard that Israel had begun bombing the Gaza Strip. I was afraid that something had happened to my brother, Osama, so I tried to call his <u>mobile</u> but he didn't answer. I later **(C)** found him dead. . . . My brother . . . didn't belong to Hamas; he was just trying to look after his family. "

—Saber Abu Reesh, Maghazi, Gaza Strip, February 3, 2009

Stop at each circled letter on the right to think about the text. Then answer the question with the same letter on the left.

D **Identify Evidence** Why does Tziona Peleg believe that peace is possible?

E **Summarize** Who does Tziona Peleg believe is responsible for her niece's death?

F **Infer** What approach does this Israeli think might help resolve the conflict?

colleague, *n.,* co-worker, peer

extremist, *n.,* a person who takes an extreme position or carries out extreme actions

bloodshed, *n.,* injury and loss of life

An Israeli Aunt

" In my work as a hospital nurse, I come into daily contact with Arabs, both patients and staff, and I have excellent relations with them. . . .

D These people are my friends and my <u>colleagues</u>. Despite the fact that [my niece] Irit is dead, I still say that there is a real possibility to reach a solution. But these are not the

E people who killed my niece. It's the <u>extremists</u> who killed my niece . . .

F [M]aybe it should be the extremists that we talk to. Otherwise, where is the end to this <u>bloodshed</u>? "

—Tziona Peleg, Ashdod, Israel,
February 3, 2009

Israelis with candles and flowers mark the end of a 7-day mourning period. ▶

Analyze the Documents

1. **Compare and Contrast** What does each of the speakers think it will take to find peace?
2. **Writing Task** Use the experiences and opinions of the two speakers to write a paragraph explaining the role of civilians in the Israeli-Palestinian conflict.

499

Chapter Assessment

Key Terms and Ideas

1. **Analyze Cause and Effect** How does the region's location help explain the many conflicts it has suffered?

2. **Summarize** Why did Palestinians begin the **Intifada?**

3. **Synthesize** How do **rain shadows** create deserts?

4. **Draw Conclusions** How are **ethics** important to the religion of Judaism?

5. **Categorize** What are the core beliefs of Christianity, including the **Trinity?**

6. **Compare and Contrast** What is life like for most Arabs in the region? Most Israelis? All people in the region?

7. **Draw Inferences** Why is the future of **aquifers** so important to the people of the region?

Think Critically

8. **Analyze Cause and Effect** How are Arabs in the region different from one another? How are they all different from most Israelis? How have differences within the groups led to greater conflict in the region?

9. **Identify Evidence** Defend the statement that if the region had more water, there would be less conflict. Use evidence from this chapter.

10. **Compare and Contrast** How are the conflicts within Lebanon similar to and different from the Palestinian-Israeli conflict?

11. **Core Concepts: Culture and Geography** What role has religion played in the history of Israel and its neighbors?

Places to Know

For each place, write the letter from the map that shows its location.

12. Syria

13. Jordan River

14. Euphrates River

15. Jerusalem

16. Lebanon

17. Gaza Strip

18. **Estimate** Using the scale, estimate the distance between Jerusalem and the Gaza Strip.

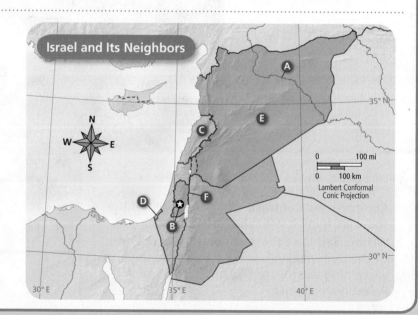

Israel and Its Neighbors

? Essential Question

myWorld Chapter Activity

History Museum Tour You want to teach other people about the history of Israel and its neighbors. Develop a stop on a history museum tour to tell about one time period. Present your tour stop and view other tour stops, then join a discussion about the entire tour.

21st Century Learning

Analyze Media Content

Find three articles about conflicts between Israelis and Palestinians. Using what you know from the chapter, analyze the articles. How accurate are the facts? Is there evidence of bias, or a favoring of one view over another? Does the article clearly explain the current conflict and connect it to the larger conflicts in the region?

Document-Based Questions

Success Tracker™
Online at myworldgeography.com

Use your knowledge of Israel and its neighbors, as well as Documents A and B, to answer questions 1–3.

Document A

Peace and Prosperity in Israel and the Palestinian Territories

How important is peace to economic prosperity?

- ■ % very
- ■ % somewhat
- ▨ % not very

Israel: 78% very, 12% somewhat, 8% not very
Palestinian Territories: 83% very, 12% somewhat, 4% not very

SOURCE: Gallup Poll, December, 2007

1. In 2007, what percentage of Israelis felt that peace was very important to their country's economic future?

A 70%

B 77%

C 78%

D 83%

Document B

"Today, many policy makers [call for] a total separation between Israel and the Palestinians. But the [Palestinians] cannot develop a prosperous economy . . . in economic isolation. Separation will result in economic ruin. . . . The fates of Israelis and Palestinians are economically intertwined."

—Daniel Doron, "Mideast Peace Can Start with Economic Growth," Wall Street Journal, March 12, 2009

2. According to Document B, what must Israeli and Palestinian economies do?

A The Israeli economy must control the Palestinian economy.

B The Palestinian economy must control that of Israel.

C The two economies should work together.

D The two economies should separate entirely.

3. Writing Task Do you think the views expressed in Document A support the views expressed in Document B? Explain.

myworldgeography.com Self-Test

Chapter 11

Iran, Turkey, and Cyprus

? Essential Question

What are the challenges of diversity?

KEY
— National border
--- Disputed border
⊕ Capital city
○ Other city

0 ___ 200 mi
0 ___ 200 km
Lambert Conformal Conic Projection

Where in the World Are Iran, Turkey, and Cyprus?

Washington, D.C., to Urfa: 5,780 miles

← Belediye

↑ Eyyüp Peygamber

↑ Harran

↑ Havaalanı ✈

Akçakale ↗

my Story

Bilal Looks Forward

Explore the Essential Question
- at my worldgeography.com
- using the myWorld Chapter Activity
- with the Student Journal

In this section, you'll read about Bilal, a young Kurdish man from Turkey who lives in Urfa. What does Bilal's story tell you about life in Iran, Turkey, and Cyprus today?

Story by Can Ertür for myWorld Geography Online

Looking out over the rooftops of Urfa, 18-year-old Bilal is proud of his town. This town, located in southeastern Turkey, has been home to Bilal and his family for most of his life.

"Urfa has a very rich history. I want people to come to see Urfa. It is a beautiful place," says Bilal.

The city of Urfa is several thousand years old. It was once called Edessa, and was one of the most important cities in the area in ancient times. Like most of Urfa's people, Bilal is a member of the Kurdish ethnic group. He is proud to be both a Kurd and a citizen of the Republic of Turkey.

Kurdish people are a minority in Turkey. For many years, the Turkish government tried to suppress Kurdish culture. Kurds were not allowed to speak the Kurdish language or even give their children Kurdish names. Many Kurds fought the Turkish government because of this. Some still do, although today the government treats Kurdish people better.

Bilal believes that Turks and Kurds are getting along well in Turkey today. "Kurds have been living here for many years. Turks and Kurds have fought in wars together side by side. There are no

my worldgeography.com On Assignment

503

Feeding the fish in the courtyard of a famous mosque in Urfa.

Bilal hard at work serving tea

problems between the Kurds and Turks."

Bilal speaks Kurdish with his parents and Turkish with his four brothers and two sisters.

"Turkish has become so widespread," he explains. "Older Kurds did not speak much Turkish, but today we speak more Turkish than Kurdish. Turkish is much more useful."

Bilal has been working since he was nine years old. He goes to school as well. "I work and go to school because it is necessary. In the morning I work in the tea house of a hospital. I serve tea. I go to school in the afternoon."

Bilal's father works day jobs during the winter and grows pistachios in the summer. "There are a lot of pistachios grown in this part of Turkey," Bilal adds with a smile. "I work on the farm all summer when I am not at school."

Bilal's family has only a small plot of land, so they mainly work in his uncle's field. Lack of water is a constant problem on the farm and across Turkey.

"Turkey is surrounded by sea, but salt water is useless," Bilal notes. "Drinking water is scarce. There will be conflict over water.

A statue of the founder of modern Turkey in Bilal's hometown

HAYATTA EN HAKİKİ MÜRŞİ İLİMDİR
K. ATATÜRK

504

Bilal in class

Bilal and his family at dinner

Something must be done about that."

Bilal is concerned about some of the things that lie ahead for his country. He follows current events closely by reading newspapers on the Internet.

"I read the Internet every day," he says. "If we want to see ahead, we have to learn from mistakes and try not repeat them."

Though Bilal worries about the future, he is encouraged by the progress he has already seen. Urfa's new mayor has brought about many changes to the city, according to Bilal.

"The roads here were awful. My younger brothers and sisters always would come home covered in mud. The mayor fixed the roads. He built new green parks and gardens. I believe he will win again next time around."

Bilal really looks forward to his weekends. "I spend most of my time playing soccer. Like everyone else, everywhere, we like to listen to music and play football." A few years ago, Bilal even made plans to move to Istanbul and become a professional soccer player.

"Back then I thought I wanted to be a soccer player," he laughs. "But as time goes by people change. At one time I wanted to become an engineer, but it was not possible. Now I would like to be a historian. As you investigate the distant past, eventually you come to the recent past. When you study the recent past, you can use it to see ahead."

➜ myStory Video

Join Bilal as he shows you more about his life in Turkey.

Meet the Journalist

Name Can Ertür
Favorite Moment Bilal's description of the peaceful world he hopes to live in

A group of young children from Urfa ▼

505

Chapter Atlas

Key Ideas
- Mountains cover much of this region and have a major effect on rainfall patterns and climate.
- The location of water resources is important to land use and settlement patterns.
- Oil and natural gas are important to Iran's economy.
- A variety of ethnic and religious groups call this region home.

Key Terms • strait • shamal • qanat • Zoroastrianism

 Visual Glossary

 Reading Skill: Label an Outline Map Take notes using the outline map in your journal.

▲ Mount Ericyes, in central Turkey

A young Turkish woman ▶

Physical Features

Iran and Turkey form a broad band stretching from the Mediterranean Sea to Afghanistan. South of Turkey, in the Mediterranean, lies the island of Cyprus. Much of this region is mountainous.

Mountains and Seas Turkey is located on two continents, Europe and Asia. Most of Turkey is made up of the peninsula of Anatolia, in Asia. Anatolia is bordered by the Black Sea to the north, the Mediterranean to the south, and a narrow waterway connecting the two seas.

Iran, Turkey, and Cyprus: Physical

Map Skills

Location Which has a higher elevation, the Elburz mountains or the Kavir desert?

Places to Know!
Label the following places on the outline map in your Student Journal: Black Sea, Zagros Mountains, Taurus Moutains, Anatolian Plateau, Cyprus.

→ Active Atlas

KEY
Elevation

Feet	Meters
6,000	1,829
3,000	914
1,000	305
500	152
Sea level	Sea level

— National border
--- Disputed border

0 — 400 mi
0 — 400 km
Lambert Conformal Conic Projection

A smaller part of Turkey is in Europe. It is divided from Asia by water. The city of Istanbul is split between the two continents. It guards a part of the waterway between the Mediterranean Sea and the Black Sea, a strait called the Bosporus. A **strait** is a narrow body of water that cuts through land, connecting two larger bodies of water. Because of its location on the Bosporus strait, Istanbul has been a major port and trading center for nearly two thousand years.

Two bands of mountains extend across Turkey from east to west along the northern and southern edges of the country.

These mountains join in eastern Turkey, where they form a rugged a landscape. The mountains surround the high Anatolian plateau. Narrow plains lie along the coasts.

Like Turkey, Iran is ringed by mountains. They surround a central plateau. Iran's plateau is larger and flatter than Turkey's. It is mostly covered by desert. Iran also has lowlands in the northwest, along the shores of the Caspian Sea, and to the south, along the Persian Gulf.

Similarly, two bands of mountains run across the north and south of Cyprus. Between them lies a highland plateau.

myWorld Activity
Trade Talk for Turkey

my worldgeography.com

Active Atlas

507

vary, *v.,* to be different

A Natural Hazard Earthquakes occur frequently in this region. In recent decades, both Iran and Turkey have been shaken by severe quakes that have killed thousands. After these earthquakes, people have rebuilt buildings or added wall supports. Most do not move away, though. Hundreds of thousands of people live in quake-prone cities, including Istanbul. Some regions that earthquakes often strike have good farmland. Turkey's government has passed laws requiring builders to construct buildings that can withstand earthquakes.

Reading Check Why is Istanbul's location so important?

Climate and Rainfall

Climates <u>vary</u> across Iran and Turkey. Both temperatures and rainfall differ from one area to another. This variation is in large part because of the mountains and the mix of inland and coastal areas.

Iran In northwestern Iran, summers are warm but winters are generally below freezing. People to the south and east have much longer, hotter summers and milder winters. In some areas of Iran, summer temperatures can reach as high as $110°F$. Adding to the summer heat are dry winds that blow across the far

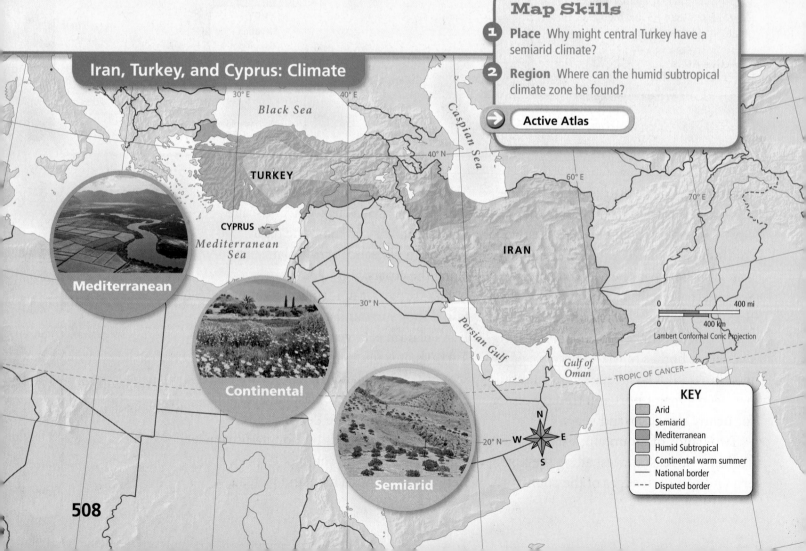

Map Skills

1. **Place** Why might central Turkey have a semiarid climate?
2. **Region** Where can the humid subtropical climate zone be found?

Active Atlas

Iran, Turkey, and Cyprus: Climate

KEY
- Arid
- Semiarid
- Mediterranean
- Humid Subtropical
- Continental warm summer
- National border
- Disputed border

508

western part of Iran from northwest to southeast. These winds are called the **shamal.** The shamal and other winds blow almost constantly during the summer. They can start powerful dust storms.

Rainfall in different parts of Iran varies. The wettest area is along the shore of the Caspian Sea. There, moist winds blowing over the sea strike the Elburz Mountains. As the air rises, it cools and drops its moisture on the coastal plain. Areas on the other side of the mountains are a desert that receives little or no rain.

Cyprus and Turkey Cyprus has a Mediterranean climate. Hot, dry summers are followed by milder, rainier winters. Farmers depend on the autumn and winter rains for their crops.

Parts of Turkey also have a typical Mediterranean climate like that of Greece or Lebanon. But seas on three sides and high mountains change climate patterns. Coastal areas tend to have milder winters than interior regions. Winter temperatures can remain around freezing in the central plateau and plunge well below freezing in the eastern mountains.

Coastal areas in Turkey receive more rain than the central plateau or the mountains—32 or more inches a year on the shores of the Black Sea and 24 to 32 inches along the western coast. As in Iran, the mountains create a rain shadow. As a result, the central plateau receives only about 16 inches a year.

Reading Check Why does the central plateau in Turkey receive little rain?

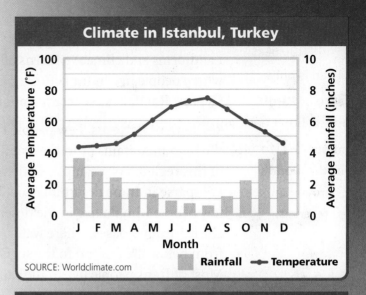

Climate in Istanbul, Turkey

SOURCE: Worldclimate.com

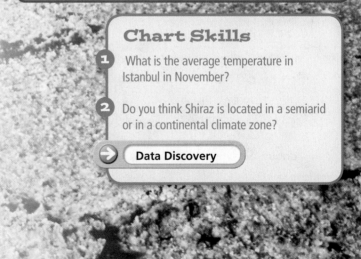

Climate in Shiraz, Iran

SOURCE: Worldclimate.com

Chart Skills

1. What is the average temperature in Istanbul in November?

2. Do you think Shiraz is located in a semiarid or in a continental climate zone?

→ **Data Discovery**

A salt flat in Iran's Kavir desert ▶

my worldgeography.com Data Discovery

509

Land Use and Energy

Landforms and climate patterns affect where people live in Iran, Turkey, and Cyprus. Rainfall is especially important.

Settlement Patterns Few people live in the high mountains or in the driest areas of this region. For example, settlements are sparse in Iran's desert interior. Those few people who do live in the desert cluster around oases, where water comes from below the ground to the surface. Most of Iran's people live in the rainier western and northern parts of the country, including the capital Tehran.

In Turkey, more than half of the people live along the narrow coastal plains, especially in the milder and wetter north. The hotter southern coast has fewer people, as does the interior. Similarly, most people in Cyprus live along the coastal plains.

Iran, Turkey, and Cyprus receive more rainfall than most other countries in Southwest Asia, but water is still scarce. In ancient times, the people of Iran developed a clever method for bringing water to their homes and fields. First, they looked in the foothills of mountains for aquifers, or underground sources of water. Then they built tunnels from the aquifers to their villages. These tunnels, called **qanats,** channeled water to their villages. They used the water to irrigate their fields.

The qanat system has an advantage over irrigation channels on the surface. Because most of the channel is below the ground, the water does not dry up, or evaporate, even in Iran's hot climate.

Although qanats are still used today, wells and above-ground irrigation are also widely practiced in Iran. They account for most of the country's water usage. But some people argue that this change has been a mistake. According to one Iranian urban planner and architect,

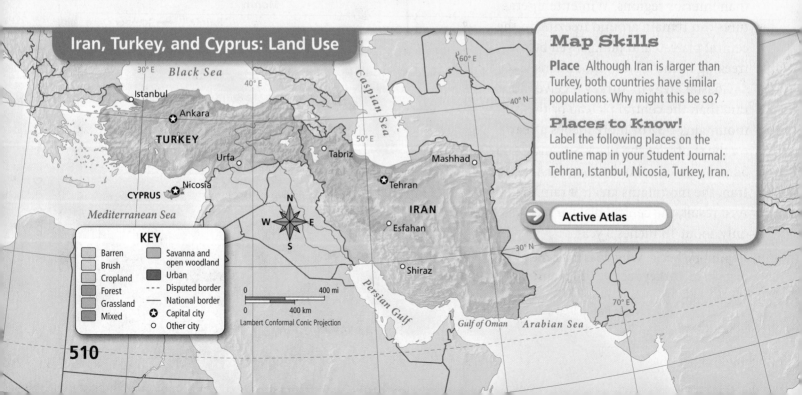

Iran, Turkey, and Cyprus: Land Use

KEY
- Barren
- Brush
- Cropland
- Forest
- Grassland
- Mixed
- Savanna and open woodland
- Urban
- --- Disputed border
- — National border
- ✪ Capital city
- ○ Other city

0 — 400 mi
0 — 400 km
Lambert Conformal Conic Projection

Map Skills

Place Although Iran is larger than Turkey, both countries have similar populations. Why might this be so?

Places to Know!
Label the following places on the outline map in your Student Journal: Tehran, Istanbul, Nicosia, Turkey, Iran.

→ **Active Atlas**

" in comparison to qanats, wells have a shorter life span (that is between 20–50 years), whereas qanats hold good for centuries. Excavation of such wells in the past half a century has further led to the drying up of wells and qanats both, contributing to drought and increasing water shortages "

—Mohammad Reza Haeri

Oil and Natural Gas In today's world, oil and natural gas are also precious resources. Iran has large deposits of both fuels. It has more oil than all but four countries, and has 10 percent of the world's natural gas. Iran's oil is a vital source of national income. Oil sales provide more than 85 percent of the government's income.

Turkey has very little oil and must import most of its fuel. It does have coal and generates hydroelectric power from mountain rivers. Cyprus has few energy resources but uses its sunny climate to make solar power.

Reading Check What important resources are plentiful in Iran?

An oil refinery in Iran. Oil is by far Iran's most important export.

Iran's Exports

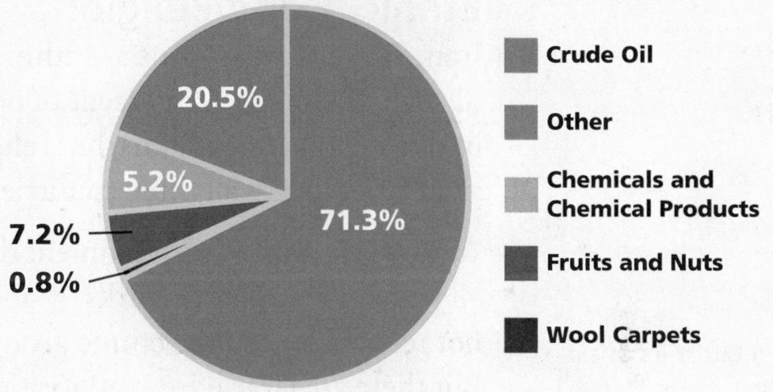

20.5%

5.2%

7.2%

0.8%

71.3%

- Crude Oil
- Other
- Chemicals and Chemical Products
- Fruits and Nuts
- Wool Carpets

SOURCE: *Time Alamanac,* 2009

Chart Skills

What percentage of Iran's exports does crude oil make up?

→ Data Discovery

◄ A rose farm in Iran

my worldgeography.com

Active Atlas

511

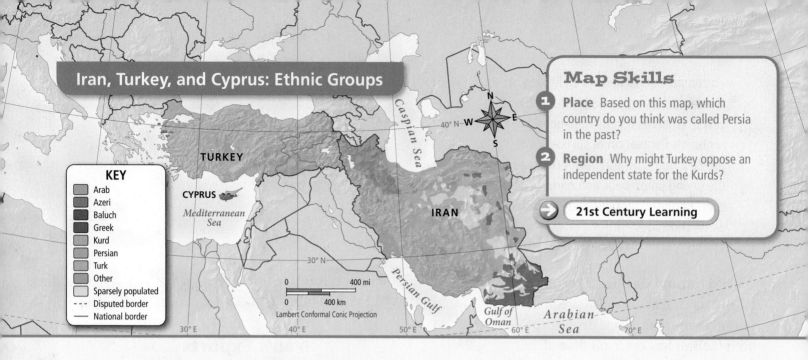

Iran, Turkey, and Cyprus: Ethnic Groups

KEY
- Arab
- Azeri
- Baluch
- Greek
- Kurd
- Persian
- Turk
- Other
- Sparsely populated
- - - Disputed border
- — National border

Lambert Conformal Conic Projection

Map Skills

1 **Place** Based on this map, which country do you think was called Persia in the past?

2 **Region** Why might Turkey oppose an independent state for the Kurds?

→ 21st Century Learning

Ethnicity and Religion

Iran, Turkey, and Cyprus are ethnically diverse. More than 97 percent of people in this region are Muslims, but religious minorities live in all three countries.

Turkey The Turkish government defines all people in Turkey as Turks. It does not recognize separate ethnic groups. But there are large ethnic minorities in

Turkey. About 80 percent of the people in Turkey are ethnic Turks, while about 20 percent are Kurds. Small numbers of people from other ethnic groups, such as Arabs and Greeks, also live in Turkey.

The Kurdish people live in a region that is split among Iran, Turkey, Iraq, and Syria. Many Kurds in these countries seek independence or self-government.

A Christian priest in Cyprus ▼

Muslim worshipers in Turkey ▼

512

In the past, Turkey banned all expressions of Kurdish culture. The government fought Kurdish rebels who wanted their own independent country. Recently, Turkey has given the Kurds more rights and the situation has improved.

Most people in Turkey are Sunni Muslims. About a quarter are Alevis, who practice a form of Shia Islam. Smaller groups include Christian Greeks and Armenians, along with Jews.

Iran In the past Iran was called Persia. Today just over half of Iranians are ethnic Persians. About a quarter of people in Iran are Azeris. They live mainly near neighboring Azerbaijan, a mostly Azeri country. Several million Kurds also live in Iran.

Nearly all people in Iran are Muslims. Almost 9 in 10 practice Shia Islam. Sunnis are a minority. Jews and Christians, who have lived in Iran since ancient times, form much smaller minorities. Today, more Jews live in Iran and Turkey

◀ A Zoroastrian fire temple in Iran

than in any other Muslim countries.

A very small number of Iranians practice **Zoroastrianism,** an Iranian religion that dates back to ancient times. Many more practice the Baha'i faith, which was founded in Iran in the 1800s.

Cyprus People who live in Cyprus are called Cypriots. About three quarters of Cypriots are Greek-speaking Christians. The rest are Turkish-speaking Muslims. Conflict between these groups has occurred in recent <u>decades</u>.

Reading Check Which large minority group is found in both Iran and Turkey?

decade, *n.,* period of ten years

Section 1 Assessment

Key Terms

1. How does the rain shadow affect climate in Iran and Turkey?

2. What are qanats, and why are they important?

Key Ideas

3. How do people in Turkey adapt to living in an earthquake-prone area?

4. How have landforms and climate influenced where people live in these countries?

5. How does the religious makeup of Iran show the long history of this region?

Think Critically

6. **Compare and Contrast** How are the landforms of Turkey and Iran similar? How are they different?

7. **Analyze Cause and Effect** Why do these countries have ethnic diversity?

Essential Question

What are the challenges of diversity?

8. What political issues have arisen from the ethnic diversity of these countries? Go to your Student Journal to record your answer.

513

Section 2

History of Iran, Turkey, and Cyprus

Key Ideas
- The countries in this region are at a cultural crossroads, blending influences from many different regions and peoples.
- Civilizations of this region have made important contributions to world culture.
- In the 1900s, empires in this region fell and were replaced by modern nations.

Key Terms
- satrap
- Ataturk
- millet
- Ayatollah
- shah
- Armenian genocide

 **Visual Glossary**

Reading Skill: Sequence Take notes using the graphic organizer in your journal.

The Persian emperor Darius ▼

As you have read, Iran used to be called Persia. Ancient Persia was influenced by Mesopotamian civilization, in modern-day Iraq.

The Persian Empire

Around 550 B.C., the Persian king Cyrus the Great conquered the Babylonian empire, in Mesopotamia, and many other lands. He created the Persian empire.

Cyrus and the rulers who followed him spread Persian control from modern Pakistan and Afghanistan in the east to modern Turkey, Cyprus, and Egypt in the west. This empire lasted about two hundred years. A Persian ruler was called the King of Kings, or the Great King.

◄ An image of archers painted on the wall in Darius' palace at Susa

514

Government and Trade To control their empire, Persian rulers sent a governor, called a **satrap,** to run each province. A general commanded the army in each area. A third official collected taxes. By splitting power, rulers made sure no satrap grew too powerful. They also regularly sent inspectors to observe these officials and report back to the king.

The Persians built a system of roads to improve communication across their empire. The roads made travel faster for soldiers and messengers sent by the government. They also made it easier for merchants to carry goods.

To help people from far-away regions trade fairly with one another, the Persians created a system of weights and measures. They also minted, or produced, coins that could be used across the empire.

Life in the Persian Empire Although they were feared conquerors, the Persians were not overly harsh rulers. They respected local traditions, though at the same time they were willing to crush revolts brutally.

Art flourished under Persian rule. Kings brought artists and craftspeople to their capital. They built large palaces decorated with sculptures and jewels.

Conquest by Alexander the Great
The Persian empire met its match in Alexander the Great. In the 330s B.C., Alexander led armies from Greece into Persia. He conquered the Persian empire.

Alexander adopted some customs of Persian rulers. For example, he wore Persian-style clothing. Alexander planned to

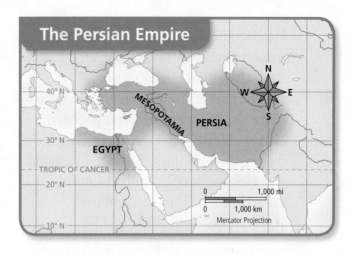

The Persian Empire

rule with Persian help. However, after his sudden death, his empire broke up into smaller kingdoms ruled by Greek kings.

These kingdoms spread Greek culture in the region. Much of modern-day Turkey became Greek-speaking. Eventually these Greek kingdoms fell too.

A new Persian empire, called the Sassanian empire, took their place. That empire dominated Iran for four hundred years. The Sassanian rulers made Zoroastrianism their official religion, though many Jews and Christians lived under their rule.

Reading Check How did the Persians govern their empire?

A gold model of a chariot from the Persian empire ▼

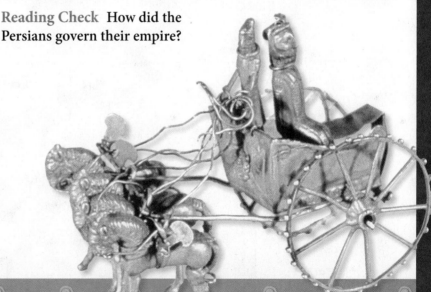

515

Romans, Arabs, and Turks

As you have read, the Roman empire conquered Turkey and Cyprus. The eastern part of the Roman empire, usually called the Byzantine empire, survived after the western part fell. It ruled parts of the region until the A.D 1400s. Its capital was Constantinople, called Istanbul today. It was a Christian empire.

establish, v., to found or build

The Arab Conquest of Iran In the 600s, Muhammad began to preach Islam in Arabia. His followers spread Islam in many regions. They defeated the Sassanian empire and conquered Iran.

Over time, most Iranians converted to Islam. Iran became a vital part of Muslim economic and cultural life. The first madrassas, or Islamic religious schools, were founded there in the 900s before spreading to other areas. However, ethnic pride remained strong in Iran. Its native language and culture survived.

The Ottoman Empire In the 1000s, Muslim Turks from Central Asia migrated into Turkey and Iran and began to gain power. They spread their language and culture. They gave the country of Turkey its name.

The Turks established kingdoms in the region. By the 1400s, the kingdom of the Turkish Ottoman family became the most powerful. The Ottomans claimed to be caliphs, or religious leaders of all Muslims. They captured Constantinople, and ended the Byzantine empire, in 1453. The Ottomans made Constantinople, now called Istanbul, their capital. They built an

Map Skills

1 **Place** Which empire ruled the Islamic holy cities of Mecca and Medina?

2 **Region** Which empire was based in Persia?

→ Active Atlas

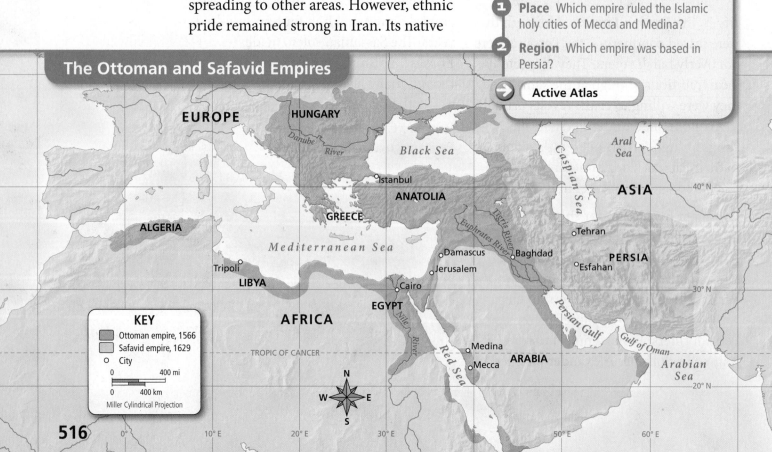

The Ottoman and Safavid Empires

KEY
- Ottoman empire, 1566
- Safavid empire, 1629
- City
- 0 — 400 mi
- 0 — 400 km
- Miller Cylindrical Projection

empire that spread over three continents.

The Muslim Ottomans ruled over many Jews and Christians. They allowed their subjects to practice their own religions. Some Jews and Christians rose to high positions in the government. Religious groups were organized into **millets,** or self-governing religious communities. Millets had their own laws and leaders.

Perhaps the greatest Ottoman ruler was Suleiman the Magnificent, who conquered much of southeastern Europe. In the 1500s, Suleiman was probably the richest ruler in the world, and one of the most powerful. He built mosques, schools, and libraries. His court was a center of art and culture.

The Safavids In the 1500s, the Safavid empire rose in Iran. It fought several large wars with the Ottomans. The Safavid ruler was called a **shah,** the Persian word for king. The Safavids made Shia Islam the official religion of Iran. This set Iran apart from its Sunni neighbors.

Iranian art and architecture reached new heights under Safavid rule. The Safavids built a magnificent capital in Esfahan. It was famous for its dazzling mosques and beautiful flower gardens.

Reading Check What religion did the Ottomans practice?

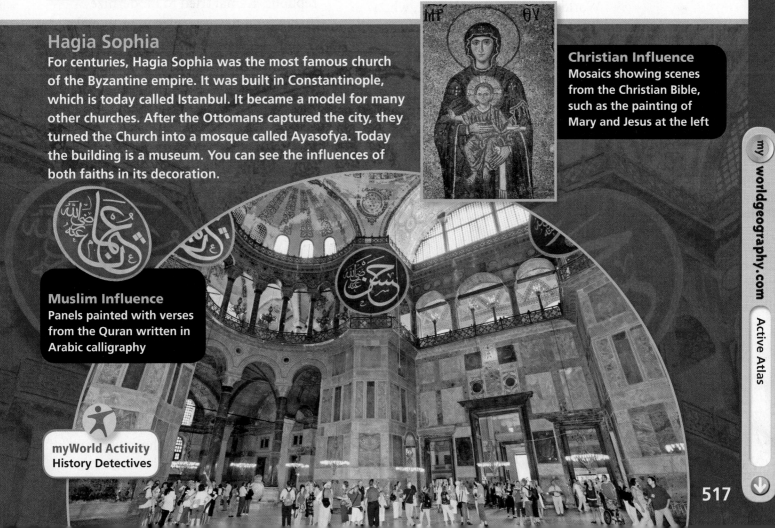

Hagia Sophia

For centuries, Hagia Sophia was the most famous church of the Byzantine empire. It was built in Constantinople, which is today called Istanbul. It became a model for many other churches. After the Ottomans captured the city, they turned the Church into a mosque called Ayasofya. Today the building is a museum. You can see the influences of both faiths in its decoration.

Christian Influence
Mosaics showing scenes from the Christian Bible, such as the painting of Mary and Jesus at the left

Muslim Influence
Panels painted with verses from the Quran written in Arabic calligraphy

myWorld Activity
History Detectives

my worldgeography.com

Active Atlas

517

Empires Collapse in the Modern Age

By the 1800s, old empires in Turkey and Iran were losing power rapidly. European countries began to influence affairs in the region. But nationalists in Turkey and Iran opposed them.

deny, *v.,* to say something is not true

Last Days of the Ottoman Empire In the early 1900s, a group of army officers called the Young Turks took power in the Ottoman empire. They wanted to create a secular nation, like those of Europe. They sided with Germany in World War I.

Though the Ottoman empire was mostly tolerant of minorities, Armenian Christians faced persecution before World War I. During the war, when some Armenians sided with Russia, the empire's enemy, Turkish soldiers forced large numbers of Armenian civilians from their homes onto long marches. The soldiers killed many, and caused

the death of others from starvation and disease. Between 600,000 and 1,500,000 Armenians died. The killing of Armenians by Turkish leaders from 1915 to 1918 is called the **Armenian genocide.** The leaders of modern Turkey do not use this term. They deny the Turkish government's responsibility for the killings.

Turkey Forms After the Ottoman empire and its allies lost World War I, the empire collapsed. European powers took control of some of its lands. They tried to take control of Turkey itself, too. But a Turkish army officer named Mustafa Kemal led forces to save Turkey's independence.

Under Kemal's rule, Turkey became a republic. Kemal tried to modernize Turkey and to westernize it, or to make it more European. Kemal made Turkey a secular state. That is, government was strictly separated from religion. Women were given more rights. People were encouraged to wear European clothes. Language and writing were reformed.

Kemal ruled using undemocratic methods. Still, many of his reforms won great respect from the Turkish people. He called himself **Ataturk,** which means "Father of the Turks." Most Turks today consider him a national hero.

A New Iran Around the beginning of the 1900s, the dynasty that ruled Iran was in trouble. It had run out of money. Russia and Britain controlled Iran's oil resources and influenced the government. Many Iranians resented this situation.

In the 1920s, a military leader named Reza Pahlavi overthrew the government

A Turkish Republic Day parade ▼

Mustafa Kemal Ataturk ▼

of Iran. He made himself shah. He tried to modernize and westernize Iran.

After 1941, his son, Mohammad Reza Pahlavi, continued this work. He became a close ally of the United States. In 1953, an elected government threw out the shah, but he returned with American help. The shah became a more oppressive ruler. He created a powerful secret police force that arrested or killed critics of his rule.

Revolution in Iran The shah's repressive policies created opposition. One leading critic of the shah was a Shia religious leader named Ayatollah Ruhollah Khomeini. **Ayatollah** is a title for high-ranking Shia leaders in Iran. Khomeini opposed the shah's efforts to make Iran more like western countries. He wanted Iran to follow Islamic law and traditions. The shah forced Khomeini to leave Iran, but the Ayatollah's attacks continued.

In 1978, a revolution broke out. Iranians took to the streets to protest the shah's rule. When the shah ordered troops to attack the protestors, this

◀ Protesters hold a poster of Khomeini during the Iranian Revolution.

provoked even more protests. Eventually, the shah and his family fled, and his government collapsed. In February 1979, Khomeini returned and took power.

Reading Check What happened to the shah's government?

Section 2 Assessment

Key Terms

1. What is a satrap? What function did satraps perform?

2. What is a secular state?

Key Ideas

3. How did the rulers of the Persian empire encourage trade?

4. How did Iran contribute to Muslim cultural life?

5. What were the goals of Mustafa Kemal Ataturk's reforms?

Think Critically

6. **Analyze Cause and Effect** What effect did Alexander's conquest have on the culture of the region?

7. **Compare and Contrast** How were the new governments formed in Turkey and Iran in the early 1900s similar? How were they different?

Essential Question

What are the challenges of diversity?

8. What role did national feeling play in the creation of modern Turkey and Iran? Go to your Student Journal to record your answer.

519

The Iranian Revolution

Key Idea
- People in Iran opposed Shah Mohammad Reza Pahlavi for different reasons, some secular and others religious.

▲ A poster from the Iranian Revolution

In 1979, the Iranian people overthrew the government of the shah. Some Iranians supported the shah because he had modernized Iran. However, many others opposed the shah's rule. Fereydoun Hoveyda had held high positions under the shah. Hoveyda blamed the monarch for bringing on the revolution. Ayatollah Ruhollah Khomeini was an even harsher critic. He criticized monarchy itself as being against Islam. When the shah threw a lavish and expensive party in honor of his own rule, Khomeini lashed out at the waste. He denounced the shah and his dynasty as evil and oppressive.

Stop at each circled letter on the right to think about the text. Then answer the question with the same letter on the left.

Ⓐ **Analyze Cause and Effect** Why might this author say there were fewer protests before 1977?

Ⓑ **Summarize** What groups objected to the shah's rule? Why did they object to it?

Ⓒ **Draw Conclusions** According to this author, what explains opposition to the shah?

flout, *v.,* to ignore or violate

nonchalance, *n.,* lack of worry, casualness

tangible, *adj.,* real

invalidate, *v.,* to make worthless

impunity, *n.,* freedom from punishment

monopolize, *v.,* to take exclusive control of

Causes of the Revolution

❝ Revolution was inevitable: during its last two years monarchy <u>flouted</u> both law and tradition with unbelievable <u>nonchalance</u>. The regime could claim many <u>tangible</u> achievements between 1965 and 1977,

Ⓐ but in the eyes of the poorer classes they were <u>invalidated</u> by the way the Shah allowed his friends and relations to line their pockets with <u>impunity</u> by <u>monopolizing</u> the nation's business. Even among the

Ⓑ more prosperous classes there was open criticism of the sovereign's person and his political choices.

Ⓒ The dictatorship was a dead weight on all sections of society, and public opinion saw the Shah as embodying everything that went wrong. That is what explains the immense hatred he aroused among the masses after 1978. ❞

—Fereydoun Hoveyda,
The Fall of the Shah, 1980

Stop at each circled letter on the right to think about the text. Then answer the question with the same letter on the left.

D Compare Viewpoints What is the source of Khomeini's opposition to the shah?

E Draw Inferences How does this explain why Khomeini would found an "Islamic Republic" instead of making himself shah?

F Identify Details What does Khomeini specifically criticize?

disgraceful, *adj.,* bringing shame or embarrassment

reactionary, *adj.,* opposed to progress

manifestation, *n.,* visible form or example

abomination, *n.,* something that is very evil, especially something that people object to for religious reasons

Islam Against the Monarchy

D 66 Islam is fundamentally opposed to the whole notion of monarchy. Anyone who studies the manner in which the Prophet [Muhammad] established the government of Islam will realize that Islam came in order to destroy these

E palaces of tyranny. Monarchy is one of the most shameful and <u>disgraceful</u> <u>reactionary</u> <u>manifestations</u>. Are millions of the people's wealth to be spent

F on these absurd celebrations? Are the people of Iran to have a festival for those whose behavior has been a scandal throughout history and who are a cause of crime and oppression, of <u>abomination</u> and corruption in the present age? 99

—Ayatollah Ruhollah Khomeini,
speech delivered in Najaf, Iraq, 1971

Protesters against the shah carrying an image of Ayatollah Ruhollah Khomeini, who became the first supreme leader of Iran after the revolution. ▼

Analyze the Documents

1. **Synthesize** What role did corruption play in the Iranian Revolution?
2. **Writing Task** Take the role of an Iranian who wanted to change the government before the revolution. Write a letter to the shah listing your complaints and the changes you urge him to make.

521

Section 3
Iran, Turkey, and Cyprus Today

Key Ideas
- Iran's government is a theocracy, while Turkey and Cyprus are democracies.
- Turkey's culture is split between tradition and modernity while it seeks greater economic ties with Europe.
- The island of Cyprus has been divided by conflict between Greeks and Turks.

Key Terms • Majlis • cleric • brain drain • coup

 Visual Glossary

Reading Skill: Identify Main Ideas Take notes using the graphic organizer in your journal.

▼ Ayatollah Ali Khamenei, Supreme Leader of Iran

After the 1979 Iranian revolution, a government that was dedicated to following Islamic law took power. The people of Iran have some say in their government, but lack many important rights.

The Islamic Republic of Iran

Iran's government is a theocracy in which religious leaders hold great power. Laws must follow Islam as it is interpreted by these leaders.

Structure of Iran's Theocracy The head of Iran's government is a religious figure called the Supreme Leader. He must approve all major government policies. He is the head of the military. Revolutionary leader Ayatollah Ruhollah Khomeini was the first Supreme Leader.

Iran's voters elect a president and a legislature, called the **Majlis**. The Majlis passes the laws for the president to carry out. The president is sometimes better known outside Iran than the Supreme Leader, but the Supreme Leader is more powerful.

The Supreme Leader names six of the twelve members of a body called the Guardian Council. All members of the council are **clerics,** or religious leaders. The Council reviews all laws passed by the Majlis. It vetoes any that it believes violate Islamic law. The Guardian Council also decides who can run for office. It uses this power to block candidates who want to change the system of government.

Rights and Restrictions on Citizens
Iranians have the right to vote. The constitution guarantees other rights as well. However, Iran's government places many limits on people's freedom. It restricts freedom of speech and freedom of the press, or newspapers and other media. The government can close newspapers and imprison journalists. It also sometimes imprisons or executes people who oppose the government.

As well, Iranian women and men do not have fully equal rights. Harsh punishments can be applied to people who violate certain moral codes established by the government.

Reform and Opposition Many Iranians are unhappy with their government. Even some clerics oppose government policies. They work within the current system to reform it. One reformist cleric, Mohammed Khatami, was elected president by a large majority in 1997. He carried out some changes, but many of his reforms were stopped by the Supreme Leader and Guardian Council. Iranians who supported reform were disappointed.

66We thought that Mr. Khatami's victory was a victory for us as well. The election of a more democratic government seemed to be a bright new beginning . . . But within less than a year of the election, the journalists, reformists and intellectuals began to be persecuted by hard-liners in the judiciary and Intelligence Ministry . . . 99

—Camella Entekhabifard, "Tehran's Eternal Youth," *The New York Times*

Some Iranians hold public protests, risking imprisonment or death. In 1999 and 2003, many students protested. In 2009, reformists claimed that an election had been rigged against their candidate. They held the largest street protests since the revolution. The government used violence against the protesters, killing many.

Reading Check Does the Supreme Leader or the president of Iran have more power?

◀ Iranian students protest against their government's restriction of the press.

523

Iran and the United States

Iran has had difficult relations with the United States. After the revolution, many Iranians were angry with the United States for supporting the shah. Iranian students attacked the American embassy and held Americans inside hostage for 444 days. Relations between the two countries have been tense ever since.

Another issue has been Iran's nuclear program. Iran says it needs nuclear energy. But the United States and other countries fear it is trying to develop nuclear weapons. The United States has tried to convince other countries to stop trading with Iran until it shows that it is not building nuclear weapons.

The United States government also accuses Iran of supporting groups that have attacked both Israel and United States troops in Iraq.

Reading Check **Why do some countries object to Iran's nuclear energy program?**

The Economy of Iran

Iran's economy is dominated by oil. Money from oil sales brings in most of the government's income. But the economy is still weak.

Economic Problems Unemployment is a major problem in Iran. In 2008, one in every eight workers was out of work. High rates of population growth contribute to unemployment. The economy has not grown fast enough to provide jobs for all of Iran's people.

In recent years, inflation, or the rise in prices from year to year, has been another problem. Rising prices mean that people can buy fewer goods with their money.

The lack of freedom and economic opportunity in Iran have a cost. Perhaps as many as 1.5 million Iranians have left their country since the 1979 revolution. Many of them are highly educated. Educated people leaving a place is called a **brain drain**. These migrants hope to find more opportunity and freedom in other places. Iranian immigrants have built prosperous communities in other countries, including the United States.

Industries A major industry in Iran is the petrochemical industry, which turns crude oil into different products. Iran also makes automobiles, appliances, steel, paper and rubber, medicines, and textiles. For centuries, craft workers in Iran have been famous for their skill in making beautiful hand-woven rugs. Weavers carry on that traditional work today.

Reading Check **Why do many educated Iranians leave their country?**

A poor neighborhood on the outskirts of Tehran, Iran.

Closer Look

Iranian Art and Architecture

A scene from the Iranian movie *Children of Heaven*

The Imam Mosque in Esfahan ▼

Iranians today are proud of the beautiful art Iran has produced throughout the ages. Iranian culture has had a large influence on the cultures of neighboring countries. For example, Iranian architecture has been widely imitated in Central and South Asia, while Iranian painting influenced Ottoman art. Today, Iranian movies receive international praise and win prestigious awards, as do movies made by Iranians living abroad.

THINK CRITICALLY   **How did Iranian culture influence the cultures of other countries?**

A man painting in a traditional style ▼

525

Turkey: Connections to Europe and the Middle East

Turkey bridges Southwest Asia and Europe. It is a mostly Muslim country with strong connections to Europe.

Turkey's Democracy Turkey is a democracy led by a president and prime minister. Its constitution forbids discrimination and guarantees important human rights for all Turkish citizens.

Voters elect the 550 members of the legislature, which passes laws. The president can challenge laws. He or she can also send laws to the constitutional court for review. If the judges of that court believe a law violates the constitution, they can strike down the law.

One issue in Turkish democracy is the power of the military. The army is a very important institution in Turkish society. It has overthrown four civilian governments since the Turkish Republic was founded in 1923. When the military uses force to overthrow a government, it is called a **coup.**

Another issue is a law that makes it a crime to "insult the Turkish nation." This law is opposed by human rights activists.

Some people who write about subjects that offend the government have been put on trial under this law. Turkish nationalism remains a very strong force in society.

A Secular State Turkey's constitution separates the nation's government from Islam. The military is strongly in favor of secularism, or nonreligious government. It helped force out a government it did not consider secular enough in 1997.

In recent years, a political party that embraces Islam more closely has grown popular. It is called the Justice and Development Party. Its initials are AKP in Turkish. In 2003, an AKP member became prime minister. Some feared that the military would overthrow the AKP government.

AKP leaders have promised they will keep Turkey a secular state. Some Turks are not convinced. In 2008, the party passed a controversial law that allowed women who wear traditional headscarves to attend universities, which the government runs. In the past the scarves had been banned at universities because they were thought to violate the government's secular character.

violate, *v.,* to break a rule or law

Istanbul Today
With more than twelve million people, Istanbul is Turkey's largest city. Istanbul and its suburbs span two continents. ▼

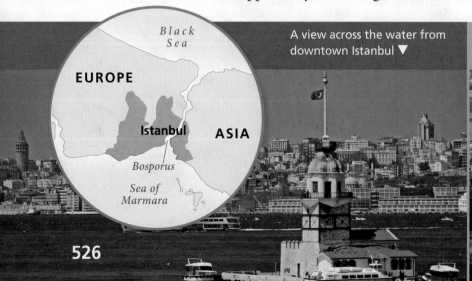

A view across the water from downtown Istanbul ▼

Hagia Sophia, Istanbul's most famous landmark ▼

526

Some Turks strongly opposed the law. One opposition leader even challenged the AKP in Turkey's constitutional court. He said that the party should be banned because it is not secular. The court disagreed and the AKP continued to govern.

Turkey's Culture Today Turkey's culture shows European and Asian influences. Most urban men and women, and most rural men, for instance, wear Western-style clothing. Rural women often wear traditional Middle Eastern clothes.

Women's roles in Turkish society show similar differences. In rural areas women generally do not work outside of their homes. In cities, women can be found in many occupations. A woman was Turkey's prime minister in the 1990s.

Life in Istanbul is very different from life in rural Turkey. Istanbul today is a modern city with skyscrapers and a busy port, though there are also traditional areas. Many people have moved to Istanbul from the countryside in search of jobs and a higher standard of living.

Reading Check What role does Turkey's military play in its government?

Turkey's Economy

Unlike Iran, Turkey does not have large deposits of oil that it can sell to bring in money. It has a more mixed economy, with agriculture, industry, and services all playing important roles.

Development For many decades, Turkey has lagged behind European nations economically. One reason is that agriculture has been a large sector in the economy, and farming does not usually lead to high incomes. In addition, the government used to run many industries. These industries were not very productive. Turkey also set up barriers to trade with other nations. These barriers prevented Turks from importing low-cost goods to improve their standard of living.

Starting in the 1980s, Turkey made changes. It removed trade barriers and became more active in importing and exporting goods. It cut the government's role in the economy and made it easier for private companies to form. As a result, the economy has grown rapidly in most recent years. People are more productive and enjoy higher incomes.

occupation, *n.,* job or profession

my **worldgeography.com** Culture Close-up

Culture Close-up

A traditional crafts market in Istanbul ▼

Modern Istanbul's business district ▼

527

Turkey's Trade Partners

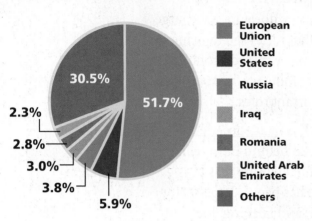

- European Union — 51.7%
- United States — 30.5%
- Russia — 2.3%
- Iraq — 2.8%
- Romania — 3.0%
- United Arab Emirates — 3.8%
- Others — 5.9%

SOURCE: European Commission

A woman weaving a decorated textile in Turkey. Textiles are one of Turkey's major exports.

Chart Skills

1. Does Turkey trade more with Russia or the United Arab Emirates?

2. Based on this graph, do you think Turkey's economy is more closely tied to Europe or to Southwest Asia?

Data Discovery

myWorld Activity
To Join or Not
To Join

The European Union Turkey's government has attempted to join the European Union (EU). Turks who support this argue that it will improve the economy by allowing Turkey to trade more freely with Europe. But not all members of the EU are willing to admit Turkey. Some criticize Turkey's record on human rights, especially its treatment of Kurds and its role in Cyprus. Many Turks resent this criticism. Some fear that joining the EU will force Turkey to change its policies. Still, Turkey continues to move slowly towards EU membership.

Reading Check Why do some EU nations object to admitting Turkey?

Divided Cyprus

Conflict between Greeks and Turks has been a problem on Cyprus for decades.

Violence and Invasion Cyprus gained its independence from Great Britain in 1960. The new republic faced difficulties from the start. Many people in the Greek majority wanted Cyprus to become a part of Greece. Turkish Cypriots feared Greece would not protect their rights. They opposed unification. They also resented Greek domination of the government of Cyprus. Greeks and Turks fought bitterly.

Events came to a boil in 1974. At that time a dictatorship held power in Greece. It sponsored an attempt to overthrow the government of Cyprus so that the island would join with Greece.

In response, Turkey invaded the island and soon controlled its northern third. The Greek-dominated Republic of Cyprus held the rest. During and after the invasion, tens of thousands of Greek and Turkish Cypriots were forced from their

Divided Cyprus

KEY
Greek Cypriot-administered area
Turkish Cypriot-administered area
British Sovereign Base Area
United Nations buffer zone

Mediterranean Sea

34° E

TURKISH REPUBLIC
OF NORTHERN CYPRUS
Nicosia

REPUBLIC
OF CYPRUS

35° N

0   20 mi
0   20 km
Lambert Conformal
Conic Projection

Mediterranean
Sea

32° E   33° E

A border guard surveys Nicosia, the divided capital of Cyprus.

homes. About one third of all people in Cyprus were displaced.

Continuing Divisions In 1983, Turkish Cypriots declared independence. They formed the Turkish Republic of Northern Cyprus. Turkey is the only nation in the world that recognizes this government.

Turkish troops remain in the northern part of the island. UN peacekeepers patrol a buffer zone that separates the two parts of the island. Movement between them was closed off until 2003.

Many efforts have been made to reunite the island. These have not yet succeeded. In 2004, Turkish Cypriots voted in favor of a reunification plan, but Greek Cypriots voted against it. Cyprus joined the EU without the Turkish north.

Reading Check How is Cyprus divided?

Section 3 Assessment

Key Terms

1. What is the role of clerics in Iran's government?

2. What happens during a military coup?

Key Ideas

3. Is Iran's government an example of rule by many, by few, or a combination? Explain your answer.

4. Why was the AKP challenged in court, and what was the result?

5. What new economic policies did Turkey adopt in the 1980s?

Think Critically

6. **Analyze Cause and Effect** What has caused Iran's brain drain?

7. **Compare and Contrast** How do women's rights compare in Iran and Turkey?

Essential Question

What are the challenges of diversity?

8. What political conflict has arisen in Turkey as a result of different views about religion? Go to your Student Journal to record your answer.

my worldgeography.com

Data Discovery

529

The Kurdish People

Key Ideas
- The Kurds are a people whose homeland has been split among four countries.
- Some Turkish Kurds want a separate Kurdish nation and have fought Turkey's government to win independence.
- Kurds who live in Iran, Iraq, and Syria have different relationships with their governments.

Key Terms • Kurdistan • peshmerga • autonomy

Kurdish people, such as Bilal, are members of a large ethnic group in Southwest Asia. The Kurds have a long history and a rich culture, but they do not have their own country. Instead, Kurdish people live in an area divided among four countries. Relations between Kurds and the governments that rule them have often been tense. Sometimes they have even been violent. Today, many Kurds hope to form an independent country.

History and Culture

The traditional homeland of the Kurdish people is often called **Kurdistan.** Most of the Kurdish homeland lies within Turkey, Iran, Iraq, and Syria. Kurdistan has never been an independent nation.

A Long History The Kurds have lived in their homeland for at least 1,400 years. Today, there are around 25 to 30 million Kurds. Traditionally, the Kurds made a living by agriculture and by herding sheep and goats. Today, many live in cities and towns. Kurdistan is a very mountainous area. In the past, high mountains made it difficult for governments based in lower areas to completely control Kurdistan. Isolation helped preserve the Kurds' language and culture.

Saladin is one of the most famous Kurds in history. He was a feared general who became sultan of Egypt in the 1100s. ▼

But, in the 1900s, modern roads and communication made Kurdistan accessible. The governments of Turkey and other countries were able to control the highlands where most Kurds lived.

A Proud Culture Kurds have long had a reputation as fierce fighters. Kurdish soldiers are called **peshmerga,** which means "those who face death." Saladin was the most famous Kurdish fighter. He was a great military leader who defeated the European Crusaders in the 1100s.

The Kurdish people have also given the world many poets and writers.

One was the poet Ehmedé Xaní. He wrote the most famous work of Kurdish literature, *Mem and Zin*, in the 1600s. *Mem and Zin* is a romance, but it also shows the author's Kurdish patriotism.

The new year's festival known as Newroz is an important part of Kurdish culture today, though Iranians and others celebrate the holiday too. For Kurdish people it is an opportunity to celebrate their culture. Today, it is also a time to promote Kurdish identity and politics.

Reading Check Is Kurdistan an independent nation?

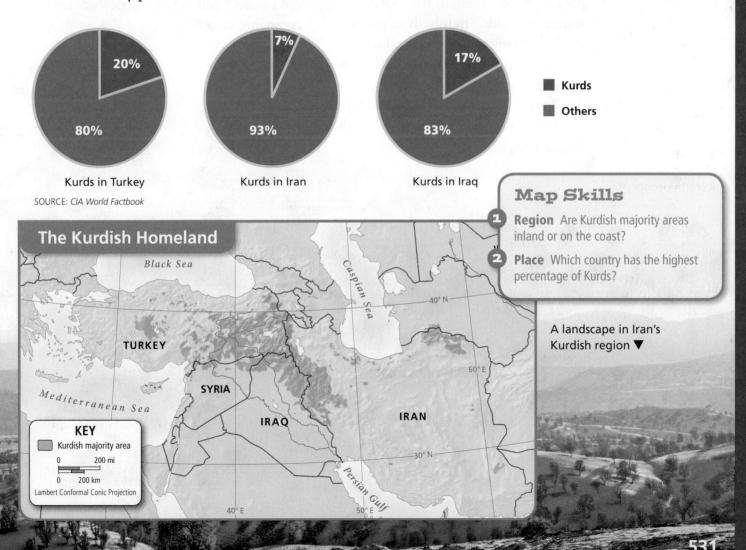

SOURCE: *CIA World Factbook*

Kurds in Turkey — 20% Kurds, 80% Others
Kurds in Iran — 7% Kurds, 93% Others
Kurds in Iraq — 17% Kurds, 83% Others

Kurds / Others

The Kurdish Homeland

KEY
Kurdish majority area
0 — 200 mi
0 — 200 km
Lambert Conformal Conic Projection

Map Skills

1 **Region** Are Kurdish majority areas inland or on the coast?

2 **Place** Which country has the highest percentage of Kurds?

A landscape in Iran's Kurdish region ▼

Tensions in Turkey

The Turkish Republic was founded in the 1920s. The new government was determined to unify the country.

Government Policies The government decided that all citizens of Turkey were to be called Turks, even if they did not belong to the Turkish ethnic group. Kurds were called "Mountain Turks." The government closed Kurdish schools and banned the use of the Kurdish language.

Kurdish Reactions These policies sparked Kurdish revolts. The government put down the rebellions with force, sometimes killing hundreds of people and destroying villages. It also forced thousands of Kurds to leave their homes and move to other parts of the country. The Turkish government hoped to fight Kurdish nationalism by breaking up the Kurdish population.

In the late 1970s, some Kurds formed the Kurdistan Workers Party, the PKK. It demanded independence for Kurds. The PKK attacked Turkish soldiers and civilians. The United Nations, the United States, and other countries consider the PKK a terrorist organization. The Turkish government fought the PKK during the 1980s and 1990s.

Other Kurds sought peaceful change. They called for economic development to address Kurdish poverty. They demanded equal rights and recognition of Kurdish language and culture. Many Kurds who did not seek full independence wanted **autonomy,** or self-rule.

Men surround the flag of the Kurdish people. ▼

532

Today's Situation Today, the situation is better. Turkey has changed some of its policies toward the Kurds. It has allowed the promotion of Kurdish cultural practices banned in the past. It now allows some use of Kurdish in radio and television broadcasts and in schools. Kurds now serve in Turkey's parliament.

Turkey's constitution protects the human rights of all citizens. Kurds in Turkey can vote and participate in politics.

Reading Check **How has the government's policy toward Kurds changed?**

Kurds in Other Countries

Many Kurdish people live in the countries neighboring Turkey. They have had different experiences in each country.

Iraq The British created the mostly Arab country of Iraq after World War I. Iraq included many Kurds, who resented being a part of this new country. They wanted independence or autonomy and fought the government. Kurdish areas in Iraq have large oil reserves. Kurds have argued with Iraqi governments over who should benefit from oil sales.

Former Iraqi dictator Saddam Hussein brutally oppressed the Kurds. He used chemical weapons against Kurdish villagers in the 1980s. However, the situation changed after the American-led invasion of Iraq in 2003. Iraqi Kurdistan gained more autonomy. Turkey has accused Iraqi Kurds of protecting PKK members. It has sent troops into Iraq to attack them.

Iran Iran's Kurdish minority freely practices its culture and speaks its language. Iran's Kurds do not have autonomy. They participate in the government like other Iranians.

When Iranian Kurds tried to become independent after the revolution in 1979, the government fought and defeated them. Today, some Kurds hope to join with Kurds in other countries to create their own state.

Iran is ruled by Shia religious leaders. However, most Kurds practice Sunni Islam. This has created some tension, since the government favors Shia Islam.

Syria For decades, Syria has been ruled by a family autocracy. The government oppresses many of its citizens. Kurdish Syrians are sometimes singled out for particularly bad treatment. The government has taken away the citizenship of some Kurds. It also seized Kurdish land along the border with Turkey and resettled Arabs there.

Reading Check **Why has Turkey sent troops into Iraq?**

Assessment

1. Among which countries is Kurdistan divided?

2. What limits did Turkey's government once place on Kurdish rights?

3. What is Newroz?

4. Why might governments in the region have tried to keep Kurds from organizing politically?

5. What is the situation of Kurds in Iraq today?

Chapter Assessment

Key Terms and Ideas

1. **Summarize** How does the location of water resources affect settlement patterns in Iran, Turkey, and Cyprus?

2. **Compare and Contrast** How is Iran's government today different than the government before the Revolution of 1979?

3. **Recall** What resources are most important to Iran's economy?

4. **Describe** Has Iran's **brain drain** been good or bad for the country?

5. **Recall** List the majority ethnic and religious group in each of Iran, Turkey, and Cyprus.

6. **Describe** How did the founding of modern Turkey affect that country's laws and culture?

7. **Explain** Why is Cyprus divided and how did the division happen?

Think Critically

8. **Compare and Contrast** What are some aspects of Turkey's government that could be considered more democratic and less democratic?

9. **Make Inferences** Why might the United States and other countries be worried by Iran seeking nuclear weapons?

10. **Solve Problems** What did the Turkish government do in the 1980s to improve its economy?

11. **Core Concepts: Cultural Diffusion and Change** How did the ancient Persians and later Arab Muslims change the region's culture?

Places to Know

For each place, write the letter from the map that shows its location.

12. Cyprus

13. Istanbul

14. Turkey

15. Iran

16. Tehran

17. Black Sea

18. **Estimate** Using the scale, estimate the distance between Istanbul and Tehran.

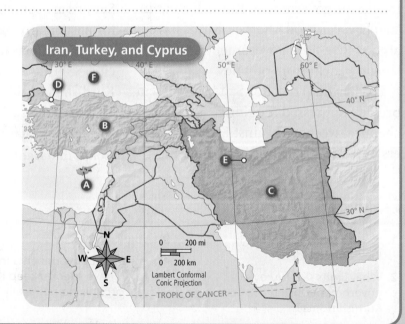

Iran, Turkey, and Cyprus

Essential Question

What are the challenges of diversity?

Regional Ethnic Cooperation Conference Suppose you represent either an ethnic group or a government in Turkey, Iran, or Cyprus. You will attend a United Nations conference to exchange ideas and present a plan of action for addressing common problems.

21st Century Learning

Solve Problems

Suppose you are working to help people in Cyprus end their conflict. Develop a list of questions you could ask people you meet in Cyprus. Focus your questions on helping those you interview to identify actions or changes in attitude that they feel would lead Greek and Turkish Cypriots to more effective efforts at peace.

Document-Based Questions

Success Tracker™
Online at myworldgeography.com

Use your knowledge of Iran, Turkey, and Cyprus, as well as Documents A and B to answer Questions 1–3.

Document A

Individual Freedom		
Country	Individual Freedom Rank*	Government Type
Israel	29	Democracy
Turkey	61	Democracy
Iran	125	Theocracy
Saudi Arabia	130	Absolute monarchy

SOURCE: The State of World Liberty Project
* The freest country in the world is ranked 1.
  The least free is ranked 159.

Document B

" There are two countries in the Middle East that offer models for the future: the democratic Republic of Turkey and the Islamic Republic of Iran."

—Bernard Lewis, Middle East historian

1. According to the table, which country provides its citizens with the least individual freedom?

   A Saudi Arabia

   B Iran

   C Turkey

   D Israel

2. Which statement best restates the views in Document B?

   A Turkey and Iran have similar governments.

   B Turkey is a theocracy and Iran is a monarchy.

   C Turkish democracy and Iranian theocracy are two paths other countries might follow.

   D Iran gives citizens more freedom than Turkey.

3. **Writing Task** Write a paragraph comparing the governments of Iran, Turkey, and one other country in Southwest Asia that you have studied.

my worldgeography.com Self-Test

535

Sharing the Wealth:

How the Oil Rich Can Help the Oil Poor

Your Mission Divide into at least two groups. Research and develop a proposal for ways that oil-rich countries can help oil-poor countries. Each group should listen to the other groups' proposals. Together, the groups then develop one proposal that everyone can accept.

Imagine a group of friends in which half the people receive very large allowances and the other half receive hardly any allowance at all. The friends who have money would be able to do activities and buy things that the others can't afford. Resentments might build up over time. Keeping friendships intact in such a group might be difficult.

Southwest Asia faces a similar situation. Several of the nations earn enormous wealth from exporting oil, while other nations in the region have much lower incomes. Because of this economic gap, the nations of this region develop at different rates. Such a situation could lead to instability in the region.

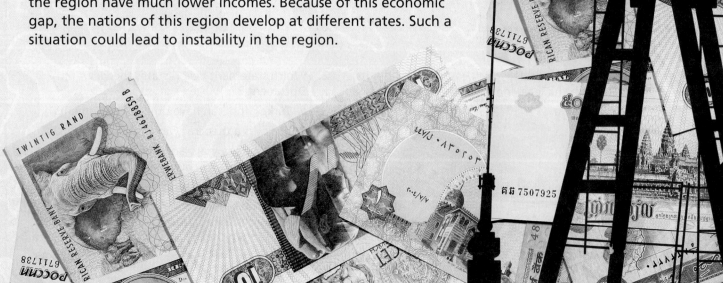

An oil refinery in
Saudi Arabia ▼

Oil Production: Jordan and Saudi Arabia

Oil Production (barrels per day)

9.2 million

0

Jordan   Saudi Arabia

SOURCE: *CIA World Factbook*

STEP 1

Research the Problem.

Identify which countries in Southwest Asia are oil-poor (OP) and which are oil-rich (OR). If your group represents an OP country, research the economic and social conditions there. Consider how an OP nation might expand existing resources or attract foreign investment. If your group represents an OR country, research how you might use your nation's advantages to help a neighbor with fewer resources. Discuss ways in which helping your neighbor will also benefit you.

STEP 2

Make a Decision.

After both groups have made their presentations, discuss the two sets of ideas. The research and the proposals from the two groups may not agree. However, before you reject a proposal entirely, think about how you might use certain elements and work them into a new solution that benefits both OP and OR nations. Remember that part of your task as a combined group is to come up with a compromise plan that both sides can accept. Discuss how to present the new proposal.

STEP 3

Present Your Ideas.

After you have finished your research and discussion, prepare a presentation with the new plan. Your presentation should explain your group's ideas about how OR countries can help OP countries. Use graphs, charts, photographs, maps, diagrams, and quotations to support your proposal. When you are ready to make your presentation, your teacher will pair OP representatives with OR representatives. The paired groups should then make their presentations to each other.

537

South and Central Asia

South and Central Asia are regions of grasslands, deserts, huge lakes, and mountains. The mountainous Himalayas dominate the area. Extremes of climate characterize these regions, with heavy monsoon rains in South Asia and desert climates in Central Asia.

What time is it there?

Washington, D.C.	Palampur, India
9 A.M. Monday	7:30 P.M. Monday

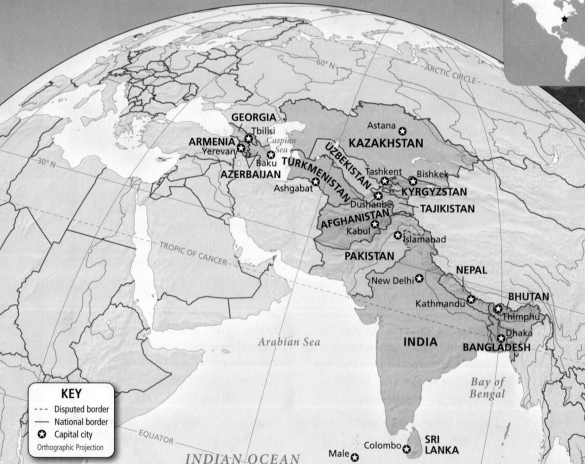

KEY
- - - Disputed border
——— National border
⊛ Capital city
Orthographic Projection

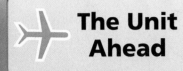

The Unit Ahead

→ **Chapter 12** Central Asia and the Caucasus

→ **Chapter 13** South Asia

my worldgeography.com

Plan your trip online by doing a Data Discovery Activity and watching the myStory Videos of the region's teens.

my **Story**

Askar

Age: 15

Home: Naryn, Kyrgyzstan

Chapter 12

my **Story**

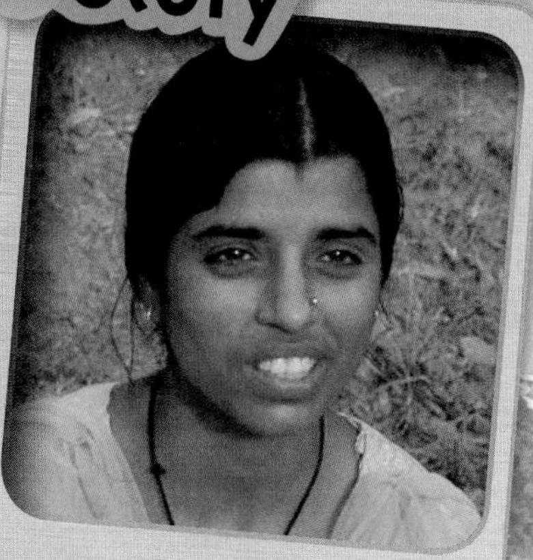

Nancy

Age: 18

Home: Palampur, India

Chapter 13

View of the Himalayas

539

Regional Overview
Physical Geography

The Caspian Sea is the largest landlocked body of water in the world.

Kirghiz Steppe

Syr Dar'ya

Aral Sea

Amu Dar'ya

Kara-Kum Desert

Caspian Sea

Himalayas

Indus River

Persian Gulf

The Kara-Kum Desert occupies most of Turkmenistan.

Arabian Sea

The Himalayas are the highest mountains on Earth.

Himalayas

Ganges River

Indo-Gangetic Plain

The Indo-Gangetic Plain stretches from the Ganges River delta to the Indus River valley.

Regional Flyover

Buckle your seatbelt for a quick flight around South and Central Asia. As your plane lifts off from Calcutta, India, look down to see the waters of the huge Ganges-Brahmaputra delta, the largest delta in the world. Traveling northwest you follow the curve of the mountains known as the Himalayas. After you've crossed the Hindu Kush mountain range, you eventually see the Syr Dar'ya River in Kazakhstan.

Now you're flying west over a vast desert that stretches to the Caspian Sea. When you reach the Caucasus on the west bank of the Caspian, your plane turns and heads back east to cross the Kara-Kum Desert in Turkmenistan. Notice how the ground rises again as you approach Afghanistan. Eventually you see this mountainous area plunging down to the lowlands of the Indus River in Pakistan and the Thar Desert. As you cross India's Deccan Plateau, see if you can glimpse the island of Sri Lanka off India's southeast coast. After your plane lands back in Calcutta, make a list of the 16 countries you have seen.

In-Flight Movie

Take flight over South and Central Asia and explore the regions from the air.

my worldgeography.com

In-Flight Movie

541

Human Geography

Economic Systems

South and Central Asia are two of the poorest regions in the world. The Central Asian nations that were once part of the communist economic system of the Soviet Union all suffer from shaky economies. In South Asia, economies are so weak that millions live in poverty and do not have enough food to eat. Despite this, in India a small minority enjoys great wealth.

However, there are signs of hope in these regions. In Central Asia, Kazakhstan has a healthier economy than its neighbors. Azerbaijan is developing its oil industry. In South Asia, India has a growing middle class and an economy that has been expanding since the 1950s.

Relief workers distribute food.

Weddings in India allow families to display their wealth.

Homelessness and poverty are widespread in these regions.

Cartogram of Regional Gross Domestic Product

A cartogram is a map that has been distorted in order to show information. In this map, the size of the country is related to its GDP, or total economic output. The map below the cartogram shows the region without distortion.

South and Central Asia GDP

Country	GDP per Person*
Afghanistan	$800
Armenia	$6,600
Bangladesh	$1,500
Georgia	$5,000
India	$2,900
Pakistan	$2,600
Turkmenistan	$5,800
Uzbekistan	$2,700
United States (for comparison)	$48,000

SOURCE: *CIA World Factbook*   *2008 Estimate

Each square represents $1 billion in GDP.

Put It Together

1. Why do you think that countries that were once part of the Soviet Union are having so many economic problems?

2. Which are the poorest countries in these regions?

3. What does the cartogram tell you about these regions?

 Data Discovery

Find your own data to make a regional data table.

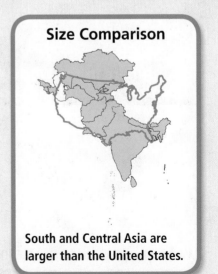

Size Comparison

South and Central Asia are larger than the United States.

my worldgeography.com   Data Discovery

543

Central Asia and the Caucasus

Essential Question

What should governments do?

KEY
— National border
⊛ Capital city
○ Other city

0 200 mi
0 200 km
Lambert Conformal Conic Projection

RUSSIA

Astana

KAZAKHSTAN

Ural River

Aral Sea

CENTRAL

Lake Balkhash

Irtysh River

THE CAUCASUS

Black Sea

GEORGIA
Tbilisi

ARMENIA
Yerevan

TURKEY

Baku

AZERBAIJAN

Caspian Sea

Syr Darya

ASIA

UZBEKISTAN
Tashkent

Samarqand

Amu Darya

TURKMENISTAN

Ashgabat

Dushanbe TAJIKISTAN

Almaty

Bishkek
KYRGYZSTAN
Naryn

CHINA

AFGHANISTAN

PAKISTAN

INDIA

Where in the World Are Central Asia and the Caucasus?

Washington, D.C., to Naryn: 6,630 miles

544

my Story

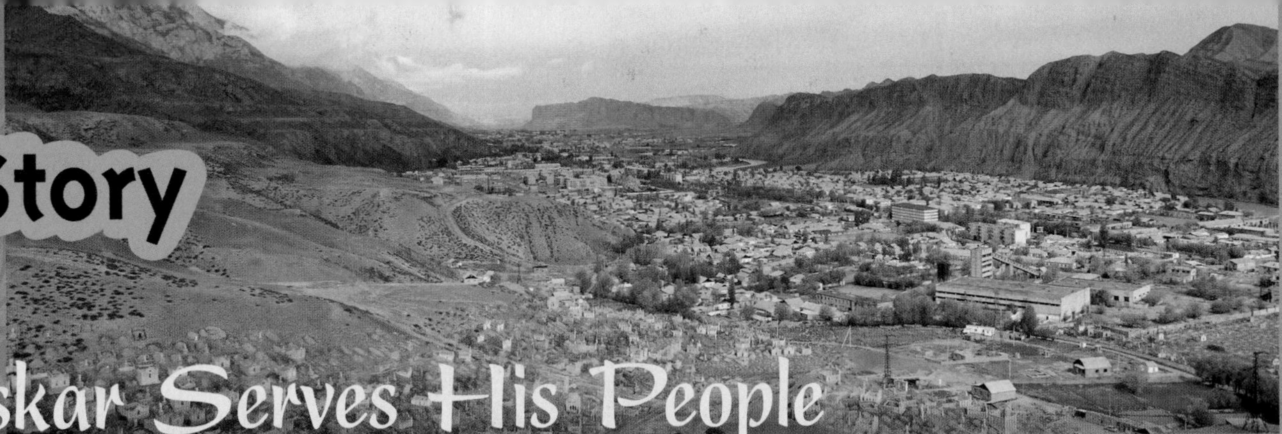

Askar Serves His People

Explore the Essential Question
- at my worldgeography.com
- using the myWorld Chapter Activity
- with the Student Journal

In this section, you'll read about Askar, a young man who lives in the mountains of Kyrgyzstan. ***What does Askar's story tell you about the people of Kyrgyzstan and their government?***

Story by Can Ertur for myWorld Geography Online

Askar lives in the mountains of Kyrgyzstan. This morning he eats two raw eggs, drinks a glass of milk, and puts on his ceremonial clothes and begins to chant lines from the Epic of Manas. This ancient poem tells the story of a legendary hero called Manas, who fought to save the Kyrgyz people and their homeland.

Like his brothers before him, Askar is trying to memorize what may be the world's longest poem. The Epic of Manas has about half a million lines and would take anywhere from 36 hours to 3 weeks to recite. It seems like an impossible task, but this hasn't stopped Askar from trying. Kyrgyz men take part every year in competitions reciting the poem.

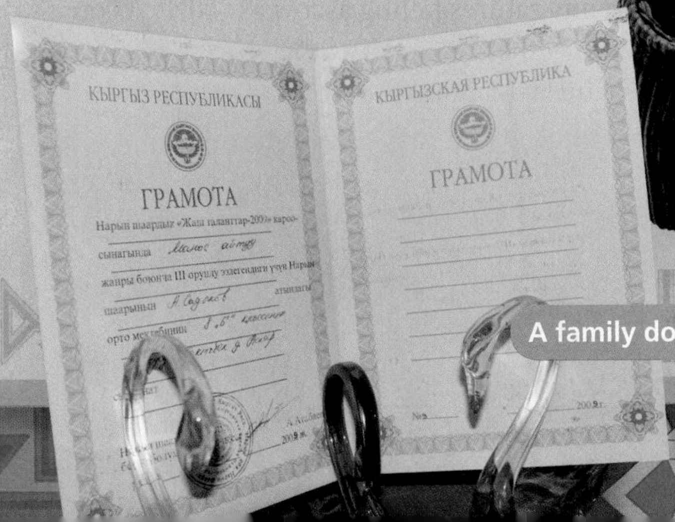

A family document

Chapter 12 Central Asia and the Caucasus

my worldgeography.com On Assignment

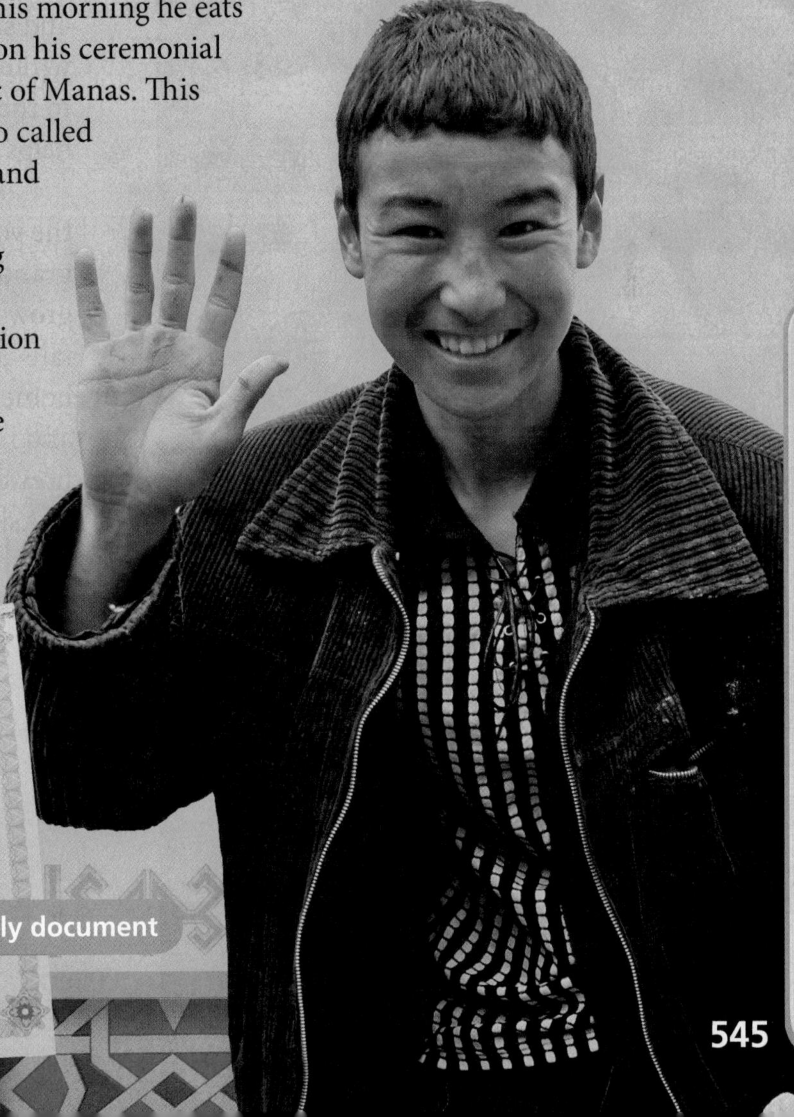

Askar recites the Epic of Manas.

Askar plays keyboard.

Askar's grandparents and extended family

Askar collects water from a spring.

Askar explains, "If it hadn't been for our ancestor Manas, we would have been enslaved as a nation." Today, Manas is a symbol of Kyrgyz pride.

Besides memorizing the Manas poem, Askar has a number of other interests. Like most Kyrgyz boys, horseback riding is at the top of the list. He also likes fishing, skiing, playing an electric keyboard, and singing and dancing the waltz at school. In the winter, he helps his father to feed the livestock, and in the summer he goes to stay with a relative and helps pick apples and apricots.

It is a tradition among the Kyrgyz people for the youngest son to look after and live with his grandparents—on his father's side— when he grows up. As the youngest of 5 brothers, this duty falls on Askar's shoulders. When his uncle is not at home to take care of his grandparents, Askar goes and helps. He cleans the house, brings in water and firewood, and takes care of anything else.

Askar's town is located in the Central Tian Shan Mountains. It is the coldest part of the country, with temperatures falling as low as -40°F. Askar likes living there but is disturbed by the problems he and his neighbors face.

546

Askar and his mother take the bus.

Celebrations for the last day of school

He believes that water is the most pressing problem. "In the villages there is no clean water to drink," he says. Furthermore, in winter, the water pipes freeze and the villagers have no running water in their homes. They have no choice but to carry water to their homes from a nearby spring. Given the extremely cold weather, some villagers must depend on their neighbors to bring them their drinking water.

But water is not the only problem these mountain people have to deal with. Despite the country's many hydropower plants, Askar was unable to attend school for 2 months last year because there wasn't enough electricity to keep the schools warm and lighted. Askar says the government told them that they couldn't provide all of Kyrgyzstan with electricity because there was a shortage of water at the power plants. Given Kyrgyzstan's plentiful water supply, Askar believes that the government should do a better job of providing a steady supply of electricity.

After graduating from high school, Askar wants to go to medical school and become a doctor. He would like to work in a big city like Bishkek, the capital of Kyrgyzstan, for a year or two. Then he plans on returning home, or to one of the mountain villages, to serve his community as a skilled doctor.

myStory Online

Join Askar as he shows you more about his life in Kyrgyzstan.

Meet the Journalist

Name Can Ertur
Favorite Moment Sharing a meal with Askar's family

my worldgeography.com   myStory Video

547

Chapter Atlas

Key Ideas
- Deserts and mountains shape farming and trade patterns.
- Herders have long grazed animals on the grasslands of Central Asia.
- Natural resources, such as oil and natural gas, are important to countries in these regions.

Key Terms • landlocked • steppe • irrigate • overgrazing • temperate • riot

→ **Visual Glossary**

Reading Skill: Label and Outline Map Take notes using the outline map in your journal.

A woman in front of her home in Tajikistan

Physical Features

Central Asia is **landlocked,** that is, cut off from direct contact with any ocean. Traveling across the region's mountains and deserts is a challenge. Yet, for thousands of years, farmers have survived in the rich mountain valleys. Nomads have grazed their herds on the vast, mostly flat grasslands.

The Caucasus (KAW kuh sus) region is the area near the Caucasus Mountains. This mountain range runs between the Black Sea and the Caspian Sea. Three countries make up this region: Georgia, Armenia, and Azerbaijan.

548

Central Asia and the Caucasus: Physical

THE STEPPES

KAZAKHSTAN

Irtysh River

Altay Shan

Ural River

Black Sea

THE CAUCASUS

Caucasus Mountains

GEORGIA

ARMENIA

Kura River

Caspian Sea

Aral Sea

CENTRAL

Lake Balkhash

Syr Dar'ya

ASIA

Kyzyl Kum Desert

KYRGYZSTAN

Tian Shan

AZERBAIJAN

Kara Kum Desert

TURKMENISTAN

Amu Dar'ya

UZBEKISTAN

TAJIKISTAN

Pamirs

50° N

40° N

KEY
Elevation

Feet	Meters
15,000	4,572
10,000	3,048
6,000	1,829
3,000	914
1,000	305
500	152
Sea level	Sea level

— National border

0   400 mi

0   400 km

Lambert Conformal Conic Projection

N W E S

50° E

60° E

Map Skills

1 **Location** What feature is found at the eastern edge of Central Asia?

2 **Place** Georgia has a coast along which sea?

3 **Places to Know!**
Label the following places on the outline map in your Student Journal: Caucasus Mountains, Caspian Sea, Aral Sea, Syr Dar'ya River, Amu Dar'ya River.

→ **Active Atlas**

Russia lies to the north of the Caucasus Mountains. Turkey, Iran, and the rest of southwest Asia stretch to the south.

Central Asia, unlike the Caucasus, is a broad expanse of land at the heart of Asia. At its eastern edge, the towering mountains of Kyrgyzstan and Tajikistan separate this region from East and South Asia.

The **steppe,** or mostly flat grasslands, of Kazakhstan lie to the northwest of the mountains. The deserts and plains of Uzbekistan and Turkmenistan spread west from these mountains to the Caspian Sea. The climate of Central Asia is mostly dry. About 70 percent of Turk-

menistan is covered by the Kara-Kum (kar a KUM) Desert.

Melting snow in the eastern mountains feeds rivers and lakes throughout Central Asia. The mighty Syr Dar'ya (sir der YAH) and Amu Dar'ya (ah MOO der YAH) rivers flow west from the mountains. Water from these rivers runs into the Aral Sea between Kazakhstan and Uzbekistan. Rainfall is scarce, so this mountain source of water is important to Central Asia.

source, *n.,* the place from which something comes

Reading Check What is a major desert found in Turkmenistan?

my **worldgeography.com**

Active Atlas

549

Climate and Land Use

The climate of Central Asia is very different from that of the Caucasus. Land use, as a result, is also different in these two regions.

Dry Central Asia Most of Central Asia has an arid or semiarid climate. The weather is hot during the summer. Agriculture is a challenge in this dry, desert climate. Farmers take water from the Amu Dar'ya and Syr Dar'ya to **irrigate,** that is, to supply water to, their crops.

In Central Asia, northern Kazakhstan and the mountain valleys of Kyrgyzstan and Tajikistan have a climate that is somewhat cooler and wetter. Farming is easier here. Kazakhstan exports the wheat grown on its vast plains.

Raising livestock is also important in Central Asia. Herders have long grazed their flocks on the steppes. In mountain areas, herders bring their animals to graze in high mountain meadows in the summer when there is no snow. They return to the lower plains in the winter.

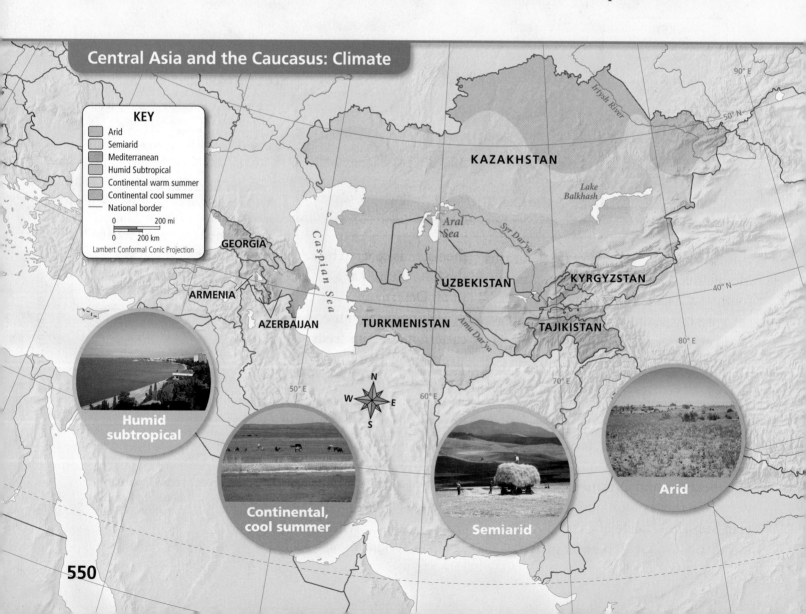

Central Asia and the Caucasus: Climate

KEY
- Arid
- Semiarid
- Mediterranean
- Humid Subtropical
- Continental warm summer
- Continental cool summer
- National border

0 — 200 mi
0 — 200 km
Lambert Conformal Conic Projection

Humid subtropical

Continental, cool summer

Semiarid

Arid

550

This protects the grassland and prevents **overgrazing,** or so much grazing that the plants are killed.

The Mild Caucasus In the Caucasus, the mountains shape the climate of the region. The mountains block cold winter winds from the north, making the climate more **temperate,** or more mild and less extreme. The mountains also leave a rain shadow to their east. Georgia receives the most rain. The land becomes drier as you move eastward toward Azerbaijan.

The valleys and plains in the Caucasus have fertile soils for agriculture. People have mainly settled in these areas. The local climate dictates the kind of crops grown. A humid climate allows Georgians to plant fruits and vegetables which are grown for export. People grow cotton, grains, and tobacco in Azerbaijan's arid climate. In addition to these crops, rich natural resources are important to the economies in the region.

Reading Check Where are fertile soils found in the Caucasus?

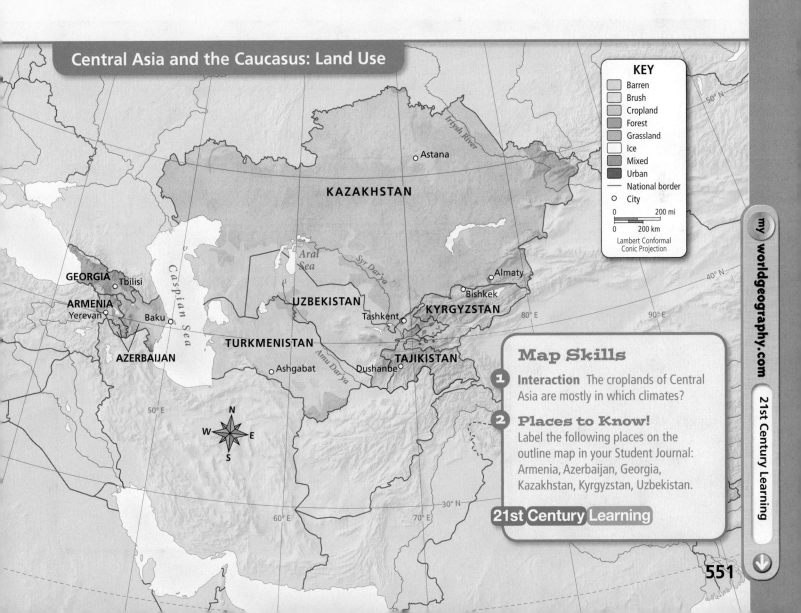

Central Asia and the Caucasus: Land Use

KEY
- Barren
- Brush
- Cropland
- Forest
- Grassland
- Ice
- Mixed
- Urban
- National border
- ○ City

0   200 mi
0   200 km
Lambert Conformal Conic Projection

Map Skills

1 **Interaction** The croplands of Central Asia are mostly in which climates?

2 **Places to Know!** Label the following places on the outline map in your Student Journal: Armenia, Azerbaijan, Georgia, Kazakhstan, Kyrgyzstan, Uzbekistan.

21st Century Learning

551

Natural Resources

These regions have many resources, including minerals, oil, and natural gas. These natural resources are not evenly distributed. Uzbekistan and Turkmenistan produce the most natural gas. Azerbaijan and Kazakhstan produce the most oil.

Oil and Minerals Several countries in the region are rich in oil. The medieval Italian explorer Marco Polo described an oil seep probably in what is now Azerbaijan.

66 This oil is not good to use with food, but 'tis good to burn ... People come from vast distances to fetch it ... 99

—Marco Polo

Oil later became a source of wealth for the region.

These countries also have important mineral deposits. For example, Armenia has copper, lead, and zinc. Gold is mined in Kyrgyzstan. Exporting minerals plays an important role in the economies of all of these countries.

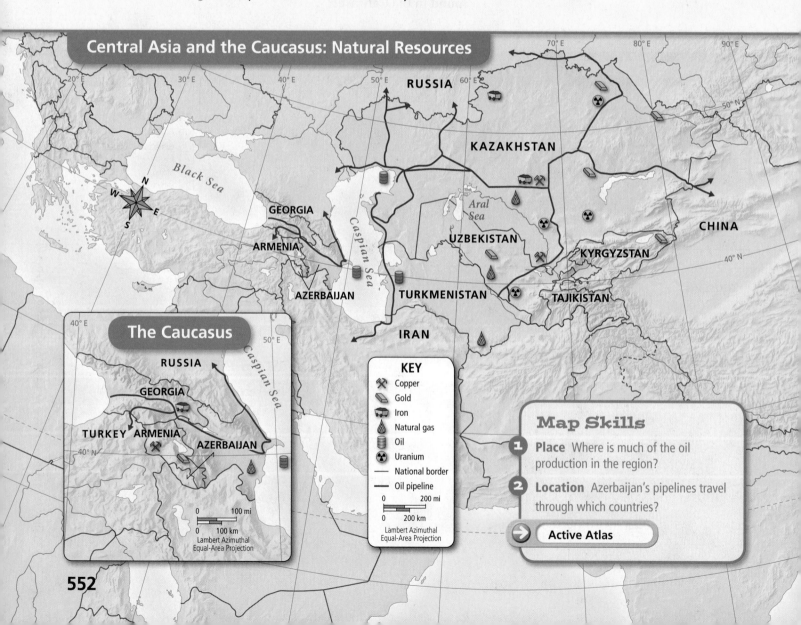

Central Asia and the Caucasus: Natural Resources

The Caucasus

KEY
- Copper
- Gold
- Iron
- Natural gas
- Oil
- Uranium
- — National border
- — Oil pipeline

Map Skills

1. **Place** Where is much of the oil production in the region?

2. **Location** Azerbaijan's pipelines travel through which countries?

→ Active Atlas

Transportation Since many of these countries are landlocked, transportation is a major challenge. Oil and gas exports must move through pipelines. One of Azerbaijan's pipelines runs through Georgia, where oil is loaded onto ships in the Black Sea. Another pipeline brings oil to Russia.

Until 2006, all of Kazakhstan's pipelines ran through Russia, which gave Russia great control. Recently, China helped build a pipeline from Kazakhstan into the west of China.

Water Water is also unevenly distributed. This is an important issue, especially in dry Central Asia. Water there comes mainly from the mountains in the east. If countries upstream use too much water, the countries downstream lose out. In 1997, Uzbekistan blocked part of the water flowing into Kazakhstan. Farmers in Kazakhstan feared their crops would die and held a **riot,** a noisy, violent public gathering.

Kyrgyzstan and Tajikistan have built dams along rivers to make electricity. Too many dams could threaten the water flow to their neighbors. Water shortages of Uzbekistan and Turkmenistan could become worse. The countries in this region must cooperate to transport and benefit from their resources.

Reading Check **Which two countries in this region produce the most oil?**

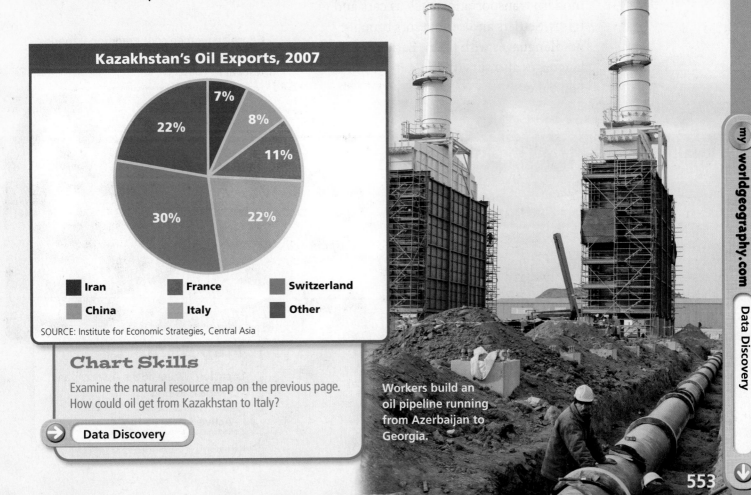

Kazakhstan's Oil Exports, 2007

- Iran 30%
- China 22%
- France 22%
- Italy 11%
- Switzerland 8%
- Other 7%

SOURCE: Institute for Economic Strategies, Central Asia

Chart Skills

Examine the natural resource map on the previous page. How could oil get from Kazakhstan to Italy?

Data Discovery

Workers build an oil pipeline running from Azerbaijan to Georgia.

553

myWorld Activity
One Side of the Coin

Cultural Diversity

Many groups of traders and invaders have passed through these regions. Each of these groups has left its mark on local cultures. As a result, these regions are very culturally diverse.

A large number of languages are spoken in the Caucasus. In total, more than 40 different languages are native to the Caucasus. Some of these languages are unique. They are not related to languages anywhere else on Earth.

The reason for this diversity of languages lies partly in the region's geography. People live in small villages separated by mountains. People in these villages were very isolated before there was modern transportation such as cars and buses. Settlers and conquerors brought new languages with them. Earlier local languages also survived in remote mountain valleys.

tension, *n.,* unease, a state of being stressed, not relaxed

All of the countries in this region have many different ethnic groups. These ethnic groups tend to live in clusters. In some cases, a minority group lives mainly in one part of a country. Some of these minorities want their own governments.

Conflict in Georgia Two areas of Georgia, Abkhazia (ab KAH zhuh) and South Ossetia (ah SEE shuh), have declared independence. The Abkhazians and Ossetians are minority ethnic groups in Georgia. They are the majority in the areas where they live. In 2008, Russian troops invaded to prevent Georgia from regaining control over these areas. Their status remains a source of <u>tension</u> in the Caucasus.

Georgian women cook traditional foods and play traditional music at a culture festival in Tblisi. ▼

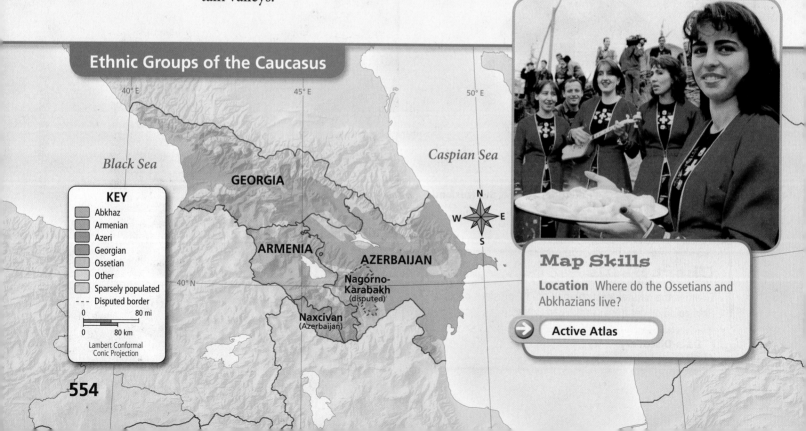

Ethnic Groups of the Caucasus

KEY
- Abkhaz
- Armenian
- Azeri
- Georgian
- Ossetian
- Other
- Sparsely populated
- - - Disputed border

0   80 mi
0   80 km
Lambert Conformal Conic Projection

Black Sea

Caspian Sea

GEORGIA

ARMENIA

AZERBAIJAN

Nagorno-Karabakh (disputed)

Naxcivan (Azerbaijan)

Map Skills

Location Where do the Ossetians and Abkhazians live?

Active Atlas

554

Nagorno-Karabakh There is a large area of southwestern Azerbaijan, called Nagorno-Karabakh (nuh GOR nuh KAHR uh bahk). Most people here are Armenian. In 1991, people in this area voted to break away from Azerbaijan.

Azerbaijan opposed this move. The government of Armenia supported the Armenians in Nagorno-Karabakh. In response, Azerbaijan blocked a natural gas pipeline that supplied fuel to Armenia. Azerbaijan also kept food and other supplies from entering Armenia. This hurt the Armenian economy. In this landlocked region, good relations with neighboring countries are important. Armenia and Azerbaijan have stopped fighting, but the conflict is unresolved.

Central Asian Crossroads As in the Caucasus, many different ethnic groups have settled in Central Asia. Tajiks are the largest ethnic group in Tajikistan. The Tajiks speak a language that is closely related to Farsi, the language of Iran. The ancestors of the Tajiks were one of the earliest groups to control this region.

Later, Arabs and Turks came to Central Asia. Arabs brought Islam to this region from southwest Asia. Now, most people in Central Asia practice Islam.

The Turks left their influence on the languages spoken across the region. Most of Central Asia's major ethnic groups, including the Kyrgyz, Uzbeks, Turkmen, and Kazakhs, speak Turkic languages. These groups have different customs, but they are all descended from the many Turkic tribes that came to the region.

The Russians are one of the latest groups to settle in Central Asia. Russia and then the Russian-dominated Soviet Union controlled this region for more than a century. As a result, many Russians made their homes here. During the years of Soviet control, many people, of all ethnic groups, learned to speak Russian. Today, both Central Asia and the Caucasus remain cultural crossroads.

Reading Check What is one reason why many languages are spoken in the Caucasus?

myWorld IN NUMBERS

If there were **100** people in the world,

Привет!

Hi!

3 would speak Russian.

Section 1 Assessment

Key Terms

1. Use the term *landlocked* to describe the location of Central Asia.

2. Use the term *temperate* to describe the climate of the Caucasus.

Key Ideas

3. In Central Asia, where do herders bring their animals to graze during the summer? Where do these animals graze during the winter?

4. Where are most farms in the Caucasus located?

5. What is the main source of water in Central Asia?

Think Critically

6. **Analyze Cause and Effect** What are the effects of the conflict in Nagorno-Karabakh?

7. **Describe** How did Russia come to dominate the region's oil and gas resources?

? Essential Question

What should governments do?

8. Should the governments of Tajikistan and Kyrgyzstan build hydroelectric dams if the dams will reduce the amount of water that flows to neighboring countries? Go to your Student Journal to record your answer.

my worldgeography.com Active Atlas

555

History of Central Asia and the Caucasus

Key Ideas
- Many groups of traders and invaders have influenced the cultures of Central Asia and the Caucasus.
- Russian, and then Soviet, control brought great changes to these regions.
- The countries in these regions became independent when the Soviet Union collapsed.

Key Terms • Silk Road • caravan • merchant • sedentary • madrassa

→ Visual Glossary

 Reading Skill: Summarize Take notes using the graphic organizer in your journal.

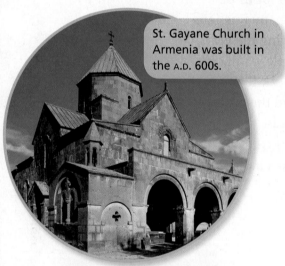
St. Gayane Church in Armenia was built in the A.D. 600s.

Throughout history, different empires fought to control Central Asia and the Caucasus. Major trade routes crossed these lands. Cities grew along these routes. In the 1800s, the Russian Empire conquered the region. Communists took over Russia in 1917, and Central Asia and the Caucasus became part of the Soviet Union.

Crossroads of the Eastern Hemisphere

Many empires have influenced the culture of this region, which is a crossroads between civilizations. Trade among empires spread ideas and technology across the region.

The Silk Road of Central Asia The **Silk Road,** which was a series of trade routes that crossed Asia, was the most important trade route in the region. The route was named for silk, a highly prized trade good from China. Many other goods traveled the route as well, including spices and fine china.

At the western edge of the Silk Road were civilizations along the Mediterranean Sea and in southwest Asia. The Silk Road connected these civilizations with China in the east. As **caravans,** or groups of people traveling together, made their way along the roads, they carried new ideas. Important technologies, such as papermaking and gunpowder, made their way from Asia to Europe.

Abdul Aziz Khan Madrassa, Bukhara, along the Silk Road

556

Merchants, or traders, relied on the banks, markets, and inns in Central Asian cities. These cities became important financial and cultural centers. For hundreds of years, the fate of these cities was tied to the Silk Road. When trade was brisk, the region prospered.

The Caucasus: Between Two Continents Many groups traveled across the Caucasus, which was a route between Europe and southwest Asia. In addition, many empires, including the Persian and Roman empires, invaded the Caucasus. These empires introduced new languages, customs, and religions.

Greek-speaking Romans, for example, brought Christianity to the kingdoms of Armenia and Georgia. Armenia soon became the first state to adopt Christianity as its official religion.

Islam Spreads Both trade and conquest brought the religion of Islam to these regions. In the early A.D. 600s, Islam spread throughout the Arab world. An Arab empire <u>expanded</u> from southwest Asia. This brought Islam to Azerbaijan and parts of Central Asia. Arabs conquered the Silk Road city of Bukhara, for example, in the early A.D. 700s.

Islam did not become the dominant religion in most of Armenia and Georgia. Yet by the 1400s, it had become the main religion throughout Central Asia. Traders and traveling scholars brought Islam to the nomads of the steppes.

Reading Check **What were some goods that were traded along the Silk Road?**

expand, *v.,* to increase in size or scope

THE SILK ROAD

Map Skills

Place Why do you think the Silk Road did not follow a straight line from Kashgar to Dunhuang?

Active Atlas

KEY
— Silk Road
— Modern border
○ City
0   600 mi
0   600 km
Miller Cylindrical Projection

Mechants sell silk in a market in the Silk Road city of Kashgar.

557

Empires Built on Horseback

Great empires also arose on the steppes of Central Asia. The vast grasslands allowed people to keep large herds of horses.

Nomads Emerge from Central Asia

Horses gave the nomads of the steppe a huge military advantage over **sedentary,** or settled, populations to the south. Nomad warriors created great empires that spanned Asia. On horseback, warriors swiftly swept down on their enemies. Armies on foot were no match for these mounted warriors.

The Huns were one early group of nomads from the western steppe. These skilled horsemen conquered the Caucasus and terrorized Europe. Attila the Hun, their most notorious leader, attacked the Roman Empire in the A.D. 400s.

The Huns were likely a Turkic-speaking people. At the time, there were many Turkic tribes in Central Asia. By the A.D. 500s, these tribes <u>dominated</u> much of Central Asia. They controlled an area from Mongolia in the east to the Amu Dar'ya River. Migration and conquest spread Turkic languages. Most of the main ethnic groups in Central Asia today speak Turkic languages.

Mighty Mongols Turkic and Persian states controlled Cenral Asia until the 1200s. At that time, Genghis Khan conquered the region and made it part of the Mongol Empire.

The Mongol warrior Genghis Khan united the Mongol tribes. He died in 1227, but his sons and grandsons continued to expand the Mongol empire. At its height, the Mongols controlled much of Asia and Eastern Europe. Their empire reached east to Korea, west into Russia, and south to northern India. No empire before the Mongol Empire was as large.

Under the Mongols, trade along the Silk Road increased. The Mongols protected caravans from bandits. Merchants moved along the route with few barriers.

Turkic tribes and descendants of the Mongol conquerors would vie for control over Central Asia for centuries until Russia took control over the entire region.

Reading Check Who was Genghis Khan?

dominate, *v.,* to rule over, control

A young woman in Kyrgyzstan performs at a festival celebrating the riding culture of the nomads of Central Asia. ▶

558

Communists Take Control

Russia, and then the communist Soviet Union, took control over Central Asia and the Caucasus. Life changed greatly under the communists.

The Russian Empire Expands During the 1700s and 1800s, the Caucasus region found itself in the middle of a struggle among three great powers: the Ottoman, Persian, and Russian empires. In Central Asia, Great Britain and Russia competed for control. By the close of the 1800s, Russia had won both of these contests. They had conquered the entire region.

Soviet Socialist Republics The communists seized power in Russia in 1917. The communist leaders took control over Central Asia and the Caucasus. They divided the regions into eight soviet republics, or states.

Changes to Culture and Daily Life Under communism, the government made decisions about economic production. Government officials told each republic what to produce. In Central Asia, many nomads were forced to settle and work on government farms. The government often did not manage the economy well. Shortages of basic goods became common.

The leaders of the Soviet Union also wanted to unify the country. They built many new schools. These schools taught in Russian instead of in local languages. The government wanted to control cultural life. It closed churches, mosques, and **madrassas,** that is, schools that teach the Islamic religion. The culture also changed as many Russians moved into both regions.

After years of growing economic problems, the Soviet Union collapsed in 1991. The eight soviet republics of these regions became independent.

Reading Check What are two ways the Soviet Union changed these regions?

myWorld Activity
Frozen in Time

Joseph Stalin, one of the Soviet Union's most powerful leaders, was born in Georgia. ▼

Section 2 Assessment

Key Terms

1. What is a madrassa?
2. Use the terms Silk Road, caravan, and merchant to describe trade routes in Central Asia.

Key Ideas

3. Who spread Christianity to the kingdoms of Armenia and Georgia?
4. What is one effect that the Silk Road had on Central Asia?
5. Which empire controlled this region at the end of the 1800s?

Think Critically

6. **Summarize** Why did nomads have a military advantage over sedentary populations in battle?
7. **Draw Inferences** Why do you think different empires fought to control these regions?

Essential Question

What should governments do?

8. Why did the Soviet government encourage the Russian language in these regions? Should the government choose the official language of the country? Go to your Student Journal to record your answers.

Samarqand: A Silk Road City

Key Idea
- Cities become centers of trade partly because of their locations.

For centuries, ideas and goods spread between the Mediterranean countries and East Asia along the Silk Road through Central Asia. In general, merchants traded along only one section of the Silk Road. Each stopped at a city along the way and traded his goods with another merchant. This merchant then carried these goods along the next section of the route. Cities grew where merchants stopped to trade. Samarqand was one of these cities along the Silk Road. It lies in the modern-day country of Uzbekistan. Below, travelers from China and Spain describe the city at two different times in its history.

▲ Historic Chinese painting of a street in Samarqand

Stop at each letter on the right and think about the text. Then answer the question with the same letter on the left.

A **Draw Conclusions** Why do you think Xuanzang mentions the landscape in his description?

B **Analyze Cause and Effect** Based on these facts, why do you think Samarqand became an important trading city?

C **Identify Bias** What impression does Xuanzang give of the people of Samarqand?

populous, *adj.,* having a large population
afford, *v.,* to provide
Shen horses, *n.,* a special breed of horses
inhabitants, *n.,* people who live in a place
trades, *n.,* crafts; types of work

A Chinese traveler on Samarqand in the A.D. 600s

66 [The city] is completely enclosed by rugged land and very <u>populous</u>. The precious merchandise of many foreign

A countries is stored up here. The soil is rich and productive, and yields abundant harvests. The forest trees <u>afford</u> a thick vegetation, and flowers and fruits are plentiful. The <u>Shen</u>

B <u>horses</u> are bred here. The <u>inhabitants</u> are skillful in the arts and <u>trades</u> beyond those of other countries. . . .

C The people are brave and energetic. . . . The king is full of courage, and the neighboring countries obey his commands. The soldiers and the horses are strong and numerous. . . . 99

—Xuanzang,
Record of the Western Regions, 646

Xuanzang

Stop at each letter on the right and think about the text. Then answer the questions with the same letter on the left.

D **Identify Evidence** What evidence does González de Clavijo give to support his opinion that Samarqand is a "great capital"?

E **Summarize** From which countries or regions did Samarqand's people come?

F **Compare and Contrast** How is this description similar to what Xuanzang saw?

district, *n.,* area surrounding the city

Moors, *n.,* Muslims from North Africa

Jacobites and Nestorians, *n.,* members of Eastern Christian churches

A Spaniard in Samarqand in the A.D. 1400s

❝ **The richness and abundance of this great capital and its <u>district</u> is such as is indeed a wonder to**

D **behold. . . . So great therefore was the population now of all nationalities gathered together in Samarqand that of men with their families the number . . . must amount to 150,000 souls.**

E **Of the nations brought here together there were . . . Turks, Arabs and <u>Moors</u> of diverse sects, with Christians who were Greeks and Armenians, Catholics, <u>Jacobites and Nestorians</u>, besides . . . [Indian] folk. . . .**

F **The markets of Samarqand further are amply stored with merchandise imported from distant and foreign countries.** ❞

—Ruy González de Clavijo, *Embassy to Tamerlane, 1403–1406*

González de Clavijo

The Sher-Dor Madrassa in modern-day Samarqand ▼

Analyze the Documents

1. **Draw Conclusions** How did Samarqand's location help it to become a center of trade?

2. **Writing Task** Suppose you were alive when one of these accounts was written. Write a list of questions you would ask the author to learn more about the city.

561

Central Asia and the Caucasus Today

Key Ideas
- Some local traditions and religious practices are being revived in this region.
- The governments of Central Asia and the Caucasus face economic, political, and environmental challenges.
- Tensions between different ethnic groups in the Caucasus have caused conflicts.

Key Terms • akyn • election fraud • repressive • demonstration • Rose Revolution

 Visual Glossary

Reading Skill: Identify Main Ideas and Details Take notes using the graphic organizer in your journal.

With the fall of the Soviet Union, the new republics of Central Asia and the Caucasus face many challenges. They must improve their economies and solve serious environmental problems. However, people in the region also are freer to reconnect to local traditions and religions.

Cultural Life of Central Asia and the Caucasus

The Soviet Union encouraged people in these regions to think of themselves as Soviet citizens. Now, people in these eight independent countries have a chance to make national identities based on the unique languages and customs of their countries.

Revival of Religion The Soviet Union did not allow religious freedom. Since independence, people have built new churches, mosques, and madrassas. The Soviets also banned customs and celebrations connected to religion. Now, Christian or Muslim holidays are public holidays in many countries.

 Culture Close-up

This man is an akyn, a traditional storyteller, from Kyrgyzstan. He memorizes long poems that tell the history of his people.

Local Culture Local languages and customs have also become more important since these countries have become independent. Many schools now teach in local languages, rather than in Russian. Also, people use local languages more often in public life. For example, after independence Islom Karimov, the president of Uzbekistan, began giving speeches in Uzbek rather than Russian. Still, there are large Russian-speaking minorities, especially in Kazakhstan.

Governments and individuals in these regions are acting to revive local arts and traditions. The government of Kyrgyzstan is helping to train traditional storytellers, called **akyn**. These storytellers recite long poems that tell the history and values of the Kyrgyz people. In Georgia and Armenia, churches have trained singers, and governments have supported dance, music, and visual arts.

Still, preserving these cultural traditions is a challenge. Knowledge of local art and literature was lost during the Soviet period. Many people do not have money to attend concerts or time to learn about the arts. Governments have limited budgets. They are trying to preserve traditional culture but also solve the serious problems that the region faces.

New Connections All of these countries now have more contact with countries besides Russia. Movies, music, and sports from the United States, China, and India have become popular in the region. Kazakhstan has also developed its own film industry. People in these regions are both connecting to local customs and sampling the cultures of other countries.

Reading Check Why is there a revival of religion in the region?

A dancer from Georgia's National Folk Song and Dance Academy performs a traditional dance.

my **Story** 📷 **Photo**

Above, the Naryn Mosque in Naryn town, Kyrgyzstan. The mosque was built in 1993.

Challenges for New Nations

People in the region must deal with new challenges as well as problems left behind by the Soviet Union.

Respecting Ethnic Diversity Different ethnic groups live side by side in these regions. Before, Russian was a common language. Now, if one group's language is more widely used, other ethnic groups must learn this language. Also, some countries now have more than one official language. Both Kyrgyz and Russian are the official languages of Kyrgyzstan.

Still, minority groups are sometimes treated unfairly. Most of the ancient Central Asian Jewish communities have moved to Israel and America due to harsh treatment. In Uzbekistan, Tajiks have a harder time finding jobs than Uzbeks. Some Tajiks claim to be Uzbek because they fear they will not be treated fairly. While the Uzbek government promotes Uzbek traditions, the Tajik people in Uzbekistan may lose their identity.

Poverty is a serious problem in many parts of Armenia. ▼

Meanwhile, in Georgia and Azerbaijan, ethnic tension has led to armed conflict when minority groups have tried to break away and form separate countries.

Joining the World Economy Before independence, each republic produced goods according to the Soviet Union's economic plan. Now, businesses in these countries must make goods to trade on the global market. Countries such as Azerbaijan and Kazakhstan have had economic success because they have valuable energy resources to trade.

Encouraging economic growth has been difficult. Many people in this region are poor and cannot find a job. Some people are frustrated and want the government to improve the economy.

66 The government says that we are independent, but people are going hungry. 99
—Young woman from Tajikistan

Inherited Environmental Problems The Soviet Union often did not manage resources well. They caused water shortages by using too much water to irrigate crops, including cotton. Industrial waste often went directly into lakes and rivers. Pollution of the Caspian Sea has damaged the fishing industry.

Cleaning up the pollution is expensive. Some Central Asian countries still rely on cotton as an important export. Governments must balance protecting the environment with their other responsibilities.

Reading Check What are two environmental problems in this region?

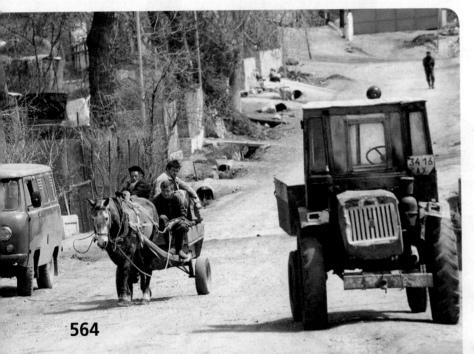

564

Closer Look

The Shrinking Aral Sea

The Aral Sea, between Kazakhstan and Uzbekistan, was once the fourth-largest lake in the world. The Amu Dar'ya and the Syr Dar'ya rivers fed the lake. The Soviet Union took water from these rivers to irrigate crops, especially cotton. They used so much water that the sea began to shrink. Local farmers still use large amounts of water for their crops. The Aral Sea is still shrinking, as the satellite photos at the right show. Scientists do not know if Kazakhstan and Uzbekistan can act fast enough to save the sea.

THINK CRITICALLY **What are some problems caused by the shrinking Aral Sea?**

1987

2008

There is a shortage of clean water for people living in the area. ▼

The water became so salty that fish could no longer live in most of the lake. Tens of thousands of people in the fishing industry lost their jobs. ▶

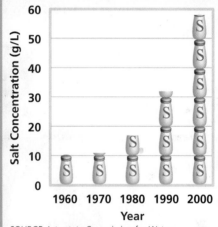

Concentration of Salt in the Aral Sea

SOURCE: Interstate Commission for Water Coordination of Central Asia

This desert used to be the bed of the Aral Sea. Kazakh villagers collect metal parts from boats that were stranded as the waters evaporated. ▼

565

task, *n.,* something that must be done, duty

Building New Governments

People of these regions face the task of overcoming political challenges. Some governments in these regions are corrupt and undemocratic.

New Governments, Old Leaders When the Soviet Union collapsed, the countries in these regions were left on their own. Often, people from within the Soviet government became leaders in the new countries. For example, both Nursultan Nazarbayev of Kazakhstan and Eduard Shevardnadze of Georgia were officials in the Soviet Union.

The leaders of the newly independent countries wrote new constitutions and laws that seemed to protect peoples' rights. Yet some of these leaders later acted to limit democracy. They have tried to stay in power as long as possible.

Limits on Democracy Elections are held in both regions, but people may not have political freedom. One common problem is **election fraud,** that is, unfair elections in which one group controls the results in order to gain power.

Often, governments have not protected the rights listed in their constitutions. Many leaders have attacked or jailed people who do not support them.

The government of Turkmenistan is one of the most **repressive,** meaning opposed to freedom. It keeps strict control over its citizens. The president holds most of the power. Saparmurat Niyazov, the country's first president, was known as Turkemenbashi, "leader of the Turks." He extended his power until his death in 2006. Even now, only one political party is allowed in Turkmenistan, and the press is not free to criticize the president.

In other countries, citizens have successfully protested against bad government. In 2003, many Georgians joined a demonstration against election fraud in a parliamentary election. A **demonstration** is a public display of group opinion, often a rally or march. Many people believed President Shevardnadze rigged the election so that candidates from his party would win.

The protests against this election came to be called the **Rose Revolution** because the demonstrators carried roses as a symbol of peace. Shevardnadze resigned

One of many golden statues of Saparmurat Niyazov, who made himself President for Life of Turkmenistan. ▶

566

because of these protests, and the country elected a new president.

Across both regions, progress has been uneven. In some countries, protests, like the Rose Revolution, have brought greater democracy. Still, the political systems of most countries are not open and democratic.

The Impact of Corruption Political problems often create problems in the economy. Corruption is a serious problem in most countries of these regions. Government officials often take money meant to build schools and hospitals and help the economy to grow. To improve their economies, many of the countries in these regions need to start by improving their schools, roads, and bridges. To make these improvements, governments will need to fight corruption.

Reading Check What is one political problem in these regions today?

Standing Up for Democracy

Kyrgyzstan
The government jailed journalist Zamira Sydykova because she reported on government corruption.

Georgia
Students protested election fraud by marching in the Rose Revolution demonstrations.

myWorld Activity
Hot Off the Press

Section 3 Assessment

Essential Question

Key Terms
1. What are akyn?
2. Use the term election fraud to describe politics in Central Asia and the Caucasus.

Key Ideas
3. Why do many countries in Central Asia and the Caucasus have more than one official language?
4. Why is Turkmenistan considered one of the most repressive countries in Central Asia?
5. What caused the Rose Revolution?

Think Critically
6. **Analyze Cause and Effect** Why has religion revived in Central Asia and the Caucasus since the fall of the Soviet Union?
7. **Compare and Contrast** Have countries in Central Asia and countries in the Caucasus faced similar problems since the fall of the Soviet Union? Explain your answer.

What should governments do?
8. Do you think the governments of Central Asia and the Caucasus should try to make farmers and businesses reduce pollution? Explain your answer.

Education: Reforming the Soviet System

Key Ideas
- Since countries gained independence from the Soviet Union, schools have made more effort to teach the languages and history of the region.
- Governments in this region are trying to improve the quality of their schools as one way to improve their economies.

Key Terms • innovative • entrepreneur

The countries of Central Asia and the Caucasus have faced many challenges since gaining independence. The new governments of these regions have taken charge of decisions that the Soviet Union used to make. One of the most important decisions for a government is how best to educate its citizens. Governments in these regions needed to change the Soviet education system to meet the needs of the market economy and to reflect each country's culture.

Investing in People

A worker with a computer can write more in an hour than someone using a pencil. However, it is harder to learn how to use a computer. If students learn to use a computer at school, they become workers with an important skill. Governments provide education to make sure the students of their country will learn the skills and knowledge that will make them good workers. The economic success of the country depends on businesses that are efficient and **innovative,** or that can develop new ideas and products.

Reading Check Why is education important?

The Soviet System

Basic education was important to the command economy of the Soviet Union. In the command economy, the government planned which products to produce. Government planners told factories and farms how much they needed to produce. The government taught workers and farmers to read, write, and do basic arithmetic. Workers kept track of what they made and reported this information back to government planners.

This Soviet farmer with a tractor can plant more crops than a farmer planting crops by hand. ▼

More Schools for More Students Many areas of Central Asia and the Caucasus did not have schools when the Soviet Union first took control of this region. The Soviet government built more schools. Also, it tried to make sure all young people attended school. The Soviet Union was successful in <u>expanding</u> basic education. By the 1980s, almost everyone in this region was literate, that is, they could read and write.

Problems of the Soviet System Still, the Soviet education system had problems. Often, the new schools in these regions did not have enough materials. It took time to train enough teachers to work in all the new schools. At some of the best schools, most students were Russians, not people native to the region.

The Soviet government required schools to teach in Russian. As a result, many never learned to read or write in their native language. Some regional languages did not develop words for new technologies.

In addition, the quality of the education was poor. Much of the learning was based on memorization. Textbooks taught the ideas of the communist leaders. Neither students nor teachers had free access to information. This limited their knowledge of new ideas and different opinions about issues.

Reading Check What were some problems of the Soviet education system?

expand, *v.,* to get larger, increase

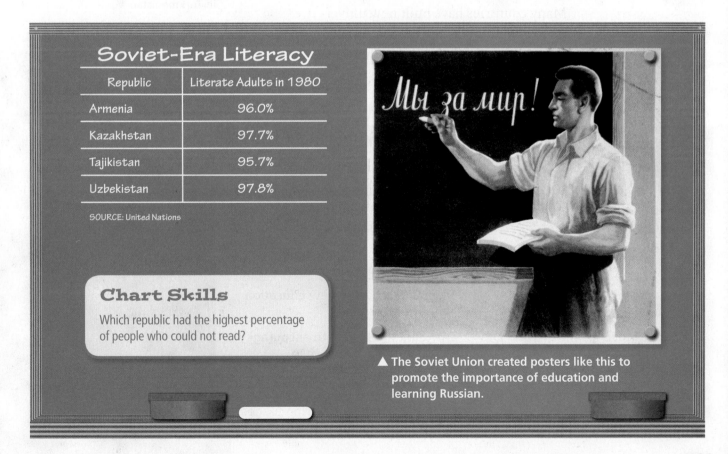

Soviet-Era Literacy

Republic	Literate Adults in 1980
Armenia	96.0%
Kazakhstan	97.7%
Tajikistan	95.7%
Uzbekistan	97.8%

SOURCE: United Nations

Chart Skills

Which republic had the highest percentage of people who could not read?

▲ The Soviet Union created posters like this to promote the importance of education and learning Russian.

569

Changing the System

The new nations of this region now face the challenge of building on the education foundations created by the Soviet Union. In addition, they need to reform the education system to meet the needs of a market economy, that is, an economy of free exchange that is not planned by the government.

New Schools and New Ideas Students in the Soviet system received training for a specific job in the planned economy. Now these countries need **entrepreneurs**, that is, people who start and manage new businesses. These countries also need people who will invent new products. Students need to learn to solve problems. They cannot just memorize information.

Many countries have built new universities to give students the more advanced training they need. In addition, they have started experimental schools that test new education methods.

Often, though, governments have been slow to make this kind of change. The government of Uzbekistan, in particular, carefully controls the education system. Citizens of Uzbekistan still do not have free access to information, nor are they free to voice their opinions.

Russian had been the major language in the Soviet education system, especially in secondary schools and in colleges. Now, in most countries in the region, the national language has become the main language used for instruction. As a result, many younger people cannot read or write Russian. They cannot use the Russian books in their school libraries.

Students in a classroom in Turkmenistan ▼

Education Reforms in Central Asia and the Caucasus

Reform	Related Problem
Change textbooks to be written in the national language and reflect national history rather than Soviet history.	Delay in getting textbooks written, produced, and printed causes a shortages of teaching materials
Obtain funding for reforms.	Governments cut spending because of economic problems.
Introduce new subjects and new teaching methods.	Training teachers in new education methods takes time.
Emphasize independent thinking and problem-solving.	Changing the system to encourage critical thinking rather than memorization takes time.
Teach about advanced technologies at school.	Words for new technologies had to be created in some national languages.

◀ A school in Tbilisi, the capital of Georgia

These nations must spend scarce money to translate books from Russian into their national languages. Shortages of teaching materials are a problem at schools across Central Asia and the Caucasus.

Funding Shortages For all countries in these regions, keeping basic levels of education high is also a challenge. The central government of the Soviet Union helped pay for the schools in these countries. Now, they must fund education on their own. The governments sometimes do not have enough money to pay teachers' salaries. Schools, especially in poor rural areas, face shortages of supplies. Some schools charge parents fees to help cover costs. When poorer parents cannot afford these fees, they take their children out of school. These children may not learn to read and write. School enrollment has decreased, especially in the poorest areas.

Wealthy parents have enough money to send their children to private schools or to schools abroad. Governments in this region are working to improve education opportunities for the children of families that are not so wealthy. They must build on the foundation created by the Soviet Union to help students succeed in a market economy.

Reading Check Why has it been difficult to improve the quality of education?

Assessment

1. What is one reason that education is important to a country's economy?

2. What was one success of the Soviet system of education?

3. Why have some children in these regions stopped going to school?

4. What is one way that the new experimental schools might be different from the old Soviet schools in this region?

5. Why are problem-solving skills important in a market economy?

Chapter Assessment

Key Terms and Ideas

1. **Describe** How do the herders of Central Asia prevent **overgrazing**?

2. **Explain** Why are pipelines important to the economies of Central Asia and the Caucasus?

3. **Compare and Contrast** What is the difference between nomads and a **sedentary** population?

4. **Recall** How did Islam spread to Central Asia?

5. **Summarize** How did the people of Georgia protest election fraud in 2003?

6. **Explain** Do you think **irrigating** crops contributes to the water shortage in Central Asia?

7. **Recall** What resource has helped the economies of Azerbaijan and Kazakhstan?

Think Critically

8. **Draw Conclusions** Why have many countries in Central Asia and the Caucasus had undemocratic governments since gaining independence?

9. **Analyze Cause and Effect** How has the geography of the Caucasus affected the cultures of the people living there?

10. **Make Decisions** Do you think Georgia should grant independence to Abkhazia and South Ossetia? Why or why not?

11. **Core Concepts: Conflict and Cooperation** Why did Silk Road trade increase under the Mongols? Why does trade decrease if there is conflict?

Places to Know

For each place, write the letter from the map that shows its location.

12. Georgia
13. Amu Dar'ya River
14. Caspian Sea
15. Kazakhstan
16. Aral Sea
17. Syr Dar'ya River
18. **Estimate** Using the scale bar, estimate the length of the Caspian Sea from northwest to southeast.

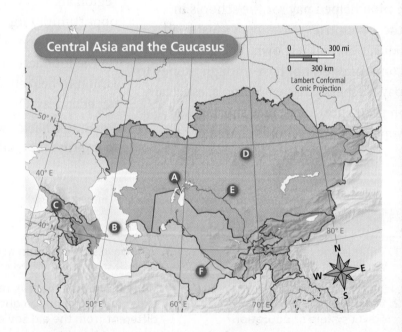

Central Asia and the Caucasus

Essential Question

myWorld Chapter Activity

Money Well Spent Work as a representative of a country from this region to decide how to spend your country's budget. Which problems are the most urgent? In addition, consider whether or not other groups in the country could address some of those problems better than the government.

21st Century Learning

Develop Cultural Awareness

Develop Cultural Awareness Draw a travel poster for a country in either Central Asia or the Caucasus. Research information that a traveler needs to understand the culture of the country. Be sure to show images that deal with the following:
- religion
- the arts
- language
- cuisine

Document-Based Questions

Success Tracker™
Online at myworldgeography.com

Use your knowledge of Kazakhstan and Documents A and B to answer questions 1–3.

Document A

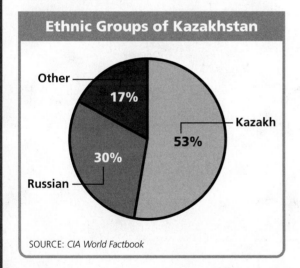

Ethnic Groups of Kazakhstan

Other 17%
Kazakh 53%
Russian 30%

SOURCE: *CIA World Factbook*

Document B

" Under Soviet rule, Russians were not just an ethnic majority, they were also the political, cultural, and social elite. . . Today, the tables have turned. Kazakhs now call the shots from the highest levels of government."

—Jessica P. Hayden, "Who Am I? Russian Identity in post-Soviet Kazakhstan," *Slate*, July 20, 2004

1. What is the largest ethnic group in Kazakhstan?
   A Russian
   B Kazakh
   C Tajik
   D Uzbek

2. What does Document B describe?
   A a change of power in favor of the Kazakhs
   B strong prejudice against Kazaks
   C Kazakhs still under Russian rule
   D Kazakhs sharing power with the Russians

3. **Writing Task** Based on Documents A and B, what has changed in Kazakhstan? Write a paragraph explaining why these changes may have taken place.

myworldgeography.com Self-Test

573

Chapter 13

South Asia

Essential Question

What makes a nation?

KEY
- - - Disputed border
—— National border
⊛ Capital city
○ Other city

0   400 mi
0   400 km
Lambert Conformal Conic Projection

Where in the World Is South Asia?

Washington, D.C., to Palampur: 7,240 miles

my Story

Nancy's Fruitful Loan

*In this section you'll read about Nancy, a young woman who is helping her mother start a new business in a mountainous region of India. **In what ways does Nancy's work help strengthen her nation?***

Explore the Essential Question
- at my **worldgeography.com**
- using the **myWorld Chapter Activity**
- with the **Student Journal**

Story by Aniruddha Das for myWorld Geography Online

It is a busy time in Nancy's hometown near Palampur, India. Next week there will be a big wedding, but in the meantime there's plenty of other work to do. Nancy already has many daily chores. She gathers food for the cattle, cleans the house, and even helps her grandfather repair her home. Now that she is 18, she has also joined the Samriddhi, a business run by a group of local women. The women of Samriddhi work together to harvest, prepare, and sell pickled fruit products. They have one of the few successful businesses in the area.

Palampur lies within a region known as the Changar belt. This is a dry, rocky area marked by ravines and gullies with a scattering of trees that provide shade and color the hills a dusty green. It is a challenging place to earn a living. The land is difficult to farm, but the women of Samriddhi have found a way to take advantage of local resources. Changar forests are rich with wild fruits. Many of these fruits can be used to make jams and chutney. A chutney is a relish made of fruits mixed with other ingredients such as vinegar and lemon juice.

"We have many different varieties of fruit . . . we have lemon, limes, Indian gooseberry, jackfruit, mango . . . " explains Nancy,

my **worldgeography.com** On Assignment

575

Nancy's home

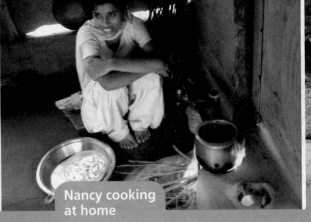
Nancy cooking at home

Nancy feeding the cows

The landscape around Nancy's home is rocky and dry.

Nancy and her family

gesturing to a range of Samriddhi jams and chutneys. The whole operation is funded by small bank loans, called microcredit loans. Thanks to these low-risk loans the Samriddhi women are able to buy the salt, spices, and sugar needed for pickling. They can also use the money for minor expenses such as renting a truck to transport their products to the Samriddhi office.

Today, Nancy is traveling with her mother and a few other Samriddhi women to the bank to apply for a new microcredit loan. "We need a loan so we can start a plantation. We want to grow some new fruit trees," Nancy explains as we walk along the dusty street to the small local bank. "It will cost us about 80,000 to 90,000 rupees," she adds, which is about $1,800.

The bank has different payment plans for different kinds of microloans. The bank manager explains to Nancy and the group that for a plantation loan, they need to show that they have plans to clear and level the land. They will also

576

Applying for a loan at the bank

Nancy at work

need to make a down payment of 15 percent of the total cost of the project. The rest of the project will be financed by the bank. Loans for things such as seeds or fertilizer require a 7-percent down payment. The money involved may not seem like much by Western standards, but the average annual income in the region is only about $300 a year.

Nancy is proud to be involved in the process and excited about helping to set up a new plantation. The older women are glad to have Nancy in the group as well. They know she is high-spirited, hardworking, and intelligent.

Later, Nancy and her mother prepare for a week-long sales trip. They fill the sales van with their products and set off. Their first stop is just outside Palampur itself, but they will also travel to several other towns before returning home.

Nancy works hard to sell as much as she can. She knows that the money they make will not only help

pay for the new loan but also provide income for her family. Some of the money will be set aside to educate Nancy and her brother. "Right now I am planning to study computer science," Nancy says. "But if there is a chance for me to join the police then I will do that. I want to serve my country."

The Samriddhi has done more for this village than just make money; it has provided hope for the future. By working together to manage the land and grow a business, the Samriddhi has brought the community together. Sometime soon they hope to see fruit growing on the new plantation that Nancy and the microcredit loan help set up. That will be something for everyone to enjoy!

Meet the Journalist

Name Sachin Singh
Favorite Moment Watching Nancy climb trees to harvest the fruit

→ **myStory Video**

Join Nancy as she shows you more about her life.

my worldgeography.com myStory Video

577

Chapter Atlas

Key Ideas

- Landforms and resources have influenced settlement in South Asia.
- People have adapted to a range of climates in South Asia.
- Physical geography plays a divisive role in South Asia.

Key Terms
- Indian subcontinent
- Green Revolution
- subsistence farming
- flood plain

Visual Glossary

Reading Skill: Label an Outline Map Take notes using the outline map in your journal.

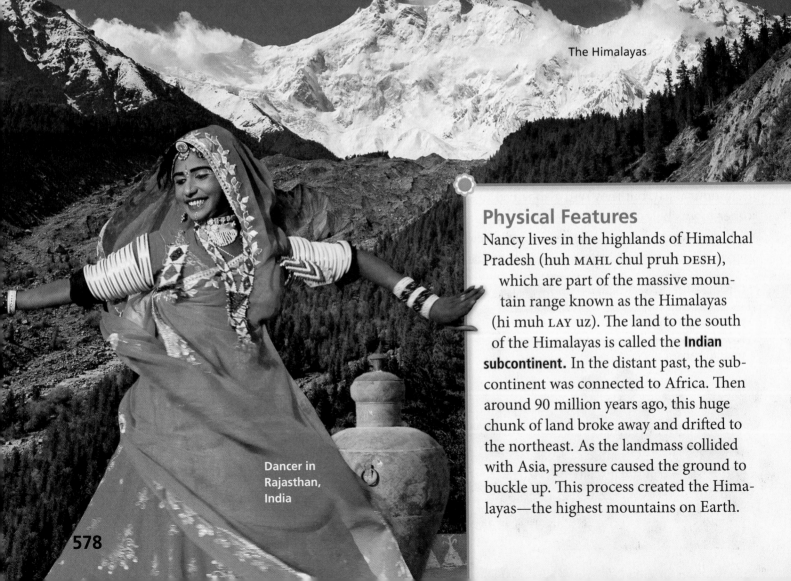

The Himalayas

Dancer in Rajasthan, India

Physical Features

Nancy lives in the highlands of Himalchal Pradesh (huh MAHL chul pruh DESH), which are part of the massive mountain range known as the Himalayas (hi muh LAY uz). The land to the south of the Himalayas is called the **Indian subcontinent.** In the distant past, the subcontinent was connected to Africa. Then around 90 million years ago, this huge chunk of land broke away and drifted to the northeast. As the landmass collided with Asia, pressure caused the ground to buckle up. This process created the Himalayas—the highest mountains on Earth.

578

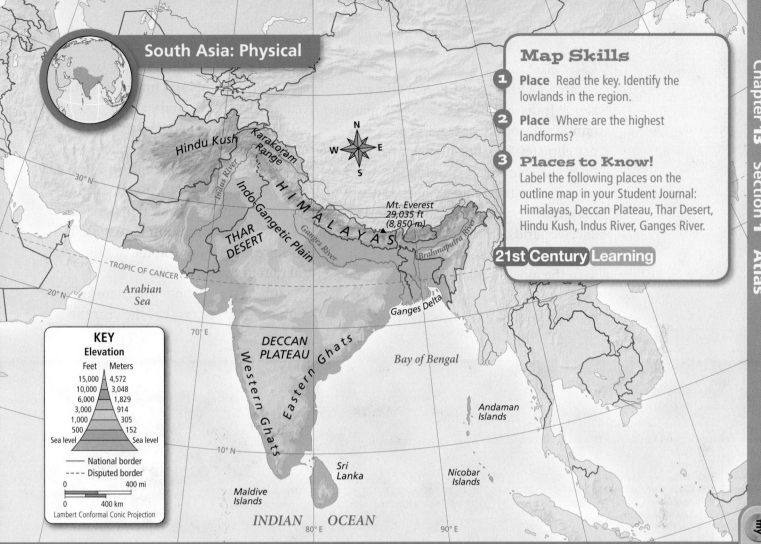

South Asia: Physical

Map Skills

1. **Place** Read the key. Identify the lowlands in the region.

2. **Place** Where are the highest landforms?

3. **Places to Know!**
Label the following places on the outline map in your Student Journal: Himalayas, Deccan Plateau, Thar Desert, Hindu Kush, Indus River, Ganges River.

21st Century Learning

KEY
Elevation

Feet	Meters
15,000	4,572
10,000	3,048
6,000	1,829
3,000	914
1,000	305
500	152
Sea level	Sea level

— National border
--- Disputed border

0 ___ 400 mi
0 ___ 400 km
Lambert Conformal Conic Projection

The Himalayas form India's northern border. They surround nearly all of Nepal and Bhutan. Smaller ranges, such as the Hindu Kush, extend this wall of mountains into western Pakistan and central Afghanistan.

Large rivers drain the melting snows of the mountains. To the south of the Himalayas, the Ganges (GAN jeez) River runs across India's northern plains and meets the Brahmaputra (brah muh POO truh) River in the heart of Bangladesh. In the west, the Indus River flows through the dry plains of Pakistan.

The southern part of South Asia is a peninsula that juts into the Indian Ocean. Much of this peninsula is a fairly flat highland area called the Deccan Plateau. It is bordered by two coastal mountain ranges known as the Western Ghats and the Eastern Ghats.

Off the southern tip of India lies the island nation of Sri Lanka. To the southwest are the Maldives, a chain of 1,190 islands formed from coral.

Reading Check What physical feature forms the northern border of India?

Climate

regulate, *v.,* to control

South Asia has many different climate zones. India and Bangladesh have mainly humid subtropical or tropical wet and dry climates. Daytime high temperatures can reach 80°F, even in the coolest months. The most intense heat, in May, can average more than 100°F. Arid and semiarid climates run through the countries of Afghanistan and Pakistan.

In the mountains of the west and far north, the high peaks are covered with snow year-round. Glaciers fill many valleys. But this area is not all snow and ice. The mountains and foothills contain fertile valleys, grasslands, and forests.

The Himalayas help to <u>regulate</u> the region's climate. They block much of the cold, dry air that would otherwise stream into South Asia from the north in winter. The mountains also draw moisture out of the warm, humid summer winds. The moisture falls as snow in the mountains and rain to the south.

South Asia's seasonal winds are known as monsoons. For most of the year the

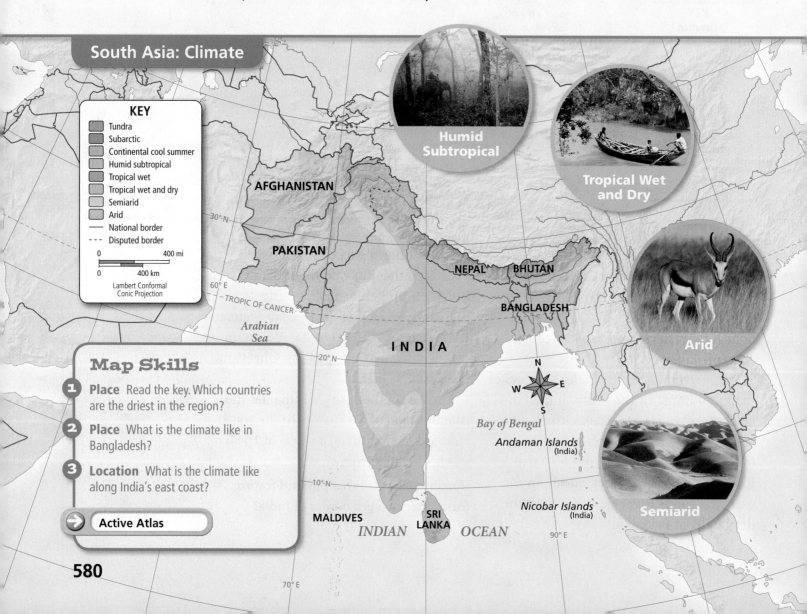

South Asia: Climate

KEY
- Tundra
- Subarctic
- Continental cool summer
- Humid subtropical
- Tropical wet
- Tropical wet and dry
- Semiarid
- Arid
- — National border
- --- Disputed border

0 — 400 mi
0 — 400 km
Lambert Conformal Conic Projection

Map Skills

1 Place Read the key. Which countries are the driest in the region?

2 Place What is the climate like in Bangladesh?

3 Location What is the climate like along India's east coast?

Active Atlas

580

monsoon blows from the northeast and brings dry air. During the wet season, lasting from June to September, the southwest winds bring drenching rain.

The warm wind of the southwest monsoon picks up moisture from the Indian Ocean. It dumps heavy rain on India's western coast, the northern plains, and the northeast. On the west coast of India, the Western Ghats block this moisture, so the land to the east of the Ghats has a semiarid climate.

The southwest monsoon can bring <u>intense</u> storms and floods. In 1988, the flooding of the Ganges and other rivers washed away crops and livestock in Bangladesh and killed some 2,000 people. A quarter of the population was left homeless.

In Afghanistan, much of the land stays dry year-round. The southwest monsoon does not penetrate far into this area.

Reading Check **How do the mountains affect climate?**

intense, *adj.,* very strong

Closer Look

Climate and Culture

People in South Asia have adapted to their environments in many ways. Their houses are well suited to local climates.

THINK CRITICALLY **Where on the climate map might you find each of these buildings? Study each house and read the description for clues.**

This haveli, or mansion, was built for a rich merchant. Its balconies and screens allow breezes to pass through the house—a relief in the hot dry area where it was built.

This stilt house is well adapted to its lowland delta environment. It can easily withstand the seasonal floods, as long as they don't get too high!

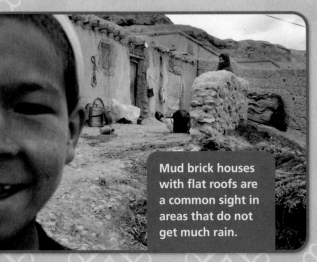

Mud brick houses with flat roofs are a common sight in areas that do not get much rain.

In cold climates, farmhouses must shelter people, animals, and grain. In this house, grain and produce are kept in the attic. Farm animals are kept on the ground floor.

myworldgeography.com Active Atlas

581

Land Use and Resources

Most South Asians work in agriculture. Farms tend to be rather small. Their owners engage mainly in **subsistence farming**, which means they use the crops they grow to feed themselves, but have little left over to send to market.

In the mid-1960s, technology created a **Green Revolution**, an increase in agricultural production. This produced more food for growing populations.

However, in some places, farmers overused chemical fertilizers and pesticides. They pumped too much water out of the ground to irrigate crops. Farming practices like these poisoned the soil, fouled rivers, and dried up wells.

The region is also rich in resources. Rivers provide hydroelectric power. Mines in the plateaus and mountains produce iron ore, bauxite, copper, and coal. Petroleum and natural gas are found in the plateaus and mountains, as well as offshore. These resources support manufacturing in India and Pakistan.

Reading Check Why are rivers an important resource?

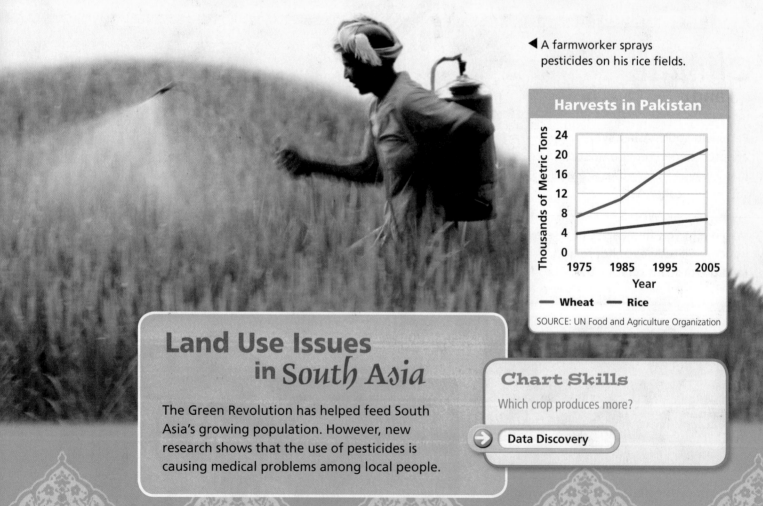

◄ A farmworker sprays pesticides on his rice fields.

Harvests in Pakistan

Thousands of Metric Tons — Year (1975, 1985, 1995, 2005)

— Wheat — Rice

SOURCE: UN Food and Agriculture Organization

Land Use Issues in South Asia

The Green Revolution has helped feed South Asia's growing population. However, new research shows that the use of pesticides is causing medical problems among local people.

Chart Skills

Which crop produces more?

→ Data Discovery

582

Population Explosion

South Asia suffers from two related problems: high population growth and poverty. Nearly half the world's poor live in this region.

The size of South Asia's population is one of the main problems. The region contains three of the ten most populous countries in the world—India, Pakistan, and Bangladesh. Just meeting people's basic needs—food, clothing, and shelter—is a monumental task.

About half of South Asia's population is located on the Indo-Gangetic plain, in the valleys of the Ganges and Brahmaputra rivers. Most of the people of this region live in rural areas.

India, for example, is only 29 percent urban, but its urban population has grown steadily. Much of this increase is made up of rural families moving to cities to improve their lives. Many Indian migrants, however, are forced to live in urban slums or on the streets.

Reading Check Which countries are the most populous in the region?

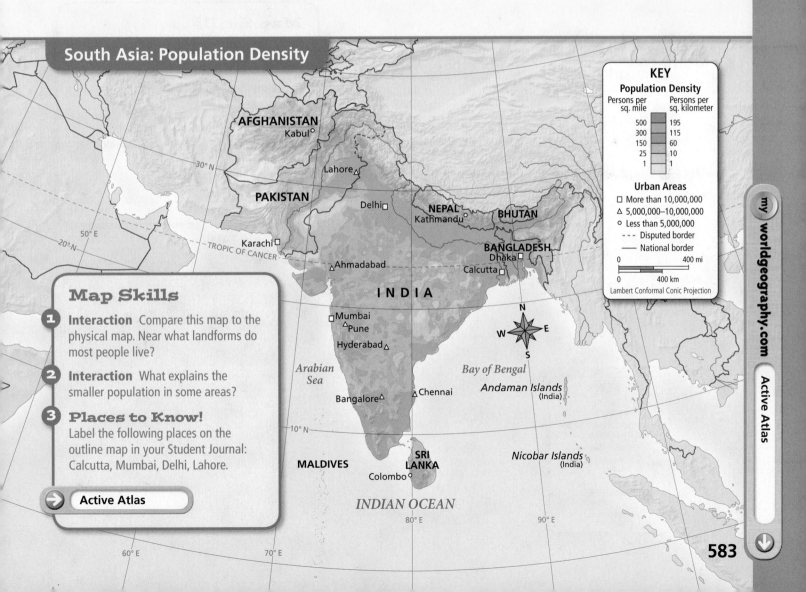

South Asia: Population Density

KEY

Population Density

Persons per sq. mile	Persons per sq. kilometer
500	195
300	115
150	60
25	10
1	1

Urban Areas
- □ More than 10,000,000
- △ 5,000,000–10,000,000
- ○ Less than 5,000,000
- --- Disputed border
- — National border

0 — 400 mi
0 — 400 km
Lambert Conformal Conic Projection

Map Skills

1 Interaction Compare this map to the physical map. Near what landforms do most people live?

2 Interaction What explains the smaller population in some areas?

3 Places to Know! Label the following places on the outline map in your Student Journal: Calcutta, Mumbai, Delhi, Lahore.

→ Active Atlas

my **worldgeography**.com

Active Atlas

Geography Shapes History

Since prehistoric times, people have migrated to the rich **flood plains**—the flat lands along the rivers. When snows melt in the mountains, rich soil is washed down onto the lowlands of the Indo-Gangetic plain. This fertile plain attracted early settlers. In time, civilization developed and rich cities arose.

The wealth of the cities attracted invaders. Although the Himalayas were too high for armies to cross, newcomers found their way into the subcontinent through mountain gorges such as the famous Khyber Pass.

Other landforms continue to shape the region's history. For example, the mountain landscapes of Afghanistan and Pakistan have always isolated communities. In both countries, fiercely independent tribes have long resisted government interference in their affairs. Today, governments struggle with rebel forces in these same tribal areas.

Reading Check How did invaders reach the rich lowlands of India?

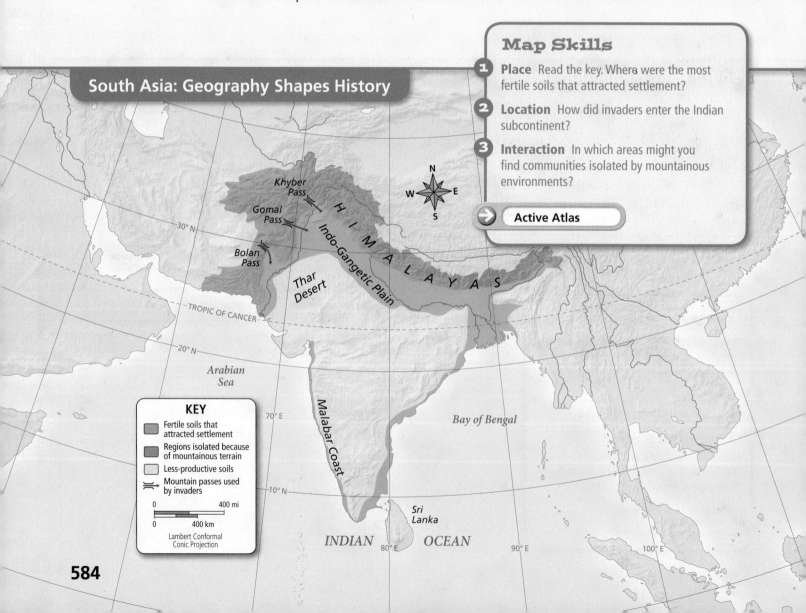

South Asia: Geography Shapes History

Map Skills

1. **Place** Read the key. Where were the most fertile soils that attracted settlement?

2. **Location** How did invaders enter the Indian subcontinent?

3. **Interaction** In which areas might you find communities isolated by mountainous environments?

→ **Active Atlas**

KEY
- Fertile soils that attracted settlement
- Regions isolated because of mountainous terrain
- Less-productive soils
- Mountain passes used by invaders

0 — 400 mi
0 — 400 km
Lambert Conformal Conic Projection

Crossroads of Culture

While some parts of South Asia were isolated by mountains, other areas have always been in contact with the wider world. Goods and ideas traveled from China to Europe along the Silk Road, which passed through northern Afghanistan. Farther south, India lay at the center of the international sea trade routes.

These trade routes brought immense wealth to the region. Indian cotton, pearls, and pepper from the Malabar coast were in worldwide demand. Sri Lanka exported cinnamon. Ancient Greek traders used the monsoon winds to sail quickly across the Arabian Sea to reach these goods. Merchants from distant lands sometimes settled in the trading ports. Meanwhile, South Asian merchants helped spread the religions and culture of South Asia to China and Southeast Asia.

As you have read, the Himalayas did not stop invaders from entering the region. Some of these invaders came to raid and others to conquer. Each set of newcomers changed the history of the Indian subcontinent. In turn, these newcomers were changed by the regions they invaded. A cultural exchange began that continues today.

The Muslim invasions brought the religion of Islam to South Asia. They also brought cultural influences from Persia and the Arab world.

Despite much peaceful cultural interaction, growing diversity also created tensions. This is a region of multiple faiths, ethnic groups, and languages. At times the tension between different groups has led to violence. However, the people of South Asia have also enjoyed periods of religious tolerance and cultural exchange. In the next section you will read how a complex and rich civilization developed in this crossroads of culture.

Reading Check How did the region become a crossroads of culture?

myWorld IN NUMBERS

If there were **100** people in the world,

17 would live in India.

Section **1** Assessment

Key Terms

1. Use the following terms to describe the geography of South Asia: Indian subcontinent, subsistence farming, Green Revolution, flood plain.

Key Ideas

2. Identify three roles that the northern mountains play in South Asia's geography.

3. What is the southwest monsoon, and how does it affect South Asia?

4. Where are the most fertile farmlands in South Asia located?

Think Critically

5. **Categorize** Some people categorize South Asia as a hot and humid region. Is that accurate? Explain.

6. **Draw Conclusions** Why are the river valleys among the most densely populated areas of South Asia?

Essential Question

What makes a nation?

7. How does the geography of a nation help create a common bond among its people and help shape its national identity? Go to your Student Journal to record your answer.

my worldgeography.com Active Atlas

History of South Asia

Key Ideas
- A series of migrations mark the history of South Asia.
- Religious diversity developed early and increased over time.
- Britain slowly gained political control of most of the region.
- After India gained independence, new nations and conflicts emerged.

Key Terms
- cultural hearth
- caste system
- Hinduism
- nirvana
- Buddhism
- partition
- nonalignment

 Visual Glossary

Reading Skill: Analyze Cause and Effect Take notes using the graphic organizer in your journal.

In ancient times, an advanced civilization developed in the Indus River Valley, in what is now Pakistan. Cities such as Mohenjo Daro and Harappa were amazingly sophisticated and well planned. Brick houses, two to three stories high, lined streets laid out on a grid pattern. The people of these cities had plumbing and clean water. They used a writing system and traded with other parts of the world.

Early History

Indus Valley civilization developed around 2500 B.C. and lasted for almost a thousand years. Its cities were spread over a huge area in the fertile Indus River basin. Here, as in other parts of the world, resources attracted settlement. Farmers in the fertile Indus flood plain grew wheat, barley, rice, cotton, and other crops. Traders set up networks to exchange goods. Soon Indus Valley products, goods, and ideas reached people in less-advanced areas. In this way, the Indus Valley served as a **cultural hearth**—a place where civilization began and spread.

Around 1900 B.C., the Indus Valley civilization went into a mysterious decline. Some believe that earthquakes or climate change may

◀ A dancing Shiva, Hindu god of creation and destruction

◀ Jain temples on Mount Girnar, a mountain that attracts Jain, Hindu, and Muslim pilgrims

586

have disrupted the food supply. But even though its cities collapsed and were abandoned, aspects of its culture survived.

A Culture Forms Around 1700 B.C., a massive migration changed the history of the region. Migrants entered the subcontinent through the mountain passes. They spread across the northern plains of the Indus and the Ganges. The newcomers blended with local peoples, forming a group we call Aryans (AYR ee unz). Out of this union came a new culture, religion, and social system.

Social Divisions The Aryan **caste system** divided society into four main groups: priests, warriors, farmers, and laborers. Priests formed the highest caste. Those in the lowest caste were scorned and considered unclean.

Reading Check **What is the caste system?**

New Religions

In South Asia the Aryans' faith merged with local beliefs. The result was **Hinduism,** the religion of most people in India today.

Hindu Beliefs The sacred texts of Hinduism are called the Vedas, a collection of hymns and instructions. The Vedic texts may date to about 1200 B.C. Later, between the years 300 B.C. and A.D. 300, great poems, known as epics, were also composed. The *Mahabharata* is the world's longest epic poem. It deals with a conflict between royal cousins.

Hindus believe in one spirit that lives in all things. In Hindu belief, this spirit, called Brahman, also takes the form of

▲ Hindu procession in Mumbai

lesser gods and goddesses. More than thirty gods are mentioned in the Rig Veda hymns.

Another principle of Hinduism is the idea that the human soul is eternal. According to Hindus, when the body dies, the soul passes into a new body. This process, known as reincarnation, can occur again and again, in an endless cycle. For believers, reincarnation is also affected by karma, the collection of good and bad deeds of a person's life. Karma determines the kind of life that will follow when the soul has been reborn.

To escape this cycle of rebirth many became ascetics—people who give up the luxuries of the world in order to try to live a spiritual life. The goal of the ascetic was to achieve salvation by uniting the individual soul with the universal soul, the Brahman.

Buddhism The Hindu search for salvation encouraged the development of a new religion. In the 500s B.C., a

587

man named Siddhartha Gautama (sih DAHR tuh gow TUH muh) taught that all suffering is caused by desire. In other words, human beings become unhappy when they cannot get what they want. In order to overcome desire, people must follow a code of conduct. According to Gautama, their goal should be to achieve **nirvana,** a state of understanding that releases the soul from the cycle of rebirth.

Gautama became known as the Buddha, or Enlightened One. His teachings developed into a religion known as **Buddhism.** Traders and Buddhist monks spread this new religion throughout Asia.

Another religion, Jainism, also emerged in South Asia. The followers of Jainism, called Jains, believed that the

soul can be perfected and purified in this world. One of the ways to reach this perfection is to practice ahimsa, or nonviolence toward all living beings.

Reading Check According to Buddhist teachings, what makes people unhappy?

Early Empires
In 327 B.C., the kingdoms of South Asia were threatened by Greek armies under Alexander the Great.

The Greek Invasion Alexander, king of Macedon, had built a huge empire over Greece and parts of Africa and Asia. His Greek army fought their way into the northern Indus Valley. Alexander's army was exhausted. Faced with a long march across the Ganges plain in monsoon rains, the soldiers forced Alexander to head home.

Shortly after Alexander's retreat, one South Asian state took control of much of the region. That state became known as the Mauryan empire. Its most famous leader was Asoka (uh SOH kuh).

Religious Tolerance Asoka led several campaigns against his enemies in the first dozen years of his reign. But after one especially brutal battle he rejected violence and adopted Buddhist beliefs. Under Asoka, Buddhism spread through the Mauryan empire.

Not long after Asoka's death, the Mauryan empire declined and smaller kingdoms arose once more. Then, around A.D. 320, a state located on the Ganges plain expanded its power to form the Gupta empire. This empire ruled territory

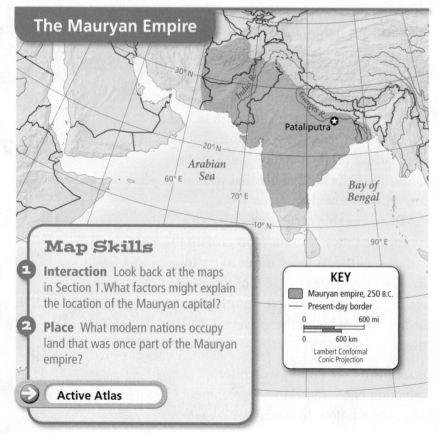

The Mauryan Empire

Map Skills

1 **Interaction** Look back at the maps in Section 1. What factors might explain the location of the Mauryan capital?

2 **Place** What modern nations occupy land that was once part of the Mauryan empire?

Active Atlas

KEY
- Mauryan empire, 250 B.C.
- Present-day border

0   600 mi
0   600 km
Lambert Conformal Conic Projection

from the Himalayas south to the Deccan Plateau. The two centuries of Gupta rule were a golden age of culture. Great advances were also made in science and mathematics. Gupta mathematicians developed the concept of zero. By A.D. 600, Indians were using a system of numbering that uses place value and numerals to represent numbers. Arab traders carried this system to Southwest Asia and Europe. Today, this system, called the Hindu-Arabic system, is used worldwide.

Reading Check **Which South Asian religion did Asoka embrace?**

Islam Arrives

Because India was such an important part of the international trade routes, new ideas and religions were spread by travelers and merchants. This is how Islam first entered the subcontinent.

Trade and Conquest Islam arrived in India in waves. The first came in the early 700s, when Arab traders introduced Islam to South Asia. The new faith spread throughout what is now Pakistan. Then, in the 900s, Turkish Muslim kingdoms began to spread through Afghanistan. Afghan kings launched raids into India to seize the wealth that was stored in the Hindu temples.

In the 1200s, one group of Muslim invaders established the Delhi Sultanate. This was a kingdom centered on the city of Delhi and led by a Muslim ruler called a sultan. Muslims would rule much of South Asia for the next 600 years. However, Hindu rajas, or rulers, controlled kingdoms in south India.

The arrival of Islam in a mainly Hindu region changed the history of South Asia. Hindus and Muslims were often rivals. Despite religious differences, there was a great deal of cultural exchange.

As Islam spread in the north, a new religion called Sikhism was born. Most followers of this religion, the Sikhs, live in an area of north India called the Punjab.

The Mughals In 1526, a Muslim from Central Asia named Babur founded the powerful Mughal empire. His grandson, Akbar, was a wise and tolerant ruler. Akbar extended Mughal control over much of South Asia. Akbar included Hindus in his army and government and protected other religions. He supported the arts and learning.

Muslim worshipers at a mosque in Lahore, Pakistan ▼

my **worldgeography.com**

Active Atlas

589

A grieving Shah Jahan built the Taj Mahal to mark the grave of his wife. ▼

The Mughal Empire

Armor of a Mughal war elephant. War elephants were the tanks of their day. They could easily smash their way through enemy lines.

Starting in the early 1500s, a Muslim dynasty called the Mughals ruled in South Asia. During much of this time the arts flourished, and both Muslims and Hindus helped govern the state.

THINK CRITICALLY Study the timeline. When did Mughal power decline?

Miniature painting showing Akbar welcoming Hindu princes and nobles

1526 Babur founds dynasty.

1628 Shah Jahan begins reign.

1707 Aurangzeb dies.

GOLDEN AGE

DECLINE

1500   1600   1700   1800

1556 Akbar begins reign.

1631 Taj Mahal is begun.

1658 Aurangzeb begins reign.

1858 British exile last Mughal.

590

Akbar's grandson, Shah Jahan, ruled at the height of Mughal power. Following the death of his beloved wife, Mumtaz Mahal, he built the Taj Mahal as a monument to her.

In 1658, Shah Jahan's son Aurangzeb seized power. Aurangzeb ended religious tolerance. He began persecuting Hindus and other non-Muslims, such as the Sikhs. Despite a series of uprisings against him, Aurangzeb continued to expand Mughal territory. However, his military campaigns weakened the empire. After Aurangzeb's death, the empire declined.

Reading Check **What was the Delhi Sultanate?**

The Colonial Period

During the Mughal period, the Portuguese, Dutch, British, and French set up trading ports. They came in search of spices, especially pepper, as well as cotton, silk, and indigo for dyeing cloth.

Trading Ports to Empire The British government sent the powerful East India Company to act as its trading agent in South Asia. By the mid-1700s, the Company had pushed its European rivals off most of the subcontinent. To protect its trade, the Company took over some Indian states by force. It also tried unsuccessfully to control Afghanistan.

In 1858, the British government took control of the East India Company's territories. Much of South Asia was now a British colony. It provided Britain with tea, coffee, grain, and raw materials such as cotton. Britain used Indian cotton to make inexpensive cloth in its factories.

India's textile industry <u>collapsed</u>. Its craftspeople could not compete with British-made cloth. Instead of exporting cloth and other finished goods, India became a market for those goods.

Struggle for Independence In the early 1900s, a movement arose to force Britain out of India. Its greatest leader was Mohandas Gandhi (moh HAHN dus GAHN dee). Gandhi organized boycotts of British goods and led protest marches. Gandhi urged nonviolent resistance, or peaceful protest.

Gandhi believed that a nation should not be built around only one religion or ethnic group. He called on Hindus and Muslims to unite as one nation.

Reading Check **What tactic did Gandhi use to force Britain out of India?**

collapse, *v.,* to break down

66 **It is my firm conviction that nothing enduring can be built upon violence.** 99
—Mohandas K. Gandhi, 1928

tense, *adj.,*
strained

South Asia After Independence

In 1947, Britain withdrew from India. But Muslims in the northwest and northeast feared that they would face discrimination if they remained in Hindu-dominated India. So India was **partitioned**—split into two states, India and Pakistan. At the time, Pakistan was made up of two regions, west and east, with 1,000 miles separating the two.

Partition With partition, a massive migration began. Millions of Hindus moved from Pakistan to India. Millions of Indian Muslims moved to Pakistan.

Many were massacred in an eruption of violence between ethnic and religious communities. In 1948, Gandhi himself was shot and killed by a Hindu extremist.

Ever since partition, relations between India and Pakistan have been tense. Both countries claim the region of Kashmir. In 1947 and again in 1965, India and Pakistan went to war over Kashmir.

India's prime minister during most of this period was Jawaharlal Nehru (juh-WAH hur lahl NAY roo). Nehru sought to modernize India. He also aimed to keep religion out of politics.

In foreign affairs, Nehru forged a policy of **nonalignment.** Nonalignment means India did not ally itself with either of the superpowers—the United States or the Soviet Union—during the Cold War.

Nehru died in 1964. Two years later his daughter, Indira Gandhi, became prime minister. She oversaw yet another war with Pakistan in 1971.

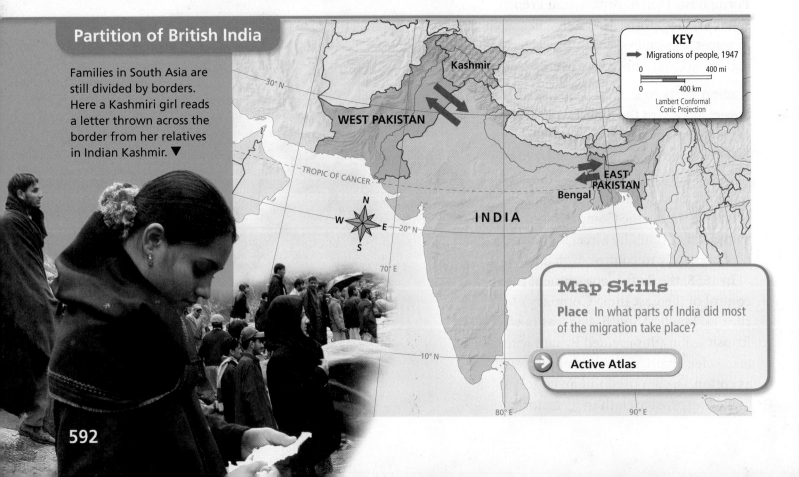

Partition of British India

Families in South Asia are still divided by borders. Here a Kashmiri girl reads a letter thrown across the border from her relatives in Indian Kashmir. ▼

KEY
→ Migrations of people, 1947

0 — 400 mi
0 — 400 km
Lambert Conformal Conic Projection

Map Skills

Place In what parts of India did most of the migration take place?

→ **Active Atlas**

592

The leading political party in East Pakistan demanded independence. The Pakistani government launched an attack on East Pakistan in March 1971. Some 10 million people, mostly Hindus, fled from East Pakistan into India.

India helped East Pakistan gain independence. In December 1971, East Pakistan became the nation of Bangladesh (BAHNG luh desh).

Other Conflicts Civil war also struck Sri Lanka. In 1983 a group of Hindu Tamils began fighting for a separate state. The war killed an estimated 70,000 people. In 2009 the government gained control of rebel areas and declared the war over.

In Afghanistan, the king was overthrown in 1973, and the country became a republic. Five years later, a communist political party seized control. In response, rebellions broke out throughout the country. To support the Afghan government, the Soviet Union invaded.

After a decade of fighting various Muslim rebel groups, the Soviet Union withdrew. One of the groups, the Taliban, took over Afghanistan. The Taliban sheltered and supported Osama bin Laden and al Qaeda, the group that planned and carried out the September 11, 2001, terrorist attacks on the United States. That year, the United States, Britain, and other NATO countries helped Afghans force the Taliban from power.

Reading Check Why did the partition of India lead to a massive migration?

Afghan rebels on a captured Soviet helicopter in 1980 ▼

Section 2 Assessment

Essential Question

What makes a nation?

Key Terms

1. Use the following terms to describe the history of South Asia: cultural hearth, caste system, Hinduism, nirvana, Buddhism, partition, nonalignment.

Key Ideas

2. How did the Aryans influence the culture of South Asia?

3. How did the colony of India serve the economic needs of Britain?

4. What three present-day countries were formed out of British India?

Think Critically

5. **Synthesize** What might have happened in South Asia if the Mughal empire had not declined?

6. **Compare Viewpoints** Why did many Hindus and Muslims in South Asia migrate during partition?

7. Do you agree or disagree with Gandhi and Nehru's idea of a nation? Explain. Go to your Student Journal to record your answer.

Nonviolent Protest

Key Idea
- Nonviolent resistance, a key strategy of the American civil rights movement, had its roots in South Asia.

Throughout history, there have always been those who rejected violence as a way of solving problems. Mohandas Gandhi was one such person. In the early 1900s, Gandhi led India's successful nonviolent resistance to British rule. Later, the American minister Dr. Martin Luther King, Jr., applied Gandhi's teachings during the civil rights movement in the American South. In the face of violent mobs and police, Dr. King led peaceful demonstrators to demand civil rights for African Americans. Study these excerpts to learn how the ideal of nonviolence linked Gandhi and King.

▲ Painting of Mohandas Gandhi

Gandhi leading a protest in India in 1930 ▼

Read the text on the right. Stop at each circled letter. Then answer the question with the same letter on the left.

A **Distinguish Between Fact and Opinion** What clue words tell you that Gandhi's first statement is an opinion?

B **Summarize** What invitation does Gandhi make to the members of his audience?

C **Identify Evidence** What evidence in this speech makes it clear that Gandhi did not want to split India into two countries?

envisage, *v.,* to form a mental picture of something

differences, *n.,* (1) qualities that are not similar; (2) disagreements

Gandhi's Ideals

66 I believe that in the history of the world, there has not been a more genuinely democratic struggle **A** for freedom than ours. . . . In the democracy which I have <u>envisaged</u>, a democracy established by nonviolence, there will be equal freedom for all. Everybody will be his own master. It is to join a struggle for such democracy that I **B** invite you today. Once you realize this, you will forget the <u>differences</u> between the Hindus and Muslims, and think of yourselves as Indians only, engaged in the common **C** struggle for independence. 99

—Mohandas Gandhi, "Quit India" speech, August 8, 1942

Read the text on the right. Stop at each circled letter. Then answer the question with the same letter on the left.

(D) Compare and Contrast Which name for King's guiding principle do you like best? Explain.

(E) Identify Main Ideas and Details In the early days of protest, how did the protesters describe their tactics?

(F) Synthesize Why do you think the Christian doctrine of love and the principle of nonviolent resistance together made such a "potent weapon"?

Christian love, *n.,* good will toward all, including one's enemies

Mahatma, *n.,* a title given to someone to show deep respect

potent, *adj.,* effective

Martin Luther King, Jr., on Nonviolence

66 **From the beginning a basic philosophy guided the movement. This guiding principle has since been referred to variously as nonviolent resistance, noncooperation, and passive resistance.**

(D) But in the first days of the protest none of these expressions was mentioned: the phrase most often heard was 'Christian love.' . . . As the days unfolded, however,

(E) the inspiration of Mahatma Gandhi began to exert its influence. I had come to see early that the Christian doctrine of love operating through the Gandhian method of nonviolence was one of the most potent weapons available to the [African American] in his struggle for freedom. 99

(F)

—Martin Luther King, Jr.,
Jubilee magazine,
September 1958

Analyze the Documents

1. **Compare and Contrast** The phrase *struggle for freedom* appears in both excerpts. What freedom did Gandhi seek? What freedom did King seek? How were their struggles similar?

2. **Writing Task** Suppose that Gandhi were still alive when King was leading the civil rights movement. What would King think of Gandhi's "Quit India" speech on the previous page? Write a letter from King to Gandhi in which King responds to the speech. In your letter, refer to specific phrases or ideas in the speech.

King leading a civil rights march in Alabama, 1965

595

South Asia Today

Key Ideas
- South Asia has a rich mix of cultures.
- Religious and ethnic divisions within countries create tensions in the region.
- Political conflict and border disputes threaten peace in the region.
- Although it has many problems, the region is playing a greater role in the global economy.

Key Terms • epic • Bollywood • secular democracy • outsourcing

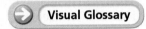 Visual Glossary

Reading Skill: Summarize Take notes using the graphic organizer in your journal.

 Culture Close-up

In India, people throw colored powder as they welcome spring during the festival of Holi. ▼

South Asia today is full of problems and promise. The region includes some of the most populated and poorest countries in the world. These nations suffer from conflicts, political instability, and terrorism. Natural disasters and rising sea levels threaten Bangladesh and the Maldives. India and Pakistan's dispute over Kashmir sometimes brings the two countries close to nuclear war.

Despite the region's troubles, South Asia holds great promise for the future. Democracy thrives in India, a land with pockets of prosperity and a growing middle class. As you have read in myStory, economic programs are helping many people, such as Nancy's family, rise out of poverty. The region's technical and scientific skills are in worldwide demand. South Asia's artistic energies fuel an exciting and influential culture.

South Asian Culture Today

Like Europe, South Asia has always been a well-defined cultural area. Many of its languages share a common ancestor. Huge parts of the region were united under Mauryan, Mughal, and British rule. In ancient times, Hinduism was another unifying force through the region. Although its religious diversity has increased, South Asians share many cultural traditions.

The Arts Ancient Hindu literature is full of stories of gods and heroes. These stories take the form of **epics,** long poems of adventure and conflict. Epics such as *The Ramayana* helped define the values of Hindu culture—values such as courage, gentleness, love, and faithfulness.

Today many of these cultural values are expressed in films. India's version of Hollywood is called "**Bollywood,**" because it first emerged in Bombay (known today as Mumbai).

Religion Most people in India and Nepal are Hindu. Muslims form a large minority in India, although in some areas, such as Kashmir, they are in the majority. In Pakistan, Afghanistan, and Bangladesh, Muslims form the largest religious group. Sikhism dominates in the Punjab area of northwest India.

Buddhism was once widespread in South Asia. Today it is strongest in the Himalayan countries of Nepal and Bhutan and on the island of Sri Lanka.

Food Food is often flavored with a variety of spices, especially in India. A typical meal throughout the region is rice mixed with vegetables and, sometimes, meat. Hindu food rules ban the eating of beef. Islam forbids the eating of pork.

Reading Check What foods make up a typical meal in South Asia?

my World IN NUMBERS

The Indian film industry, known as Bollywood, produces as many as **1,000** films a year.

Closer Look

Bollywood

Bollywood is one of the largest film industries in the world. Like Hindu epics, Bollywood films tell tales of heroes, love, and adventure, and are full of music and dancing. Some Bollywood films tell the stories of the Hindu epics.

THINK CRITICALLY In what ways might Bollywood films differ from Hollywood films?

Bollywood is famous for its dance scenes.

my worldgeography.com Culture Close-up

597

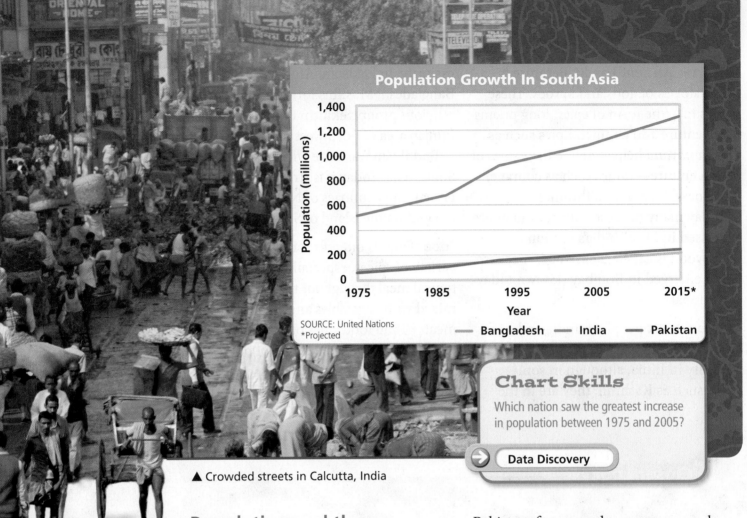

Population Growth In South Asia

Population (millions) vs Year (1975, 1985, 1995, 2005, 2015*)

SOURCE: United Nations
*Projected

Bangladesh — India — Pakistan

▲ Crowded streets in Calcutta, India

Chart Skills

Which nation saw the greatest increase in population between 1975 and 2005?

→ Data Discovery

Population and the Environment

South Asia is home to more than 1.5 billion people. It is a region of dense populations and high birthrates. These factors are associated with poverty and with environmental problems.

Population Growth Today India has some 1.2 billion people. By 2050, India is expected to add 500 million more people and overtake China as the world's most populous country. This increase will probably happen even though India's birthrate has <u>dramatically</u> slowed in recent decades.

The populations of other nations in South Asia are also growing rapidly. In

dramatically, *adv.,* greatly, strongly

Pakistan, for example, a woman can be expected to have an average of four children during her lifetime. Afghanistan's population is growing the fastest. On average nearly seven children are born to each woman.

Search for Resources As in other parts of the world, rising populations are putting pressure on shrinking resources. In Bangladesh, people are moving onto the delta in order to farm. The delta is covered with rich sediment that has washed down from the Himalayas. However, the delta is also prone to cyclones and flooding.

Throughout the region, existing farmland may not be able to provide people with enough food to eat. In addition, the food that is available may not be very nutritious. In densely populated Bangladesh, some 30 percent of the population is undernourished.

People's health depends on vitamin-rich food and clean water. Clean water is another scarce resource in much of South Asia. Rivers are being dammed and water is being pumped out of the ground to irrigate crops. Such actions reduce the amount of drinking water available for the growing population.

Pollution South Asia's rivers are also polluted. Industries dump chemicals and other waste into them. Cities and villages foul them with raw sewage. For this reason, South Asians face a high risk of waterborne diseases. The Ganges is one of the most heavily polluted rivers in the world. Yet people wash clothes in it, bathe in it, and drink from it.

Much of the air pollution in South Asia comes from factories, power plants, and vehicles. But a significant amount comes from the burning of forests to make way for farms and the burning of wood and coal for cooking and heating.

As a result, a blanket of pollution hovers over South Asia. Some call it the "Asian Brown Cloud." By reflecting sunshine, it cools the land below and warms the air in the mountains. This could <u>alter</u> the monsoon to reduce rainfall in the dry northwest. Some scientists believe it is helping speed the melting of Himalayan glaciers by adding to climate change.

Reading Check What are the main causes of air pollution in South Asia?

▲ Protest against a dam project in India

Social Problems

South Asia is a mix of the old and the new. It is often caught between traditional ways of life and the demands of the modern world.

Social Issues The caste system is a very ancient feature of society in India. A caste is a social group into which people are born. In the past, it was very difficult to leave one's caste. People were expected to marry within their caste, and their jobs were usually linked to that caste. People in the lower castes, who did forms of labor such as cleaning toilets, were considered unclean. So were those outside the caste system. In the past,

alter, *v.,* to change

my worldgeography.com

Data Discovery

599

these people, or dalits, were forced to live outside town or village boundaries.

Gandhi and other South Asian leaders hoped to create a "casteless society." Toward that end, the constitutions of both India and Pakistan forbid discrimination based on caste. Today, the people who were once called untouchable now call themselves Dalit, meaning oppressed.

India's constitution also bans other common forms of discrimination:

> 66 The State shall not discriminate against any citizen on grounds only of religion, race, caste, sex, place of birth or any of them. 99
>
> —Constitution of India, Part III, Article 15, Clause 1

The legal ban on discrimination has not stopped the practice. Women, for example, still face unequal treatment. Throughout South Asia, a man is considered the head of the household. In some rural areas, girls are prevented from attending school. Women's social and political roles are limited.

Another social issue in South Asia is unemployment. The region's economies are growing. But they are not growing fast enough to put everyone to work. Unemployment is worst in Afghanistan, where as much as 40 percent of workers do not have paying jobs.

Reading Check What kinds of discrimination exist in South Asia?

Closer Look

Women in South Asia

Women enjoy some rights but also endure many restrictions and problems in South Asia. In Pakistan, India, and Bangladesh, women have been elected to powerful leadership positions. However, in many places they suffer from lack of food, poor medical care, and discrimination.

THINK CRITICALLY Read the chart of literacy rates. What might explain the difference between men and women's literacy in the region?

President Patil of India helps lead the region's largest country.

In rural Afghanistan, women who go out in public are expected to cover themselves almost completely. They are often kept from getting an education and may be forced into marriage.

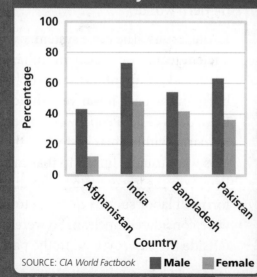

Literacy Rates

Bar chart showing Percentage (y-axis, 0 to 100) by Country (x-axis). Afghanistan: Male ~43, Female ~12. India: Male ~73, Female ~48. Bangladesh: Male ~54, Female ~41. Pakistan: Male ~63, Female ~36.

SOURCE: *CIA World Factbook*   ■ Male   ■ Female

600

Conflicts in South Asia

Political and ethnic conflicts often have a religious aspect in South Asia. In India, rivalry between Hindus and Muslims sometimes explodes into violence. In 2002, Hindu-Muslim violence in India's Gujarat province left more than 1,000 people dead.

In Afghanistan, the government is under threat from the Taliban, a religious group that follows a fundamentalist form of Islam. In the 1990s, the Taliban ruled the country. Although the United States and its allies forced them from power in 2001, the Taliban fight on. An American-led coalition is fighting Taliban rebels in the south and in the eastern mountains.

But extremist groups like the Taliban can easily cross the Pakistan border to safe havens in the mountainous areas of northwest Pakistan.

Tensions between India and Pakistan often threaten the peace. The main cause of friction is Kashmir, an Indian state with a large Muslim population. In the past, Pakistan's government has backed Kashmiri groups fighting for independence. These armed rebel forces often clash with Indian troops. Both India and Pakistan possess nuclear weapons. When tensions rise between these two neighbors, the world holds its breath.

Reading Check Which South Asian countries possess nuclear weapons?

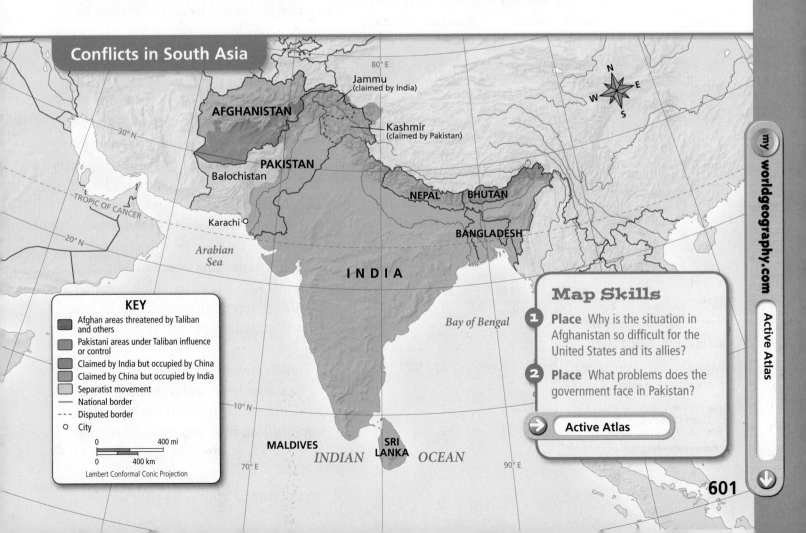

Conflicts in South Asia

KEY
- Afghan areas threatened by Taliban and others
- Pakistani areas under Taliban influence or control
- Claimed by India but occupied by China
- Claimed by China but occupied by India
- Separatist movement
- — National border
- --- Disputed border
- ○ City

0 — 400 mi
0 — 400 km
Lambert Conformal Conic Projection

Map Skills

1 **Place** Why is the situation in Afghanistan so difficult for the United States and its allies?

2 **Place** What problems does the government face in Pakistan?

→ **Active Atlas**

my **worldgeography.com** Active Atlas

Governments and Economies

South Asia has a mix of governments. India enjoys a long-lasting parliamentary democracy. However, other South Asian governments have been unstable.

A Variety of Governments India is a representative democracy. People elect nearly all the members of one house of India's parliament, or legislature. One member of parliament is chosen as the prime minister to head the government.

Bangladesh and Sri Lanka have had democratic rule for a long time. But their citizens do not always enjoy the same level of rights and freedoms as citizens do in India. Nepal recently ended its monarchy. It is now a democratic republic. Bhutan also holds democratic elections.

India is a **secular democracy,** which is a democracy not based on religion. In other nations, religion defines the state. For example, the nations of Pakistan, Afghanistan, and the Maldives are all Islamic republics. In Pakistan, the prime minister must be Muslim.

After a coup by the military in 1999, an army general ran Pakistan for nine years. The courts, the press, and the people all suffered a loss of rights. In 2008, civilians once more gained power.

In Afghanistan, much has changed since the United States helped overthrow the Taliban in 2001. Afghanistan has a constitution and holds elections. However, the central government is weak. The United States and its allies continue to send troops to maintain order.

Economies Much of the region remains very poor, despite efforts to industrialize and diversify economies. Although Pakistan's economy has grown in recent years, its increasing population cuts into these economic gains. Many of its citizens live in poverty. Industrialized areas around Karachi and Lahore contrast sharply with the poverty of Balochistan and the North-West Frontier Province.

Bangladesh is the poorest country in South Asia. However, it has a strong textile industry. Microcredit banks have helped pull many people in that nation out of poverty.

Indian government policies have emphasized trade and technology. The government has lowered trade barriers, but tariffs on food products are high. It

India's Exports, 1990–2006

A line chart showing India's exports in Billions of Dollars (y-axis, 0 to 140) versus Year (x-axis: 1990, 1994, 1998, 2002, 2006). Exports rise gradually from about 15 billion in 1990 to about 30 billion in 1998, then sharply increase to about 123 billion by 2006.

SOURCE: United Nations

Chart Skills

Which four-year period shows a sharp increase in exports?

→ Data Discovery

has also signed trade agreements with other countries in South Asia. Trade has helped give India one of the world's fastest-growing economies. Today, about 100 million Indians can afford goods like televisions and washing machines.

In the 1990s, the government began building software technology parks. Here, workers create computer software for worldwide export.

India is also providing software services to companies all over the world. For example, companies in Europe and the United States have found it cheaper to send many computer-related tasks to workers outside the company. This practice is called **outsourcing.** India's economy and its skilled workforce have benefited from this practice.

India has put its high-tech skills to work in another area—space. The country has launched many satellites into orbit around Earth for many nations. In 2008,

India successfully landed a space probe on the moon.

Reading Check In which South Asian country do citizens have the most democratic freedoms?

▲ India has a highly skilled technology workforce.

Section 3 Assessment

Key Terms

1. Use the following terms to describe life in South Asia today: epic, Bollywood, secular democracy, outsourcing.

Key Ideas

2. What are the two most commonly practiced religions in South Asia?

3. Why is Kashmir one of the main trouble spots in South Asia?

4. What actions by India's government opened up trade with the rest of the world?

Think Critically

5. **Draw Inferences** What is the connection between dense population, poverty, and environmental problems?

6. **Summarize** How is India's economy tied to the world economy?

Essential Question

What makes a nation?

7. What problems threaten the national unity of each nation in South Asia? Go to your Student Journal to record your answer.

my worldgeography.com Data Discovery

Governments and Citizens in South Asia

Key Ideas
- The relationship between government and citizens varies throughout South Asia.
- Cultural values affect issues of justice and injustice in the region.
- In parts of South Asia, geography has a strong influence on political life.

Key Terms • secular • judiciary

The relationship between government and citizens varies throughout South Asia. In a democratic country like India, citizens have specific rights that are defined in the constitution. When citizens are protected by constitutions, it is harder for governments to take these rights away.

While India has a strong democratic tradition, in other nations, democracy is new or unstable. However, there are many signs of hope in the region.

Defining the Nation

For thousands of years, nations in the modern sense did not exist. Instead, the lands of South Asia were divided into many small kingdoms. Sometimes strong rulers would succeed in creating larger kingdoms or empires. These empires included people of many different ethnic groups and religions.

New Governments Under the British, much of South Asia was united under colonial rule. But by the late 1800s, South Asians were demanding independence. For a time, people from many different religions worked together to protest against British rule. But even as they struggled for independence, they argued about the kind of nation they wanted to create. Political leaders such as Gandhi

◀ The wheel symbol on India's flag comes from a column set up by the emperor Asoka. The wheel represents Buddha's teachings.

and Nehru wanted a nation that was **secular,** meaning religion and politics were separated. They believed that they could create a nation that was united by democratic ideals. However, many Muslims knew that they would become a minority in this new nation. As a minority, they feared that they would be vulnerable to discrimination. Because of this, Muslims wanted a separate country.

So as India gained independence, the entire area was partitioned, or divided, between a largely Hindu India and a mainly Muslim Pakistan.

Religious Tolerance Even without a large Muslim minority, India's new leaders were in control of a nation that was ethnically diverse. They banned discrimination based on religion.

India's Federal State The new Indian government also organized the country into a federal state, with power distributed through individual states. This system was partly influenced by the constitution of the United States, which allows for power to be shared between the federal government and the states. The Indian government controls foreign policy, defense, and some forms of taxation. The states have power over public health and local government.

Reading Check How is India's government like that of the United States?

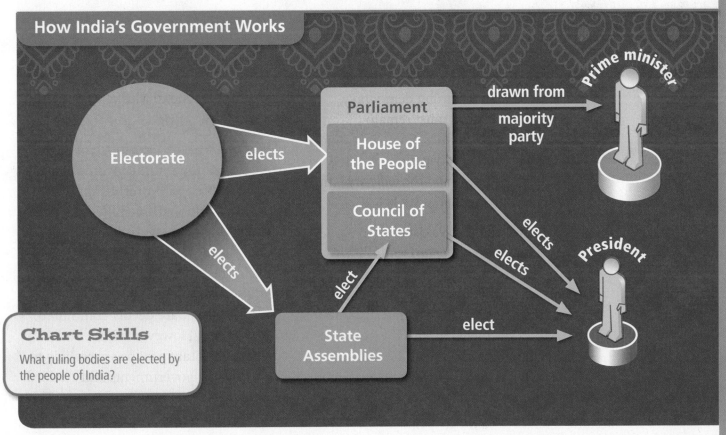

How India's Government Works

Chart Skills
What ruling bodies are elected by the people of India?

605

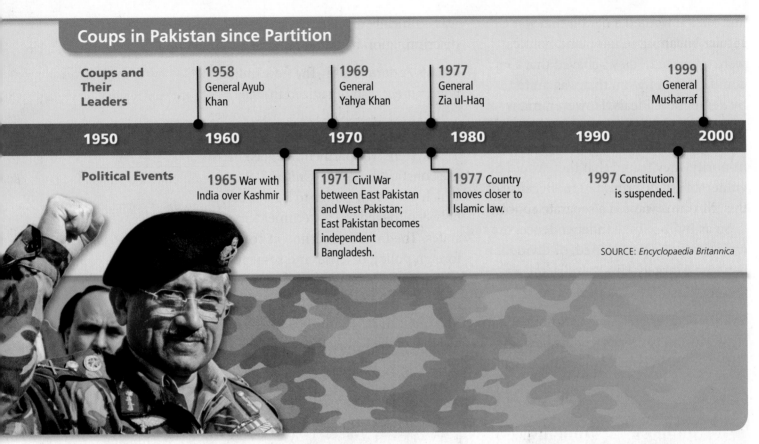

Coups in Pakistan since Partition

Coups and Their Leaders	1958 General Ayub Khan	1969 General Yahya Khan	1977 General Zia ul-Haq	1999 General Musharraf

1950	1960	1970	1980	1990	2000

Political Events

1965 War with India over Kashmir

1971 Civil War between East Pakistan and West Pakistan; East Pakistan becomes independent Bangladesh.

1977 Country moves closer to Islamic law.

1997 Constitution is suspended.

SOURCE: *Encyclopaedia Britannica*

▲ Former President of Pakistan, General Pervez Musharraf

Political Problems

In Afghanistan and Pakistan, democracy is very weak. In a strong democracy, certain institutions must remain independent of politics. Some institutions that must remain independent are the military, the press, and the **judiciary**—the system of courts that provide justice.

Coups in Pakistan Pakistan has repeatedly suffered coups, or military takeovers. Generals, who often promise a return to civilian rule, quickly become dictators, people who assume absolute power. They interfere with the judiciary and censor the press. In 2007 the president, General Musharraf, got rid of the chief justice and several other judges of the Supreme Court for political reasons. However, this led to a pro-democracy movement that eventually helped push General Musharraf and the military from power.

Militants Threaten Governments In Afghanistan, the central government is weak in the face of powerful warlords. Although a national assembly—the Loya Jirga—exists, the real power in the country lies at the local level.

In contrast to the Indian government's secular policies, both Pakistan and Afghanistan are deeply committed to Islamic law. However, within both countries, militant groups are seeking to overthrow the governments and establish an extremist version of Islamic rule. This would threaten their citizens' civil rights.

606

Corruption and Censorship Besides ongoing conflicts, other problems plague governments in South Asia. One is corruption. Too many officials take bribes from businesses in return for special favors. Another problem is the lack of press freedom. Journalists are often kept from investigating or reporting events that the government or religious leaders do not want revealed. Rooting out corruption and ensuring a free press are just two tasks facing countries seeking to promote a democratic system.

Reading Check **What kind of institutions help support democracy?**

Strengthening Democracy

In spite of lingering political problems, there are signs that democracy in South Asia is growing stronger.

Pakistan and Afghanistan Pakistan recently emerged from a period of military rule. During that time, citizens protested actions by the government that went against the rule of law. In 2008, they forced their leaders to hold fair elections for parliament.

Afghans are also eager to participate in their new democracy. In the 2004 presidential election, voter turnout reached more than 80 percent.

Bhutan and India In Bhutan, democracy was established in 2008. The country is now a constitutional monarchy.

India is the world's largest democracy. It is also the most stable democracy in South Asia. Gandhi dreamed of a secular democracy, based on religious tolerance. Although violence between religious groups occurs from time to time, extremists have not been able to gain power. By working to fulfill Gandhi's dream, India has kept its democracy strong.

Reading Check **When was democracy established in Bhutan?**

Political rally in Bhutan during the 2008 election campaign ▼

Assessment

1. What are some ingredients of a strong democracy?

2. Which governments are threatened by militants?

3. What was Gandhi's vision of democracy?

4. What is the status of freedom of the press in South Asia?

5. What are some signs that democracy is growing stronger in South Asia?

Chapter Assessment

Key Terms and Ideas

1. **Recall** What areas in South Asia have good soil and why?

2. **Describe** What benefits has the **Green Revolution** brought to South Asia?

3. **Recall** What religions first emerged in South Asia?

4. **Explain** Why did **partition** take place in India?

5. **Describe** What problems are caused by South Asia's growing population?

6. **Compare and Contrast** What is the difference between the **secular democracy** of India and the Islamic republics of Pakistan and Afghanistan?

7. **Summarize** What are some hopeful signs of economic growth in South Asia?

Think Critically

8. **Draw Conclusions** Why are some areas of South Asia more populated than others?

9. **Synthesize** What factors help slow economic growth in South Asia?

10. **Compare Viewpoints** Why did Gandhi want the British to leave India?

11. **Core Concepts: Human–Environment Interaction** How does South Asia's population growth affect the environment?

Places to Know

For each place, write the letter from the map that shows its location.

12. Ganges River

13. Kabul

14. Himalayas

15. Lahore

16. Indus River

17. Sri Lanka

18. **Estimate** Using the scale, estimate the distance between Kabul and Lahore.

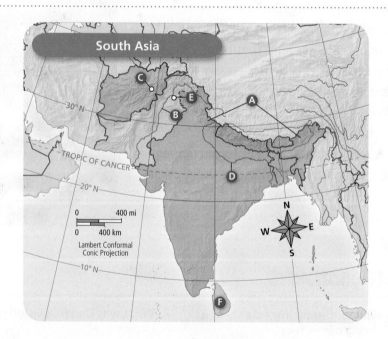

608

Essential Question
myWorld Chapter Activity

Microloan Assessment Follow your teacher's instructions to study the countries of South Asia in order to recommend a microloan to a group in need. Discuss your findings and decide who should get the loan. Then write a proposal that includes your reasons for granting the loan.

21st Century Learning
Search for Information on the Internet

With a partner, search for sites that give information on the economies of South Asia today. You may want to select three countries before you begin your search. Then do a Web search about each country's trade, manufacturing, exports, and so on.

Document-Based Questions

Success Tracker™
Online at myworldgeography.com

Use your knowledge of South Asia and Documents A and B to answer Questions 1–3.

Document A

Arable Land	
Country	Arable Land
Pakistan	24.44%
India	48.33%
Afghanistan	12.13%

SOURCE: *CIA World Factbook*

Document B

" India has become a key market for many information communication technology products made in the U.S., while the U.S. is an important consumer of Indian [information technology]-enabled services."

—U.S. State Department

1. Which of the following best describes the information about the three countries shown in Document A?

   A Afghanistan has the highest percentage of land that can be farmed.

   B Pakistan has less farmland than Afghanistan.

   C India has the highest percentage of farmland.

   D Afghanistan has more farmland than Pakistan.

2. Which of the following best describes the meaning of the quote in Document B?

   A India buys products made in South Asia.

   B India and the United States have an important economic relationship.

   C The United States does not use Indian products.

   D The United States buys Indian products.

3. **Writing Task** Compare the economic strengths of India and Pakistan, using Documents A and B.

my worldgeography.com Self-Test

609

Getting to the Truth:
Fact or *Opinion?*

Your Mission In groups, research Web sites for information on one South or Central Asian nation. As you read, look for examples of facts and opinions and develop a presentation evaluating the Web sites you have visited.

When researching on the Internet, it is important to be able to evaluate the reliability of Web sites. One way to do this is to know how to distinguish between facts and opinions. Facts are claims that can be confirmed by evidence.

Opinions are claims that cannot be confirmed by evidence, even if you agree with them. Your friend may say that basketball is better than baseball, but that claim cannot be confirmed by evidence, as it is merely your friend's opinion.

Web sites can present facts, opinions, or both. When researching, learn to spot the differences by evaluating the evidence that is presented to support any claims.

It's raining.

If it were raining, I would do better in math class.

610

STEP 1

Break It Down.

First, break down the different elements of your group's task. You will investigate information about your nation in order to make a presentation. As you do so, note where you find information. Then, check another site for the same data and note any discrepancies. For example, India's population figures might differ between two sites. Why might this be? As you research, look for clues to whether or not the Web site is reliable and the data on it are based on fact or based on opinion.

STEP 2

Look for Clues.

Think about the purpose of the Web site. Consider how the site functions. Is it easy to use? Look for the author of the site and how often the site is updated. Also, try to determine if the site has any affiliations. Some sites share content or republish content without reviewing it. Errors may be transferred from site to site in this way. As you read, you should also be aware that Web sites may have certain points of view and are designed to reinforce certain attitudes.

STEP 3

What's the Truth Factor?

Focus your group's presentation on the reliability of the information you found on the sites you visited. As you present your nation's data, discuss what the data mean as well as any conflicting information you discovered. Read aloud at least one quote from each of the news Web sites you visited. Point out specific word clues that led you to believe the quote was fact or opinion. Also, discuss your overall impression of the reliability of the content on these sites.

Regional Overview

East and Southeast Asia

East and Southeast Asia are regions of rugged mountains, vast plains, dense forests, and crowded coastlines. These regions are heavily populated. The largest country in these regions is China, which has more inhabitants than any other country on Earth.

What time is it there?

Washington, D.C.	Wuxi, China
9 A.M. Monday	10 P.M. Monday

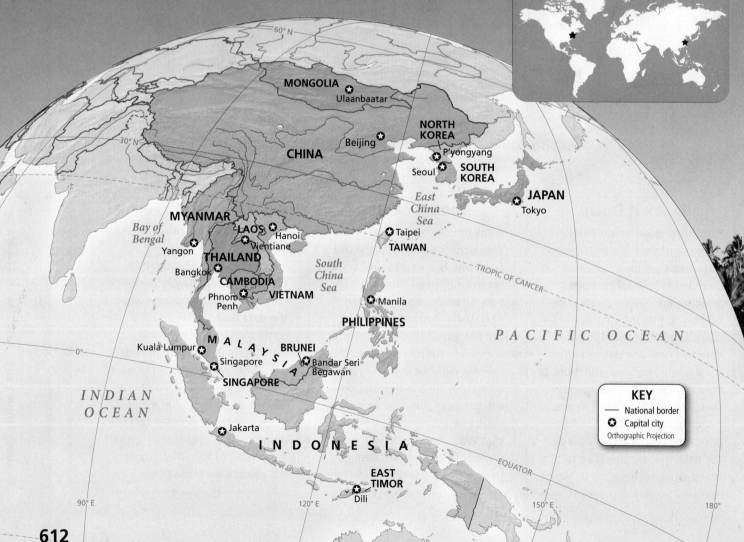

KEY
— National border
✪ Capital city
Orthographic Projection

The Unit Ahead

→ Chapter 14 China and Its Neighbors

→ Chapter 15 Japan and the Koreas

→ Chapter 16 Southeast Asia

my worldgeography.com

Plan your trip online by doing a Data Discovery Activity and watching the myStory Videos of the region's teens.

my Story

Xiao
Age: 18
Home: Wuxi, China
Chapter 14

my Story

Asuka
Age: 18
Home: Yokohama, Japan
Chapter 15

my Story

Ridwan
Age: 19
Home: Bukittinggi, Indonesia
Chapter 16

Rice fields in Bali, Indonesia

613

Physical Geography

The Himalayas are one of the many mountain ranges in East Asia.

Tian Shan
Taklimakan Desert
Kunlun Shan

Plateau of Tibet
Mt. Everest
29,035 ft (8,850 m)

Himalayas

Gobi

Huang (Yellow) River

North
China Plain

Chang (Yangtze) River

Malay Peninsula

Gulf of
Thailand

South China Sea

INDIAN
OCEAN

Java Sea

Active volcanoes lie throughout the islands of Southeast Asia.

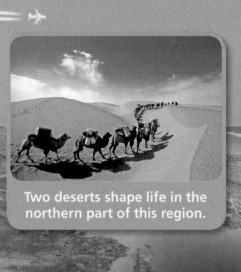

Two deserts shape life in the northern part of this region.

Manchurian Plain

Korean Peninsula

Sea of Japan (East Sea)

Philippine Sea

Mountains give way to plains in China and, on a smaller scale, in Taiwan, the Koreas, and Japan.

P A C I F I C O C E A N

Regional Flyover

Beginning your flight in the west, you enter China's airspace high above the Himalayas. Then, you face the high Plateau of Tibet.

To the north of this plateau lie two vast deserts, the Gobi and the Taklimakan. As you fly north over the Gobi Desert, you come to Mongolia, a dry land of deserts, plateaus, and mountains.

Circling south from Mongolia, along the eastern coast of Asia, you see a mountainous peninsula, home to North and South Korea. As you continue south the climate becomes warmer, and soon your eyes glimpse the tropical forests of Vietnam, Laos, Thailand, Cambodia, and the island nations of Malaysia, Singapore, Indonesia, East Timor, Brunei, and the Philippines. As the plane turns north, you pass over the small island nation of Taiwan. When you reach Japan, count the countries you have seen—17!

 In-Flight Movie

Take flight over East Asia and Southeast Asia and explore the regions from the air.

my **worldgeography**.com | In-Flight Movie

615

Regional Overview
Human Geography

Downtown Tokyo is lit up brightly every night.

Where People Live

East and Southeast Asia's physical features have influenced where people in the region live. Many nations in these regions do not have much land that is good for farming or settlement. Not very many people live in the rugged mountains and dry deserts. The dry climate in the north of these regions is particularly challenging. Even in the south, where water is more plentiful, there are many hills and very little land that is flat enough to farm.

As a result, the huge population of these regions is packed into the areas where life is easier—on the plains and along rivers and flat coastal areas. Japan, the Koreas, and many of the nations of Southeast Asia have forested mountains running through their centers, so in those countries people live mainly in valleys and in coastal cities. China and Mongolia both have large plains where people can farm or raise livestock.

This map shows where people live in East and Southeast Asia.

The lights in this satellite photo show electricity use in heavily populated areas of East and Southeast Asia.

KEY
· 100,000 people

my World
IN NUMBERS

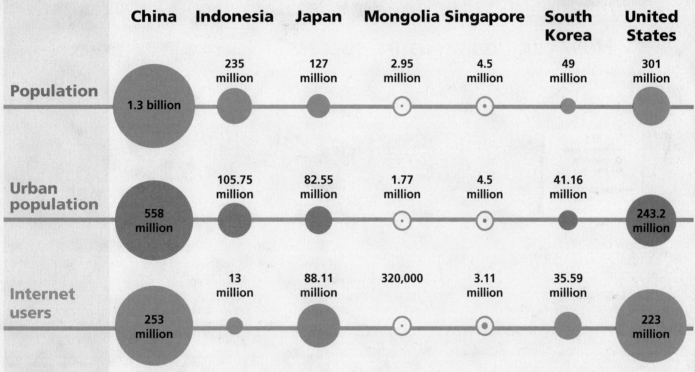

	China	Indonesia	Japan	Mongolia	Singapore	South Korea	United States
Population	1.3 billion	235 million	127 million	2.95 million	4.5 million	49 million	301 million
Urban population	558 million	105.75 million	82.55 million	1.77 million	4.5 million	41.16 million	243.2 million
Internet users	253 million	13 million	88.11 million	320,000	3.11 million	35.59 million	223 million

SOURCE: *CIA World Factbook, Encyclopaedia Britannica*

Put It Together

1. What physical features prevent western China from being heavily settled?

2. Where do many of the rivers in China and Southeast Asia begin?

3. Compare the number of Internet users to the number of urban dwellers. Which country has more Internet users than urban residents?

 Data Discovery

Find your own data to make a regional data table.

Size Comparison

East and Southeast Asia are more than twice as large as the United States but have 7 times the population.

my **worldgeography.com** Data Discovery

617

Chapter 14

China and Its Neighbors

Essential Question

How can you measure success?

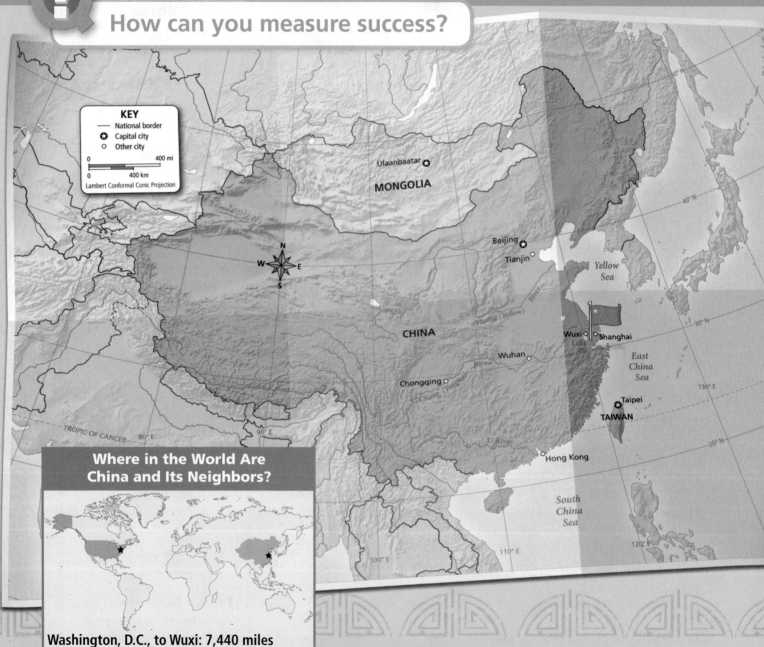

KEY
- National border
- ⊛ Capital city
- ○ Other city

400 mi
400 km
Lambert Conformal Conic Projection

MONGOLIA
Ulaanbaatar ⊛

Beijing ⊛
Tianjin ○

Yellow Sea

Huang (Yellow) River

CHINA

Wuxi ○ ○ Shanghai
Lake Tai

Wuhan ○

East China Sea

Chongqing ○
Chang (Yangtze) River

Taipei ⊛
TAIWAN

TROPIC OF CANCER

Xi River

Hong Kong ○

South China Sea

Where in the World Are China and Its Neighbors?

Washington, D.C., to Wuxi: 7,440 miles

my Story

Xiao's Lake

Explore the Essential Question
- at **my worldgeography.com**
- using the **myWorld Chapter Activity**
- with the **Student Journal**

In this section you'll read about Xiao, a young man helping to care for his family. He lives in eastern China. What does his story tell you about the challenges China faces?

Story by Megan Shank for myWorld Online

Xiao lives with his father, mother, grandmother, and older brother in a tiny village near Wuxi (woo shee), an ancient city in the east of China. After learning of his father's diabetes diagnosis, 17-year-old Xiao found a full-time job to help support his family.

Xiao (whose name is pronounced show, as in *shower*) and his brother both work at a factory that produces machines that make ice cream. His mother works at a different factory and tends the family's orange and peach orchard. His father is a part-time driver.

Every morning at 7 A.M., Xiao rides his motorcycle to Wuxi. There are many factories in this area. They have easy access to railways and canals that transport goods to large cities, such as Shanghai. Xiao works 10 hours a day, five days a week. Many local youth leave to make their fortunes, but Xiao wants to stay close to his family.

Life has changed as China has become wealthier. Meat used to be too expensive to eat every day. Thirty years ago, few people could afford a television. Now, most families in Xiao's village own one.

Xiao rides home from work.

my worldgeography.com On Assignment

619

A street in Xiao's village

Xiao's mother prepares dinner in a large wok.

Xiao's family shares these dishes at dinner.

Xiao's mother applies pesticides to the orange trees in the family orchard.

Unlike his parents' generation, which suffered famine and shortages of many goods, Xiao doesn't remember a time when food was scarce.

He does remember when the waters of Lake Tai were clean and clear. Lake Tai is China's third-largest body of fresh water. It is just a five-minute jaunt from Xiao's house. As a boy, he learned to swim there. He collected snails in the lake and had mud fights with friends.

Walking through the family's fruit orchard, it's hard to imagine this place ever smelled like anything other than sun-ripened oranges. Yet in the summer of 2007 a terrible odor crept from the lake across the orchard and into their home.

An algae bloom covered the lake with green slime. The algae bloom was caused, in part, by pollution and pesticides from the farms and factories around the lake. The algae used up the oxygen in the lake. Suffocated fish floated to the surface, belly up.

"You didn't even want to use the water to bathe, much less to drink," says Xiao.

Thirty million people rely on Lake Tai for drinking water. That summer, families in Xiao's village avoided the lake water. They drew water from local wells or bought bottles of water. Bottled water was rushed to Wuxi during the crisis.

Xiao's family shut the windows and put up with the stench. Flies and mosquitoes swarmed.

A factory by the lake is torn down.

Algae and trash float on this small pond near Xiao's home.

Small ponds where neighbors had once washed their fruit and rinsed their rice filled with algae and muck. People started to throw their garbage into these pools, as well.

"If the environment is better, people behave better," says Xiao. "When there's pollution, people throw their garbage where they shouldn't."

The city of Wuxi has started to solve the problem. They hired people to remove the algae. They have also shut down some factories around the lake to reduce the pollution.

Towns are also being bulldozed. Citizens in the village next to Xiao's village were forced to move when the government claimed the area for a park. Xiao has never lived anywhere else and worries the government will make his family move, too.

He has mixed feelings about his parents' use of pesticides and fertilizers in their orchard. He knows these chemicals run off into the lake and cause more harm. He also knows that the factory where he works may be adding to the pollution. Still, Xiao needs his job. He hopes to save money, marry, and start a family—preferably, he says, by the time he's 23— so there are no easy answers.

"How can you choose between your family and your home?"

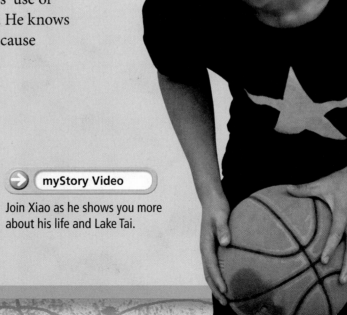

Meet the Videographer

Name Carl Thelin

Favorite Moment Eating dinner with Xiao's family

→ **myStory Video**

Join Xiao as he shows you more about his life and Lake Tai.

my worldgeography.com myStory Video

621

Chapter Atlas

Key Ideas
- Most people live on the plains and in the coastal areas of this region.
- Climate, especially rainfall, influences the economic activities in this region.
- Cities have grown rapidly in China in recent years.

Key Terms
- loess
- staple crop
- nomadic herder
- arable land
- one-child policy

 Visual Glossary

 Reading Skill: Label an Outline Map Take notes using the outline map in your journal.

A fisherman uses a cormorant bird to catch fish on the Li River, China.

622

Physical Features

Travelers who enter China from the west must struggle over a barrier of high mountains. The Himalayas, along China's southwest border, are the highest mountain range in the world.

North of the Himalayas, travelers cross the Tibetan Plateau, the highest and largest plateau in the world. Many rivers begin here. They flow south and east to many countries, providing drinking water for one third of the world's population.

China's largest rivers—the Chang (or Yangtze) and the Huang (or Yellow)—begin on the Tibetan Plateau. These rivers

China and Its Neighbors: Physical

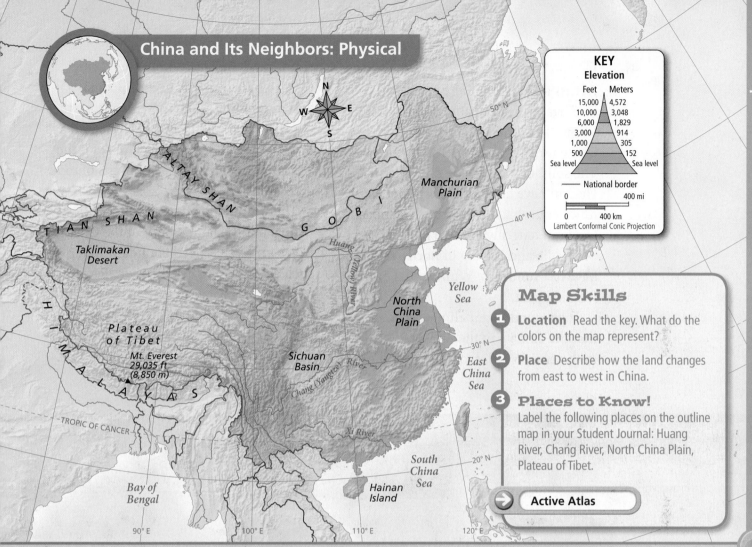

KEY
Elevation

Feet	Meters
15,000	4,572
10,000	3,048
6,000	1,829
3,000	914
1,000	305
500	152
Sea level	Sea level

National border

0   400 mi
0   400 km
Lambert Conformal Conic Projection

ALTAY SHAN
TIAN SHAN
Taklimakan Desert
GOBI
Manchurian Plain
Huang (Yellow) River
HIMALAYAS
Plateau of Tibet
Mt. Everest 29,035 ft (8,850 m)
Sichuan Basin
Chang (Yangtze) River
Xi River
North China Plain
Yellow Sea
East China Sea
South China Sea
Hainan Island
Bay of Bengal
TROPIC OF CANCER
50° N
40° N
30° N
20° N
90° E   100° E   110° E   120° E

Map Skills

1 Location Read the key. What do the colors on the map represent?

2 Place Describe how the land changes from east to west in China.

3 Places to Know! Label the following places on the outline map in your Student Journal: Huang River, Chang River, North China Plain, Plateau of Tibet.

➜ Active Atlas

tumble from the highlands down to the plains on the east coast. The island of Taiwan, by contrast, has mountains on the east and <u>fertile</u> plains on the west side.

Mountains and highland plateaus cover much of Mongolia. A huge desert called the Gobi stretches from southern Mongolia toward the Huang River. Winds from the desert carry **loess** (LOH es) into China. Loess is a dustlike material that can form soil. It can pile up more than 100 feet deep. People carve caves into the loess hills and build their homes in them.

The Huang River cuts through these deposits, picking up the loess. Huang means "yellow" in Chinese. If you hopped on board a boat along the river, you would see that the loess makes it look yellow and muddy. The Huang created the North China Plain by flooding many times. Each flood left behind fertile soil. For thousands of years, Chinese people have farmed the flat lands along the country's rivers.

Landforms, such as rivers, affect where people live. Climate is also important when people decide how to use the land.

Reading Check What physical feature do China and Mongolia share?

fertile, *adj.*, rich in nutrients, capable of growing many plants

623

Climate and Land Use

Across this region, there are two important climate patterns. The first is that the climate is generally colder in the north and warmer in the south. The southern islands of Taiwan and Hainan have hot, humid summers and mild winters. Cities such as Ulaanbaatar (oo lahn BAH tawr) in the north of Mongolia and Beijing in northern China have hot summers. Winters there are freezing cold.

The second major climate pattern is that the climate in the west is drier than in the east. Winds blowing from the south carry moisture from the Pacific Ocean to Taiwan and eastern China. Tall mountains block these winds, so the climate of Mongolia and western China is dry. Two great deserts, the Gobi and the Taklimakan, stretch for hundreds of miles across this area.

These climate patterns influence how people use the land. South of the Chang River, crops that need abundant water, such as tea and rice, are grown. People here, such as Xiao's family, generally eat rice with their daily meals. Taiwan's wet western plains grow rice and other tropical crops, such as sugar and bananas.

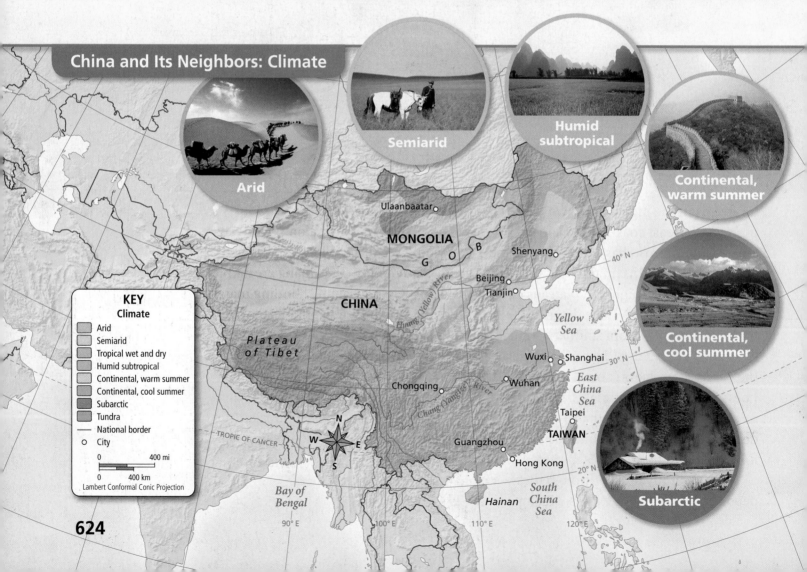

China and Its Neighbors: Climate

KEY
Climate
- Arid
- Semiarid
- Tropical wet and dry
- Humid subtropical
- Continental, warm summer
- Continental, cool summer
- Subarctic
- Tundra
- National border
- o City

0 — 400 mi
0 — 400 km
Lambert Conformal Conic Projection

Between the Chang River and the Huang River both rice and wheat are grown. The fertile North China Plain north of the Huang River is too dry for rice. Here, wheat is the **staple crop,** that is, the major crop that is the basis of the diet. Common foods in northern China include steamed bread, dumplings, and noodles made of wheat flour.

Still farther north and west, the climate is usually too dry for growing crops. People in these regions have lived mainly as **nomadic herders,** that is, they herd flocks and do not settle in one place. They must move their herds to find sources of water and grassland. This nomadic lifestyle is especially common in Mongolia and Tibet. Like the cowboys of the American West, Mongolian herders become skilled horseback riders at a young age.

In recent years, industry has expanded in China, Taiwan, and Mongolia. More people have moved to the cities to work in offices and factories, rather than working as farmers or nomadic herders. Large industrial areas have grown around the cities of the region. Peoples' lives across the region are changing.

Reading Check What are the two major climate patterns in this region?

my World IN NUMBERS

China has **10%** of the world's good farmland to feed **20%** of the world's population.

China and Its Neighbors: Land Use

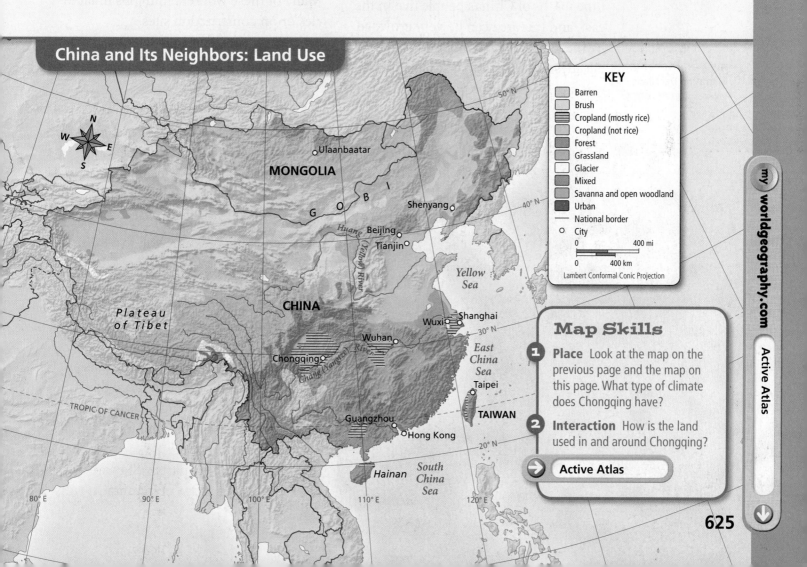

KEY
- Barren
- Brush
- Cropland (mostly rice)
- Cropland (not rice)
- Forest
- Grassland
- Glacier
- Mixed
- Savanna and open woodland
- Urban
- — National border
- ○ City

0 400 mi
0 400 km
Lambert Conformal Conic Projection

Map Skills

1. **Place** Look at the map on the previous page and the map on this page. What type of climate does Chongqing have?

2. **Interaction** How is the land used in and around Chongqing?

→ **Active Atlas**

my worldgeography.com Active Atlas

625

Growing Cities, Crowded Coasts

People are not evenly spread across the countries in this region. People have settled where it is easiest to make a living. Today, this is a region on the move with millions of people migrating to find work.

More people live in China than in any other country. Yet China's resources are limited. Deserts and mountains cover much of the country. Only about 15 percent of China's land is **arable land,** that is, land that can be used to grow crops. Most of the arable land is in the eastern part of the country. More than nine tenths of China's people live in the east, and this area can be very crowded.

The Chinese government realized decades ago that China's large population was a problem. If the population contin-

ued to grow quickly, there would not be enough food in the country for everyone.

In the late 1970s, the government started a **one-child policy.** Under this law, many married couples are only allowed to have one child. Couples who have more children are punished. There are some exceptions to this rule. Couples in rural areas may sometimes have more than one child. In the cities the one-child policy has been strictly <u>enforced</u>.

Still, China's cities are large and are growing quickly. This is because millions of people are leaving rural areas and moving to the cities to look for work. Many of these workers find jobs in factories or on construction sites.

A migrant worker in Chengdu explains why she and her husband moved to the city to work:

> 66 We lived in a village that's surrounded by big mountains. Where we were, you really can't make a cent. . . you raise a little livestock, some crops, but that's really not sufficient [enough]. 99
>
> —Cai Zisheng, Chinese migrant

Most people in China still live in rural areas. Only about 45 percent of Chinese people live in cities—in the United States almost 80 percent of people live in cities. China's population is much larger than that of the United States, and so many cities in China are very large. China's capital, Beijing, is home to more than 14 million people. Shanghai is the largest city in the country with more than 16 million people.

Like China, some parts of Taiwan are very crowded. A ridge of mountains runs

enforce, *v.,* to make someone follow a rule or law

**myWorldActivity
Migration Decisions**

In 1990, parts of the Pudong area of Shanghai were covered by farmland (inset). Now, towering skyscapers and even an airport have been built over the fields.

626

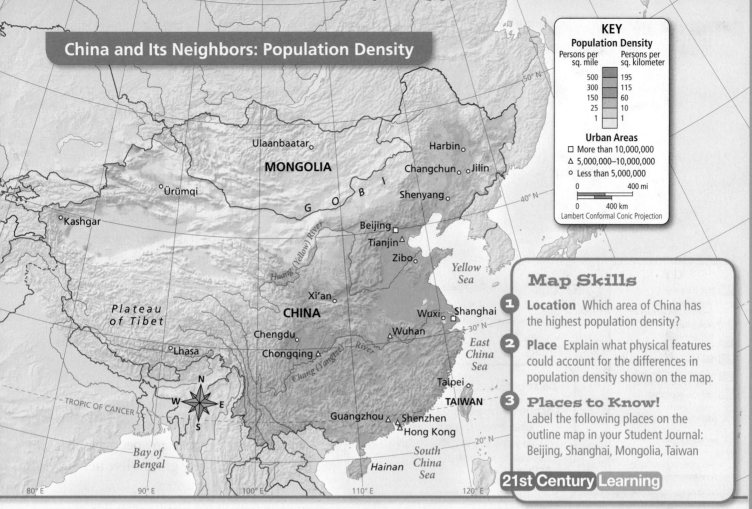

China and Its Neighbors: Population Density

KEY

Population Density

Persons per sq. mile	Persons per sq. kilometer
500	195
300	115
150	60
25	10
1	1

Urban Areas

□ More than 10,000,000
△ 5,000,000–10,000,000
○ Less than 5,000,000

0   400 mi
0   400 km
Lambert Conformal Conic Projection

Map Skills

1 **Location** Which area of China has the highest population density?

2 **Place** Explain what physical features could account for the differences in population density shown on the map.

3 **Places to Know!**
Label the following places on the outline map in your Student Journal: Beijing, Shanghai, Mongolia, Taiwan

21st Century Learning

along the east coast of the island, so most cities and farms are on the flatter west coast of the island. Almost three quarters of Taiwan's population lives in these coastal cities.

In contrast, Mongolia is a landlocked nation, or a nation without a coastline. About half of all Mongolians are nomadic, moving their homes to follow herds of livestock across the country's grassy plains. The nomads live in tents called gers (gehrz). Most of the rest of the population lives in cities. Almost a third of the population lives in the capital city of Ulaanbaatar.

In Mongolia, cities grow or shrink depending on the weather. When a hard winter strikes, livestock may die from a lack of food. Nomadic herders must go to the cities to find work, and the cities grow. During mild winters, some city workers give up their jobs to return to herding. In this region, as in many others, many people move to find of work.

Reading Check Why do many people in both China and Taiwan live along the coast?

Mongolian nomads often live in gers, which can be easily moved. ▼

Culture Close-up

627

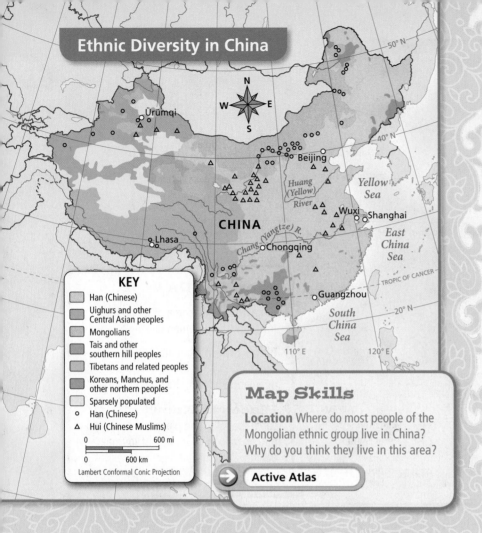

Ethnic Diversity in China

KEY
- Han (Chinese)
- Uighurs and other Central Asian peoples
- Mongolians
- Tais and other southern hill peoples
- Tibetans and related peoples
- Koreans, Manchus, and other northern peoples
- Sparsely populated
- ○ Han (Chinese)
- △ Hui (Chinese Muslims)

0 ——— 600 mi
0 ——— 600 km
Lambert Conformal Conic Projection

Map labels: Ürümqi, Beijing, Huang (Yellow) River, Yellow Sea, Wuxi, Shanghai, Lhasa, CHINA, Chang (Yangtze) R., Chongqing, East China Sea, TROPIC OF CANCER, Guangzhou, South China Sea

Map Skills

Location Where do most people of the Mongolian ethnic group live in China? Why do you think they live in this area?

➜ **Active Atlas**

Hello! I'm Tibetan. I live in Tibet. I am a Buddhist. Here is what "hello" looks like written in my language:
བཀྲ་ཤིས་བདེ་ལེགས།

Hello! I'm Han Chinese. Most people in China are Han, like me. Here is what "hello" looks like written in my language: 你好

Hello! I'm Korean. I live in the northeast of China. Here is what "hello" looks like written in my language:
안녕 하세요

Ethnic Diversity in China

About 92 percent of Chinese people today belong to the Han ethnic group. More than 50 ethnic groups make up the rest of the population.

Some of the larger minority groups are the Uighurs (WEE goorz) of northwestern China and the Tibetans.

These groups have their own languages, traditional clothing, and holidays. Some of these groups are closely identified with a religion. For example, many Uighurs are Muslim. Many Tibetans practice a unique form of Buddhism.

China's many ethnic groups are not evenly spread across the country. People of the Han ethnic group live mostly in the east. Many people who belong to minority groups live near the borders of the country.

The reason for this pattern lies in China's history. The Han people built their earliest kingdoms in the east along the Huang River. Later, these kingdoms joined together and created a powerful Chinese empire.

The Chinese emperors conquered new lands. They came to control regions whose people were not Han. These people kept many of their own customs and stayed near their traditional homelands.

People from all ethnic groups have played an important role in China's history. Some emperors were not from the Han ethnic group. Mongolian lead-

➜ **Language Lesson**

628

ers ruled China for almost a hundred years. The last emperor and his ancestors belonged to a people called the Manchu.

China's current government has tried to protect the country's rich cultural heritage. For example, the one-child policy only applies to Han Chinese people. Families of other ethnic groups are allowed to have more than one child.

However, the Chinese government has made other rules that control cultural and religious life in China. People cannot freely form groups to practice religion. The government limits the number of churches and religious organizations.

All Chinese people, including the Han, must follow these restrictions. However, these rules make it harder for groups with special religious traditions to preserve their cultures.

Tibetans and Uighurs have protested against the government. Some have called for more autonomy from China. The Chinese government has attacked and imprisoned people who protest against its policies. The government is trying to improve the economy of borderland areas, but conflict continues because of its rules controlling cultural life.

Reading Check Why are many minority groups found along China's borders?

Uighur schoolgirls in China's western province of Xinjiang ▼

Section **1** Assessment

Key Terms

1. Use the following terms to describe land use in this region: loess, staple crop, nomadic herder, arable land.

Key Ideas

2. Why is there little farming in Mongolia?
3. Why did the Chinese government introduce the one-child policy?
4. Where were the early Han kingdoms in China?

Think Critically

5. **Analyze Information** Look at the population density map. Which areas have the highest population density? Why do so many people live in these areas?
6. **Summarize** Why are cities growing in China?

Essential Question

How can you measure success?

7. How can the Chinese government measure whether or not the one-child policy has been successful? Go to your Student Journal to record your answer.

Section 2

History of China and Its Neighbors

Key Ideas
- For much of its history, China was an advanced, powerful empire.
- Communists created command economies in both China and Mongolia.
- In recent years, Mongolia and China have changed to market economies to increase economic growth.

Key Terms • dynasty • Confucianism • Daoism • command economy • famine

→ **Visual Glossary**

Reading Skill: Main Ideas and Details Take notes using the graphic organizer in your journal.

A statue of a warrior from the tomb of Emperor Qin Shi Huangdi ▼

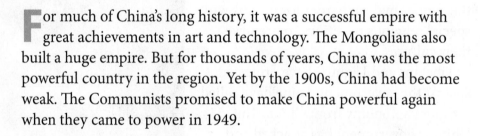

For much of China's long history, it was a successful empire with great achievements in art and technology. The Mongolians also built a huge empire. But for thousands of years, China was the most powerful country in the region. Yet by the 1900s, China had become weak. The Communists promised to make China powerful again when they came to power in 1949.

The Empires of China and Mongolia

The great empires of China and Mongolia were very different. The Chinese empire was based on agriculture. The Mongols' power came from their skill as warriors on horseback.

The Powerful Chinese Empire
China's civilization began when farming villages formed on the North China Plain thousands of years ago. Geographic features

→ **Timeline**

Major Chinese Dynasties

				Qin	
Shang	Zhou			Han	
1500 B.C.	1000 B.C.	500 B.C.	A.D. 1		

■ Period of war or division

630

isolated China from other early civilizations. High mountains limited communication to the west. By sea, all but a few neighbors were too far to reach. Around 1800 B.C., a series of emperors began to rule China. Usually, emperors were members of a **dynasty,** or a ruling family that held power for many years.

Powerful emperors unified and protected China. The Qin (chin) emperor Shi Huangdi (shur hwahng DEE) created a uniform written language for the whole empire. This made communication easier and helped unite the country. It is the basis of China's written language today.

Shi Huangdi also began to connect scattered walls to build the Great Wall, which still stands. The wall was meant to protect farmers from nomadic invaders. Later rulers added to it, extending it more than 4,000 miles.

Chinese Achievements Under the Dynasties The Chinese had many accomplishments during their history. They built roads and canals to make trade and travel easier. The Grand Canal is the longest man-made waterway in the world. It stretches for over a thousand miles from Beijing to Hangzhou. It passes Wuxi where Qian Xiao works.

Chinese inventions include paper, silk, and the magnetic compass. In the Song dynasty, the Chinese developed gunpowder. At first they used it for fireworks. Later, they began to use it in weapons.

A Mongolian Empire Many groups of nomads have lived on the plains north of China. One group, called the Mongols, united under the leadership of Genghis Khan in the 1200s. They were the ancestors of today's Mongolians. They swept over the Great Wall and conquered China. They also rapidly took control of much of Asia. The Mongol empire was the largest empire the world had ever seen, but it was short-lived. In 1368, the Chinese overthrew the Mongols, and the Ming dynasty came to power.

Reading Check **Why did the Chinese build the Great Wall of China?**

uniform, *adj.,* the same, consistent

Today, tourists climb the Great Wall of China. ▼

my **worldgeography.com** Timeline

	Sui				Mongol Rule		Republican Era	Communist Era
	Tang		Song		Ming	Qing		
A.D. 500	A.D. 750		A.D. 1000	A.D. 1250	A.D. 1500	A.D. 1750	A.D. 2000	

631

Important Ideas and Beliefs

As dynasties rose and fell, three belief systems strongly influenced this region's culture. **Confucianism** (kuhn FYOO shuh niz um), is based on the ideas of the thinker Confucius. **Daoism** (DOW iz um) is a philosophy of seeking the natural way of the universe. The third philosophy, Buddhism, grew from the teachings of Siddhartha Gautama. He taught that people can become free from suffering if they give up selfish desires.

Confucianism Confucius (551–479 B.C.) believed society could be peaceful and harmonious if people acted strictly according to their roles. In the family,

the young should respect the old. In government, the ruler should care for his subjects. In return, subjects had a duty to respect and obey the ruler.

Three hundred years after Confucius's death, the influence of his teaching increased. It was then that Emperor Wudi of the Han dynasty began to use Confucianism in government. Dynasties after the Han also supported the ideas of Confucius. Confucianism was taught in schools throughout China. This system of values greatly influenced Chinese culture.

Daoism The ideas of Daoism developed at around the time Confucius was teaching. The word *dao* (dow) means "the

Belief Systems of China

Confucianism

Based on the teachings of Confucius (551–479 B.C.)

Goal To act according to one's role in society. Education teaches values and duties.

◀ Statue of Confucius in a temple in Nanjing, China

Statue of the Buddha meditating. The concentration of meditation helps Buddhists reach enlightenment. ▼

Buddhism

Based on the teachings of Siddhartha Gautama, the Buddha, 500s B.C.

Goal To become free from the pain and suffering of the world. This mental state is enlightenment.

Daoism

Based on the teachings of Laozi, 500s B.C.

Goal To follow the dao. For Daoists, the dao is the rhythm of the universe. They studied nature to harmonize with this rhythm.

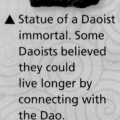

▲ Statue of a Daoist immortal. Some Daoists believed they could live longer by connecting with the Dao.

632

path" or "the way." Daoists believe people should try to find this path. Often, they see evidence of the Dao in natural things, such as water.

66 There is nothing in the world more soft and weak than water, and yet for attacking things that are firm and strong, nothing is better than water ... 99

—Laozi

Water, through patient effort over time, is even stronger than rock. By acting like water, people were following the Dao.

Buddhism Monks and other travelers from India brought Buddhism to China during the Han dynasty. Over time, Buddhism attracted a wide following. Buddhists built monasteries and temples across the country. Buddhism also became popular in Mongolia. Buddhism was much more influential than Daoism and Confucianism on Mongolia's culture.

Reading Check **What did Confucius think people should do to bring order to society?**

The End of the Dynasties

China's last dynasty, the Qing (ching), fell early in the 1900s. New, communist governments took control in both China and Mongolia.

The Qing Dynasty Struggles In 1839, the Qing dynasty fought with Britain over the opium trade. Opium is an addictive drug that Britain had been trading for Chinese tea. The Qing saw the bad effects of the drug and tried to stop the trade. The British sent warships to bombard some Chinese cities. China's weak military could barely put up a fight.

The British won. They forced the Chinese to accept the opium trade and foreign domination.

This was just the beginning of the Qing dynasty's troubles. It lost Taiwan to Japan after a brief war in 1895. Taiwan stayed under Japanese control through World War II. The Chinese people were shocked that their country could be defeated by the small island nation of Japan.

Revolution, Civil War, and Invasion
Many Chinese people blamed the Qing for the country's weakness. In 1911 and 1912, revolutionaries took power from the Qing dynasty.

The revolutionary leaders hoped to make China a strong, modern nation. Yet, they could not bring peace. China suffered nearly 30 years of almost constant fighting followed by a Japanese invasion during World War II.

Nationalists under Jiang Jieshi (jahng jeh shur), also know as Chiang Kai-shek, fought Communists led by Mao Zedong (mow dzuh doong) for control of the country. Finally, in 1949, the Communists won the long civil war. They set up a stable government on mainland China.

The Nationalists fled to Taiwan. There, they set up a rival government, which continues to this day.

Mongolia's Revolution The Qing dynasty controlled much of Mongolia. Mongolia's Communist leaders won independence from China in 1921 after the Qing dynasty fell. Mongolia became a new nation.

Reading Check **Why did the Chinese overthrow the Qing dynasty?**

Dr. Sun Yixian served as the first president of China's republic after revolutionaries overthrew the Qing dynasty.

633

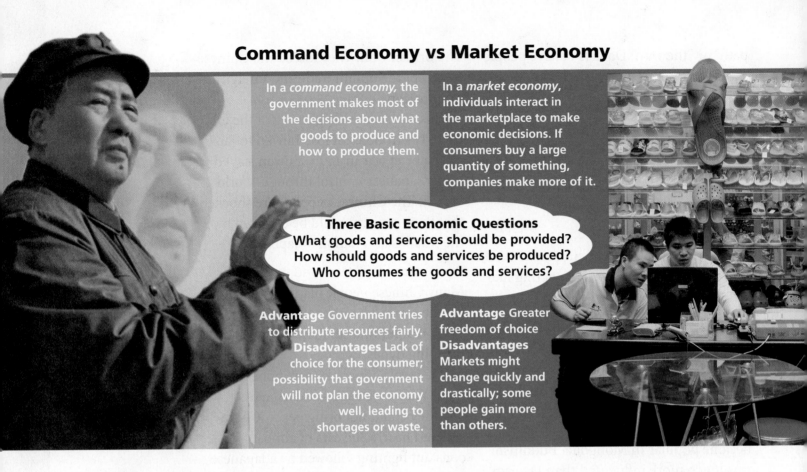

Command Economy vs Market Economy

In a *command economy*, the government makes most of the decisions about what goods to produce and how to produce them.

In a *market economy*, individuals interact in the marketplace to make economic decisions. If consumers buy a large quantity of something, companies make more of it.

Three Basic Economic Questions
What goods and services should be provided?
How should goods and services be produced?
Who consumes the goods and services?

Advantage Government tries to distribute resources fairly.
Disadvantages Lack of choice for the consumer; possibility that government will not plan the economy well, leading to shortages or waste.

Advantage Greater freedom of choice
Disadvantages Markets might change quickly and drastically; some people gain more than others.

myWorldActivity
Command Economy vs. Market Economy

resource, *n.,* something, such as coal, timber, or land, that a country can use

China and Mongolia Under Communism

Communist leaders in China and Mongolia brought great change to their countries. They had little economic success, though, and had to make major changes to their economic systems.

The Command Economy Communism is based on the idea that everyone should share a country's wealth equally. The Communists argued that a society could not reach this goal with a market economy. Instead, the Communists created a **command economy,** an economic system based on government planning and control.

In a command economy, the government owns the land, businesses, and resources of the country. The government makes an economic plan for the country. It decides which goods and services will be produced. People have jobs based on this plan, and the government has great control over the lives of the people. The Communists did not create a democracy. People could not vote. A small number of Communist Party leaders held power.

In both Mongolia and China, the Communists took land, livestock, and businesses away from their owners. These resources were supposed to be managed fairly according to the government's economic plan.

These governments also started programs to help people. Doctors, for example, traveled to small villages to provide basic healthcare.

634

Command Economy Problems The command economy often did not work well. When the Mongolian government tried to take livestock away from nomads to create the command economy, many herders decided to kill their animals rather than give them to the government. In part because of this, a **famine**, or severe food shortage, followed.

Poor planning by the Communists in China also led to famine. In 1958, Mao introduced the Great Leap Forward. This policy called for the country to rapidly increase production of steel, as part of an effort to make China's economy more modern.

Making steel took farmers away from their fields. The shift in focus away from agriculture combined with poor weather created food shortages. Historians believe that as many as 30 million Chinese people may have died of hunger between 1958 and 1962. This tragedy took place because the economic plan ignored the needs of the people.

New Leaders Leave the Command Economy Behind When Mao Zedong died in 1976, a Communist leader named Deng Xiaoping (dung show PING) rose to power. He began reforms that opened China up to international trade.

He also started to move China toward a market economy. New businesses opened. They competed with one another to make the best, cheapest goods. China's economy began to grow rapidly.

At the same time, Deng and other Communist leaders had no intention of allowing political power to slip out of their hands. The Chinese Communist Party's hold on the government stayed as strong as ever.

By contrast, political and economic reforms came at almost the same time in Mongolia. Both the political and economic systems changed in the 1990s. Mongolia became a democracy with a market economy.

Reading Check How did China change after Deng Xiaoping took power?

Section 2 Assessment

Key Terms

1. Describe the beliefs of Confucianism and Daosim.

2. What is a command economy?

Key Ideas

3. **Draw Conclusions** Why was China the most powerful country in the region for much of its history?

4. **Cause and Effect** What policies caused famine in China and Mongolia in the 1900s?

Think Critically

5. **Sequence** What was the sequence of events from China's war with Britain to the formation of a new government led by Mao Zedong?

Essential Question

How can you measure success?

6. Do you think the Qing dynasty was unsuccessful? Go to your Student Journal to record your answer.

635

Confucianism and Imperial Law

Key Idea
- The ideas of Confucius have influenced many aspects of Chinese society, including the legal system of the Qing dynasty.

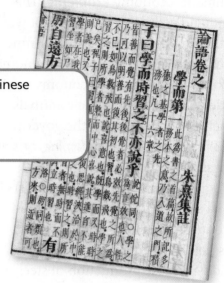

Confucius did not write any books. His students wrote down his ideas. A book called *The Analects* is a collection of his teachings. This book includes his ideas for maintaining an orderly society. Those ideas have influenced Chinese life and government for hundreds of years. For example, Confucius emphasized the value of filial piety, that is, love and respect for one's parents and ancestors. The court case of Fan Gui, from the Qing dynasty, China's last imperial dynasty, shows how the idea of filial piety was part of the law.

▲ A copy of *The Analects*, compiled by 200 B.C.

Stop at each circled letter on the right to think about the text. Then answer the question on the left with the same letter.

A Infer How might adult children cause their parents "anxiety"?

B Summarize Why is providing only for parents' physical needs treating them like farm animals?

C Synthesize What does Confucius mean by *filial piety*?

anxiety, *n.,* upset or worry
filial, *adj.,* proper for a son or daughter
piety, *n.,* devotion, dutiful respect

Filial Piety

66 [A student] asked about the treatment of parents. The Master said, behave in such a way that your father and mother have no <u>anxiety</u>

A about you. . . .

'<u>Filial</u> sons' are people who see to

B it that their parents get enough to eat. But even dogs and horses are cared for to that extent. If there is no feeling of respect, wherein lies the difference?

Filial <u>piety</u> does not consist merely in young people undertaking the

C hard work. It is something much more than that. 99
—Confucius, *The Analects*

Confucius

636

Stop at each circled letter on the right to think about the text. Then answer the question on the left with the same letter.

(D) Summarize Why was Fan Gui sentenced to death?

(E) Paraphrase What is one reason that a criminal could be released according to Chinese law?

(F) Analyze How did Fan Yuan's behavior influence the Board's decision about Fan Gui?

petition, *v.,* to make a formal, written request

provisionally, *adv.,* until a final arrangement is made

deport, *v.,* to send away by force

Filial Piety in the Court

66 Mrs. Fan . . . <u>petitioned</u> to have her eldest son, Fan Gui, released from his criminal sentence to care for her. Fan Gui accidentally wounded his mother when quarreling with his younger brother. Fan Gui was tried and **(D)** <u>provisionally</u> sentenced to immediate death. . . .

[W]e again received a petition [from] Mrs. Fan [stating] that her third son had died, and Fan Yuan, her second son, had been **(E)** <u>deported</u>. Moreover, he is truly an unfilial rascal. Hence, she requests that her eldest son, Fan Gui, be allowed to remain at home.

This Board . . . submitted a palace memorial to the emperor proposing approval of the petition. . . .

(F) Fan Gui [was able] to remain at home. 99
—The Case of Fan Gui, Qing Dynasty, 1821

▲ A magistrate in a Chinese court during the Qing dynasty

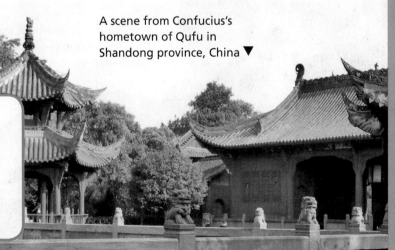

A scene from Confucius's hometown of Qufu in Shandong province, China ▼

Analyze the Documents

1. **Draw Inferences** In what way might Fan Yuan have caused his mother anxiety?
2. **Writing Task** Write a paragraph explaining how Fan Gui's sentence and pardon both show the importance of filial piety.

637

Section 3
China and Its Neighbors Today

Key Ideas
- The governments of Mongolia and Taiwan have become more democratic, but China's has not.
- Exports have been important to the economies of all three countries.
- China's economy has grown rapidly, but it faces many challenges.

Key Terms
- single-party state
- hydroelectricity
- wage
- life expectancy
- illiterate

 **Visual Glossary**

 Reading Skill: Compare and Contrast Take notes using the outline map in your journal.

Protests in Mongolia led to political reform. ▼

The Chinese government used the army to stop protests in Tiananmen Square. ▼

In recent years, China, Taiwan, and Mongolia have all experienced great changes. For Taiwan and Mongolia, the changes have been both political and economic. China, by contrast, has seen impressive economic growth with less change in the country's government.

Politics: One Party or Many?

Since the 1980s, Taiwan and Mongolia have changed their governments. In both countries, many parties can compete in elections. People in China, by contrast, do not have the freedom to create new parties. The people of Taiwan and Mongolia also enjoy more freedom in their religious and private lives than the people of China.

Reforms in Mongolia In 1989, protesters in Mongolia demanded change in the political system. The country's leaders responded and made many reforms. New parties could join free elections. Mongolian leaders also wrote a new constitution. This constitution states that the people directly elect the president and the parliament makes the laws.

638

The Communist Party is still important in Mongolia. Candidates from this party have won many elections. Now, though, this party competes with other parties for control of the government.

The new constitution also protects certain freedoms, such as religious freedom. In the past, the communists did not allow people to worship freely. Now, many people are again practicing Buddhism and other religions.

Democracy Grows in Taiwan After China's civil war, Jiang Jieshi left China and set up a government in Taiwan. He created a **single-party state,** that is, a country in which one political party controls the government. Jiang's Nationalist Party controlled the government. In the 1980s, some Taiwanese people began to push the government to become more open.

Finally in 1989, the Nationalists allowed other parties to take part in elections. Like the communists in Mongolia, the Nationalists Party is still important in Taiwan. Now, though, the Taiwanese can choose from more than one party when they vote.

Limited Freedom in China China's leaders have not made major political changes. It continues to be a single-party state. The Chinese Communist Party (CCP) controls the government.

The CCP no longer controls the economy. It does control peoples' lives in other ways. For example, China does not have freedom of the press. That is, journalists are not free to report the news

as they see it. The CCP also blocks many Web sites. Chinese people do not have <u>access</u> to all information on the Internet.

access, *n.,* ability to be used

Chinese people also do not have freedom of speech. The government may imprison people who say or do things to oppose the government.

In 1989, tens of thousands of people gathered in Tiananmen Square (tyen ahn mun skwehr) in Beijing. They called for more freedom and changes to the government. They refused to leave the square. China's leaders sent in tanks and troops to break up the demonstration. Thousands of people were killed or wounded.

The government refused to make any of the changes that the protesters had demanded. The freedoms of the Chinese people remain very limited.

Reading Check **Is Taiwan a single-party state today?**

Political and Economic Systems: China and Its Neighbors

	China	Taiwan	Mongolia
Political Parties	Single-party system	Several parties	Several parties
Elections	Few elections, very limited	Open elections	Open elections
Freedoms	Freedoms limited by government	Religious freedom, freedom of the press	Religious freedom, freedom of the press
Economic System	Market system	Market system	Market system

Chart Skills

How is China different from Taiwan and Mongolia? How are all three countries similar?

⊙ **Data Discovery**

The skyscaper Taipei 101 towers over Taiwan's capital. ▼

Economic Growth: The Importance of Exports

Trade is important for the economies of all three countries in this region. Taiwan and China have had rapid economic growth. Mongolia struggles to strengthen its economy.

Taiwan: An Asian Tiger Taiwan has been called an "Asian Tiger" because for decades its economy had strong growth. In the mid-1900s, Taiwan began to manufacture more goods. At the time, many people still worked on farms. The country was relatively poor.

People were paid a low **wage,** that is, their pay was low. Factories paid their workers less than factories paid in wealthier countries. As a result, factories in Taiwan could make their products more cheaply. Other countries were happy to buy Taiwan's cheaper goods. Soon, the country was exporting goods. Its economy began to grow quickly.

As money from exports came into the country, Taiwanese people became wealthier and wages increased. The price of making goods in Taiwan went up.

The Taiwanese economy continued to grow even as wages went up. One reason is because the government improved the education system. Better education helped Taiwan to produce new, technologically advanced products, such as chemicals, medicines, and electronics. Taiwan now exports these complex, expensive products. By making this change, the economy continued to grow.

Mongolia's Mineral Resources Early in the 1990s, Mongolia changed to a market economy. This change was difficult. In the past, the Soviet Union gave Mongolia economic support. Mongolia struggled without this help.

Wages are not high in Mongolia, but transportation is difficult. This increased the cost of making goods in Mongolia. The country is landlocked. This means it has no coastline. Moving goods long distances across land is more expensive than shipping them the same distance by sea.

Railroads connect Mongolia to Russia and China. Now, China is one of Mongolia's major trading partners. Mongolia's main exports are its mineral resources. In addition, raising livestock is still important to Mongolia's economy.

With the market economy, Mongolia's economy has grown. More Mongolians now have cellphones and access to the Internet. Still, many people remain poor. The country has not had the strong growth of Taiwan and China.

China's Economic Miracle China's economic reforms began much earlier than Mongolia's. In the late 1970s, the Chinese government told farmers in some areas that they did not have to follow the government's economic plan. The farmers could decide what they wanted to grow. They could sell their harvest and keep the profits. Some farmers figured out how to use their land more efficiently than the government plan. They produced more than before.

Because these farmers were successful, the government expanded the policy. Farmers across the country could make their own decisions. The government also let more people start private businesses. Slowly, the government gave up the command economy.

As with Taiwan, trade became important to China's economic growth. Wages in China continue to be relatively low. Companies make their products cheaply and sell them abroad.

The Chinese government also encouraged foreign companies to come to China. These companies had money to build new factories. Most of these factories are along China's long coastline. Here, it is easy for companies to ship their goods around the world. The companies need many workers. People have moved to coastal cities to find jobs in these factories. Shenzhen is one coastal city where many factories have been built. In 1980, it was a town of 30,000 people. By 2006 it had become a city of more than 8 million people!

Now, China's economy is one of the largest in the world. Toys, clothing, and many other goods sold in the United States are made in China.

Reading Check Why is trade more difficult for Mongolia?

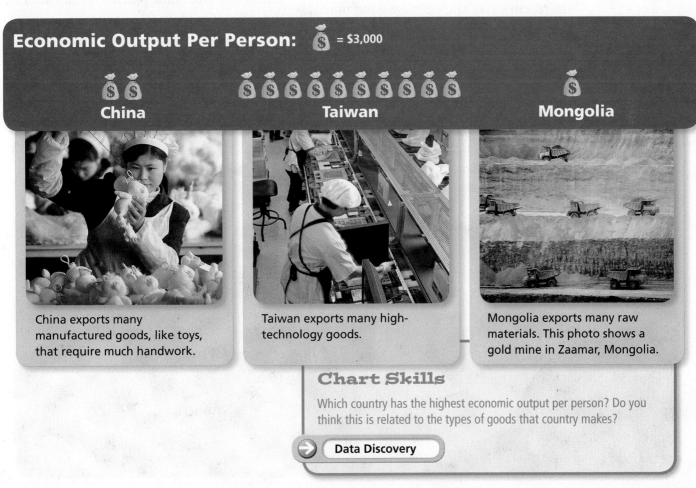

Economic Output Per Person: 💰 = $3,000

China 💰💰

Taiwan 💰💰💰💰💰💰💰💰💰💰

Mongolia 💰

China exports many manufactured goods, like toys, that require much handwork.

Taiwan exports many high-technology goods.

Mongolia exports many raw materials. This photo shows a gold mine in Zaamar, Mongolia.

Chart Skills

Which country has the highest economic output per person? Do you think this is related to the types of goods that country makes?

➔ Data Discovery

641

A More Unequal Society

The economic growth in China has made many people wealthier. Now, more families can afford products such as televisions, refrigerators, and even cars. Still, some people have <u>benefited</u> from this new wealth more than others have.

benefit, *v.*, to help, be of service to

Greater Wealth in the East Trade has helped bring growth to coastal cities. Many factories are located along the south and east coasts. This area produces 60% of the nation's industrial output.

Areas in the west and center of China face many of the same challenges as Mongolia. Companies far from the coast find it expensive to transport their goods. In recent years, the Chinese government has tried to increase investment in the west and center of China. Still, growth there lags behind eastern China.

Many Rural Areas Struggle Many rural communities have also faced difficulties. Under the command economy, the national government provided some services to rural areas. They sent doctors to rural areas to give everyone basic medical care. The **life expectancy,** that is, the number of years that people live on average, rose rapidly.

Now, individuals or local governments often must pay for these services. Less wealthy areas struggle to pay the costs of basic services. For example, some villages do not have enough money to have their own school. Parents, then, have to pay to send their children to a school in a different town. Some parents cannot afford these fees. Children from rural areas are less likely than those from urban areas to go to college and get higher-paying jobs.

Many villages in rural China cannot afford to have their own school. Five small villages share this primary school. Mr. Dai teaches all classes at the school.

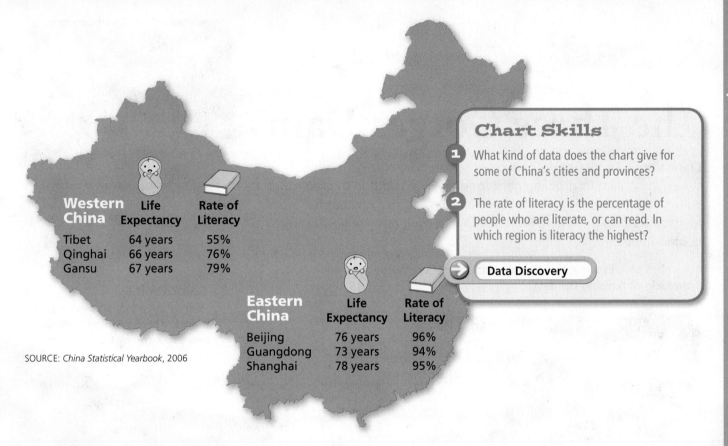

Western China	**Life Expectancy**	**Rate of Literacy**
Tibet	64 years	55%
Qinghai	66 years	76%
Gansu	67 years	79%

Eastern China	**Life Expectancy**	**Rate of Literacy**
Beijing	76 years	96%
Guangdong	73 years	94%
Shanghai	78 years	95%

SOURCE: *China Statistical Yearbook*, 2006

Chart Skills

1 What kind of data does the chart give for some of China's cities and provinces?

2 The rate of literacy is the percentage of people who are literate, or can read. In which region is literacy the highest?

→ Data Discovery

The Floating Population Because there are fewer opportunities for education and employment in rural areas, millions of people have been moving to cities.

These migrants are known as the "floating population." It is estimated at over 140 million people, or one tenth of China's total population. That is nearly half the population of the United States.

This floating population is moving illegally. The Chinese government has a rule allowing people to live only where they are registered, usually their birthplace. The government limits new registration in cities. Migrants who work in a city without registration often cannot receive healthcare or other government services. This is another challenge for people from rural areas as they try to improve life for their families.

Opportunities for Women Traditionally, couples live with the husband's family. The son takes care of his parents as they grow older. Therefore, many parents want to have at least one son.

The one-child policy changes this situation. If a couple has a daughter, they cannot have a son. They will help their daughter to be as successful as possible. Now, many daughters support their elderly parents.

Still, parents who have more than one child may send their son to school and keep their daughter at home to work. More women than men are **illiterate,** that is, more women than men do not know how to read. Women still do not have equal education and job opportunities.

Reading Check Why are migrant workers described as a floating population?

643

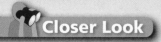

The Three Gorges Dam

China's huge Three Gorges Dam produces clean electricity. This helps the country meet its growing need for energy. In addition to producing energy, the project created thousands of jobs. It also changed the landscape along the Chang River. A 400-mile-long resevoir now extends behind the dam.

THINK CRITICALLY **Examine the diagram below. What are the benefits and drawbacks of building the dam?**

▲ Relocation
More than a million people had to move because their homes were covered by the reservoir.

◄ Lost History
The rising waters of the reservoir covered many historic sites along the river.

The dam can hold back high waters and help control flooding along the river.

Turbines in the dam produce electricity.

myWorldActivity
Three Gorges Dam

Newly built locks make transport along the river easier.

644

Environmental Challenges

As the Chinese economy has grown, pollution has become a major problem. China also uses many resources to feed, clothe, and house its large population.

Facing Environmental Problems Chinese cities have some of the worst air pollution in the world. Millions of cars, buses, and coal-burning electricity plants contribute to the smog around Chinese cities.

Water pollution is also a serious problem. Factories and farms dump dangerous chemicals into rivers and lakes near cities. Lake Tai near Xiao's home is one of many lakes affected by this issue.

Drier areas in the north and west are struggling with shortages of water. Factories, farms, and citizens compete to use this limited resource. At times, the Huang River dries up before reaching the sea. The land around Beijing is so dry that sandstorms blow into the city.

China has laws to limit pollution, but local governments do not want to punish polluters too harshly. People would lose their jobs if factories closed down.

Searching for Energy In the past, China could produce all the energy it needed. Now, more energy is needed to run its many new businesses. China has started importing oil. Also, it has been building more coal-burning power plants.

Burning oil and coal makes China's air pollution even worse, so China is looking for cleaner forms of energy. In western China, wind power produces electricity. The Chinese government also built the Three Gorges Dam along the Chang River to produces **hydroelectricity** (hy droh ee lek TRIH suh tee), or electricity made by water power. Building this dam was disruptive and expensive. China's leaders have to balance these costs with the need for new sources of energy.

Reading Check What kinds of environmental challenges does China face?

my **Story** 📷 Photo

Xiao, like many Chinese people, boils his water to make it safe to drink.

Section 3 Assessment

Key Terms

1. What is a single-party state?

2. What is illiteracy?

Key Ideas

3. **Compare and Contrast** How has reform been different in China and Mongolia?

4. What is one problem that China faces, and how might China solve it?

Thinking Critically

5. **Analyze Cause and Effect** What effect does geography have on Mongolia's economic growth?

Essential Question

How can you measure success?

6. What is one way that China has been successful? Give evidence from the text and from figures to support your point. Go to your Student Journal to record your answer.

645

Information Control in China

Key Ideas
- When Mao Zedong led China, the Communist Party controlled information as a way to change Chinese society.
- Today, the Communist Party still controls information on political issues.

Key Terms
- liberate
- propaganda
- Cultural Revolution

The Communist Party won a civil war and took control of China in 1949. The leaders of the Party claimed that they **liberated** China, or made it free, but the Communist Party limited the political freedoms of the Chinese people. The Party tightly controlled information, and China entered a period of isolation. Since economic reforms in the 1980s, China has become less isolated. The Communist Party allows more freedom of expression but still controls political information.

Chairman Mao ▼

Victorious Communist troops march into Beijing in 1949 ▼

The Communist Transformation of China

The leaders of the Communist Party hoped to transform, or completely change, China. They took control of the economy. In addition, they wanted to sweep away many traditional beliefs and practices in China. For example, women had fewer rights than men. The Communists created laws to improve equality between men and women. They encouraged parents to send not only their sons but also their daughters to school. They gave women jobs in government-owned businesses, and more women began to work outside the home.

Despite new opportunities for some, the Communists did not create a free and open society. They wanted to change society quickly. The Party punished people who criticized its policies and began to control the information that people received. The Party took over newspapers and companies that published books. In addition, the Party began to supervise schools and colleges. Teachers had to use textbooks approved by the Party. Meanwhile, China became more isolated. News and information from foreign countries was strictly controlled.

Much of the information that Chinese people received was **propaganda,** that is, information that supported the policies of the government. Posters and newspaper articles showed the positive side of the changes taking place in China and hid the serious problems in the country.

Reading Check **Why did the Party take over newspapers in the country?**

The Cultural Revolution

China's leader, Mao Zedong, felt that cultural change was happening too slowly. He thought people who supported his ideas about communism should fight against people who held traditional values. In the 1960s, Mao called for a **Cultural Revolution.** This was a period of sometimes violent upheaval in China.

The "soldiers" in this revolution were students called Red Guards. Mao thought that respect for teachers and education was not a communist value. He closed schools across the country and encouraged students to join the Guards. Mao told them to rid the country of the traditional, Confucian ideas.

The Red Guards broke into people's homes looking for old books and art. They criticized and even attacked people who had these things. In addition, the Guards damaged temples and monuments to destroy traditional culture.

During this time, artists and performers had to show support for Mao and the ideas of the Cultural Revolution. People could only go to a few approved movies and plays.

The Cultural Revolution began to disrupt life across China. Workers joined the Revolution. Production at factories slowed. In addition, different groups of Red Guards began to fight with each other. Finally, Mao had to bring in the army to end the fighting between these groups and restore order to the country.

Reading Check **Who were the Red Guards?**

Chairman Mao's Little Red Book

Mao's "Little Red Book" was handed out to the Red Guards. The book contained quotes from Mao. These quotes were meant to build support for the Communist Party among soldiers.

647

Shutting Down Culture

In the early 1960s, Mao believed that China had not lived up to its communist ideals. Mao believed that educated people and artists were part of an elite group who maintained divisions between rich and poor. During the Cultural Revolution, Mao's government controlled the media, books were destroyed, and artists, teachers, and others were jailed.

During the Cultural Revolution, people read news distributed by the Communist Party. ▶

Information and the Arts: Change Since the Time of Chairman Mao

	Cultural Revolution	China Today
Books	Few books are published. People study Chairman Mao's ideas for building a new society.	There are more choices as books on many topics are published. The Communist Party still bans books.
Arts	Old buildings and works of art are destroyed. New art must support communism and Chairman Mao's ideas.	Old buildings are being restored. Some artistic freedom is allowed, but artwork critical of the Party is often banned.
News	The Party controls news. News from foreign sources is not allowed.	The Party controls news. Only limited foreign news is allowed.
Education	Schools are shut down. Many teachers are criticized for encouraging old thinking.	New schools open. Education is respected but still faces Communist Party control.

This newsstand in China's capital, Beijing, can sell only material approved by the Communist Party.

The Party After the Cultural Revolution

Mao died in 1976. Deng Xiaoping and some other Party leaders did not agree with the goals of Mao's Cultural Revolution. These leaders ended the disruption of the Cultural Revolution, but they wanted to maintain Party control.

Deng opened universities that Mao had closed. In addition, the government has restored historic palaces and temples damaged by the Red Guards. Deng also ended China's isolation. Today, Chinese students study abroad, and many people travel to China each year. Chinese people also have more choices for news and entertainment. Magazines on a wide range of topics are now published. Television stations show comedies, drama, and even reality shows—not just the few plays allowed by the Communist Party during the Cultural Revolution.

Still, the Chinese government tries to control how people think and how much they know. The Communist government decides which books can be published. The government also continues to control news and entertainment. Every week, the Party gives newspapers a list of topics that must be covered and other topics that must be avoided. The Party still makes large posters to support its policies, such as the one-child policy.

Journalists who report news against the wishes of the Party may be fined, fired, or imprisoned. One event the media are forbidden to mention is the 1989 killings in Tiananmen Square. Journalists do not discuss it, and textbooks say nothing about it. An Internet search launched in China might yield hits about the square as a tourist site but nothing about the events of 1989.

The Internet is tightly controlled in other ways as well. Many Web sites are blocked. Those who run Web sites are expected to censor their content and are punished if they do not.

Even with these restrictions, Chinese people now pursue hobbies and interests that were not allowed in the past, especially during the Cultural Revolution. However, access to information, especially about many political issues, is limited.

Reading Check **How do the Chinese government and Communist Party control information on the Internet?**

Assessment

1. What was Mao's goal for the Cultural Revolution?

2. What was the government's attitude toward education during the Cultural Revolution?

3. How does the government force journalists to report events from the government's point of view?

4. How does the government stop Internet users from looking up the events in Tiananmen Square in 1989?

5. Why do you think that the Chinese government still tries to control its people's access to information about politics?

China and Its Neighbors

Chapter Assessment

Key Terms and Ideas

1. **Discuss** Why are people migrating from villages to cities in China?

2. **Summarize** How has the government of China helped and hurt China's minority groups?

3. **Compare and Contrast** How are men and women treated differently in China?

4. **Explain** What are the important beliefs of Confucianism and Daoism?

5. **Recall** What are some of the main physical features of China?

6. **Compare and Contrast** How do a command economy and a market economy differ?

7. **Describe** How and when did the Mongols conquer China?

Think Critically

8. **Problem Solving** What are some causes of air and water pollution in China? How could you lower pollution in China without forcing many people out of work?

9. **Identify Evidence** What might explain why China's population density is higher than Mongolia's?

10. **Draw Conclusions** Why is it easier for a country to export its goods if wages are low?

11. **Core Concepts: Economics** What three basic questions do economists ask when studying economies? How have the answers to these questions changed for China?

Places to Know

For each place, write the letter from the map that shows its location.

12. Beijing

13. Chang River

14. Huang River

15. Mongolia

16. Shanghai

17. Taiwan

18. **Estimate** Using the scale, estimate the distance between Beijing and Shanghai.

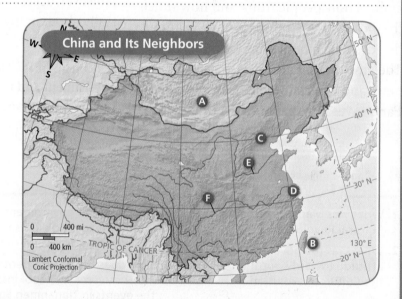

650

Essential Question

How can you measure success?

A Changing China: Who Benefits the Most? Gather data about the changes taking place in China. Answer the question *How do these changes affect different people in different ways?* Organize your findings and write a report to an economic leader.

21st Century Learning

Evaluating Web Sites

Search for three different Web sites that give information on the Three Gorges Dam. Examine each site and answer the following questions. Create a table to record your answers.
- Who is the source of the information?
- How up-to-date is the information?
- Does the information seem accurate?
- Is the information easy to understand?

Document-Based Questions

Success Tracker™
Online at myworldgeography.com

Use your knowledge of the region and Documents A and B to answer Questions 1–3.

Document A

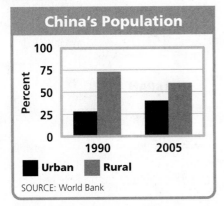

China's Population

SOURCE: World Bank

Document B

" There are no social benefits—all I get is my salary. Hands stop, mouth stops. If I get sick, I just have to keep my eyes open and sit here."

—a migrant worker in urban China

1. Which of the following might explain the change seen in Document A?

   A better health care in rural areas

   B better schools in rural areas

   C better-paying jobs in urban areas

   D natural disasters in urban areas

2. Which of the following best describes the worker quoted in Document B?

   A a member of the "floating population"

   B a person who was born in a big city and has health benefits

   C a government official in a city

   D a farmer in western China

3. **Writing Task** Do you think the situation described in Document B is common? Explain your answer.

myworldgeography.com Self-Test

651

Chapter 15

Japan and the Koreas

Essential Question

How much does geography shape a country?

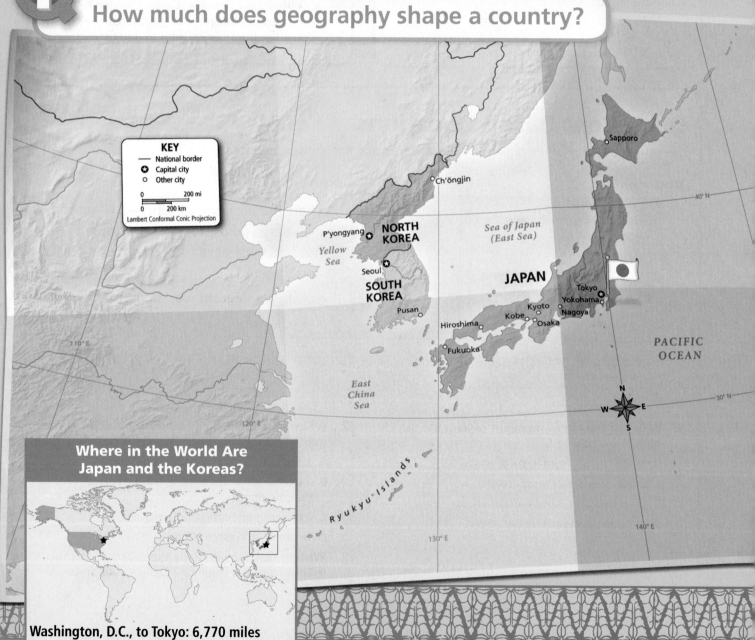

KEY
- National border
- Capital city
- Other city

0 — 200 mi
0 — 200 km
Lambert Conformal Conic Projection

Where in the World Are Japan and the Koreas?

Washington, D.C., to Tokyo: 6,770 miles

my Story

Asuka: A Girl on the Go

Explore the Essential Question
- at my worldgeography.com
- using the myWorld Chapter Activity
- with the Student Journal

In this section you'll read about Asuka. She is a senior in high school and lives with her family in Yokohama, Japan. Life has not been easy for Asuka, but that has not stopped her from wanting to make the world a better place to live. **What does Asuka's story tell you about the challenges young people face living in Japan?**

Story by Michael Condon for MyWorld Geography Online

In the bamboo- and concrete-covered hills of Yokohama, a cluster of identical apartment blocks stands out. The drab, box-shaped buildings have numbers stenciled onto the top of their walls to identify them. On the third floor of one of the apartment buildings, in a small apartment no bigger than an average American living room, lives Asuka. The third-year high school student shares the apartment with her father, her grandmother, her 15-year-old brother, the family's pet turtle, and Max, a pet rabbit.

More than 35 million people live in the Greater Tokyo-Yokohama metropolitan area. This is almost twice as many people as live in Greater New York. With so many people needing housing, space is scarce. Most people live in small apartments. About 2,500 people live in this four-block square area of Yokohama. It is very crowded, and the cost of living in Yokohama is high.

my worldgeography.com On Assignment

653

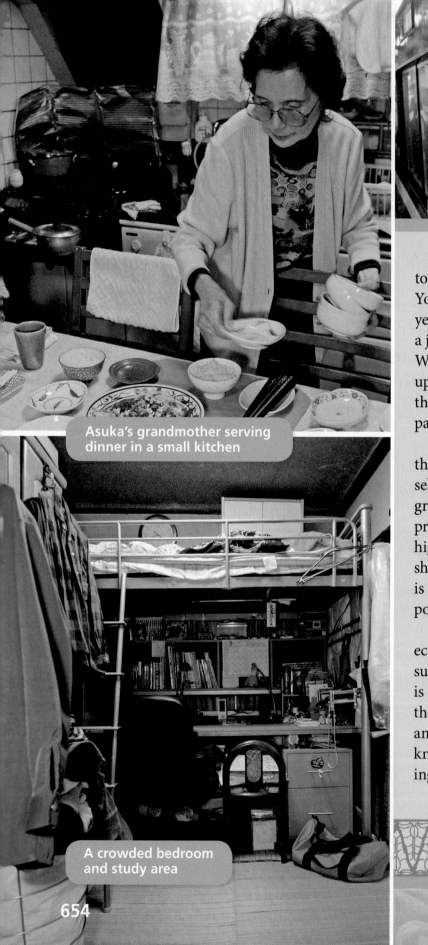

Asuka's grandmother serving dinner in a small kitchen

A crowded bedroom and study area

654

Standing room only on the train to school

For a single-parent family, it can be a struggle to make ends meet. Asuka's family moved to Yokohama after her parents divorced. She was three years old. To support the family, her father took a job as a salesman in the construction industry. With money short, Asuka also helps out by working up to 20 hours a week after school. She gives one third of her wages to the family and uses the rest to pay her other expenses.

Though her family does not have a lot of money, the 18-year-old high school senior considers herself fortunate. Every day she wakes up at 6:30 A.M., grabs the "bento" lunch box her grandmother has prepared, and heads off to school. She attends a high school in the middle of Yokohama, where she studies international affairs. Her curriculum is demanding. It includes courses in world history, politics, economics, Japanese, English, and Korean.

Asuka has developed a keen interest in politics, economics, and history. She plans to major in these subjects when she goes to college. Asuka thinks it is important to study politics and history because they explain how various countries have developed and the way their governments work. With that knowledge, she believes, "We can improve the living conditions of people and make things better."

A Glocally field trip

Class is just about to begin.

Asuka is a high-energy person. In addition to her studies and her job, she takes part in extracurricular activities. These activities range from volunteer work to playing drums in a rock band. Asuka is also the leader of the school's "Glocally" Club. (The club's name is a combination of the words "global" and "locally.") As part of the club's activities, the students go on field trips to observe war ruins. They also learn how wars affect people and look for ways to achieve peace in the modern world.

The teacher in charge of the club has introduced the students to some serious issues that are far from the minds of the average high school student in most developed countries. Asuka is glad he challenges them to think about real-world issues.

Over the last couple of years, Asuka has also taken part in the Yokohama Student Forum. Last year she became a student leader and put together a forum on child labor—an issue that touches the lives of families across Asia.

Asuka appreciates all the opportunities she has had. "I have [led] a privileged life," she says, "while others are suffering elsewhere." After graduating from college, Asuka says she wants to do something to help others less privileged.

Judging by what she has achieved so far, the promising young student will be sure to put her talents to good use in the future.

myStory Video

Join Asuka as she shows you about her life in Yokohama.

Meet the Journalist

Name Heath Cozens
Favorite Moment My favorite memory was Asuka doing karaoke.

my worldgeography.com
myStory Video

655

Chapter Atlas

Key Ideas
- Mountains cover much of this region.
- A dense population requires careful use of resources.
- People have adapted to sudden natural disasters.

Key Terms
- foliage
- scarcity
- comparative advantage
- interdependent

 Visual Glossary

 Reading Skill: Label an Outline Map Take notes using the outline map in your journal.

A hiker at the base of Mt. Fuji in Japan ▼

Physical Features

Japan, at the far eastern edge of Asia, is sometimes called the "land of the rising sun." The Japanese see each day's sunrise before most parts of Asia. North and South Korea lie just to the west of Japan.

Japan is a 1,500-mile-long chain of islands made up of four large islands and about 3,000 smaller islands. The countries of North and South Korea together form the Korean peninsula.

Four tectonic plates are close to Japan and the Koreas. The plates are slowly moving together. The result is

656

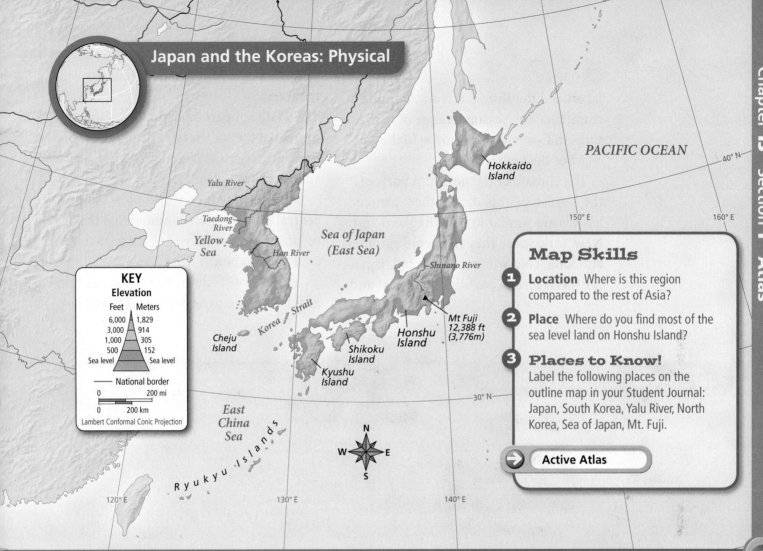

Japan and the Koreas: Physical

PACIFIC OCEAN

Hokkaido Island

Yalu River

Taedong River

Yellow Sea

Han River

Sea of Japan (East Sea)

Shinano River

KEY
Elevation

Feet		Meters
6,000		1,829
3,000		914
1,000		305
500		152
Sea level		Sea level

— National border

0   200 mi
0   200 km
Lambert Conformal Conic Projection

Cheju Island

Korea Strait

Kyushu Island

Shikoku Island

Honshu Island

Mt Fuji 12,388 ft (3,776m)

East China Sea

Ryukyu Islands

40° N
150° E   160° E
30° N
120° E   130° E   140° E

Map Skills

1 **Location** Where is this region compared to the rest of Asia?

2 **Place** Where do you find most of the sea level land on Honshu Island?

3 **Places to Know!** Label the following places on the outline map in your Student Journal: Japan, South Korea, Yalu River, North Korea, Sea of Japan, Mt. Fuji.

Active Atlas

great pressure that causes earthquakes. Earthquakes that <u>occur</u> under the sea can make huge waves that slam into the towns along the shore. As the Pacific Plate sinks beneath Japan, it melts and is called molten rock. The molten rock then rises to Earth's surface, creating volcanic eruptions. Japan has 108 active volcanoes.

Both North Korea and South Korea are mountainous countries. In both countries, there are a wide coastal plain in the west and smaller plains in the east. South Korea has more flat land suitable for farming than North Korea.

Japan is more rugged than the Koreas. Mountains and hills cover about 70 percent of the country's surface. In Japan and the Koreas, most people live in the valleys and coastal plains. In Japan, the largest level area is on Honshu Island.

The mountains in these countries are popular sites for hiking. Mount Fuji, the highest peak in Japan, is particularly popular. The mountain is a volcano, but it has not erupted for centuries. Thousands of people climb Mount Fuji every year.

Reading Check Why are there earthquakes and volcanoes in Japan and the Koreas?

occur, v., to take place; to happen

myworldgeography.com   Active Atlas

657

Climate

Japan and the Koreas are mid-latitude countries. The seasonal range of temperatures in this region is similar to the east coast of the United States.

The climate of the northern parts of the Korean peninsula and the Japanese islands are similar to New England and New York State. They have cool summers and long, cold winters. In the fall, Japan's northern forests are bright with red and yellow foliage. **Foliage** is the leaves on the trees.

The southern part of Japan has a climate more like the southeast coastal region of the United States. Winters are mild, and summers are hot and humid.

During the winter, winds blow from central Asia into Korea and across the Sea of Japan. These cold winds are very dry, especially in North Korea.

About three fifths of North Korea's rain falls from June to September. By contrast,

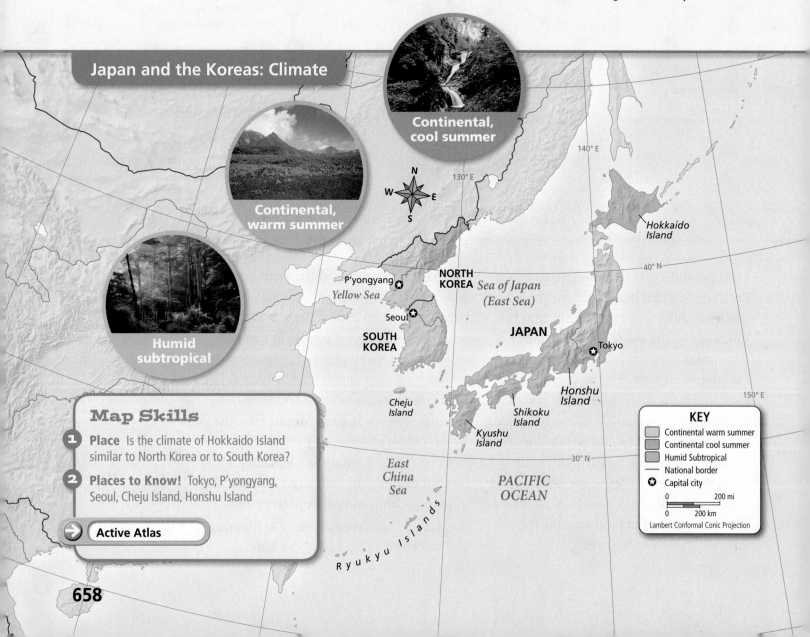

Japan and the Koreas: Climate

Continental, cool summer

Continental, warm summer

Humid subtropical

Map Skills

1. **Place** Is the climate of Hokkaido Island similar to North Korea or to South Korea?

2. **Places to Know!** Tokyo, P'yongyang, Seoul, Cheju Island, Honshu Island

→ Active Atlas

KEY
- Continental warm summer
- Continental cool summer
- Humid Subtropical
- National border
- Capital city

0 — 200 mi
0 — 200 km
Lambert Conformal Conic Projection

658

the sea brings some moisture all year to South Korea and Japan.

Summer seasonal winds, or monsoons, can drop as much as 80 inches of rainfall a year. They sometimes bring powerful tropical cyclones or hurricanes. In this part of the world, these storms are referred to as typhoons. Because of the warm, moist air, summers are humid in this region.

After a dry winter, the Koreas may experience a spring drought. The heavy summer rains that follow these droughts can cause flooding and mudslides. When this happens, houses are buried, and farmers may lose their crops.

Summer monsoon rainfall supports lush forests. As a result, most of the uplands of Japan and the Koreas are wooded. Particularly in Japan, people have worked hard to preserve their forests. It is one of the few industrialized countries that is heavily forested.

Reading Check Why are wind patterns important to climate in this region?

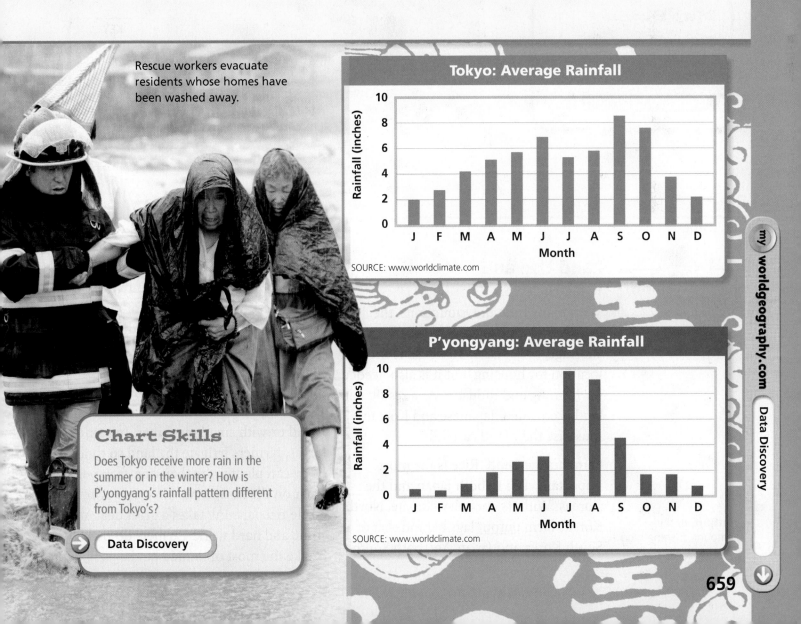

Rescue workers evacuate residents whose homes have been washed away.

Tokyo: Average Rainfall

SOURCE: www.worldclimate.com

P'yongyang: Average Rainfall

SOURCE: www.worldclimate.com

Chart Skills

Does Tokyo receive more rain in the summer or in the winter? How is P'yongyang's rainfall pattern different from Tokyo's?

→ Data Discovery

my worldgeography.com Data Discovery

659

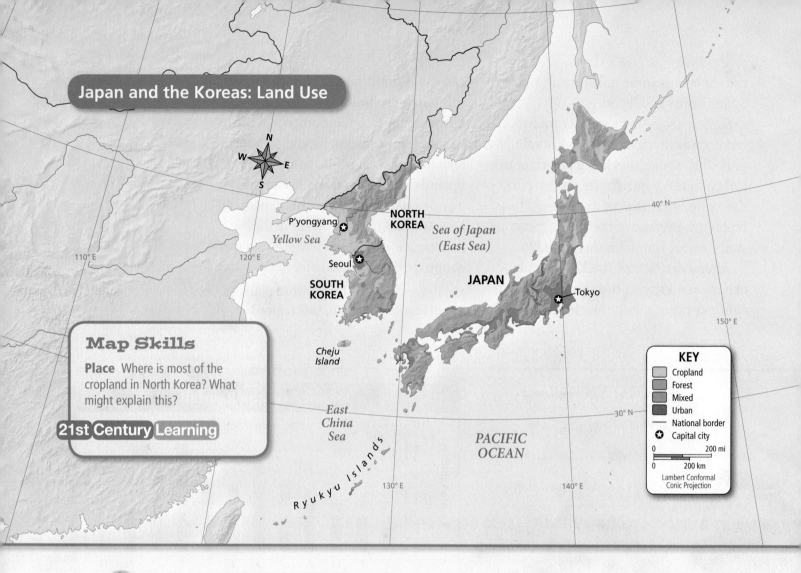

Japan and the Koreas: Land Use

N W E S

P'yongyang ☆
Yellow Sea

NORTH KOREA

Sea of Japan (East Sea)

Seoul ☆

SOUTH KOREA

JAPAN

Tokyo ☆

Cheju Island

East China Sea

PACIFIC OCEAN

Ryukyu Islands

40° N
30° N
150° E
140° E
130° E
120° E
110° E

KEY
- Cropland
- Forest
- Mixed
- Urban
- —— National border
- ☆ Capital city

0 ___ 200 mi
0 ___ 200 km
Lambert Conformal Conic Projection

Map Skills

Place Where is most of the cropland in North Korea? What might explain this?

21st Century Learning

myWorld Activity
Trade Off

output, *n*, the amount of something produced

Land Use and Natural Resources

With many hills and mountains, the countries of this region face a **scarcity,** or shortage, of flat land. This land is the best location for housing, but it is also needed for farming and industry. As a result, flat land is crowded. Japanese and Koreans must use their land carefully.

Farming the Land Rice is the most important crop in both Japan and the Koreas. With its cool, dry climate, North Korea's farm output lags behind that of South Korea and Japan. Yet, both South

Korea and Japan are highly urbanized. Large cities in these two countries take up space. Less land is available for farming. Farmers often must work on difficult, hilly land. Terraces are used to create flat fields on sloping ground. Large tractors are too big to plow the narrow terraces. Instead, rice is planted and harvested by hand or with small machines. In some areas, farmers irrigate the land so that they can plant more than one crop per year on the same land. This type of small-scale rice farming takes a great deal of time and hard work. Farmers do this to make the most of limited land.

660

Food Imports and Exports Many other countries can produce farm goods more cheaply than Japan and the Koreas. These other countries have a comparative advantage over Japan and the Koreas in agriculture. **Comparative advantage** is the ability to produce goods at a lower cost than your competitors.

Because farming is costly in Japan and the Koreas, these countries import food. Still, people in this region continue to farm so that they will not be dependent on other countries for all their food.

The sea is also an important resource. Fish products are an important export for North Korea. The ocean currents near Japan create an environment that is good for many kinds of fish. Fish is also an important export for Japan as well as an important part of the Japanese diet.

Scarce Resources Mineral resources are not evenly spread across this region. Both Japan and South Korea have few mineral resources. North Korea, by contrast, is rich in mineral resources including coal, lead, iron ore, copper, gold, and salt.

Scarcity makes countries **interdependent,** which means they depend on each other. Japan and South Korea trade with each other to acquire some of the raw materials they need for industry.

In addition, all three countries need energy resources. Hydroelectricity is one source of energy. Because of the hilly land, there are many fast flowing rivers. These rivers are good for hydroelectric dams because the falling waters carry large amounts of energy that can be used to create electricity.

To meet their energy needs, South Korea and Japan have built nuclear power plants and also produce small amounts oil. Still, it is not enough. These countries must import oil and other resources to meet their energy needs.

Reading Check Which country is richest in mineral resources?

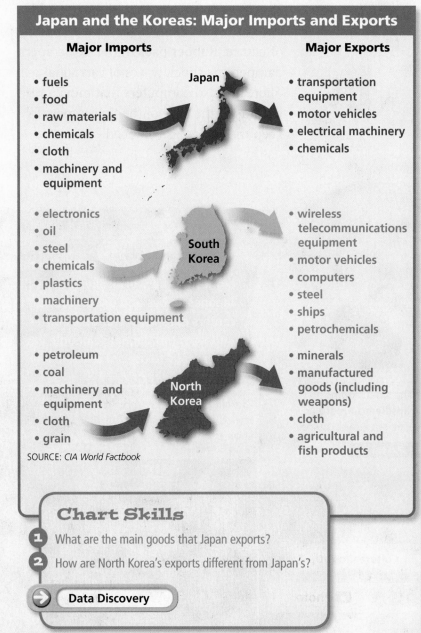

Japan and the Koreas: Major Imports and Exports

Major Imports

Japan
- fuels
- food
- raw materials
- chemicals
- cloth
- machinery and equipment

South Korea
- electronics
- oil
- steel
- chemicals
- plastics
- machinery
- transportation equipment

North Korea
- petroleum
- coal
- machinery and equipment
- cloth
- grain

Major Exports

Japan
- transportation equipment
- motor vehicles
- electrical machinery
- chemicals

South Korea
- wireless telecommunications equipment
- motor vehicles
- computers
- steel
- ships
- petrochemicals

North Korea
- minerals
- manufactured goods (including weapons)
- cloth
- agricultural and fish products

SOURCE: *CIA World Factbook*

Chart Skills

1. What are the main goods that Japan exports?
2. How are North Korea's exports different from Japan's?

→ **Data Discovery**

661

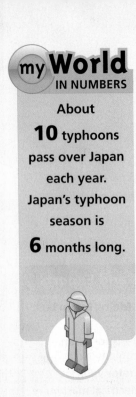

Adapting to Challenges

The people of the region have learned to live in a challenging environment. In the past, most buildings in Japan and the Koreas were made of wood. Fires, earthquakes, and floods might destroy them, but these wooden structures could be quickly rebuilt.

Today, the people of Japan and the Koreas use modern technology to build structures that can withstand the forces of nature. Rubber pads under skyscrapers dampen the shock waves of earthquakes. There are also computers that move weights in the base of the skyscrapers to keep the buildings balanced.

Safety Alerts Early warning systems also help people to take safety measures during earthquakes. One system developed in Japan can give people as much as 30 seconds warning. This might not seem like very much time. But every extra second is important when an earthquake is about to hit.

> 66 School children will be able to take shelter under their desks in classrooms if they have five seconds. In fact . . . if we have 10 seconds to prepare for major tremors, we can reduce the number of deaths caused by quakes significantly. 99
> —Yoshinori Sugihara

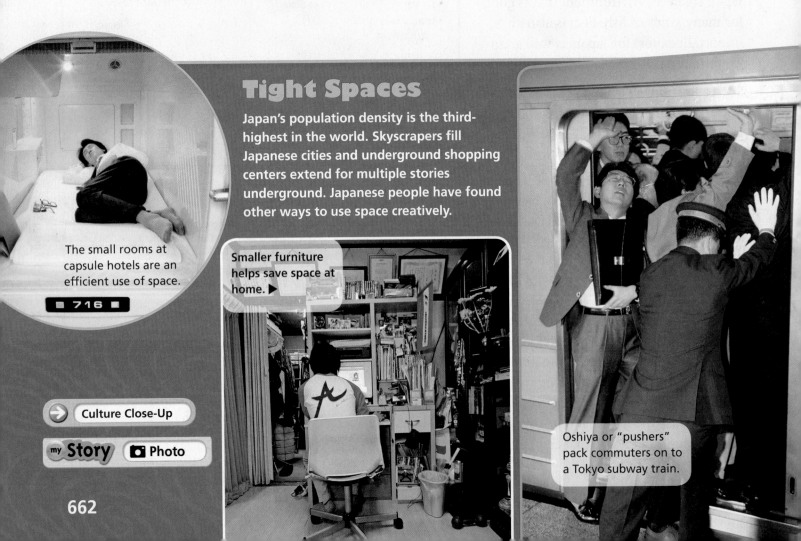

Tight Spaces

Japan's population density is the third-highest in the world. Skyscrapers fill Japanese cities and underground shopping centers extend for multiple stories underground. Japanese people have found other ways to use space creatively.

The small rooms at capsule hotels are an efficient use of space.

■ 716 ■

Smaller furniture helps save space at home. ▶

Oshiya or "pushers" pack commuters on to a Tokyo subway train.

⊙ Culture Close-Up

my **Story** 📷 Photo

662

Environmental Threats Managing resources is another challenge. With so many people crowded together, it is easy to use limited resources too quickly.

North Korea and South Korea have lost much of their forest land by cutting trees faster than they can grow back. Without tree cover, rain water washes quickly into rivers and streams and flooding becomes worse. As a result, soil needed for farming is washed away.

Overfishing is also a problem in the region. Near Japan, fish were taken from coastal waters too quickly. Now, ships must go far out to sea to find fish.

Intensive use of the land has resulted in serious pollution in all three countries. Factories, cars, and farms create air and water pollution.

While much remains to be done, the people in South Korea and Japan have pushed their governments to make changes. Their governments are working to reduce air and water pollution, find cleaner fuels, and recycle more waste.

The North Korean government has made less progress addressing these problems. The shortage of clean water for drinking and bathing is still a problem in that country.

Reading Check What are two ways people in Japan and the Koreas have adapted to their environment?

Overfishing threatens to drive the tuna fish into extinction. ▼

Section 1 Assessment

Key Terms

1. What is foliage?

2. What does scarcity mean?

3. Use the term *comparative advantage* to describe the products that Japan imports.

Key Ideas

4. How do physical features affect land use in this region?

5. How have Japan and the Koreas used technology to adapt to the forces of nature?

6. What environmental problems have Japan and the Koreas faced?

Think Critically

7. **Analyze Cause and Effect** How does scarcity make countries interdependent?

8. **Compare and Contrast** Why does North Korea have less agricultural production than Japan and South Korea?

Essential Question

How much does geography shape a country?

9. How much does geography affect the problems that countries in this region face? Are there other factors that influence pollution in these countries? Go to your Student Journal and record your answer.

663

Section 2
History of Japan and the Koreas

Key Ideas
- Japan and the Koreas all have long histories.
- Japan built an empire early in the 1900s but lost this empire at the end of World War II.
- Korea was divided into two countries, North Korea and South Korea, after the Korean War.
- Japan's economy grew rapidly after World War II.

Key Terms • shogun • samurai • Meiji Restoration • Korean War • constitutional monarchy

 **Visual Glossary**

Reading Skill: Identify Main Ideas and Details Take notes using the graphic organizer in your journal.

The imperial palace in Seoul, South Korea ▼

The people of Japan and the Koreas have adapted to their environment by building skyscrapers that survive the tremors of earthquakes. These nations have also needed to survive political and cultural tremors, such as wars and invasions. Japan and the Koreas have changed since their beginnings, but they are still standing.

Historical Roots

People have lived in this region for about 30,000 years. Powerful kingdoms have influenced the history of these countries, but each has charted its own course.

Korean Dynasties For thousands of years, kingdoms rose and fell on the Korean peninsula. At times, Chinese empires controlled parts of the peninsula. Ideas from China, especially Confucianism and Buddhism, influenced the Korean kingdoms.

In A.D. 668, the kingdom of Silla conquered the other Korean kingdoms. They pushed the Chinese empire off the peninsula and created a strong government. This dynasty, rulers in the same family, lasted until A.D. 935. After that, a series of dynasties kept the peninsula united for centuries.

664

Korean Achievements Under the various emperors, a unique society developed. Emperor Sejong called for a new writing system to be created in the 1400s. The system, called Hangul, is still used today. The Koreans also invented moveable metal type. This made printing easier. Korean potters also made delicate porcelain that is valued throughout the world.

Emperors and Shoguns in Japan
Around the time of the Silla dynasty in Korea, Japan became a unified country under an emperor. People believed the emperor was descended from a goddess.

For much of Japan's history, however, the emperors were not strong. Powerful military leaders called **shoguns** controlled Japan's government.

At times, neither the emperor nor the shoguns had complete control over all of the country. Some powerful landowners had their own armies. They granted land to **samurai**, or warrior lords, who supported them. These landowners fought each other to gain power. This created a lot of conflict in Japanese society.

grant, *v.,* to give

In 1603, a shogun called Tokugawa Ieyasu (toh koo GAH wah ee yay AH soo) came to power. Ieyasu and the Tokugawa shoguns that followed him tried to bring peace to Japan. The Tokugawa brought the powerful landowners under the shogun's control.

The Tokugawa closed the country off from contact with most other countries. They wanted to keep outside forces from disrupting Japanese society.

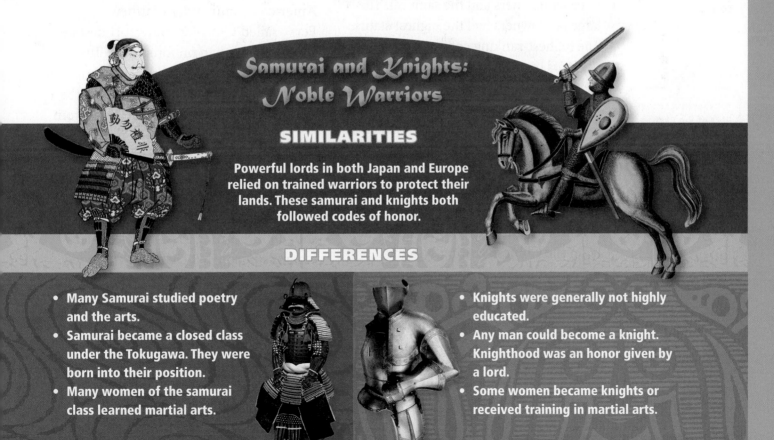

Samurai and Knights: Noble Warriors

SIMILARITIES

Powerful lords in both Japan and Europe relied on trained warriors to protect their lands. These samurai and knights both followed codes of honor.

DIFFERENCES

- Many Samurai studied poetry and the arts.
- Samurai became a closed class under the Tokugawa. They were born into their position.
- Many women of the samurai class learned martial arts.

- Knights were generally not highly educated.
- Any man could become a knight. Knighthood was an honor given by a lord.
- Some women became knights or received training in martial arts.

665

▲ A dinner at the palace of Emperor Meiji. Western-style clothing became popular in the Meiji court.

myWorld Activity
Best of the Best

The Tokugawa created strict divisions between nobles and commoners. People were not allowed to move between these two groups. The nobles were mostly the large landowners and the samurai. The large landowners had the highest status. The highest-ranking commoners were peasants (or small farmers). Below them were craftspeople and merchants. Peasants made up 80 percent of the population.

Before the Tokugawa, Japan had close ties with other countries, particularly China and Korea. Buddhism had spread from Korea into Japan. Many Japanese studied Chinese literature and art. The Japanese writing system was based mainly on the Chinese writing system.

New forms of art developed during the Tokugawa period. The country was prosperous. Wealthy nobles and merchants supported artists who created new styles of theater and painting.

Reading Check How did The Tokugawa try to bring stability to Japanese society?

International Conflicts and Connections

Early in the 1800s, both Japan and Korea were largely cut off from the rest of the world. By the beginning of the 1900s, both nations had been pulled into international conflicts and trade networks.

Early Contact with Europeans Ships from Europe first arrived in Japan and Korea around 1600. Both kingdoms had decided to keep Western merchants and missionaries away. Korea allowed only Chinese and Japanese traders. It attacked American and French ships trying to enter its ports. This isolation, or lack of contact, continued until the mid-1800s in Japan and even longer in Korea.

Changes Come to Japan In 1854, the American commander Matthew C. Perry sailed into a Japanese port despite the Tokugawa ban on foreigners. The Japanese knew that Perry's ship carried powerful weapons. So they accepted the trade agreement that Perry brought from the United States. Soon other nations pushed Japan to sign similar treaties.

Many Japanese people thought that these trade agreements were unfair to Japan. They blamed the Tokugawa shogun for signing these treaties. Many Japanese people felt change was needed to make Japan a more powerful country.

In 1868, new leaders arose and pushed out the Tokugawa shogun. They brought back the emperor, but they told him what to do. This time in Japanese history is called **Meiji Restoration.** It marks the return to power of Emperor Meiji.

The Rise of Japan Japan's new leaders expanded its industry and military. They also increased its power in the region.

In 1910, the Japanese took control over Korea. It was a difficult time for Koreans. They were forced to do hard work in new Japanese industries. They had to learn to speak Japanese, and many were forced to take Japanese sounding names. Japanese control of Korea was harmful to both the Korean people and culture.

Later Japan also invaded other countries. It took over large areas in the north of China as well as Formosa or Taiwan.

When World War II broke out, Japan joined on the side of Germany. Japan soon invaded Southeast Asia. The United States and Japan grew further apart. In 1941, Japan attacked the United States Navy at Pearl Harbor, Hawaii. As a result, the United States entered World War II.

In 1945, the United States dropped atomic bombs on the Japanese cities of Hiroshima and Nagasaki. The resulting casualtes were huge, and Japan surrendered. It lost all the lands it had invaded, including Korea.

Reading Check How did Japan's empire grow and then shrink?

A Japanese fighter plane called a "Zero" ▼

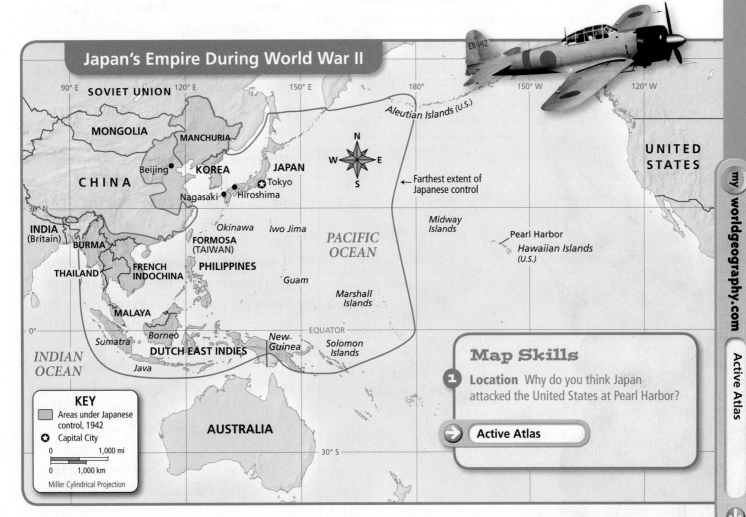

Japan's Empire During World War II

Map Skills

1 **Location** Why do you think Japan attacked the United States at Pearl Harbor?

Active Atlas

KEY
- Areas under Japanese control, 1942
- ✪ Capital City

0 — 1,000 mi
0 — 1,000 km
Miller Cylindrical Projection

Japan and the Koreas Since World War II

After World War II, Japan focused on rebuilding its government and its economy. In Korea, conflict quickly resumed. This conflict would divide a country that had been united for centuries.

The Korean War Japan's control of Korea ended after Japan surrendered at the end of World War II. At that time, the United States occupied the southern part of Korea. The Soviet Union occupied the northern part of the country. The United States and the Soviet Union disagreed about how to unite the two parts of Korea. They asked the United Nations to help, but they could not reach agreement.

Two new governments developed. One was a communist government in the north, which the Soviet Union supported. The other was a democratic government in the south, which the United States supported. Both governments claimed to rule Korea.

North Korea invaded South Korea in 1950. This marked the beginning of the **Korean War.** Hoping to limit the spread of communism, the United States led United Nations troops sent to defend South Korea. The Soviet Union and China aided North Korea.

Neither side won. Instead, they agreed to stop fighting in 1953. The two sides drew a new border. A strip along the border was declared a demilitarized zone, an area that neither army is allowed to enter. The peninsula was split into two countries: the communist Democratic People's Republic of Korea in the north—or North Korea, and the Republic of Korea in the south—or South Korea.

Japan's Recovery The United States occupied Japan after World War II. With the help of the United States, the Japanese created a new system of government. Japan is now a constitutional monarchy. A **constitutional monarchy** is a system of government in which the constitution limits the powers of the emperor or the monarch. Power lies in the hands of the voters, who elect their leaders.

Japan also needed to rebuild its economy after the war. Bombing had destroyed nearly all of the country's industry. The Korean War helped Japan's recovery to get started.

U.S. and U.N. troops were based in Japan. They needed supplies and labor.

occupy, *v.,* to take over, control

South Korean soldiers patrol the border along the demilitarized zone. ▼

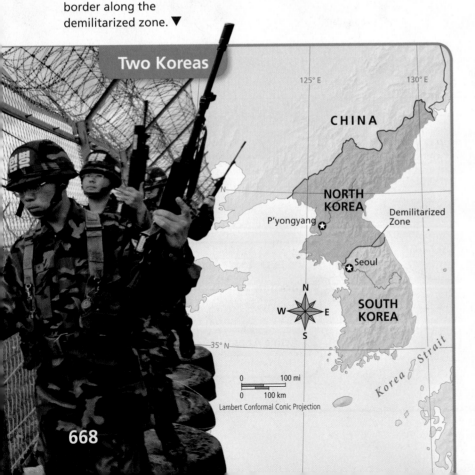

Two Koreas

CHINA

NORTH KOREA

P'yongyang

Demilitarized Zone

Seoul

SOUTH KOREA

Korea Strait

125° E

130° E

35° N

0   100 mi
0   100 km
Lambert Conformal Conic Projection

The Japanese people went to work to meet those needs.

The Japanese built new factories to replace the ones destroyed during the war. These factories had the most modern technology. They produced goods better and cheaper than the old factories.

The Japanese government supported education and job training. It also encouraged people to work hard and save their money. Banks used these savings to make loans to businesses. This helped the economy to grow.

Japan had a well-educated workforce and modern equipment in its factories. Japan produced and exported well-made products such as cars, electronics, and cameras. Those products attracted buyers in many parts of the world. Exports helped Japan's economy grow very quickly for the following 30 years, and the Japanese people grew wealthier.

Reading Check How did the Korean War affect Japan?

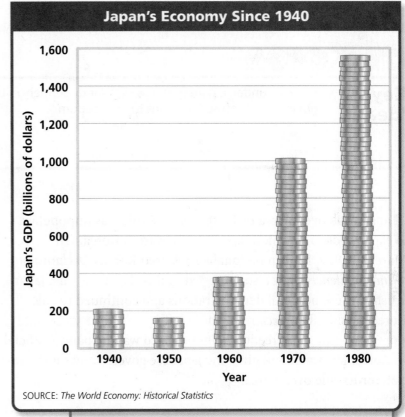

Japan's Economy Since 1940

SOURCE: *The World Economy: Historical Statistics*

Chart Skills

In which decade did Japan's economy grow the most?

 **Data Discovery**

Section 2 Assessment

Essential Question

Key Terms

1. Who were the shogun and the samurai?

2. What happened during the Meiji Restoration?

3. What is a constitutional monarchy?

Key Ideas

4. How did China influence the culture of Japan and Korea?

5. How did the Tokugawa change Japanese society?

6. Why was Korea divided after World War II?

Think Critically

7. **Draw Inferences** Why might the Koreans have wanted to create their own writing system rather than continuing to use the Chinese system?

8. **Analyze Cause and Effect** What factors helped the Japanese rebuild their economy after World War II?

How much does geography shape a country?

9. Both Japan and Korea chose to limit contact with outsiders at certain times during their histories. How do you think their geography helped them to do that? Go to your Student Journal and record your answers.

669

Japan's Occupation of Korea

Key Idea
- Koreans under Japanese rule wanted independence, but Japan's government refused to grant them freedom.

▲ Independence Declaration Day celebration in Korea

Japan took over Korea in 1910. Japanese rule was unpopular. Japan took large amounts of resources from Korea. On March 1, 1919, Korean nationalists released Korea's *Declaration of Independence*. They also protested against Japanese rule. Japan crushed these peaceful demonstrations and continued to rule Korea harshly. The *Declaration of Independence* gives voice to Korea's yearning for freedom. Nitobe Inazo was a Japanese official in Korea. His statement gives the Japanese government's justification for its rule over Korea.

Statue of a Korean independence activist ▼

Stop at each circled letter on the right to think about the text. Then answer the question on the left with the same letter.

Ⓐ **Main Idea** What does Korea announce to the world in the declaration?

Ⓑ **Summarize** What are the grievances, or charges, of the Korean people against Japan?

Ⓒ **Infer** The March 1, 1919, protests remain important to Koreans today. Why do you think this is the case?

proclaim, *v.,* announce
agony, *n.,* pain, torment
oppression, *n.,* harsh, unjust rule

Korea Proclaims Its Independence

66 We herewith <u>proclaim</u> the independence of Korea and the liberty of the Korean
Ⓐ people. We tell it to the world in witness of the equality of all nations. . . . [W]e have come after these long thousands of years to experience the <u>agony</u> of ten years of foreign <u>oppression</u>, with every loss to the right to live, every restriction of the freedom of thought, every damage done to the
Ⓑ dignity of life, every opportunity lost for a share in the intelligent advance of the
Ⓒ age in which we live. 99
—Korea's *Declaration of Independence*, March 1, 1919

670

Stop at each circled letter on the right to think about the text. Then answer the question on the left with the same letter.

D **Identify Bias** What does Nitobe Inazo think of the Korean people?

E **Paraphrase** In your own words, state Nitobe Inazo's reasons for Japanese rule in Korea.

F **Synthesize** Based on Nitobe Inazo's statement, what was Japan's attitude toward Korea during the colonial period?

tutelage, *n.,* instruction, guidance

conviction, *n.,* confidence, belief

steward, *n.,* guardian, supervisor

devolve, *v.,* to fall (to)

uplifting, *n.,* improvement, inspiration

Nitobe Inazo's Argument

Nitobe **Inazo**

❝ I count myself among the best and truest friends of Koreans. I like them . . . . I think they are a capable people who can be trained to a large measure of self-government, for which the present is a period **D** of <u>tutelage</u>. Let them study what we are doing in Korea, and this I say not to . . . boast of some of our achievements. In all humility, but with a firm <u>conviction</u> that Japan is a <u>steward</u> on whom **E** <u>devolves</u> the gigantic task of the <u>uplifting</u> of the Far East, I cannot think that the young Korea is yet **F** capable of governing itself. ❞

—Nitobe Inazo, colonial administrator, 1919

Japanese troops invading Korea, around 1900 ▼

Analyze the Documents

1. **Compare Viewpoints** Would the Koreans who wrote the *Declaration of Independence* agree that Nitobe Inazo is "among the best and truest friends of Koreans"? Explain.

2. **Writing Task** How would a signer of the Korean declaration respond to Nitobe Inazo's statement? Use both documents to write a paragraph from the signer's viewpoint.

Japan and the Koreas Today

Key Ideas
- South Korea's economy has grown, and its democracy has become stronger.
- North Korea is a communist dictatorship.
- North Korea's nuclear program is a source of conflict in the region.
- Japan has struggled with economic problems in recent years.

Key Terms • limited government • unlimited government • dictator • recession • Shinto

Visual Glossary

Reading Skill: Set a Purpose for Reading Take notes using the graphic organizer in your journal.

◀ 63 Building, the tallest building in Seoul, South Korea

Japan and the Koreas have faced challenges in recent years. Yet, the people of South Korea and Japan have a good standard of living. These countries have become more influential in the world. By contrast, North Korea is largely isolated. Its people have suffered severe hardship.

Prosperity and Democracy in South Korea

South Korea has become more democratic over the years. It has also become a world economic power.

Growing Democracy The leaders of South Korea approved a constitution in 1948 and began building a new government. They created a **limited government**, that is, a government with powers that are limited by law. However, the constitution also stated that leaders did not have to follow those limits or protect individual rights if the country faced serious problems.

As a result, South Korea's political system was not always democratic. More than once, the military took over the country. Freedom of speech and freedom of the press was not always protected. In 1987, people began to call for change. Many South Koreans joined huge political protests. That year, the leaders changed the constitution.

Under the new constitution, the government cannot take away freedoms even when there are political or economic troubles. Citizens have more rights. The military is less powerful. It has not taken over the government since those reforms.

Economic Boom After the Korean War, the leaders of South Korea focused on producing industrial goods for export to other countries. The government supported a number of large companies. It helped them get the money and equipment they needed to make more products. The government also improved the education system.

Now, South Korea exports many high-technology goods, such as cell phones and computers. Its economy is one of the largest in the world. People now live more comfortably and have more belongings.

Still, the growth of South Korea's economy has not been stable. The government borrowed large sums of money from abroad. In the late 1990s, the country had too much debt. This hurt the economy. The economy improved, but the government will have to work to avoid this problem in the future.

Daily Life and Culture As the economy has grown, daily life for the people of South Korea has changed. In the past, most Koreans were farmers. Now, most people live in cities. In addition, South Korea now has contact with many countries. This has changed Korean culture. It has also introduced Korean culture to people throughout the world.

For example, the popular Korean sport of tae kwon do has become very popular outside the country. Tae kwon do became an official Olympic sport in 2000. At the same time, the Koreans have become fans of many sports from abroad. Soccer, in particular, is very popular. Almost every town has its own team. Other sports such

▲ Winner of a gold medal in tae kwon do, South Korea's Hwang Kyungseon (left) at the Beijing Olympics in 2008

as baseball, basketball, and volleyball have a wide following.

Religious life in South Korea has also changed. Christianity spread rapidly through the country after the Korean War. About one quarter of South Korea's population is Christian. In addition, about one quarter of the population is Buddhist. The Buddha's birthday is a national holiday in South Korea. More than ten thousand Buddhist temples dot the landscape. Both foreign visitors and Koreans study Buddhism at these colorful temples. South Koreans enjoy complete religious freedom.

Reading Check How has the South Korean government changed since the 1980s?

673

STANDARD OF LIVING: NORTH AND SOUTH KOREA

A standard of living measures the health of a country by the goods and services its people can buy.

	North Korea	South Korea
Ecomonic output per person	$1,800	$27,100
Number of phone lines	1.2 million	24 million
Number of cell phones	0	43.5 million
Undernourished people	36%	1.6%
Life expectancy	64 years	79 years

SOURCE: *CIA World Factbook*, 2008, UN Common Database, 2001

Chart Skills

From the information in this table, which country has a higher standard of living?

→ **Data Discovery**

Repression and Hardship in North Korea

North Korea is very different from South Korea. North Korea is one of the most isolated countries in the world. The people of North Korea face a hard life with little political freedom.

Dictatorship and Isolation North Korea is not a democracy. Its government is an example of an **unlimited government,** which is a government that, by law, may take any action it wants. Kim Jong-il is the country's leader. Kim is a dictator. A **dictator** has total control over the government. Kim Jong-il came to power when his father, Kim Il-sung, died in 1994.

Kim Il-sung rose to power in 1948. He was the leader of the Communist Party. Other parties were not allowed. Communist Party leaders tightly controlled the North Korean people. Like his father, Kim Jong-il is also a Communist and has kept this system.

The government controls the information reported by newspapers, radio, and television. The news supports Kim's policies. In addition, the leadership limits information from the outside world. Very few North Koreans have cell phones or Internet access.

People are not free to express their opinions. People who disagree with the leadership are punished. The North Korean government may have jailed up to 200,000 people for their political actions.

The North Korean government controls cultural and religious life. People cannot worship freely. Only a few churches and temples are allowed in the country.

The government promotes Korean culture by funding museums and the arts. Still, it controls the work of these writers, dancers, and musicians. It can ban any art that goes against the ideas of the leaders. North Koreans have few of the freedoms that South Koreans now enjoy.

▲ Kim Jong-il

Dancers in North Korea perform at a ceremony for the 95th anniversary of Kim Il-sung's birth.

A Crippled Economy North Korea is a communist country with a command economy. The government controls much of the economy and decides what goods are made. Often, it has not managed the economy well. As a result, the economy has not grown.

The leadership has focused on building a strong military. As a result, it does not spend enough to update machines on farms or in factories. Food production has fallen because of shortages of tractors, fertilizer, and fuel.

Natural disasters have added to these problems. Starting early in the 1990s, frequent floods and droughts damaged crops. More than two million people died of starvation in the late 1990s.

Foreign counties have given food <u>aid</u> to help North Koreans survive. Still, the population suffers. The government has focused on keeping control rather than solving its serious economic problems.

A Tense Border Many people in North and South Korea hope the Koreas can be reunited. In recent years, South Korea has given aid, in the form of food, to North Korea. In addition, leaders from North and South Korea have met and agreed to try to improve relations.

However, despite earlier promises not to develop nuclear weapons, North Korea has continued to build them. This has hurt North Korea's relationship with South Korea and many other countries around the world.

World leaders have met with North Koreans and tried to persuade the government to stop developing nuclear weapons. The United States and other countries have pressured North Korea to give up these weapons, but its leaders refuse. Peace and prosperity seem far away for North Korea.

Reading Check Who is the leader of North Korea?

aid, *n.,* help, assistance

my **worldgeography.com** Data Discovery

675

Challenges and Changes in Japan

Japan's growth in the decades after World War II made it an important economic power. Japan builds many high-technology goods, such as computers and video games. Today, Japan faces new challenges, including slower economic growth and an aging population.

Economic Woes Japan has one of the largest economies in the world. Still, the country's economy has not grown as quickly in recent years.

After the World War II, the Japanese sold more goods abroad. They invested the money they earned to make more advanced products. The Japanese people became wealthier.

At the start of the 1980s, the Japanese economy was doing very well. Each year stock prices went higher and higher. Then in the early 1990s, the Japanese economy started heading downward.

Due to bad bank practices, Japan's economy entered a **recession**, a time when the economy becomes weaker and does not grow. Businesses produced less. They laid off many workers. In 2003, Japan's economy began to improve. In 2008, however, it fell back into recession. Japan continues to face challenges that may make future economic growth difficult.

An Aging Population One of these challenges is supporting a large population of retired people. Japanese people, on average, live longer than people in any other country. They have healthy eating habits and a good healthcare system.

In addition, couples in Japan have fewer children now. As a result, there are

Chart Skills

Will the percentage of elderly people increase or decrease in the future?

Data Discovery

Japan's Aging Population

17% / 83% — 2000

32% / 68% — 2030*

■ People 64 years and younger
■ People 65 years and older

SOURCE: Japan Statistics Bureau
*Projected

676

fewer young people to support the elderly population. With fewer young people entering the workforce, Japan may not be able to produce as many goods. Its economy may remain weak.

Some companies in Japan are building new kinds of robots as one way to avoid a possible shortage of future workers. By taking over jobs that people currently do, robots may help keep Japan's economic production high. They can even care for the elderly:

66 There are robots [in Japan] serving as receptionists, vacuuming office corridors, spoon-feeding the elderly. They serve tea, greet company guests, and chatter away at public technology displays. 99

—Associated Press

Changing Family Life Most Japanese people now live in cities. People are more likely to live in small family groups than with their extended families.

When the economy was growing quickly, many companies could provide excellent pay and benefits. Often only the husband worked. Wives generally stayed at home to care for children and older family members. Children were expected to study hard to get into college.

These family roles have changed in many families. During the recession, more women found jobs to help support their families. Also, some companies started hiring women as their older employees retired. These companies also encourage women to return to work after having children rather than becoming stay-at-home mothers.

Now, women have more job opportunities, but they still may not be treated equally to men. For example, women may find it difficult to be hired for the highest levels of management in a company.

School life has also changed in Japan. Many schools had classes six days a week to prepare students for difficult college entrance exams. Now, most schools have classes just five days a week.

Yet, the competition to get into the best colleges is as tough as ever. Many students attend extra classes during weekends and evenings in hopes of getting into one of Japan's best universities.

Reading Check How did economic problems change Japanese family life?

In an emergency, this security guard robot can put out a fire. *How might society change if robots could do many jobs that people now do?* ▼

my worldgeography.com Data Discovery

677

JAPAN'S POPULAR CULTURE

Japan's entertainment industry grew after World War II. People had more time and money for entertainment, such as movies and video games. Japan now has the largest comic book industry in the world, and entertainment is one of Japan's major exports.

CRITICAL THINKING: Why do you think Japanese entertainment has become popular in other countries?

▲ Video games that started in Japan, such as the dancing game above, have become popular across the world.

Manga, or Japanese comics, are reaching a wider audience in the United States. ▼

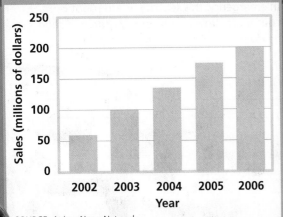

Sales of Manga in the United States

SOURCE: Anime News Network

▲ An anime, or cartoon, character from the Japanese video game Dragon Ball Z

This character is from the famous anime series Yu Gi Oh! The show is popular in Japan and also Australia, Germany, and Britain. ▶

Shoppers in Tokyo browse manga. ▼

myWorld Activity
Political Manga

678

A Rich Cultural Life

Most people in Japan belong to the same ethnic group and speak Japanese. There are not many immigrants. Yet, like South Korea, Japan is not cut off from the world. It influences and has been influenced by the cultures of many countries.

Spiritual Beliefs More than 80 percent of all Japanese people practice a combination of Buddhism and Shinto. **Shinto** is a traditional Japanese religion. In Shinto, kami are worshiped. Kami are gods or spirits that may live on earth in animals, trees, rocks, or other natural objects.

Today, many Japanese people practice both Buddhism and Shinto. For example, many Japanese people may have a Shinto marriage ceremony. Yet they will choose a Buddhist funeral.

Many traditions and holidays in Japan are connected to one of these two religions. At New Year's celebrations, Japanese people traditionally visit a Shinto shrine to pray to kami for a good harvest in the coming year.

Recent Cultural Borrowing In recent years, Japan has borrowed from the culture of many countries. Cultural imports, such as baseball and soccer, have been popular for many years in Japan.

At the same time, cultures around the world have borrowed from Japanese culture. Japanese martial arts, such as karate, are now popular around the world. So are Japanese foods such as sushi, or raw fish served with rice. Japanese artists have influenced artists in Europe, the United States, and other countries.

Japan has also had a big impact on the world of entertainment. It has had a large video-game industry for decades. Also, Japanese movies and television programs have a wide audience, especially in Asia.

More recently, Japanese anime—or cartoons—and manga—or comics—have attracted more and more fans throughout the world. Japan has added these products to its long list of successful exports.

Reading Check How have Shinto and Buddhism influenced Japanese culture?

Section 3 Assessment

Essential Question

How much does geography shape a country?

Key Terms

1. What is Shinto?
2. What is a limited government?
3. Is Kim Jong-il a dictator? Explain.

Key Ideas

4. Why has North Korea's nuclear program created conflict in the region?
5. How did Japan's economy change beginning in the 1990s?
6. Why is Japan's aging population causing economic problems?

Think Critically

7. **Draw Inferences** Why does the North Korean government limit access to outside information?
8. **Analyze Cause and Effect** What caused South Korea's political system to become more democratic in recent years?

9. How important is geography to the differences between North Korea and South Korea? Go to your Student Journal and record your answers.

Governments and Citizens in Japan and the Koreas

Key Ideas
- Both South Korea and Japan are democracies.
- South Korea has a presidential system, while Japan has a parliamentary system.
- Citizens in North Korea have very few rights.

Key Terms
- presidential system
- parliamentary system

Emperor Akihito at the imperial palace in Tokyo ▼

The citizens of Japan and South Korea enjoy political and economic freedom. Their governments are democracies that protect their rights. Their economies are free markets with limited government control. In stark contrast, North Koreans have very little freedom. Their government is a communist dictatorship. North Korea's Communist Party controls the country's politics and economy. Citizens of North Korea have little influence over their government.

Two Democratic Systems, One Dictatorship

The organization of the Japanese and South Korean governments is different. However, in both systems, citizens actively choose their leaders. By contrast, Kim Jong-il and North Korea's Communist Party control the government of North Korea.

South Korea's political system is a **presidential system.** In this form of government, citizens elect the president, who heads the executive branch of government. The president also serves as the head of state, or the country's symbolic leader. The United States also has a presidential system. Citizens also vote for the members of the legislative branch of government. The legislative branch, much like Congress in the United States, makes the country's laws. In South Korea, the legislature is called the National Assembly.

Japan's government is a **parliamentary system.** In this system, people directly elect representatives to the legislative branch, or legislature. The legislature then selects the prime minister, who heads the executive branch. Since Japan is a constitutional monarchy, the emperor is the head of state. However, the emperor's powers are symbolic.

Political Systems of Japan and South Korea

Japan and South Korea are both democracies, but each country organizes its government differently. People in South Korea elect their president and members of the National Assembly. Japanese voters elect only the members of the legislature.

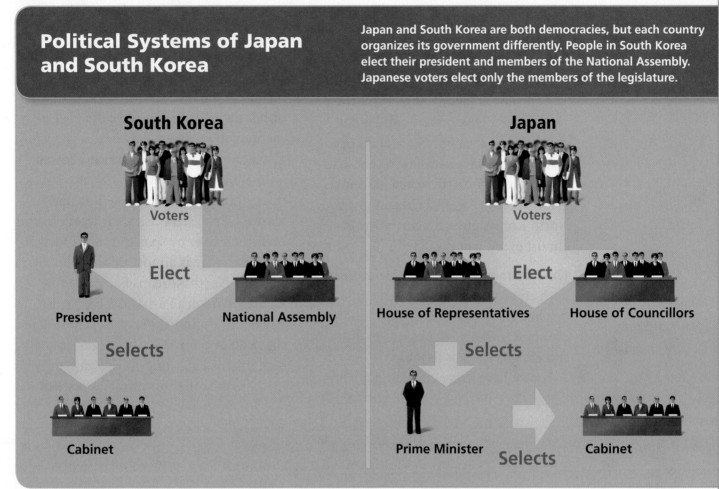

Real power lies with the prime minister and the legislature. In Japan, the legislature is called the Diet. It has two parts, the House of Councillors and the House of Representatives. Japan's prime minister leads the Diet's largest party, so he also controls the Diet.

North Korea's citizens can also vote in elections, but they do not have a real choice. The Communist Party creates a list of candidates for each position in the government. No one runs against these candidates.

People cannot vote for someone else if they do not support the choice of the party. For example, no one ran against Kim Jong-il in the last election. He controls North Korea's Communist Party and makes sure that his supporters are chosen for the legislature.

In North Korea, the courts do not review the laws made by the government. In both South Korea and Japan, the highest levels of the court can review the laws. The courts can challenge laws that violate the constitutions of these countries. The courts help ensure that new laws do not violate the rights listed in the constitutions of these two countries.

Reading Check How are the political systems of Japan and South Korea different?

681

Rights and Responsibilities of Citizens

The citizens of Japan and South Korea control their governments and enjoy many rights. By contrast, citizens of North Korea have very few rights. The government of North Korea has much greater control over its citizens' lives. North Korea's government controls almost every aspect of life in the country.

The Communist System Communism is both an economic system and a political system. The government plans the economy, owns most businesses and land, and assigns citizens to jobs.

People have fewer choices in a com-munist system. For example, a person in North Korea cannot simply decide to quit his or her job and start a business of his or her own. That is because the government owns most businesses, and very few privately owned businesses are allowed.

In a dictatorship such as North Korea, opposition to the government is not allowed. Protesters risk their freedom and even their lives by speaking out. Organizing for change is almost impossible.

Many North Koreans belong to the Korean Worker's Party (KWP), North Korea's Communist Party. Kim Jong-il is the head of the KWP. This organization strengthens Kim Jong-il's dictatorship.

There are other political parties, but

A campaign poster for a candidate running for office in Japan ▼

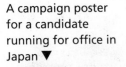

Citizens Get Involved:
Japan and South Korea

In South Korea and Japan, citizens are free to create organizations to express their opinions and protect their interests.

Labor Unions Workers may create unions to protect their interests. Unions often call for better wages and working conditions.

Environmental Groups The people in this photograph are celebrating the passage of an important environmental bill.

682

they must closely follow the policies of the KWP, and they cannot challenge the KWP leadership. In elections, North Koreans only have one choice—a KWP candidate. They can vote against this candidate but risk harsh punishment if they do so.

Democratic Systems In Japan and South Korea, there are several political parties. No political party in these countries holds powers like the KWP's. When the citizens of Japan and South Korea vote, they choose between candidates from different parties. Representatives must work hard on issues important to their voters if they want to win reelection.

Like the United States, political parties express the needs and points of view of different groups of people, but citizens can also form groups and speak out when they do not agree with their leaders. Unlike North Korea's dictatorship, these democracies have freedom of speech.

In South Korea, citizen organizations are growing in size and power. Human rights organizations, churches, and labor unions have worked for civil and economic rights.

Japan also has many activist groups. Labor unions have struggled there for years to improve working conditions and pay. Activists in both countries have rallied citizens in support of many causes. In a democracy, lawmakers must listen to citizens.

Reading Check **Why don't citizen groups organize in North Korea?**

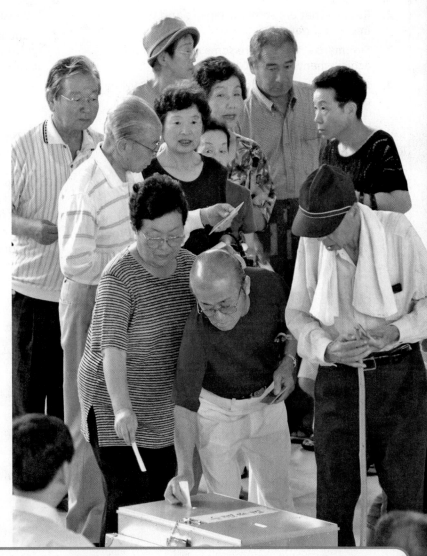

Japanese voters in a recent election for members of the House of Representatives ▼

Assessment

1. Which officials do voters elect in South Korea's political system?

2. Which officials do voters elect in Japan's political system?

3. How does the Communist Party control elections in North Korea?

4. What kinds of citizen organizations influence politics in South Korea and Japan?

5. What kinds of things do unions struggle to improve for their members?

Chapter Assessment

Key Terms and Ideas

1. **Explain** During what season do Japan and the Koreas get the most rain? Why is rain heaviest in this season?

2. **Recall** What are some of Japan's and the Koreas important natural resources?

3. **Summarize** What were some of the cultural achievements of the Koreans?

4. **Discuss** What was the Meiji restoration? What changes took place in Japan after this event?

5. **Compare and Contrast** How are the governments of North Korea and South Korea different?

6. **Recall** What were some of the effects of the recession in Japan during the 1990s?

7. **Summarize** What are examples of Japanese culture that have become popular in other countries?

Think Critically

8. **Solve Problems** How has Japan attempted to prepare for earthquakes?

9. **Making Inferences** Under Tokugawa rule, farmers had a higher social status than merchants. Why do you think farming was so highly valued?

10. **Comparing Viewpoints** How does North Korea view culture and the arts? How is this different from Japan?

11. **Core Concepts: Land Use** How does this region's geography create challenges for land use?

Places to Know

For each place, write the letter from the map that shows its location.

12. Japan

13. North Korea

14. South Korea

15. P'yongyang

16. Seoul

17. Mt. Fuji

18. **Estimate** Using the scale, estimate the length of the border between North Korea and South Korea.

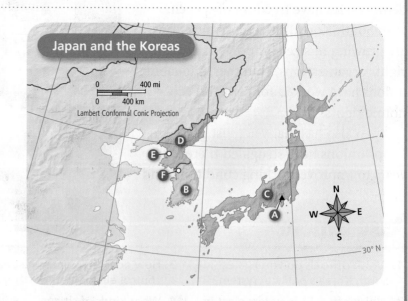

Japan and the Koreas

684

Essential Question

How much does geography shape a country?

Demonstrate Understanding Plan a multimedia presenstation that shows how Japan and the Koreas have adapted to and changed their environment. Make recommendations to the United Nations Environment Programme to help these countries solve environmental problems.

21st Century Learning

Search for Information on the Internet

Search for information on the culture of Japan, North Korea, or South Korea. Then write a report about that country's culture. Include pictures with your report. Be sure to include information on:
- religion
- the arts
- recreation
- food

Document-Based Questions

Success Tracker™
Online at myworldgeography.com

Use your knowledge of Japan and Documents A and B to answer the questions below.

Document A

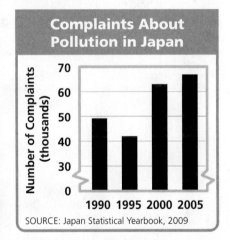

Complaints About Pollution in Japan

SOURCE: Japan Statistical Yearbook, 2009

Document B

" Japan's greenhouse gas emissions [releases] surged [increased rapidly] last year . . . Emissions of carbon dioxide and other greenhouse gases blamed for global warming spiked 2.3 percent to 1.37 billion tons in the 2007 . . . "

—CBS News, November 12, 2008

1. In Document A, which of the following years shows a drop in complaints about pollution?

   A 1990

   B 1995

   C 2000

   D 2005

2. Which of the following BEST describes the information presented in Document B?

   A Pollution decreased in 2007, which was encouraging.

   B Pollution stayed about the same in 2007.

   C Pollution increased a small amount in 2007, which is cause for some concern.

   D Pollution increased sharply in 2007, which is cause for alarm.

3. **Writing Task** Based on Document A and B, did Japan handle its pollution better in the 1990s or in the 2000s? Explain your answer.

my worldgeography.com Self-Test

Chapter 16

Southeast Asia

Essential Question

What are the challenges of diversity?

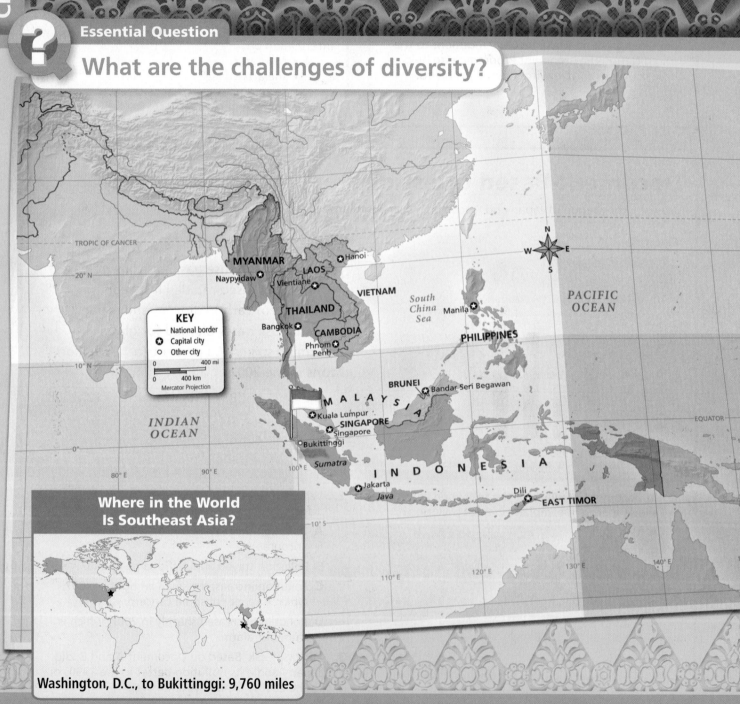

KEY
- National border
- ☆ Capital city
- ○ Other city

0   400 mi
0   400 km
Mercator Projection

Where in the World Is Southeast Asia?

Washington, D.C., to Bukittinggi: 9,760 miles

686

my Story

A Minangkabau Wedding

In this section you will read about Ridwan, a young man helping his family and friends prepare for his cousin's wedding on the island of Sumatra in Indonesia. What does Ridwan's story tell you about the culture of Southeast Asia?

Explore the Essential Question
- at **my worldgeography.com**
- using the **myWorld Chapter Activity**
- with the **Student Journal**

Story by Millie Phuah for myWorld Geography Online

Laughing voices drift through the cool air as nineteen-year-old Ridwan works with the men. They are busily moving furniture and cleaning the house where a wedding ceremony will take place. Meanwhile, in the kitchen, dozens of women are preparing chili peppers, onions, garlic, ginger, and a host of other spices. The spices will go into the meat and vegetable dishes of the day-long wedding feast. Although it is still early in the morning, there is not a moment to lose. Soon hundreds of relatives, friends, and neighbors will start arriving to honor the happy couple getting married today.

Ridwan looks out over the rice fields and the sea that surround this village called Bukittinggi, a name meaning "high hill." He can't wait to see his cousin, Nentis, who is the bride, begin her life with Al, her groom.

"Weddings are happy and important events that everyone looks forward to because it's a time for relatives

my worldgeography.com On Assignment

687

Bride and groom in one pair of wedding costumes. The photo on the facing page shows them wearing another set of costumes.

688

Preparing the wedding feast

and friends to get together. Today is especially meaningful to me, not only because my cousin is getting married, but it's also the first time I've attended a Minangkabau wedding," says Ridwan. (The Minangkabau are the main ethnic group in West Sumatra.) "And according to Minangkabau practice, Al is moving into Nentis' home, which belongs to the bride's grandmother."

Minangkabau culture is unique. Minangkabau houses often have upward-curved roofs that look like the horns of a water buffalo. The resemblance is not a coincidence. For centuries the Minangkabau depended on the buffalo for food and to help them plow the rice fields. In fact, the name *Minangkabau* means "winning buffalo." The Minangkabau are also one of the few ethnic groups in the world in which family homes are passed down from mothers to daughters, instead of from fathers to sons.

Nentis starts dressing early, because her wedding costume consists of layers of silk and other fabric woven with gold thread, gold jewelry, and a glittering Minangkabau headdress. Meanwhile, Al dons his suit. He looks like an Indian raja, or king, as he slips on a kris, an ornamental dagger. Such costumes reveal the Chinese and Indian influences that have helped shape Minangkabau culture.

Some wedding guests visit the buffet outside.

Musicians entertain the guests.

Later in the day, as a band plays, the couple moves to the wedding dais, or platform. Everyone lines up to congratulate the smiling pair. It is a long day for the couple as they rise repeatedly to greet new arrivals. During the feast, long-separated relatives laugh and exchange news. Many have traveled from distant parts of Indonesia to be here today.

Traveling and moving away from home are common among the Minangkabau. In fact, Ridwan's parents left Bukittinggi years ago to run a textile shop in East Java. Ridwan helps at his family's textile business and lives in his maternal grandmother's house. The house will one day be passed down to Ridwan's mother and aunt, and then to his sister. When the time comes for Ridwan and his brothers to marry, they will move into their wives' homes. It is the Minangkabau way.

"This is part of Minangkabau culture and I totally accept it, just as all the other men do. It just makes me work harder at my vocation," says Ridwan. "I'd like to further my studies in the Indonesian language and be a theatre performer. My father, of course, hopes I'll take over his business one day, but I think I'll deal with that later," he smiles shyly.

Ridwan returns to his video camera, using modern technology to record an ancient tradition and the scenes that his family will enjoy throughout their lives.

→ **myStory Video**

Join Ridwan as he shows you more about his life.

Meet the Journalist

Name Millie Phuah
Favorite Moment Talking to Ridwan's grandmother

my worldgeography.com myStory Video

689

Chapter Atlas

Key Ideas
- Southeast Asia is a region of varied landforms.
- Location and climate affect both agricultural production and natural resources.
- Geography has influenced Southeast Asian history and settlement patterns.

Key Terms • peninsula • archipelago • tsunami • monsoon • typhoon

 Visual Glossary

 Reading Skill: Label an Outline Map Take notes using the outline map in your journal.

Mount Mayon erupts in the Philippines.

Balinese dancers from Indonesia

Physical Features

Ridwan's cousin's wedding took place on the island of Sumatra in Indonesia. Indonesia is one of the 11 nations that make up Southeast Asia. The region has two parts: a mainland and an island area, part of which lies on the Equator.

The mainland of Southeast Asia is a **peninsula**—a land area almost surrounded by water. It extends from the Shan Plateau down to the narrow Malay peninsula. Among the major rivers are the Mekong, the Irrawaddy, and the Red River. These rivers carry rich soil to fertilize the deltas before they empty into the sea.

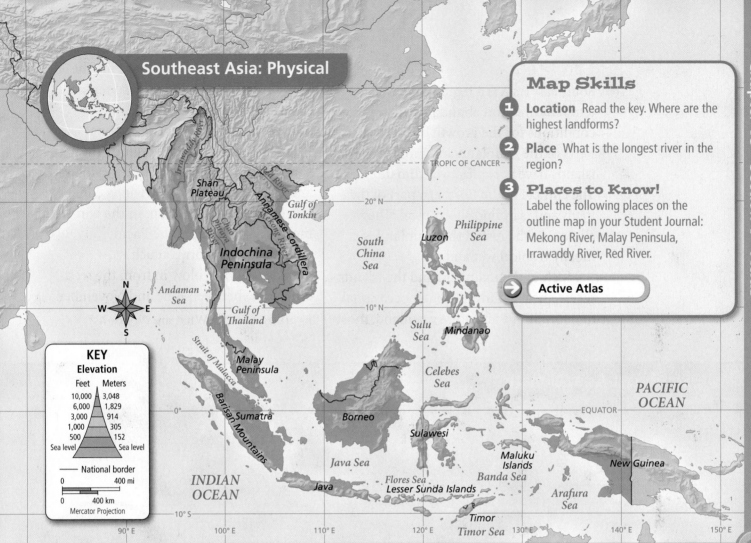

Southeast Asia: Physical

Map Skills

1 **Location** Read the key. Where are the highest landforms?

2 **Place** What is the longest river in the region?

3 **Places to Know!** Label the following places on the outline map in your Student Journal: Mekong River, Malay Peninsula, Irrawaddy River, Red River.

→ **Active Atlas**

KEY
Elevation

Feet	Meters
10,000	3,048
6,000	1,829
3,000	914
1,000	305
500	152
Sea level	Sea level

— National border

0 — 400 mi

0 — 400 km

Mercator Projection

The rest of the region is made up of **archipelagoes,** or groups of islands. The sizes of the islands vary greatly, from huge Borneo to tiny islands that may not even appear on some maps. Many island landscapes are breathtaking. Beyond beautiful sandy beaches, mountains and volcanoes tower over narrow coastal plains. Short, fast-flowing rivers run through rain forests filled with great biodiversity, or variety of living things.

Many islands in Indonesia and the Philippines are part of the Ring of Fire, a string of active volcanoes that encircles the Pacific Ocean.

Most of Southeast Asia is part of the Eurasian Plate, which is colliding with the Indo-Australian Plate. When these plates shift deep underground, destructive earthquakes can occur. In December 2004, an earthquake just 150 miles west of the island of Sumatra created a huge **tsunami,** or tidal wave. This tsunami killed more than 230,000 people living around the Indian Ocean. An early warning system has been <u>launched</u> to try to prevent such a disaster from happening again.

launch, *v.,* to set in operation

Reading Check What are the two main parts of Southeast Asia?

691

Climate

Southeast Asia is a region of hot temperatures and abundant rain—perfect conditions for the growth of rain forests. Parts of the mainland and most of the islands have a tropical wet climate. The climate in the northern part of the mainland is humid subtropical. The climate in the rest of the mainland is mostly tropical wet and dry.

Much of the mainland and the islands receive heavy rain. Although occasional dry conditions affect the mainland, most of the islands have no dry season. The islands are near the Equator, so temperatures are hot everywhere.

Every year **monsoons,** or seasonal winds, blow through the region. The summer monsoons carry heavy rain and cause flooding. These winds come in from the Indian Ocean. In the winter, monsoons blow from the Pacific.

Typhoons are storms much like hurricanes. They blow in from the western Pacific between June and November.

Reading Check What are typhoons?

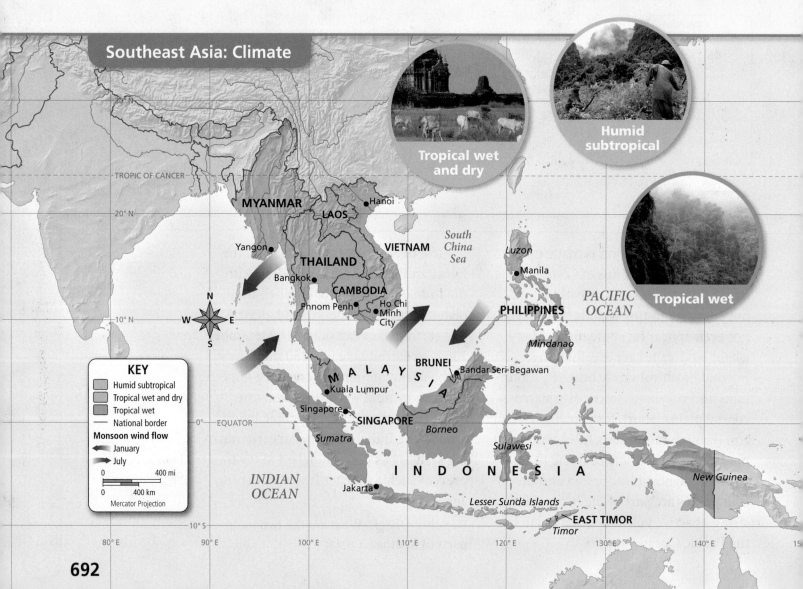

Southeast Asia: Climate

KEY
- Humid subtropical
- Tropical wet and dry
- Tropical wet
- National border

Monsoon wind flow
- January
- July

0 — 400 mi
0 — 400 km
Mercator Projection

692

People and Geography

Geography has shaped the history and culture of Southeast Asia. In the north, mountains separated mainland Southeast Asia from the rest of Asia. Within the region itself, north-south cordilleras, or parallel mountain ranges, isolated early societies. Later, the cordilleras helped define national borders. The rivers that carried rich sediment to the deltas also played an important role, for it was in the <u>fertile</u> river valleys that the first civilizations emerged.

The mostly gentle seas of Southeast Asia allowed trade, much of which traveled through the narrow Malacca Strait. For centuries pirates and kings fought to control the riches of this waterway. Another rich prize lay to the east in the Maluku Islands. Here, in the volcanic soil, grew rare spices such as nutmeg and cloves. At one time, these spices could be found nowhere else on Earth. The spice trade attracted Europeans—who came first to trade and then to colonize.

Reading Check **Where did spices grow?**

fertile, *adj.,* rich, fruitful

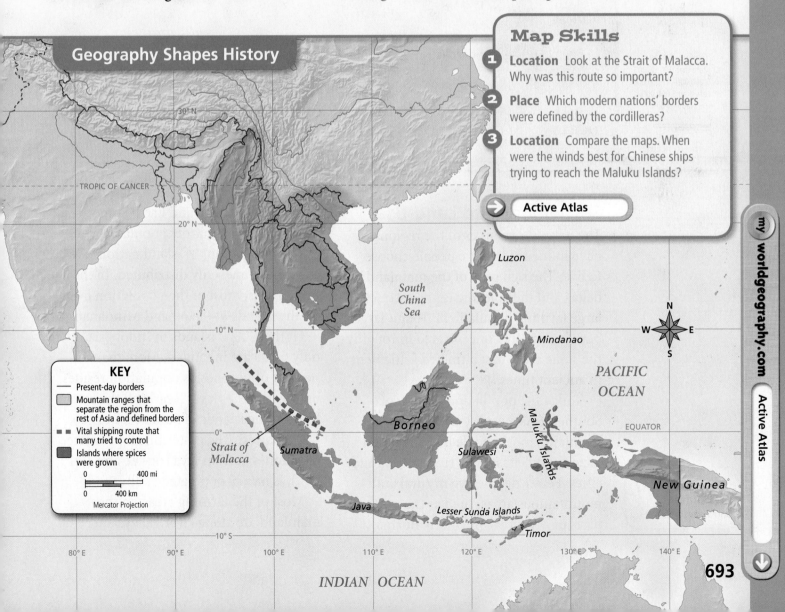

Geography Shapes History

Map Skills

1 Location Look at the Strait of Malacca. Why was this route so important?

2 Place Which modern nations' borders were defined by the cordilleras?

3 Location Compare the maps. When were the winds best for Chinese ships trying to reach the Maluku Islands?

→ **Active Atlas**

KEY
- Present-day borders
- Mountain ranges that separate the region from the rest of Asia and defined borders
- Vital shipping route that many tried to control
- Islands where spices were grown

0 — 400 mi
0 — 400 km
Mercator Projection

693

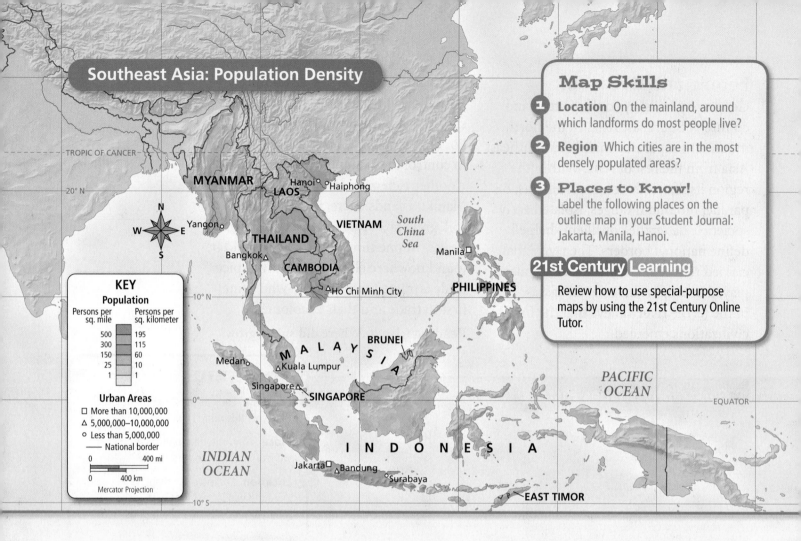

Southeast Asia: Population Density

Map Skills

1. **Location** On the mainland, around which landforms do most people live?

2. **Region** Which cities are in the most densely populated areas?

3. **Places to Know!** Label the following places on the outline map in your Student Journal: Jakarta, Manila, Hanoi.

21st Century Learning

Review how to use special-purpose maps by using the 21st Century Online Tutor.

KEY — Population

Persons per sq. mile	Persons per sq. kilometer
500	195
300	115
150	60
25	10
1	1

Urban Areas
- □ More than 10,000,000
- △ 5,000,000–10,000,000
- ○ Less than 5,000,000
- — National border

0 — 400 mi
0 — 400 km
Mercator Projection

Settlement and Land Use

The natural resources of the region have influenced where people choose to live. The rich soils of the mainland deltas and the volcanic islands attracted large farming populations. Today, large populations are concentrated in roughly the same areas that attracted settlement in ancient times.

Today the population density of Southeast Asia is very uneven. On the mainland, most people live on coastal plains and deltas, or in river valleys and cities. Fewer people live in rural and mountainous areas, such as the northern parts of Myanmar (formerly Burma), Thailand, Vietnam, and Laos. Some areas of rain forest are hardly populated at all.

The populations of island nations are even more unevenly distributed. In the Philippines, most of the population live on the islands of Luzon and Mindanao.

Of the 17,000 islands in Indonesia, only 6,000 are inhabited. More than 60 percent of Indonesia's population resides on the island of Java. Nearly all the rest lives on the islands of Sumatra, Borneo, and Sulawesi. The easternmost province of Indonesia, Irian Jaya (IRH ee ahn JAH yuh), is hardly populated at all.

Most of the farming areas on the mainland are along river valleys and

myWorld Activity
Why Settle in Southeast Asia?

694

deltas where plentiful water and good soil allow people to grow rice. Thailand's rice is some of the best in the world. Because Southeast Asia has very little land that is level enough for farming, the peoples of this mountainous region have cleverly altered their landscape to meet their needs. By sculpting the hillsides into steps, or terraces, they have turned mountain slopes into farmland for rice crops. On the higher slopes, cool temperatures provide the perfect conditions for growing tea.

Southeast Asian forests are a great natural resource. Exported lumber from the rain forests is a major source of income for some nations. The lumber is exported mainly to Japan and the United States.

Reading Check Why did large populations develop in the deltas?

Urban Problems

Even though there are many large cities, the region as a whole is mainly rural. However, more people are moving to urban areas in search of jobs and higher living standards. This migration has turned Jakarta, Bangkok, Manila, and Phnom Penh into huge cities with growing urban problems.

The increase in population places great strains on the cities' infrastructures, such as water supplies, electricity, and sewage facilities. Housing, healthcare, and other services also suffer. There are many environmental problems, such as air pollution and traffic congestion. The monsoon rains bring floods that cause sewage overflow and water contamination.

Reading Check What urban problems can be traced to population increases?

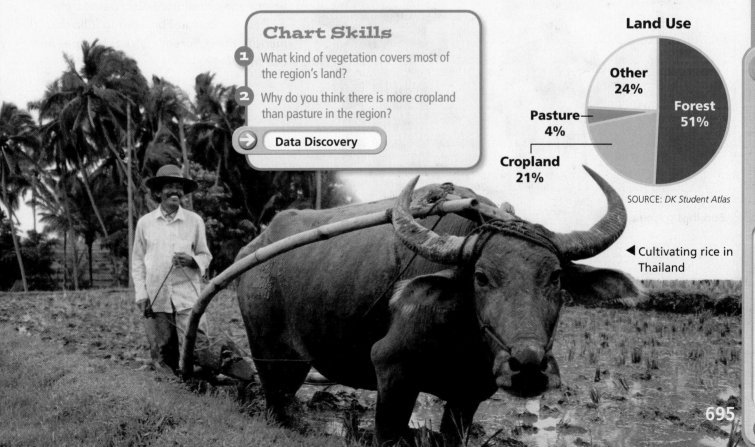

Chart Skills

1. What kind of vegetation covers most of the region's land?
2. Why do you think there is more cropland than pasture in the region?

→ Data Discovery

Land Use

- Other 24%
- Pasture 4%
- Forest 51%
- Cropland 21%

SOURCE: *DK Student Atlas*

◀ Cultivating rice in Thailand

my worldgeography.com 21st Century Learning

A History of Diversity

Southeast Asia has a history of cultural and religious diversity. Waves of migrations from the north have brought Burmese, Thai, and Lao peoples onto the mainland. Other ancient migrations brought settlers to the region by sea. Today, Chinese, Indians, Malays, Burmese, Indonesians, Vietnamese, Filipinos, Thai, Khmer, and Hmong all call the region home. In addition, there are indigenous peoples who live in remote, isolated rain forest communities.

There has always been a strong Chinese presence in Southeast Asia. In ancient times, China was ruling parts of what is now Vietnam by 100 B.C. This started a long history of Chinese involvement in Vietnam.

Today, Chinese communities thrive in every country in the region. Many Chinese immigrated into the region in the 1800s when demand for labor was high. The Chinese population ranges from less than 1 percent in East Timor to 77 percent in Singapore. There are also large Indian communities in Malaysia and Myanmar.

Cultural Borrowing

Southeast Asia's location on the international trade routes has created a lively cultural exchange. In Vietnam the Cao Dai religion mixes elements of several major religions. Cao Dai temples express this cultural borrowing. *Can you identify the different cultural features in this building?*

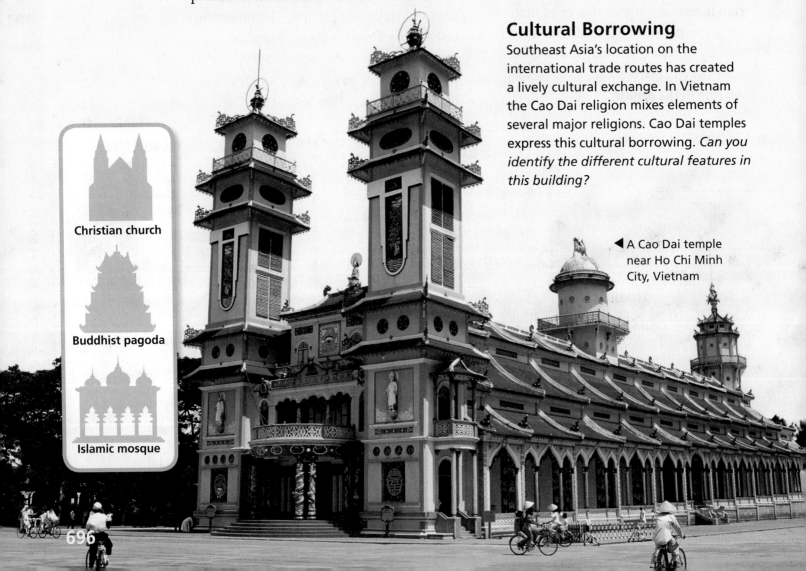

Christian church

Buddhist pagoda

Islamic mosque

◄ A Cao Dai temple near Ho Chi Minh City, Vietnam

696

In a region of such ethnic diversity, it is not surprising that there is much religious diversity as well. Most of mainland Southeast Asia was influenced by two different forms of Buddhism that spread from India and China.

Islam became the major religion in large parts of island Southeast Asia. On most of the islands it replaced Buddhism and Hinduism. However, islands such as Bali remained Hindu. Today Bali is part of Indonesia, a country that has the largest Muslim population in the world.

While most people of the islands are Muslim, the majority of people in the Philippines are Roman Catholic due to Spanish colonization in the 1500s. However, there are Muslims in the Philippines as well, especially on the two islands of Mindanao and Palawan.

Many religious communities blend customs and traditions from more than one faith. This cultural mixing is a feature of Southeast Asian life. Ridwan's Minangkabau are a good example of this cultural openness, which began in ancient times. From their homeland in the mountains of Sumatra, the Minangkabau traveled downriver to trade. In time they became merchants and travelers, pursuing the knowledge and wealth of the wider world. Along the way they absorbed Indian, Chinese, and Western customs and beliefs. They married their old traditions to the new ways of Islam that they embraced. Later, they enthusiastically adopted the educational system of the Dutch. Their openness to other cultures has served them well. Today the Minangkabau are among the wealthiest, most educated, and most powerful groups in Indonesia.

Southeast Asia's location, which attracted international trade, helped the Minangkabau achieve economic success. In the next section you will see how the story of the Minangkabau connects with Southeast Asia's history of economic trade and cultural exchange.

Reading Check Why is Southeast Asia populated with such a great diversity of ethnic groups?

my World IN NUMBERS

If there were **100** people in the world,

4 would come from Indonesia.

Section 1 Assessment

Essential Question
What are the challenges of diversity?

Key Terms

1. Use the following terms to describe the geography and climate of Southeast Asia: peninsula, archipelago, tsunami, monsoon, typhoon.

Key Ideas

2. What are some differences between the landscapes of the mainland and the islands?

3. Where do most Southeast Asians live?

4. How have Southeast Asians adapted the landscape to meet their needs?

Think Critically

5. **Synthesize** Compare the population density map with the physical map. What patterns do you see?

6. **Draw Conclusions** Why might the coastal areas and islands have had more contact with the outside world?

7. Why did the geography of the region help create such a diverse population? Go to your Student Journal to record your answer.

History of Southeast Asia

Key Ideas
- Southeast Asia's location encouraged trade and cultural and ethnic diversity.
- Europeans transformed the cultural geography of the region.
- Wars of independence were followed by civil wars on mainland Southeast Asia.

Visual Glossary

Key Terms • reservoir • surplus • maritime • exploit

Reading Skill: Sequence Take notes using the graphic organizer in your journal.

If the history of Southeast Asia were a video, it would show you a story of migrations and trade. First you would see people living on the volcanic island of Java tens of thousands of years ago. Running the video forward would show newcomers migrating to the region by land and sea. Soon you would notice Indonesian boats carrying the earliest trade goods between India and China.

Ancient Southeast Asia

As the video reached 500 B.C., you would see fields of rice growing in the lowlands of Cambodia and Vietnam. Everywhere you would notice populations increasing because of plentiful harvests. Soon you would see villages specializing in particular crafts and trading goods with one another as societies became more complex.

More than 2000 years ago, civilizations grew up in the river valleys, where rice crops kept the populations well fed. In the north of what is now Vietnam, the city of Co Loa grew rich. Its wealth attracted the Chinese, who conquered the city by 100 B.C. In the south, port cities bustled with foreign merchants, traders, and traveling priests. The famous ethnic diversity of Southeast Asian cities had emerged.

Reading Check Why did populations increase in ancient times?

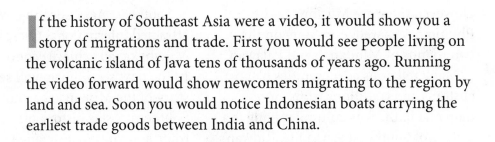

◀ A strangler fig tree creeps over the ruins of Angkor Thom, Cambodia.

Culture Close-up

The Great Kingdoms

Between A.D. 500 and 1500 kingdoms grew and trade expanded. Southeast Asians blended foreign influences into their own culture.

Controlling the Strait The region's location on international trade routes led to contact with India and China. Local kingdoms adopted religions from India, such as Hinduism and Buddhism.

Commerce created such wealth that coastal states fought to control trade. One of the busiest trade routes went through the Strait of Malacca. Srivijaya, a Hindu-Buddhist kingdom on Sumatra, controlled the strait from A.D. 600 to 1300.

Agricultural Empires On the mainland, a civilization rose in what is now Cambodia. The Khmers (kuh MEHRZ) used the landscape to meet their needs.

They built **reservoirs,** or storage pools, of rainwater to irrigate rice fields. This produced huge harvests. They grew rich by selling their extra, or **surplus,** food.

The Khmer empire was a kind of "seed culture" from which many Southeast Asian traditions grew. The Khmers had a strong influence on the culture of Cambodia and Thailand.

As the Khmer empire declined, fierce invaders entered the region. In 1287 the Mongols destroyed the Burmese empire of Bagan (Pagan). But the invaders suffered from the tropical heat and rains. They were also startled by Southeast Asian war elephants, which hurled enemy soldiers into the air with their trunks! During their invasion of Java, the Mongols lost three thousand men.

Reading Check Which civilizations influenced culture in Southeast Asia?

invader, *n.,* person who enters a place by force

Ancient Trade Routes

In ancient times, goods from the Mediterranean, China, India, and Southeast Asia were exchanged along the trade routes. Southeast Asia occupied an important position on these routes.

Map Skills

1. **Interaction** Why would traders have wanted to travel such great distances?

2. **Interaction** Why did ancient trade routes hug the coast?

3. **Interaction** Where might you have seen the busiest shipping lanes in ancient times?

→ **Active Atlas**

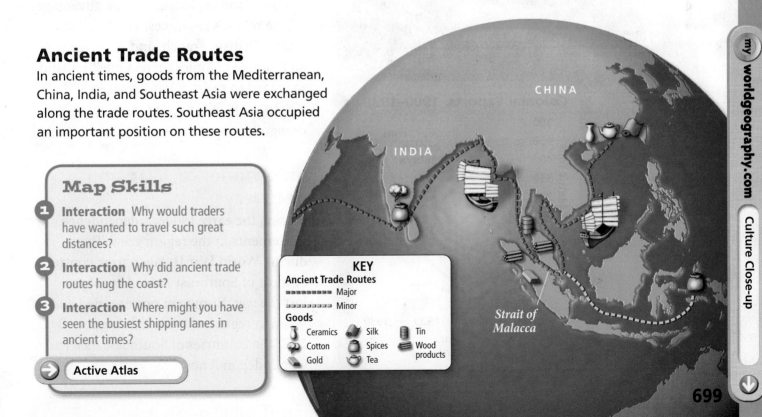

CHINA

INDIA

KEY
Ancient Trade Routes
▬▬▬▬▬ Major
▭▭▭▭▭ Minor
Goods
Ceramics — Silk — Tin
Cotton — Spices — Wood products
Gold — Tea

Strait of Malacca

Closer Look

EFFECTS OF COLONIZATION

Between the 1850s and the 1950s, Southeast Asia was colonized first by Western nations and then occupied by Japan. During that hundred-year period the region changed forever. Large plantations replaced small farms. The demand for cheap labor attracted workers from India and China.

THINK CRITICALLY *Study the graph. Which export increased dramatically around 1910?*

The Dutch built plantations like this one in Indonesia. ▼

▲ Western governments introduced export crops such as rubber and coffee. The region still exports these goods.

Colonial Exports, 1900–1930

Rubber from British Malaya

Coffee from Dutch Indonesia

(y-axis: Thousands of Metric Tons, 0 to 500; x-axis: Year, 1900 to 1930)

SOURCE: *International Historical Statistics*

The Age of Commerce

By the 1400s, the old agricultural empires of Bagan and the Khmer had declined. New regional powers had emerged, based on **maritime,** or sea, trade. Meanwhile, the religion of Islam was spreading along the trade routes, carried by Muslim merchants. After the ruler of the rich port of Malacca converted to Islam in 1414, the religion spread through the islands. Ridwan's Minangkabau ancestors were some of the people who converted to the faith.

The famous wealth of Malacca and its control of the spice trade excited the envy of Europeans. For centuries, Europeans had been trying to gain control of the trade in spices, many of which grew on the Maluku Islands. Then, in 1511, the Portuguese conquered Malacca.

During the following centuries, Western powers tightened their grip on Southeast Asia and **exploited,** or took advantage of, the region's resources. The Spanish, Dutch, British, French, and Americans all founded colonies there. Only Thailand managed to resist colonization.

Reading Check How did Western powers change Southeast Asia?

Independence, War, and Recovery

During the early 1900s, independence movements in the region grew. Then, during World War II, Japan took control of most of Southeast Asia. After Japan lost the war, European powers tried and failed to regain control of the region. By 1957 the countries of Southeast Asia had won independence.

Mainland Conflicts For some nations, the fight for independence was long and bloody. In Vietnam, communist forces under Ho Chi Minh fought the French. War lasted until 1954, when France gave up control. Vietnam was divided into two republics: a communist north and a non-communist south.

However, fighting soon developed between north and south. The United States first sent advisers and then troops to South Vietnam to stop the spread of communism. The fighting spread to neighboring nations. This war dragged on until 1975, when the country was united under communist rule, following the departure of United States troops from the area.

Cambodia, which gained independence in 1953, also suffered conflict. As the Vietnam War heated up, Cambodia was dragged into the fight. This led to years of suffering. Under the brutal communist government of the Khmer Rouge, people who lived in the cities were forced into the countryside, where millions of them were murdered.

Southeast Asia Recovers The 1900s had been a violent century for Southeast Asia. The communist nations of Vietnam, Laos, and Cambodia all suffered terribly from the wars of the mainland. In addition, some communist economic policies had been disastrous. In the late 1980s Vietnam, Laos, and Cambodia adopted some capitalist practices that finally turned their economies around. However, today the communist countries of Southeast Asia remain the poorest nations in the region.

The capitalist countries such as Indonesia and Malaysia approached the new century in better shape. They marketed their resources and varied their economies. Rather than relying on agricultural exports, these economies now include manufacturing. Some Southeast Asian nations, like Singapore, were so successful that by the 1990s they were called "Asian Tigers." In the next section, you will read more about Southeast Asia today.

Reading Check What changes did World War II bring to Southeast Asia?

resource, *n.,* something that a country can use to its advantage

myWorld Activity
Historical Cartoon

Section 2 Assessment

Key Terms

1. Use the following terms to describe the history of Southeast Asia: reservoir, surplus, maritime, exploit.

Key Ideas

2. Why was there so much trade in Southeast Asia?

3. How did Europeans transform Southeast Asia?

4. How did Southeast Asians gain independence?

Think Critically

5. **Draw Conclusions** Why did different states want to control the Strait of Malacca?

6. **Make Inferences** Why are the communist countries the poorest in the region?

? Essential Question

What are the challenges of diversity?

7. How did Southeast Asians react to contact with many different religions? Go to your Student Journal to record your answer.

701

Southeast Asia in the 1200s

Key Idea
- The people of Southeast Asia developed sophisticated civilizations that grew rich from natural resources.

▲ Marco Polo

Marco Polo traveled widely in Asia, and his accounts include descriptions of life in the many lands that he visited. On a mission for Kublai Khan, he visited Southeast Asia. The first text comes from his description of a Southeast Asian kingdom.

Zhou Daguan was a member of a diplomatic mission from China to the Khmer empire in the late 1200s. Upon his return, Zhou Daguan wrote a book, *Notes on the Customs of Cambodia*, describing the land and the people.

An ancient pagoda in Laos ▼

Read the text on the right. Stop at each circled letter. Then answer the question with the same letter on the left.

A **Summarize** What is the relationship between Kaugigu and China?

B **Draw Conclusions** What other valuable goods does Kaugigu produce?

C **Infer** What are the body decorations described?

submitted, *v.,* gave in to another country's power

tribute, *n.,* payment a weaker nation makes to a stronger one

game, *n.,* animals hunted for food

The Travels of Marco Polo

66 Kaugigu has its own king. The people . . . have <u>submitted</u> to the Great Khan and pay him a yearly **A** <u>tribute</u>. . . . This province is rich in gold. It also abounds in precious **B** spices of many sorts . . . There are plenty of elephants and animals of many other kinds and no lack of <u>game</u>. The people live on meat, milk, and rice. . . . All the people alike, male and female, have . . . their flesh covered all over with pictures of lions and dragons and birds and **C** other objects. . . . 99
—Marco Polo, *The Travels of Marco Polo*

Read the text on the right. Stop at each circled letter. Then answer the question with the same letter on the left.

D Summarize Who leads the procession?

E Analyze Who is the procession meant to honor?

F Infer What does the gold on the elephants' tusks and the parasols show?

procession, *n.*, group of people moving in a slow, formal manner

tapers, *n.*, tall, thin candles

sovereign, *n.*, ruler

parasols, *n.*, umbrellas that protect from strong sunlight

The Customs of Cambodia

66 When the King leaves his palace, the <u>procession</u> is headed by the **D** soldiery; then come the flags, the banners, the music. Girls of the palace, three or five hundred in number, gaily dressed, with flowers in their hair and <u>tapers</u> in their hands, are massed together in a separate column. . . . Finally **E** the <u>Sovereign</u> appeared, standing erect on an elephant and holding in his hand the sacred sword. This elephant, his tusks sheathed in gold, was accompanied by bearers of twenty white <u>parasols</u> with golden shafts. All around was a bodyguard of elephants drawn **F** close together. 99

—Zhou Daguan, *Notes on the Customs of Cambodia*

▲ Khmer carving showing the king in procession

The Khmer temple of Angkor Wat in Cambodia ▼

Analyze the Documents

1. **Categorize** What social groups does each passage describe?
2. **Writing Task** What impression of Kaugigu and Cambodia do the passages give? Write a short essay explaining how the details in each passage give that impression.

703

Section 3

Southeast Asia Today

Key Ideas
- Southeast Asia is a culturally diverse region.
- Southeast Asian countries have differing political goals, human rights records, and economies.
- Population and environmental issues affect economies throughout the region.

Key Terms • secular • military junta • insurgency • separatist group • ASEAN

 Reading Skill: Identify Main Idea and Details Take notes using the graphic organizer in your journal.

◀ The Petronas Towers, Kuala Lumpur, Malaysia

Southeast Asia is one of the world's most diverse regions. Its wide range of governments and income levels sets it apart from other places in the world. Its varied geography is home to many cultures and ethnic groups, such as Ridwan's Minangkabau. Today this diverse region is developing new industries and has an important role to play in international trade.

Southeast Asian Culture Today

Southeast Asia's culture was formed by geography and history. The region's location on international trade routes attracted merchants and immigrants, new customs, and new religions. Southeast Asia's unique culture astonished a famous Indian poet during his visit to Indonesia. He observed,

❝ I see India everywhere, but I do not recognize it. ❞
—Rabindranath Tagore

Today, the culture of Southeast Asia is still being shaped by a diversity of peoples and the environment they share.

Religion

Over the centuries, Indian traders from the East brought Hinduism and Buddhism from India and Sri Lanka. From China to the north, Mahayana Buddhism and Confucian thought entered Vietnam. These religions and ideas mixed with the local beliefs in spirits.

Later, Arab and Indian traders brought Islam, which took root in Malaysia and most of Indonesia. As the region came under European influence, Christianity gained <u>converts</u>, especially in the Philippines and Vietnam.

Religious traditions are woven through Southeast Asian culture. On most of the mainland, Buddhism is the main religion. However, Islam dominates on most of the islands and on the Malay Peninsula. In Malaysia, there are two systems of justice. One system is **secular,** or nonreligious,

and the other is Islamic. Some Malaysian Muslims prefer to seek justice in courts that use Islamic, or Sharia, law.

Indonesia has the world's largest Muslim population. However, its mixed population of Muslims, Buddhists, Hindus and Christians has created a tolerant society. Through the region there is also much cultural blending, as customs and ideas from different religions are fused.

Reading Check What religion is most popular on the mainland of Southeast Asia?

convert, *n.,* a person who changes from one religion to another

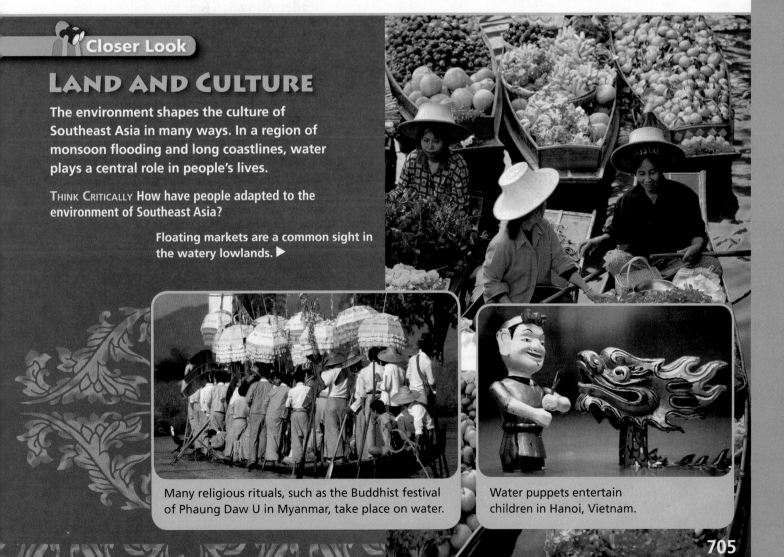

Closer Look

LAND AND CULTURE

The environment shapes the culture of Southeast Asia in many ways. In a region of monsoon flooding and long coastlines, water plays a central role in people's lives.

THINK CRITICALLY How have people adapted to the environment of Southeast Asia?

Floating markets are a common sight in the watery lowlands. ▶

Many religious rituals, such as the Buddhist festival of Phaung Daw U in Myanmar, take place on water.

Water puppets entertain children in Hanoi, Vietnam.

705

Governments and Citizens

The governments of Southeast Asia are as diverse as the region's population and religions. Citizens' rights also vary.

Types of Governments Republics such as Indonesia, the Philippines, Singapore, and East Timor have constitutions that provide citizens with some protections and freedoms. Like the United States, these countries have legislative, executive, and judicial branches of government. In Indonesia, democracy has been growing stronger ever since the fall of the dictator Suharto in 1998.

considerable, *adj.,* large

Chinese festival in Singapore ▼

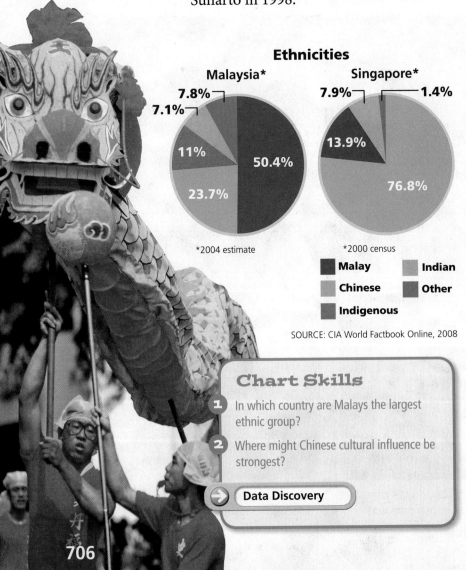

Ethnicities

Malaysia*

- 50.4%
- 23.7%
- 11%
- 7.1%
- 7.8%

*2004 estimate

Singapore*

- 76.8%
- 13.9%
- 7.9%
- 1.4%

*2000 census

Legend:
- Malay
- Chinese
- Indigenous
- Indian
- Other

SOURCE: CIA World Factbook Online, 2008

Chart Skills

1. In which country are Malays the largest ethnic group?
2. Where might Chinese cultural influence be strongest?

→ Data Discovery

Malaysia, Cambodia, the kingdom of Thailand, and the sultanate of Brunei are all constitutional monarchies in which one person rules as head of state. Yet, there is a <u>considerable</u> degree of democracy in some of these nations.

In other nations governments allow much less democracy. The Communist nations of Laos and Vietnam are one-party states ruled by an oligarchy, or a small group of people. Myanmar is ruled by a brutal **military junta,** a committee of military leaders. The junta punishes its critics and has placed the political leader Aung San Suu Kyi under house arrest. In 2008 the junta blocked disaster relief intended for victims of a cyclone.

Political Tensions In Myanmar, political frustration sometimes erupts into demonstrations. However, political tensions afflict every nation in the region.

In the Philippines, the government is fighting an **insurgency,** or rebellion, from a Muslim **separatist group** on islands in the south and east. A separatist group is a group of people who want to establish an independent state.

In Thailand, the Constitutional Court brought down the government in 2008, after months of anti-government protests.

Even in more democratic countries, such as Malaysia and Indonesia, disputes rage over economic issues, corruption, election fraud, and crime rates. In this ethnically diverse region, there are also constant concerns over income inequalities between ethnic groups.

Reading Check Which nations are one-party states?

706

Air Pollution

In 1997 an environmental disaster struck Southeast Asia as fires meant to clear land burned out of control. The fires created a huge cloud of smoke that threatened economies and public health. The fires were stopped by a certain Southeast Asian weather pattern. *Can you identify the weather pattern?*

◀ People in cities like Jakarta and Bangkok wore breathing masks.

▲ The fires of 1997 destroyed millions of acres of forest.

Population and Environment

Some environmental problems in Southeast Asia have emerged when there are too many people living in an area for its resources to support.

Population Issues Countries with higher rates of population growth must worry about feeding a growing population. Countries with low population growth are also concerned about the future. If there are not enough younger people in the work force, who will pay the taxes that support social security and medical benefits for the elderly? Singapore's population is hardly growing at all. To encourage growth, the government has offered citizens tax rebates of thousands of dollars for every child that is born.

In contrast, Indonesia is dealing with overcrowding on the island of Java, where 60 percent of Indonesians live. Overpopulation strains resources. It also damages the environment.

The government of Indonesia encourages families to migrate to the outer islands such as Sulawesi by providing money and land. However, there are no jobs or social services on the islands. The land must be cleared and the soil is poor.

The Environment Today Because of the global demand for wood products, Southeast Asian forests are disappearing. Countries such as Indonesia are having difficulty stopping this destruction. A weak central government has been unable to enforce regulations.

Reading Check What are some environmental problems in Southeast Asia?

my **worldgeography**.com Data Discovery

707

Diverse Economies

Southeast Asia includes some of the richest and poorest nations in the world. There are many factors that can hinder economic growth. As you have read, the poorer nations all suffered wars in recent times.

Uneven Development A successful economy depends on certain conditions. There must be a stable government, natural resources, skilled workers, banks, and transportation and communication systems. Singapore and Brunei meet these conditions and are the most successful countries economically. More than half of Brunei's income comes from oil and natural gas production. Singapore's economy is based on exports of consumer electronics and information technology.

The economies of Southeast Asia are as diverse as other aspects of the region. Although international trade is bringing changes to countries such as Indonesia, nations such as Myanmar and Cambodia continue to resist globalization.

Countries without transportation networks, stable government, or freedom for their citizens—such as Myanmar— have difficulty in attracting foreign investments. Nations with oil and natural gas such as Indonesia are more attractive to investors.

Southeast Asian Economies
This graph shows the gross domestic product (GDP) for most countries in Southeast Asia.

Below: Searching through trash in Phnom Penh, Cambodia
Lower right: The modern skyline of wealthy Singapore

Chart Skills

1 Which country has the highest GDP in the region?

2 Which countries have the lowest?

→ Data Discovery

GDP per Capita of Selected Southeast Asian Nations

Country	GDP per Capita
Brunei	$51,000
Singapore	$49,700
Malaysia	$13,300
Thailand	$7,900
Indonesia	$3,700
Philippines	$3,400
Vietnam	$2,600
East Timor	$2,500
Laos	$2,100
Myanmar	$1,900
Cambodia	$1,800
United States (for comparison)	$45,800

SOURCE: CIA World Factbook Online, 2008

708

Southeast Asia and the World Today Southeast Asia is once again a center of international trade. The Strait of Malacca is a major global shipping lane. The ports of Singapore, Malaysia, and Indonesia benefit greatly from such traffic. But there are also enormous dangers along the strait. Modern-day pirates have attacked merchant ships. And since the al-Qaeda attack on September 11 and later attacks in Indonesia, there is a new fear. Attacks by militant groups on shipping could endanger the world's oil supply. In the words of one writer,

❝ With 60,000 vessels transiting through the Strait each year, carrying half of the world's oil supplies and a third of its trade, the stakes are high in maintaining stability along these sea lanes. ❞

—Chietigj Bajpaee

All the countries in the region have the potential for economic growth. Tourism is an important source of income in all of Southeast Asia. Malaysia is developing a high-technology complex near its capital, Kuala Lumpur. This complex is called the Multimedia Super Corridor. Thailand is attempting to develop high-technology industries, but the lack of skilled labor may be an obstacle.

ASEAN, the Association of Southeast Asian Nations, is a trade group working to promote growth and social progress. The organization has reduced regional tariffs and has created a free-trade area.

Today Southeast Asia's problems and strengths are tied to its geography and history. Many of its people, such as the Minangkabau, continue to welcome foreign culture and new ideas. With its ancient traditions of cultural diversity and international trade, Southeast Asia is well positioned to play an important role in the modern world.

Reading Check Why is the Strait of Malacca so important to the world's economy?

my World IN NUMBERS

In 2007, Thailand had a labor force of about **37** million people. In 2008, this figure rose to about **38** million.

myWorld Activity
Facing Challenges

Section 3 Assessment

Key Terms

1. Use the following terms to describe Southeast Asia today: secular, military junta, insurgency, separatist group.

Key Ideas

2. What role does Southeast Asia play in the world economy?

3. What kinds of governments exist in Southeast Asia?

4. Why are Southeast Asian rain forests under threat?

Think Critically

5. **Draw Conclusions** Why is religious tolerance valued in Indonesia, where there are so many religious faiths?

6. **Synthesize** Why is it so difficult for Southeast Asian nations to solve environmental problems?

Essential Question

What are the challenges of diversity?

7. Why has "Unity in Diversity" become the motto of Indonesia? Go to your Student Journal to record your answer.

Geography of a Disaster

Key Ideas
- Undersea earthquakes cause tsunamis in South and Southeast Asia.
- People in the region are finding ways to prepare for natural disasters.

Key Terms • tsunami • plate • evacuate • tsunameter

Natural disasters strike populations all over the world. Floods and earthquakes in heavily populated areas often lead to much loss of life and destruction of property. One kind of natural disaster is called a **tsunami,** a series of huge waves. Tsunamis can be triggered by underwater earthquakes. When these powerful waves reach land, they may rise to more than 50 feet. The water, weighing millions of tons, can destroy buildings, farms, and forests.

The Tsunami of 2004

The worst tsunami in history struck 14 countries around the Indian Ocean on December 26, 2004. It was set off by a 9.1-magnitude earthquake near Sumatra. Sumatra was hit within minutes of the earthquake. Two hours later, thirty-foot waves reached India and Sri Lanka, 750 miles from the quake. Almost 230,000 people died, around three quarters of them in Indonesia. Survivors lost their homes and livelihoods, as farms and fishing grounds were destroyed.

Reading Check What set off the Indian Ocean tsunami of 2004?

Cause of the Tsunami

Earthquakes are caused by the movement of tectonic **plates**, huge blocks of rock that form the outermost layer of the earth. This movement is very slow, but over time, enormous pressure builds up as plates are forced against each other. Eventually one plate will suddenly shift under another. When the Indo-Australian plate slid under the Philippine plate on December 26, 2004, the planet shook. The shifting plates caused an underwater earthquake that set off the tsunami. According to the U.S. Geological Survey, the force of the

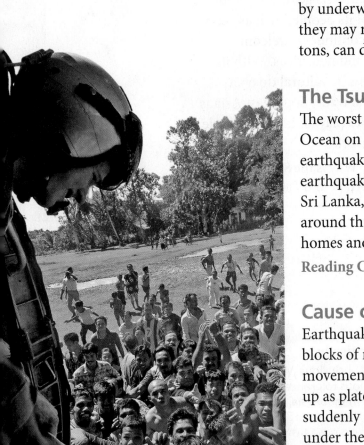

◀ U.S. Navy helicopter crew distributes food and water to tsunami victims in Indonesia.

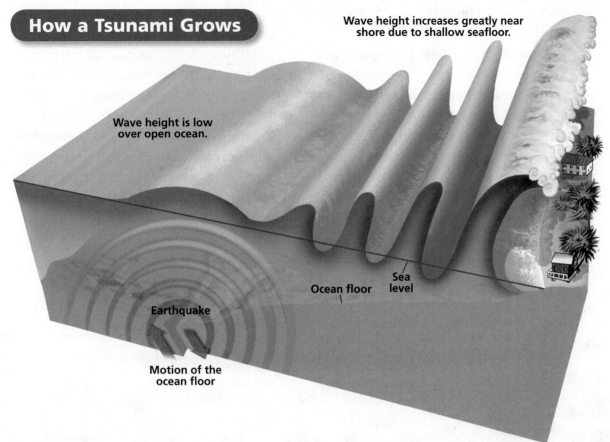

How a Tsunami Grows

Wave height increases greatly near shore due to shallow seafloor.

Wave height is low over open ocean.

Ocean floor

Sea level

Earthquake

Motion of the ocean floor

2004 tsunami was comparable to the power of 23,000 atomic bombs.

For people on the beaches, there was little warning. Many reported seeing animals fleeing for higher ground shortly before the tsunami struck. In some areas, the ocean receded, exposing fish on the sand. Then came the sound of the approaching tsunami like the rush of a jet. In some places the tsunami arrived in waves. In other places, water rose like a flood. Many were killed by the force of the waves. As the sea retreated, it swept thousands of people out with it. Miles of coastline were destroyed and many islands were submerged.

Reading Check What were some signs of the approaching disaster?

Preparing for a Disaster

In the tsunami of 2004, many deaths might have been prevented if people had been **evacuated,** or moved to other areas. However, tsunamis rarely occur in the Indian Ocean, and there was no system in place for detecting them or alerting people.

There are two parts to preparing for a natural disaster: mitigation and response. Mitigation includes taking steps to limit the damage a disaster can cause. Buildings, bridges, and other structures must be built in safe locations and with the right materials to withstand damage. Mitigation also includes creating systems for detecting and warning about disasters. Finally, mitigation includes teaching the

711

public how to prepare for and respond to an emergency.

One of the best ways to prepare for a disaster is to know how to respond to one. Rehearsals and drills can help people meet the emergency when a disaster strikes. In such a situation, experts would rush to the site to assess damage and decide what needs to be done. Police officers, firefighters, and medical personnel would work together to save lives. Government officials at different levels would communicate with each other and with relief agencies, like the Red Cross.

Supplies and equipment would be brought to the stricken area.

Southeast Asian nations are learning from disaster preparations in other regions. Countries bordering the Pacific Ocean have had long experience with tsunamis. Instruments called **tsunameters** can detect a tsunami when it passes. A tsunameter sits on a floating platform and is anchored by a line to the ocean floor. These devices send a signal to warning centers, which then issue alerts.

Reading Check How have countries on the Pacific Rim prepared for tsunamis?

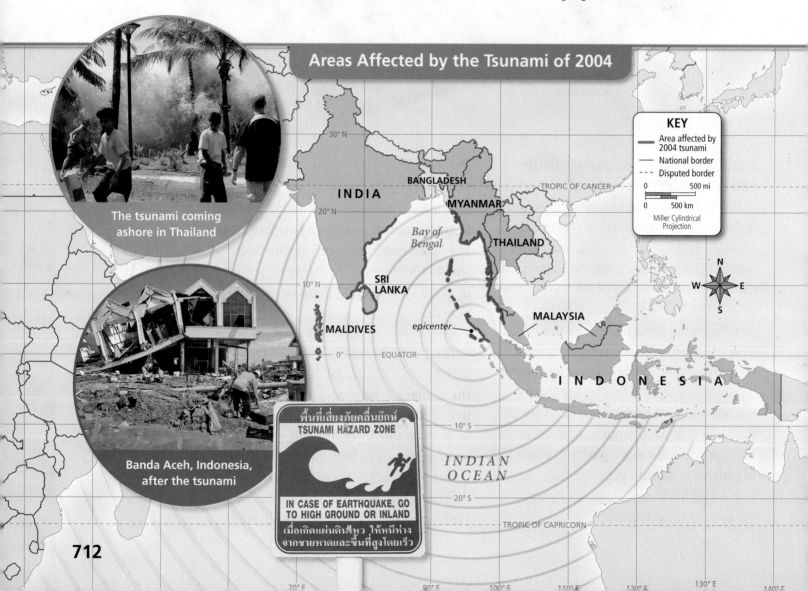

Areas Affected by the Tsunami of 2004

The tsunami coming ashore in Thailand

Banda Aceh, Indonesia, after the tsunami

KEY
— Area affected by 2004 tsunami
— National border
--- Disputed border

Miller Cylindrical Projection

Disaster Preparation in Indian Ocean Nations

Since 2006, the Indian Ocean Tsunami Warning System has been set up to monitor the Indian Ocean. Because of this new system, the entire region of the Indian Ocean has a way of tracking tsunamis and issuing warnings. The Indian government also began placing detectors in the Indian Ocean. International groups have helped countries in the area with mitigation and response systems.

Since 2004, countries in the area affected by the tsunami have focused more on disaster preparedness. In Southeast Asia, Indonesia is teaching its people how to respond to a disaster. In South Asia, Sri Lanka and other countries have moved people from the coast to safer areas inland. But many worry about densely populated countries bordering the Bay of Bengal, where millions of people live. Bangladesh, also prone to cyclones, has built a warning system and hundreds of shelters along the coast.

The potential for a future disaster remains, however. Cyclones frequently strike in the Indian Ocean. Some scientists think the region is likely to suffer

▲ Worker in the tsunami early-warning center that has recently opened in India

another major earthquake and tsunami in the next 30 years. There are new concerns about an area along the coast of Myanmar. In 1762, a serious earthquake damaged parts of this coast. A similar quake today could have a disastrous effect on the region. Faced with these concerns, United Nations officials believe the countries of the region are not completing mitigation work rapidly enough.

Reading Check What is Indonesia doing to prepare for possible disasters?

Assessment

1. What causes a tsunami?
2. What is the difference between mitigation and response?
3. Why are many countries in the Pacific region prepared for natural disasters?
4. Why might the United Nations want the nations around the Indian Ocean to put more stress on mitigation?
5. Why are some scientists concerned about the coast of Myanmar?

713

Chapter Assessment

Key Terms and Ideas

1. **Discuss** How did physical geography determine where people settled in Southeast Asia?

2. **Explain** What kinds of weather conditions do the summer **monsoons** create?

3. **Recall** Which civilizations influenced Southeast Asia?

4. **Explain** How did the ancient Khmer create a food **surplus**?

5. **Summarize** What were the causes and effects of Western colonialism in the region?

6. **Recall** What is the goal of the **insurgency** in the Philippines?

7. **Explain** Why is the Strait of Malacca so important today?

8. **Describe** Which are the richest and the poorest countries in Southeast Asia?

Think Critically

9. **Draw Conclusions** How have the people of Southeast Asia used the environment to meet their needs?

10. **Synthesize** How did geography contribute to the diversity of the region?

11. **Make Inferences** Why did Islam spread through the islands?

12. **Core Concepts: Culture and Geography** How has the environment shaped culture in Southeast Asia?

Places to Know

For each place, write the letter from the map that shows its location.

13. **Mekong River**

14. **Singapore**

15. **Strait of Malacca**

16. **Bangkok**

17. **The Philippines**

18. **South China Sea**

19. **Estimate** Using the scale, estimate the distance between Bangkok and the Philippines.

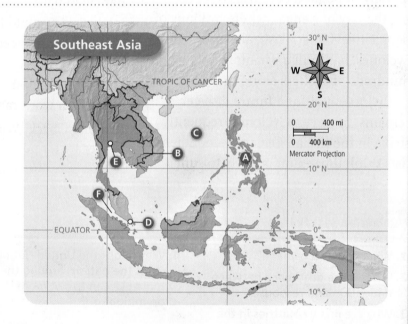

714

Essential Question
myWorld Chapter Activity

Gaining Wealth Through History
Follow your teacher's instructions to investigate the geographical factors that have contributed to the economic success of each historical character. Then rank the characters on an economic assessment scale and explain the reasons for your assessment.

21st Century Learning
Develop Cultural Awareness

Look back over the chapter and make a list of features that make Southeast Asian culture unique. Then consider why each feature might have developed—was it because of geography, climate, or history? Create a table that lists each feature and your theory about its origin.

Document-Based Questions

Success Tracker™
Online at myworldgeography.com

Use your knowledge of Southeast Asia and Documents A and B to answer Questions 1–3.

Document A

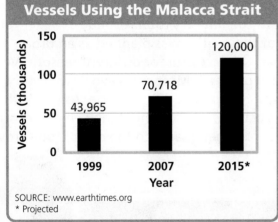

Vessels Using the Malacca Strait

(Vessels in thousands)
- 1999: 43,965
- 2007: 70,718
- 2015*: 120,000

SOURCE: www.earthtimes.org
* Projected

Document B

" He who is lord of Malacca has his hand on the throat of Venice."

—Duarte Barbosa describing world trade in the 1400s and 1500s

1. What does Document A tell you about shipping in the Strait of Malacca?

   A The number of vessels is decreasing every decade.

   B The number of vessels peaked in the 1990s and then declined.

   C The projected number of vessels will have nearly tripled in a 16-year span.

   D The projected number of vessels will decline sharply by 2015.

2. Which of the following best describes the meaning of Document B?

   A The European trading city of Venice depends on goods traveling through the Malacca Strait.

   B The trading city of Venice is being attacked by the lord of Malacca.

   C The cities of Venice and Malacca have little contact with each other.

   D Venice defeated Malacca after a long war.

3. **Writing Task** Use Documents A and B to write a short paragraph explaining the role of the Malacca Strait in world trade.

myworldgeography.com Self-Test

715

Plan the City of Tomorrow

Your Mission Study the effects of population change on a city in East or Southeast Asia. Then present a plan for how to manage more growth in your city, including predictions for its future needs.

The skyline of Kuala Lumpur, the capital of Malaysia, is dominated by the twin spires of the Petronas Towers (left). Architects and urban planners designed the building to be a destination for both workers and their families. North of Kuala Lumpur, across the Gulf of Thailand, lies Ho Chi Minh City, the economic center of Vietnam. Historic and elegant, Ho Chi Minh City boasts some 300,000 businesses and contributes as much as 20 percent to the nation's total revenue.

Neither of these cities was planned as an urban success story, yet each is successful for different reasons. Very few cities are planned. Most cities evolve as history, governments, and populations change. As you investigate cities in this activity, consider how their characteristics might be useful when planning the city of tomorrow.

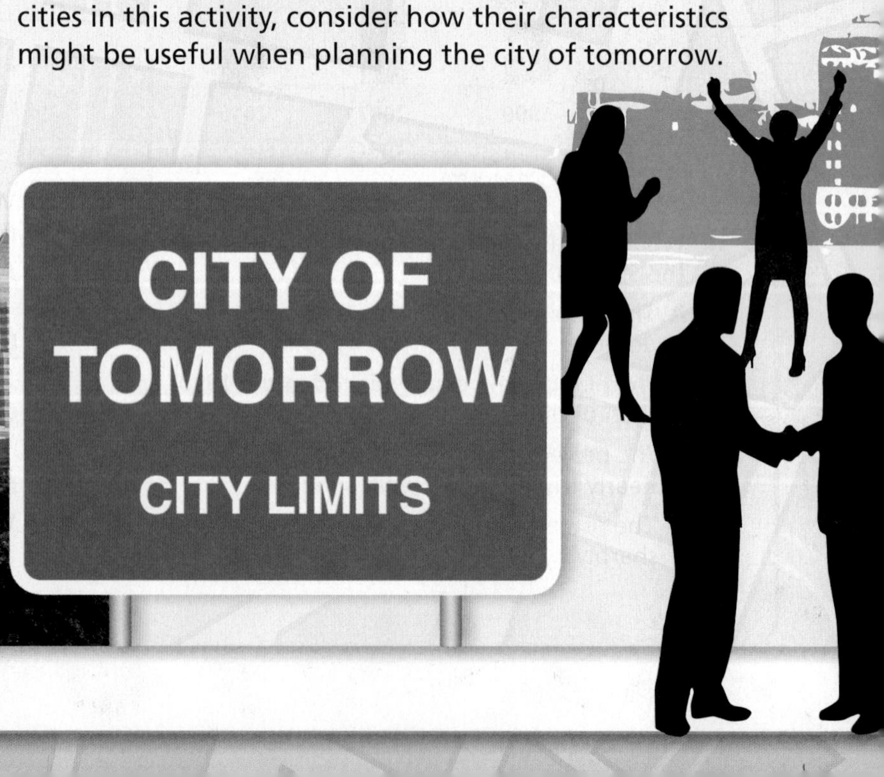

CITY OF
TOMORROW

CITY LIMITS

716

STEP 1

What's in a Name?

The name of the city you are researching may have changed over the years. City names can change, for example, if the country was once a colony that later declared independence. When this happens, large groups of people may move in or out of a region. Investigate the history of your city's name and begin your presentation with this brief overview—it will engage your listeners right from the start.

STEP 2

What's Your Plan?

Your main goal is to improve life for the people of your city. But you need a solid plan. Gather facts and figures about population trends. Identify areas where your city functions well and areas that need improvement. Remember that you are offering a solution for the future and that you can't always predict what will happen. Thus, your plan should offer reasonable expectations for implementing your ideas.

STEP 3

The Big Finale

An effective presentation ends with a summary of what you have already said. If you have any final arguments, make them with confidence. Avoid arrogance. Chances are that your audience will agree with your proposals— after all, they live in this city!—but they may be concerned with the costs associated with your plan. Keep in mind that planning the city of tomorrow begins with understanding cities of today.

Australia and the Pacific

Australia, New Zealand, and tens of thousands of other Pacific islands are spread across a vast area of ocean to the south and east of Asia. The people of these islands are as diverse as their geography, which includes high mountains, arid deserts, and icy glaciers.

What time is it there?

Washington, D.C.	Auckland, New Zealand
9 A.M. Monday	2 A.M. Tuesday

KEY
— National border
✪ Capital city
Orthographic Projection

The Unit Ahead

→ **Chapter 24** Australia and the Pacific

my worldgeography.com

Plan your trip online by doing a Data Discovery Activity and watching the myStory Video of the region's teen.

my Story

Jack
Age: 17
Home: Auckland, New Zealand

Chapter 24

New Zealand's South Island has many mountains and thick forests.

Regional Overview
Physical Geography

Most of Australia is very dry. Australians use the continent's dry plains for mining and raising livestock.

Melanesia has many high volcanic islands with fertile soil and mineral resources.

Mount Wilhelm
14,790 ft (4,509 m)

Arafura Sea

Gulf of Carpentaria

Cape York Peninsula

Coral Sea

Great Barrier Reef

Timor Sea

Great Dividing Range

Kimberley Plateau

INDIAN OCEAN

Great Sandy Desert

Simpson Desert

Great Artesian Basin

Darling River

Mt. Kosciuszko
7,310 ft (2,228 m)

Murray River

Gibson Desert

Great Victoria Desert

Nullarbor Plain

Bass Strait

Great Australian Bight

Tasmania

Darling Range

Many Pacific islands are low-lying atolls, islands formed by coral reefs.

PACIFIC OCEAN

North Island

Cook Strait

Southern Alps

Aoraki (Mt. Cook)
12,316 ft (3,754 m)

South Island

New Zealand's Southern Alps are home to more than 20 mountains higher than 10,000 feet.

Regional Flyover

You begin your flight at Easter Island, the easternmost settlement in Polynesia. From here you fly west across the Pacific Ocean, traveling over the thousands of high volcanic islands and low coral atolls that form the Pacific islands. These islands are spread out over 116 million square miles of ocean.

Flying low over the ocean, your airplane reaches Papua New Guinea, a nation on the eastern half of the island of New Guinea. Although it is just south of the Equator, Papua New Guinea has peaks high enough to receive snow. As your plane circles back to the southeast, you fly over New Zealand's icy glaciers, tall mountains, and thick rain forests.

Then you travel west across the Tasman Sea to Australia, following the 1,250-mile-long Great Barrier Reef along Australia's northeast coast. Finally you circle south, landing on the deserts of central Australia. Here you find Uluru, or Ayers Rock, an enormous sandstone rock rising about 1,100 feet above the surrounding land.

→ In-Flight Movie

Take flight over Australia and the Pacific and explore the region from the air.

my worldgeography.com   In-Flight Movie

Regional Overview
Human Geography

People, Land, and Resources

The Pacific region's physical features have shaped where people in the region live. Most Australians and New Zealanders live in dense urban areas near the ocean. Few people live in Australia's dry deserts or in New Zealand's rugged mountains. The population of the smaller Pacific islands is generally more rural. Most people live in small villages.

Some countries in the region have many natural resources. Others are less fortunate. Australia and New Zealand's many resources have led to strong industrial economies. However, the economies of the smaller islands are generally limited by a lack of resources. Most smaller islands have developing economies, and many islanders fish or farm.

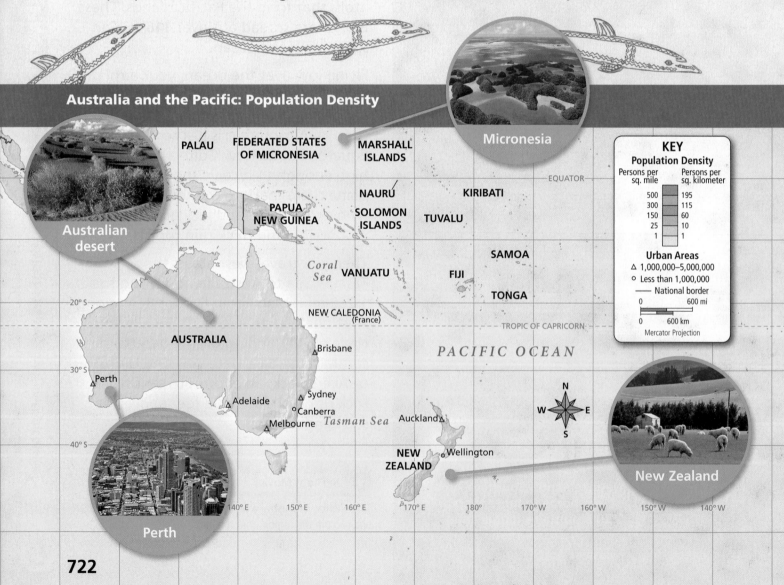

Australia and the Pacific: Population Density

KEY
Population Density

Persons per sq. mile	Persons per sq. kilometer
500	195
300	115
150	60
25	10
1	1

Urban Areas
△ 1,000,000–5,000,000
○ Less than 1,000,000
— National border

0   600 mi
0   600 km
Mercator Projection

my World IN NUMBERS

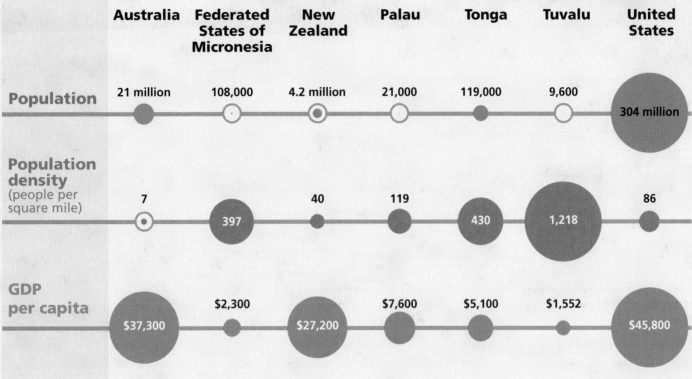

	Australia	Federated States of Micronesia	New Zealand	Palau	Tonga	Tuvalu	United States
Population	21 million	108,000	4.2 million	21,000	119,000	9,600	304 million
Population density (people per square mile)	7	397	40	119	430	1,218	86
GDP per capita	$37,300	$2,300	$27,200	$7,600	$5,100	$1,552	$45,800

SOURCE: *CIA World Factbook, Encyclopaedia Britannica*

Put It Together

1. What might be the advantages and disadvantages of living on a small Pacific island?

2. Remember that GDP per capita is the total economic output per person in a country. What geographic factors might influence the numbers for this region?

3. What seems to be the relationship between land and population? Between land and economy?

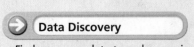
Data Discovery

Find your own data to make a regional data table.

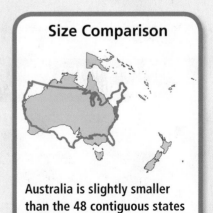
Size Comparison

Australia is slightly smaller than the 48 contiguous states of the United States.

Chapter 17

Australia and the Pacific

Essential Question

What makes a nation?

Where in the World Are Australia and the Pacific?

Washington, D.C., to Auckland: 8,620 miles

KEY
— National border
✪ Capital city
○ Other city

0 — 600 mi
0 — 600 km
Mercator Projection

my Story

Jack Connects to His Culture

In this section, you'll read about Jack, a young man from New Zealand trying to keep in touch with his Maori culture. What does Jack's story tell you about life in Australia and the Pacific?

Story by Tui Ruwhiu for myWorld Geography Online

It is early one weekday morning, and 17-year-old Jack is busy getting ready for another day at school. Jack lives in Auckland, New Zealand's largest city. By 7:30, Jack is on the bus for the 50-minute ride to his school, Avondale College.

Jack lives with his two younger brothers and his mother, father, and grandmother. Jack's father is a television actor and comedian. His mother manages the household and works in a television production company.

Jack is part Maori (MAow ree), descended from the original inhabitants of New Zealand. The Maori migrated to New Zealand—which they call Aotearoa (AOW tee AR roh uh)—from other parts of the Pacific region about 1,000 years ago.

Explore the Essential Question
- at **my worldgeography.com**
- using the **myWorld Chapter Activity**
- with the **Student Journal**

Facial expressions like Jack's were often used by Maori to frighten enemies before battle. Today, Maori people make this expression as part of a traditional greeting on important occasions. ▶

my **worldgeography.com** On Assignment

725

Jack and his brothers

Maori students make up about 8 percent of the 2,600 students at Avondale College. They have their own wharenui (meeting house) and wharekai (dining hall) at school. At breaks, lunchtimes, and after school, Maori students gather at the wharekai to talk and share food with friends.

But Maori people like Jack and his friends once faced many obstacles in New Zealand. During the 1800s, British colonization of New Zealand led to a series of wars with the Maori. Eventually, the British defeated the Maori. Many Maori moved to cities and lost touch with their culture.

Interest in Maori culture has grown since the mid-1900s. Today, many Maori study their language, history, and customs. Jack feels a strong connection to his culture and to his homeland on New Zealand's North Island. "I know the blood of my ancestors is in that soil," he says quietly, "because they gave their lives fighting for that land."

Jack takes a Maori language class at school every day. He hopes to become a skilled Maori speaker like his father, who grew up speaking Maori.

Jack and his horse

726

Jack's class practices kapa haka.

Jack's waka ama team

Although Jack went to a Maori-language day care center as a child, his parents decided to send him to English-language schools. English is the language most commonly spoken in New Zealand. At home, the family speaks English.

Jack stays connected to Maori culture in other ways. He is one of the leaders of his school's kapa haka team. Kapa haka is a performance art that combines singing and dancing. It uses parts of traditional Maori songs, dances, and combat techniques.

Each year, New Zealand holds a national competition for high school students of kapa haka. This competition is part of Polyfest, a celebration of Polynesian culture and dance. To prepare for the competition, Jack's kapa haka team practices each day at lunchtime and after school. It also practices for at least one full day each weekend.

Jack is also a member of his school's waka ama team. Waka ama are Maori canoes designed for use on the open ocean. Avondale has male, female, and mixed waka ama teams. Students of all ethnic backgrounds take part in the sport.

Jack plans to continue studying the Maori language and participating in kapa haka after he finishes school. He hopes to increase his understanding of his culture. "If you're interested, it's a lot easier to learn," Jack says. "There are a lot of people out there who have the knowledge. You've just got to be willing to go out and grab it."

myStory Video

Join Jack as he shows you more about his life in New Zealand.

Meet the Journalist

Name Tui Ruwhiu
Favorite Moment Watching Jack's kapa haka team practice

my worldgeography.com myStory Video

727

Chapter Atlas

Key Ideas
- The physical geography of Australia and the Pacific region is diverse and unusual.
- The Pacific Ocean includes thousands of islands with different sizes, climates, and resources.
- Climate, location, and resources have affected where and how people live.

Key Terms • Outback • coral reef • atoll • plate tectonics

 Visual Glossary

 Reading Skill: Label an Outline Map Take notes using the outline map in your journal.

Children in Papua New Guinea play in an outrigger canoe designed for ocean travel. ▼

Physical Features

The physical geography of Australia and the Pacific region is diverse. The region has tens of thousands of islands of varying sizes. Each has different resources, climates, and ecosystems. The great distance between these islands and other land areas has helped make them unique.

Australia lies at the southwest edge of the Pacific Ocean between Southeast Asia and Antarctica. It is the largest country in the huge Pacific region. The Pacific region also includes three separate subregions of islands: Melanesia, Micronesia, and Polynesia.

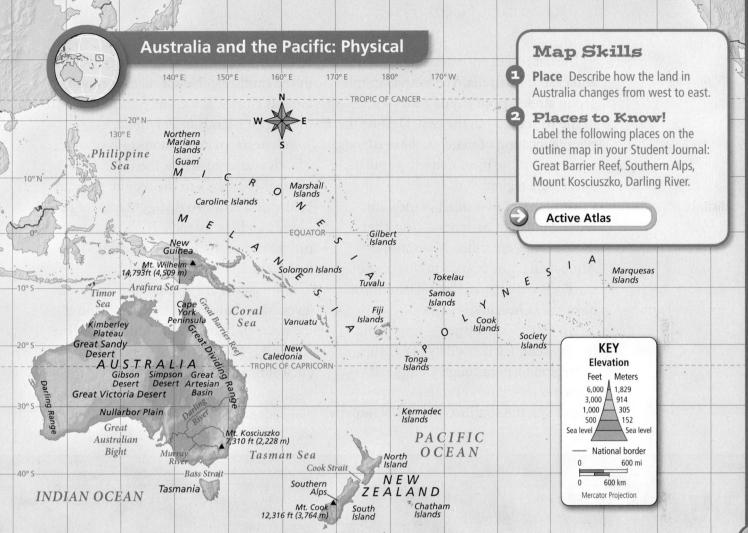

Australia and the Pacific: Physical

Map Skills

1 Place Describe how the land in Australia changes from west to east.

2 Places to Know! Label the following places on the outline map in your Student Journal: Great Barrier Reef, Southern Alps, Mount Kosciuszko, Darling River.

→ Active Atlas

KEY
Elevation

Feet	Meters
6,000	1,829
3,000	914
1,000	305
500	152
Sea level	Sea level

— National border

0 — 600 mi
0 — 600 km
Mercator Projection

Australia is completely surrounded by water, just like an island. But because of its large size, it is considered a continent. It is Earth's smallest continent.

Australia has wide, flat stretches of dry land, especially in its central and western portions. The interior of Australia is known as the **Outback,** a sparsely inhabited region with low plateaus and plains. The Outback is home to a large rock formation known as Uluru, or Ayers Rock. Central and western Australia include three large deserts—the Great Victoria Desert, the Great Sandy Desert, and the Simpson Desert. Eastern Australia, on the other hand, is covered by low mountains, valleys, and a large river system. Australia's coasts also include fertile plains.

Australia's dramatic physical features are not limited to land. The Great Barrier Reef, located off Australia's northeast coast, is the world's largest grouping of coral reefs. A **coral reef** is a formation of rock-like material made up of the skeletons of tiny sea creatures. The Great Barrier Reef is more than 1,250 miles (2,000 kilometers) long. It is home to many different underwater plants and animals. It is also a popular place for surfing and scuba diving.

my worldgeography.com Active Atlas

The subregion Melanesia lies just north and east of Australia. The islands in this group stretch from Papua New Guinea in the west to Fiji in the east. Despite the remote location of many of these islands, Melanesia is the most densely populated part of the region.

distinct, *adj.*, different

More than 2,000 small islands are located north of Melanesia. Together, these islands are called Micronesia. Almost all of the islands in this part of the Pacific are made of coral, and most have sandy beaches.

The third—and largest—subregion in the South Pacific is Polynesia. This subregion forms a rough triangle. It stretches thousands of miles from New Zealand in the southwest to the Hawaiian Islands in the north and to Easter Island in the southeast. New Zealand's mountainous North Island and South Island are the largest islands in Polynesia.

Polynesia includes thousands of small islands scattered across the Pacific Ocean. Like other islands in the region, they can be divided into two <u>distinct</u> types: high islands and low islands. High islands are mountainous, rocky, and volcanic. They have very fertile soil.

Low islands are located just above sea level. Most have poor, sandy soil and little fresh water. Many low islands are atolls. An **atoll** is a ring-shaped coral island enclosing a body of water.

Reading Check What are the three subregions of the Pacific region?

Atoll Formation

The diagram below shows how an atoll (right) is formed. **1** An atoll begins as a coral reef around a volcanic island. **2** The coral builds as the island wears away over time. **3** Finally, only a ring of coral remains.

730

Plate Tectonics

Plate tectonics helps us understand the forces that have shaped Australia and the Pacific. **Plate tectonics** is the theory that explains how huge blocks of Earth's crust called "plates" move. Hundreds of millions of years ago, the region was part of a giant continent. This ancient continent also included the land that now makes up South America, Africa, and India. Over time, Earth's plates separated. The giant continent slowly broke apart.

Australia and the Pacific include the Indo-Australian and Pacific plates. These two plates move toward each other at a rate of a few inches per year. Although this movement is slow, it has important effects on the region. As the plates <u>collide</u>, they push the ocean floor up above sea level. This creates many islands and volcanoes along the plate boundaries.

Plate movement and volcanic action have formed the two main islands of New Zealand. North Island has a series of high volcanic peaks that tower over green valleys below. South Island's Southern Alps are even higher mountains running along the island's western edge.

The movement of tectonic plates also helps explain the region's unique plant and animal populations. After the region broke away from other areas millions of years ago, its plants and animals were cut off from the rest of the world.

collide, *v.,* to come together

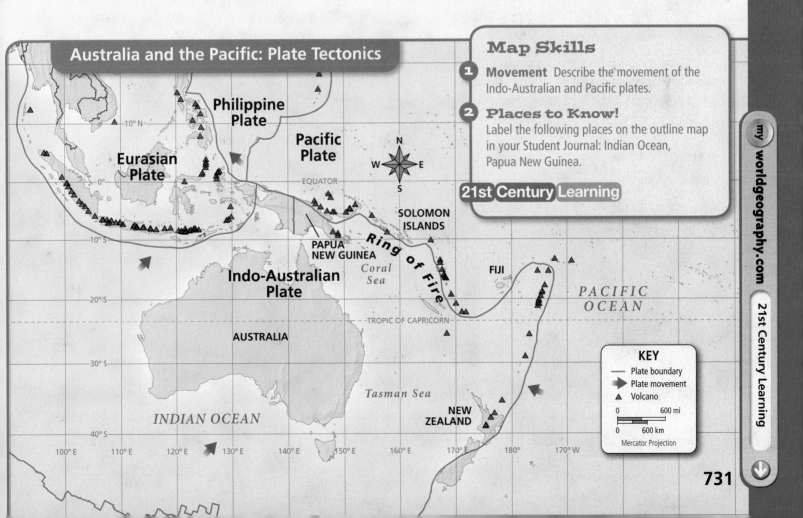

Australia and the Pacific: Plate Tectonics

Map Skills

1 **Movement** Describe the movement of the Indo-Australian and Pacific plates.

2 **Places to Know!** Label the following places on the outline map in your Student Journal: Indian Ocean, Papua New Guinea.

21st Century Learning

KEY
- Plate boundary
- Plate movement
- ▲ Volcano

0 — 600 mi
0 — 600 km
Mercator Projection

731

Over time, small changes have occurred naturally in the region's plants and animals. Because of the area's isolation, these changes have not spread to other places. As a result, Australia and the Pacific islands have many plant and animal species that cannot be found anywhere else in the world.

However, people have brought new plants and animals to the region. In some areas, the spread of nonnative species such as rabbits, snakes, and wild pigs has harmed the region's ecosystems.

Reading Check How has plate movement affected the region?

Climate

Weather and climate patterns vary widely across the Pacific region. Even opposite sides of the same island can have very different weather patterns due to differences in elevation, wind, and ocean currents.

Australia Australia's climate changes dramatically from one area to another. Its southeast and southwest coasts have temperate climates. The eastern coast has plentiful rainfall. In far northern Australia, heavy monsoon rains are common in the summer months. A winter dry season follows this wet season. However, most

Pacific Ecosystems

The Pacific region is so far from other places that many of its animals and plants are not found anywhere else on Earth. At right, a boab, a tree found only in Australia.

Koalas sleep for about 19 hours a day.

The platypus is a mammal that lays eggs.

A baby kangaroo lives in its mother's pouch.

732

of central Australia has arid and semiarid climates. This region has warm temperatures and little rain year-round.

New Zealand and the Pacific Islands New Zealand has a mild and wet maritime climate. It is cooler than Australia. Most other Pacific islands are located in the tropics. They tend to have tropical wet climates, with heavy precipitation and high temperatures year-round. On some mountainous islands, such as New Guinea, precipitation and temperature vary with elevation. Places at higher elevations usually have less rain and lower temperatures.

Water and Wildfires Although many of the Pacific islands receive heavy rainfall, some places still do not have enough fresh water for drinking or other human use. Low-lying atolls and low, sandy islands can collect very little rainwater.

Wildfires are a serious challenge in dry parts of the region. In Australia, fires can spread rapidly across the countryside during the winter dry season. These destructive fires are made worse by the grasses that grow during the summer wet weather and dry out during the winter.

Reading Check How do climates vary within Australia?

myWorld Activity
Traveling Tips

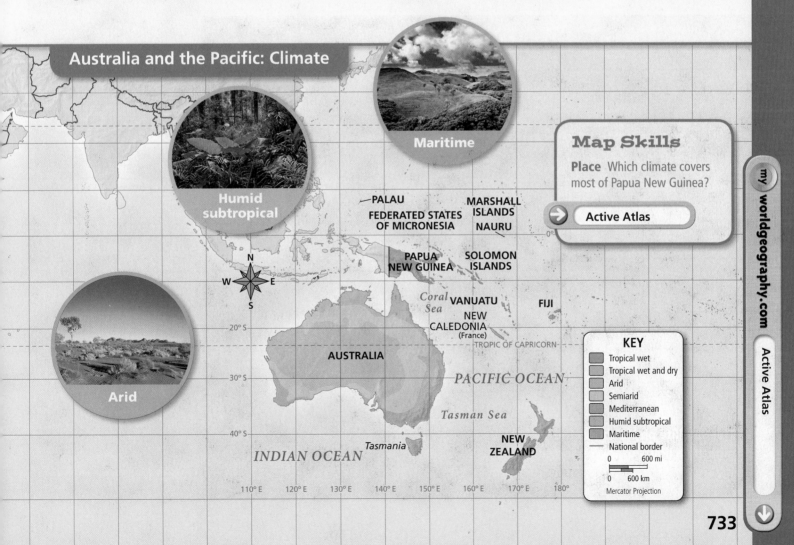

Australia and the Pacific: Climate

Maritime

Humid subtropical

Arid

Map Skills

Place Which climate covers most of Papua New Guinea?

Active Atlas

PALAU
FEDERATED STATES OF MICRONESIA
MARSHALL ISLANDS
NAURU
PAPUA NEW GUINEA
SOLOMON ISLANDS
Coral Sea
VANUATU
NEW CALEDONIA (France)
FIJI
AUSTRALIA
PACIFIC OCEAN
TROPIC OF CAPRICORN
Tasman Sea
Tasmania
NEW ZEALAND
INDIAN OCEAN

KEY
- Tropical wet
- Tropical wet and dry
- Arid
- Semiarid
- Mediterranean
- Humid subtropical
- Maritime
- National border

0   600 mi
0   600 km
Mercator Projection

myworldgeography.com Active Atlas

733

my **World** IN NUMBERS

If there were **100** people in the world,

51 would live in cities.

People and Resources

The region's population patterns vary widely. The availability of natural resources also differs from place to place.

Australia and New Zealand Most Australians and New Zealanders live in urban areas. Most Australians live on the country's mild east coast. Nearly 90 percent of the country's 22 million people live in coastal cities such as Sydney and Melbourne. The hot, dry central area of Australia has fewer people.

Most of New Zealand's 4 million people live on North Island. This island includes Auckland and other cities.

Australia is rich in natural resources, including bauxite, iron, and diamonds. It also has energy resources such as coal and natural gas. New Zealand, however, has relatively few mineral resources.

Both Australia and New Zealand have many large farms and ranches. Australia produces cotton, wheat, and sheep, although lack of water is a big challenge

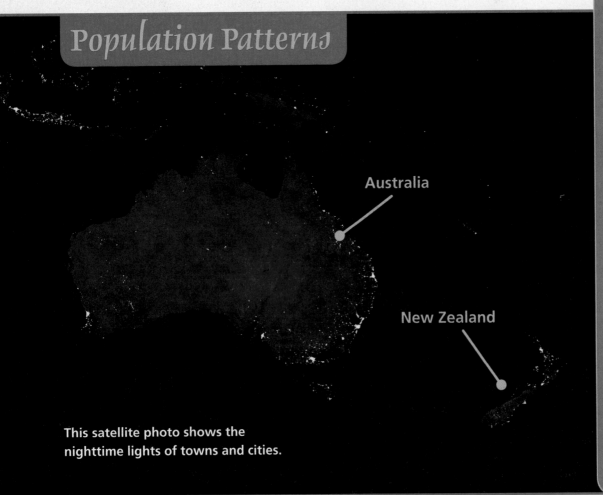

Population Patterns

This satellite photo shows the nighttime lights of towns and cities.

Australia

New Zealand

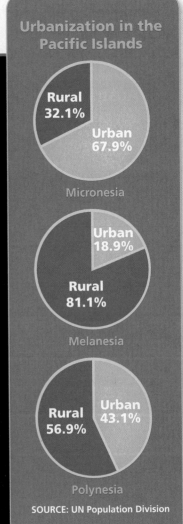

Urbanization in the Pacific Islands

Rural 32.1%
Urban 67.9%
Micronesia

Urban 18.9%
Rural 81.1%
Melanesia

Rural 56.9%
Urban 43.1%
Polynesia

SOURCE: UN Population Division

734

for farmers and ranchers. Much of central Australia is too dry for agriculture or grazing. Irrigation is very important.

New Zealand's fertile farmland and supplies of fresh water support its successful agriculture. Wool production is important.

Pacific Islands The population of the Pacific islands is generally less urban than that of Australia and New Zealand. Many people live in small villages in hilly regions or on coastlines.

The availability of natural resources varies. Most of the low islands have poor soil, little vegetation, and few mineral or energy resources. As a result, the low islands have relatively small populations.

High islands have fertile soil and many natural resources. Their farms produce bananas, cacao, and other crops. Some high islands also have resources such as gold, copper, and petroleum.

Reading Check How does the availability of resources affect population in the region?

▲ Many Pacific economies rely on natural resources. Above, oil workers drill in Papua New Guinea.

Section 1 Assessment

Key Terms

1. How has the movement of tectonic plates affected the region?

2. Describe Australia's Outback region.

Key Ideas

3. How have Australia's geography and climate influenced where people live?

4. How do high islands differ from low islands?

5. How does the geography of the region vary from one place to another?

Think Critically

6. **Compare and Contrast** How do population and resources vary in different parts of the region?

7. **Draw Conclusions** Why are many Pacific species found nowhere else on Earth?

Essential Question

What makes a nation?

8. How have climate, location, and resources affected the development of Australia, New Zealand, and the Pacific islands?

735

Section 2

History of Australia and the Pacific

Key Ideas
- The Pacific region was one of the last places on Earth settled by people.
- By the late 1800s, Australia and the Pacific were under the control of European and other colonial powers.
- Colonization transformed the region.

Key Terms • Aborigines • Maori • assimilation • ethnocentrism • missionary   Visual Glossary

Reading Skill: Sequence Take notes using the graphic organizer in your journal.

This Maori woman's chin is marked with the traditional Maori tattoos known as moko. ▼

The Pacific region was one of the last areas on Earth to be settled by people. When European settlers arrived in large numbers in the 1800s, they made the region's native peoples change their ways of life.

Migration and Settlement

People settled the region in three waves of migration, shown on the map in this section. Around 60,000 years ago, the first people settled Australia and New Guinea. By 1,000 years ago, people had sailed across the ocean to New Zealand and other Pacific islands.

Australia The original inhabitants of Australia are known as **Aborigines.** Aborigines lived throughout the continent, but most lived in the temperate southeast part of Australia. Early Aborigines were nomadic. They moved together in small groups, hunting animals and gathering plants. Aborigines had a complex society without chiefs or other formal leaders. They had strong religious convictions about nature, believing that it was their responsibility to care for the land.

The Pacific Islands In Melanesia, the great number of islands led to the development of isolated cultural groups over thousands of years. Most island people relied on the ocean for fishing, but Melanesians also developed agriculture about 10,000 years ago. In Polynesia, kingdoms extended over entire groups of islands.

736

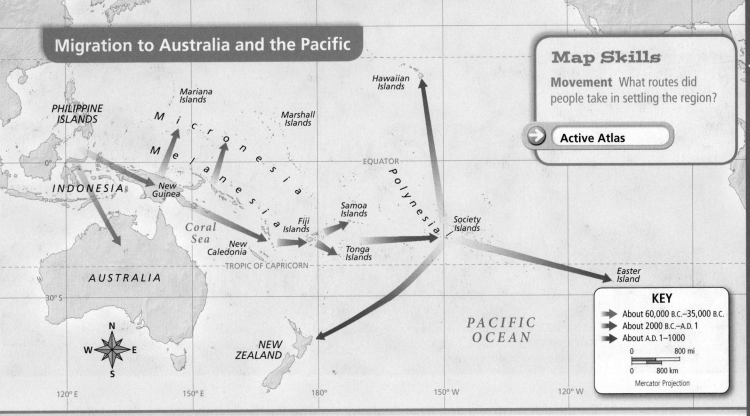

Migration to Australia and the Pacific

Map Skills

Movement What routes did people take in settling the region?

Active Atlas

KEY
➤ About 60,000 B.C.–35,000 B.C.
➤ About 2000 B.C.–A.D. 1
➤ About A.D. 1–1000

0   800 mi
0   800 km
Mercator Projection

Frequent conflict led people to live in protected settlements. Polynesians often went on long-distance ocean trips.

Like other Polynesians, the Maori lived in small settlements. The **Maori** are the original inhabitants of New Zealand and the Cook Islands. The Maori fished, hunted, and farmed. Chiefs were at the top of Maori society. At the bottom of society were slaves, usually captured during warfare.

The center of Maori society is a marae, an enclosed area of land that includes a meeting house and other buildings. Art is an important part of Maori culture. The Maori carve decorations into their buildings, canoes, weapons, and other objects.

Reading Check How did people settle Australia and the Pacific region?

Exploration and Colonization

In the late 1700s, British explorer James Cook claimed Australia and New Zealand for Great Britain. Cook's expeditions increased European interest in the region.

66 In this Extensive Country it can never be doubted but what most sorts of Grain, Fruits, Roots … of every kind would flourish … and here [is food] for more Cattle at all seasons of the year than ever can be brought into this Country. 99

—James Cook, journal entry, 1770

Colonization Begins British settlement of Australia began in 1788. Many early settlers were convicted criminals who had been <u>exiled</u> to Australia. Colonists farmed and ranched. In 1851, colonists discovered gold, and the British population soared.

exile, *v.,* to force out of one's own home

my worldgeography.com Active Atlas

737

A Changing Region

Lieutenant James Cook was an early British explorer of the region.

British colonization led to conflict with native peoples.

Conflict in Australia and New Zealand

As British colonists forced Aborigines off their lands, fighting broke out. In addition, many Aborigines died from European diseases.

The British also practiced forced assimilation. **Assimilation** is the process by which one group takes on the cultural traits of another. British ethnocentrism led settlers to force Aborigines to adopt British customs. **Ethnocentrism** is the attitude that one's own social or cultural group is better than all others. British colonists took Aboriginal children away from their families and forced them to live in institutions or with white families. This practice continued into the 1960s.

British settlers began to arrive in New Zealand in the early 1800s. They were attracted by New Zealand's harbors and fertile soil. Conflict with the Maori led to a series of wars eventually won by Britain.

strategic, *adj.,* important to military or action plans

The Pacific Islands

By the early 1900s, the United States, France, Great Britain, and Japan controlled most of the Pacific islands. Colonizers claimed some islands because of their natural resources. Other islands were taken for their location. For example, the Micronesian islands served as a <u>strategic</u> midpoint between the United States and Japan.

Britain ruled its colonies with colonial governors. Other countries controlled their colonies with military forces or through commercial companies.

Colonizers brought many new ideas and customs. For example, colonizers introduced the concept of owning land instead of using land collectively. Some colonizers were **missionaries,** or people sent to another country by a church to spread its religious beliefs.

Reading Check How did the British treat the region's native people?

738

Left, Aborigines were forced to adopt British ways.
Above, Aborigines protest government policies.

myWorld Activity
Before and After

Independence

Australia and New Zealand gained their independence peacefully in the early 1900s. Today, both belong to the British Commonwealth of Nations, which includes many former British colonies.

Most Pacific islands won independence peacefully in the second half of the 1900s. Independence movements played a role on some islands. In Western Samoa (now Samoa), the nonviolent Mau movement worked for independence, which Samoa won in 1962. Still, not all of the Pacific region has been decolonized. The United States, France, and New Zealand still control some Pacific islands.

Reading Check How did the region win independence from colonizers?

Section 2 Assessment

Essential Question

Key Terms

1. How did the British policy of forced assimilation affect Aborigines?

2. What did missionaries to the region seek to do?

Key Ideas

3. Why did countries seek to colonize the region?

4. How did people first settle the region?

5. How did the British colonization of Australia and New Zealand affect native peoples there?

Think Critically

6. **Compare and Contrast** How were the region's people alike and different before British colonization began?

7. **Sequence** In what order were Australia and the three subgroups of Pacific islands settled?

What makes a nation?

8. Does the history of colonization explain the formation of present-day nations in this region? Explain.

Aborigines Under British Rule

Key Idea
- When Britain colonized Australia, British settlers forced Aborigines off their lands and took control of many aspects of their lives.

The British settlement of Australia increased rapidly in the 1800s. British officials often forced Aborigines to give up their lands to colonists. They sometimes made Aborigines adopt British customs and live on settlements controlled by British officials. Living conditions in these settlements are described in a letter written by a group of Aborigines to Britain's Queen Victoria in 1846. British officials also passed laws that gave themselves the power to control Aborigines' lives. These excerpts will help you understand how Aborigines and British officials interacted in the 1800s.

▲ British officials and soldiers interacting with Aborigines, about 1790

Aborigines in the 1800s ▼

Read the text on the right. Stop at each circled letter. Then answer the question with the same letter on the left.

A Summarize How has the population of the Aborigines' community changed?

B Paraphrase In your own words, explain how the British official treated the Aborigines.

C Infer How do you think British officials felt about the Aboriginal settlements they created?

vermin, *n.,* animal pests, especially insects

rations, *n.,* food allowances

Petition to Queen Victoria

66 [W]hen we left our own place we

A were plenty of People, we are now but a little one … Our houses were let fall down [and] they were never cleaned but were covered with

B vermin … We were often without Clothes … [and the settlement's British official] did not care to mind us when we were sick until we were very bad. Eleven of us died when he was here. He put many of us into Jail … because we would not be his

C slaves. He kept us from our Rations when he pleased [and] sometimes gave us bad Rations of Tea [and] Tobacco. 99

—Aborigines on Flinders Island, Tasmania, Australia, 1846

Read the text on the right. Stop at each circled letter. Then answer the question with the same letter on the left.

(D) **Identify** What is the governor able to do?

(E) **Paraphrase** In your own words, explain the governor's powers over Aborigines.

(F) **Analyze** Why do you think British officials wanted to control Aborigines' labor and earnings?

prescribe, *v.,* to choose, decide
reside, *v.,* to live
exertions, *n.,* work
apportion, *v.,* to divide, distribute

Aboriginal Protection Act

(D) 66 **It shall be lawful for the Governor from time to time to make regulations and orders for any of the purposes hereinafter mentioned …** (I.) For <u>prescribing</u> the place where any aboriginal or any tribe of aborigines shall <u>reside</u>.

(E) (II.) For prescribing the terms on which contracts for and on behalf of aboriginals may be made with Europeans, and upon which certificates may be granted to aboriginals who may be able and willing to earn a living by their own <u>exertions</u>.
(III.) For <u>apportioning</u> amongst aboriginals the earnings of

(F) aboriginals under any contract, or where aboriginals are located on a reserve, the net produce of the labor of such aboriginals. 99

—Victoria, Australia, Act of Parliament, 1869

Aboriginal children were sometimes taken away from their homes. ▼

An Aboriginal man examining a rock painting ▼

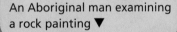

Analyze the Documents

1. **Synthesize** Explain how the 1846 petition shows that British attempts to control Aborigines existed long before the 1869 Aboriginal Protection Act.
2. **Writing Task** Examine the two documents. How do you think Aboriginal culture and society were affected by British treatment? Explain in a poem.

Australia and the Pacific Today

Key Ideas

- The region has a great deal of cultural diversity.
- Countries in the region have different forms of government and different levels of economic development.
- Protecting the environment is a major concern for the region's people.

Key Terms
- indigenous
- coup
- secondary industry
- primary industry
- drought
- climate change
- nuclear weapon

 Visual Glossary

Reading Skill: Identify Main Ideas and Details
Take notes using the graphic organizer in your journal.

Most Australians, such as the man below, are descended from British settlers. ▼

 Culture Close-up

Australia and the Pacific region are home to many cultures and ethnic groups, such as Jack's Maori people in New Zealand. A shared history and a blend of different cultures and traditions have shaped life in the region. Today, Australia and New Zealand are wealthy, highly developed nations with modern industrial economies. The smaller Pacific islands are less developed, with economies based largely on tourism and the use of natural resources.

People and Culture

Australia, New Zealand, and the Pacific islands include people from many different ethnic groups and cultures. As a result, the population of the region is diverse.

Australia and New Zealand Most Australians and New Zealanders have British ancestors. Since the 1970s, growing numbers of Asians and Pacific islanders have moved to these two countries.

Smaller numbers of Australians and New Zealanders are descended from **indigenous** people, or people native to the region. Only about 1 percent of Australia's 22 million people are Aboriginal. As you learned in Section 2, British settlers and the Australian government mistreated Aborigines for many years. In 2008, the Australian government officially apologized for this unjust treatment of Aborigines.

One Region, Many Cultures

Australia and the Pacific region are home to people from many different cultures. These cultures developed independently because of the great distances separating them.

→ Language Lesson

An Aboriginal girl from Australia

A man from Papua New Guinea takes part in a traditional celebration.

Samoan girls wearing woven grass dresses and beaded headbands

Jack, who is from New Zealand, is part Maori.

my Story 📷 Photo

New Zealand has a larger population of indigenous people: about 8 percent of New Zealand's 4 million people are Maori. Like the Aborigines, the Maori were forced to adopt many British ways of life. Still, Maori culture has survived. In recent years, Maori people have gained more political power. Since the 1970s, the New Zealand government has paid hundreds of millions of dollars to Maori groups to <u>compensate</u> them for having taken Maori land in the past.

In general, Australians and New Zealanders are healthy and well educated, with long average life expectancies. However, many Aborigines and Maori have lower standards of living and levels of education than other Australians and New Zealanders. Government leaders are working to improve the political and economic status of indigenous peoples.

Pacific Islands Over time, Pacific islanders developed many different languages, religions, and customs. European colonization reduced this cultural diversity. For example, Pacific people once practiced hundreds of different religions. Today, most are Christian. Still, most Pacific islanders are indigenous people.

Although modern culture has spread throughout the region, some islanders have kept traditional customs. For example, many Pacific islanders practice traditional forms of art, dance, and music.

Reading Check What is the name of New Zealand's indigenous people?

compensate, *v.,* pay

my worldgeography.com Culture Close-up

743

Government

Australia and New Zealand were once British colonies. As a result, both have governments that are similar to the British system of government.

Australia and New Zealand Australia and New Zealand are parliamentary democracies. In these systems, citizens elect representatives to a parliament, or legislature. The parliament then chooses a prime minister as the head of the government. The prime minister and the parliament govern the country.

Australia has six states. As in the United States, these states have a great deal of power to govern themselves. They also have their own legislatures and court systems. New Zealand does not have any provinces or states, but it does have local and regional governments.

Citizens of Australia and New Zealand have rights and responsibilities similar to those of U.S. citizens. For example, Australians have freedom of religion and freedom of speech. There are also differences. Australians who are registered to vote can be fined for failing to vote, for example.

Pacific Islands The Pacific islands have a variety of governments, although most are democratic. A few of these countries have suffered from political <u>corruption</u> or unstable governments. For example, Fiji's military has led four coups since 1987. A **coup** is the sudden, violent overthrow of a government, often by the military.

Reading Check How does Australia select leaders and establish laws?

corruption, *n.,* improper use of power

Queen Elizabeth II of the United Kingdom is the official head of state of Australia, New Zealand, and several other former British colonies. She has little real power, however. ▼

Pacific Governments

Many of the region's countries are parliamentary democracies. Above, a Papua New Guinea man waits to vote in a national election. Left, Australia's Parliament

744

Economy

The region's levels of economic development vary greatly. While Australia and New Zealand have highly developed market economies, most smaller Pacific islands have developing economies.

Australia and New Zealand Australia's major industries are agriculture, mining, tourism, and manufacturing. Although Australia exports natural resources to many countries in Asia, many Australian businesses are secondary industries. A **secondary industry** involves the use of resources to create new products, as occurs in manufacturing. Australia's highly educated population and advanced technology have helped its industries modernize and succeed. As a result, Australia has a wealthy economy with a high economic output per person.

New Zealand's economy is similar to Australia's, although it is smaller. Services, industry, and tourism are the most valuable elements of New Zealand's economy. New Zealand farmers raise cows and sheep for meat, dairy, and wool products.

Pacific Islands Many island economies rely on primary industries such as fishing. A **primary industry** involves the collection of resources from nature. Agriculture and fishing are important primary industries.

Many islands have joined together in trade and business groups, such as the Pacific Islands Forum. By working together, islanders hope that they can attract international business and tourism to their islands, improving their economies and standards of living.

Reading Check Which countries in the region are wealthiest?

my **World** IN NUMBERS

The region's countries catch about **1.4** million fish per year—less than **1%** of the world's total fish catch.

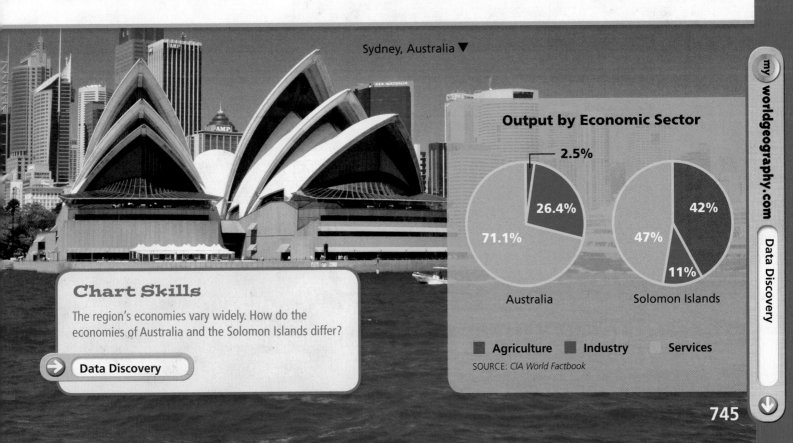

Sydney, Australia ▼

Chart Skills

The region's economies vary widely. How do the economies of Australia and the Solomon Islands differ?

Data Discovery

Output by Economic Sector

Australia: 71.1%, 26.4%, 2.5%

Solomon Islands: 47%, 42%, 11%

■ Agriculture ■ Industry ■ Services

SOURCE: *CIA World Factbook*

my worldgeography.com Data Discovery

Disappearing Islands

myWorld Activity
Take Action on the Pacific Environment

A melting Antarctic glacier ▼

In recent years, higher global temperatures have led to the melting of glaciers. Also, as water warms, it expands. Melting ice and expanding water have raised global sea levels. In the Pacific region, many people live close to sea level. For example, Tuvalu is a group of nine tiny islands about 2,500 miles (4,000 kilometers) northeast of Australia. Its highest point is only 15 feet (4.5 meters) above sea level, and most land is just a few feet above the water. As global sea level rises, Tuvalu—with its 9,600 residents—is slowly sinking below the ocean.

THINK CRITICALLY How is the sea level rise affecting Tuvalu?

Effects on Tuvalu

- High tides regularly flood Tuvalu.
- Waves from strong storms can wash completely over Fongafale, Tuvalu's largest island.
- Rising levels of salt water kill Tuvalu's crops and threaten livestock.
- Some residents are making plans to migrate to Australia or other countries in order to flee the rising seas.

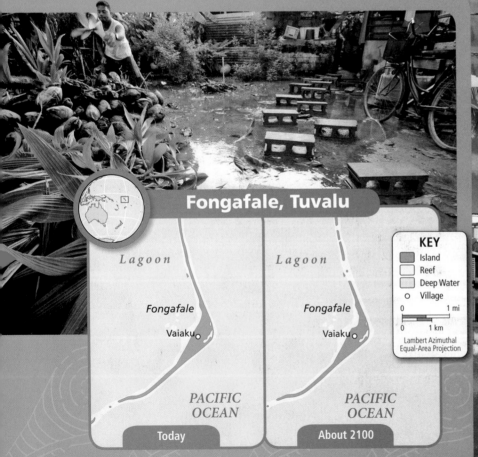

Fongafale, Tuvalu

Lagoon

Fongafale

Vaiaku

PACIFIC OCEAN

Today

Lagoon

Fongafale

Vaiaku

PACIFIC OCEAN

About 2100

KEY
- Island
- Reef
- Deep Water
- ○ Village

0 ___ 1 mi
0 ___ 1 km
Lambert Azimuthal Equal-Area Projection

▲ Parts of Tuvalu flood often, forcing people and animals to adapt.

746

Environment

Pacific economies often depend on the environment. For example, tourism relies on the region's sandy beaches and clear blue water. Agriculture and fishing involve the use of natural resources. Today, people are working to protect the environment and use resources carefully. But the Pacific region still faces environmental challenges.

Drought Australia is the driest inhabited continent. In recent years, many areas of the country have been affected by drought. A **drought** is a long period of extremely dry weather. Drought has caused Australia's farms to produce fewer and smaller harvests.

Climate Change Climate change is another major environmental problem. **Climate change** is a long-term, significant change to a region's average weather. Natural processes can cause climate change. However, many scientists believe that human activity—such as air pollution—is a major factor.

Perhaps the most important effect of climate change in the Pacific region is a rise in sea level. This rise is caused by the melting of glaciers and the warming and expansion of water due to higher global temperatures. Many scientists believe that the sea level will continue to rise in coming years, perhaps by as much as two feet or more by 2100.

Since many of the people in the Pacific region live near sea level, the sea level rise is a serious concern. Even a small rise can affect low-lying areas. Storms can push higher water farther onto land, causing widespread erosion.

Other Issues Some economic activities can cause environmental harm. For example, mining can cause water and soil pollution. In addition, the United States, France, and the United Kingdom tested nuclear weapons in the region from the 1940s to the 1990s. A **nuclear weapon** is a powerful explosive device that can cause widespread destruction. This testing may have harmful long-term effects on the region's people and ecosystems.

Reading Check How is sea level rise affecting the Pacific region?

Section 3 Assessment

Essential Question

What makes a nation?

Key Terms

1. How is climate change affecting Australia and the Pacific region?

2. What are primary and secondary industries?

Key Ideas

3. Why are the region's people concerned about the environment?

4. Describe the region's economies.

5. Why does the region have such a wide variety of cultures?

Think Critically

6. **Summarize** Summarize the present-day conditions of Australia's indigenous people.

7. **Draw Conclusions** Why might people who live on an island be able to preserve their culture for a long time without change?

8. How do governments and economies vary among the region's nations?

747

The Economy of the Pacific Islands

Key Ideas
- Many Pacific islands have developing economies that depend on the use of natural resources.
- Pacific leaders are working to improve the region's economy and build new industries for the future.

Key Terms
- subsistence farming
- copra
- Pacific Islands Forum
- Pacific Island Countries Trade Agreement

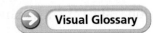 Visual Glossary

The economy of the Pacific islands has changed dramatically in recent years. Pacific islanders have worked hard to modernize their traditional economies. They seek to increase trade with other countries and to develop new industries. But many of the islands have small populations and very limited resources. They are located far from most customers. Pacific islanders have yet to fully overcome these challenges.

Using Natural Resources

For thousands of years, the people of the Pacific islands have used the region's natural resources to support themselves. Islanders have fished, hunted animals, and gathered fruits and nuts.

In recent decades, Pacific islanders have begun using the region's resources in new ways. Some islands have many mineral resources. (For example, Papua New Guinea has gold.) On these islands, mining for minerals is an important part of the economy. On other islands, cutting trees for timber is a major economic activity. Tourism is also important. Many tourists travel to the region because of its sandy beaches and clear blue waters. Its rich diversity of plant and animal life also attracts visitors.

Still, fishing and agriculture are the two most important economic activities for most islands. Many farmers practice **subsistence farming,** or farming with little left over to sell. Other farmers grow crops for export. Coffee, cocoa, squash, and **copra**—dried coconut meat—are common export crops.

Reading Check What are the most important economic activities in the Pacific islands?

▼ Papua New Guinea gold miners

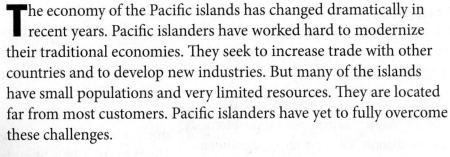

748

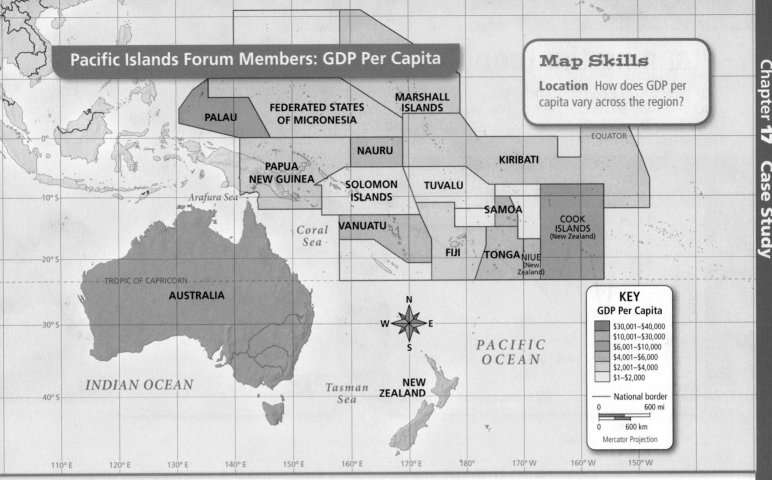

Pacific Islands Forum Members: GDP Per Capita

Map Skills

Location How does GDP per capita vary across the region?

KEY
GDP Per Capita
- $30,001–$40,000
- $10,001–$30,000
- $6,001–$10,000
- $4,001–$6,000
- $2,001–$4,000
- $1–$2,000

National border

0   600 mi

0   600 km

Mercator Projection

Working Together

With their small sizes and limited resources and manufacturing, most Pacific islands import more goods than they export. In recent years, the region's economy has grown more slowly than the economies of many other regions.

Today many of the region's countries belong to the Pacific Islands Forum. The **Pacific Islands Forum** is an intergovernmental organization that aims to increase cooperation between and represent the interests of Pacific countries. Members discuss regional issues, such as education, tourism, and trade.

In recent years, the Forum has worked to increase economic growth in the region. Some proposals have involved making it easier for Pacific islanders to move from their homes to other islands in order to to find work.

Many Forum members have signed the **Pacific Island Countries Trade Agreement** (PICTA), an agreement intended to form a free-trade area among member nations. PICTA is designed to gradually reduce trade barriers in the region. Pacific islanders hope that making trade easier will improve the region's economies. They also hope that the agreement will help them increase trade with larger markets, such as Europe and the United States.

Reading Check How are the Pacific islands working to improve their economies?

749

Planning the Economic Future

For years, the Pacific islands' economies have grown more slowly than the rest of the world's economy. Pacific leaders are working to improve education and build new industries for the future.

Pacific Islands and World: GDP Growth, 1995–2008

SOURCE: World Economic Outlook, 2008

■ Pacific Islands   ■ World

▲ Government leaders seek to develop the region's economy.

Chart Skills

How does the rate of GDP growth in the Pacific islands compare to the world's GDP growth?

21st Century Learning

Looking to the Future

As Pacific islanders plan for the future, they hope to increase economic growth. Many also wish to reduce their reliance on foreign aid from Australia, the United States, Japan, and other nations. Today, a number of poor islands depend on this aid. For example, more than 20 percent of Kiribati's income comes from foreign aid.

Protecting the Environment Pacific economies often depend on the environment, for example, through fishing, tourism, or mining. As a result, protecting the environment is an important economic issue. In some areas, overfishing has reduced the supply of sea resources. Logging has caused deforestation and the near extinction of animal and plant species. Some of

the beaches and coral reefs that attract tourists have been harmed by pollution.

But limiting activity that harms the environment may also affect economic growth. For example, limiting fishing in order to protect sea life also limits the amount of money that the region's people can make from fishing.

Working for Change Government leaders are seeking to replace traditional economic practices with new industries and new technologies. They are also trying to improve existing industries. For example, cellphones and better access to the Internet will improve communications and make business easier to conduct. Improving air transport will make it easier to ship goods and for tourists to visit the region.

▲ Tourism is a major part of the region's economy.

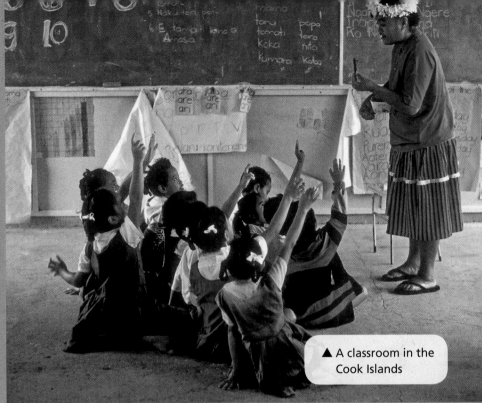

▲ A classroom in the Cook Islands

The small nation of Tuvalu provides an example of a creative use of technology for economic growth. Tuvalu's national Internet domain name is ".tv." The country rents the use of this name to people and businesses interested in starting video- or entertainment-related Web sites. In 2006, Tuvalu earned more than $2 million from renting .tv—about 13 percent of its total GDP.

Technological improvements may only happen if islanders are able to improve their education and training. In some countries, children often end their schooling before graduating from high school. A number of governments and international organizations are working to provide education and training that will prepare residents for new economic activities. They hope that better education will lead to new opportunities.

Reading Check Why are educational issues a concern for the region's economic future?

Assessment

1. How do Pacific islanders use natural resources?

2. In what ways do people hope to change the region's economies?

3. How are Pacific islanders working together?

4. Why is environmental protection an important economic issue?

5. Why has the Pacific economy generally grown more slowly than the economy of the rest of the world?

Section 4
Antarctica

Key Ideas
- Antarctica is the most remote and least populated continent on Earth.
- Antarctica has a harsh climate.
- People first ventured to Antarctica to claim land and resources, but now the continent is set aside for science.

Key Terms • ice sheet • glacier • iceberg • pack ice • Antarctic Treaty • ozone layer

 Visual Glossary

Reading Skill: Summarize Take notes using the graphic organizer in your journal.

▲ Adelie penguins on an iceberg off Antarctica

Physical Geography

Covered by a glittering sheet of ice and surrounded by stormy seas, Antarctica is Earth's least populated continent. It is located directly south of Australia, Africa, and South America. It is the coldest and windiest region on Earth.

An Icy Landscape Antarctica is a place unlike anywhere else on Earth. A thick **ice sheet**—a large mass of compressed ice—covers 98 percent of the continent. This ice sheet holds most of the world's fresh water. **Glaciers,** or slow-moving bodies of ice, form in Antarctica's valleys

752

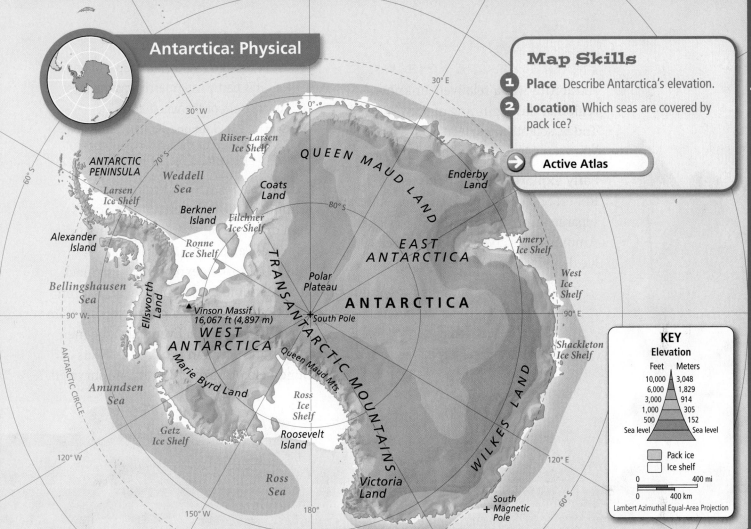

Antarctica: Physical

Map Skills

1 **Place** Describe Antarctica's elevation.

2 **Location** Which seas are covered by pack ice?

→ **Active Atlas**

KEY
Elevation

Feet	Meters
10,000	3,048
6,000	1,829
3,000	914
1,000	305
500	152
Sea level	Sea level

Pack ice
Ice shelf

0 — 400 mi
0 — 400 km
Lambert Azimuthal Equal-Area Projection

and flow toward the coast. When glaciers reach the sea, the ice breaks off into **icebergs,** or large floating masses of ice.

In winter, the surface of the sea around Antarctica freezes, forming pack ice. **Pack ice** is seasonal ice that floats on the water rather than being attached to land.

The Transantarctic Mountains divide Antarctica into two regions, a large, flat area called East Antarctica and a smaller region called West Antarctica. At the tip of West Antarctica, the Antarctic Peninsula extends toward South America. The Transantarctic Mountains have glaciers and dry valleys free of snow and ice.

Climate, Life, and Resources Antarctica's interior is a high, dry plateau. It receives little precipitation, less than two inches per year. The snow that does fall does not melt. Instead, it piles up year after year, eventually turning into glacial ice.

Antarctica's mineral resources include coal and iron ore. Its harsh climate limits vegetation to simple plants such as algae and mosses. Penguins, seals, and other animals spend much of their time in the ocean. The seas are home to a variety of fish, whales, and other marine life.

Reading Check How do Antarctica's climate and landscape affect life there?

my worldgeography.com Active Atlas

753

Exploration and Research

Antarctica was a relatively unknown region at the beginning of the 1900s. Today, scientists use Antarctica as a giant laboratory to examine the natural world.

Early Explorers In 1910, explorers Robert Scott and Roald Amundsen began separate expeditions to the South Pole. Amundsen reached it in December 1911. He described part of the journey:

“ Our walk across this frozen lake was not pleasant. The ground under our feet was evidently hollow, and it sounded as if we were walking on empty barrels. First a man fell through, then a couple of dogs … This part of our march was the most unpleasant of the whole trip. ”

–Captain Roald Amundsen, *The South Pole: An Account of the Norwegian Antarctic Expedition in the* Fram, *1910–1912*

Scott reached the Pole a month after Amundsen. On the return trip, Scott's team died in a blizzard. Still, their studies helped advance Antarctic science.

In 1915, British explorer Ernest Shackleton set out to cross Antarctica. His ship was destroyed by pack ice, forcing his team to live on an ice floe. Eventually, the men crossed the ocean in three small boats and found help. Amazingly, everyone survived.

The Frozen Continent

Early explorers mapped Antarctica by foot and dogsled. At left, Robert Scott (standing) and Edward Wilson at the South Pole in 1912.

myWorld Activity
Dear Antarctica

Today, scientists use Antarctica to study a range of topics. Below, a group of biologists. Right, a marker near the South Pole

A shelter used by Antarctic explorer Ernest Shackleton in 1907

Antarctica and Science Early explorers often claimed land in Antarctica. By the 1940s, these competing land claims led to international conflict. In 1959, twelve countries signed the **Antarctic Treaty,** an agreement that preserves Antarctica for peaceful and scientific use. Other protections were adopted in later years.

Today, Antarctica has no permanent human settlement. It does have several scientific research stations scattered across the continent. Scientists from a number of countries study topics such as oceans, glaciers, and climate.

Climate and the Ozone Layer To study climate, scientists drill deep into the ice sheet to gather ice samples. By examining the samples, they can learn more about the climate at the time when the ice was formed. By studying past climates, scientists hope to understand more about how climate might change in the future.

Scientists in Antarctica also study the ozone layer. The **ozone layer** is a layer of the atmosphere that filters out most of the sun's harmful ultraviolet rays. Over time, the ozone layer over Antarctica has grown thinner. This area of reduced ozone, called the ozone hole, allows more ultraviolet radiation to reach Earth. A major cause of the hole in the ozone layer has been certain human-made chemical <u>compounds</u>. Today, most uses of these compounds have been banned. Scientists predict that the ozone layer will eventually recover if this ban is maintained.

Reading Check How do people use Antarctica today?

compound, *n.,* something formed by two or more parts

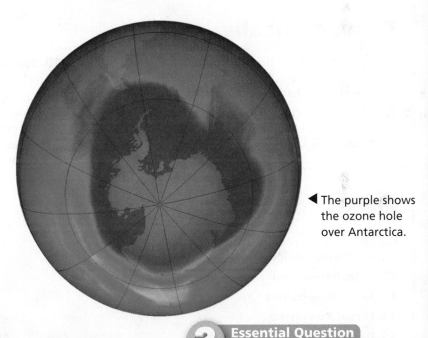

◄ The purple shows the ozone hole over Antarctica.

Section 4 Assessment

Essential Question
What makes a nation?

Key Terms

1. How does the Antarctic Treaty affect Antarctica?

2. Give short definitions of each of the following terms: ice sheet, glacier, iceberg, and pack ice.

Key Ideas

3. Why is Antarctica the least populated continent?

4. How does Antarctica's climate affect its environment?

5. Why are scientists interested in studying Antarctica?

Think Critically

6. **Draw Conclusions** How might its geography explain why Antarctica was not explored or settled until relatively recently?

7. **Synthesize** What challenges might Antarctica face in the future?

8. Why have no nations formed in Antarctica?

Chapter Assessment

Key Terms and Ideas

1. **Describe** How does **plate tectonics** explain the creation of volcanic islands in the Pacific?

2. **Recall** How did people settle the Pacific region?

3. **Summarize** What environmental issues does the region face?

4. **Compare and Contrast** Describe population density in Australia, New Zealand, and the Pacific islands.

5. **Paraphrase** Explain **ethnocentrism** in your own words.

6. **Summarize** What do **Aborigines** and the **Maori** have in common?

7. **Recall** How does the **Antarctic Treaty** protect Antarctica?

Think Critically

8. **Draw Inferences** How do you think Australia and New Zealand would be different today if British colonization had never taken place?

9. **Draw Conclusions** How might early explorers' experiences have helped to inspire the Antarctic Treaty?

10. **Synthesize** If drought continues in Australia, how might its population and economy change?

11. **Core Concepts: Climates and Ecosystems** How do you think the introduction of nonnative plant species has affected the Pacific region's ecosystem? What do you think can be done to better protect native species?

Places to Know

For each place, write the letter from the map that shows its location.

12. Great Barrier Reef

13. Papua New Guinea

14. Mount Kosciuszko

15. Darling River

16. Southern Alps

17. Indian Ocean

18. **Estimate** Using the scale, estimate the distance between the northwest tip of Papua New Guinea and the Southern Alps.

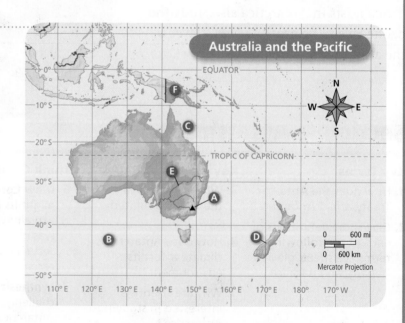

Australia and the Pacific

Essential Question

What makes a nation?

Reporting Back: A Voyage to the Pacific Follow your teacher's instructions to investigate geographic features of Australia and New Zealand as a member of explorer James Cook's crew. Work with your team members to collect and organize information on your field of expertise. Then prepare a multimedia presentation on the region to present to the British king.

21st Century Learning

Search for Information on the Internet

Imagine that you work at a U.S. zoo planning an exhibit on Antarctic penguins, leopard seals, and other animals. Use the Internet to research how to create an accurate exhibit. Then use this information to write a brief report. Remember to consider the following:

- Antarctica's climate and landscape
- Antarctica's land and sea temperatures
- the needs of Antarctic animals

Document-Based Questions

Success ⭐ Tracker™
Online at myworldgeography.com

Use your knowledge of Australia and the Pacific and Documents A and B to answer Questions 1–3.

Document A

Internet Users	
Country	Users per 100 People
Australia	75.1
New Zealand	78.8
Papua New Guinea	1.8
Tonga	3.0
Vanuatu	3.5

SOURCE: United Nations Statistics Division

Document B

" I was definitely not told that I was Aboriginal. What [they] told us was that we had to be white. It was drummed into our heads that we were white … We were prisoners from [the moment] we were born."

—John, an Aboriginal man who was taken away from his family as a child in the 1940s

1. Examine Document A. What can you conclude about Pacific economies based on these data?

   A Australia and New Zealand are less developed than other countries in the region.

   B Australia and New Zealand are more developed than other countries in the region.

   C Countries in the region are equally developed.

   D Smaller countries are more developed than larger countries.

2. Read Document B. What does the quotation describe?

   A climate change

   B forced assimilation

   C migration

   D missionaries

3. **Writing Task** Do you think the situation described in Document B was common? Explain your answer.

my worldgeography.com   Self-Test

757

Meet the Islanders

Your Mission Working in groups, you will research the indigenous peoples of Australia, New Zealand, and the Pacific islands. Then you will choose a person from one of those groups, research his or her life, and develop a multimedia biography.

One memorable moment of the 2000 Olympic Games in Sydney, Australia, came when Cathy Freeman won the 400-meter race. She was the first person of Aboriginal descent to win an Olympic medal. She took her victory lap proudly waving both the Australian and Aboriginal flags.

Many indigenous groups are found in Australia, New Zealand, and the Pacific islands. The indigenous people of Australia are known as Aborigines. The Maori are the indigenous people of New Zealand. The Pacific islands have a variety of indigenous cultures.

STEP 1

Choose a Subject.

Assign each person in your group to research one of these groups: Aborigines, Maori, and indigenous Pacific islanders. As you learn about these peoples, make a list of well-known or prominent individuals with that heritage. Try to include people from the arts, politics, sports, entertainment, science, and other fields. Share your findings and, as a group, choose one person to be the subject of your multimedia biography.

STEP 2

Research the Subject.

Do additional research on your subject's life and achievements. Divide up the tasks of finding out about the subject's family and childhood, adult life and achievements, historical events from his or her lifetime, and the customs and heritage of his or her ethnic group. Try to find lively details to enhance your presentation. Share your research with your group, and together decide what you will include in the biography.

STEP 3

Make a Presentation.

Plan and present a multimedia biography about your subject. Consider using written materials, photographs, videos, music, and other elements. Your biography should be thorough and focused. It should include interesting details as well as accurate facts. Your presentation to the class may take the form of a multimedia slideshow, a podcast, a radio broadcast, a documentary, or an interactive Web site.

The World: Political

760

The World: Physical

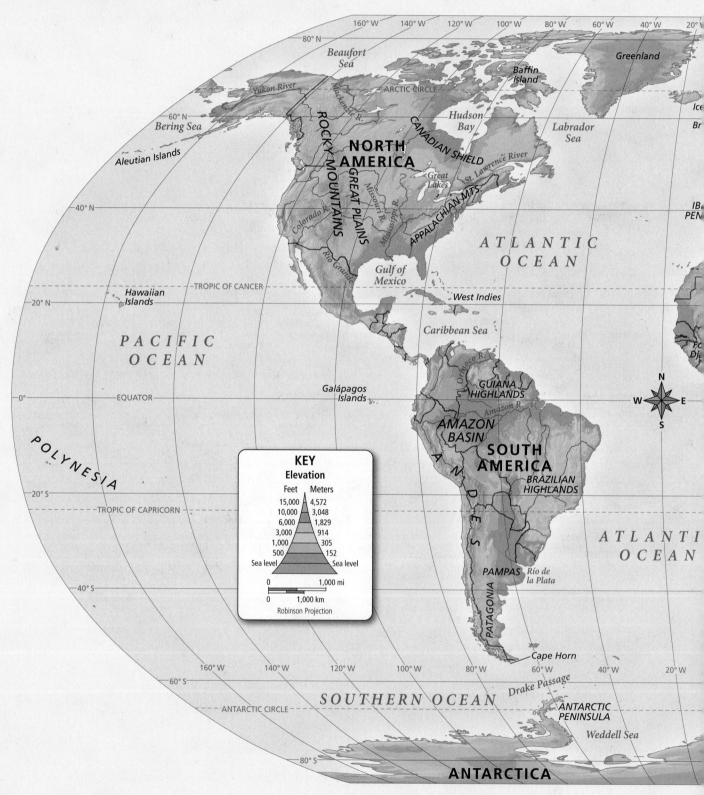

KEY
Elevation

Feet	Meters
15,000	4,572
10,000	3,048
6,000	1,829
3,000	914
1,000	305
500	152
Sea level	Sea level

0   1,000 mi
0   1,000 km
Robinson Projection

North and South America: Political

North and South America: Physical

United States: Political

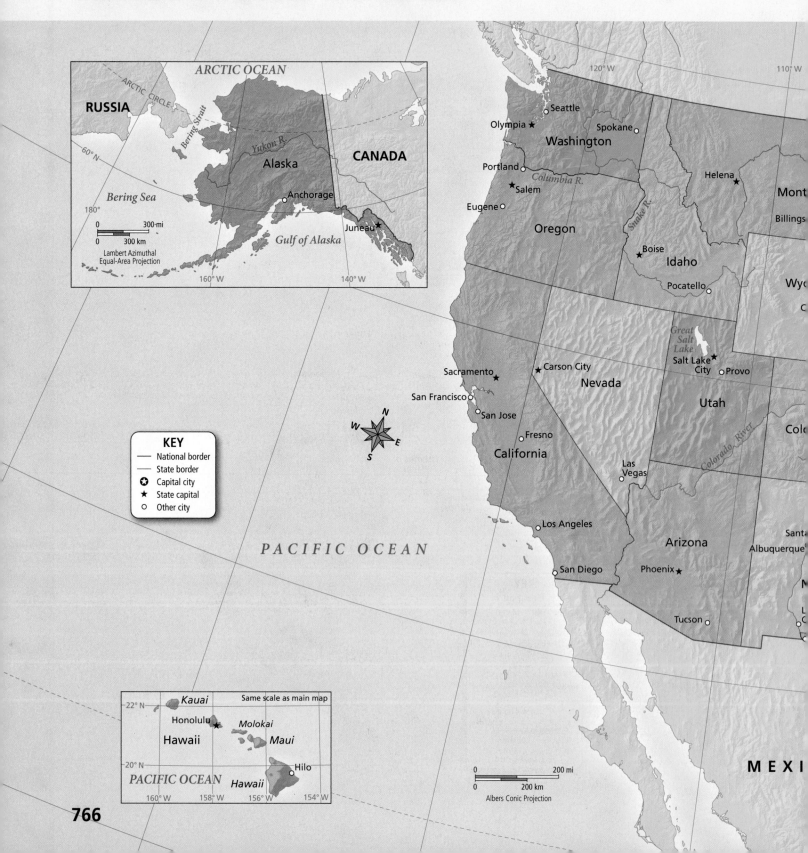

ARCTIC OCEAN
RUSSIA
CANADA
Alaska
Bering Sea
Anchorage
Juneau
Gulf of Alaska
Yukon R.
Bering Strait
ARCTIC CIRCLE
60° N
180°
160° W
140° W
0 300 mi
0 300 km
Lambert Azimuthal Equal-Area Projection

KEY
— National border
— State border
⊛ Capital city
★ State capital
○ Other city

Seattle
Olympia ★
Washington
Spokane
Portland
Salem ★
Eugene
Oregon
Columbia R.
Helena ★
Mont
Billings
120° W
110° W
Boise
Idaho
Snake R.
Pocatello
Wyo
Great Salt Lake
Salt Lake City ★
Provo
Sacramento ★
Carson City ★
Nevada
Utah
Col
San Francisco
San Jose
Fresno
California
Colorado River
Las Vegas
Los Angeles
San Diego
Phoenix ★
Arizona
Santa
Albuquerque
N
Tucson
PACIFIC OCEAN

Kauai
Honolulu ★
Hawaii
Molokai
Maui
Hilo
Hawaii
PACIFIC OCEAN
Same scale as main map
22° N
20° N
160° W 158° W 156° W 154° W

0 200 mi
0 200 km
Albers Conic Projection

MEXI

766

Europe: Political

Europe: Physical

ARCTIC OCEAN

Barents Sea

Kola Peninsula

Iceland

Norwegian Sea

Kjølen Mountains

SCANDINAVIAN PENINSULA

White Sea

Northern Dvina R.

URAL MOUNTAINS

Faroe Islands

Shetland Islands

Gulf of Bothnia

Lake Ladoga

Lake Vänern

Gulf of Finland

Gotland

Baltic Sea

Volga River

North Sea

Jutland

Sjælland

Elbe R.

NORTH EUROPEAN PLAIN

Vistula R.

Central Russian Upland

Ireland

Great Britain

Thames R.

English Channel

Rhine R.

Oder R.

Dnieper River

Volga River

Seine R.

Dniester R.

Carpathian Mountains

Don River

Caspian Sea

ATLANTIC OCEAN

Bay of Biscay

Loire R.

Danube R.

A L P S

Mont Blanc 15,781 ft (4,810 m)

Transylvanian Alps

Danube River

Sea of Azov

Crimea

CAUCASUS MTS.

Mount Elbrus 18,510 ft (5,642 m)

Massif Central

Garonne R.

Rhône R.

Po River

Dinaric Alps

Adriatic Sea

Black Sea

Pyrenees

Apennines

Balkan Mts.

Bosporus

ASIA

Meseta

Douro R.

Ebro R.

Corsica

BALKAN PENINSULA

Tagus R.

IBERIAN PENINSULA

ITALIAN PENINSULA

Pindus Mts.

Dardanelles

Guadalquivir R.

Balearic Islands

Sardinia

Tyrrhenian Sea

Aegean Sea

M e d i t e r r a n e a n

Sicily

Ionian Sea

Peloponnisos

Maltese Islands

Crete

S e a

AFRICA

KEY

Elevation

Feet	Meters
10,000	3,048
6,000	1,829
3,000	914
1,000	305
500	152
Sea level	Sea level

0   200 mi

0   200 km

Lambert Conformal Conic Projection

70° N

ARCTIC CIRCLE

60° N

20° W

50° N

10° W

ATLANTIC OCEAN

0°

30° N

10° E

20° E

30° E

40° E

Africa: Political

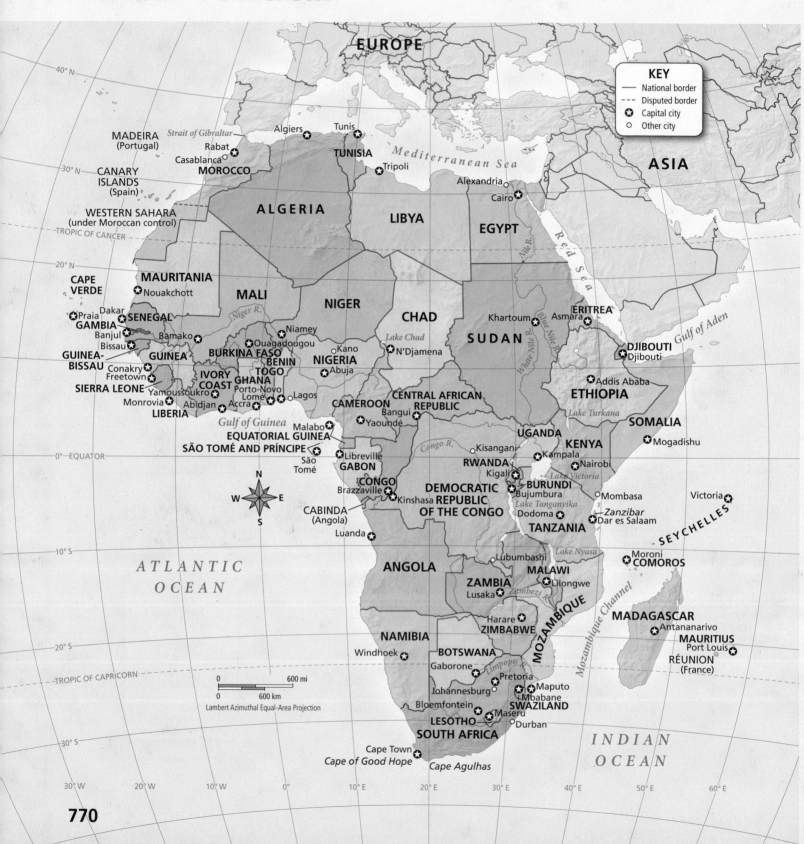

Africa: Physical

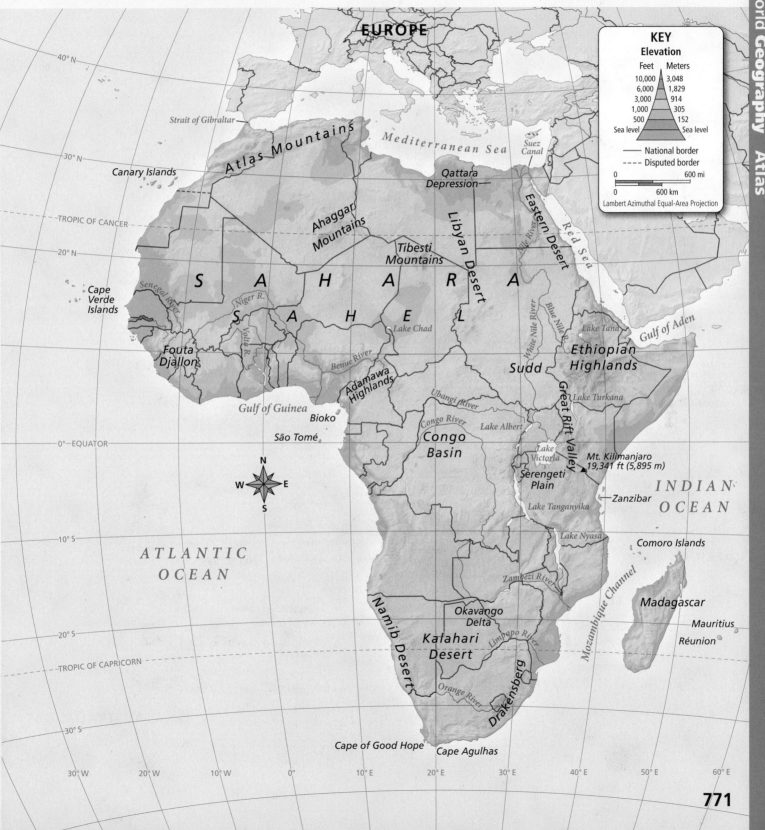

KEY
Elevation

Feet	Meters
10,000	3,048
6,000	1,829
3,000	914
1,000	305
500	152
Sea level	Sea level

National border
Disputed border

0   600 mi
0   600 km
Lambert Azimuthal Equal-Area Projection

Asia: Political

KEY
- - - Disputed border
—— National border
⊛ Capital city
○ Other city

772

Asia: Physical

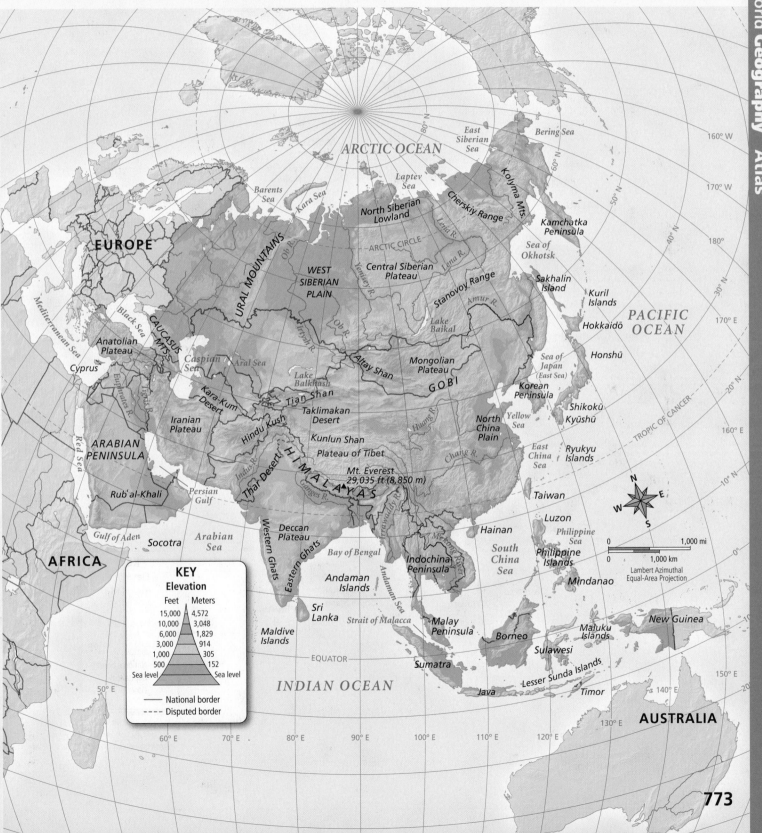

KEY
Elevation

Feet	Meters
15,000	4,572
10,000	3,048
6,000	1,829
3,000	914
1,000	305
500	152
Sea level	Sea level

—— National border
- - - Disputed border

Lambert Azimuthal Equal-Area Projection

Australia and the Pacific

The Arctic

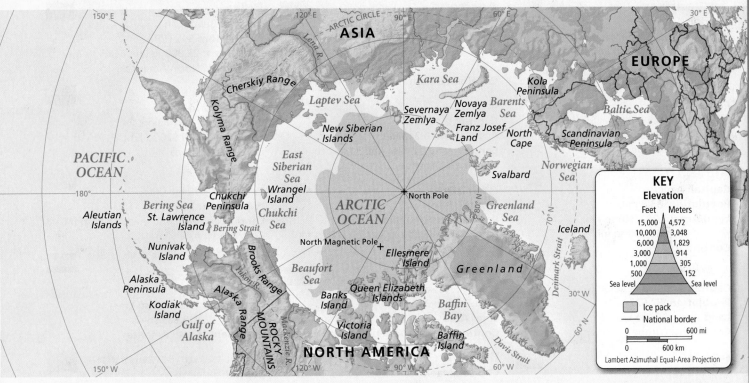

Antarctica

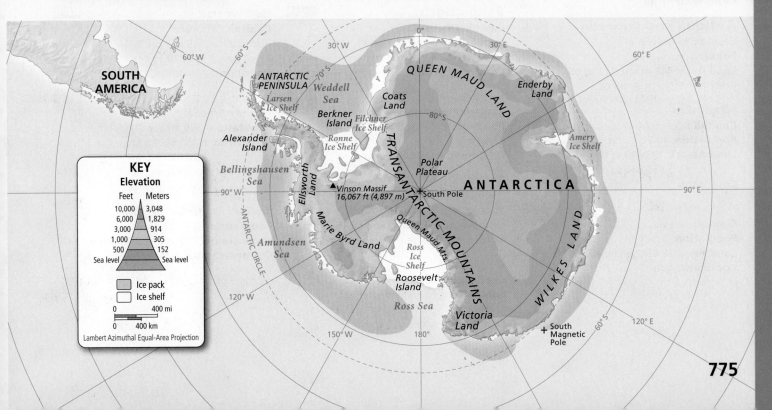

775

Country Databank

Afghanistan
Capital: Kabul
Population: 32.7 million
Land Area: 647,500 sq km; 250,000 sq mi
Continent: Asia

Albania
Capital: Tirana
Population: 3.6 million
Land Area: 27,398 sq km; 10,578 sq mi
Continent: Europe

Algeria
Capital: Algiers
Population: 33.8 million
Land Area: 2,381,740 sq km;
919,590 sq mi
Continent: Africa

Andorra
Capital: Andorra la Vella
Population: 82,627
Land Area: 468 sq km; 181 sq mi
Continent: Europe

Angola
Capital: Luanda
Population: 12.5 million
Land Area: 1,246,700 sq km;
481, 551 sq mi
Continent: Africa

Antigua and Barbuda
Capital: Saint John's
Population: 84,522
Land Area: 442 sq km; 171 sq mi
Continent: North America

Argentina
Capital: Buenos Aires
Population: 40.5 million
Land Area: 2,736,690 sq km;
1,056,636 sq mi
Continent: South America

Armenia
Capital: Yerevan
Population: 3 million
Land Area: 28,454 sq km; 10,986 sq mi
Continent: Asia

Australia

Capital: Canberra
Population: 21 million
Land Area: 7,617,930 sq km;
2,941,283 sq mi
Continent: Australia and Oceania

Austria
Capital: Vienna
Population: 8.2 million
Land Area: 82,444 sq km; 31,832 sq mi
Continent: Europe

Azerbaijan

Capital: Baku
Population: 8.2 million
Land Area: 86,100 sq km; 33,243 sq mi
Continent: Asia

Bahamas
Capital: Nassau
Population: 307,541
Land Area: 10,070 sq km; 3,888 sq mi
Continent: North America

Bahrain
Capital: Manama
Population: 718,306
Land Area: 665 sq km; 257 sq mi
Continent: Asia

Bangladesh

Capital: Dhaka
Population: 153.5 million
Land Area: 133,910 sq km; 51,705 sq mi
Continent: Asia

Barbados
Capital: Bridgetown
Population: 281,968
Land Area: 431 sq km; 166 sq mi
Continent: North America

Belarus
Capital: Minsk
Population: 9.7 million
Land Area: 207,600 sq km; 80,154 sq mi
Continent: Europe

Belgium
Capital: Brussels
Population: 10.4 million
Land Area: 30,278 sq km; 11,690 sq mi
Continent: Europe

Belize

Capital: Belmopan
Population: 301,270
Land Area: 22,806 sq km; 8,805 sq mi
Continent: North America

Benin

Capital: Porto-Novo
Population: 8.5 million
Land Area: 110,620 sq km; 42,710 sq mi
Continent: Africa

Bhutan
Capital: Thimphu
Population: 682,321
Land Area: 47,000 sq km; 18,147 sq mi
Continent: Asia

Bolivia

Capitals: La Paz and Sucre
Population: 9.2 million
Land Area: 1,084,390 sq km;
418,683 sq mi
Continent: South America

Bosnia and Herzegovina

Capital: Sarajevo
Population: 4.6 million
Land Area: 51,197 sq km; 19,767 sq mi
Continent: Europe

Botswana

Capital: Gaborone
Population: 1.8 million
Land Area: 585,370 sq km; 226,011 sq mi
Continent: Africa

Brazil

Capital: Brasília
Population: 196 million
Land Area: 8,456,510 sq km;
3,265,059 sq mi
Continent: South America

Brunei
Capital: Bandar Seri Begawan
Population: 381,371
Land Area: 5,270 sq km; 2,035 sq mi
Continent: Asia

Bulgaria
Capital: Sofía
Population: 7.3 million
Land Area: 110,550 sq km; 42,683 sq mi
Continent: Europe

Burkina Faso
Capital: Ouagadougou
Population: 15.3 million
Land Area: 273,800 sq km; 105,714 sq mi
Continent: Africa

Burundi
Capital: Bujumbura
Population: 8.7 million
Land Area: 25,650 sq km; 9,903 sq mi
Continent: Africa

Cambodia
Capital: Phnom Penh
Population: 14.2 million
Land Area: 176,520 sq km; 68,154 sq mi
Continent: Asia

Cameroon
Capital: Yaoundé
Population: 18.5 million
Land Area: 469,440 sq km; 181,251 sq mi
Continent: Africa

Canada
Capital: Ottawa
Population: 33.2 million
Land Area: 9,093,507 sq km;
        3,511,009 sq mi
Continent: North America

Cape Verde
Capital: Praia
Population: 426,998
Land Area: 4,033 sq km; 1,557 sq mi
Continent: Africa

Central African Republic
Capital: Bangui
Population: 4.4 million
Land Area: 622,984 sq km; 240,534 sq mi
Continent: Africa

Chad
Capital: N'Djamena
Population: 10.1 million
Land Area: 1,259,200 sq km;
        486,177 sq mi
Continent: Africa

Chile
Capital: Santiago
Population: 16.5 million
Land Area: 748,800 sq km; 289,112 sq mi
Continent: South America

China
Capital: Beijing
Population: 1.33 billion
Land Area: 9,326,410 sq km;
        3,600,927 sq mi
Continent: Asia

Colombia
Capital: Bogotá
Population: 45 million
Land Area: 1,038,700 sq km;
        401,042 sq mi
Continent: South America

Comoros
Capital: Moroni
Population: 731,775
Land Area: 2,170 sq km; 838 sq mi
Continent: Africa

Congo, Democratic Republic of the
Capital: Kinshasa
Population: 66.5 million
Land Area: 2,267,600 sq km;
        875,520 sq mi
Continent: Africa

Congo, Republic of the
Capital: Brazzaville
Population: 3.9 million
Land Area: 341,500 sq km; 131,853 sq mi
Continent: Africa

Costa Rica
Capital: San José
Population: 4.2 million
Land Area: 50,660 sq km; 19,560 sq mi
Continent: North America

Croatia
Capital: Zagreb
Population: 4.5 million
Land Area: 56,414 km; 21,781 sq mi
Continent: Europe

Cuba
Capital: Havana
Population: 11.4 million
Land Area: 110,860 sq km; 42,803 sq mi
Continent: North America

Cyprus
Capital: Nicosia
Population: 792,604
Land Area: 9,240 sq km; 3,568 sq mi
Continent: Europe

Czech Republic
Capital: Prague
Population: 10.2 million
Land Area: 77,276 sq km; 29,836 sq mi
Continent: Europe

Denmark
Capital: Copenhagen
Population: 5.5 million
Land Area: 42,394 sq km; 16,368 sq mi
Continent: Europe

Djibouti
Capital: Djibouti
Population: 506,221
Land Area: 22,980 sq km; 8,873 sq mi
Continent: Africa

Dominica
Capital: Roseau
Population: 72,514
Land Area: 754 sq km; 291 sq mi
Continent: North America

Dominican Republic
Capital: Santo Domingo
Population: 9.5 million
Land Area: 48,380 sq km; 18,679 sq mi
Continent: North America

Ecuador
Capital: Quito
Population: 13.9 million
Land Area: 276,840 sq km; 106,888 sq mi
Continent: South America

Country Databank (continued)

Egypt
Capital: Cairo
Population: 81.7 million
Land Area: 995,450 sq km; 384,343 sq mi
Continent: Africa

El Salvador
Capital: San Salvador
Population: 7.1 million
Land Area: 20,720 sq km; 8,000 sq mi
Continent: North America

Equatorial Guinea
Capital: Malabo
Population: 616,459
Land Area: 28,051 sq km; 10,831 sq mi
Continent: Africa

Eritrea
Capital: Asmara
Population: 5.5 million
Land Area: 121,320 sq km; 46,842 sq mi
Continent: Africa

Estonia
Capital: Tallinn
Population: 1.3 million
Land Area: 43,211 sq km; 16,684 sq mi
Continent: Europe

Ethiopia
Capital: Addis Ababa
Population: 82.5 million
Land Area: 1,119,683 sq km; 432,310 sq mi
Continent: Africa

Fiji
Capital: Suva
Population: 931,741
Land Area: 18,270 sq km; 7,054 sq mi
Continent: Australia and Oceania

Finland
Capital: Helsinki
Population: 5.2 million
Land Area: 304,473 sq km; 117,557 sq mi
Continent: Europe

France
Capital: Paris
Population: 64 million
Land Area: 545,630 sq km; 310,668 sq mi
Continent: Europe

Gabon
Capital: Libreville
Population: 1.5 million
Land Area: 257,667 sq km; 99,489 sq mi
Continent: Africa

The Gambia
Capital: Banjul
Population: 1.7 million
Land Area: 10,000 sq km; 3,861 sq mi
Continent: Africa

Georgia
Capital: T'bilisi
Population: 4.6 million
Land Area: 69,700 sq km; 26,911 sq mi
Continent: Asia

Germany
Capital: Berlin
Population: 82.4 million
Land Area: 349,223 sq km; 134,835 sq mi
Continent: Europe

Ghana
Capital: Accra
Population: 23.4 million
Land Area: 230,940 sq km; 89,166 sq mi
Continent: Africa

Greece
Capital: Athens
Population: 10.7 million
Land Area: 130,800 sq km; 50,502 sq mi
Continent: Europe

Grenada
Capital: Saint George's
Population: 90,343
Land Area: 344 sq km; 133 sq mi
Continent: North America

Guatemala
Capital: Guatemala City
Population: 13 million
Land Area: 108,430 sq km; 41,865 sq mi
Continent: North America

Guinea
Capital: Conakry
Population: 9.8 million
Land Area: 245,857 sq km; 94,925 sq mi
Continent: Africa

Guinea-Bissau
Capital: Bissau
Population: 1.5 million
Land Area: 28,000 sq km; 10,811 sq mi
Continent: Africa

Guyana
Capital: Georgetown
Population: 770,794
Land Area: 196,850 sq km; 76,004 sq mi
Continent: South America

Haiti
Capital: Port-au-Prince
Population: 8.9 million
Land Area: 27,560 sq km; 10,641 sq mi
Continent: North America

Holy See (Vatican City)
Capital: Vatican City
Population: 824
Land Area: 0.44 sq km; 0.17 sq mi
Continent: Europe

Honduras
Capital: Tegucigalpa
Population: 7.6 million
Land Area: 111,890 sq km; 43,201 sq mi
Continent: North America

Hungary
Capital: Budapest
Population: 9.9 million
Land Area: 92,340 sq km; 35,652 sq mi
Continent: Europe

Iceland
Capital: Reykjavík
Population: 304,367
Land Area: 100,250 sq km; 38,707 sq mi
Continent: Europe

India
Capital: New Delhi
Population: 1.15 billion
Land Area: 2,973,190 sq km; 1,147,949 sq mi
Continent: Asia

Indonesia
Capital: Jakarta
Population: 237.5 million
Land Area: 1,826,440 sq km; 705,188 sq mi
Continent: Asia

Iran
Capital: Tehran
Population: 65.9 million
Land Area: 1,636,000 sq km; 631,660 sq mi
Continent: Asia

Iraq
Capital: Baghdad
Population: 28.2 million
Land Area: 432,162 sq km; 166,858 sq mi
Continent: Asia

Ireland
Capital: Dublin
Population: 4.2 million
Land Area: 68,890 sq km; 26,598 sq mi
Continent: Europe

Israel
Capital: Jerusalem
Population: 7.1 million
Land Area: 20,330 sq km; 7,849 sq mi
Continent: Asia

Italy
Capital: Rome
Population: 58.2 million
Land Area: 294,020 sq km; 113,521 sq mi
Continent: Europe

Ivory Coast
Capital: Yamoussoukro
Population: 20.2 million
Land Area: 318,000 sq km; 122,780 sq mi
Continent: Africa

Jamaica
Capital: Kingston
Population: 2.8 million
Land Area: 10,831 sq km; 4,182 sq mi
Continent: North America

Japan
Capital: Tokyo
Population: 127.3 million
Land Area: 374,744 sq km; 144,689 sq mi
Continent: Asia

Jordan
Capital: Amman
Population: 6.2 million
Land Area: 91,971 sq km; 35,510 sq mi
Continent: Asia

Kazakhstan
Capital: Astana
Population: 15.3 million
Land Area: 2,669,800 sq km; 1,030,810 sq mi
Continent: Asia

Kenya
Capital: Nairobi
Population: 38 million
Land Area: 569,250 sq km; 219,787 sq mi
Continent: Africa

Kiribati
Capital: Bairiki (Tarawa Atoll)
Population: 110,356
Land Area: 811 sq km; 313 sq mi
Continent: Australia and Oceania

Korea, North
Capital: Pyongyang
Population: 23.5 million
Land Area: 120,410 sq km; 46,490 sq mi
Continent: Asia

Korea, South
Capital: Seoul
Population: 48.4 million
Land Area: 98,190 sq km; 37,911 sq mi
Continent: Asia

Kosovo
Capital: Pristina
Population: 2.1 million
Land Area: 10,887 sq km; 4,203 sq mi
Continent: Europe

Kuwait
Capital: Kuwait City
Population: 2.6 million
Land Area: 17,820 sq km; 6,880 sq mi
Continent: Asia

Kyrgyzstan
Capital: Bishkek
Population: 5.4 million
Land Area: 191,300 sq km; 73,861sq mi
Continent: Asia

Laos
Capital: Vientiane
Population: 6.7 million
Land Area: 230,800 sq km; 89,112 sq mi
Continent: Asia

Latvia
Capital: Riga
Population: 2.3 million
Land Area: 63,589 sq km; 24,552 sq mi
Continent: Europe

Lebanon
Capital: Beirut
Population: 4 million
Land Area: 10,230 sq km; 3,950 sq mi
Continent: Asia

Lesotho
Capital: Maseru
Population: 2.1 million
Land Area: 30,355 sq km; 11,720 sq mi
Continent: Africa

Liberia
Capital: Monrovia
Population: 3.3 million
Land Area: 96,320 sq km; 37,189 sq mi
Continent: Africa

Libya

Capital: Tripoli
Population: 6.2 million
Land Area: 1,759,540 sq km; 679,358 sq mi
Continent: Africa

Liechtenstein
Capital: Vaduz
Population: 34,498
Land Area: 160 sq km; 62 sq mi
Continent: Europe

Lithuania
Capital: Vilnius
Population: 3.6 million
Land Area: 65,300 sq km; 25,212 sq mi
Continent: Europe

Luxembourg
Capital: Luxembourg
Population: 486,006
Land Area: 2,586 sq km; 998 sq mi
Continent: Europe

Macedonia
Capital: Skopje
Population: 2.1 million
Land Area: 24,856 sq km; 9,597 sq mi
Continent: Europe

Country Databank (continued)

Madagascar
Capital: Antananarivo
Population: 20 million
Land Area: 581,540 sq km; 224,533 sq mi
Continent: Africa

Malawi
Capital: Lilongwe
Population: 13.9 million
Land Area: 94,080 sq km; 36,324 sq mi
Continent: Africa

Malaysia
Capital: Kuala Lumpur
Population: 25.3 million
Land Area: 328,550 sq km; 126,853 sq mi
Continent: Asia

Maldives
Capital: Malé
Population: 385,925
Land Area: 300 sq km; 116 sq mi
Continent: Asia

Mali
Capital: Bamako
Population: 12.3 million
Land Area: 1,220,000 sq km; 471,042 sq mi
Continent: Africa

Malta
Capital: Valletta
Population: 403,532
Land Area: 316 sq km; 122 sq mi
Continent: Europe

Marshall Islands
Capital: Majuro
Population: 63,174
Land Area: 181.3 sq km; 70 sq mi
Continent: Australia and Oceania

Mauritania
Capital: Nouakchott
Population: 3.4 million
Land Area: 1,030,400 sq km; 397,837 sq mi
Continent: Africa

Mauritius
Capital: Port Louis
Population: 1.3 million
Land Area: 2,030 sq km; 784 sq mi
Continent: Africa

Mexico
Capital: Mexico City
Population: 110 million
Land Area: 1,923,040 sq km; 742,486 sq mi
Continent: North America

Micronesia, Federated States of
Capital: Palikir (Pohnpei Island)
Population: 107,665
Land Area: 702 sq km; 271 sq mi
Continent: Australia and Oceania

Moldova
Capital: Chisinau
Population: 4.3 million
Land Area: 33,371 sq km; 12,885 sq mi
Continent: Europe

Monaco
Capital: Monaco
Population: 32,796
Land Area: 1.95 sq km; 0.75 sq mi
Continent: Europe

Mongolia
Capital: Ulaanbaatar
Population: 3.0 million
Land Area: 1,554,731 sq km; 600,283 sq mi
Continent: Asia

Montenegro
Capital: Podgorica
Population: 678,177
Land Area: 13,812 sq km; 5,333 sq mi
Continent: Europe

Morocco
Capital: Rabat
Population: 34.3 million
Land Area: 446,300 sq km; 172,316 sq mi
Continent: Africa

Mozambique
Capital: Maputo
Population: 21.3 million
Land Area: 784,090 sq km; 302,737 sq mi
Continent: Africa

Myanmar (Burma)
Capital: Yangon (Rangoon)
Population: 47.8 million
Land Area: 657,740 sq km; 253,953 sq mi
Continent: Asia

Namibia
Capital: Windhoek
Population: 2.1 million
Land Area: 825,418 sq km; 318,694 sq mi
Continent: Africa

Nauru
Capital: Yaren District
Population: 13,770
Land Area: 21 sq km; 8 sq mi
Continent: Australia and Oceania

Nepal
Capital: Kathmandu
Population: 29.5 million
Land Area: 143,181 sq km; 55,282 sq mi
Continent: Asia

Netherlands
Capital: Amsterdam
Population: 16.7 million
Land Area: 33,883 sq km; 13,082 sq mi
Continent: Europe

New Zealand
Capital: Wellington
Population: 4.2 million
Land Area: 268,021 sq km; 103,483 sq mi
Continent: Australia and Oceania

Nicaragua
Capital: Managua
Population: 5.8 million
Land Area: 120,254 sq km; 46,430 sq mi
Continent: North America

Niger
Capital: Niamey
Population: 13.3 million
Land Area: 1,226,700 sq km; 489,073 sq mi
Continent: Africa

Nigeria
Capital: Abuja
Population: 146.3 million
Land Area: 910,768 sq km; 351,648 sq mi
Continent: Africa

Norway
Capital: Oslo
Population: 4.6 million
Land Area: 307,442 sq km; 118,704 sq mi
Continent: Europe

Oman
Capital: Muscat
Population: 3.3 million
Land Area: 212,460 sq km; 82,030 sq mi
Continent: Asia

Pakistan
Capital: Islamabad
Population: 172.8 million
Land Area: 778,720 sq km; 300,664 sq mi
Continent: Asia

Palau
Capital: Koror
Population: 21,093
Land Area: 458 sq km; 177 sq mi
Continent: Australia and Oceania

Panama
Capital: Panama City
Population: 3.3 million
Land Area: 75,990 sq km; 29,340 sq mi
Continent: North America

Papua New Guinea
Capital: Port Moresby
Population: 5.9 million
Land Area: 452,860 sq km; 174,849 sq mi
Continent: Australia and Oceania

Paraguay
Capital: Asunción
Population: 6.8 million
Land Area: 397,300 sq km; 153,398 sq mi
Continent: South America

Peru
Capital: Lima
Population: 29.2 million
Land Area: 1,280,000 sq km; 494,208 sq mi
Continent: South America

Philippines
Capital: Manila
Population: 96.1 million
Land Area: 298,170 sq km; 115,123 sq mi
Continent: Asia

Poland
Capital: Warsaw
Population: 38.5 million
Land Area: 304,459 sq km; 117,552 sq mi
Continent: Europe

Portugal
Capital: Lisbon
Population: 10.7 million
Land Area: 91,951 sq km; 35,502 sq mi
Continent: Europe

Qatar
Capital: Doha
Population: 824,789
Land Area: 11,437 sq km; 4,416 sq mi
Continent: Asia

Romania
Capital: Bucharest
Population: 22.3 million
Land Area: 230,340 sq km; 88,934 sq mi
Continent: Europe

Russia
Capital: Moscow
Population: 140.7 million
Land Area: 16,995,800 sq km; 6,592,100 sq mi
Continent: Europe and Asia

Rwanda
Capital: Kigali
Population: 10.2 million
Land Area: 24,948 sq km; 9,632 sq mi
Continent: Africa

Saint Kitts and Nevis
Capital: Basseterre
Population: 39,817
Land Area: 261 sq km; 101 sq mi
Continent: North America

Saint Lucia
Capital: Castries
Population: 159,585
Land Area: 606 sq km; 234 sq mi
Continent: North America

Saint Vincent and the Grenadines
Capital: Kingstown
Population: 118,432
Land Area: 389 sq km; 150 sq mi
Continent: North America

Samoa
Capital: Apia
Population: 217,083
Land Area: 2,934 sq km; 1,133 sq mi
Continent: Australia and Oceania

San Marino
Capital: San Marino
Population: 29,973
Land Area: 61 sq km; 24 sq mi
Continent: Europe

São Tomé and Príncipe
Capital: São Tomé
Population: 206,178
Land Area: 1,001 sq km; 386 sq mi
Continent: Africa

Saudi Arabia
Capital: Riyadh and Jiddah
Population: 28.2 million
Land Area: 2,149,690 sq km; 829,997 sq mi
Continent: Asia

Senegal
Capital: Dakar
Population: 12.9 million
Land Area: 192,000 sq km; 74,131 sq mi
Continent: Africa

Serbia
Capital: Belgrade
Population: 10.2 million
Land Area: 77,474 sq km; 29,913 sq mi
Continent: Europe

Seychelles
Capital: Victoria
Population: 82,247
Land Area: 455 sq km; 176 sq mi
Continent: Africa

Sierra Leone
Capital: Freetown
Population: 6.3 million
Land Area: 71,620 sq km; 27,652 sq mi
Continent: Africa

Singapore
Capital: Singapore
Population: 4.6 million
Land Area: 683 sq km; 264 sq mi
Continent: Asia

Slovakia
Capital: Bratislava
Population: 5.5 million
Land Area: 48,800 sq km; 18,842 sq mi
Continent: Europe

Country Databank (continued)

Slovenia
Capital: Ljubljana
Population: 2 million
Land Area: 20,151 sq km; 7,780 sq mi
Continent: Europe

Solomon Islands
Capital: Honiara
Population: 581,318
Land Area: 27,540 sq km; 10,633 sq mi
Continent: Australia and Oceania

Somalia
Capital: Mogadishu
Population: 9.6 million
Land Area: 627,337 sq km; 242,215 sq mi
Continent: Africa

South Africa
Capitals: Cape Town, Pretoria, and Bloemfontein
Population: 48.8 million
Land Area: 1,219,912 sq km; 471,008 sq mi
Continent: Africa

Spain
Capital: Madrid
Population: 40.5 million
Land Area: 499,542 sq km; 192,873 sq mi
Continent: Europe

Sri Lanka
Capital: Colombo
Population: 21.1 million
Land Area: 64,740 sq km; 24,996 sq mi
Continent: Asia

Sudan
Capital: Khartoum
Population: 40.2 million
Land Area: 2,376,000 sq km; 917,374 sq mi
Continent: Africa

Suriname
Capital: Paramaribo
Population: 475,996
Land Area: 161,470 sq km; 62,344 sq mi
Continent: South America

Swaziland
Capital: Mbabane
Population: 1.1 million
Land Area: 17,203 sq km; 6,642 sq mi
Continent: Africa

Sweden
Capital: Stockholm
Population: 9 million
Land Area: 410,934 sq km; 158,662 sq mi
Continent: Europe

Switzerland
Capital: Bern
Population: 7.6 million
Land Area: 39,770 sq km; 15,355 sq mi
Continent: Europe

Syria
Capital: Damascus
Population: 19.8 million
Land Area: 184,050 sq km; 71,062 sq mi
Continent: Asia

Taiwan
Capital: Taipei
Population: 22.9 million
Land Area: 32,260 sq km; 12,456 sq mi
Continent: Asia

Tajikistan
Capital: Dushanbe
Population: 7.2 million
Land Area: 142,700 sq km; 55,096 sq mi
Continent: Asia

Tanzania
Capitals: Dar es Salaam and Dodoma
Population: 40.2 million
Land Area: 886,037 sq km; 342,099
Continent: Africa

Thailand
Capital: Bangkok
Population: 65.5 million
Land Area: 511,770 sq km; 197,564 sq mi
Continent: Asia

Timor-Leste
Capital: Dili
Population: 1.1 million
Land Area: 15,007 sq km; 5,794 sq mi
Continent: Asia

Togo
Capital: Lomé
Population: 5.9 million
Land Area: 54,385 sq km; 20,998 sq mi
Continent: Africa

Tonga
Capital: Nuku'alofa
Population: 119,009
Land Area: 718 sq km; 277 sq mi
Continent: Australia and Oceania

Trinidad and Tobago
Capital: Port-of-Spain
Population: 1.2 million
Land Area: 5,128 sq km; 1,980 sq mi
Continent: North America

Tunisia
Capital: Tunis
Population: 10.4 million
Land Area: 155,360 sq km; 59,984 sq mi
Continent: Africa

Turkey
Capital: Ankara
Population: 71.9 million
Land Area: 770,760 sq km; 297,590 sq mi
Continent: Asia

Turkmenistan
Capital: Ashgabat
Population: 5.2 million
Land Area: 488,100 sq km; 188,455 sq mi
Continent: Asia

Tuvalu
Capital: Funafuti
Population: 12,177
Land Area: 26 sq km; 10 sq mi
Continent: Australia and Oceania

Uganda
Capital: Kampala
Population: 31.4 million
Land Area: 199,710 sq km; 77,108 sq mi
Continent: Africa

Ukraine
Capital: Kyiv (Kiev)
Population: 46 million
Land Area: 603,700 sq km; 233,090 sq mi
Continent: Europe

United Arab Emirates

Capital: Abu Dhabi
Population: 4.6 million
Land Area: 83,600 sq km; 32,278 sq mi
Continent: Asia

United Kingdom
Capital: London
Population: 60.9 million
Land Area: 241,590 sq km; 93,278 sq mi
Continent: Europe

United States
Capital: Washington, D.C.
Population: 303.8 million
Land Area: 9,161,923 sq km;
        3,537,424 sq mi
Continent: North America

Uruguay
Capital: Montevideo
Population: 3.5 million
Land Area: 173,620 sq km; 67,100 sq mi
Continent: South America

Uzbekistan
Capital: Tashkent
Population: 27.3 million
Land Area: 425,400 sq km; 164,247 sq mi
Continent: Asia

Vanuatu
Capital: Port-Vila
Population: 215,446
Land Area: 12,200 sq km; 4,710 sq mi
Continent: Australia and Oceania

Venezuela
Capital: Caracas
Population: 26.4 million
Land Area: 882,050 sq km; 340,560 sq mi
Continent: South America

Vietnam
Capital: Hanoi
Population: 86.1 million
Land Area: 325,360 sq km; 125,622 sq mi
Continent: Asia

Yemen
Capital: Sanaa
Population: 23 million
Land Area: 527,970 sq km; 203,849 sq mi
Continent: Asia

Zambia
Capital: Lusaka
Population: 11.7 million
Land Area: 740,724 sq km; 285,994 sq mi
Continent: Africa

Zimbabwe
Capital: Harare
Population: 11.4 million
Land Area: 386,670 sq km; 149,293 sq mi
Continent: Africa

SOURCE: *CIA World Factbook Online, 2009*

Landforms and Water Features

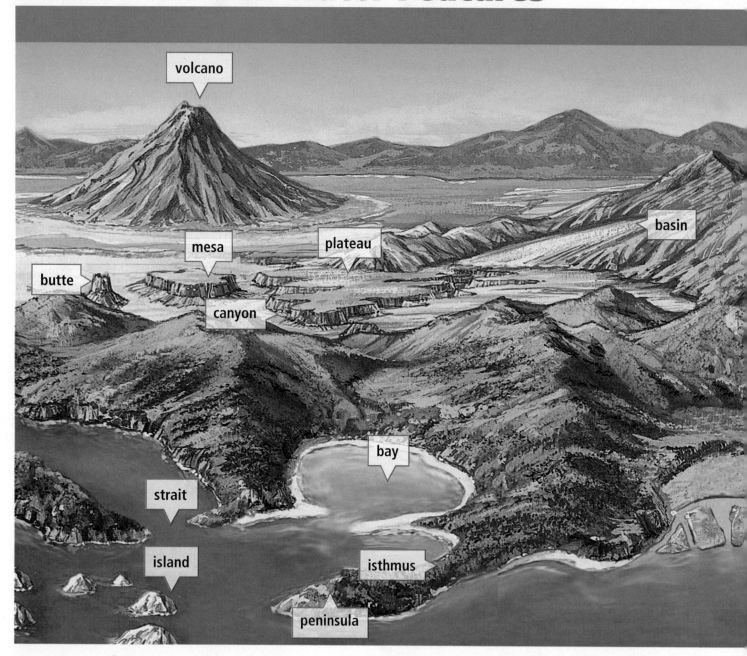

volcano

mesa · plateau · basin

butte

canyon

bay

strait

island · isthmus

peninsula

basin an area that is lower than surrounding land areas; some basins are filled with water

bay a part of a larger body of water that extends into the land

butte a small, high, flat-topped landform with cliff-like sides

canyon a deep, narrow valley with steep sides; often has a stream flowing through it

cataract a large waterfall or steep rapids

delta a plain at the mouth of a river, often triangular in shape, formed when material is deposited by flowing water

flood plain a broad plain on either side of a river, formed when sediment settles during floods

glacier a huge, slow-moving mass of snow and ice

hill an area that rises above surrounding land and has a rounded top; lower and usually less steep than a mountain

island an area of land completely surrounded by water

isthmus a narrow strip of land that connects two larger areas of land

mesa a high, flat-topped landform with cliff-like sides; larger than a butte

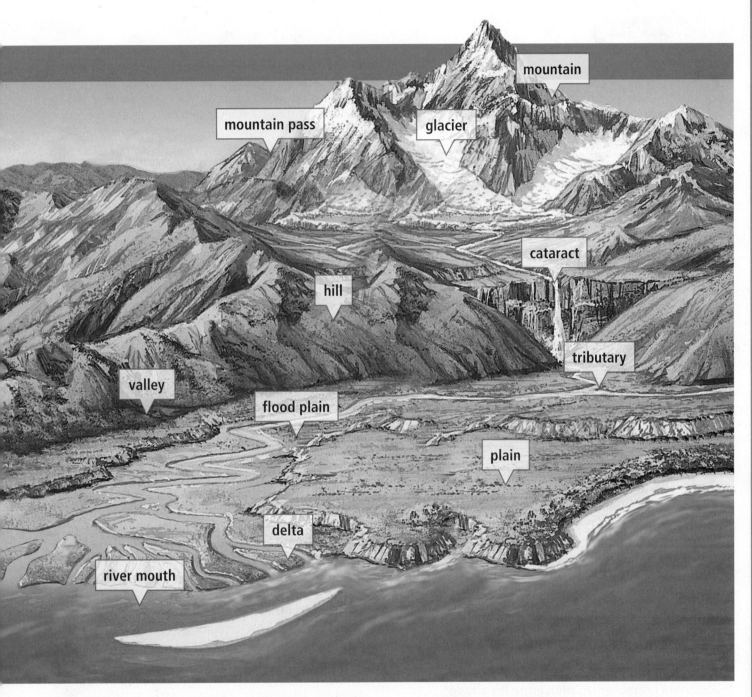

mountain

mountain pass

glacier

cataract

hill

tributary

valley

flood plain

plain

delta

river mouth

mountain a landform that rises steeply at least 2,000 feet (610 meters) above surrounding land; usually wide at the bottom and rising to a narrow peak or ridge

mountain pass a gap between mountains

peninsula an area of land almost completely surrounded by water and connected to the mainland by an isthmus

plain a large area of flat or gently rolling land

plateau a large, flat area that rises above the surrounding land; at least one side has a steep slope

river mouth the point where a river enters a lake or sea

strait a narrow stretch of water that connects two larger bodies of water

tributary a river or stream that flows into a larger river

valley a low stretch of land between mountains or hills; land that is drained by a river

volcano an opening in Earth's surface through which molten rock, ash, and gases from Earth's interior escape

Glossary

A

abolish to put an end to (p. 387)
  abolir anular, derogar

Aborigines the original inhabitants of Australia (p. 736)
  aborígenes habitantes indígenas de Australia

absolute location exact position on Earth in terms of longitude and latitude (p. 6)
  ubicación absoluta posición exacta en la Tierra según la longitud y la latitud

absolute monarchy system of government in which the monarch has unlimited power over the government (p. 461)
  monarquía absoluta sistema de gobierno en el que el poder del monarca es ilimitado

absolutism centralized and unlimited government power (p. 192)
  absolutismo poder ilimitado y centralizado del gobierno

acid rain rain, snow, or mist that is acidic (p. 267)
  lluvia ácida lluvia, nieve o neblina con ácidos disueltos

aerial photograph photographic image of Earth's surface taken from the air (p. 8)
  fotografía aérea imagen fotográfica de la superficie de la Tierra que se tomó desde el aire

African National Congress South African organization that worked for black civil rights (p. 377)
  Congreso Nacional Africano organización sudafricana que laboró por los derechos civiles de los negros

African Union organization formed in 2002 to promote unity among African states and to foster development and end poverty (p. 354)
  Unión Africana organización que se formó en 2002 para promover la unión entre los estado africanos, fomentar el desarrollo y acabar con la pobreza

agriculture the raising of plants and animals (p. 478)
  agricultura cultivo de plantas y crianza de animales

AIDS often-deadly disease that attacks the immune system and is caused by the HIV virus (p. 384)
  SIDA enfermedad causada por el virus VIH, y generalmente de carácter mortal, que ataca el sistema inmunológico

akyn traditional storyteller in Kyrgyzstan (p. 563)
  akyn narrador de relatos épicos de Kirguistán

Alawite a person who follows a form of Islam similar to Shia Islam (p. 477)
  alauí persona que sigue una rama del islam semejante al islam chiita

altitude height above sea level (p. 35)
  altitud altura sobre el nivel del mar

Antarctic Treaty agreement signed by twelve countries in 1959 that preserves Antarctica for peaceful and scientific use (p. 755)
  Tratado Antártico acuerdo firmado en 1959 entre doce países, que designa a la Antártida como un territorio de uso pacífico y científico

anthropology study of humankind in all aspects, especially development and culture (p. 123)
  antropología estudio de todos los aspectos de la humanidad, especialmente el desarrollo y la cultura

anti-Semitism discrimination against Jews (p. 484)
  antisemitismo discriminación hacia los judíos

apartheid official South African government policy of keeping white and black South Africans apart (p. 376)
  apartheid política oficial del gobierno sudafricano que separa a los sudafricanos blancos y negros

aqueduct channel that moves water over a long distance (p. 151)
  acueducto canal que transporta agua por largas distancias

aquifer an underground layer where water collects (p. 474)
  acuífero capa subterránea donde se acumula el agua

arable land land that can be used for farming (pp. 336, 626)
  tierra fértil terreno que se puede usar para cultivos

archaeology scientific study of ancient cultures through the examination of artifacts and other evidence (p. 123)
arqueología estudio científico de las culturas antiguas a través del análisis de artefactos y otros tipos de evidencia

archipelago group of islands (p. 691)
archipiélago grupo de islas

architect person who designs buildings (p. 94)
arquitecto persona que diseña edificios

architecture the design and construction of buildings (p. 94)
arquitectura diseño y construcción de edificios

arid climate very dry desert climate (p. 41)
clima árido clima desértico muy seco

Armenian genocide the killing of Armenians in the Ottoman empire in 1915–1918 (p. 518)
genocidio armenio exterminio de armenios que se llevó a cabo desde 1915 hasta 1918 durante el Imperio Otomano

artifact object made by a human being (p. 120)
artefacto objeto hecho por un ser humano

ASEAN Association of Southeast Asian Nations, an organization working to promote growth and social progress in Southeast Asia (p. 709)
Asociación de Naciones del Sureste Asiático (ASEAN, por sus siglas en inglés) organización que promueve el crecimiento y progreso social en el sudeste asiático

assimilation process by which one group takes on the cultural traits of another (p. 738)
asimilación proceso en el que un grupo adquiere los rasgos culturales de otro grupo

Ataturk name taken by Mustafa Kemal, the founder of modern Turkey, meaning "Father of the Turks" (p. 518)
Ataturk nombre adoptado por Mustafá Kemal, el fundador de la Turquía moderna, que significa "padre de los turcos"

Atlantic slave trade process by which Europeans brought enslaved Africans to the Americas (p. 342)
comercio de esclavos del Atlántico proceso mediante el cual los europeos trajeron esclavos africanos a las Américas

atmosphere thick layer of gases or air (p. 23)
atmósfera capa gruesa de gases o aire

atoll a ring-shaped coral island enclosing a body of water (p. 730)
atolón isla de coral en forma de anillo que rodea una masa de agua

authoritarian government in which all power is held by a single person or a small group (p. 107)
autoritario gobierno en el que todo el poder yace en un individuo o grupo pequeño

autocracy a government controlled by one person who has not won a free election (p. 491)
autocracia tipo de gobierno bajo el control de una persona que no participó en elecciones libres

autonomy self-rule (p. 532)
autonomía gobernarse a sí mismo

axis imaginary line running through Earth between the North and South Poles (p. 18)
eje línea imaginaria que atraviesa la Tierra y que corre entre los polos Norte y Sur

ayatollah title for high-ranking Shia Muslim leaders in Iran (p. 519)
ayatolá título otorgado a los líderes de alta postura dentro del clero chiita musulman en Irán

B

Baath Party Iraqi political party formed after Iraq won independence from Britain (p. 462)
Partido Socialista Árabe Baath partido político iraquí que se formó tras obtener la independencia de la Gran Bretaña

Benin city in present-day southwestern Nigeria that was a powerful empire from around 1300 to the 1800s (p. 349)
Benín ciudad de la actual Nigeria sudoccidental que albergó un poderoso imperio entre los siglos XIV y XIX

Berbers indigenous people of western North Africa (p. 407)
bereberes grupo indígena que habita el oeste de África del Norte

Glossary (continued)

Berlin Wall a wall built by the East German government in 1961 to divide East and West Berlin; this wall came to symbolize Cold War divisions (p. 209)
Muro de Berlín muralla construida por el gobierno de la antigua República Democrática Alemana (RDA) en 1961 para dividir las partes este y oeste de Berlín; se convirtió en un símbolo de la divisiva Guerra Fría

bias unfair preference for or dislike of something (p. 121)
prejuicio preferencia injusta o disgusto por algo

biodiversity variety of living things in a region or ecosystem (p. 52)
biodiversidad variedad de clases diferentes de seres vivos de una región o ecosistema

biofuel fuel from organic material (p. 233)
biocombustible combustible proveniente de material orgánico

birth rate number of live births per 1,000 people in a year (p. 74)
tasa de natalidad número de nacimientos por cada mil habitantes durante un año

Boers Dutch, French, and other European farmers in colonial South Africa (p. 374)
bóer granjeros europeos de origen holandés y francés, entre otros, que habitaban la Sudáfrica colonial

Bollywood Indian film industry (p. 597)
Bollywood industria del cine indio

Bolsheviks Russian political group that called for worker control (p. 302)
bolcheviques grupo político ruso que defiende el control por parte del proletariado

bond certificate issued by a company or government promising to pay back borrowed money with interest (p. 69)
bono certificado emitido por una compañía o un gobierno que promete pagar el dinero prestado con intereses

Book of the Dead ancient Egyptian collection of prayers and other writings meant to help the dead find their way during the afterlife (p. 413)
Libro de los Muertos colección de plegarias y otros escritos del antiguo Egipto que sirve de guía para la vida después de la muerte

brain drain situation when large numbers of educated people migrate out of a country (p. 524)
fuga de cerebros situación en la que un gran número de personas con alta capacitación emigran de un país

Buddhism religion that developed out of the teachings of Siddhartha Gautama, the Buddha (p. 588)
budismo religión que se desarrolló a partir de las enseñanzas de Siddhartha Gautama, el Buda

budget plan that shows income and expenses over a period of time (p. 68)
presupuesto plan que muestra los ingresos y los costos para un período de tiempo

bureaucracy set of hired government officials (p. 461)
burocracia grupo de funcionarios gubernamentales

C

caliph Muslims' political and religious leader (p. 447)
califa líder religioso y político musulman

calligraphy artistic lettering (p. 489)
caligrafía dibujar letras artísticamente con precisión y belleza

capital money or goods that are used to make products (pp. 275, 492)
capital dinero o bienes que se usan para crear productos

caravan group of people traveling together (p. 556)
caravana grupo de personas que viajan juntas

caravel a small, light ship developed by the Portuguese that performed well on long voyages (p. 188)
carabela nave pequeña y ligera diseñada por los portugueses, especialmente efectiva en viajes largos

cardinal directions north, east, south, and west (p. 4)
puntos cardinales norte, sur, este y oeste

cartography the science of making maps and globes (p. 188)
cartografía técnica de trazar mapas y globos terráqueos

788

caste system system that divides society into groups (p. 587)
sistema de castas sistema que divide a la sociedad en grupos

Catholic Reformation changes made by the Catholic Church to keep Catholicism strong; response to the Reformation (p. 184)
Reforma Católica (o Contrarreforma) cambios que la Iglesia Católica hizo para fortalecer al catolicismo; fue una respuesta a la Reforma Protestante

censor to suppress or delete anything considered objectionable (p. 311)
censurar ocultar o borrar cualquier cosa que se considere ofensiva

chronology list of events arranged in the order in which they occurred (p. 118)
cronología lista de sucesos organizados en el orden en que ocurrieron

citizen legal member of a country (p. 112)
ciudadano miembro legal de un país

city-state independent state consisting of a city and its surrounding territory (pp. 106, 139)
ciudad estado estado independiente que consiste en una ciudad y el territorio aledaño

civic life activities having to do with one's society and community (p. 113)
vida cívica actividades relacionadas con nuestra sociedad o comunidad

civic participation taking part in government (p. 113)
participación cívica tomar parte en asuntos del gobierno

civilization culture with a written language in which people have many different kinds of jobs (p. 444)
civilización cultura que lleva un lenguaje escrito y en la que las personas desempeñan muchos trabajos diferentes

cleric religious leader (p. 522)
clérigo líder religioso

climate average weather of a place over many years (p. 32)
clima tiempo promedio de un lugar a lo largo de muchos años

climate change long-term significant change to a region's average weather (p. 747)
cambio climático cambio significativo y de largo plazo en el tiempo promedio de una región

Cold War post-World War II period of hostility between the United States and its allies on one side and the Soviet Union and its allies on the other side (p. 208)
Guerra Fría período de hostilidad entre los Estados Unidos y la Unión Soviética, más aliados los de ambos, posterior a la Segunda Guerra Mundial

collectivization control shift to a group, or collective, from an individual or single entity (p. 302)
colectivismo social cambio del control a un grupo o colectivo de un individuo o entiedad individual

colonialism policy by which one country seeks to rule other areas (p. 342)
colonialismo política por medio de la cual un país intenta gobernar otras áreas

colonization movement of new settlers and their culture to an area (p. 51)
colonización mudanza de pobladores nuevos y la cultura de éstos a un área

command economy economy in which the central government makes all basic economic decisions (pp. 63, 314, 634)
economía dirigida sistema económico en el que el gobierno central toman todas las decisiones básicas

communism political and economic system in which government owns all property and makes all economic decisions (pp. 107, 203)
comunismo sistema político y económico en el que el Estado posee toda propriedad y toma todas las decisiones económicas

comparative advantage ability of one person or country to produce a good at a lower cost than another (p. 661)
ventaja comparativa capacidad de una persona o país para producir un bien a un costo menor que otra persona o país

compass rose diagram of a compass showing direction (p. 10)
rosa de los vientos diagrama de una brújula que indica la dirección

competition struggle among producers for consumers' money (p. 60)
competencia rivalidad entre los productores por el dinero del consumidor

Glossary (continued)

Confucianism a belief system based on the ideas of the Chinese thinker Confucius (p. 632)
confucianismo sistema de creencias basadas en la ideología del filósofo chino Confucio

coniferous tree tree that produces cones to carry seeds (p. 42)
árbol conífero árbol que produce frutos en forma de conos que contienen las semillas

consensus agreement (p. 460)
consenso acuerdo

constitution system of basic rules and principles by which a government is organized (p. 105)
constitución sistema de reglas y principios básicos que establece la organización de un gobierno

constitutional monarchy system of government in which the laws in the constitution limit the monarch's or emperor's powers (pp. 236, 461, 668)
monarquía constitucional sistema de gobierno en el que las leyes de la constitución limitan los poderes del monarca o emperador

consumer person or business that buys, or consumes, products (p. 59)
consumidor persona o negocio que compra o consume productos

copra dried coconut meat (p. 748)
copra pulpa de coco seca

Copts minority group in Egypt that practices Christianity (p. 415)
coptos grupo minoritario en Egipto que practica el cristianismo

coral reef a formation of rock-like material made up of the skeletons of tiny marine creatures (p. 729)
arrecifes de coral conjunto de material rocoso compuesto de restos de criaturas marinas pequeñas

core sphere of very hot metal at the center of Earth (p. 22)
núcleo esfera de metal muy caliente en el centro de la Tierra

corruption use of power for personal gain (p. 351)
corrupción uso del poder para beneficio personal

coup sudden violent overthrow of a government, often by the military (pp. 526, 744)
golpe de estado derrocamiento repentino y violento de un gobierno, generalmente por parte de las fuerzas armadas

cradle-to-grave system system of basic services provided to citizens at every stage of life by Scandinavian governments (p. 239)
sistema "desde la cuna hasta la tumba" sistema de servicios básicos que les ofrecen los gobiernos escandinavos de por vida a sus ciudadanos

credit arrangement in which a buyer can purchase something and pay for it over time (p. 69)
crédito arreglo que permite al consumidor comprar algo y pagarlo durante un plazo de tiempo

Crusades religious wars in which Christian soldiers from Europe aimed to stop the spread of Islam and to retake control of Palestine, also called the Holy Land (pp. 164, 483)
Cruzadas guerras de índole religiosa en las que los soldados cristianos de Europa buscaban frenar la difusión del islam y retomar el control de Palestina, también conocida como la Tierra Santa

crust thin layer of rocks and minerals that surrounds Earth's mantle (p. 22)
corteza capa fina de rocas y minerales que rodea el manto de la Tierra

cuisine style of food (p. 277)
cocina estilo de comida

cultural borrowing absorbing ideas or customs from other cultures (p. 241)
préstamo cultural absorción de ideas y costumbres de otras culturas

cultural diffusion spread of cultural traits from one culture to another (pp. 96, 251)
difusión cultural diseminación de los rasgos culturales de una cultura a otra

cultural hearth place where cultural traits begin and from which they spread to surrounding cultures and regions (pp. 96, 140, 586)
corazón cultural lugar donde nacen los rasgos culturales y desde donde se difunden hacia las culturas y regiones aledañas

cultural landscape geographic area that has been shaped by people (p. 86)
paisaje cultural área geográfica moldeada por la gente

Cultural Revolution violent attempt at cultural change in China begun by Mao Zedong in the 1960s (p. 647)
revolución cultural proletaria violento intento de transformación cultural ordenado por Mao Zedong en China durante la década de 1960

cultural trait idea or way of doing things that is common in a certain culture (p. 86)
rasgo cultural idea o manera de hacer las cosas que es común en una cultura determinada

culture beliefs, customs, practices, and behavior of a particular nation or group of people (p. 86)
cultura creencias, costumbres, prácticas y comportamientos de una nación o un grupo de personas determinado

culture region area in which a single culture or cultural trait is dominant (p. 86)
región cultural área en la que predomina una sola cultura o rasgo cultural

D

Daoism a philosophy of following the Dao, that is, the natural way of the universe (p. 632)
taoísmo filosofía que sigue el Tao, es decir, el orden natural del universo

death rate number of deaths per 1,000 people in a year (p. 74)
tasa de mortalidad número de muertes por cada mil habitantes durante un año

deciduous tree tree that loses its leaves in the fall (p. 42)
árbol de hoja caduca árbol que pierde sus hojas en el otoño

deforestation the loss of forest cover in a region that results from the trees in a forest being destroyed faster than they can grow back (pp. 52, 337)
deforestación destrucción acelerada de los árboles de un bosque que impide su regeneración y resulta en la pérdida de una región boscosa

degree unit that measures angles (p. 4)
grado unidad que se utiliza para medir ángulos

delta a flat plain formed on the seabed where a river deposits material over many years (pp. 25, 397)
delta llanura plana que se forma en el lecho marino donde un rio deposita sedimento a través de los años

demand desire for a particular good or service (p. 59)
demanda interés en un bien o servicio determinado

democracy form of government in which citizens hold political power (p. 106)
democracia tipo de gobierno en el que los ciudadanos tienen el poder político

demographer scientist who studies human populations (p. 74)
demógrafo científico que estudia las poblaciones humanas

demonstration a public display of group opinion, often a rally or march (p. 566)
manifestación demostración pública de la opinión de un grupo, generalmente un mitin o una marcha

deportation being sent back to one's home country (p. 255)
deportación acción que consiste en devolver a alguien a su país de origen

deposition process of depositing material eroded and carried by water, ice, or wind (p. 25)
depósito proceso de depositar material que ha sido erosionado y transportado por el agua, hielo o viento

desalination removal of salt from seawater (p. 440)
desalinización proceso de quitar la sal del agua del mar

desertification the change when arable land dries out and becomes desert (p. 337)
desertización transformación de la tierra fértil al secarse y convertirse en desierto

developed country country with a strong economy and a high quality of life (p. 64)
país desarrollado país con una economía fuerte y un alto nivel de vida

developing country country with a less-productive economy and a lower quality of life (p. 64)
país en vías de desarrollo país con una economía menos productiva y un nivel de vida más bajo

development country's economic growth and quality of life (p. 64)
desarrollo el crecimiento económico y la calidad de vida de un país

dictator leader with complete control over government (pp. 450, 674)
dictador líder con control total del gobierno

diplomacy managing communication and relationships between countries (p. 111)
diplomacia manejo de las comunicaciones y relaciones entre países

791

Glossary (continued)

direct democracy government in which citizens take part directly in the day-to-day affairs of government (p. 141)
democracia directa tipo de gobierno en el que los ciudadanos participan directamente en los asuntos diarios del gobierno

disposable income money left after taxes are paid (p. 309)
ingreso disponible dinero restante después de pagar los impuestos

distortion loss of accuracy (p. 9)
distorsión pérdida de exactitud

diversify to add variety (p. 253)
diversificar agregar variedad

diversity cultural variety (p. 97)
diversidad variedad cultural

drought long period of extremely dry weather (p. 747)
sequía largo período de tiempo extremadamente seco

Druze a person who follows a religion related to Islam (p. 477)
druso persona que sigue una religión semejante al islam

dynasty a series of rulers from the same family (p. 631)
dinastía serie de reglas pertenecientes a la misma familia

E

economics study of how people meet their wants and needs (p. 58)
economía estudio de cómo la gente satisface sus deseos y necesidades

ecosystem group of plants and animals that depend on each other and their environment for survival (p. 43)
ecosistema grupo de plantas y animales cuya sobrevivencia depende de la relación entre sí y con su medio ambiente

ecotourism tourism that focuses on the environment and seeks to minimize environmental impact (p. 367)
ecoturismo tipo de turismo que se enfoca en el medio ambiente y trata de minimizar el impacto ambiental

election fraud unfair elections in which one group controls the results to gain power (p. 566)
fraude electoral elecciones injustas en las que un grupo controla los resultados para adueñarse del poder

elevation height above sea level (p. 12)
elevación altura sobre el nivel del mar

emigrate to migrate out of a place (pp. 79, 269)
emigrar dejar un lugar

empire state containing several countries or territories (p. 106)
imperio estado que incluye a varios países o territorios

English Bill of Rights an act passed in 1689 that limited the power of the English monarch and increased Parliament's power (p. 196)
Declaración de Derechos inglesa ley aprobada en 1689 que limitaba el poder del monarca inglés y aumentaba el poder del Parlamento

Enlightenment a period during the 1600s and 1700s when scholars studied culture and society by applying reason and natural laws (p. 195)
Ilustración período del siglo XVII al siglo XVIII en que los eruditos estudiaron la cultura y la sociedad a partir de la razón y las leyes naturales

entrepreneur person who organizes and manages his or her own business (pp. 456, 570)
empresario dícese de la persona que organiza y maneja su propia empresa

entrepreneurship starting a business (p. 456)
espíritu empresarial el establecimiento de un negocio

epic long poem of adventure and conflict (p. 597)
poema épico poema largo que trata de aventuras y conflictos

equinox point at which, everywhere on Earth, days and nights are nearly equal in length (p. 18)
equinoccio momento en el que la duración de los días y las noches es casi la misma en todos los rincones de la Tierra

erosion process in which water, ice, or wind remove rock and soil (p. 24)
erosión proceso en el que el agua, hielo o viento desgasta la roca y tierra

ethics beliefs about what is right and wrong (pp. 92, 480)
ética creencias sobre el bien y el mal

ethnic cleansing attempt to create an area with only one ethnic group by removing or attacking other ethnic groups (p. 278)
limpieza étnica intento de crear un área donde sólo habite un grupo étnico por medio del ataque o el traslado de otros grupos étnicos

ethnocentrism attitude that one's own social or cultural group is better than all others (pp. 375, 738)
etnocentrismo tendencia a valorar la cultura o el grupo social propios por encima de otros

European Union economic and political partnership among member nations (p. 211)
Unión Europea asociación económica y política de países miembros

evacuate to move to another area (p. 711)
evacuar desalojar de un lugar

evaporation process in which a liquid changes to a gas (p. 37)
evaporación proceso en el que un líquido se convierte en gas

exploit take advantage of (p. 700)
explotar aprovecharse de algo o alguien

export good or service produced within a country and sold outside the country's borders (p. 67)
exportación bien o servicio que se produce en un país y se vende fuera de los confines del país

extended family family that includes parents, children, and other family members such as grandparents, aunts, uncles, and cousins (p. 88)
familia extensa familia que incluye a los padres, los hijos y otros parientes como los abuelos, los tíos y los primos

F

family two or more people who are closely related by birth, marriage, or adoption (p. 88)
familia dos o más personas que están estrechamente vinculadas por los lazos de sangre, el matrimonio o la adopción

famine a huge food shortage (p. 635)
hambruna gran escasez de comida

fascism a political system that stresses national strength, military might, and the belief that the state is more important than individuals (p. 203)
fascismo sistema político que enfatiza la fuerza nacional, el poderío militar y la creencia de que el estado es más importante que el individuo

fasting limited eating (p. 273)
ayuno alimentación limitada

fault seam in Earth's crust (p. 26)
falla quiebra en la corteza terrestre

federal system system of government in which power is divided among central, regional, and local governments (p. 108)
sistema federal sistema de gobierno en el que el poder se divide entre los gobiernos centrales, regionales y locales

Fertile Crescent a region with good conditions for growing crops that stretches from the Mediterranean coast east through Mesopotamia (modern Iraq) to the Persian Gulf (p. 471)
Creciente Fértil región con buenas condiciones para cultivos que se extiende desde las áreas de la costa del Mediterráneo hacia el este por Mesopotamia (que hoy se conoce como Iraq) hasta el Golfo Pérsico

feudalism in medieval Europe, a system in which land was owned by lords but held by vassals in return for their loyalty (p. 160)
feudalismo sistema que se practicó en Europa durante la Edad Media en el que la tierra era propiedad de los señores nobles, quienes se la concedían a vasallos a cambio de su lealtad

Five-Year Plan one of a series of plans introduced by Josef Stalin that was intended to transform the Soviet Union's economy (p. 314)
Plan Quinquenal uno de una serie de planes para la transformación económica de la Unión Soviética introducido por Josef Stalin

flood plain flat lands along a river (p. 584)
terreno inundable tierras llanas adyacentes a un río

793

Glossary (continued)

foliage leaves on trees (p. 658)
follaje hojas en árboles

foreign policy set of goals outlining how a country plans to interact with other countries (p. 110)
política exterior conjunto de metas que describe cómo un país planea interactuar con otros

fossil preserved remains of ancient human, animal, or plant (p. 372)
fósil restos conservados de personas, animales o plantas de la antigüedad

fossil fuel nonrenewable resource formed over millions of years from the remains of ancient plants and animals (pp. 49, 233, 438)
combustible fósil recurso no renovable formado durante millones de años de los restos antiguos de plantas y animales

free trade removal of trade barriers (p. 67)
libre comercio eliminación de las barreras comerciales

French Revolution a political movement that removed the French king from power and formed a republic (p. 197)
Revolución Francesa movimiento político que derrocó al rey francés y estableció una república

fundamentalism belief that holy books should be taken literally, word for word (p. 455)
fundamentalismo idea que sugiere que las escrituras religiosas deben interpretarse literalmente, al pie de la letra

G

genocide attempt to destroy a whole people (p. 382)
genocidio exterminio de todo un grupo social

geographic information system (GIS) computer-based system that stores and uses information linked to geographic locations (p. 8)
sistema de información geográfica (SIG) sistema computarizado que archiva y usa información relacionada con sitios geográficos

geography study of the human and nonhuman features of Earth (p. 4)
geografía estudio de las características humanas y no humanas de la Tierra

glacier slow-moving body of ice (pp. 225, 752)
glaciar masa de hielo que se desliza lentamente

government group of people who have the power to make and enforce laws for a country or area (p. 104)
gobierno grupo de personas de un país o área que tiene el poder de crear y hacer cumplir las leyes

Great Depression worldwide economic slump during the 1930s (p. 202)
Gran Depresión crisis económica mundial durante la década de 1930

Great Rift Valley long, unusually flat area of land between areas of higher ground in eastern Africa (p. 364)
Gran Valle del Rift franja de terreno larga y plana ubicada entre terrenos elevados en África oriental

Great Trek during the late 1700s, the migration of Boers inland from the Cape Colony to escape British rule (p. 388)
El Gran Trek movimiento migratorio a finales del siglo XVIII que condujo a los bóers tierradentro desde la Colonia del Cabo para escapar del régimen británico

Green Revolution increase in agricultural production created by improved technology (p. 582)
Revolución Verde gran aumento en la producción agrícola debido a avances en la tecnología

griot African musician-storyteller who uses music to track heritage and record history as well as entertain (p. 353)
griot músico y narrador de la tradición oral africana; usa la música para entretener y preservar su historia y cultura

gross domestic product (GDP) total value of all goods and services produced in a country in a year (pp. 64, 240, 416)
producto interno bruto (PIB) valor total de todos los bienes y servicios que produce un país durante un año

gross domestic product per capita a country's GDP divided by the number of people who live in the country (p. 416)
producto interno bruto per cápita PIB de un país dividido por la población del país

gross national product (GNP) annual income of a country's companies and residents (p. 245)
producto nacional bruto (PNB) ingreso anual de las empresas y los residentes de un país

794

guild association of people who have a common interest (p. 168)
gremio asociación de personas que comparten un interés común

gulag Soviet forced-labor camp (p. 314)
gulag antiguo campo de concentración de la Unión Soviética

H

heavy industry the manufacture of steel, equipment, or weapons (p. 314)
industria pesada aquella que requiere procesar grandes cantidades de materias primas, por ejemplo la fabricación del acero, de máquinas o de armas

hemisphere one half of Earth (p. 5)
hemisferio una mitad de la Tierra

hereditary monarch a ruler from a traditional ruling family who is the son, daughter, or younger relative of the last ruler (p. 491)
monarca heredero soberano perteneciente a una familia gobernante tradicional que es hijo, hija o un familiar joven del soberano anterior

hieroglyphics Egyptian system of writing using pictures and other symbols (p. 405)
jeroglíficos sistema de escritura egipcia que utiliza figuras y símbolos

high latitudes areas north of the Arctic Circle and south of the Antarctic Circle; also known as polar zone (p. 34)
latitudes altas áreas al norte del Círculo Polar Ártico y al sur del Círculo Polar Antártico

hijab concealing, baggy garments worn by many Arab women (p. 459)
hiyab prendas de vestir holgadas que muchas mujeres árabes usan para cubrirse

Hinduism religious system of beliefs and practices that emerged in South Asia (p. 587)
hinduismo sistema de creencias y prácticas religiosas que emergieron del sur asiático

historian person who studies the past (p. 118)
historiador persona que estudia el pasado

historical map special-purpose map that provides information about a place at a certain time in history (p. 125)
mapa histórico mapa con el propósito especial de dar información acerca de un lugar en un momento determinado de la historia

Holocaust the mass murder of Jews by the Nazis during World War II (p. 205)
Holocausto exterminio masivo de judíos por el régimen nazi durante la Segunda Guerra Mundial

human development index a measure of living conditions using factors such as life expectancy, education, and income (p. 417)
índice de desarrollo humano medición de las condiciones de vida basada en factores como la expectativa de vida, la educación y el ingreso económico

human–environment interaction how people affect their environment and how their environment affects them (p. 7)
interacción humanos–medio ambiente manera en la que los seres humanos afectan su medio ambiente y viceversa

humanism the study of secular, or nonreligious, subjects such as history (pp. 179, 270)
humanismo estudio de temas laicos, o no religiosos, como la historia

humid subtropical climate climate with year-round precipitation, mild winters, and hot summers (p. 40)
clima subtropical húmedo clima de precipitación continua durante todo el año, inviernos templados y veranos cálidos

hurricane tropical cyclone that forms over the tropical Atlantic Ocean (p. 39)
huracán ciclón tropical que se forma sobre el Océano Atlántico tropical

hydroelectricity electricity power made by water (p. 645)
hidroelectricidad electricidad producida por la fuerza del agua

hydropower power generated by flowing water (p. 234)
energía hidráulica energía que genera la corriente del agua

795

Glossary (continued)

I

Iberian Peninsula Spain and Portugal (p. 250)
Península Ibérica España y Portugal

ice age time of lower temperatures when much of the land was covered with snow and ice (p. 263)
edad de hielo período de temperaturas bajas donde gran parte de la tierra estaba cubierta de nieve y hielo

iceberg large floating mass of ice (p. 753)
iceberg gran masa de hielo flotante

ice sheet large mass of compressed ice (p. 752)
capa de hielo gran masa de hielo compacto

icon image of important Christian figures, such as Jesus Christ, his mother, Mary, or various saints and Biblical events (p. 488)
ícono imagen de una figura cristiana importante como Jesucristo, su madre, la Virgen María, o de un santo o acontecimiento bíblico

illiterate not able to read and write (p. 643)
analfabeta que no sabe leer y escribir

illumination art of decorating books with elaborate designs and sometimes with pictures in gold, silver, and bright colors (p. 487)
iluminación arte de decorar libros con diseños complicados o ilustraciones de oro, plata y colores brillantes

immigrate to migrate into a place (p. 79)
inmigrar llegar a un lugar

imperialism process of creating an empire by taking over other areas (p. 342)
imperialismo creación de un imperio por medio del dominio de otras áreas

import good or service sold within a country that is produced in another country (p. 67)
importación bien o servicio que se vende en un país pero es producido en otro

incentive factor that encourages people to behave in a certain way (p. 59)
incentivo factor que motiva a la gente a actuar de cierta manera

Indian subcontinent land to the south of the Himalayas (p. 578)
subcontinente indio territorio al sur de los Himalayas

indigenous native to a region (pp. 380, 742)
indígena nativo de una región

industrialization growth of machine-powered production and manufacturing (pp. 51, 314)
industrialización aumento de la producción a máquina y la manufactura

Industrial Revolution a time in which new technologies transformed manufacturing and changed society forever (p. 198)
Revolución Industrial período en el que nuevas tecnologías transformaron la industria manufacturera en particular y la sociedad en general

infant mortality rate number of infant deaths per 1,000 births (p. 75)
tasa de mortalidad infantil número de muertes infantiles por cada mil nacimientos

inflation general increase in prices (p. 61)
inflación alza general de los precios

infrastructure body of public works, such as roads, bridges, and hospitals, that a country needs to support a modern economy (p. 350)
infraestructura conjunto de elementos o servicios públicos como carreteras, puentes y hospitales que un país necesita para mantener una economía moderna

innovative characterized by an ability to develop new ideas and products (p. 568)
innovador se caracteriza por la habilidad de desarrollar nuevas ideas y productos

insurgency rebellion (p. 706)
insurgencia rebelión

interdependent dependent on one another (p. 661)
interdependiente que depende uno de otro

interest price paid for borrowing money (p. 69)
interés precio que se paga por el dinero prestado

interest group group that seeks to influence public policy on certain issues (p. 113)
grupo de interés grupo que busca influir en la política pública en relación a cuestiones particulares

intertropical convergence zone belt of rising air near the Equator (p. 38)
zona de convergencia intertropical cinturón de aire ascendente cerca del ecuador

Intifada a Palestinian campaign of violent resistance against Israeli control (p. 495)
Intifada campaña revolucionaria palestina en contra del control israelí

796

investing act of using money in the hopes of making a future profit (p. 69)
invertir usar el dinero con la esperanza de obtener ganancias futuras

irrigate to supply water to (pp. 99, 550)
irrigar aportar agua

Islamism belief that politics and society should follow Islamic teachings (p. 455)
islamismo creencia según la cual la política y la sociedad deben seguir las enseñanzas del islam

Israeli settlements places in the West Bank and Gaza Strip where Israelis have settled (p. 494)
asentamientos israelíes áreas de Cisjordania y la franja de Gaza donde se han establecido los israelíes

J

jihad Arabic word meaning "struggle for reform" (p. 455)
yihad palabra de origen árabe que significa "luchar por la reforma"

judiciary system of courts of law (p. 606)
poder judicial conjunto de tribunales de justicia

K

Kamchatka Peninsula a peninsula in the Russian far east known for its volcanic activity (p. 293)
Península de Kamchatka península del lejano oriente ruso conocida por su estado volcánico

key section of a map that explains the map's symbols and shading (p. 10)
leyenda sección de un mapa que explica el significado de sus símbolos y áreas sombreadas

KGB the Soviet-era secret police (p. 309)
KGB policía secreta de la era soviética

Korean War war between North Korea and South Korea and their allies during the early 1950s (p. 668)
Guerra de Corea guerra entre Corea del Norte y Corea del Sur, más sus aliados, durante los primeros años de la década de 1950

Kremlin a great complex of Russian official buildings, including palaces, state offices, and churches (p. 300)
Kremlin gran recinto de edificios oficiales rusos que incluye palacios, oficinas del Estado e iglesias

Kurdistan traditional homeland of the Kurdish people southwest of the Caspian Sea (p. 530)
Curdistán hogar histórico del pueblo curdo localizado al suroeste del mar Caspio

L

Lake Baikal a huge lake in Siberia that is more than one mile deep and holds about 20 percent of Earth's fresh water (p. 293)
lago Baikal gran lago localizado en Siberia que tiene más de una milla de profundidad y contiene aproximadamente 20 por ciento del agua dulce de la Tierra

landform shapes and types of land (p. 23)
accidente geográfico formas y tipos de terreno

landlocked cut off from direct access to the ocean (p. 548)
sin litoral sin acceso directo al mar

language set of sounds or symbols that make it possible for people to communicate (p. 90); also, the language of a community or nation
lenguaje conjunto de sonidos o símbolos que hace posible la comunicación entre las personas; **idioma**, lengua de una comunidad o una nación

latitude distance north or south of the Equator measured in degrees (p. 4)
latitud distancia en grados que se mide al norte o al sur desde el ecuador

liberate to free (p. 646)
liberar dar libertad a alguien o algo

life expectancy the average number of years a person is expected to live (p. 642)
esperanza de vida número promedio de años que se espera que viva una persona

limited government government structure in which government actions are limited by law (pp. 105, 672)
gobierno limitado estructura gubernamental cuyas acciones están limitadas por la ley

Glossary (continued)

literature written work such as fiction, poetry, or drama (p. 95)
literatura obras escritas como la ficción, la poesía o el drama

locator map section of a map that shows a larger area than the main map (p. 10)
mapa localizador sección de un mapa que amplía un área del mismo

loess a dustlike material that can form soil (pp. 226, 623)
loes material polvoroso que puede formar tierra

longitude distance east or west of the Prime Meridian measured in degrees (p. 5)
longitud distancia en grados que se mide al este o al oeste desde el Primer meridiano

lords in medieval Europe, noblemen who gave land to other noblemen in return for services (p. 160)
señores en la Europa medieval, señores nobles que cedían terrenos a otros señores nobles a cambio de sus servicios

low latitudes area between the Tropic of Cancer and the Tropic of Capricorn; also known as tropics (p. 34)
latitudes bajas área entre el Trópico de Cáncer y el Trópico de Capricornio; también se le llama trópico

M

madrassa school, especially one that teaches the Islamic religion (p. 559)
madraza escuela, especialmente una que enseña la religión islámica

magma stream of soft, nearly molten rock (p. 26)
magma flujo de roca blanda y casi fundida

Magna Carta document that limited the English king's power (p. 169)
Carta Magna documento que limitaba el poder del rey de Inglaterra

Majlis Iranian legislature (p. 522)
Majlis asamblea legislativa de Irán

majority more than half (p. 442)
mayoría más de la mitad

malaria life-threatening disease spread by mosquitoes and caused by parasites (p. 339)
malaria enfermedad grave causada por parásitos y propagada por mosquitos

manorialism in medieval Europe, the economic relationship between a lord and the peasants who worked for him (p. 161)
señorío en la Europa medieval, relación económica entre un señor y sus trabajadores campesinos

mantle thick, rocky layer around Earth's core (p. 22)
manto capa rocosa gruesa alrededor del núcleo de la Tierra

Maori the original inhabitants of New Zealand and the Cook Islands (p. 737)
maorí habitantes nativos de Nueva Zelanda y las islas Cook

maritime having to do with navigation or shipping on the sea (p. 700)
marítimo pertinente a la naútica o la navegación por mar

maritime climate climate that is wet year-round, with mild winters and cool summers (p. 40)
clima marítimo clima que es húmedo todo el año, con inviernos templados y veranos frescos

market organized way for producers and consumers to trade goods and services (p. 60)
mercado intercambio organizado de bienes y servicios entre productores y consumidores

market economy economy in which individual consumers and producers make all economic decisions (p. 62)
economía de mercado economía en la que los consumidores y los productores toman todas las decisiones económicas

Marshall Plan an economic program initiated by the United States to help Europe recover from World War II (p. 208)
Plan Marshall programa económico iniciado por los Estados Unidos para la reconstrucción europea tras la Segunda Guerra Mundial

Mau Mau Kenyan independence movement during the 1950s (p. 376)
Mau Mau movimiento por la independencia de Kenya durante la década de 1950

mechanized farming farming with machines (p. 265)
mecanización agrícola uso de maquinaria en la industria agrícola

Meiji Restoration time period when Japan's Emperor Meiji was returned to power (p. 666)
Restauración Meiji período en el cual el emperador japonés Meiji retomó el poder

798

merchant trader (p. 557)
comerciante negociante

messiah a leader chosen by God who would restore the Jewish nation and help create God's kingdom in the world (p. 481)
mesías líder enviado de Dios que restauraría el pueblo judío y ayudaría a establecer el reino de Dios en la Tierra

microcredit small loan (p. 355)
microcrédito préstamo pequeño

middle latitudes areas between the high and low latitudes; also known as temperate zone (p. 34)
latitudes medias (zona templada) áreas entre las latitudes altas y bajas

middle passage voyage across the Atlantic from Africa to the Americas that formed the middle leg of the triangular trade among Europe, American colonies, and Africa (p. 342)
paso central viaje a través del océano Atlántico desde África hasta las Américas que constituía el trayecto medio del comercio triangular entre Europa, las colonias americanas y África

migration movement of people from one place to another (p. 78)
migración desplazamiento de personas de un lugar a otro

military junta committee of military leaders (p. 706)
junta militar comité de líderes militares

millet self-governing religious community in the Ottoman empire (p. 517)
millet comunidad religiosa del Imperio Otomano de índole autónoma

minority group making up less than half of a population (p. 449)
minoría grupo que constituye menos de la mitad de una población

missionary a person sent to another country by a church to spread its religious beliefs (p. 738)
misionero persona enviada a otro país por una iglesia con el propósito de diseminar sus creencias religiosas

mixed economy economy that combines elements of traditional, market, and command economic systems (p. 63)
economía mixta economía que combina elementos de los sistemas económicos tradicional, de mercado y dirigida

monarchy form of government in which the state is ruled by a monarch (p. 107)
monarquía tipo de gobierno en el que el Estado está regido por un monarca

monotheism the belief in a single God (p. 446)
monoteísmo creencia en un solo Dios

monsoon seasonal winds (p. 692)
monzón vientos estacionales

mosque Islamic house of worship (p. 449)
mezquita lugar de culto islámico

movement how people, goods, and ideas get from one place to another (p. 7)
movimiento manera en la que las personas, los bienes y las ideas van de un lugar a otro

mummy a body that has been preserved so it will not decompose (p. 406)
momia cadáver preservado sin descomponerse

music art form that uses sound, usually produced by instruments or voices (p. 95)
música arte que usa sonidos, normalmente producidos por instrumentos o voces

Muslim Brotherhood an Islamist party that opposes the Egyptian government (p. 418)
Hermandad Musulmana partido islamista que se opone al gobierno egipcio

N

nationalism strong devotion to one's nation (p. 271)
nacionalismo gran devoción de un individuo hacia su nación

nation-state state that is independent of other states (p. 107)
estado-nación Estado que es independiente de otros

natural resource useful material found in the environment (p. 48)
recurso natural material útil que se encuentra en el medio ambiente

nirvana in Hinduism, a state of understanding that releases the soul from the cycle of rebirth (p. 588)
nirvana según el hinduismo, estado de claridad que libera el alma del ciclo de renacimiento

nomad person who moves from place to place without a permanent home (p. 398)
nómada persona que se desplaza de un lugar a otro sin un hogar permanente

Glossary (continued)

nomadic herder a person who raises livestock for a living and has no settled home but moves from place to place (p. 625)
pastor nómada persona cuyo oficio es criar ganado y que se desplaza de un lugar a otro sin un hogar permanente

nonalignment not becoming an ally of either the United States or the Soviet Union during the Cold War (p. 592)
sin alineación no tener alianzas ni con los Estados Unidos ni con la Unión Soviética durante la Guerra Fría

nongovernmental organization (NGO) group that operates with private funding (p. 385)
organización no gubernamental (ONG) grupo que funciona gracias al financiamiento privado

nonrenewable energy energy that cannot be replaced (p. 233)
energía no renovable energía que no se puede reemplazar

nonrenewable resource resource that cannot be replaced in a relatively short period of time (p. 49)
recurso no renovable recurso que no se puede reemplazar en un período de tiempo relativamente corto

norm behavior that is considered normal in a particular society (p. 86)
norma comportamiento que se considera normal en una sociedad determinada

northwest passage hypothetical North American passage between the Atlantic and Pacific Oceans (p. 192)
paso del noroeste ruta marítima hipotética en Norteamérica que conecta los océanos Atlántico y Pacífico

nuclear family family that consists of parents and their children (p. 88)
familia nuclear familia constituida por los padres y sus hijos

nuclear weapon powerful explosive device that can cause widespread destruction (p. 747)
arma nuclear explosivo de alto poder que puede causar gran destrucción

O

oasis place in the desert where water can be found (p. 397)
oasis lugar del desierto donde se halla agua

oligarchy government in which a small group of people rule (p. 139)
oligarquía tipo de gobierno en el que un grupo pequeño de personas tiene el poder

one-child policy China's family planning policy; under this law, many married couples are only allowed to have one child (p. 626)
política de hijo único política de planeación familiar china; esta ley permite a muchas parejas casadas tener sólo un hijo o una hija

oni Yoruba religious leader (p. 348)
ooni líder espiritual de los yoruba

opportunity cost cost of what you have to give up when making a choice (p. 59)
costo de oportunidad costo de lo que se pierde al elegir una opción

oral tradition community's cultural and historical background, passed down in spoken stories and songs (p. 123)
tradición oral trasfondo cultural e histórico de una comunidad, trasmitido por cuentos hablados y canciones

orbit path one object makes as it circles around another (p. 18)
órbita trayectoria que traza un cuerpo al desplazarse alrededor de otro

Outback a sparsely inhabited region of Australia with low plateaus and plains (p. 729)
outback territorio escasamente poblado de Australia que tiene mesetas y llanuras

outsourcing sending tasks to be done by workers outside a company (p. 603)
subcontratación práctica que consiste en enviar trabajo a trabajadores de otra compañía

overgrazing so much grazing that plants are killed (p. 551)
pastoreo excesivo pastoreo a un nivel tan intenso que causa la muerte de las plantas

ozone layer layer of the atmosphere that filters out most of the sun's harmful ultraviolet rays (p. 755)
capa de ozono capa de la atmósfera que bloquea la mayoría de los nocivos rayos ultravioleta del sol

P

Pacific Island Countries Trade Agreement (PICTA) agreement intended to form a free-trade area among member nations (p. 749)
Acuerdo de Comercio de los Países Insulares del Pacífico (PICTA por sus siglas en inglés) acuerdo que fomenta el libre comercio entre los países miembros

Pacific Islands Forum inter-governmental organization that aims to increase cooperation between and represent the interests of Pacific countries (p. 749)
Foro de las Islas del Pacífico organización intergubernamental que busca fomentar la cooperación entre las naciones del Pacífico y representar sus intereses

pack ice seasonal ice that floats on water rather than being attached to land (p. 753)
banquisa hielo flotante que no está conectado a la tierra

Pan-Africanism political and social movement that sought to unite black Africans across the globe (p. 344)
panafricanismo movimiento sociopolítico que promueve la hermandad de los africanos de raza negra alrededor del mundo

Pan-Arabism idea that all Arabic-speaking countries should cooperate and join together (p. 409)
panarabismo ideología que promueve la cooperación y unión de todos los países de habla árabe

Parliament British legislature (p. 237)
Parlamento asamblea legislativa británica

parliamentary democracy a democracy in which parliament chooses the government (p. 490)
democracia parlamentaria democracia en la que el parlamento escoge al gobierno

parliamentary system system of government in which voters elect representatives to the legislature, which then selects the prime minister (p. 680)
sistema parlamentario sistema de gobierno en el que los votantes eligen a los representantes de la asamblea legislativa encargada de elegir al Primer Ministro

partition splitting a country into two states (p. 592)
división separación de un país en dos estados

patricians wealthy aristocrats in ancient Rome (p. 149)
patricios aristócratas adinerados de la antigua Roma

Pax Romana period of stability in the Roman empire under Augustus (p. 151)
Paz Romana período de estabilidad del Imperio Romano bajo el mandato de Augusto

peninsula area of land almost completely surrounded by water but connected to a mainland (pp. 224, 690)
península área de tierra rodeada en su mayoría por agua pero conectada a un territorio más extenso

period length of time singled out because of a specific event or development that happened during that time (p. 118)
período lapso de tiempo resaltado debido a un suceso o desarrollo específico que sucedió durante ese tiempo

permafrost permanently frozen soil (p. 294)
permafrost tierra permanentemente congelada

perspective a technique that allows artists to portray a three-dimensional space on a flat surface (p. 179)
perspectiva técnica que permite al artista crear un espacio tridimensional en una superficie plana

peshmerga Kurdish fighter (p. 531)
peshmerga guerrillero kurdo

pharaoh king of ancient Egypt (p. 405)
faraón rey del antiguo Egipto

philosophy general study of knowledge and the world; Greek for "love of wisdom" (p. 143)
filosofía estudio general sobre el conocimiento y el mundo; en griego significa "amor por la sabiduría"

physical map map that shows physical, or natural, features (p. 12)
mapa físico mapa que muestra las características físicas o naturales

pictogram picture symbol (p. 412)
pictograma signo de las figuras o símbolos

pilgrimage religious journey (p. 271)
peregrinación viaje por motivos religiosos

place mix of human and nonhuman features at a given location (p. 6)
lugar combinación de características humanas y no humanas en un sitio determinado

Glossary (continued)

plain large area of flat or gently rolling land (p. 25)
llanura área extensa de terreno ondulado o llano

plantation large commercial farm (p. 190)
plantación granja grande con fines comerciales

plate block of rock and soil that makes up Earth's crust (pp. 26, 437, 710)
placa bloque de roca y tierra que forma la corteza terrestre

plateau large, mostly flat area that rises above the surrounding land (p. 25)
meseta gran extensión de terreno, generalmente plano, que se eleva sobre la tierra circundante

plate tectonics theory that explains how huge blocks of Earth's crust called "plates" move (pp. 26, 731)
tectónica de placas teoría que explica el movimiento de las placas de la corteza terrestre

plebeian nonpatrician citizen of ancient Rome (p. 149)
plebeyo ciudadano de la antigua Roma que no se consideraba patricio

poaching illegal hunting (p. 367)
furtivismo caza ilegal

polar zone areas north of the Arctic Circle and south of the Antarctic Circle; also known as high latitudes (p. 34)
zona polar áreas al norte del Círculo Polar Ártico y al sur del Círculo Polar Antártico; también se le llama áreas de latitudes altas

polders areas of dry land reclaimed from lake bottoms or the seabed (p. 245)
pólderes áreas de tierra seca ganadas a los lechos laguneros o marinos

political map map that shows political units, such as countries or states (p. 13)
mapa político mapa que muestra las unidades políticas, como países o estados

political party group that supports candidates for public offices (p. 113)
partido político grupo que apoya a los candidatos que postulan a cargos públicos

pollution waste that makes the air, soil, or water less clean (pp. 53, 229)
contaminación desechos que alteran la pureza del aire, el suelo o el agua

polytheist person who believes in more than one god (p. 410)
politeísta persona que adora a más de un dios

population density measure of the number of people per unit of land (p. 77)
densidad de población medida del número de personas por unidad de territorio

population distribution spreading of people over an area of land (p. 76)
distribución de población dispersión de las personas a lo largo de un área geográfica

precipitation water that falls to the ground as rain, snow, sleet, or hail (p. 32)
precipitación agua que cae sobre la tierra en forma de lluvia, nieve, aguanieve o granizo

prehistory time before humans invented writing (p. 119)
prehistoria época anterior a la invención de la escritura

presidential system system of government in which voters directly elect the president (p. 680)
sistema presidencial sistema gubernamental en el que los votantes eligen al presidente

primary industry industry involving the collection of resources from nature, such as fishing (p. 745)
sector primario industria relacionada con la recolección de recursos naturales, como la pesca

primary source information that comes directly from a person who experienced an event (p. 120)
fuente primaria información sobre un suceso que proviene directamente de una persona que experimentó el suceso

privatization individual and private group ownership of businesses (p. 244)
privatización situación en la que individuos o grupos privados son los dueños de las empresas

producer person or business that makes and sells products (p. 59)
productor persona o negocio que fabrica y vende productos

productivity amount of goods and services produced given the amount of resources used (p. 65)
productividad cantidad de bienes y servicios producidos en relación a la cantidad de recursos empleados

profit money a company has left over after subtracting the costs of doing business (p. 60)
ganancias dinero que sobra después que una compañía deduce los costos de operar el negocio

projection way to map Earth on a flat surface (p. 9)
proyección manera de trazar un mapa de la Tierra sobre una superficie plana

propaganda information created or distributed by governments in order to influence public opinion (p. 647)
propaganda información creada o distribuida por un gobierno con el fin de influenciar la opinión pública

prophet a messenger of God (p. 479)
profeta mensajero de Dios

pull factor cause of migration that pulls, or attracts, people to new countries (p. 79)
factor de arrastre causa de la migración que arrastra o atrae a la gente a países nuevos

push factor cause of migration that pushes people to leave their home country (p. 79)
factor de empuje causa de la migración que empuja a la gente a dejar su país de origen

Q

qanat tunnel that provided water to Persian villages by bringing water from an aquifer (p. 510)
qanat túnel que transportaba agua de un acuífero a las aldeas persas

Quran holy book of Islam (p. 446)
Corán libro sagrado del islam

R

rain shadow a dry area that forms behind a highland that captures rainfall and snow (p. 472)
sombra orográfica área árida que se forma detrás de una zona montañosa donde cae lluvia y nieve

recession zero or negative economic growth for six or more months in a row (pp. 61, 540)
recesión cero o crecimiento económico negativo por un período continuo de seis meses o más

Reconquista reconquering of Spain by Christians beginning in the 1000s (p. 166)
Reconquista la conquista cristiana de España que comenzó en el siglo XI

Reformation a religious movement in which calls for reform led to the emergence of non-Catholic, or Protestant, churches (p. 182)
Reforma Protestante movimiento religioso cuya convocación de la reforma de la Iglesia Católica conllevó a la creación de iglesias protestantes o no católicas

region area with at least one unifying physical or human feature such as climate, landforms, population, or history (p. 7)
región área con al menos una característica física o humana que es unificadora, como el clima, los accidentes geográficos, la población o la historia

relative location location of a place relative to another place (p. 6)
ubicación relativa ubicación de un lugar con respecto a otro

religion people's beliefs and practices about the existence, nature, and worship of a god or gods (p. 92)
religión creencias y prácticas de los seres humanos acerca de la existencia, la naturaleza y la adoración de un dios o dioses

Renaissance a time of a renewed interest in art and learning in Europe; "rebirth" (p. 178)
Renacimiento período de renovado interés en el arte y el aprendizaje en Europa; "un nuevo nacimiento"

renewable energy energy sources that can be replaced (p. 232)
energía renovable recursos de energía que se pueden reemplazar

renewable resource a resource that Earth or people can replace (p. 49)
recurso renovable recurso que la Tierra o las personas pueden reemplazar

repressive opposed to freedom (p. 566)
represivo que se opone a la libertad

reservoir storage pool of water (p. 699)
embalse depósito donde se almacena agua

reunification process of becoming unified again (p. 246)
reunificación proceso para volver a unificar

revenue money earned by selling goods and services and through taxes (p. 60)
ingresos dinero recaudado de la venta de bienes y servicios y impuestos

803

Glossary (continued)

revolution circular journey around the sun (p. 18)
revolución vuelta alrededor del Sol

riot noisy, violent public gathering (p. 553)
motín reunión pública de carácter violento y ruidoso

ritual object object used in religious practices (p. 487)
objeto ritual objeto usado en las prácticas religiosas

Rose Revolution peaceful protests against the results of the 2003 Georgia election (p. 566)
Revolución de las Rosas protestas pacíficas contra el resultado de las elecciones nacionales de Georgia en 2003

rotation complete turn (p. 20)
rotación vuelta completa

rural settlement in the country (p. 80)
rural poblado del campo

S

Sahel a semiarid area that lies between the Sahara and moister regions to the south in northern Africa (p. 333)
Sáhel área semiárida ubicada entre el desierto del Sahara y las regiones más húmedas al sur del norte de África

salt trade exchange between West Africans selling gold and Arab traders selling salt, beginning around A.D. 750 (p. 341)
comercio de la sal intercambio comercial del oro de África occidental por la sal de los mercaderes árabes, que comenzó alrededor del 750 d. C.

samurai Japanese warrior lord (p. 665)
samurái guerrero japonés miembro de la nobleza

satellite image picture of Earth's surface taken from a satellite in orbit (p. 8)
imagen de satélite fotografía de la superficie de la Tierra que tomó un satélite en órbita

satrap Persian governor (p. 515)
sátrapa gobernador persa

savanna parklike landscape of grasslands with scattered trees that can survive dry spells, found in tropical areas with dry seasons (pp. 42, 334)
sabana pradera con árboles dispersos que pueden sobrevivir periodos de sequía; se encuentra en las áreas tropicales que tienen estaciones secas

saving setting aside money for future use (p. 68)
ahorrar reservar dinero para el uso futuro

scale relative size (p. 8)
escala tamaño relativo

scale bar section of a map that shows how much distance on the map represents a given distance on the land (p. 10)
barra de escala sección de un mapa que muestra la correspondencia entre las distancias del mapa y las distancias reales sobre la Tierra

scarcity having a limited quantity of resources to meet unlimited wants (pp. 58, 660)
escasez tener una cantidad limitada de recursos para satisfacer deseos ilimitados

schism split (p. 157)
cisma división

science knowledge of the natural world (p. 98)
ciencia conocimientos sobre el mundo natural

Scientific Revolution a series of major advances in science during the 1500s and 1600s (p. 194)
Revolución Científica serie de grandes avances científicos durante los siglos XVI y XVII

Scramble for Africa period during the late 1800s when European powers raced to seize control of African territory (p. 386)
Reparto de África período entre 1880 y 1890 durante el que las potencias imperialistas europeas se disputaron el control de los territorios africanos

scribe ancient Egyptian trained to write hieroglyphics (p. 413)
escriba escritor de jeroglíficos del antiguo Egipto

secede to break away (p. 278)
separarse desprenderse

secondary industry industry involving the use of resources to create new products, such as manufacturing (p. 745)
sector secundario industria relacionada con el uso de recursos para crear nuevos productos, como la industria manufacturera

804

secondary source information about an event that does not come directly from a person who experienced that event (p. 120)
fuente secundaria información sobre un suceso que no proviene directamente de una persona que experimentó el suceso

secular not religious (pp. 270, 605, 705)
laico no religioso

secular democracy democracy not based on religion (p. 602)
democracia laica tipo de democracia que no se basa en la religión

secularism idea that government should be separate from religion (p. 418)
laicismo idea que promueve la separación entre el Estado y la Religión

sedentary settled (p. 558)
sedentario asentado

semiarid climate dry climate (p. 41)
clima semiárido clima seco

separatist group group of people who want to establish an independent state (p. 706)
grupo separatista grupo de personas que quieren establecer un estado independiente

Serengeti Plain a part of the savanna in Kenya and Tanzania, home to many animals such as elephants and gazelles (p. 366)
Llanura del Serengeti parte de la sabana de Kenya y Tanzania donde habitan animales como elefantes y gacelas

serf a peasant who is legally bound to live and work on land owned by a lord (p. 300)
siervo persona que está legalmente forzada a vivir y trabajar en la tierra de su noble

shah Persian word for king (p. 517)
sah término persa para rey

shamal hot, dry winds that blow across Iran from west to east (p. 509)
shamal viento seco y cálido que atraviesa Irán de oeste a este

Shinto traditional religion that originated in Japan (p. 543)
sintoísmo religión tradicional que se originó en Japón

shogun powerful Japanese military leader, who often had more power than the emperor (p. 665)
shogún poderoso líder militar japonés que por lo general tenía más poder que el emperador

Siberia Asiatic Russia (p. 290)
Siberia Rusia asiática

Silk Road series of trade routes that crossed Asia (p. 556)
Ruta de la Seda red de rutas comerciales que atravesaban Asia

single-party state a country in which one political party controls the government (p. 639)
estado de un solo partido país en donde un partido político controla el gobierno

slum poor, overcrowded urban neighborhood (p. 81)
barrio marginal vecindario urbano pobre y sobrepoblado

social class group of people living in similar economic conditions (p. 89)
clase social grupo de personas que tienen una condición económica similar

social structure pattern of organized relationships among groups of people within a society (p. 89)
estructura social patrón de las relaciones organizadas entre los grupos de personas de una sociedad

society group of humans with a shared culture who have organized themselves to meet their basic needs (p. 88)
sociedad grupo de personas con una cultura compartida que se han organizado para satisfacer sus necesidades básicas

solstice point at which days are longest in one hemisphere and shortest in another (p. 18)
solsticio momento en el que la duración de los días es más larga en un hemisferio y más corta en el otro

sovereignty supreme authority (p. 110)
soberanía autoridad suprema

soviet a republic or unit of government under a central communist government (p. 302)
sóviet república o unidad gubernamental bajo un gobierno central comunista

specialization act of concentrating on a limited number of goods or activities (p. 60)
especialización concentrarse en una cantidad limitada de bienes o actividades

special-purpose map map that shows the location or distribution of human or physical features (p. 13)
mapa temático o de propósito particular mapa que muestra la ubicación o distribución de características humanas o físicas

805

Glossary (continued)

sphere round-shaped body (p. 4)
esfera cuerpo geométrico de forma redonda

spillover an effect on someone or something not involved in an activity (p. 53)
externalidad efecto sobre alguien o algo que no participa en una actividad

standard of living level of comfort enjoyed by a person or society (p. 99)
nivel de vida nivel de comodidad que posee un individuo o una sociedad

staple crop the most important crop produced or consumed in a region (p. 625)
alimento básico el producto alimenticio más importante que se produce o se consume en una región

state region that shares a common government (p. 106)
estado región que tiene un gobierno común

steppe vast area of grasslands (pp. 293, 549)
estepa territorio extenso de llanuras

stock share of ownership in a company (p. 69)
acción porción de la propiedad de una compañía

strait narrow body of water that cuts through land, connecting two larger bodies of water (p. 507)
estrecho cuerpo de agua angosto que pasa por tierra para conectar a dos cuerpos de agua más grandes

subarctic climate climate with limited precipitation, cool summers, and very cold winters (p. 41)
clima subártico clima de precipitación limitada, veranos frescos e inviernos muy fríos

subsistence farming farming with little left over to send to market (pp. 582, 748)
agricultura de subsistencia tipo de agricultura en el que casi no sobran productos para el mercado

suburb residential area on the edge of a city or large town (p. 51)
suburbio área residencial ubicada en los límites de una ciudad o un pueblo

suburban sprawl spread of suburbs away from the core city (p. 81)
dispersión suburbana extensión de los suburbios lejos del centro de la ciudad

superpower an extremely powerful nation (p. 311)
superpotencia nación sumamente poderosa

supply amount of a good or service that is available for use (p. 59)
oferta cantidad disponible de un bien o servicio

surplus extra (p. 699)
superávit excedente

Swahili Bantu language that has many Arabic elements and words from other languages (p. 381)
swahili lengua bantú que contiene muchos elementos del idioma árabe y palabras de otras lenguas

T

taiga thick forest of coniferous trees (p. 227)
taiga bosque denso de árboles coníferos

tariff tax on imports or exports (p. 67)
arancel impuesto a las importaciones o las exportaciones

technology practical application of knowledge to accomplish a task (p. 65)
tecnología aplicación práctica del saber para ejecutar una tarea

temperate moderate in terms of temperature (p. 551)
templado de temperatura moderada

temperate zone areas between the high and low latitudes; also known as middle latitudes (p. 34)
zona templada área entre las latitudes altas y bajas; también se le llama latitudes medias

temperature measure of how hot or cold the air is (p. 32)
temperatura medida de cuán caliente o fría se encuentra la atmósfera

terrorism use of violence to create fear for political reasons (p. 455)
terrorismo actos violentos destinados a crear un clima de temor para fines políticos

theocracy a government run by religious power (p. 405)
teocracia gobierno en el que rige el poder religioso

time zones areas sharing the same time (p. 20)
husos horarios áreas que comparten la misma hora

timeline line marked off with a series of events and their dates (p. 118)
línea cronológica línea marcada con una serie de sucesos y sus fechas

Tombouctou city founded around A.D. 1100 in modern-day Mali; for centuries, one of the most important cities in West Africa (p. 341)
Tombuctú (o Tombouctou) ciudad fundada alrededor del año 1100 d. C. en la actual República de Mali; por siglos, ha sido una de las ciudades más importantes de África occidental

tornado swirling funnel of wind that can reach 200 miles (320 km) per hour (p. 39)
tornado túnel de aire giratorio que puede alcanzar una velocidad de 200 millas (320 km) por hora

trade exchange of goods and services in a market (p. 66)
comercio intercambio de bienes y servicios en un mercado

trade barrier something that keeps goods and services from entering a country (p. 67)
barrera comercial obstáculos para la entrada de bienes y servicios a un país

traditional economy economy in which people make economic decisions based on their customs and habits (p. 62)
economía tradicional economía en la que la gente toma decisiones económicas de acuerdo a sus costumbres y hábitos

treaty formal agreement between two or more countries (p. 111)
tratado acuerdo formal entre dos o más países

triangular trade three-stage trade pattern that carried goods and enslaved people among Europe, Africa, and the Americas (p. 192)
comercio triangular sistema comercial de tres partes que transportó bienes y personas esclavizadas entre Europa, África y las Américas

tribune representative of plebeians in ancient Rome (p. 149)
tribuno representante de los plebeyos de la antigua Roma

Trinity the three persons, or forms, of God according to Christian belief: God the Father, God the Son, and the Holy Spirit (p. 482)
Trinidad dícese de las tres personas o formas de Dios de acuerdo con las creencias cristianas: Dios padre, Dios hijo y el Espíritu Santo

tropical cyclone intense rainstorm with strong winds that forms over oceans in the tropics (p. 39)
ciclón tropical aguacero intenso con vientos fuertes que se forma sobre el océano en los trópicos

tropical wet and dry climate climate with a wet season in summer and a dry season in winter (p. 40)
clima tropical húmedo y seco clima de temporada húmeda durante el verano y temporada seca en el invierno

tropical wet climate climate with hot temperatures and heavy rainfall year-round (p. 40)
clima tropical húmedo clima de temperaturas cálidas y lluvia abundante durante todo el año

tropics areas between the Tropic of Cancer and the Tropic of Capricorn; also known as low latitudes (p. 34)
trópico área comprendida entre el Trópico de Cáncer y el Trópico de Capricornio (latitudes bajas)

tsar ruler of imperial Russia; a term used by Byzantine rulers, derived from the Latin *caesar*, or king (p. 300)
zar gobernador del Imperio Ruso; término derivado del latín *césar*, o rey, que usaban los gobernadores del Imperio Bizantino

tsunameter scientific instrument that can detect when a tsunami passes (p. 712)
tsunámetro instrumento científico que puede detectar el acercamiento de un tsunami

tsunami series of huge waves (pp. 691, 710)
maremoto serie de olas enormes

tundra area with limited vegetation, such as moss and shrubs (p. 226)
tundra área con vegetación limitada, como musgos y arbustos

tundra climate climate with cool summers and bitterly cold, dry winters (p. 41)
clima de tundra clima de veranos frescos e inviernos gélidos y secos

typhoon storm much like a hurricane (p. 692)
tifón tormenta parecida a un huracán

tyranny unjust use of power (p. 105)
tiranía uso injusto del poder

Glossary (continued)

U

unitary system system of government in which a central government has the authority to make laws for the entire country (p. 108)
  sistema unitario sistema de gobierno en el que un gobierno central tiene la autoridad de hacer leyes para todo el país

universal theme subject or theme that relates to the entire world (p. 94)
  tema universal materia o tema que se relaciona con todo el mundo

unlimited government government structure in which there are no effective limits on government actions (pp. 105, 674)
  gobierno ilimitado tipo de gobierno en el que no existen límites sobre las acciones del gobierno

Ural Mountains low-lying mountains that separate European Russia from Asiatic Russia (p. 291)
  Montes Urales cadena montañosa de poca elevación que separa a Rusia europea de Rusia asiática

urban located in cities (p. 80)
  urbano localizado en la ciudad

urbanization movement of people from rural to urban areas (pp. 80, 399)
  urbanización desplazamiento de personas de las áreas rurales a las áreas urbanas

urbanized place where most people live in cities (p. 441)
  urbanizado lugar donde la mayoría de las personas viven en la ciudad

V

valley stretch of low land between mountains or hills (p. 25)
  valle extensión de terreno bajo ubicado entre montañas o colinas

vassals in medieval Europe, noblemen who received land from other noblemen in return for their services (p. 160)
  vasallos en la Europa medieval, señores nobles que recibían terrenos de otros señores nobles a cambio de sus servicios

visual arts art forms such as painting, sculpture, and photography (p. 94)
  artes visuales expresiones artísticas como la pintura, la escultura y la fotografía

W

wage money paid to an employee (p. 640)
  sueldo dinero que se le paga a un empleado

water cycle the movement of water from Earth's surface into the atmosphere and back (p. 37)
  ciclo del agua movimiento del agua desde la superficie de la Tierra hacia la atmósfera y viceversa

weather condition of the air and sky at a certain time (p. 32)
  tiempo condiciones del aire y el cielo en un momento determinado

weathering process that breaks rocks down into tiny pieces (p. 24)
  meteorización proceso que rompe la roca en pedazos muy pequeños

wind turbines giant windmills that use large baldes to collect the wind's energy (p. 234)
  turbinas eólicas grandes molinos que utilizan grandes palas para recoger la energía del viento

World War I 1914–1918, sometimes called the Great War, the first truly global conflict (p. 200)
  Primera Guerra Mundial 1914 a 1918, a veces llamada La Gran Guerra, fue el primer verdadero conflicto global

World War II 1939–1945, the second major global conflict (p. 204)
  Segunda Guerra Mundial 1939 a 1945, segundo gran conflicto global

Y

Yoruba ethnic groups living mainly in present-day Nigeria that share a common language, culture, and history (p. 347)
  yoruba grupos étnicos que viven principalmente en la actual Nigeria y que tienen la misma historia, cultura e idioma

808

Z

Zionism a movement to create a Jewish state in the Jews' historic homeland (p. 484)
sionismo movimiento que busca la creación de un estado judío en la patria histórica en Palestina de los judíos

Zoroastrianism an Iranian religion that dates back to ancient times (p. 515)
zoroastrismo religión iraní que data de tiempos antiguos

Index

The letters after some page numbers refer to the following: c = chart; g = graph; m = map; p = picture; q = quotation.

A

Abdullah II, king of Jordan, 491, 491p
Abkhazia, 554
abolish, 387, 786
Aboriginal culture, 736, 738, 739p, 742, 743, 743p, 758, 786
under British rule, 740–741, 740p, 740q, 741p, 741q
language of, 91
Aboriginal Protection Act, 740, 741q
Aborigines, 736, 786
Abraham, 479, 481, 496
absolute location, 6, 786
absolute monarchy, 107, 450, 461, 462m, 786
absolutism, 192–193, 192m, 193p, 786
Abu Bakr, 447
acid rain, 229, 229p, 267, 786. See also air pollution
A.D. See anno Domini
adobe, 97c
advertising, 61
Aegean World, 138, 139m
Aeneas, 148
Aeneid (Virgil), 148
aerial photographs, 8, 8p, 786
Aeschylus, 143
Aesop's Fables, 146, 146q
Afghanistan, 574m
climate of, 580, 580m, 581
culture of, 585
economy of, 600
government of, 602, 606–607
history of, 584, 593, 593p
Islam in, 589
literacy in, 600g
population of, 598
religion in, 597
Soviet Union and, 593, 593p
United States and, 593, 601, 602
women in, 600p
Africa
archaeology in, 122p
human geography, 326–327
physical geography, 324–325
population density in, 326m
regional flyover, 325
regional overview, 322–327

tourism in, 424–425
urbanization in, 80
water resources in, 326, 326m
See also North Africa; Southern and Eastern Africa; West and Central Africa
African Americans, 79
African National Congress (ANC), 377, 786
African Union (AU), 354–355, 385, 419, 786
Afrikaans language, 381
Afrikaners, 381, 388
Afro-Asiatic language, 90
Age of Absolutism, 192–193, 192m, 193p
Age of Empires, 190–192
Age of Exploration, 188–190, 188p, 189m
agora, 144
agriculture, 478, 786
in Arabia and Iraq, 440
arable land, 626
in China, 625, 626, 635, 640
culture and, 98–99
plantations, 700, 700g
in Scandinavia, 239
in Southeast Asia, 694–695, 695p, 699
staple crops, 625
subsistence farming, 351, 351p
in West and Central Africa, 336, 340, 351, 351p
See also farming
Agrippina the Younger, 151
ahimsa, 588
AIDS (disease), 354, 371, 371c, 384–385, 786
air circulation, 38, 38p, 39, 39m, 41
air pollution, 53, 747
in China, 645
in South Asia, 599
in Southeast Asia, 695, 707, 707p
in Western Europe, 215, 229, 229p, 245, 267
See also acid rain
Akbar, 589, 590
Akihito, emperor of Japan, 680p
Aksum kingdom, 373
akyn, 562p, 563, 786
Al-Aqsa Mosque, 486, 486p
al-Assad, Bashar, 491, 491p
Alawite Muslims, 477, 786
Albania, 258m, 265, 268, 268m, 279, 279p

al-Bashir, Omar, 383
Albéniz, Isaac, 252
Alevis, 513
Alexander the Great, 135–137, 135p, 136p, 137p, 141, 144m, 145, 145p, 445p, 446, 515, 588
algebra, 449
Algeria, 392m
culture of, 415, 415p
economy of, 416–417, 416g
environmental concerns in, 401
France and, 408, 408m, 409
government of, 418
population of, 398, 399
Ali, 447
Al-Khwarizmi, 179
alliances, 200
Allied Powers, 204–205, 204m
alphabets, 148, 157, 157p
Alps, 130p, 225, 225m
al-Qaeda, 214, 455, 593, 709
Altaic language, 91
altitude, 35, 213, 786
America, 189m, 190–192, 191m
American Samoa, 724m
Amnesty International, 111
Amu Dar'ya, 549, 549m, 550, 558
Amundsen, Roald, 754, 754q
Amur River, 292
Anabaptist, 183
Analects, 636, 636p, 636q
Anatolia, 506, 507m
ANC. See African National Congress
Angkor Wat, 703p
Anglican Church, 184
Anglo-Saxons, 158, 169
Angola, 336m, 337, 352, 353
animal life
in Africa, 366–367, 367p
in Antarctica, 752p, 753
in Australia, 732, 732p
in Russia, 294
anime, 678, 678p
Ankara River, 292
Annan, Kofi, 383q
anno Domini (A.D.), 119
Antarctica, 8, 8p, 9m, 746, 746p, 747
animal life of, 752p, 753
climate of, 753, 755
natural resources of, 753
physical features of, 752p, 753m, 852–853
research in, 754–755, 754p, 755p
Antarctic Circle, 34, 34m

Antarctic Treaty, 755, 786
anthropology, 123, 786
anti-Semitism, 203, 484, 786
apartheid system, 362, 376–377, 377p, 383, 389, 389p, 786
Appalachian Mountains, 25
appanage system, 299
aqueducts, 151p, 223, 786
aquifer, 474, 475, 510–511, 786
Arabia
Arab culture of, 458, 458p
atlas of, 432m, 436–443, 437m, 438m, 439g, 441m, 442m
economy of, 439, 456–457, 457g
ecosystems in, 440, 440m
government in, 460–463, 460p, 461p, 462m, 463p
history of, 444–451, 444p, 445m, 445p, 446p, 447p, 448m, 449p, 450p, 451p
natural resources in, 438–439, 438m, 456
oil in, 438–439, 438m, 438p, 439g, 450, 456–457, 457g
population density in, 441, 441m
religion in, 442–443, 442m, 442p, 446–449, 446p, 447p, 448m, 454–455, 455p
traditions in, 454–455
water resources in, 440, 440m, 440p
Arabian Peninsula, 429p, 436, 437m, 441
Arabian Plate, 437, 438
Arabian Sea, 436, 437m
Arabic numerals, 179, 589
Arab-Israeli conflicts, 484–485
arable land, 336, 626, 786
Arabs, 476–477, 476m, 476p
Aral Sea, 549, 565, 565g, 565p
archaeology, 116p, 117, 117p, 122–123, 122p, 372p, 787
archipelagoes, 691, 787
architect, 94, 787
architecture, 94, 94p, 787
of ancient Greece, 143
in Byzantine empire, 158
of Iran, 525, 525p
Islamic, 489, 489p
of Jerusalem, 486, 486p
Muslims and, 165
of North Africa, 407p
in the Renaissance, 178p, 179
of Roman empire, 152
Arctic Circle, 34, 34m, 226, 239

Index (continued)

812

Index (continued)

814

decimal system, 589
Declaration of Human Rights, U.N., 111
Declaration of Independence, 196c
Declaration of Korean Independence, 670, 670q
deforestation, 52, 337, 337p, 791
degree, 4, 791
DeKlerk, F. W., 377
Delhi Sultanate, 589
delta, 25, 25p, 397, 791
demand, 59, 59g, 791
democracy, 106, 791
    in ancient Greece, 140–141, 142, 142p, 250
    in Central Asia and the Caucasus, 566
    in India, 596, 607
    in Iraq, 463
    in Poland, 274
    Primary Source, 216–217, 216p, 216q, 217p, 217q
    representative, 106, 112, 149, 602
    in Southeast Asia, 706
    in Southern and Eastern Africa, 383
    in South Korea, 672–673
    in Turkey, 526–527
Democratic People's Republic of Korea. See North Korea
Democratic Republic of the Congo, 335g, 335m, 383
    history of, 351–352, 352p, 354
    literacy rate, 354g
    resources of, 336m, 337
demographers, 74, 791
demokratia, 142
demonstration, 566, 567p, 791
Deng Xiaoping, 635, 649
Denmark, 231, 232, 235, 238, 239, 240
De Pisan, Christine, 162, 163q
deportation, 255, 791
deposition, 25, 791
desalination, 440, 440p, 441, 457, 474, 475, 791
Descartes, René, 194
De Ségur, Philippe Paul, 206
desert and desert brush ecosystem, 42m–43m, 43, 43p
desertification, 75, 337, 338, 401, 401p, 791
deserts
    in Arabia and Iraq, 440, 440m
    in Australia, 729, 729m
    in Central Asia, 549, 549m
    in North Africa, 396–397, 397m

    in Southern and Eastern Africa, 365, 365m
    in Southwest Asia, 473
developed country, 64, 64p, 791
developing country, 64, 64p, 791
development, 64, 384–385, 385g, 791
diamonds, 368, 368m, 368p
Dias, Bartolomeu, 188
Díaz, Porfirio, 226, 226p
dictator, 450, 674, 791
dictatorships, 450, 461p, 462
    in North Korea, 674, 675p, 680, 681, 682–683
    in Southern and Eastern Africa, 383
Diet, 681
dikes, 245
Dinaric Alps, 262, 263m
Diocletian, 153
diplomacy, 111, 791
direct democracy, 106, 141, 792
directions, 4
diseases
    Black Death, 170–171, 170p
    Industrial Revolution and, 198, 199
    in Russian Federation, 310
    in Southern and Eastern Africa, 361, 371, 371c, 384–385
    in West and Central Africa, 339, 354
disposable income, 309, 792
distortion, 9, 9m, 792
diversified economies, 457
diversify, 253, 792
diversity, 97, 792
Djenné, 341
Djibouti, 360m
Document-Based Questions
    Arabia and Iraq, 465
    Australia and Pacific region, 757
    climate and ecosystems, 45
    culture, 101
    Democratic Republic of the Congo, 359
    Eastern Europe, 285
    economics, 71
    Europe, 219, 257
    geography tools, 15
    government, 115
    historical maps, 127
    human-environment interaction, 55
    infant mortality, 359g
    Iran, Turkey, and Cyprus, 535
    Israel, 501
    Japan, 685

    Kazakhstan, 573
    Malacca Strait, 715
    Middle Ages, 173
    North Africa, 423
    plates, 29
    population and movement, 83
    population of China, 651
    Russia, 319
    secondary sources, 127
    South Asia, 609
    Southern and Eastern Africa, 391
Dome of the Rock, 483p, 486, 486p
domestic trade, 67
dominion, 792
Don River, 292
drainage basins, 333, 333m
Drake, Francis, 188p
Dravidian language, 90
drought, 384, 659, 747, 792
Druze, 477, 792
Dubai, 457
Dürer, Albrecht, 181
Dutch East India Company, 374
Dvina River, 292
dynasty, 630–631, 792

Earth
    air circulation and, 38, 38p, 39, 39m
    axis, 18
    climates of, 32–41, 33g, 34m, 35m, 36m, 37c, 38m, 39m, 40m–41m
    directions, 4
    ecosystems of, 42–43, 42m–43m, 42p–43p
    forces on, 24–25, 24p, 25m, 25p
    hemispheres of, 4m, 5, 5m
    inside of, 26–27, 26p, 27m, 27p
    latitude, 4–5, 4m
    longitude, 5, 5m
    rotation of, 20, 20p
    seasons of, 18–19, 18p–19p, 35
    structure of, 22–23, 22p–23p
    study of, 4–7, 4m, 5m
    sun and, 18–19, 18p–19p, 20, 20p, 34, 34m, 37, 37p, 38, 38p
    surface of, 8–9, 8p, 9m
    temperatures of, 34–35, 34m, 35m
    time zones, 20–21, 21c

earthquakes, 17, 17p, 26–27, 27p, 225, 691, 710–713, 710p, 711c, 712m, 713p
    in Asia, 657, 662
    in Iran and Turkey, 508
East Asia
    human geography, 614–615
    physical geography, 614–615
    population of, 616m, 616p
    regional flyover, 615
    regional overview, 612–617
East Berlin, 246
Eastern Europe, 258m
    atlas, 262–269, 263m, 264m, 265p, 266p, 267p, 269p
    Case Study, 270–273, 270p, 271p, 272p, 273p
    climate of, 264–265, 264m
    Cold War and, 209
    communism in, 209, 211–213, 212p, 213p
    energy choices in, 266, 266m, 266p, 267
    environmental concerns in, 267
    European Union and, 214
    farming in, 265, 265p
    migration from, 214
    mountains of, 262, 263m, 264–265
    natural resources in, 266, 267
    physical features of, 262–263, 262p, 263m
    Primary Source, 216–217, 216p, 216q, 217p, 217q
    religion in, 268–269, 268m, 269p, 270, 271, 271p
    See also individual countries
Eastern Ghats, 579, 579m
Eastern Hemisphere, 5, 5m
Eastern Orthodox Church, 157, 159, 268–269, 268m, 269p, 272, 272p, 299, 488
East India Company, 591
East Pakistan, 592–593, 592m
East Slavs, 298–299, 298p
East Timor, 696, 706
Ecclesia, 142p
economic development, 64–65, 64p, 65m
economic organizations, 111, 111p
economics and economic systems, 62–63, 62p, 63c, 63p, 792
    capital, 58
    command economy, 634–635, 634p, 675
    definition of, 58
    demand, 59, 59g
    entrepreneurs and, 57, 57p, 58, 58p, 62

Index (continued)

Index (continued)

818

Index (continued)

820

Institutes of the Christian Religion (Calvin), 183
insurgents and insurgency, 706, 796
interdependent, 661, 796
interest, 69, 796
interest groups, 113, 796
intermediate directions, 4
International Monetary Fund (IMF), 111
international trade, 67, 67c, 111
International Tsunami Information Center, 713
Internet
    in China, 99, 649
    cultural diffusion and, 97
    evaluating sources on, 15, 121, 285, 610–611, 651
intertropical convergence zone (ITCZ), 38, 334, 796
Intifada, 495, 796
inventions, 631
investing, 69, 797
investments, 69, 69p
Ionia, 138, 139m
Iran, 414, 502m
    Arab conquest of, 516
    art and architecture of, 525, 525p
    atlas, 506–513, 507m, 508m, 509g, 510m, 511c, 511p, 512m, 513p
    Britain and, 518
    climate of, 508–509, 508m, 509c
    earthquakes in, 508
    economy of, 524
    ethnic groups in, 512–513, 512m
    government of, 522–523, 522p, 523p
    history of, 514–516, 514p, 515m, 515p, 516m, 517, 518–519, 519p
    Iraq and, 451, 462
    irrigation in, 510–511
    Kurdish people in, 512–513, 512m, 531c, 533
    land use in, 510–511, 510m, 511c
    oil in, 510, 511, 511c, 511p
    physical features of, 506–508, 507m
    population of, 510
    religion in, 512–513, 512m, 516
    revolution in, 519, 519p, 520–521
    Russia and, 313, 518
    terrorism and, 524
    United States and, 519, 524

    voting rights in, 523
    women in, 523
Iran-Iraq War, 451
Iraq
    agriculture in, 440
    Arab culture of, 458, 458p, 459
    Arab-Israeli conflicts, 484–485
    atlas of, 432m, 436–443, 437m, 438m, 439g, 441m, 442m
    Britain and, 449
    democracy in, 463
    dictatorship in, 461p, 462
    economy of, 439, 456–457, 457g
    ecosystems in, 440, 440m
    ethnic groups in, 442
    government in, 450, 451, 460–463, 460p, 461p, 462m, 463p
    history of, 444–451, 444p, 445m, 445p, 446p, 447p, 448m, 449p, 450p, 451p
    Iran and, 451, 462
    Kurdish people and, 531c, 533
    Kuwait and, 451, 462
    natural resources in, 438–439, 438m, 456
    oil in, 438–439, 438m, 438p, 439g, 450, 451, 456–457, 457g
    population density in, 441, 441m
    religion in, 442–443, 442m, 442p, 446–449, 446p, 447p, 448m, 454–455, 455p
    rivers of, 445, 445m
    traditions in, 454–455
    water resources in, 440, 440m, 440p
    women in, 459
Ireland, 174m, 236
    currency in, 237
    economy of, 240, 240g
    trade in, 237
    Vikings in, 159
Irian Jaya, 694
iron, 368, 368m, 373
Iron Curtain, 210m, 210p
Irrawaddy River, 690, 691m
irrigate, 99, 796
irrigation, 99c
    in Central Asia, 550
    in Egypt, 405
    in Iran, 510–511
    See also water resources
Isabella of Castile, 166
Isis (Egyptian goddess), 410, 411, 411p
Islam, 92, 92m–93m

    in Afghanistan, 589
    in Arabia and Iraq, 442m, 443, 454–455, 455p
    art of, 489, 489p
    beliefs of, 447, 447p
    in Byzantine empire, 157–158
    calendar of, 119
    in the Caucasus, 557
    Crusades and, 164–166, 165m, 167
    in Eastern Europe, 268–269, 268m, 269p, 270, 273, 273p
    fundamentalism, 455
    government and, 461, 462
    Hinduism and, 589, 591, 601
    history of, 164, 444, 446–449, 483
    in India, 589–591
    in Iran, 516
    mosques and, 486, 486p
    in North Africa, 407, 407p, 414, 414p
    in Pakistan, 589, 589p
    in South Asia, 585, 589–591, 589p, 597
    in Southeast Asia, 697, 700, 705
    in Southern and Eastern Africa, 373, 381, 381c
    in Southwest Asia, 430, 430p, 476m, 476p, 477
    in Tibet, 628
    in West and Central Africa, 353
    women and, 452–453, 452p, 452q, 453p, 453q, 454
Islamic law, 483, 519, 522, 606
Islamism, 455, 797
islands, 26
Israel, 403, 414, 466m
    Arabs in, 477
    atlas, 470–477, 471m, 473m, 474m, 475p, 476m
    climate of, 472–473, 472m
    conflicts in, 484–485, 494–496, 494m, 495p, 496p
    economy of, 493, 493g, 493p
    Egypt and, 409
    Gaza Strip, 498, 498q, 499q
    government of, 490–491, 490p
    history of, 479, 479p, 484–485
    myStory, 467–469, 467p, 468p, 469p
    parliamentary democracy in, 490
    people of, 498, 499p, 499q
    physical features of, 470–471, 471m
    population density of, 473m
    religion in, 476–477, 476m,

    476p, 496
    standard of living in, 492
    trade in, 492, 496–497, 497
    United States and, 485
    water resources in, 474–475, 474m, 475p
Israeli settlements, 494–495, 797
Istanbul, 158, 507, 516, 517p, 526p, 527, 527p
Italy, 211, 211m, 225
    culture of, 251–252, 251p
    economy of, 252–253, 252p, 253g, 254
    in European Union, 253
    fascism in, 203
    government of, 197
    immigrants in, 254–255, 254p
    population of, 229
    religion in, 178p, 251
    in the Renaissance, 178, 180
    trade centers in, 168
    in World War II, 204–205, 204m
    See also Roman empire; Roman Republic
ITCZ. *See* intertropical convergence zone
Ivan III, prince of Russia, 300
Ivan the Terrible, 299p
Ivory Coast, 337, 337p

J
Jainism, 588
Jakarta, 695
Jamestown, 191
Jani festival, 275, 275p
Japan, 652m
    art in, 666
    atlas of, 652m, 656–663, 656p, 657m, 658m, 659g, 659p, 660m, 661c, 662p, 663p
    China and, 633, 667, 667m
    citizenship in, 682–683, 682p
    class system in, 666
    climate of, 658–659, 658m, 659g, 659p, 662
    constitutional monarchy of, 668
    culture of, 677, 678, 678g, 678p, 679
    culture regions, 87
    as developed country, 64p
    economic system of, 63
    economy of, 669, 669g, 676
    education in, 677
    emperors of, 665–666
    energy resources in, 661
    environmental concerns in, 662–663, 663p

Index (continued)

822

physical features of, 549, 549m

water resources in, 553

L

labor, as factor of production, 58

Lake Baikal, 291m, 293, 797

Lake Chad, 333, 333m

Lake Nasser, 400, 400p

Lake Tai, 620–621, 645

Lake Victoria, 365, 365m

land, as factor of production, 58

landform regions, 25

landforms, 23, 25, 25p, 797

landlocked, 548, 553, 798

landslides, 27

land use

in the Caucasus, 551, 551m

in Central Asia, 550, 551m

in China, 624–625, 625m

in Cyprus, 510–511, 510m

human–environment interaction and, 50–51, 50m, 51p

in Iran, 510–511, 510m, 511c

in Japan and the Koreas, 660–661, 660m, 661c

in Kazakhstan, 550, 551m

in South Asia, 582, 582g

in Southeast Asia, 694–695, 695c

in Turkey, 510–511, 510m

languages, 90, 797

Bantu, 373, 381

in Byzantine empire, 157

of the Caucasus, 554, 563, 564, 570–571

of Central Asia, 555, 563, 564, 570–571

of China, 628p, 631

cultural diffusion and, 97c

culture and, 90–91, 90m–91m

of Hungary, 277

of Korea, 628p

of Luxembourg, 245

of Morocco, 414

of New Zealand, 727

of North Africa, 403, 407, 414, 415

of Russia, 296

of Southern and Eastern Africa, 381

of Southern Europe, 250

of Tibet, 628p

Turkic, 555

of United Kingdom, 237

of Western Europe, 227–228, 228m

Laos, 694, 694m, 696, 701, 702, 706

Laozi, 633q

Late Middle Ages, 178

Latins, 148

latitude, 4–5, 4m, 6, 34, 34m, 797

Latium, 148

Latvia, 213, 258m, 268, 268m, 275, 275p

lava, 26, 26p, 657

laws

common law, 169

Justinian's Code, 156

Roman, 149, 151

See also justice system

League of Nations, 449, 484

Leakey, Louis and Mary, 122p

Lebanon, 406, 466m

Arab-Israeli conflicts, 484–485

atlas, 470–477, 470p, 471m, 472m, 473m, 474m, 476m

climate of, 472m

economy of, 493g

government of, 491, 491p

history of, 484–485

physical features of, 470–471, 471m

population density of, 473m

religion in, 476, 476m, 482p

standard of living in, 492, 492p

water resources in, 474, 475m

legislative branch, 109

Lenin, Vladimir, 302, 302p, 306p, 306q, 307

Leningrad, 296

Leo III, Pope, 158

Leo X, Pope, 184

Lesotho, 360m

Levi, Primo, 207q

Leviathan (Hobbes), 195, 195q

liberate, 646, 797

Liberia, 336m, 337

Libya, 392m

economy of, 416–417, 416g

environmental concerns in, 400–401

government of, 418

natural resources in, 402, 402m

population of, 398, 399

Liechtenstein, 242

life expectancy, 797

in China, 642, 643c

economic development and, 64

in North Africa, 416

limited government, 105, 105c, 672, 797

Limpopo River, 365, 365m

literacy

in Afghanistan, 600g

in Bangladesh, 600g

economic development and, 64

in India, 600g

in Pakistan, 600g

in Southern and Eastern Africa, 385g

in Tunisia, 417

in West and Central Africa, 354g

literature, 95, 95p, 797

of ancient Egypt, 412–413, 413p

of ancient Greece, 143, 146–147, 146p, 146q, 147p, 147q

of Ethiopia, 378, 378p, 378q

Hindu, 597

Muslims and, 165

in the Renaissance, 181

in Roman empire, 152

of South Africa, 378, 379p, 379q

of Southern and Eastern Africa, 378–379, 378p, 378q, 379p, 379q

Lithuania, 174m, 213, 258m, 274, 275

"Little Red Book" (Mao), 647, 647p

Livia, 148p, 151

loans, 69

local government, 108

location, theme of, 6

locator map, 10, 798

Locke, John, 196

loess, 226, 623, 798

London, 77p, 132p, 237, 240

longbows, 169, 169p

longitude, 5, 5m, 6, 798

lords, 160, 160c, 161, 798

Louisiana, 30p, 31, 31p

Louis XIV, king of France, 193, 193p

Louis XVI, king of France, 197

Low Countries, 245, 245p

lower class, 89

low islands, 730

low latitudes, 34, 798

Loya Jirga, 606

Lukashenko, Aleksandr, 280

lumber, 695

Luther, Martin, 182–183, 184

Lutheran Church, 183, 184

Luxembourg, 211, 211m, 242, 245

Luzon, 694

M

Maasai people, 380

Maastricht Treaty (1992), 211

Macedonia, 135–137, 258m, 278

Machiavelli, Niccolò, 186, 186p, 186q

Machu Picchu, 122p

Madagascar, 360m, 367

madrassas, 556g, 559, 562, 798

magistrates, 142p

magma, 26, 798

Magna Carta, 168p, 169, 196c, 236, 798

Magyars, 159, 298

Mahabharata, 587

Maijuna tribe, 2p, 3, 3p

maize, 222

Majlis, 522, 798

majority, 442, 798

majority rule, 108

Malacca Strait, 693, 693m, 699, 699m, 700, 709, 715

malaria, 339, 354, 371, 798

Malawi, 360m

Malay Peninsula, 705

Malaysia, 705

ethnic diversity in, 696, 706c

global trade and, 709

government of, 706

high-technology in, 709

Maldives, 579, 579m, 596

Mali, 341, 341p, 353

Malta, 174m

Maluku Islands, 693, 693m, 700

Mandela, Nelson, 377, 377p

manga, 678, 678g

Manila, 695

manorialism, 161, 171, 798

Mansa Musa, 341

mantle, 22, 798

Maori culture, 123p, 725–727, 725p, 726p, 727p, 736p, 737, 738, 743, 743p, 798

Mao Zedong, 633, 635, 646p, 647

maps and mapping

Earth's surface and, 8–9, 9m

keys, 10, 11

physical, 10, 10m, 12, 12m

political, 13m

projections, 9, 9m

reading, 10m, 11, 11m

road maps, 11, 11m

special purpose, 13m, 124–125, 125m

types of, 12–13, 12m, 13m

Map Skills, 14m, 28, 44, 54, 82

ancient Europe, 139m, 144m, 150m, 152m

Antarctica, 753m

Arabia and Iraq, 437m, 438m, 441m, 442m

Australia and the Pacific, 729m, 731m, 733m, 737m

Central Asia and Caucasus, 549m, 551m, 552m, 554m, 557m

823

Index (continued)

824

Muhammad, 119, 446–448, 483, 496, 516
Multimedia Super Corridor, 709
mummy, 406, 406p, 799
Mumtaz Mahal, 591
Muscovy, 299p
Musharraf, Pervez, 606, 606p
music, 95, 95p, 799
  of Algeria, 415, 415p
  of Arabia and Iraq, 458, 458p
  of Southern Europe, 252
Muslim Brotherhood, 418, 418p, 799
Muslim empire, 448–449, 448m
Muslims
  in Arabia and Iraq, 442–443, 442m, 442p
  Crusades and, 483
  in Israel, 496
  mathematics and, 179
  See also Islam
Muslumovo, 316p
Mussolini, Benito, 203
mutual funds, 69
Myanmar, 713
  economy of, 708, 708c
  environment of, 705, 705p
  ethnic diversity in, 696
  government of, 706
  population of, 694, 694m
  See also Burma
Mycenaean civilization, 139
mystics, 185
myStory
  Alexander the Great, 135–137, 135p, 136p, 137p
  China, 619–621, 619p, 620p, 621p
  Egypt, 393–395, 393p, 394p, 395p
  Elizabeth I, queen of England, 175–177
  Ghana, 329–331, 329p, 330p, 331p
  India, 575–577, 575p, 576p, 577p
  Indonesia, 687–689, 687p, 688p, 689p
  Israel, 467–469, 467p, 468p, 469p
  Japan, 653–655, 653p, 654p, 655p
  Kyrgyzstan, 545–547, 545p, 546p, 547p
  New Zealand, 725–727, 725p, 726p, 727p
  Palestinians, 467–469, 467p, 468p, 469p
  Russia, 287–289, 287p, 288p, 289p
  Saudi Arabia, 433–435, 433p,

434p, 435p
  South Africa, 361–363, 361p, 362p, 363p
  Spain, 175–177
  Spanish Armada, 175–177
  Sumatra, 687–689, 687p, 688p, 689p
  Turkey, 503–505, 503p, 504p, 505p
  Ukraine, 259–261, 259p, 260p, 261p
  West and Central Africa, 329–331, 329p, 330p, 331p
  Western Europe, 221–223, 221p, 222p, 223p
mythology, 143, 411
myWorld in Numbers
  Africa, 327
  Albania, 265
  Arabia and Iraq, 456
  Australia, 723
  Black Death, 171
  Bollywood, 597
  Britain, 198
  Central Asia, 543
  China, 625
  democracy, 277
  East Asia, 617
  Egypt, 327
  Ethiopia, 327
  Europe, 133
  fishing, 745
  France, 133, 244
  India, 585, 597
  Indonesia, 697
  Iran, 510
  Italy, 133
  Ivory Coast, 339
  language in Central Asia and Caucasus, 563
  mosquito nets, 339
  Nigeria, 327
  Pacific region, 723
  population in cities, 734
  religions, 477
  Russia, 133, 311
  Russian language, 555
  South Africa, 327
  South Asia, 543
  Southeast Asia, 617
  Southwest Asia, 431
  Suez Canal, 403
  Sweden, 133
  Tanzania, 367
  Thailand, 709
  typhoons in Japan, 662
  Ukraine, 133
  United Kingdom, 133
  world populations, 676

N

Nagasaki, 667
Nagorno-Karabakh, 555
Namib Desert, 365, 365m
Namibia, 352, 360m, 369, 374m, 376
Naples, 174m
Napoleon Bonaparte, 197, 225
Napoleonic Wars, 197
Nasr, Seyyed Hossein, 452q
Nasser, Gamal Abdel, 409, 409p
nationalism, 200, 213, 271, 799
  in Europe, 197
  in North Africa, 408
  in Southeast Asia, 700
  in Soviet Union, 304
  in Turkey, 526
nation-states, 107, 799
Native Americans
  dance, 84p, 85, 85p
  horses and, 96
  language of, 91
NATO. *See* North Atlantic Treaty Organization
natural disasters, 27
  preparing for, 711–713, 713p
  tsunami, 710–713, 710p, 711c, 712m, 713p
natural gas, 214, 214m, 233g, 235, 267, 438–439, 438m, 511
natural hazards, 27
naturalization, 112, 112p
natural resources, 799
  of Antarctica, 753
  of Arabia and Iraq, 456
  of Australia, 734–735
  of Central Asia and Caucasus, 552, 552m
  definition of, 48
  of Eastern Europe, 266, 267
  human–environment interaction and, 48–49, 48p, 49c, 52–53
  of Japan and the Koreas, 660–661, 660m, 661c
  of New Zealand, 734–735
  of North Africa, 402, 402m
  of Pacific region, 735, 735p, 748, 748p
  of Russia, 294–295, 295m
  of South Asia, 582
  of Southern and Eastern Africa, 368–369, 368m, 369p, 370, 370m
  of West and Central Africa, 336–337, 336m
  of Western Europe, 227, 227m, 229
Nauru, 724m

Navajo culture, 84p, 85, 85p
navigation, 195
Nazarbayev, Nursultan, 566
Nazi Party, 203–205, 203c, 204m
Ndebele people, 381p
Nefertiti (Egyptian queen), 412p
Nehru, Jawaharlal, 592, 605
Nepal, 574m, 597, 602
Netherlands, 193, 211, 211m, 242, 245, 245p
  in Africa, 374, 374m
  explorations by, 189, 189m, 191
Nevada, 85
Nevi'im, 480
New Caledonia, 724m
Newcomen, Thomas, 195
New England, 191
New Guinea, 724m, 733, 733m
New Mexico, 85
New Orleans, 30p, 31, 31p
Newroz, 531
New Testament, 482
Newton, Isaac, 195
New York, 709
New York Stock Exchange, 69p
New Zealand, 721p, 724m
  climate of, 733, 733m
  economy of, 745
  ethnic groups of, 742–743, 743p
  government of, 744
  Great Britain and, 737–738
  history of, 737, 737m, 738, 739
  indigenous people of, 123p
  language of, 727
  myStory, 725–727, 725p, 726p, 727p
  natural resources in, 734–735
  physical features of, 729m, 730, 731, 731m
  plate tectonics and, 731, 731m
  population of, 734, 734p
NGO. *See* nongovernmental organizations
Nicholas II, tsar of Russia, 301, 302
Niger, 62, 62p, 335g, 335m
Niger-Congo language, 90
Niger Delta, 336m, 337
Nigeria, 327
  agriculture in, 351p
  ethnic diversity in, 345
  history of, 344–345, 345p
  oil in, 351
  population of, 338, 338m
  resources of, 336, 336m, 337
Niger River, 332p, 333, 333m

Index *(continued)*

826

P

Pacific Coastal Lowlands, 211, 211*m*

Pacific Island Countries Trade Agreement (PICTA), 749, 801

Pacific Islands Forum, 745, 749, 749*m*, 801

Pacific Ocean, 724*m*, 729*m*

Pacific plates, 657, 731, 731*m*

Pacific region
- atlas, 724*m*, 728–735, 728*p*, 729*m*, 730*p*, 731*m*, 732*p*, 733*m*, 735*p*
- climate of, 732–733, 733*m*
- culture of, 743, 743*p*
- economy of, 745, 745*c*, 748–751, 748*p*, 749*m*, 750*g*, 750*p*, 751*p*
- ecosystem of, 732, 733
- environmental concerns of, 746–747
- ethnic groups of, 743, 743*p*, 758
- exports of, 748–749
- government of, 744, 744*p*
- history of, 736–739, 736*p*, 737*m*, 738*p*–739*p*
- human geography, 722–723
- indigenous people of, 758
- migration to, 736–737, 737*m*
- natural resources in, 735, 735*p*, 748, 748*p*
- physical features of, 728–731, 728*p*, 729*m*, 730*p*, 731*m*
- physical geography, 720–721
- plate tectonics and, 731–732, 731*m*
- population of, 734*c*, 735
- regional flyover, 721
- regional overview, 718–723
- water resources in, 733

Pacific Tsunami Warning Center, 713

pack ice, 753, 801

pagans, 159

Pahlavi, Reza, 518–519

Pakal (Maya leader), 122*p*

Pakistan, 574*m*
- climate of, 580, 580*m*
- coups in, 606
- discrimination in, 600
- economy of, 602
- government of, 602, 606–607, 606*p*
- history of, 584
- India and, 601, 601*m*, 605
- Kashmir and, 596
- land use in, 582, 582*g*
- literacy in, 600*g*
- partition of, 592–593, 592*m*

population of, 583, 583*m*, 598, 598*g*
religion in, 589, 589*p*, 597

Palau, 722, 724*m*

Palawan, 697

Palestine, 164, 483, 484

Palestine Liberation Organization (PLO), 495

Palestinian Authority, 490, 495

Palestinian people, 475, 498, 498*p*, 498*q*
- myStory, 467–469, 467*p*, 468*p*, 469*p*

Palestinian Territories, 470, 476, 478, 492, 496

Pan-Africanism, 344, 801

Panama, 80, 80*p*

Pan-Arabism, 409, 801

Papal States, 174*m*

paper, 167

Papua New Guinea, 724*m*, 729*m*, 730, 735*p*, 743*p*, 744*p*, 748, 748*p*

Paris, 244

Parliament, 169, 196, 196*c*, 236–237, 801

parliamentary democracy, 463, 490, 491, 491*p*, 680, 744, 801

parliamentary system, 680, 801

Parmenio, 137

Parthenon, 143

partition, 592–593, 592*m*, 801

Passover, 479

Pasteur, Louis, 199

Patil, Pratibha, 600*p*

patricians, 149, 801

Paul (follower of Jesus), 481

Paul III, Pope, 184

Pax Romana, 151, 801

Pearl Harbor, 667, 667*m*

peasants, 161, 161*p*, 167

Peloponnesian Wars, 143, 145

peninsula, 224, 690, 801

People's Court (ancient Greece), 142*p*

perestroika, 304, 308

Pericles, 141*q*

period (time), 118, 801

permafrost, 294, 801

Perry, Matthew C., 666

Persia, 513, 514. *See also* Iran

Persian empire, 446, 448, 514–515, 514*p*, 515*m*, 515*p*, 559

Persian Gulf, 436, 437, 437*m*, 451, 451*p*, 497, 507

Persian Wars, 145

perspective, 801

Peru, 3, 122*p*, 190

peshmerga, 531, 801

Peter the Great, 300–301, 300*p*

Petition of Right, 196

petroleum, 49, 52, 214, 214*m*, 215*c*, 215*p*. *See also* oil

Petronas Towers, 716

phalanx, 136*p*, 148

pharoah, 405, 801

Philip II, king of Macedonia, 135

Philip II, king of Spain, 176, 192–193

Philippine plate, 710

Philippines, 690*p*
- government of, 706
- physical features of, 691, 691*m*
- population of, 694, 694*m*
- religion in, 697, 705

philosophy, 143, 801

Phnom Penh, 695

Phoenicia, 406, 478

physical maps, 10, 10*m*, 12, 12*m*, 801

Picasso, Pablo, 251

PICTA. *See* Pacific Island Countries Trade Agreement

pictograms, 412–413, 413*p*, 801

pilgrimages, 271, 801

pirates and piracy, 384, 384*p*, 709

Pizarro, Francisco, 190

place, theme of, 6, 801

plains, 25, 224, 225, 225*m*, 802

planets, 18

planned economy, 570

plantations, 190, 191, 802

plate, 26, 27, 27*m*, 437, 802

plateau, 25, 25*p*, 332, 437, 622, 623*m*, 802

plate tectonics, 26, 656–657, 710–711, 731–732, 731*m*, 802

Platiensis, Michael, 171*q*

platinum, 368

Plato, 143

plebeians, 149, 802

PLO. *See* Palestine Liberation Organization

Plymouth Colony, 191

poaching, 367, 802

Poland, 174*m*, 232, 258*m*, 274*m*, 274*p*, 300
- culture of, 275
- democracy in, 274
- economy of, 274–275
- European Union and, 275
- government of, 274–275
- natural resources in, 267
- religion in, 268, 268*m*, 269*p*, 271, 271*p*
- Solidarity in, 212, 212*p*
- World War I and, 201, 201*m*
- World War II and, 204–205, 204*m*

polar zones, 34, 34*m*, 802

polders, 245, 802

political maps, 13, 13*m*, 802

political parties, 113, 231, 802

political structures, 108–109, 108*p*, 109*p*

political systems, 106–107, 106*p*, 107*p*
- communism, 302–303, 303*c*
- in Europe, 203, 203*c*
- *See also* government

pollution, 53, 229–230, 229*p*, 802
- in Central Asia, 564
- in China, 645, 645*p*
- in Eastern Europe, 267
- in Egypt, 400
- energy resources and, 232
- in Europe, 215
- human–environment interaction and, 53
- in Japan and the Koreas, 663
- oil spills, 46*p*, 47, 47*p*
- population growth and, 75
- in South Asia, 599
- in Southern and Eastern Africa, 369
- *See also* air pollution; water pollution

Polynesia, 729*m*, 730
- culture of, 727
- history of, 736–737, 737*m*
- population in, 734*c*

polytheist, 410, 802

population
- of Australia, 722, 734, 734*p*
- of Britain, 198
- of China, 617
- of East Asia, 616*m*, 616*p*
- of Egypt, 398, 399, 399*p*
- of Federated States of Micronesia, 722*m*
- of Indonesia, 617
- of Iran, 510
- of Japan, 617
- measuring, 74–75, 74*g*, 75*p*
- migration and, 78–79, 78*p*, 79*p*
- of Mongolia, 617
- movement of, 72*p*, 73, 73*p*
- of New Zealand, 734, 734*p*
- of North Africa, 398–399, 399*p*
- of Pacific region, 734*c*, 735
- of Palau, 722*m*
- of Singapore, 617
- of Southeast Asia, 616*m*, 616*p*
- of South Korea, 617
- of Tonga, 722*m*
- of Turkey, 510
- of Tuvalu, 722*m*

827

Index (continued)

828

Index (continued)

830

Index (continued)

in Muslim empire, 448, 448m
in North Africa, 403, 407
in Persian empire, 515
in the Renaissance, 178–179, 180
in Roman empire, 151
slave, 192, 342, 342p, 397
in Southeast Asia, 693, 693m, 698–700, 699m, 700g
in Southern and Eastern Africa, 373, 374
in Sumatra, 699
in Turkey, 527–528, 528c, 528p
types of, 67, 67c
in United Kingdom, 237
in West and Central Africa, 340–341, 342
trade barrier, 67, 807
traditional economy, 62, 62p, 807
Trajan, emperor of Rome, 150p
Transantarctic Mountains, 753, 753m
Transdniestria, 281
transportation
in Central Asia and Caucasus, 553
culture and, 97
in Industrial Revolution, 198
population distribution and, 77
in Russia, 294g, 294p, 295
technology and, 98p–99p
in Western Europe, 231, 231m
Trans-Siberian Railroad, 294g, 294p, 295
Transylvanian Alps, 262, 263m
treaty, 111, 807
Treaty of Versailles, 201, 203
trees, 42, 42p
triangular trade, 192, 342, 342p, 807
tribal government, 460, 460p
tribunes, 149, 807
Trinity, 482, 807
trireme, 140, 140p
Trojan War, 148
tropical cyclones, 39, 807
tropical or subtropical forest ecosystem, 42, 42m–43m, 42p
tropical or subtropical grassland ecosystem, 42, 42m–43m, 42p
tropical rain forest, 332, 334, 335m
tropical wet and dry climate, 40, 40m–41m, 334, 335m, 807
tropical wet climate, 40, 40m–41m, 334, 335m, 807

Tropic of Cancer, 34, 34m
Tropic of Capricorn, 34, 34m
tropics, 34, 34m, 36, 807
tsar, 300–302, 300p, 807
tsetse belt, 371
tsetse fly, 338p, 339, 371
tsunameters, 712, 807
tsunami, 225, 691, 710–713, 710p, 711c, 712m, 713p, 807
tundra, 226, 226m, 293, 807
tundra climate, 40m–41m, 41, 807
tundra ecosystem, 42m–43m, 43, 43p
Tunisia, 392m, 397m, 406, 417p
government of, 419
literacy in, 417
natural resources in, 402, 402m
population of, 398, 399
religion in, 407
Turkey, 414, 502m
atlas, 506–513, 506p, 507m, 508m, 509g, 510m, 511c, 512m, 512p
climate of, 508–509, 508m, 509c
culture of, 527
Cyprus and, 528–529, 529m, 529p
earthquakes in, 508
economy of, 527–528, 528c, 528p
ethnic groups in, 512–513, 512m, 512p
European Union and, 528
government of, 526–527
history of, 449, 516–517, 516m, 517p, 518, 518p
Kurdish people in, 503–505, 503p, 504p, 505p, 512–513, 528, 530, 531, 531c, 531m, 532–533
land use in, 510–511, 510m
myStory, 503–505, 503p, 504p, 505p
nationalism in, 526
oil in, 511
physical features of, 506–508, 507m
population of, 510
religion in, 512–513, 512m, 512p
as secular state, 526
trade in, 527–528, 528c, 528p
water resources in, 475
women in, 527
See also Ottoman empire
Turkic languages, 555
Turkish Republic of Northern Cyprus, 529

Turkmenistan, 540p, 544m, 570p
government of, 566, 566p
natural resources in, 552, 552m
physical features of, 549, 549m
water resources in, 553
Tutankhamen (Egyptian pharoah), 412, 412p
Tutsi people, 380, 383
Tuvalu, 722, 724m, 746, 746m, 746p, 749m, 751
Twelve Tables, 149
Twenty-first Century Learning
analyze media content, 83, 115, 239, 320–321, 391, 501
communication, 219
community awareness, 29
creativity, 173
cultural awareness, 127, 465, 573, 715, 758–759
cultural differences, 257
evaluate Web sites, 15, 285, 610–611, 651
generate new ideas, 424–425
giving presentations, 45, 716–717
Internet information, 55, 71, 319, 423, 609, 685, 757
make a difference, 536–537
research aid organizations, 359
solve problems, 535
work in teams, 101
typhoons, 692, 807
tyranny, 105, 105c, 807

U

Uganda, 352, 360m
AIDS in, 385
animal life in, 367p
ethnic groups of, 380
population of, 75p
water resources in, 370, 370c, 370m
Uighur ethnic group, 628, 628m, 629, 629p
Ukraine, 213, 258m, 300, 303, 312m, 313
energy resources in, 235
government of, 280, 280p
myStory, 259–261, 259p, 260p, 261p
natural resources in, 267
religion in, 268–269, 268m, 269p
Vikings in, 159
Ulaanbaatar, 624
Uluru, 729

UN. See United Nations
unemployment, 600. See also unemployment
Union of Soviet Socialist Republics (USSR). See Soviet Union
unitary system, 108, 808
United Arab Emirates, 438, 438m, 439g
economy of, 457
ethnic groups in, 442
government of, 450
history of, 449
water resources in, 440, 440m
United Kingdom
economy of, 240, 240g
government of, 107, 236–237
immigrants to, 237
languages of, 237
population of, 230, 230m
tourism in, 238
See also Britain; England; Great Britain
United Nations (UN), 111, 111p, 247
Balkan Nations and, 279
formation of, 209
Korean War and, 668, 668m
Rwanda and, 383
United States
Afghanistan and, 593, 601, 602
citizenship in, 102p, 103, 103p, 112–113, 112p, 113p
Cold War and, 345
democracy in, 141
as developed country, 64
economic system of, 63
government of, 105, 105c, 106, 108
Great Depression in, 202
immigration to, 73, 78p, 79, 79p
Iran and, 519, 524
Iraq and, 451, 451p, 462
Israel and, 485
Japan and, 666, 667, 668–669
landforms of, 25, 25p
NAFTA and, 234, 237
nation-states and, 107
North Korea and, 675
physical map of, 12m
political map of, 13m
Soviet Union and, 303
special-purpose map of, 13m
terrorism in, 593
trade and, 67c
Vietnam War and, 701
World War I and, 201
World War II and, 204, 205
universal theme, 94, 808
Universal Time (UT), 21

Index (continued)

Acknowledgments

The people who made up the myWorld Geography team—representing composition services; core design, digital, and multimedia production services; digital product development; editorial; editorial services; materials management; and production management—are listed below.

Leann Davis Alspaugh, Sarah Aubry, Deanna Babikian, Paul Blankman, Alyssa Boehm, Peter Brooks, Susan Brorein, Megan Burnett, Todd Christy, Neville Cole, Bob Craton, Michael Di Maria, Glenn Diedrich, Frederick Fellows, Jorgensen Fernandez, Thomas Ferreira, Patricia Fromkin, Andrea Golden, Mary Ann Gundersen, Christopher Harris, Susan Hersch, Paul Hughes, Judie Jozokos, Lynne Kalkanajian, John Kingston, Kate Koch, Stephanie Krol, Karen Lepri, Ann-Michelle Levangie, Salena LiBritz, Courtney Markham, Constance J. McCarty, Anne McLaughlin, Rich McMahon, Mark O'Malley, Alison Muff, Jen Paley, Gabriela Perez Fiato, Judith Pinkham, Paul Ramos, Charlene Rimsa, Marcy Rose, Rashid Ross, Alexandra Sherman, Owen Shows, Melissa Shustyk, Jewel Simmons, Ted Smykal, Emily Soltanoff, Frank Tangredi, Simon Tuchman, Elizabeth Tustian, Merle Uuesoo, Alwyn Velásquez, Andrew White, Heather Wright

Maps
XNR Productions, Inc.

Illustration
Kerry Cashman, Marcos Chin, Dave Cockburn, Jeremy Mohler

Photography
FRONT MATTER: Pages vi–xxix, Bkgrnd sky, Image Source/Getty Images; viii, T, ZZ/Alamy; LB, Jim Sugar/Corbis; RB, GoGo Images Corporation/Alamy; ix, SuperStock/age Fotostock; x, B, Jeff Greenberg/PhotoEdit; xi, LB, RB, Pearson Education, Inc.; xii–xix, All, Pearson Education, Inc.; xx, LB Bkgrnd, Ebru Baraz/iStockphoto.com; LB, iStockphoto.com; RB, Miodrag Gajic/Shutterstock; xxi, LB, Pearson Education, Inc.; xxii–xxiii, Pearson Education, Inc.; xxiv, Shutterstock; xxv, LB, Shutterstock; RB, Pearson Education, Inc.; xxvi, LB, Thaier Al-Sudani/Reuters/Corbis; RB, javarman/Shutterstock; xxvii, B, Laurence Mouton/PhotoLibrary; xxviii–xxix, Shutterstock; xxx, Bkgrnd, Michele Falzone/JAI/Corbis; LT, Pearson Education, Inc.; TM, Pearson Education, Inc.; RT, Pearson Education, Inc.; xxxi, iStockphoto.com.

CORE CONCEPTS: Pages xxxii–1, Bkgrnd sky, Image Source/Getty Images; xxxii, L, Shutterstock; LM, Jim Sugar/Corbis; M, Fabian Gonzales/Alamy; RM, All Canada Photos/Alamy; R, Gavin Hellier/Getty Images; 1, L, Reed Kaestner/Corbis/JupiterImages; LM, Gavin Hellier/Getty Images; RM, Todd Gipstein/Corbis; R, Digital Vision/Getty Images; 2, LT, Shutterstock; RT, Photo courtesy of Jason Young; B, Beth Wald/Aurora/Getty Images; LB, Harley Couper/Alamy; 3, LT, Photo courtesy of Jason Young; RT, Photo courtesy of Jason Young; 4, LM, Mike Agliolo/Corbis; 6, Saul Loeb/AFP/Getty Images; 8, RT, Silver Burdett Ginn; LM, Bill Curtsinger/National Geographic Stock; 16, RT, Jim Sugar/Corbis; LT, Shutterstock; M, Jerry Driendl/Getty Images; 17, RT, Stephen Alvarez/Getty Images; Inset, Courtesy of Tamsen Buriak; LT, Hyogo Prefectural Government/epa/Corbis; 24, Goodshoot/Corbis; 25, RT, Shutterstock, Inc.; RM, Digital Vision/Alamy; 26, L, Jim Sugar/Corbis; 27, RM, Hyogo Prefectural Government/epa/Corbis; RB, AP Photo/Ric Francis; 30, RT, NOAA; M, David J. Phillip/AP Images; LT, NASA/Corbis; 31, RT, Photo courtesy of Airin McGhee; LT, Alex Brandon/Newhouse News Service/Landov; TM, Smiley N. Pool/Dallas Morning News/Corbis; 32, LB, Paul Zahl/National Geographic/Getty Images; 33, LT, AP Photo/M. Spencer Green; RB, Indranil Mukherjee/AFP/Getty Images; 39, B, Wave RF/Photolibrary; 40, Francisco González/age Fotostock; 41, RT, JTB Photo/JTB MEDIA CREATION, Inc./Alamy; RB, James L. Stanfield/National Geographic Stock; 42, T, Fabian Gonzales/Alamy; LM, Joseph Sohm-Visions of America/Getty Images; TM, John Glover/Getty Images; LB, Jake Rajs/Getty Images; M, David Ball/Getty Images; 42–43, B, Macduff Everton/Corbis; 43, TM, Radius Images/Photolibrary; M, Mike Tittel/Getty Images; T, Ruth Tomlinson/Getty Images; LM, Ron Sanford/Photo Researchers, Inc.; RB, Bill Curtsinger/National Geographic Stock; 46, LT, Jon Holloway/Stock Connection; RT, Marilyn Humphries/The Image Works; M, Ashley Cooper/Picimpact/Corbis; 47, RT, Photo courtesy of Lauren Hexilon; TM, Frank Perry/AFP/Getty Images; LT, Atlantide Phototravel/Corbis; 48, LM, Melanie Stetson Freeman/The Christian Science Monitor/Getty Images; B, vario images GmbH & Co./KG/Alamy; 50–51, All,

Pearson Education, Inc.; 52, B, Paul Hanna/Reuters/Corbis; 53, RT, All Canada Photos/Alamy; 56, RT, San Rostro/age Fotostock; LT, Alexey U/Shutterstock; B, Jim Russi/age Fotostock; 57, RT, Photo courtesy of Chris Krestner; TM, Imagebroker/Alamy; LT, J. R. Bale/Alamy; MT, James A.Isbell/Shutterstock; 58, LB, LWA/Getty Images; BM, Ariel Skelley/Blend Images/Corbis; BM, fotog/Getty Images; RB, Getty Images; 59, RT, Brigitte Sporrer/zefa/Corbis; 62, B, Dennis MacDonald/PhotoEdit; M, Bruno Morandi/age Fotostock; 63, T, Reuters/KNS Korean News Agency; 64, LB, Gavin Hellier/Getty Images; RB, Mike Cohen/Shutterstock; 66, B, SuperStock/age Fotostock; 67, LB, The Seattle Times/Newscom; RB, Photo by Wang Kai/ChinaFotoPress/Newscom; 68, LB, Ed Kashi/Corbis; 69, RT, Hou Jun/Newscom; 72, M, Reed Kaestner/Corbis/JupiterImages; LT, DDCoral/Shutterstock; RT, Mark Gabrenya/Shutterstock; 73, RT, Photo courtesy of Ludwig Barragan; TM, Pearson Education, Inc.; LT, Steven Senne/AP Images; 74–75, B, Shutterstock; 75, RT, ©2008 by Ira Lippke/Newscom; LB, Thony Belizaire/AFP/Getty Images; 76, B, Travelpix Ltd/Getty Images; 77, B, PCL/Alamy; 78, LT, Private Collection/The Bridgeman Art Library; B, Bettmann/Corbis; 79, RT, Jack Kurtz/Newscom; 80, LT, Paul Almasy/Corbis; LB, iStockphoto.com; 81, RT, Bettmann/Corbis; RB, Fly Fernandez/zefa/Corbis; 84, B, Interfoto/Alamy; RT, Sylvain Grandadam/age Fotostock; LT, Sergei Bachlakov/Shutterstock, Inc.; 85, TM, Photo courtesy of Joanna Baca; RT, mikenorton/Shutterstock; RT, Photo courtesy of Joanna Baca; 86, LT, Gavin Hellier/Getty Images; LB, Pearson Education, Inc.; BM, Pearson Education, Inc.; RB, Pearson Education, Inc.; 87, All, Pearson Education, Inc.; 88, LM, Glenda M. Powers/Shutterstock; B, GoGo Images Corporation/Alamy; 89, RB, Rubberball/Getty Images; RM, Kuzma/Shutterstock; RT, Silver Burdett Ginn; TM, Kokhanchikov/Shutterstock; TM, Lebedinski Vladislav/Shutterstock; M, George Doyle & Ciaran Griffin/Getty Images; M, Pearson Education, Inc.; TM, Cecile Treal and Jean-Michel Ruiz/Dorling Kindersley; 90, LT, Pearson Education, Inc.; LT, Pearson Education, Inc.; LM, Pearson Education, Inc.; LM, Pearson Education, Inc.; LB, Pearson Education, Inc.; LB, dbimages/Alamy; 91, RT, Pearson Education, Inc.; RT, Pearson Education, Inc.; RM, Rubberball/age Fotostock; RM, Jaime Mota/age Fotostock; RB, Pearson Education, Inc.; RB, Pearson Education, Inc.; 94, LT, Carp (1848), Taito. Woodcut/The Granger Collection, New York; B, Jarno Gonzalez Zarraonandia/Shutterstock; 95, BM, Hellestad Rune/Corbis Sygma; T, Bob Krist/eStock Photo; 96, Stephane De Sakutin/AFP/Getty Images; 97, TM, Dmitry Kosterev/Shutterstock; RT, Dave King/Dorling Kindersley; RM, Luchschen/Shutterstock; RB, Dorling Kindersley; BM, Owen Franken/Corbis; RB, James Marshall/Corbis; 98, L, Alistair Duncan/Dorling Kindersley; LB, Michael Holford/Dorling Kindersley; RB, Bruce Forster/Dorling Kindersley/Courtesy of the National Historic Oregon Trail Interpretive Center; 99, LB, Swim Ink 2, LLC/Corbis; RB, Matthew Ward/Dorling Kindersley; 102, RT, Kim Sayer/Dorling Kindersley; B, Tom Sliter/The Stennis Center for Public Service Leadership; RT, Phil Sandlin/AP Images; 103, LT, Reuters/Hans Deryk; RT, Photo courtesy of Anne Marie Sutherland; 104, LB, Art Resource/Musée du Louvre; RB, Spc Katherine M. Roth/HO/epa/Corbis. All Rights Reserved; 105, L, Todd Gipstein/Corbis; R, Imaginechina via AP Images; 106, R, Pool/Anwar Hussein Collection/Getty Images; L, Karel Prinsloo/AP Images; 107, John Leicester/AP Images; 108, T, Kim Sayer/Dorling Kindersley; M, L. Clarke/Corbis; B, AP Photo/Douglas Healey; 109, M, White House Photo Office; T, Wally McNamee/Corbis; B, The Collection of the Supreme Court of the United States; 110, Alan Gignoux/age Fotostock; 111, B, Kote Rodrigo/EFE/Corbis; T, Karel Prinsloo/AP Images; 112, B, Jeff Greenberg/PhotoEdit; T, William Whitehurst/Corbis; 113, RB, Wally McNamee/Corbis; 116, RT, Jim Zuckerman/Corbis; LT, Digital Vision/Getty Images; B, El Comercio Newspaper, Dante Piaggio/AP Images; 117, RT, Photo courtesy of Brian McCray; LT, Ira Block/National Geographic/Getty Images; TM, University of Oregon/AP Images; 118, LB, The British Museum/Dorling Kindersley; LB, O. Louis Mazzatenta/National Geographic Stock; RB, Ivonne Wierink/Shutterstock; M, Giles Stokoe/Felix deWeldon/Dorling Kindersley; 119, RT, Image Asset Management Ltd./Alamy; M, Andy Crawford/Dorling Kindersley, Courtesy of the University Museum of Archaeology and Anthropology, Cambridge; RB, Getty Images/De Agostini Editore Picture Library; 120, LB, Bettmann/Corbis; LM, Bettmann/Corbis; 121, RB, Hulton Archive/Getty Images; L, The Granger Collection, New York; 122, LT, Sean Hunter/Dorling Kindersley; B, Martin Gray/National Geographic Stock; R,

837

Acknowledgments (continued)

B, Matthew Septimus/Getty Images; **325, T**, Gavin Hellier/Photolibrary; **B**, Roger De La Harpe/Photolibrary; **M**, Eric Isselée/Shutterstock; **326**, Hugh Sitton/zefa/Corbis; **327, R**, Pearson Education, Inc.; **L**, Pearson Education, Inc.; **M**, Pearson Education, Inc.

CHAPTER 6: Pages 328–331, All, Pearson Education, Inc.; **332**, Bruno Morandi/Getty Images; **334**, Bruno Morandi/Getty Images; **335, LM**, Pearson Education, Inc.; **L**, Nigel Bean/naturepl.com; **RM**, Atlantide Phototravel/Corbis; **R**, Bruno Fert/Corbis; **337**, Inset, Bruce Dale/National Geographic/Getty Images; **Bkgrnd**, George Steinmetz/Corbis; **338**, Martin Dohrn/Photo Researchers, Inc.; **340**, Frans Lemmens/zefa/Corbis; **R**, Joan Webb/The Art Archive; **R**, Joan Pollock/Alamy; **342**, Courtesy of the Wilberforce House Museum, Hull/Dorling Kindersley; **343, T**, National Archives Image Library, UK/Dorling Kindersley; **B**, Popperfoto/Getty Images; **344, L**, Bettmann/Corbis; **R**, AFP/Getty Images; **345**, AP Images; **346, T**, Corbis/Photolibrary; **346, B**, Hugh Sitton/zefa/Corbis; **347, R**, Sebastien Cailleux/Corbis; **348**, Paul Almasy/Corbis; **349, Inset**, Werner Forman/Corbis; **349, Bkgrnd**, iStockphoto.com; **350**, Gideon Mendel/ActionAid/Corbis; **351**, Jacob Silberberg/Getty Images; **352, L**, AFP/Getty Images; **R**, George Osodi/AP Images; **353**, Cloth, Dorling Kindersley; **LT**, Comstock Images/Jupiter Unlimited; **RT**, Paul Almasy/Corbis; **LB**, Studio Patellani/Corbis; **RB**, Philippe Lissac/Godong/Corbis; **355**, Pearson Education, Inc.; **356**, Werner Forman/Art Resource, NY; **357, B**, Newscom; **357, T**, Eye Ubiquitous/Alamy.

CHAPTER 7: Pages 360–361, Ksenia Khamkova/iStockphoto.com; **360, B**, Pearson Education, Inc.; **361, T**, Pearson Education, Inc.; **B**, Pearson Education, Inc.; **362–363, All**, Pearson Education, Inc.; **364, Bkgrnd**, SuperStock; **B**, Steve Outram/Mira.com; **367, L**, Tim Laman/Getty Images, Inc.; **L Inset**, Oleg Znamenskiy/Fotolia; **M Inset**, Beckman/Dorling Kindersley; **R Inset**, meoita/Fotolia; **R**, Image Source/Photolibrary; **368, L**, Ian Murphy/Getty Images; **M**, Charles O'Rear/Corbis; **R**, Kulka/zefa/Corbis; **369, Bkgrnd**, Franco Pizzochero/age Fotostock; **B**, F.A.O. Food and Agriculture Organization of the United Nations; **370, T**, Reza/Webistan/Getty Images; **TM**, Peter Martell/AFP/Getty Images; **BM**, Andrew Holt/Getty Images; **B**, Jenny Matthews/Alamy; **371**, Liba Taylor/Corbis; **372, T**, David Boyer/National Geographic/Getty Images; **B**, Gallo Images/Corbis; **373, B**, Peter Groenendijk/age Fotostock **T**, Yadid Levy/age Fotostock; **375, RT**, The Granger Collection, New York; **LT**, The Granger Collection, New York; **B**, Bettmann/Corbis; **376**, Bettmann/Corbis; **377**, David Turnley/Corbis; **378**, The Art Archive/Collection Antonovich/Dagli Orti; **379**, Nicole Duplaix/Corbis; **380**, PCN Photography/PCN/Corbis; **381, T**, Patrick Robert/Sygma/Corbis; **B**, Lindsay Hebberd/Corbis; **382**, Alfred De Montesquiou/AP Images; **384, B**, AFP Photo/HO/US Navy/Jason R. Zalasky/Newscom; **T**, epa/Corbis; **385**, Wolfgang Schmidt/Peter Arnold, Inc.; **386**, Peter Groenendijk/age Fotostock; **387**, Hulton-Deutsch Collection/Corbis; **388, R**, D Barnett/Hulton Archive/Getty Images; **C**, The Stapleton Collection/Art Resource, NY; **389, R**, Peter Horree/Alamy; **L**, David Turnley/Corbis; **Inset**, Keystone/Getty Images.

CHAPTER 8: Pages 393–395, All, Pearson Education, Inc.; **396, Bkgrnd**, Franck Guiziou/Hemis/Corbis; **B**, Hugh Sitton/zefa/Corbis; **398**, Jacques Descloitres, MODIS Land Science Team/NASA; **399, LB**, Tony Craddock/zefa/Corbis; **RB**, Sylvain Grandadam/age Fotostock; **LT**, Aristidis Vafeiadakis/Alamy; **RT**, R. Matina/age Fotostock; **400, B**, Otto Lang/Corbis; **T**, Otto Lang/Corbis; **401**, Cecile Treal and Jean-Michel Ruiz/Dorling Kindersley; **404**, Roger Wood/Corbis; **405, T**, Bojan Brecelj/Corbis; **M**, Peter Hayman/The British Museum/Dorling Kindersley; **B**, The Gallery Collection/Corbis; **Bkgrnd**, Yanta/Shutterstock; **406, LB**, Peter Hayman/The British Museum/Dorling Kindersley; **BM**, John Hepver/The British Museum/Dorling Kindersley; **Bkgrnd**, Hydromet/Shutterstock; **LT**, Peter Hayman/The British Museum/Dorling Kindersley; **RB**, Kazuyoshi Nomachi/Corbis; **RT**, Pearson Education, Inc.; **407, R**, Gavin Hellier/Robert Harding World/Corbis; **L**, The Gallery Collection/Corbis; **M**, Pearson Education, Inc.; **408**, Interpress/Interpress/Kipa/Corbis; **409**, Bettmann/Corbis; **410**, Alistair Duncan/Dorling Kindersley; **411, L**, Roger Wood/Corbis; **R**, The Art Archive/Egyptian Museum Cairo/Gianni Dagli Orti; **412 ML**, JupiterImages/Brand X/Alamy; **LT**, The Print Collector/Alamy; **LB**, British Museum/Dorling Kindersley; **L**, N-a-s-h/Shutterstock; **TM**, Stephanie Pilick/epa/Corbis; **413, M**, N-a-s-h/Shutterstock; **414**, Brakefield Photo/Brand X/Corbis; **415, T**, Claudia Wiens/Das Fotoarchiv/Peter Arnold, Inc.; **B**, Hekimian Julien/Corbis; **M**, Franck Guiziou/Hemis/Corbis; **417, R**, Olivier Martel/Corbis; **L**, Alan Hills/Dorling Kindersley; **418**, Mona Sharaf/Reuters; **419**, John Chiasson/Liaison/Getty Images; **420, RT**, David Kay/Shutterstock; **RB**, Abdelhak Senna, Pool/AP Images; **421, TR**, Abdelhak Senna/AFP/Getty Images.

UNIT 2 CLOSER: Page 424, RT, Shutterstock; **B**, iStockphoto.com; **424–425, B**, Pearson Education, Inc.; **425, LM**, Shutterstock; **RM**, Christian Musat/Shutterstock; **RT**, Pearson Education, Inc.; **Bkgrnd**, iStockphoto.com; **LT**, Shutterstock; **M**, Shutterstock.

UNIT 3: Pages 426–431, Bkgrnd sky, Image Source/Getty Images; **427, B**, Polly Wreford/Photolibrary; **LT**, Pearson Education, Inc.; **RM**, Pearson Education, Inc.; **LM**, Pearson Education, Inc.; **RT**, Pearson Education, Inc.; **428**, Yvan Travert/Photononstop/Photolibrary; **429, T**, Nik Wheeler/Corbis; **B**, Ray Ellis/Photo Researchers, Inc.; **430, L**, Christian Kober/Photolibrary; **M**, Ahmad Al-Rubaye/AFP/Getty Images/Newscom; **R**, Mark Hannaford/Photolibrary; **431, L**, Pearson Education, Inc.; **RM**, Pearson Education, Inc.; **LM**, Pearson Education, Inc.; **R**, Pearson Education, Inc.

CHAPTER 9: Pages 432–435, All, Pearson Education, Inc.; **436, Bkgrnd**, John Warburton-Lee Photography/Photolibrary; **B**, Patrick Robert/Sygma/Corbis; **439**, Essam Al-Sudani/AFP/Getty Images; **440, T**, Homer Sykes Archive/Alamy; **B**, Ed Kashi/Aurora Photos; **442, T**, Thaier Al-Sudani/Reuters/Corbis; **B**, Marwan Ibrahim/AFP/Getty Images; **M**, David Turnley/Corbis; **444, Bkgrnd**, Georg Gerster/Photo Researchers, Inc.; **L**, Robert Harding World Imagery/Robert Harding Picture Library Ltd/Alamy; **M**, The London Art Archive/Alamy; **R**, Accounts table with cuneiform script (about 2400 B.C.), Mesopotamia, terracotta. Louvre, Paris, France/The Bridgeman Art Library; **445**, Erich Lessing/Art Resource, NY; **446**, Picture Partners/Alamy; **447, T**, Sucheta Das/Reuters/Corbis; **TM**, World Religions Photo Library/Alamy; **BM**, Akhtar Soomro/epa/Corbis; **B**, Hassan Ammar/AFP/Getty Images; **449, L**, VIVIENNE SHARP/Imagestate Media Partners Limited - Impact Photos/Alamy; **RB**, Turkish School/Getty Images; **RT**, General Photographic Agency/Getty Images; **450, R**, Bettmann/Corbis; **L**, AP Photo; **451, LT**, Jacques Langevin/Sygma/Corbis; **452, T**, Library of Congress; **B**, Photo by Alex Wong/Getty Images for Meet the Press; **453, .T**, Albert Gea/Reuters; **B**, Mohammed Sehety/AP Photo; **454**, Jose Fuste Raga/Corbis; **455**, JTB Photo/Photolibrary; **456, L**, Karim Sahib/AFP/Getty Images; **R**, AFP/Getty Images; **458, RB**, Photopqr/La Voix Du Nord/karine Delmas/Newscom; **T**, Khaled Desouki/AFP/Getty Images; **LB**, Safin Hamed/AFP/Getty Images; **459**, Pearson Education, Inc.; **460**, Reza/National Geographic/Getty Images; **461, T**, Hulton-Deutsch Collection/Corbis; **C**, AP Photo; **B**, Karim Kadim/AP Photo; **463**, Khaled Fazaa/AFP/Getty Images; **460**, Reza/National Geographic/Getty Images; **461, T**, Hulton-Deutsch Collection/Corbis; **C**, AP Photo; **B**, Karim Kadim/AP Photo; **463**, Khaled Fazaa /AFP/Getty Images.

CHAPTER 10: Pages 466–469, All, Pearson Education, Inc.; **470, Bkgrnd**, Grapheast/Photolibrary; **B**, Ali Kabas/Alamy; **472, B**, Josef F. Stuefer/Shutterstock; **M**, Sami Sarkis Travel/Alamy; **T**, Israel images/Alamy; **475**, Mike Abrahams/Alamy; **476, T**, Rosebud Pictures/Getty Images; **B**, Chris Hondros/Getty Images; **M**, Anwar Amro/Getty Images; **478**, Ancient Art & Architecture/DanitaDelimont.com; **479**, The Art Archive/University Library Istanbul/Dagli Orti; **480, L**, Image Asset Management Ltd./SuperStock; **R**, Menahem Kahana/AFP/Getty Images; **481**, Bridgeman-Giraudon/Art Resource, NY; **482**, Megapress/Alamy; **483**, Magnus Rew/Dorling Kindersley; **485**, Rolls Press/Popperfoto/Getty Images; **486, LT**, Jupiter Unlimited; **C**, Steve Allen/age Fotostock; **B**, Natalia Bratslavsky; **487, R**, Getty Images; **L**, Richard T. Nowitz/Corbis; **488, R**, Geopix/Alamy; **L**, Philippe Lissac/GODONG/Corbis; **489, T**, The Print Collector/age Fotostock; **M**, The Art Archive/Dagli Orti; **490**, David Silverman/Getty Images; **491, L**, Hussein Malla/AP Photo; **M**, Julian Herbert/Getty Images; **R**, AFP Photo/Louai Beshara/Newscom; **492, R**, Alan Keohane/Photolibrary; **L**, Salah Malkawi/Getty Images; **493, T**, Israel images/Alamy; **M**, AFP/Getty Images; **B**, An Qi/Alamy; **495**, Alexandra Boulat/VII/AP Images; **496, L**, Ricki Rosen/Corbis; **R**, Shawn Baldwin/Corbis; **497**, Pearson Education, Inc.; **498, RT**, Wissam Nassar/Xinhua/SipaPress/Newscom; **C**, Wissam Nassar/Xinhua/Sipa Press/Newscom; **499**, Reuters.

CHAPTER 11: Page 502, Bkgrnd, Ebru Baraz/iStockphoto.com; **B**, Pearson Education, Inc.; **502–503**, Sufi70/iStockphoto.com; **503, RT**, Pearson Education, Inc.; **RB**, Pearson Education, Inc.; **LT**, Cokeker/Shutterstock; **504–505, All**, Pearson Education, Inc.; **506, Bkgrnd**, Alistair Duncan/Dorling Kindersley; **B**, Chris Rout/Alamy; **508, L**, Kate Clow, Terry Richardson, Dominic Whiting/Dorling Kindersley; **R**, David Poole/Robert Harding Word Imagery; **M**, Rainer Jahns/Alamy; **509**, Ryan Pyle/Corbis; **511, B**, Arthur Thévenart/Corbis; **T**, Raheb Homavandi CJF/KS/Reuters; **512, R**, SuperStock/age Fotostock; **L**, Peter Guttman/Corbis; **513**, Robert Preston Photography/Alamy; **514, L**, Berni/Fotolia; **R**,

838

Acknowledgments (continued)

Color lithograph. Private Collection/The Stapleton Collection/The Bridgeman Art Library International; **739, L,** Cannon Collection/Australian Picture Library/Corbis; **Bkgrnd,** Lawrence Manning/Corbis; **R,** Mark Baker/AP Photo; **740,** *Mssrs. White, Harris, and Laing With a Party of Soldiers Visiting Botany Bay Colebee at that Place When Wounded near Botany Bay* (c. 1790), Port Jackson Painter. Watercolor on paper. British Museum, London, UK/The Bridgeman Art Library International; **B,** The Print Collector/age Fotostock; **741, T,** Cannon Collection/Australian Picture Library/Corbis; **B,** Oliver Gerhard/age Fotostock; **742,** Barry Lewis/Corbis; **743, R,** Pearson Education, Inc.; **LM,** Bob Krist/Corbis; **RM,** James Davis Photography/Alamy; **L,** Penny Tweedie/Corbis; **744, LT,** Rob Griffith/epa/Corbis; **RB,** Palani Mohan/AP Photo/SMH; **LB,** Jonathan Marks/Corbis; **745,** Bruce Martin/Alamy; **746, RB,** Ashley Cooper/Corbis; **LB,** Richard Vogel/AP Photo; **T,** Vladimir Melnik/Shutterstock; **M,** Ashley Cooper/Corbis; **748,** Neil Duncan/Photolibrary New York; **750, L,** dpaint/Shutterstock; **R,** Chris Skelton/Reuters; **751, R,** Jeremy Hoare/Alamy; **L,** Reinhard Dirscherl/age Fotostock; **752,** Sea World of California/Corbis; **754, RT,** Courtesy: Anthony Gibson/National Science Foundation; **LB,** Handout/Getty Images Entertainment/Getty Images; **LT,** Bettmann/Corbis; **RB,** blickwinkel/Baesemann/Alamy; **755,** NASA.

UNIT 6 CLOSER: Page 758, L, R McKown/Shutterstock; **758–759, All,** Shutterstock

Text Acknowledgments
Grateful acknowledgment is made to the following for copyrighted material:

Page 162 Excerpt from "Hildegard to Odo Soissons," from *Hildegard of Bingen: Selected Writings,* translated by Mark Atherton. Translation copyright © Mark Atherton 2001. Penguin Group. All rights reserved. Used by permission.

Page 212 Address at the Institute of Contemporary Arts, London; quoted in *The Independent, March 22, 1990.*

Page 314 Excerpt from "Russia Close-Up: Overcoming Soviet Industrial Legacy," from *Russia Today, July 29, 2007.*

Page 317 Excerpt from "Russia Rising," by Fen Montaigne, from *National Geographic, November 2001.* Copyright © National Geographic Society.

Page 626 Excerpt from "Migrant Couple Struggles to Earn in New China," from *NPR, May 20, 2008.* Copyright © National Public Radio.

Page 651 Excerpt from "Voices from Modern China: Fu Ansi, Migrant Worker," from *bbc.com.* Copyright © BBC.

Note: Every effort has been made to locate the copyright owner of material reproduced in this publication. Omissions brought to our attention will be corrected in subsequent editions.